A HANDBOOK OF ALTERNATIVE MONETARY ECONOMICS

A Handbook of Alternative Monetary Economics

Edited by

Philip Arestis

University Director of Research, Cambridge Centre for Economic and Public Policy, Department of Land Economy, University of Cambridge, UK

and

Malcolm Sawyer

Professor of Economics, University of Leeds, UK

Edward Elgar
Cheltenham, UK • Northampton, MA, USA

Published by
Edward Elgar Publishing Limited
Glensanda House
Montpellier Parade
Cheltenham
Glos GL50 1UA
UK

Edward Elgar Publishing, Inc.
William Pratt House
9 Dewey Court
Northampton
Massachusetts 01060
USA

A catalogue record for this book
is available from the British Library

Library of Congress Cataloguing in Publication Data
A handbook of alternative monetary economics / edited by Philip Arestis, Malcolm Sawyer.
    p. cm. — (Elgar original reference)
Includes bibliographical references and index.
1. Money. 2. Monetary policy. 3. Finance. 4. Economics. I. Arestis, Philip, 1941–
II. Sawyer, Malcolm C. III. Series.

HG221.H236   2006
332.4′01—dc22   2005033750

ISBN-13: 978 1 84376 915 6 (cased)
ISBN-10: 1 84376 915 8 (cased)

Printed and bound in Great Britain by MPG Books Ltd, Bodmin, Cornwall

Contents

Contributors

Philip Arestis, University of Cambridge, UK

Santonu Basu, Queen Mary, University of London, UK

Jörg Bibow, Skidmore College, New York, USA

Suzanne de Brunhoff, Centre National de la Recherche Scientifique, Paris, France

Paul Davidson, New School University, New York, USA

Elisabetta De Antoni, University of Trento, Italy

Sheila C. Dow, University of Stirling, UK

Gary A. Dymski, University of California, Riverside and University of California Center Sacramento, USA

Korkut A. Erturk, University of Utah, and The Levy Economics Institute, Annandale-on-Hudson, New York, USA

Duncan K. Foley, New School for Social Research, New York, USA

Giuseppe Fontana, University of Leeds, UK and Università del Sannio, Benevento, Italy

James Forder, Balliol College, Oxford, UK

Ilene Grabel, University of Denver, Colorado, USA

Claude Gnos, Université de Bourgogne, Dijon, France

Greg Hannsgen, The Levy Economics Institute, Annandale-on-Hudson, New York, USA

Mark Hayes, Northumbria University, Newcastle upon Tyne, UK

Gunnar Heinsohn, Universität Bremen, Germany

Peter Howells, University of the West of England, Bristol, UK

Dorene Isenberg, University of Redlands, California, USA

Michael Knittel, Hohenheim University, Germany

Marc Lavoie, University of Ottawa, Ontario, Canada

Thomas I. Palley, Economist, Washington, USA

Riccardo Realfonzo, Università del Sannio, Italy

Sergio Rossi, University of Fribourg, Switzerland

Roy J. Rotheim, Skidmore College, New York, USA

Malcolm Sawyer, University of Leeds, UK

John Smithin, York University, Toronto, Canada

Sybille Sobczak, Hohenheim University, Germany

Peter Spahn, Hohenheim University, Germany

Otto Steiger, Universität Bremen, Germany

Pavlina R. Tcherneva, University of Missouri–Kansas City, USA

Éric Tymoigne, California State University, Fresno, USA

Matías Vernengo, University of Utah, Salt Lake City, Utah, USA

L. Randall Wray, University of Missouri–Kansas City, USA

Preface

This Handbook seeks to cover the range of exciting and interesting work on money and finance that is taking place within heterodox economics. There are many themes and facets of alternative monetary and financial economics. The contributions below will also show that there is not always agreement among heterodox economists. There are, though, two major themes, which run through many of the chapters. The first comes directly from the nature of money: money is credit money created through the financial system in the process of loan creation. Money is endogenous and not exogenous money (represented by the usual textbook assumption of 'helicopter money'). The book opens with a chapter on the origins and nature of money, and the theme of endogenous money comes through the detailed analyses of money in a number of contributions, but especially in the survey of empirical work on endogenous money and in a chapter on the nature of monetary policy when money is endogenous.

The second theme focuses on the financial system, and the perception that this system is generally subject to volatility, instability and crisis. This theme recurs in a number of chapters, but more concretely in the chapters on deregulation of the financial system and on financial liberalization.

We do not attempt to summarize the 29 contributions in this volume, but offer them as a broad-ranging coverage of alternative monetary economics. We thank the authors for their enthusiastic response to the invitation to contribute to this volume. We also wish to thank the publisher of the series, Edward Elgar, for suggesting it in the first place, and his staff for the enormous and efficient work they have provided in the production of this Handbook.

Philip Arestis, University of Cambridge
Malcolm Sawyer, University of Leeds

1 Money: an alternative story
Éric Tymoigne and L. Randall Wray

Overview

To be sure, we will never 'know' the origins of money. First, the origins are lost 'in the mists of time' – almost certainly in pre-historic time (Keynes, 1930, p. 13). It has long been speculated that money pre-dates writing because the earliest examples of writing appear to be records of monetary debts – hence we are not likely to uncover written records of money's 'discovery'. Further, it is not clear what we want to identify as money. Money is social in nature and it consists of complex social practices that include power and class relationships, socially constructed meaning, and abstract representations of social value (Zelizer, 1989). There is probably no single source for the institution of modern capitalist economies that we call 'money'. When we attempt to discover the origins of money, we are identifying institutionalized behaviours that appear similar to those today that we wish to identify as 'money'. This identification, itself, requires an underlying economic theory. Most economists focus on market exchanges, hypothesizing that money originated as a cost-reducing innovation to replace barter, and highlighting the medium of exchange and store of value functions of money. While this is consistent with the neoclassical preoccupation with market exchange and the search for a unique equilibrium price vector, it is not so obvious that it can be adopted within heterodox analysis.

If money did not originate as a cost-minimizing alternative to barter, what were its origins? It is possible that one might find a different 'history of money' depending on the function that one identifies as the most important characteristic of money. While many economists (and historians and anthropologists) would prefer to trace the evolution of the money used as a medium of exchange, our primary interest is in the unit of account function of money.[1] Our alternative history will locate the origin of money in credit and debt relations, with the unit of account emphasized as the numeraire in which they are measured. The store of value function could also be important, for one stores wealth in the form of others' debts. On the other hand, the medium of exchange function and the market are de-emphasized as the source of money's origins; indeed, credits and debits can exist without markets and without a medium of exchange.

Innes (1913; 1914; 1932) suggested that the origins of credit and debt can be found in the elaborate system of tribal wergild designed to prevent blood feuds (see also Grierson, 1977; 1979; Goodhart, 1998; Wray, 2004). As Polanyi put it: 'the debt is incurred not as a result of economic transaction, but of events like marriage, killing, coming of age, being challenged to potlatch, joining a secret society, etc.' (Polanyi, 1957 [1968], p. 198). Wergild fines were paid by transgressors directly to victims and their families, and were established and levied by public assemblies. A long list of fines for each possible transgression was developed, and a designated 'rememberer' would be responsible for passing it down to the next generation. As Hudson (2004b) reports, the words for debt in most languages are synonymous with sin or guilt, reflecting these early reparations for personal injury. Originally, until one paid the wergild fine, one was 'liable', or 'indebted', to the victim. It is almost certain that wergild fines were gradually converted to payments made to an authority. This could not occur in an egalitarian tribal society, but had to await the rise of some sort of ruling class. As Henry (2004) argues for the case of Egypt, the earliest ruling classes were probably religious officials, who demanded tithes. Alternatively, conquerors required payments of tribute by a subject population. Tithes and tribute thus came to replace wergild fines, and eventually fines for 'transgressions against society' (that is, against the Crown), paid to the rightful ruler, could be levied for almost any conceivable activity. (See Peacock, 2003–4.)

Later, taxes would replace most fees, fines and tribute (although this occurred surprisingly late – not until the nineteenth century in England) (Maddox, 1969). These could be self-imposed as democracy gradually replaced authoritarian regimes. In any case, with the development of civil society and reliance mostly on payment of taxes rather than fines, tithes, or tribute, the origin of such payments in the wergild tradition have been forgotten. A key innovation was the transformation of what had been a debt to the victim to a universal 'debt' or tax obligation imposed by and payable to the authority. The next step was the standardization of the obligations in terms of a unit of account – a money. At first, the authority might have levied a variety of in-kind fines (and tributes, tithes and taxes), in terms of goods or services to be delivered, one for each sort of transgression (as in the wergild tradition). When all payments are made to the single authority, however, this became cumbersome. Unless well-developed markets already existed, those with liabilities denominated in specific goods or services could find it difficult to make such payments. Or, the authority could find itself blessed with an overabundance of one type of good while short of others. Further, in-kind taxes provided an incentive for the taxpayer to provide the lowest-quality goods required for payment of taxes.

Denominating payments in a unit of account would simplify matters – but would require a central authority. As Grierson (1977; 1979) realized, development of a unit of account would be conceptually difficult (see also Henry, 2004). It is easier to come by measures of weight or length – the length of some anatomical feature of the ruler (from which, of course, comes our term for the device used to measure short lengths like the foot), or the weight of a quantity of grain. By contrast, development of a money of account used to value items with no obvious similarities required more effort. Hence the creation of an authority able to impose obligations transformed wergild fines paid to victims to fines paid to the authority and at the same time created the need for and possibility of creation of the monetary unit.

Orthodoxy has never been able to explain how individual utility maximizers settled on a single numeraire (Gardiner, 2004; Ingham, 2004). While use of a single unit of account results in efficiencies, it is not clear what evolutionary processes would have generated the numeraire. According to the conventional story, the higgling and haggling of the market is supposed to produce the equilibrium vector of relative prices, all of which can be denominated in the single numeraire. However, this presupposes a fairly high degree of specialization of labour and/or resource ownership – but this pre-market specialization, itself, is hard to explain (Bell et al., 2004). Once markets are reasonably well developed, specialization increases welfare; however, without well-developed markets, specialization is exceedingly risky, while diversification of skills and resources would be prudent. Thus it seems exceedingly unlikely that either markets or a money of account could have evolved out of individual utility-maximizing behaviour.

In fact, it has long been recognized that early monetary units were based on a specific number of grains of wheat or barley (Wray, 1990, p. 7). As Keynes argued, 'the fundamental weight standards of Western civilization have never been altered from the earliest beginnings up to the introduction of the metric system' (Keynes, 1982, p. 239). These weight standards were then taken over for the monetary units, whether the livre, sol, denier, mina, shekel, or the pound (Keynes, 1982; Innes, 1913, p. 386; Wray, 1998, p. 48). This relation between the words used for weight units and monetary units generated speculation from the time of Innes and Keynes that there must be some underlying link. Hudson (2004a) explains that the early monetary units developed in the temples and palaces of Sumer in the third millennium BC were created initially for internal administrative purposes: 'the public institutions established their key monetary pivot by making the shekel-weight of silver (240 barley grains) equal in value to the monthly consumption unit, a "bushel" of barley, the major commodity being disbursed' (Hudson, 2004b, p. 111). Hence, rather than the intrinsic value (or even the exchange-value) of precious metal giving rise to the numeraire, the authorities established the monetary value of precious metal by setting it equal to the numeraire that was itself derived from the weight of the monthly grain consumption unit. This leads quite readily to the view that the unit of account was socially determined rather than the result of individual optimization.

To conclude our introduction, we return to our admission that it is not possible to write a definitive history of money. We start from the presumption that money is a fundamentally social phenomenon or institution, whose origins must lie in varied and complex social practices. We do not view money as a 'thing', a commodity with some special characteristics that is chosen to lubricate a pre-existing market. Further, we believe that the monetary unit almost certainly required and requires some sort of authority to give it force. We do not believe that a strong case has yet been made for the possibility that asocial forces of 'supply and demand' could have competitively selected for a unit of account. Indeed, with only very rare exceptions, the unit of account throughout all known history and in every corner of the globe has been associated with a central authority. Hence we suppose that there must be some connection between a central authority – what we will call 'the state' – and the unit of account, or currency. In the next section we will lay out the scope of the conceptual issues surrounding the term 'money', before turning to a somewhat more detailed examination of the history of money.

What is money? Conceptual issues
Before telling any story about the history of money, one should first identify the essential characteristics of a monetary system:

1. The existence of a method for recording transactions, that is, a *unit of account* and *tools* to record transactions.
2. The *unit of account* must be social, that is, recognized as the unit in which debts and credits are kept.
3. The *tools* are *monetary instruments* (or (monetary)[2] debt instruments): they record the fact that someone owes to another a certain number of units of the unit of account. Monetary instruments can be of different forms, from bookkeeping entries to coins, from bytes in a hard drive to physical objects (like cowrie shells). Anything can be a monetary instrument, as long as, first, it is an acknowledgement of debt (that is,

something that has been issued by the debtor, who promises to accept it back in payment by creditors) and, second, it is denominated in a unit of account.

4.　Some monetary instruments are *money-things* that are transferable ('circulate'): they must be impersonal from the perspective of the receiver (but not the issuer) and transferable at no or low discount to a third party. A cheque is a monetary instrument but not usually a money-thing because it is not transferable (it names the receiver). Currency is a money-thing because it is transferable and impersonal from the perspective of the receiver but it is a debt of the issuer (treasury or central bank).

5.　There is a hierarchy of monetary instruments, with one debt issuer (or a small number of issuers) whose debts are used to clear accounts. The monetary instruments issued by those high in the hierarchy will be the money-things.

These five characteristics imply that a history of money would be concerned with at least three different things: the history of debts (origins of debts, nature and types of debts before and after the emergence of a legal system), the history of accounting (origins, unit(s) used, evolution of units, purpose), and the history of monetary and non-monetary debt instruments (forms, issuers, name, value in terms of the unit of account, and their use (emergency, special types of transactions like shares, daily commercial transactions, etc.)). Behind each of these histories lie politico-socioeconomic factors that are driving forces and that would also need to be studied carefully.

In addition, while telling the story of money one has to avoid several pitfalls. First, the dangers of ethnocentrism are always present when one studies societies that are totally different from current modern societies (Dalton, 1965). Second, one should not concentrate the analysis on specific debt instruments: as Grierson (1975; 1977) notes, the history of money and the history of coins are two different histories. Focusing on coins would not only limit the study to one type of debt instrument, but would also avoid a detailed presentation of units of account – and, indeed, could be highly misleading regarding the nature of money.[3] Third, the nature of money cannot be reduced to the simple functions of medium of exchange or means of payment. Using a physical object for economic transactions does not necessarily qualify it as a money-thing, and one risks confusing monetary payment with payment in kind. Fourth, and finally, the existence and use of money does not imply that an economy is a monetary economy, that is an economy in which the accumulation of money is the driving force of economic decisions.

Thus, looking at the history of money is a gigantic and very difficult task. In addition, it is an interdisciplinary subject because it involves, among others, the fields of politics, sociology, anthropology, history, archaeology and economics. There is no doubt that progress in all those disciplines will bring new light to the dark story of money.

Money in primitive, archaic and modern societies

A brief history of money can be begun by dividing the history of humanity into three analytically different types of society, along the lines posed by Polanyi, Dalton and others: primitive, archaic and modern economies (Dalton, 1971; Bohannan and Dalton, 1962). This analytical framework does not exclude the possibility that there is some transition and overlap; however, such a division is useful for telling a story about the evolution of money.

Primitive

In primitive societies, there is no notion of private property[4] in the sense of ownership of the means of production (agricultural land, forests, fisheries) and so no possibility of a society based on barter (in the economic sense of the term) or commercial exchange: these are marketless economies. However, there is a well-defined system of obligations, offences and compensations. Obligations are 'pre-legal obligations' (Polanyi, 1957 [1968], p. 181), defined by tradition (marriage, providing help, obtaining favours, making friends, etc.), with magic and the maintenance of social order playing a central role in their existence. Their fulfilment can be qualitative (dancing, crying, loss of social status or role, loss of magical power, etc.) or quantitative (transfer of personal objects that can be viewed as a net transfer of wealth) (ibid., p. 182). In addition, payment of wergild compensation is not standardized but rather takes the form of in-kind payment, with type and amount of payment established socially – as discussed previously.

In primitive societies there is, therefore, no economic or social need for accounting, even if debts are present, because they are egalitarian societies in which exchange is usually reciprocal (the purpose of exchange is not to better one's position, but rather to bring members of the society closer together – often by redistribution), accumulation of wealth is repressed or non-existent (Schmandt-Besserat, 1992, p. 170), and the fulfilment of obligations is not standardized. Some methods of computing existed, for example, to record time (ibid., p. 160) in order to calculate the phases of the moon, the seasons, and other natural phenomena, or to count numbers and measure volume. That is why one can find notches on different objects like bones that date at least back to 60 000 BC (ibid., p. 158). However, there was no need to keep detailed records of debts.

Archaic

One can date the emergence of money to the development of large archaic societies between 3500 and 3000 BC in the Ancient Near East. In this type of society, market transactions exist but are peripheral and mostly developed for external commercial transactions. Given the relatively low importance of trade (and/or its control by the ruling authorities) and the minimal power of merchants, one should not search for the origins of money in this direction. Trade was subsumed under a larger socioeconomic framework based on the redistribution of the economic output (mainly crops but also handicrafts, tools, and other finished products (Hudson and Wunsch, 2004)). This centralization emerged as the rules of primitive tribal societies were progressively weakened, bringing profound social changes (Henry, 2004). A highly organized and stratified society with a religious upper class (king, princes and high-rank priests) was progressively formed, while reciprocity was progressively weakened. Religion replaced magic and led to the emergence of sacral obligations, that is, obligations under the sanction of religion.

With the emergence of a powerful administration, a legal system also developed, and, with it, legal obligations. These differ from tribal obligations in that the former are generalized, compulsory and standardized. These obligations, by allowing the concentration of a large portion of the economic output, were essential to the redistributive nature of the economic system. With the progressive standardization and generalization of compulsory obligations, several innovations had to be developed to enforce them. Among them, the counting and recording of debts was essential and it apparently took several millennia to develop a uniform numerical system: starting from 8000 BC with concrete counting via plain tokens used as calculi, to 3100 BC with the creation of abstract counting (and writing) via pictographic tablets (Schmandt-Besserat, 1992; Nissen et al., 1993; Englund, 2004). This transition from concrete counting (each thing is counted one by one, with a different method of counting for different things) to abstract counting (the same number can represent different types of items) was central to development of the unit of account. Several units of account might exist in the beginning:

> Depending on the economic sector, the means of comparison or the measure of standardized norms and duties could be silver, barley, fish, or 'labourer-day,' that is, the product of the number of workers multiplied by the number of days they worked. (Nissen et al., 1993, pp. 49–50)

But the units were progressively reduced to two (silver and barley), and apparently silver eventually became the single unit of account. Archaeologists are still not sure why silver was chosen (Hudson and Wunsch, 2004, p. 351); maybe it played a central role in the gift giving to the palace and temple (Hudson, 2004a). In any case, 'money-things' were not needed, even though these early societies used markets and had recorded debts and credits – most famously on clay 'shubati' tablets. Rather, purchases were made 'on credit' at prices set by the authorities on the basis of credit. The merchants would keep a running tally for customers, which would be settled later (usually at harvest). For example, tallies of debts for beer consumed would be kept, with the tally settled at harvest by delivery of barley at the official price and measured in the money of account. Hudson (2000; 2004a) documents such widespread use of money for accounting purposes as well as sophisticated understanding of compound interest on debt in these archaic societies.

To sum up the argument to this point, early money units appear to have been derived from weight units, created to simplify accounting. The palace authorities also had to establish price lists to value items in the money of account. Initially all of this may have been undertaken only to facilitate internal record-keeping, but eventually use of the internal unit of account spread outside the palace. Commercial transactions, rent payments, and fees, fines and taxes came to be denominated in the money of account. Use of the money of account in private transactions might have derived from debts owed to the palaces. Once a money rent, tax or tribute was levied on a village, and later on individuals, the palace would be able to obtain goods and services by issuing its own money-denominated debt in the form of tallies.

Modern: tallies and coins
Historical evidence suggests that most 'commerce' from the very earliest times was conducted on the basis of credits and debits – rather than on the basis of precious metal coins. Innes writes of the early European experience: 'For many centuries, how many we do not know, the principal instrument of commerce was neither the coin nor the private token, but the tally' (1913, p. 394). This was a 'stick of squared hazel-wood, notched in a certain manner to indicate the amount of the purchase or debt', created when the 'buyer' became a 'debtor' by accepting a good or service from the 'seller' who automatically became the 'creditor' (ibid.). 'The name of the debtor and the date of the transaction were written on two opposite sides of the stick, which was then split down the middle in such a way that the notches were cut in half, and the name and date appeared on both pieces of the tally' (ibid.). The split was stopped about an inch from the base of the stick so that one piece,

the 'stock', was longer than the other, called the 'stub' (also called the 'foil'). The creditor would retain the stock (from which our terms capital and corporate stock derive) while the debtor would take the stub (a term still used as in 'ticket stub') to ensure that the stock was not tampered with. When the debtor retired his debt, the two pieces of the tally would be matched to verify the amount of the debt.

Tallies could circulate as 'transferable, negotiable instruments' – that is, as money-things. One could deliver the stock of a tally to purchase goods and services, or to retire one's own debt. 'By their means all purchases of goods, all loans of money were made, and all debts cleared' (Innes, 1913, p. 396). A merchant holding a number of tally stocks of customers could meet with a merchant holding tally stocks against the first merchant, 'clearing' his tally stub debts by delivery of the customers' stocks. In this way, great 'fairs' were developed to act as 'clearing houses', allowing merchants 'to settle their mutual debts and credits'; the 'greatest of these fairs in England was that of St. Giles in Winchester, while the most famous probably in all Europe were those of Champagne and Brie in France, to which came merchants and bankers from all countries' (ibid.). Debts were cleared 'without the use of a single coin'; it became common practice to 'make debts payable at one or other of the fairs', and '[a]t some fairs no other business was done except the settlement of debts and credits', although retail trade was often conducted at the fairs. While conventional analysis views the primary purpose of the fairs as retail trade, Innes postulated that the retail trade originated as a sideline to the clearing-house trade.[5] Boyer-Xambeu et al. (1994) concur that twelfth- and thirteenth-century European medieval fairs were essential in the trading and net settling of bills of exchange, the latter being done in several ways, from the (rare) use of coins, to bank transfers, the carrying forward of net positions to the next fair (one of the most frequently used techniques), and the use of transferable bills of exchange (ibid., pp. 34, 38–9, 65). These bills of exchange were, along with debenture bills for intra-nation trade between cities, the preferred debt instruments used by merchants in commerce. Coins were of less significance.

Even if one accepts that much or even most trade took place on the basis of credits and debts, this does not necessarily disprove the story of the textbooks, according to which credits and debits follow the invention of coin, with paper 'fiat' money an even later invention. Perhaps coins existed before these tallies (and other records of debts), and surely the coins were made of precious metals. Perhaps the debts were made convertible to coin; indeed, perhaps such debt contracts were enforceable only in legal tender coin. If this were the case, then the credits and debts merely substituted for coin, and net debts would be settled with coin, which would not be inconsistent with the conventional story according to which barter was replaced by a commodity money (eventually, a precious metal) that evolved into stamped coins with a value regulated by embodied precious metal. However, there are several problems with such an interpretation.

First, the credits and debts are at least 2000 years older than the oldest known coins – with the earliest coins appearing only in the seventh century BC. Second, the denominations of most (but not all – see Kurke, 1999) early precious metal coins were far too high to have been used in everyday commerce. For example, the earliest coins were electrum (an alloy of silver and gold) and the most common denomination would have had a purchasing power of about ten sheep, so that 'it cannot have been a useful coin for small transactions' (Cook, 1958, p. 260). They might have sufficed for the wholesale trade of large merchants, but they could not have been used in day-to-day retail trade.[6]

Furthermore, the reported nominal value of coins does not appear to be closely regulated by precious metal content, nor was the value even stamped on the coins until recently, but rather was established through official proclamation (see below).

And, finally, it is quite unlikely that coins would have been invented to facilitate trade, for 'Phoenicians and other peoples of the East who had commercial interests managed satisfactorily without coined money' for tens of centuries (Cook, 1958, p. 260). Indeed, the introduction of coins would have been a less efficient alternative in most cases. While the textbook story argues that paper 'credit' developed to economize on precious metals, we know that lower-cost alternatives to full-bodied coin were already in use literally thousands of years before the first coins were struck. Further, hazelwood tallies or clay tablets had lower non-monetary value than did precious metals; thus it is unlikely that metal coins would be issued to circulate competitively (for example, with hazelwood tallies) unless their nominal value were well above the value of the embodied precious metal.[7]

What then are coins, what are their origins, and why are they accepted? Coins appear to have originated as 'pay tokens' (in Knapp's colourful phrase), as nothing more than evidence of debt. Many believe that the first coins were struck by government, probably by Pheidon of Argos about 630 BC (Cook, 1958, p. 257). Given the large denomination of the early coins and uniform weight (although not uniform purity – which probably could not have been tested at the time), Cook argues that 'coinage was invented to make a large number of uniform payments of considerable value in a portable and durable form, and that the person or authority making the payment was the king of Lydia' (ibid., p. 261). Further, he suggests, 'the purpose of coinage was the payment of mercenaries' (ibid.).[8] This thesis was modified 'by Kraay (1964) who suggested that governments minted coins to pay mercenaries only in order to create a medium for the payment of taxes'[9] (Redish, 1987, pp. 376–7). Crawford has argued that the evidence indicates that use of these early coins as a medium of exchange was an 'accidental consequence of the coinage', and not the reason for it (Crawford, 1970, p. 46). Instead, Crawford argued that 'the fiscal needs of the state determined the quantity of mint output and coin in circulation'; in other words, coins were intentionally minted from the beginning to provide 'state finance' (ibid.).

Similarly, Innes argued that '[t]he coins which [kings] issued were tokens of indebtedness with which they made small payments, such as the daily wages of their soldiers and sailors' (1913, p. 399). This explains the relatively large value of the coins – which were not meant to provide a medium of exchange, but rather were evidence of the state's debt to 'soldiers and sailors'. The coins were then nothing more than 'tallies' as described above – evidence of government debt.

What are the implications of this for our study of money? In our view, coins are mere tokens of the Crown's (or other issuer's) debt, a small proportion of the total 'tally' – the debt issued in payment of the Crown's expenditures.

> Just like any private individual, the government pays by giving acknowledgments of indebtedness – drafts on the Royal Treasury, or some other branch of government. This is well seen in medieval England, where the regular method used by the government for paying a creditor was by 'raising a tally' on the Customs or some other revenue-getting department, that is to say by giving to the creditor as an acknowledgment of indebtedness a wooden tally. (Ibid., pp. 397–8)[10]

But why would the Crown's subjects accept hazelwood tallies or, later, paper notes or token coins? Another quote from Innes is instructive:

> The government by law obliges certain selected persons to become its debtors. It declares that so-and-so, who imports goods from abroad, shall owe the government so much on all that he imports, or that so-and-so, who owns land, shall owe to the government so much per acre. This procedure is called levying a tax, and the persons thus forced into the position of debtors to the government must in theory seek out the holders of the tallies or other instrument acknowledg- ing a debt due by the government, and acquire from them the tallies by selling to them some commodity or in doing them some service, in exchange for which they may be induced to part with their tallies. When these are returned to the government Treasury, the taxes are paid. (Ibid., p. 398)

Each taxpayer did not have to seek out individually a Crown tally to pay taxes, for match- ing the Crown's creditors and debtors was accomplished 'through the bankers, who from the earliest days of history were always the financial agents of government' (ibid., p. 399). That is, the bank would intermediate between the person holding Crown debt and the tax- payer who required Crown debt in order to pay taxes.[11] The Exchequer began to assign debts owed to the king whereby 'the tally stock held in the Exchequer could be used by the king to pay someone else, by transferring to this third person the tally stock. Thus the king's creditor could then collect payment from the king's original debtor' (Davies, 1997, p. 150). Further, a brisk business developed to 'discount' such tallies so that the king's creditor did not need to wait for payment by the debtor.

The inordinate focus of economists on coins (and especially on government-issued coins), market exchange and precious metals, then, appears to be misplaced. The key is debt, and specifically, the ability of the state to impose a tax debt on its subjects; once it has done this, it can choose the form in which subjects can 'pay' the tax. While govern- ment could in theory require payment in the form of all the goods and services it requires, this would be quite cumbersome. Thus it becomes instead a debtor to obtain what it requires, and issues a token (hazelwood tally or coin) to indicate the amount of its indebt- edness; it then accepts its own token in payment to retire tax liabilities.[12] Certainly its tokens can also be used as a medium of exchange (and means of debt settlement among private individuals), but this derives from its ability to impose taxes and its willingness to accept its tokens, and indeed is necessitated by imposition of the tax (if one has a tax liability but is not a creditor of the Crown, one must offer things for sale to obtain the Crown's tokens).

Modern: the gold standard
In the transition from feudalism (a system in which money is used, however, not a system that one would identify as a 'monetary production economy', as Keynes put it) to capit- alism (an economic system based on production for market to realize profits), there is a period of the emergence and consolidation of national spaces of sovereignty during which kings progressively gained power over the multiple princes and lords of their territory, and battled with kings of other sovereign areas. This 'transition' period recorded several periods of monetary anarchy because of the lack of control (but also the lack of understanding – Boyer-Xambeu et al., 1994) of the monetary system by the kings and their administration. For complex reasons, the value of coins became more closely

associated with precious metal content. What had begun as merely a 'token', indicating the issuer's debt, took on a somewhat mysterious form whose value was supposed to be determined by embodied metal. Hence, while use of precious metal in coinage began for technical reasons (to reduce counterfeiting through limited access to the metal – see Heinsohn and Steiger, 1983) or cultural reasons (use of high-status material – see Kurke, 1999), regulation of the metal content came to be seen as important to maintain the coin's value. This created a problem, however, by producing an incentive to clip coins to obtain the valuable metal. When the king received his clipped coins in payment of taxes, fees and fines, he lost bullion in every 'turnover'. This made it difficult to maintain metal content in the next coinage. And, because international payments by sovereigns could require shipment of bullion, this reduced the king's ability to finance international payments. Hence began the long history of attempts to regulate coinage, to punish clippers, and to encourage a favourable flow of bullion (of which Mercantilism represents the best known example – see Wray, 1990).

The right to coin was usually delegated to private masters who worked under contract (Boyer-Xambeu et al., 1994, p. 45). The profit motive that drove the masters (but also the money-changers, who were central intermediaries in the trafficking of coins – ibid., pp. 62, 123) – led to conflicts between the king and the rest of the agents involved in the monetary system, and widespread infractions existed: clipping, debasement, billonage.[13] The coins were rude and clumsy and forgery was easy, and the laws show how common it was in spite of penalties of death, or the loss of the right hand. Every local borough could have its local mint and the moneyers were often guilty of issuing coins of debased metal or short weight to make an extra profit.

> [Henry I] decided that something must be done and he ordered a round-up of all the moneyers in 1125. A chronicle records that almost all were found guilty of fraud and had their right hands struck off. Clipping was commoner still, and when (down to 1280) the pennies were cut up to make halfpennies and farthings, a little extra clip was simple and profitable. . . . Clipping did not come to an end before the seventeenth century, when coins were machine-made with clear firm edges. . . . (Quigguin, 1964, pp. 57–8)

Thus kings actively fought any alteration of the intrinsic value of coins which represented an alteration of the homogeneous monetary system that they tried to impose. This preoccupation also fuelled the belief that intrinsic value determines the value of money.

However, kings were actually responsible for the nominal value of coins, and sometimes were forced to change that (Boyer-Xambeu et al., 1994), by crying them up or down. Crying down the coinage (reducing the value of a coin as measured in the unit of account – recall that nominal values were not usually stamped on coins until recently) was a common method of increasing taxes. If one had previously delivered one coin to pay taxes, now one had to deliver two if the sovereign lowered the nominal value of coins by half (also representing an effective default on half the Crown's debt). Any nominal change in the monetary system 'was carried out by royal proclamation in all the public squares, fairs, and markets, at the instigation of the ordinary provincial judges: bailiffs, seneschals, and lieutenants' (ibid., p. 47). The higher the probability of default by the sovereign (of which crying down the coinage represented just one example) on his debts (including coins and tallies), the more desirable was an embodied precious metal to be used in recording those debts. In other words, coins with high precious metal content would be demanded of sovereigns that could not be trusted.[14] This probably explains, at least in part, the attempt to operate gold (or silver) standards during the transition from monarchies to democracies that occurred with the rise of capitalism and the modern monetary production economy. Unfortunately, this relatively brief experiment with gold has misled several generations of policymakers and economists who sought the essence of money in a commodity – precious metals – and ignored the underlying credits and debts.

Modern: the return to 'fiat' money

Eventually, we returned to the use of 'pure token' money, that is, use of 'worthless' paper or entries on balance sheets as we abandoned use of precious metal coins and then even use of a gold reserve to 'back up' paper notes. Those who had become accustomed to think of precious metal as 'money' were horrified at the prospect of using a 'fiat money' – a mere promise to pay. However, all monetary instruments had always been debts. Even a gold coin really was a debt of the Crown, with the Crown determining its nominal value by proclamation and by accepting it in payment of fees, fines and taxes at that denomination. The 'real' or relative value (that is, purchasing power in terms of goods and services) of monetary instruments is complexly determined, but ultimately depends on what must be done to obtain them. The monetary instruments issued by the authority (whether they take the form of gold coins, green paper, or balance sheet entries) are desired because the issuing authority will accept them in payment (of fees, fines, taxes, tribute and tithes) and because the receivers need to make these payments. If the population does not need to make payments to the authority, or if the authority refuses to accept the monetary instruments it has issued, then the value of those monetary instruments will fall toward their value as commodities. In the case of entries on balance sheets or paper notes, that is approximately zero; in the case of gold coins, their value cannot fall much below the value of the bullion. For this reason, the gold standard may have been desirable in an era of monarchs who mismanaged the monetary system – even though the gold standard represents something of an aberration with respect to money's history.

Through the nineteenth and early twentieth centuries, governments frequently faced crises that forced them off gold; they would attempt to return but again face another crisis. In the aftermath of the Second World War, the Bretton Woods system adopted a dual gold–dollar standard that offered more flexibility than the gold standard. However, this system ultimately proved to also have significant flaws and effectively came to an end when the USA abandoned gold. We thus came full circle back to a system based on 'nothing' but credits and debits – IOUs. With the rise of modern capitalism and the evolution of participatory democracy, elected representatives could choose the unit of account (the currency), impose taxes in that currency, and issue monetary instruments denominated in the currency in government payments. The private sector could accept these monetary instruments without fear that the government would suddenly refuse them in payment of taxes, and (usually) with little fear that government would 'cry down' the currency by reducing the nominal value of its debts. At this point, a gold standard was not only unnecessary, but also hindered operation of government in the public interest. Unfortunately, substantial confusion still exists concerning the nature of money and the proper policy to maintain a stable monetary system.

This brief history of money makes several important points. First, the monetary system did not start with some commodities used as media of exchange, evolving progressively toward precious metals, coins, paper money, and finally credits on books and computers. Credit came first and coins, latecomers in the list of monetary instruments, are never pure assets but are always debt instruments – IOUs that happen to be stamped on metal. Second, many debt instruments other than coins were used, and preferred, in markets. Third, even if debt instruments can be created by anybody, the establishment of a unit of account was (almost always) the prerogative of a powerful authority. Without this unit of account, no debt instruments could have become monetary instruments because they could not have been recorded in a generalized unit of account but rather only as a specific debt.

Conclusion: modern money
In this chapter we briefly examined the origins of money, finding them in debt contracts and more specifically in tax debt that is levied in money form. Similarly, we argued that coins were nothing more than tokens of the indebtedness of the Crown, or, later, the government's treasury. Significantly, even though coins were long made of precious metal, it was only relatively recently that gold standards were adopted in an attempt to stabilize gold prices to try to stabilize the value of money. It would be a mistake to try to infer too much about the nature of money from the operation of a gold standard that was a deviation from usual monetary practice. Throughout history, monetary systems relied on debts and credits denominated in a unit of account, or currency, established by the authority. Adoption of a gold standard merely meant that the authority would then have to convert its debts to gold on demand at a fixed rate of conversion. This did not really mean that gold was money, but rather that the official price of gold would be pegged by the authority. Hence even the existence of a gold standard – no matter how historically insignificant it might be – is not inconsistent with the alternative view of the history of money.

In truth, we can probably never discover the origins of money. Nor is this crucial for understanding the nature of the operation of modern monetary systems, which have been variously called state money or Chartalist money systems (Knapp, 1924; Keynes, 1930; Goodhart, 1998; Wray, 1998). Most modern economies have a state money that is quite clearly defined by the state's 'acceptation' at 'public pay offices' (Knapp, 1924). The operation of a state money can be outlined succinctly: the state names the unit of account (the dollar), imposes tax liabilities in that unit (a five-dollar head tax), and denominates its own 'fiat money' liabilities in that account (a one-dollar note). It then issues its own liabilities in payment, and accepts those in payment of taxes. As Davies notes, this necessary link between public spending and money was far more obvious in the Middle Ages:

> Minting and taxing were two sides of the same coins of royal prerogative, or, we would say, monetary and fiscal policies were inextricably connected. Such relationships in the Middle Ages were of course far more direct and therefore far more obvious than is the case today. In the period up to 1300 the royal treasury and the Royal Mint were literally together as part of the King's household. (Davies, 2002, p. 147)

There are two real-world complications that require some comment. First, most payments in modern economies do not involve use of a government-issued (state, 'fiat') currency; indeed, even taxes are almost exclusively paid using (private, 'fiat') bank money. Second, government money is not emitted into the economy solely through treasury purchases.

In fact, the central bank supplies most of our currency (paper notes), and it is the proximate supplier of almost all of the bank reserves that are from the perspective of the non-banking public perfect substitutes for treasury liabilities. Obviously if we simply consolidate the central bank and the treasury, calling the conglomerate 'the state', we eliminate many complications. When one uses a bank liability to pay 'the state', it is really the bank that provides the payment services, delivering the state's fiat money, resulting in a debit of the bank's reserves. When the state spends, it provides a cheque that will be deposited in a bank, leading to a reserve credit on the books of the bank. Hence, as Innes long ago argued, banks act as 'intermediaries' between government and the public.

We will not pursue here any of this accounting in more detail; readers are referred to Wray (1998) and Bell (2000). (See also Chapter 5 on tax-driven money in this volume.) The only thing that must be understood is that the sovereign state 'spends' by emitting its own liability (mostly taking the form of a credit to banking system reserves). A tax payment is just the opposite: the state taxes by reducing its own liability (mostly taking the form of a debit to banking system reserves). In reality, the state cannot 'spend' its tax receipts, which are just reductions of outstanding state liabilities. When a household issues an IOU to a neighbour after borrowing a gallon of milk, it will receive back the IOU when the debt is repaid. The household cannot then 'spend' its own IOU; rather, it simply tears up the note (this was also true with gold coins, which were government liabilities: once received in payment of taxes, coins were usually melted down to verify the gold content and ensure that clipping did not occur – Grierson, 1975, p. 123). This is effectively what the state does with its tax 'receipts'. Essentially, then, the state spends by crediting bank accounts and taxes by debiting them. And all of this works only because the state has first exerted its sovereignty by imposing a tax liability on the private sector.

It is important to note that there is a whole other story about the rise of banks and the evolution of the private banking system. Orthodoxy presents banks as intermediaries between 'savers' and 'borrowers', and posits a 'deposit multiplier' that constrains bank lending to the quantity of reserves supposedly controlled by the central bank. We do not have the space to explore these issues in any detail, but reject the orthodox approach (see Wray, 1990). Above we noted the intermediary function played by banks, used by government to accomplish its fiscal activities. In addition, banks play a critical function in all capitalist economies as 'creators of credit' – that is, banks accept IOUs of borrowers and issue their own IOUs in the form of bank deposits. These are used by the non-bank public as means of payment and stores of value. In most cases, credits and debits are cleared on the balance sheets of these private banks, while banks use the liabilities of the government only for net clearing (among banks and with the government). In truth, banks are never reserve constrained – indeed, all modern central banks ensure that banks have the reserves required or desired. All of this is critically important for the operation of modern 'monetary production economies', but is not so essential for our study of the origins of money. In a sense, the activities of the private banks can be seen as 'derivative', as their credits and debits are all denominated in the state money of account, and as the money-things issued by the state are used for ultimate clearing. (See Gardiner, 2004; Wray, 1990; 1998.)

We thus conclude this story about the origins and nature of money. Money is a complex social institution, not simply a 'thing' used to lubricate market exchanges. What is most important about money is that it serves as a unit of account, the unit in which debts and credits (as well as market prices) are denominated. It must be social – a socially recognized measure, almost always chosen by some sort of central authority. Monetary instruments are never commodities; rather, they are always debts, IOUs, denominated in the socially recognized unit of account. Some of these monetary instruments circulate as 'money-things' among third parties, but even 'money-things' are always debts – whether they happen to take a physical form such as a gold coin or green paper note. While one can imagine a 'free market' economy in which private participants settle on a unit of account and in which all goods and assets circulate on the basis of private debts and credits, in practice in all modern monetary systems the state plays an active role in the monetary system. It chooses the unit of account; it imposes tax liabilities in that unit; and it issues the money-thing that is used by private markets for ultimate clearing. Any story of money that leaves out an important role for the state represents little more than fantasy, a story of what might have been, that sheds little light on the operation of real-world monetary systems.

Notes

1. See also Grierson (1977, p. 16) and Keynes (1930 (1976), p. 3; 1982, p. 252).
2. Of course not all acknowledgements of debt are monetary in nature; that is, they do not respect the following characteristics. One may, for example, give to another person a piece of rock and promise to take it back, but, if no relation to a unit of account is established, the piece of rock is just a reminder that someone owes someone else something. In this sense, the famous 'stone-money' does not seem to qualify as a monetary debt instrument.
3. Early coins do not have any value in terms of unit of account written on them. They have names (like 'gros tournois', 'penny', or 'dime') but this does not say anything about the unit of account. A full description requires the statement of the unit of account: a 'penny of 2 pence' or a 'gros of 4 deniers', etc. (Grierson, 1975, p. 88).
4. See Heinsohn and Steiger (1983; 2000) for the importance of private property for the history of money.
5. Admittedly, the view expounded by Innes is controversial and perhaps too extreme. What is important and surely correct, however, is his recognition of the importance of the clearing-house trade to these fairs. He also noted that such clearing-house fairs were held in ancient Greece and Rome, and in Mexico at the time of the conquest.
6. It is true that there are coins of base metal with much lower nominal value, but it is difficult to explain why base metal was accepted in retail trade when the basis of money is supposed to be precious metal.
7. It is often asserted that coins were invented to facilitate long-distance trade. 'The evidence, however, is against the earliest coins having been used to facilitate trade of such a kind, for the contents of hoards points overwhelmingly to their local circulation' (Grierson, 1977, p. 10).
8. Grierson (1977, p. 10) also advances this thesis.
9. Crawford (1970, p. 46) suggests that '[c]oinage was probably invented in order that a large number of state payments might be made in a convenient form and there is no reason to suppose that it was ever issued by Rome for any other purpose than to enable the state to make payments . . . [o]nce issued, coinage was demanded back by the state in payment of taxes.'
10. The wooden tallies were supplemented after the late 1670s by paper 'orders of the exchequer', which in turn were accepted in payment of taxes (Grierson, 1975, p. 34). The 'tallia divenda' developed to allow the king to issue an exchequer tally for payment for goods and services delivered to the court.
11. This poses the interesting question of the origins of the word 'bank'. As Kregel (1998, pp. 15ff.) notes, 'It is generally believed that the English word "bank" is derived from the Italian "banco", which is thought to derive from the bench or long table used by money changer. . . . The similarity between the two words is misleading, and most probably mistaken. Rather, the historical evidence suggests that the origin of the English "bank" comes from the German "banck." This is the German equivalent of the Italian "monte", which means a "mound" or a "store" where things are kept for future use. . . . The modern English equivalent would be "fund", which is the name used in England for the public debts of the English sovereign.'
12. That is, even most private transactions took place on credit rather than through use of coin as a medium of exchange. McIntosh (1988, p. 561) notes in a study of London of 1300–1600; 'Any two people might build up a number of outstanding debts to each other. As long as goodwill between the individuals remained firm, the balances could go uncollected for years. When the parties chose to settle on an amicable basis, they normally named auditors who totaled all current unpaid debts or deliveries and determined the sum which had to be paid to clear the slate.'

13. Billonage is defined as: '1) sale of coins at their legal value after buying them at the price of unminted metal; 2) taking coins of a better intrinsic out of circulation' (Boyer-Xambeu et al., 1994, p. 209).
14. Indeed, the creation of the Bank of England can be traced to a default by the Crown on tally debts that made merchants reluctant to accept the king's promises to pay. Hence the Bank of England was created specifically to buy Crown debt and to issue its own notes, which would circulate (with the help of laws that effectively eliminated circulation of bank notes issued by rivals). See Wray (1990).

References

Bell, Stephanie (2000), 'Do taxes and bonds finance government spending?', *Journal of Economic Issues*, **34**: 603–20.

Bell, Stephanie, John F. Henry and L. Randall Wray (2004), 'A Chartalist critique of John Locke's theory of property, accumulation, and money: or is it moral to trade your nuts for gold?', *Review of Social Economy*, **LXII**(1): 51–65.

Bohannan, Paul and George Dalton (1962), *Markets in Africa*, Evanston, IL: Northwestern University Press.

Boyer-Xambeu, Marie-Thérèse, Ghislain Deleplace and Lucien Gillard (1994), *Private Money and Public Currencies*, New York: M.E. Sharpe.

Cook, Robert M. (1958), 'Speculation on the origins of coinage', *Historia*, **7**: 257–62.

Crawford, Michael H. (1970), 'Money and exchange in the Roman world', *Journal of Roman Studies*, **60**: 40–48.

Dalton, George (1965), 'Primitive money', *American Anthropologist*, **67**: 44–65. Reprinted in G. Dalton (ed.), *Tribal and Peasant Economies*, 254–81, Austin, TX: University of Texas Press.

Dalton, George (1971), *Primitive, Archaic, and Modern Economies*, Boston: Beacon Press.

Davies, Glynn (1997), *A History of Money from Ancient Times to the Present Day*, 2nd edn, Cardiff: University of Wales Press.

Davies, Glynn (2002), *A History of Money from Ancient Times to the Present Day*, 3rd edn, Cardiff: University of Wales Press.

Englund, Robert K. (2004), 'Proto-Cuneiform account books and journals', in M. Hudson and C. Wunsch (eds), *Creating Economic Order*, 23–46, Bethesda, MD: CDL Press.

Gardiner, Geoffrey W. (2004), 'The primacy of trade debts in the development of money', in L.R. Wray (ed.), *Credit and State Theories of Money: The contributions of A. Mitchell Innes*, 128–72, Cheltenham, UK and Northampton, MA, USA: Edward Elgar.

Goodhart, Charles A.E. (1998), 'Two concepts of money: implications for the analysis of optimal currency areas', *European Journal of Political Economy*, **14**: 407–32.

Grierson, Philip (1975), *Numismatics*, London: Oxford University Press.

Grierson, Philip (1977), *The Origins of Money*, London: Athlone Press. Reprinted in G. Dalton (ed.), *Research in Economic Anthropology*, Vol. 1, Greenwich, CT: JAI Press, 1978.

Grierson, Philip (1979), *Dark Age Numismatics*, London: Variorum Reprints.

Heinsohn, Gunnar and Otto Steiger (1983), 'Private property, debts and interest, or: the origin of money and the rise and fall of monetary economics', *Studi Economici*, **21**: 3–56.

Heinsohn, Gunnar and Otto Steiger (2000), 'The property theory of interest and money', in J. Smithin (ed.), *What is Money?*, 67–100, London: Routledge.

Henry, John F. (2004), 'The social origins of money: The case of Egypt', in L.R. Wray (ed.), *Credit and State Theories of Money*, 79–98, Cheltenham, UK and Northampton, MA, USA: Edward Elgar.

Hudson, Michael and Cornelia Wunsch (2004), *Creating Economic Order*, Bethesda, MD: CDL Press.

Hudson, Michael (2000), 'Reconstructing the origins of interest-bearing debt and the logic of clean slates', in M. Hudson and M. Van De Mieroop (eds), *Debt and Economic Renewal in the Ancient Near East*, 7–58, Bethesda, MD: CDL Press.

Hudson, Michael (2004a), 'The development of money-of-account in Sumer's temples', in M. Hudson and C. Wunsch (eds), *Creating Economic Order*, 303–29, Bethesda, MD: CDL Press.

Hudson, Michael (2004b), 'The archaeology of money: debt versus barter theories of money's origins', in L.R. Wray (ed.), *Credit and State Theories of Money: The contributions of A. Mitchell Innes*, 99–127, Cheltenham, UK and Northampton, MA, USA: Edward Elgar.

Ingham, Geoffrey (2004), 'The emergence of capitalist credit money', in L.R. Wray (ed.), *Credit and State Theories of Money: The contributions of A. Mitchell Innes*, 173–222, Cheltenham, UK and Northampton, MA, USA: Edward Elgar.

Innes, A. Mitchell (1913), 'What is money?', *Banking Law Journal*, **30**(5): 377–408. Reprinted in L.R. Wray (ed.), *Credit and State Theories of Money*, 14–49, Cheltenham, UK and Northampton, MA, USA: Edward Elgar, 2004.

Innes, A. Mitchell (1914), 'The credit theory of money', *Banking Law Journal*, **31**(2): 151–68. Reprinted in L.R. Wray (ed.), *Credit and State Theories of Money*, 50–78, Cheltenham, UK and Northampton, MA, USA: Edward Elgar, 2004.

Innes, A. Mitchell (1932), *Martyrdom in our Times*, London: Williams & Norgate.

Keynes, John M. (1930), *A Treatise on Money*, Vols I and II (1976), New York: Harcourt, Brace & Co.

Keynes, John M. (1982), *The Collected Writings of John Maynard Keynes, Volume XXVIII*, Moggridge, D. (ed.), London: Macmillan.

Knapp, Georg F. (1924), *The State Theory of Money*. Partially reprinted by Augustus M. Kelley, 1973.

Kraay, Colin M. (1964), 'Hoards, small change and the origin of coinage', *Journal of Hellenic Studies*, **84**: 76–91.

Kregel, Jan A. (1998), *The Past and Future of Banks*, Quaderni di Ricerche, No. 21, Rome: Ente 'Luigi Einaudi'.

Kurke, Leslie (1999), *Coins, Bodies, Games, and Gold*, Princeton, NJ: Princeton University Press.

Maddox, Thomas, Esq. (1969), *The History and Antiquities of the Exchequer of the Kings of England in Two Periods*, Vols 1 & 2, 2nd edn, New York: Greenwood Press.

McIntosh, Marjorie K. (1988), 'Money lending on the periphery of London, 1300–1600', *Albion*, **20**(4): 557–71.

Nissen, Hansen J., Peter Damerow and Robert K. Englund (1993), *Archaic Bookkeeping*, Chicago, IL: Chicago University Press.

Peacock, Mark S. (2003–4), 'State, money, catallaxy: underlabouring for a Chartalist theory of money', *Journal of Post Keynesian Economics*, **26**(2): 205–25.

Polanyi, Karl (1957), 'The semantics of money-uses', reprinted in G. Dalton (ed.), *Primitive, Archaic and Modern Economies*, 175–203, Boston, MA: Beacon Press, 1968.

Quigguin, A. Hingston (1964), *The Story of Money*, New York: Roy Publisher.

Redish, Angela (1987), 'Coinage, development of', in J. Eatwell, M. Murray and P. Newman (eds), *The New Palgrave Dictionary of Money and Finance*, 376–7, London: Macmillan.

Schmandt-Besserat, Denise (1992), *Before Writing*, Vol. 1, Austin, TX: University of Texas Press.

Wray, L. Randall (1990), *Money and Credit in Capitalist Economies: The Endogenous Money Approach*, Aldershot, UK and Brookfield, USA: Edward Elgar.

Wray, L. Randall (1998), *Understanding Modern Money: The Key to Full Employment and Price Stability*, Cheltenham, UK and Lyme, USA: Edward Elgar.

Wray, L. Randall (2004), *Credit and State Theories of Money: The Contributions of A. Mitchell Innes*, Cheltenham, UK and Northampton, MA, USA: Edward Elgar.

Zelizer, Viviana A. (1989), 'The social meaning of money: "special money"', *American Journal of Sociology*, **95**(2): 342–77.

2 Endogenous money: accommodationist
Marc Lavoie*

Endogenous money is a key feature of post-Keynesian monetary economics. Kaldor (1970; 1982) and Moore (1988) were the most vocal advocates of a theory of endogenous money in the Anglo-Saxon world. Their ideas were mainly developed in the 1980s, although such ideas were also outlined as early as the 1950s. One could also go back to earlier 'heterodox' classical authors, such as Tooke and Fullarton in the early nineteenth century, as well as members of the Austrian school in the early twentieth century, among whom we may include Wicksell, whose pure credit economy now benefits from an extraordinary revival among mainstream economists.

Both Kaldor and Moore drew graphs representing either the money supply or the credit supply as completely flat curves in the credit-money and interest rate space. Both argued that the supply of high-powered money and money ought to be considered as endogenous and demand-determined. By contrast, (short-term) interest rates were viewed as exogenous, under the control of the central bank, rather than market-determined, and liquidity preference explanations were relegated to the sideline. Both asserted that there could never be any excess money supply, and hence that inflation could not be caused by an excessively high growth rate of the money supply. In addition, these authors claimed that the central bank could not directly control the supply of money, and could not exert quantity constraints on the reserves of banks. These positions came to be known as 'accommodationism' or 'horizontalism'. We shall stick to the term 'horizontalism', which we believe is the more correct way to characterize authors belonging to this tradition.[1]

As the endogenous money point of view became more popular among post-Keynesian authors, the opinions expressed by the originators of these views came under tight scrutiny in the 1990s, and a slightly different stance, which came to be known as the 'structuralist' or 'liquidity preference' version of endogenous money, emerged from these criticisms. Structuralists claimed that horizontalists over-simplified the money supply process.

From various sides, structuralists made the following critiques. First, central banks could not always accommodate the need for reserves; surely, in some circumstances, they would only partially accommodate. This would bring on structural changes, such as liability management, not analysed by proponents of horizontalism – a second critique. Third, horizontalists did not and could not take into account credit rationing and the lack of commercial bank accommodation to credit demand. Fourth, even if central banks did fully accommodate the demand for reserves, this did not mean that the supply for credit would be horizontal, since endogenous forces would push interest rate markups upwards as economic activity increased, as a result of rising debt or illiquid ratios, either from the borrower's or the lender's side. Thus, in general, the supply for reserves and the supply of loans ought to be represented as upward-sloping curves. Fifth, horizontalists paid insufficient attention to the impact of market forces on long-term rates of interest but also on the short-term rate of interest targeted by the central bank. In other words, issues of liquidity preference had been ignored. Finally, it was pointed out that endogenous money had only been considered within the framework of a closed economy.

The 'structuralists' helped to put in the limelight some issues that had been discussed only sketchily by Kaldor and Moore. Indeed, in a sense, as Fontana (2003, p. 309) has put it, 'structuralists took over where the accommodationists have stopped'. However, in doing so, some 'structuralists' have set up a 'horizontalist strawman', attributing to horizontalists opinions that they have never held. On most issues, I will argue that the horizontalist viewpoint is still preferable, and that it has been vindicated by recent changes in the operating procedures of central banks. At the very least, critics must recognize that the horizontalist story is highly relevant to the current monetary process put in place in the more important central banks.

In the early 1990s, most post-Keynesian or Marxist authors considered that the approach advocated by Moore was controversial and 'extreme' (Davidson, 1989, p. 490; Isaac, 1991, p. 104; Wray, 1992, p. 297; Targetti, 1992, p. 275; Musella and Panico, 1995, p. xxvii). The few post-Keynesian economists that could said to be in sync with Moore and Kaldor on monetary theory were Godley and Cripps (1983), Smithin (1994), Rogers (1989), Arestis and Eichner (1988), Eichner (1987), Thirlwall (1994), Hicks (1982, ch. 19), myself (Lavoie, 1992; 1996), as well as a few Sraffian (Pivetti, 1998) and circuitist authors (Parguez and Seccareccia, 2000), plus the iconoclast central banker, Goodhart (1989).

I would argue that horizontalism is once again a reputable version of endogenous money, for a variety of reasons. First, the weaknesses of some structuralist claims have been highlighted (Fullwiler, 2006). Second, new authors have given some energetic impetus to the horizontalist position, by showing that horizontalist authors had responded to many of their critiques from the very start (Rochon, 1999; 2001a), or by adopting a horizontalist approach to modelling (Hein and Ochsen, 2003; Zezza and Dos Santos, 2004; Docherty, 2005). Third, the study of some well-known earlier post-Keynesian authors, such as Robinson, Kahn and Kalecki, has shown that these authors did give some support to the horizontalist viewpoint (Rochon, 2001b; Sawyer, 2001). Fourth, formal comprehensive post-Keynesian models have provided support for some horizontalist claims (Godley, 1999). Fifth, new developments in New Keynesian monetary theory, based on endogenous money, have helped to show that the horizontalist position was far from 'extreme'.[2] And finally, the new operating procedures pursued by central banks, which are much more transparent now, pierce through the veil of rhetoric and seem to indicate that 'horizontalism' is a most appropriate description of the money supply process. This, with the renewed study of the link between government expenditures and central bank money, has led some previously sceptic post-Keynesian authors to offer their support to (most) horizontalist claims (Wray, 1998; 2004a).

Modern operating procedures vindicate the horizontalist position

There are two kinds of monetary systems: *asset-based* and *overdraft* financial systems. Asset-based financial systems, also called *financial markets economy* or the *auto-economy*, are systems where producing firms and financial firms hold stocks of financial assets that allow them to face fluctuations in their income and capital needs, without the obligation to borrow. By contrast, in an overdraft economy, firms are always in need of advances from banks, and banks are always indebted to the central bank. In such overdraft systems – which is relevant to most financial systems in the world – commercial banks hold no or very small amounts of Treasury bills. The only means to acquire banknotes or compulsory reserves is to borrow them from the central bank (Le Bourva, 1992). The central bank has no choice but to provide these on demand, at the cost of its choice, however. By contrast, structuralists insist that reserves are quantity-constrained in the case of an asset-based economy (Pollin, 1991, 1996).

The purpose of this section is to show that the supply of high-powered money is equally endogenous in the asset-based Anglo-Saxon financial systems. 'The logic of a monetary production economy is such that the consequences of an overdraft economy also apply to an economy with open market operations . . . whatever the actual financial institutions' (Lavoie, 1992, p. 179). This was more difficult to demonstrate previously, because in the Anglo-Saxon asset-based financial systems, more complex institutional features as well as monetarist rhetoric used to hide the reversed causality and the essential mechanisms at work. However, the new operating procedures put in place by central banks in North America and elsewhere help to cut through the veil of complexities inherent to asset-based financial systems. We first examine the Canadian system, which, being a pure example of the newly fashionable *channel* (*tunnel* or *corridor*) system, contains some features of the overdraft system.[3] This will help us to understand the American system, which has not yet reached the channel system stage.

Zero-reserve requirements at the Bank of Canada
Before 1991, Canada had a nearly textbook monetary system: chartered banks faced reserve ratios on their deposits, advances to banks at the discount window were strongly discouraged, and open market operations by the Bank of Canada were frequent. There are now no reserve requirements. Banks may borrow freely from the Bank at the bank rate if they so desire (provided they have some collateral), and banks can deposit excess reserves at a positive rate, 50 basis points below the bank rate. There is an official target overnight rate, which is in the middle of the horizontal band delineated by the first two rates.

In Canada, as in Sweden, Switzerland, Australia and New Zealand, there are no compulsory reserves, and banks hold virtually no free reserves. The amount of high-powered money is limited to the amount of banknotes held by the general public or in the vaults of commercial banks. The supply of high-powered money is obviously fully endogenous since, as noted by a researcher at the Bank of Canada, 'withdrawals of bank notes from the central bank are made as needed by the clearing institutions' (Clinton, 1991, p. 7).

In Canada, as in many other countries, banks and other direct clearers are required by law to settle their payment obligations on accounts at the Bank of Canada. If there were no transactions with the public sector, or with the foreign exchange fund, the level of net settlement balances would always be zero (in Canada there are no *reserves*, only *settlement balances*, which are called *clearing balances* in the USA and *working balances* in Europe). Since a debit for any bank corresponds to a credit for some other bank, the *net* amount of settlement balances in this pure credit economy cannot be any different from zero (Black, 1970). By contrast, the *gross* amount of settlement balances would vary according to the dispersion in incoming and outgoing payment flows between banks. A given amount of transactions can give rise to widely different amounts of gross settlement balances.

However, the situation is modified when government transactions are entered into the clearing system, or when the central bank intervenes on foreign exchange markets (Mosler, 1997–98; Wray, 1998). As is well known, when the central bank purchases foreign currency to keep the exchange rate fixed, this adds to the reserves or the settlement balances of commercial banks. Similarly, when governments pay for their expenditures, by making cheques on their central bank account, which are later deposited at banks, these transfers add to reserves. On the other hand, when private agents pay their taxes by writing a cheque to the government, this transaction withdraws reserves or settlement balances from the financial system once the cheque is deposited in the government account at the central bank. Similarly, when banks acquire banknotes, this reduces their settlement balances.

The Bank of Canada normally acts in such a way that the level of settlement balances in the financial system by the end of the day is exactly equal to zero. 'To maintain the level of settlement balances at zero, the Bank must neutralize the net impact of any public sector flows between the Bank of Canada's balance sheet and that of the financial system' (Howard, 1998, p. 59). To achieve this, the Bank transfers government deposits in and out of its own accounts, towards or from, government deposit accounts held at various commercial banks, or it engages into repo operations. In terms of standard terminology, one could say that these actions are part of the *defensive* operations of the Bank of Canada. The extent and the importance of these *defensive* operations are nothing new, however; under the old procedures, they were already at the centre of the money supply process (Clinton, 1991, pp. 7–8).

The Bank effects most of its neutralization operations late in the afternoon, after *all* settlement transactions with the government are completed. When the Bank makes its final cash management decisions, it knows with perfect certainty the amounts that need to be transferred between government accounts at the Bank and government accounts at commercial banks to achieve complete neutralization of the public sector flows. On the other hand, when banks are given the opportunity to have a last go on the overnight market in the evening, they know with certainty what their clearing balances are.

The new procedures ensure a determinate demand for net settlement balances – equal to zero. In normal times, as confirmed by Whitesell (2003, p. 10), both the supply and the demand for settlement balances are given by a vertical line arising from the zero level of settlement balances. 'Since equality of demand and supply is represented by the intersection of two vertical lines (at zero quantity), on any given day the precise overnight rate at which the market settles is indeterminate within the 50-basis-point operating band. The actual rate will be influenced by a variety of technical factors, such as the size and distribution of clearing imbalances among the banks' (Clinton, 1997, p. 11).

The overnight rate of interest could thus be any rate within the operating band. One would expect, however, the overnight rate to be right in the middle of the operating band on average. If the target overnight rate is set as the mid-point of the operating band, there is some likelihood that it will be exactly realized. In reality, it turns out that the overnight market rate is systematically equal to the target rate set by the Bank of Canada. With the new procedures, tied to zero-reserve requirements, near-perfect certainty on the demand for settlement balances and absolute control over the supply of settlement balances, the Bank is able to control the overnight rate to the tune of one basis point.

Another feature that is worth noting is that overnight rates change in response to target rates without central banks having to add or subtract any amount of settlement balances. As Woodford (2002a, p. 89) points out, in channel systems such as the Canadian one, 'the central bank can shift the rate at which the interbank market is likely to clear by shifting the interest rates associated with the two standing facilities without any immediate need for an adjustment of the supply of clearing balances'. The target rate set by the central bank, with its operating band, provides an anchor to the financial system. The anchor is credible because the Bank of Canada has the capacity to enforce it. If the overnight rate were to wander away from the target, the Bank could get it back on track (Rogers and Rymes, 2000).

In systems such as the Canadian one, which is an asset-based financial system, the veil of open market operations is superseded by the transparency of the zero-reserve requirement. It becomes nearly as obvious that the day-to-day role of the central bank is to provide on demand the required level of high-powered money. It is a fully endogenous variable, while the overnight rate is the exogenous interest rate, determined by the target rate set by the Bank of Canada. Within an overdraft or zero-reserve system, commercial banks cannot be reserve-constrained. This part of the structuralist story just does not hold up.

The defensive operations of the Fed
The American financial system obeys the same logical requirements that rule overdraft economies or financial systems with zero-reserve requirements. The Fed is mainly pursuing *interest maintenance operations* (Mosler, 1997–98, p. 170; Wray, 1998, p. 87). Neo-Chartalist post-Keynesians have made this quite clear over the last years. For instance, Wray (1998, p. 115) claims that 'Fed actions with regards to quantities of reserves are necessarily defensive. The only discretion the Fed has is in interest rate determination.' Similarly, Mosler (2002, p. 422) writes that 'loans (which create deposits) have not been constrained by reserve availability per se, but only by the interest rate that results from Fed action.'

This has been recently confirmed by an institutional analysis of the daily actions and tactics of the Fed, more specifically those of the Trading Desk at the New York Fed. Fullwiler (2003, p. 857) argues that 'the Desk's actions are generally defensive in nature', attempting to provide the adequate supply of balances based on the intra-day, average maintenance period and seasonal needs of the banks. Indeed, this is also how the European Central Bank operates (Bindseil and Seitz, 2001, p. 11). Fullwiler (2003, p. 869) concludes that 'the primary objective of the Desk's open market operations has never been to "increase/decrease reserves to provide for expansion/contraction of the money supply" but rather to maintain the integrity of the payments system through provision of sufficient quantities of Fed balances such that the targeted funds rate is achieved'. Thus the full endogeneity of the supply of high-powered money does not in general arise from the 'lender of last resort' role of the central bank or from its willingness to engage into open market operations; rather it arises from the procedures through which the central bank can operate the clearinghouse.

Some post-Keynesians have pointed out long ago that open market operations had little or nothing to do with monetary policy. For instance,

> It is usually assumed that a change in the Fed's holdings of government securities will lead to a change, with the same sign attached, in the reserves of the commercial banking system. It was the failure to observe this relationship empirically which led us, in constructing the monetary-financial block of our model, to try to find some other way of representing the effect of the Fed's open market operations on the banking system. (Eichner, 1986, p. 100)

That other way is that 'the Fed's purchases or sales of government securities are intended primarily to offset the flows into or out of the domestic monetary-financial system' (Eichner, 1987, p. 849).

The weak exogeneity of the federal funds rate
Still, in the USA there have been important fluctuations in the overnight rate, relative to the federal funds rate target. Similar deviations between the target rate and the actual overnight rate can be observed with the new European Central Bank. None the less, over recent years, the *average* federal funds rate is virtually equal to its average target rate.

In view of these results, it is easier to understand why some American post-Keynesians are reluctant to recognize that reserves are fully endogenous and that interest rates are set exogenously by central banks. In the USA, as in Europe, the central bank does not appear to have full control over the shortest of the rates – the overnight rate. Interest rates under the control of the central bank do not appear to be truly exogenous. Their levels seem to depend on the interaction between the demand for and the supply of reserves. It should be noted that this feature of the American system was underlined by Moore (1988, p. 124) from the outset, when he wrote that 'the federal funds rate is predetermined within a small range, ordinarily within fifty or sixty basis points . . . It is not *directly* set by the Fed.'

Some economists (Pollin, 1996; Dow, 1997, p. 73) have taken advantage of this institutional feature to argue that the Fed is somehow constrained by market forces when setting the federal funds rate. But this interpretation was rejected by Moore (1988, p. 124): 'It is . . . disingenuous and misleading to declare that the funds rate is now "market-determined". Market forces are really attempting to forecast the behavior of the Fed itself.' However, there may be circumstances where central bankers, lacking strong views regarding the direction monetary policy should take, will change the target interest rate in the way expected by market opinion (Wray, 2004b). Notwithstanding the above, the Fed instructs the Desk to achieve its target rate.

Thus the Fed is pursuing essentially defensive operations, just like the Bank of Canada. The difference is that the Fed does not have perfect information about the drains on reserves that must be compensated for, nor does it have perfect information about the daily or even hourly demand for free reserves or for discount window borrowing; as a result, the Fed cannot perfectly equate supply to demand at the target funds rate (or at the actual rate). In the USA, over the reserve-averaging period, the Fed supplies high-powered money on demand, as in overdraft economies or in zero-reserve financial systems, but it is unable to do so perfectly on a day-to-day basis. In other words, the apparent *non-defensive* operations arise inadvertently. They are an artefact.

Thus perhaps it would be best to distinguish between 'defensive' and 'accommodating' behaviour, as done by Eichner (1987, p. 847) and Rochon (1999, p. 164). In my opinion, central banks pursue 'defensive' or 'neutralizing' operations at all times. High-powered money is thus always fully endogenous. This is a key feature of horizontalism. On the other hand, central banks can be accommodating or not. When they are, they will peg the interest rate, whatever the economic conditions. When they are not accommodating, i.e., when they are pursuing 'dynamic' operations, as Chick (1977, p. 89) calls them, central banks will increase (or reduce) interest rates. As shown above, to do so, they now need simply announce a new higher target overnight rate. The actual overnight rate will gravitate towards this new anchor within the day of the announcement. Indeed, the prime rate has been following suit, with a nearly constant 300-basis-points premium (Atesoglu, 2003–4). No open market operation and no change whatsoever in the supply of high-powered money are required.

A depiction of the supply of high-powered money

Horizontalist authors claim that the supply of high-powered money should be represented by a 'set of horizontal lines, representing different stances of monetary policy' (Kaldor, 1983, p. 22). A line represents, in modern parlance, the target overnight rate set by the central bank, usually for a period of approximately one month. This rate, as we have seen, will not change simply because there is an increase in the level or growth rate of high-powered money. The size of M0 is totally irrelevant to central bankers.

As pointed out by Moore (1991, p. 125), the customary criticism against horizontalism is that 'monetary endogeneity does not imply that the money supply curve is horizontal. "Let it slope upwards just a little" (and preferably discontinuously) is the usual refrain.' Thus various authors have picked up on this idea and drawn upward-sloping curves (either continuous, such as Palley, 1994; 1996, or discontinuous, such as Fontana, 2003) that illustrate non-accommodation by the central bank, and that lead to upward-sloping LM curves. For these structuralist authors, 'the horizontal slope of the money supply must be considered a *simplifying* analytical device' (Musella and Panico, 1995, p. xxviii). But for horizontalists, the *best* depiction of the high-powered money supply curve remains a horizontal line, at the target overnight rate.

This of course does not mean that the rate of interest is set forever. Central banks, as time moves on, may decide to modify the target, on the basis of various economic conditions. If central banks give themselves a target growth rate of M0, or if they always 'lean against the wind', the short-run (static) high-powered money supply curve will be horizontal while the long-run (dynamic) curve, 'arising from a set of temporally-ordered horizontal lines which, *when money demand is taken into consideration*, will constitute a positively-sloped money supply curve.[4] *The upward-sloping curve is thus a special case, based on a particular feedback rule*' (Lavoie, 1996, p. 280).

The recent New Keynesian literature on monetary policy, the so-called New Consensus of Romer (2000), Taylor (2000) and Woodford (2002b), based on central bank reaction functions, has reinforced the horizontalist stance. Whether the LM curve is horizontal or upward-sloping in these New Consensus models depends on the exact specification taken by the central bank reaction function. If the rate of interest set by the central bank only depends on the inflation rate, the short-run (static) LM curve is flat; if the reaction function also incorporates output levels or capacity utilization rates, then the short-run (static) LM curve is upward-sloping, nearly by definition. A careful reading of Moore (1988, ch. 11) shows that he had Taylor's rule (before it was spelled out) in mind when writing his book on endogenous money. However, statements by central bankers clearly demonstrate that decisions about target interest rates are neither mechanical nor automatic (cf. Rochon, 1999, p. 174). This is certainly the point of view of Sraffian authors: 'Interest rate determination is not subject to any general law' (Pivetti, 1988, p. 282). Interest-setting decisions are bureaucratic decisions, taken on the basis of a variety of factors and hence the most we know for certain is that the central bank pegs the target overnight rate for a month, meaning that the supply of high-powered money is perfectly flat for a month (as in Cecchetti, 2006, p. 463).

New Consensus authors also give credence to the beliefs expressed by horizontalists regarding the ability of central banks to fix short-term *real* interest rates (see the contributions in Lavoie and Seccareccia, 2004). Horizontalists believe in addition that these short rates will eventually impact on *real* long rates. Smithin (1994, p. 112) argues that the central bank 'sets the pace for real interest rates, and not just nominal rates'.

Credit rationing and the liquidity preference of banks
Creditworthiness
Besides non-accommodation by the central bank to the demand for high-powered money, structuralists have also emphasized non-accommodation by banks to the demand for loans by firms. This is the issue of the liquidity preference of banks and that of credit rationing. Some post-Keynesian authors have depicted horizontalist banks as 'passive' (Dow, 1996, p. 497), or 'mere ciphers' (Cottrell, 1994, p. 599). There is now a wide body of evidence to show that this never was the case (Rochon, 1999, pp. 169–73 and ch. 8). Horizontalists such as Moore and Kaldor did emphasize the elasticity of the supply of credit by banks and their accommodating behaviour (*non-discretionary*), through overdraft arrangements for instance, rather than the credit-rationing aspects. But this is to be expected since these authors were initially trying to convince their readers that money was endogenous. However, both Kaldor (1981, p. 15) and Moore (1988, pp. 24 and 57) did underline the possibility of credit rationing and the importance of finding creditworthy borrowers, as did other horizontalist advocates, such as Godley and Cripps, who point out that 'changes in the stock of loans and money are governed solely by the demand for loans and the *credit-worthiness* of would-be-borrowers' (1983, p. 77). Indeed creditworthiness is a crucial explaining feature of the horizontalist depiction of credit-money endogeneity, and it ties in with the property and collateral requirements of Heinsohn and Steiger (2000).

Structuralists represent credit rationing through rising credit supply curves (Dow, 1996). How do horizontalists represent credit rationing? Horizontalists consider that credit rationing acts as a shift variable in regression analysis (Arestis and Eichner, 1988, p. 1010). Thus credit rationing has nothing to do with the slope of the credit supply curve. This was pointed out in Lavoie (1985, p. 845), where the conditions being imposed on borrowers ('profitability, collateral and the like') were being considered as 'shift parameters'. In Lavoie (1992, pp. 177–8), there is a reference to the *effective* demand for credit curve, based on the 'existing collateral and risk requirements for borrowing. When these requirements are modified, say relaxed, they shift upwards the effective demand curve for credit.'

Wolfson (2003, p. 79) argues similarly in his attempt 'to develop a framework to analyse credit rationing that incorporates a horizontal endogenous money supply curve'. For a borrower of a given risk class, Wolfson (1996) draws a horizontal credit supply curve. There are then two credit demand curves, in analogy with the notional and effective labour demand curves as developed by some French Keynesians. There is a *notional* demand curve, which corresponds to the demand for loans by entrepreneurs, according to their own expectations. There is then another demand curve, the *effective* demand curve, which only takes into account the demand that responds to the conditions and expectations of the bankers.[5] The horizontal distance, at the existing lending rate, between the notional and the effective demand curves is a measure of the extent of credit rationing. In other words, from the perspective of the bankers, the effective demand curve for credit is the demand curve arising from creditworthy borrowers. It is '*creditworthy* demand' (Wolfson, 2003, p. 80). Horizontalists claim that banks will always fulfil such demand. Credit supply is demand-led, but subject to the assessment of creditworthiness, which depends on both objective and subjective criteria. We may say that it depends on the liquidity preference of bankers or their animal spirits. Except for credit controls that would be directly imposed by the monetary authorities, there are no supply constraints on the amount of loans that can be granted by the banking system.

Debt ratios
The supply of credit, for a given risk classification, is a horizontal line. This risk classification depends on the debt and liquidity ratios, but it also depends on the solidity of collaterals and the size of the firm. A firm with a high debt ratio will get loans at a cost higher than the prime lending rate. This is not the issue at stake. It has been argued by some critics of horizontalism, for instance Dow (1996), that the supply of credit has to be upward-sloping because one should expect expanding activity and balance sheets to be associated with rises in either the overall debt ratios of firms or the overall debt ratios of banks, that is with greater borrower's and/or lender's risk. As a result, lending interest rates should rise relative to the base rate set by the central bank. This analysis is usually based on some version of Kalecki's principle of increasing risk and on Minsky's financial fragility hypothesis. The argument is that, as activity picks up, firms and banks will be willing to engage in more and more fragile balance sheet structures, that is, essentially, they will act to increase their debt ratio. In the case of banks, they would end up with higher loans to own funds ratios, or with higher loan to bills ratios, or higher loans to deposit ratios.

My argument (Lavoie, 1996; Lavoie and Seccareccia, 2001) has always been that these claims are essentially based on partial equilibrium graphical analyses, or based on microeconomic analyses. As soon as one takes a macroeconomic stance, and especially a *comprehensive* macroeconomic stance, it then becomes clear that debt to equity ratios, or loans to bills ratios, become endogenous variables that are not really under the control of individual agents. In other words, we enter the possible realm of 'fallacies of composition'. The attempt by *all* firms to achieve higher rates of capacity utilization may in fact lead to lower such rates in the aggregate. The attempt by firms to increase their profit margins may lead to reduced realized profit rates. And finally, as identified by Steindl (1952, pp. 113–21), there is the paradox of debt, according to which the efforts of individual firms to reduce their debt ratios might in fact lead to rising debt ratios. We just don't know what will happen to debt ratios until we have a comprehensive model. Until then, isn't it better to assume a flat credit supply curve at the macro level?

Implications of stock–flow consistent monetary macroeconomics
Debt ratios again
Fontana (2003, p. 309) claims that structuralists 'have explored the complexities and interdependencies of the complex nature of money'. This is true, but in doing so structuralists have relied on comparative statics or partial equilibrium analysis. By contrast, some horizontalists have constructed multi-sectorial comprehensive stock–flow consistent macroeconomic models, all of which take into account changes in economic activity, changes in the liquidity preference of households and changes in the behaviour of the central bank, while some also entertain changes in the liquidity preference of banks. These dynamic models can track the evolution *through time* of a large number of real and financial aggregates or financial ratios, as well as the behaviour of some endogenously determined interest rates (beyond simple marked-up rates). In other words, the models track in discrete time the evolution of these variables during the transition (the traverse) towards steady states, if these exist.[6] Indeed it can be verified on a number of occasions that the short-run behaviour of a variable is quite distinct from its long-run behaviour, when comparing two steady states.

Two examples may be given. In the growth model of Lavoie and Godley (2001–2), firms invest according to capacity utilization rates and inversely with the weight of interest payments relative to gross profitability; they take bank loans and issue stock market shares; households decide on the proportions in which they wish to hold their wealth in the form of deposits and equities; and banks set interest rates. Various experiments were conducted with this stock–flow consistent model. Depending on the parameter that was changed to start the simulation, the relationship between the steady-state rate of accumulation and the steady-state debt ratio could be either positive or negative. Since Kaleckians generally believe that the long run is simply a succession of short runs, readers may be more interested in what occurs during the transition from one state to another. In almost all cases, there is a *negative* relationship between growth rates and debt ratios at the start of the traverse. By contrast, in all cases, there is a *positive* relationship between the rate of accumulation and the debt ratio towards the end of the traverse, when the economy is actually converging towards its new steady state. The lesson to be drawn is that no general statement, valid for all parameter changes and at all times, can be made. It can certainly not be asserted that there is a *necessary* positive connection between economic activity and the debt ratios of firms.[7] This dismisses one reason for which the supply of credit could be upward-sloping. What about the second reason?

Interest rates set by banks and economic activity
The model of Godley (1999) contains over 60 equations, many of which refer to the portfolio choice of households and to the behaviour and constraints of the banking system. In Godley's model, banks are driven by the need to remain profitable and by two liquidity constraints. Because of the profitability constraint, interest rates on loans must reflect the main cost of funds, that of time deposits. In addition banks must maintain a fractional reserve requirement, by holding in cash a given fraction of their total deposits (the primary reserve ratio). Banks also target a liquidity ratio: a Treasury bills to deposits ratio (a kind of secondary reserve ratio). To achieve this norm, banks gradually raise the rate of interest on time deposits relative to the Treasury bill rate as long as the ratio is below the norm.[8]

Godley (1999, pp. 400–401) reports an experiment that he conducted. Starting from a full equilibrium at the steady state, there is an exogenous expansion of inventories. This increase requires an immediate and equal increase in bank loans and money balances. However, as the various agents react to their new situation, loans rise faster than deposits, and eventually, despite the fact that interest rates on bills and bonds are fixed by assumption, banks must raise the rates of interest on time deposits (and hence loans) to recover the target norm on secondary reserve requirements. In the end, the balance sheet of banks has grown in size, and higher interest rates are associated with a higher level of loans and of money deposits.[9]

At first sight, these results are rather congruent with the structuralist story and Godley's stock–flow comprehensive model would seem to provide ammunition against horizontalism. But contrary to expectations, it does not. First, it should be pointed out that in the experiment conducted by Godley, the increase in inventories leads to a *fall* in the new steady-state level of income. The higher level of interest rates on loans and deposits, resulting from the higher loans, is thus associated with a lower level of income. The experiment generates a rising credit supply curve, *but a downward-sloping LM curve*!

But a second, more damaging experiment can be conducted with Godley's model (see Lavoie, 2001a). Impose an exogenous (permanent) increase in government expenditures. This entails, in the short run and in the stationary state, a higher level of activity, accompanied by larger inventories, and larger banking balance sheets, more precisely larger loans and deposits. All this, however, is accompanied by *lower* rates of interest on loans and time deposits in the short and medium run. This is because a larger proportion of wealth has to be retained in the form of government debt, bills and bonds, instead of money deposits. We have a short-run *downward-sloping* supply curve of credit, and again a *downward-sloping* LM curve. Across stationary states, both of these curves are flat: neither the loan rate nor the deposit rate rises. We can thus conclude, as Sawyer (2001, p. 497) suggests, that no conclusion can be drawn regarding the 'co-movements of interest rates and loans (or the stock of money) over the cycle'. It follows, once more, that the least misguiding assumption is to suppose that the credit supply curve is horizontal.

Strong exogeneity of interest rates and financial innovation
Godley's (1999) model allows us to deal with a few more issues. In his model, both the Treasury bill rate and the interest rate on long-term government bonds are constant, set by the monetary authorities with help from the Treasury.[10] In that sense, from the point of view of central bank accommodation, one could say that the model is fully in the horizontalist tradition. Indeed, according to Parguez (2001, p. 92), 'an exogenous long-run rate would be deemed the ultimate break-up of all the established theories of interest rates'. Parguez calls this 'the strong exogeneity theory', by contrast with the weak exogeneity theory, which would only involve short-term rates. Still, despite this 'strong' horizontalist position, it is possible to assess the effects of changes in the liquidity preference of households in Godley's model. There is no incompatibility between this horizontalist framework and the study of liquidity preference (as confirmed by Brown, 2003–4). Indeed, an interest rate adjustment affecting lending rates, not much different from Dow's (1997), is being proposed in Lavoie (1984b, pp. 243–4, 251–2), when households desire to hold a larger proportion of their assets in the form of money balances, or when they desire to hold a larger proportion of their assets in the form of government-issued bonds.

A similar comment can be made regarding financial innovation. It was never denied by horizontalists that banks would attempt to economize on reserves and that high interest costs would exacerbate these innovations.

> If such pressures were exercised, the various economic units would use all sort of subterfuges to avoid the utilization of money (currency or checking accounts). There would be a move from banking activities toward non-banking financial activities, as explained by John Gurley and Edward Shaw: Banks would encourage the transformation of demand deposits for term deposits; large firms would start acting as banking institutions and credits between companies would be extended . . . As a consequence the velocity of money as defined by the authorities would be on the rise. (Lavoie, 1984a, p. 779)

Thus many of the points later raised by structuralists were actually discussed in the earlier horizontalist works, although with less detail. However, the standard structuralist endogeneity claim (Pollin, 1991, p. 375) that financial innovation and liabilility management mainly arise from central bank restraints on bank reserves becomes ever more dubious. Indeed, Mosler (2002, p. 420) says that such a claim 'makes little sense . . . since bankers will *always* do their utmost to minimize their reserve requirements'. In a world with zero-reserve requirements, hence without reserve restraints, we shall still observe both liability management and financial innovation. These are features of any banking system, even when the central bank is pegging interest rates.

The impossibility of an excess supply of money

Kaldor and Trevithick's (1981) and Moore's (1988) intuition – that there can never be an excess supply of money, a claim often associated with the reflux principle – has often been questioned from various quarters, but this claim is vindicated by Godley's model and method. Some authors have noted that, because money deposits are created as a result of loans being granted to firms, money supply could exceed money demand. Coghlan (1978, p. 17), for instance, says that: 'If we accept that advances can be largely exogenous . . . then the possibility must exist that bank deposits can grow beyond the desires of money holders.' It has sometimes been claimed that the horizontalist assertion regarding the impossibility of an excess supply of credit-money should be attributed to the absence of a proper portfolio demand for money (Goodhart, 1989, p. 33; Howells, 1995, p. 92).

But in Godley's models, there is both an *explicit* demand for money function, and an apparently completely independent supply for money function, which depends in particular on the supply of loans. Still, in Godley's models, there is never any excess supply of money, despite deposit rates being given at a moment of time. The reason for this is that the overall constraints imposed by a coherent double-entry financial bookkeeping framework imply an additional equality, which is not part of the model *stricto sensu* – the equality between the supply for and the demand of money. Hence in a fully coherent accounting framework, the portfolio demand for money can only be an *apparently* independent function. So, Moore (1997, p. 427) is right when he states that: '*there is no separate and independent demand for money* that must somehow be "reconciled" with the demand for credit'. As a result, when banks do not entertain a target liquidity ratio, changes in the liquidity preference of households could occur without any change in the structure of interest rates. On the other hand, when the monetary authorities let the long-term rate float, and when banks set a range of target ratios, such a change in liquidity preference could modify the structure of interest rates. In addition, in general, changes in liquidity preference will modify the prices and the rates of return on stock market shares, as shown in the Lavoie and Godley (2001–2) model, since these prices are fully market-determined.

The belief that there can be an excess supply of money has also arisen in another context. It has been claimed by various mainstream and heterodox authors that government deficits could lead to an excess money supply. This claim arises because the authors assume that the central bank (or government) decides arbitrarily on the proportion of the deficit that will be financed by bond issues and by the creation of high-powered money. In the models of these authors, this proportion is an exogenous variable.

In the horizontalist view, cash is provided on demand to the public. The government, or the central bank, does not decide in advance on the proportion of the deficit that will be 'monetized'. This proportion depends on the portfolio decisions of the households, taken on the basis of the rate of interest set from the onset by the monetary authorities. As is noted by Bertocco (2001, p. 104), this post-Keynesian view was clearly spelled out by Kaldor (1982, p. 14) when he claimed that neither the government nor the central bank could decide what portion of the government deficit would be held in the form of cash or in various forms of public sector debt. The proportion of the deficit that is financed by security issues is an endogenous variable, in line with the theory of endogenous money.

Endogenous money in an open economy
It is sometimes claimed that demand-led endogenous money, with interest rates set by the central bank, finds its limits within the context of an open economy. With flexible exchange rates, some mainstream economists claim that expectations about future changes in spot exchange rates determine (nominal and real) domestic interest rates relative to those ruling in the rest of the world. The argument is that changes in expected future spot exchange rates determine the forward rate relative to the current spot rate. This differential, through the covered interest parity condition, which is known to hold at all times, would then determine domestic interest rates relative to those ruling abroad. The post-Keynesian answer to such a claim has been provided by Smithin (1994) and Lavoie (2000; 2002–3). Their argument is that the causality of the covered interest parity condition must be reversed, as in the so-called *cambist* approach to exchange rates. Banks set the forward premium on the basis of existing interest rates. The interest spread determines, i.e., *causes*, the differential between forward and spot exchange rates, and hence the forward rate is no indicator of the future spot rate, as empirical studies have shown (Moosa, 2004). In models with imperfect capital substitution, interest differentials only lead to a one-time adjustment in portfolios; as a result, interest rates remain exogenous, under the control of monetary authorities which can set domestic rates at levels that are different from those in the rest of the world in a flexible exchange rate economy. The conclusion that monetary policy is possible within a flexible exchange regime is also accepted by a large number of mainstream economists.

What about fixed exchange regimes (gold standard regime or dollar standard regime)? Mainstream economists argue that monetary policy is then impossible. Balance of payments deficits (surpluses) lead to foreign reserve losses (gains), and hence either lead or should lead to reductions (increases) in the monetary base and in the money supply, followed by endogenous hikes (cut-backs) in interest rates. In such a context, the money supply is endogenous, but it is supply-led, no longer demand-led. It is thus totally at odds with the post-Keynesian approach. It is also at odds with empirical facts.

Studies devoted to both gold standard periods have shown that the rules of the game did not apply whatsoever (Lavoie, 2001b). Increases or decreases in central bank foreign assets were compensated by fluctuations of central bank domestic assets in the opposite direction. This is the 'compensation' thesis, advocated in particular by French central bankers and Le Bourva (1992, pp. 462–3). Compensation is the rule rather than the exception. In standard terminology, fluctuations in foreign reserves were 'sterilized' or 'neutralized'. Neutralization arose either automatically, at the initiative of the private sector, or naturally, as a result of the normal behaviour of the central bank to sustain the payment system. Thus, even in the gold standard period, fixed exchange rates did not prevent central banks from setting interest rates, while money creation was still demand-led.

Things are even more transparent in the modern context. Central banks target overnight rates. Their 'normal' behaviour is to act in such a way that the target will be realized. In overdraft economies, where commercial banks take advances from the central bank, a balance of payment surplus allows these banks to reduce their debt towards the central bank. On the balance sheet of the latter, the increase in foreign reserves is then compensated by a reduction in domestic credit, and no increase in the monetary base needs to occur. In the case of asset-based economies, the flow of additional foreign reserves acts like any government net flow into the financial system. As a result, as pointed out by the Bank of Canada, 'To "sterilize" the effect of the Bank's sale of Canadian dollars (and prevent downward pressure on Canadian interest rates), the same amount of Canadian-dollar balances are withdrawn from the financial system.' The increase in foreign reserves is thus once more fully compensated, either by a reduction in domestic credit, or through a shift in government deposits from the accounts of commercial banks to the government account at the central bank, thus wiping out the banks' excess settlement balances.

Thus, as noted by Arestis and Eichner (1988, p. 1004), 'Any money creation emanating from fiscal or debt management operations initiated by the authorities or from a favourable balance of payments, can be neutralized through an equivalent reduction in commercial bank credit brought about by the actions of private economic agents.' It can then be concluded, as was done by Arestis and Eichner (1988, p. 1015), that 'so long as it is recognized that money supply is credit-driven and demand-determined, the exchange rate regime is of absolutely no consequence in the determination of money and credit'.

Stock–flow consistent comprehensive two-country models depicting a fixed exchange rate regime have been built by Godley and Lavoie (2004; 2005–6). These models show that central banks in both countries can set different interest rates, while running balance of payments deficits or surpluses. The compensation mechanism arises from the decision of central banks to keep short-term interest rates constant. Despite the inflow or outflow of reserves, the monetary base remains entirely determined by the demand for money arising from the portfolio household decisions. In a stationary state with constant income flows and constant private wealth, for instance, the money supply remains constant despite the continuous increase in the stock of foreign reserves. The money supply is still endogenous and demand-led in a fixed exchange regime. Similar models show that, even in a currency board, as long as minimum foreign reserves are fulfilled, interest rates are still under the control of the monetary authorities, thanks to a compensation mechanism that operates through variations in government deposits at the central bank (Lavoie, 2006).

Conclusion

The 'horizontalist' or 'accommodationist' view of endogenous money was considered 'extreme' for a while. I have shown that horizontalist authors had already taken on board most of the realistic features that they were later accused of having ignored. In addition, recent developments in central banking operating procedures, which make more transparent the money creation process, have vindicated the horizontalist approach. There are now formal comprehensive models that put together a horizontalist approach to endogenous money and a generalized liquidity preference framework, showing that these two strands can be synthesized. These models can be modified at will to tackle new questions or to formalize different behaviours.

Notes

*   Usual acknowledgments and disclaimers apply to comments kindly provided by Alain Parguez, John Smithin and the editors.
1.   Indeed, the word *accommodation* is nowhere to be found in the index of Moore's (1988) book.
2.   Regretfully, New Keynesian authors never make any acknowledgment of the previous post-Keynesian literature on endogenous money – out of ignorance or dishonesty?
3.   The current Swedish monetary framework, which arose from an overdraft system, was put in place by the

Riksbank in 1994 and features many similarities with the Canadian framework. A highly pedagogical presentation of the Swedish operating procedures is provided by Mitlid and Vesterlund (2001).

4. From Meulendyke's (1988) testimony, it seems that this reaction function, akin to the arguments of Pollin and Palley, could have been relevant only between 1979 and 1982 in the USA, although even this is disputed by Poole (1982).

5. Hewitson (1997, p. 132) also uses the terms 'notional and effective demand for loans' in a similar context.

6. Thus Fontana's (2003) assessment that horizontalism is limited to single-period analysis is only valid within the framework of a central bank reaction function, a point also made by Palley (1996, p. 585); otherwise, it is utterly mistaken.

7. In Canada, for instance, the debt to equity ratio of corporate non-financial firms moved down progressively from 80 per cent to 55 per cent between 1996 and 2004, during years of high growth (2005 Federal budget document, 23 February).

8. This mechanism would seem to be in line with the empirical evidence brought out by Eichner (1986) and Arestis and Driver (1988), who show that interest rates on loans rise when the loans to deposits ratio rises (and hence the Treasury bills to deposit ratio falls) compared to its trend value.

9. The similarities between Godley's (1999) time-discrete model and Palley's (1994) analytical model are remarkable, but they are not surprising since both models take their inspiration from Tobin. Indeed the mechanism by which banks react to changes in the structure of their balance sheet is nearly identical. These similarities highlight the fact that the only true distinction between Moore's horizontalist model and Palley's structuralist model is that the latter assumes that central banks 'lean against the wind', letting federal funds move somewhat, whereas the former assumes that central banks manage to keep the federal funds rate at its target level. Moore (2001, p. 13) may be quite right when he speaks of a 'storm in a teacup'!

10. This is possible as long as all assets are not perfect substitutes. Naturally, other hypotheses regarding the behaviour of the long-term interest rate can be modelled.

References

Arestis, P. and Driver, C. (1988), 'The endogeneity of the UK money supply: a political economy perspective', *Économies et Sociétés*, **22**(9), 121–38.

Arestis, P. and Eichner, A.S. (1988), 'The Post-Keynesian and Institutionalist theory of money and credit', *Journal of Economic Issues*, **22**(4), 1003–22.

Atesoglu, H.S. (2003–4), 'Monetary transmission – federal funds rate and prime rate', *Journal of Post Keynesian Economics*, **26**(3), 357–62.

Bertocco, G. (2001), 'Is Kaldor's theory of money supply endogeneity still relevant?', *Metroeconomica*, **52**(1), 95–120.

Bindseil, U. and Seitz, B. (2001), 'The supply and demand for eurosystem deposits: the first 18 months', Working papers series No. 44, European Central Bank, Frankfurt.

Black, F. (1970), 'Banking and interest rates in a world without money', *Journal of Banking Research*, **1**(3), 8–20.

Brown, C. (2003–4), 'Toward a reconcilement of endogenous money and liquidity preference', *Journal of Post Keynesian Economics*, **26**(2), 325–40.

Cecchetti, S.G. (2006), *Money, Banking, and Financial Markets*, New York: McGraw-Hill Irwin.

Chick, V. (1977), *The Theory of Monetary Policy*, Oxford: Parkgate Books.

Clinton, K. (1991), 'Bank of Canada cash management: the main technique for implementing monetary policy', *Bank of Canada Review*, January, 3–32.

Clinton, K. (1997), 'Implementation of monetary policy in a regime with zero reserve requirements', Working Paper 97-8, Bank of Canada.

Coghlan, R. (1978), 'A new view of money', *Lloyds Bank Review*, July, 12–27.

Cottrell, A. (1994), 'Post-Keynesian monetary theory', *Cambridge Journal of Economics*, **18**(6), 587–605.

Davidson, P. (1989), 'On the endogeneity of money once more', *Journal of Post Keynesian Economics*, **11**(3), 488–90.

Docherty, P. (2005), *Money and Employment: A Study of the Theoretical Implications of Endogenous Money*, Cheltenham, UK and Northampton, MA, USA: Edward Elgar.

Dow, S.C. (1996), 'Horizontalism: a critique', *Cambridge Journal of Economics*, **20**(4), 497–508.

Dow, S.C. (1997), 'Endogenous money', in G.C. Harcourt and P. Riach (eds), *The Second Edition of Keynes's General Theory*, London: Routledge, pp. 61–78.

Eichner, A.S. (1986), 'The demand for money further considered', *Toward a New Economics: Essays in Post-Keynesian and Institutionalist Theory*, London: Macmillan, pp. 98–112.

Eichner, A.S. (1987), *The Macrodynamics of Advanced Market Economics*, Armonk, NY: M.E. Sharpe.

Fontana, G. (2003), 'Post Keynesian approaches to endogenous money: a time framework explanation', *Review of Political Economy*, **15**(3), 291–314.

Fullwiler, S.T. (2003), 'Timeliness and the Fed's daily tactics', *Journal of Economic Issues*, **37**(4), 851–80.

Fullwiler, S.T. (2006), 'Setting interest rates in the modern era', *Journal of Post Keynesian Economics*, **28**(4), 495–526.

Godley, W. (1999), 'Money and credit in a Keynesian model of income determination', *Cambridge Journal of Economics*, **28**(4), 393–411.

Godley, W. and Cripps, F. (1983), *Macroeconomics*, London: Fontana.

Godley, W. and Lavoie, M. (2004), 'Two-country stock–flow consistent macroeconomics using a closed model within a dollar exchange regime', Working Paper 10, CERF, University of Cambridge.

Godley, W. and Lavoie, M. (2005–6), 'Comprehensive accounting in simple open economy macroeconomics with endogenous sterilization or flexible exchange rates', *Journal of Post Keynesian Economics*, **28**(2), 241–76.

Goodhart, C. (1989), 'Has Moore become too horizontal?', *Journal of Post Keynesian Economics*, **12**(1), 29–34.

Hein, E. and Ochsen, C. (2003), 'Regimes of interest rates, income shares, savings and investment: a Kaleckian model and empirical estimation for some advanced OECD economies', *Metroeconomica*, **54**(4), 404–33.

Heinsohn, G. and Steiger, O. (2000), 'The property theory of interest and money', in J. Smithin (ed.), *What is Money?*, London: Routledge, pp. 67–100.

Hewitson, G. (1997), 'The post-Keynesian "demand for credit" model', *Australian Economic Papers*, **36**(68), 127–43.

Hicks, J. (1982), *Money, Interest and Wages*, Cambridge, MA: Harvard University Press.

Howard, D. (1998), 'A primer on the implementation of monetary policy in the LVTS environment', *Bank of Canada Review*, Fall, 57–66.

Howells, P.G.A. (1995), 'The demand for endogenous money', *Journal of Post Keynesian Economics*, **18**(1), 89–106.

Isaac, A.G. (1991), 'Economic stabilization and money supply endogeneity in a conflicting-claims environment', *Journal of Post Keynesian Economics*, **14**(1), 93–110.

Kaldor, N. (1970), 'The new monetarism', *Lloyds Bank Review'* July, 1–17.

Kaldor, N. (1981), *Origins of the New Monetarism*, Cardiff: University College Cardiff Press.

Kaldor, N. (1982), *The Scourge of Monetarism*, Oxford: Oxford University Press.

Kaldor, N. (1983), 'Keynesian economics after fifty years', in D. Worswick and J. Trevithick (eds), *Keynes and the Modern World*, Cambridge: Cambridge University Press, pp. 1–28.

Kaldor, N. and Trevithick, J. (1981), 'A Keynesian perspective on money', *Lloyds Bank Review*, January, 1–19.

Lavoie, M. (1984a), 'The endogenous credit flow and the Post Keynesian theory of income', *Journal of Economic Issues*, **18**(3), 771–97.

Lavoie, M. (1984b), 'Un modèle post-keynésien d'économie monétaire fondé sur la théorie du circuit', *Économies et Sociétés*, **18**(4), 233–58.

Lavoie, M. (1985), 'The Post Keynesian theory of endogenous money: a reply', *Journal of Economic Issues*, **19**(3), 843–8.

Lavoie, M. (1992), *Foundations of Post-Keynesian Economic Analysis*, Aldershot, UK and Brookfield, US: Edward Elgar.

Lavoie, M. (1996), 'Horizontalism, structuralism, liquidity preference and the principle of increasing risk', *Scottish Journal of Political Economy*, **43**(3), 275–301.

Lavoie, M. (2000), 'A Post Keynesian view of interest parity theorems', *Journal of Post Keynesian Economics*, **23**(1), 163–79.

Lavoie, M. (2001a), 'Endogenous money in a coherent stock–flow framework', Working Paper 325, The Levy Economics Institute of Bard College.

Lavoie, M. (2001b), 'The reflux mechanism and the open economy', in L.P. Rochon and M. Vernengo (eds), *Credit, Interest Rates and the Open Economy: Essays on Horizontalism*, Cheltenham, UK and Northampton, MA, USA: Edward Elgar, pp. 215–42.

Lavoie, M. (2002–3), 'Interest parity, risk premia, and Post Keynesian analysis', *Journal of Post Keynesian Economics*, **25**(2), 237–50.

Lavoie, M. (2006), 'A fully coherent post-Keynesian model of currency boards', in C. Gnos and L.P. Rochon (eds), *Post-Keynesian Principles of Economic Policy*, Cheltenham, UK and Northampton, MA, USA: Edward Elgar, pp. 185–207.

Lavoie, M. and Godley, W. (2001–2), 'Kaleckian models of growth in a coherent stock–flow monetary framework: a Kaldorian view', *Journal of Post Keynesian Economics*, **24**(2), 253–76.

Lavoie, M. and Seccareccia, M. (2001), 'Minsky's financial fragility: a missing macroeconomic link?', in R. Bellofiore and P. Ferri (eds), *Financial Fragility and Investment in the Capitalist Economy: The Economic Legacy of Hyman Minsky, Volume II*, Cheltenham, UK and Northampton, MA, USA: Edward Elgar, pp. 76–96.

Lavoie, M. and Seccareccia, M. (eds) (2004), *Central Banking in the Modern World: Alternative Perspectives*, Cheltenham, UK and Northampton, MA, USA: Edward Elgar.

Le Bourva, J. (1992), 'Money creation and credit multipliers', *Review of Political Economy*, **4**(4), 447–66.

Meulendyke, A.M. (1988), 'Can the Federal Reserve influence whether the money supply is endogenous? A comment on Moore', *Journal of Post Keynesian Economics*, **10**(3), 390–97.

Mitlid, K. and Vesterlund, M. (2001), 'Steering interest rates in monetary policy – how does it work?, *Riksbank Economic Review*, (1), 19–41.

Moore, B.J. (1988), *Horizontalists and Verticalists: The Macroeconomics of Credit Money*, Cambridge: Cambridge University Press.

Moore, B.J. (1991), 'Has the demand for money been mislaid? A reply to "has Moore become too horizontal?"', *Journal of Post Keynesian Economics*, **14**(1), 4125–33.

Moore, B.J. (1997), 'Reconciliation of the supply and demand for endogenous money', *Journal of Post Keynesian Economics*, **19**(3), 423–8.

Moore, B.J. (2001), 'Some reflections on endogenous money', in L.P. Rochon and M. Vernengo (eds), *Credit, Interest Rates and the Open Economy: Essays on Horizontalism*, Cheltenham, UK and Northampton, MA, USA: Edward Elgar, pp. 11–30.

Moosa, I.A. (2004), 'An empirical examination of the Post Keynesian view of forward exchange rates', *Journal of Post Keynesian Economics*, **26**(3), 395–418.

Mosler, W. (1997–98), 'Full employment and price stability', *Journal of Post Keynesian Economics*, **20**(2), 167–82.

Mosler, W. (2002), 'A critique of John B. Taylor's "Expectations, open market operations, and changes in the federal funds rate"', *Journal of Post Keynesian Economics*, **24**(3), 419–22.

Musella, M. and Panico, C. (1995), 'Introduction', in *The Supply of Money in the Economic Process: A Post Keynesian Perspective*, Aldershot, UK and Brookfield, US: Edward Elgar, pp. xiii–xli.

Palley, T.I. (1994), 'Competing views of the money supply process: theory and evidence', *Metroeconomica*, **45**(1), 67–88.

Palley, T.I. (1996), 'Accommodationism versus structuralism: time for accommodation', *Journal of Post Keynesian Economics*, **18**(4), 585–94.

Parguez, A. (2001), 'Money without scarcity: from the horizontalist revolution to the theory of the monetary circuit', in L.P. Rochon and M. Vernengo (eds), *Credit, Interest Rates and the Open Economy: Essays on Horizontalism*, Cheltenham, UK and Northampton, MA, USA: Edward Elgar, pp. 69–103.

Parguez, A. and Seccareccia, M. (2000), 'The credit theory of money: the monetary circuit approach', in J. Smithin (ed.), *What is Money?*, London: Routledge, pp. 101–23.

Pivetti, M. (1988), 'On the monetary explanation of distribution: a rejoinder to Nell and Wray', *Political Economy: Studies in the Surplus Approach*, **4**(2), 275–83.

Pollin, R. (1991), 'Two theories of money supply endogeneity: some empirical evidence', *Journal of Post Keynesian Economics*, **13**(3), 366–96.

Pollin, R. (1996), 'Money supply endogeneity: what are the questions and why do they matter?', in G. Deleplace and E.J. Nell (eds), *Money in Motion: The Post Keynesian and Circulation Approaches*, London: Macmillan, pp. 490–515.

Poole, W. (1982), 'Federal Reserve operating procedures: a survey and evaluation of the historical record since October 1979', *Journal of Money, Credit and Banking*, **14**(2), 575–95.

Rochon, L.P. (1999), *Credit, Money and Production: An Alternative Post-Keynesian Approach*, Cheltenham, UK and Northampton, MA, USA: Edward Elgar.

Rochon, L.P. (2001a), 'Horizontalism: setting the record straight', in L.P. Rochon and M. Vernengo (eds), *Credit, Interest Rates and the Open Economy: Essays on Horizontalism*, Cheltenham, UK and Northampton, MA, USA: Edward Elgar, pp. 31–68.

Rochon, L.P. (2001b), 'Cambridge's contribution to endogenous money: Robinson and Kahn on credit and money', *Review of Political Economy*, **13**(3), 287–307.

Rogers, C. (1989), *Money, Interest and Capital: A Study in the Foundations of Monetary Theory*, Cambridge: Cambridge University Press.

Rogers, C. and Rymes, T.K. (2000), 'The disappearance of Keynes's nascent theory of banking between the *Treatise* and the *General Theory*', in J. Smithin (ed.), *What is Money?*, London: Routledge, pp. 257–69.

Romer, D. (2000), 'Keynesian macroeconomics without the LM curve', *Journal of Economic Perspectives*, **14**(2), 149–69.

Sawyer, M. (2001), 'Kalecki on money and finance', *European Journal of the History of Economic Thought*, **8**(4), 487–508.

Smithin, J. (1994), *Controversies in Monetary Economics: Ideas, Issues and Policy*, Aldershot, UK and Brookfield, US: Edward Elgar.

Steindl, J. (1952), *Maturity and Stagnation in American Capitalism*, Oxford: Basil Blackwell; New York: New Monthly Press (1976).

Targetti, F. (1992), *Nicholas Kaldor: The Economics and Politics of Capitalism as a Dynamic System*, Oxford: Clarendon Press.

Taylor, J.B. (2000), 'Teaching modern macroeconomics at the principles level', *American Economic Review*, **90**(2), May, 90–94.

Thirlwall, A.P. (1994), 'Talking about Kaldor', in J.E. King (ed.), *Economic Growth in Theory and Practice: A Kaldorian Perspective*, Aldershot, UK and Brookfield, US: Edward Elgar, pp. 70–83.

Whitesell, W. (2003), 'Tunnels and reserves in monetary policy implementation', Finance and Discussion Papers 2003-28, Federal Reserve Board, http://www.federalreserve.gov/pubs/feds/2003/200328/200328pap.pdf

Wolfson, M.H. (1996), 'A Post Keynesian theory of credit rationing', *Journal of Post Keynesian Economics*, **18**(3), 443–70.

Wolfson, M.H. (2003), 'Credit rationing', in J. King (ed.), *The Elgar Companion to Post Keynesian Economics*, Cheltenham, UK and Northampton, MA, USA: Edward Elgar, pp. 77–82.

Woodford, M. (2002a), 'Financial market efficiency and the effectiveness of monetary policy', *FRBNY Economic Policy Review*, May, 85–94.

Woodford, M. (2002b), *Interest and Prices: Foundations of a Theory of Monetary Policy*, Princeton, NJ: Princeton University Press.

Wray, L.R. (1992), 'Commercial banks, the central bank, and endogenous money', *Journal of Post Keynesian Economics*, **14**(3), 297–310.

Wray, L.R. (1998), *Understanding Modern Money: The Key to Full Employment and Price Stability*, Cheltenham, UK and Northampton, MA, USA: Edward Elgar.

Wray, L.R. (2004a), 'When are interest rates exogenous ?', Working Paper 30, Center for Full Employment and Price Stability, University of Missouri–Kansas City.

Wray, L.R. (2004b), 'The Fed and the new monetary consensus', Public Policy Brief 80, The Levy Economics Institute of Bard College.

Zezza, G. and Dos Santos, C. (2004), 'The role of monetary policy in post-Keynesian stock–flow consistent macroeconomic growth models', in M. Lavoie and M. Seccareccia (eds), *Central Banking in the Modern World: Alternative Perspectives*, Cheltenham, UK and Northampton, MA, USA: Edward Elgar, pp. 183–208.

3 Endogenous money: structuralist
*Sheila C. Dow**

1. Introduction

It is now a widely held view that the money supply is not under the full control of the monetary authorities, that is, that it is (at least in part) endogenous to real private sector economic processes. This has long been the view of those who study the actual workings of banking systems. But the inability of the authorities to control the money supply became most evident during the 1980s when attempts were made at such control in the name of monetarist theory. The practice of monetary policy now, in the USA, the UK and the Euro-zone, is therefore explicitly focused on setting the rate charged on borrowed reserves (in the form of the repo rate[1]) rather than targeting a particular rate of growth of the money supply. It is therefore now increasingly (though by no means universally) accepted that the money supply should be treated as an endogenous variable in monetary theory. This is the case across a wide spectrum of modern theoretical approaches, including the neoclassical theory of monetary policy (as in Goodhart, 1984) and new classical business cycle theory (as in McCallum, 1986), as well as, more traditionally, in the post-Keynesian approach.

The view that the money supply is endogenous has a long pedigree,[2] which, contrary to popular belief, includes Keynes (Moore, 1988; Dow, 1997a). The literature is rich, reflecting the several senses in which the money supply may be seen to be endogenous (Rousseas, 1986: chs 4 and 5), although all refer to the capacity of the banks to create deposits as a by-product of credit creation. In one sense endogeneity refers to the capacity of the banks to determine how much deposits they create on the basis of an exogenous quantity of reserves. Tobin's (1963) portfolio theory identified endogeneity with the liabilities side of the banks' balance sheet; while the authorities might control the volume of reserves, the multiplier applied to those reserves was endogenous to the non-bank sector. Bank customers could alter their preferences for cash and different types of deposit, particularly in response to changes in the interest rate. But this endogeneity was still predictable and so could simply be factored into money supply targeting.

Most long-standing endogenous money theories, however, have put the focus more on the asset side of the banks' balance sheet, putting credit creation at the centre of the analysis. Bank deposits (the major component of the money supply) come into being as the vehicle through which credit is extended. The significance of these theories is that the supply of reserves is itself endogenous (as well as the multiplier). This follows from the central bank's lender-of-last resort facility, whereby the central bank stands ready to supply additional reserves as required. Further, sophisticated modern banking systems have the capacity to innovate in the face of constraints on their capacity to increase portfolios, and thus profit potential. Central banks do not have the instruments to control directly the volume of either money or credit. The focus in endogenous money theory is therefore instead on the demand for credit, and the expectations and expenditure plans which underpin it, as the primary causal process out of which arises the stock of money and the general price level. The scope for the monetary authorities to alter these outcomes arises from the setting of the cost of borrowing reserves, in so far as it influences the supply of and demand for credit through the responses of the banking system.

A theory of endogenous money has long been one of the defining characteristics of post-Keynesianism, and formed the core of early critiques of monetarism (Davidson and Weintraub, 1973; Kaldor, 1982). Indeed, Cottrell (1994) identifies endogenous money along with non-neutral money as the two pillars of post-Keynesian monetary theory. But within that endogenous money theory there have been some important differences, notably over the nature and extent of central bank influence on monetary conditions, relative to the influence of the banking sector and the non-bank sector respectively. These ideas fall into two broad groups. The horizontalist, or accommodationist, view, most closely associated with Kaldor (1982) and Moore (1988), emphasizes the two driving forces as the private sector demand for credit and the central bank short-term interest rate (see Chapter 2 of this volume). Other views focus more on the (interrelated) roles of the structure of the financial system, including central banking arrangements and the evolving market strategies of the banks, as well as credit demand and liquidity preference, in determining the volume of credit and thus money. It is these latter views we consider here under the heading of 'structuralism'.

It was Pollin (1991) who first characterized the two alternative endogenous money approaches as 'accommodative theory' and the 'theory of structural endogeneity', respectively. As a proponent of structuralism, Pollin puts the emphasis on the structure of the banking system (including liability structure) and the consequent influence both of the monetary authorities and the banks on interest rates and the volume of credit. This contrasts with the more passive role of the banking system (both the central bank and the private sector banks) in the horizontalist, or accommodationist approach. Cottrell (1994) subsequently identified the two strands of endogenous money theory as the radical and Keynesian approaches, respectively; Hewitson (1995) identified them as the mark-up and liquidity preference approaches, respectively, while Palley (1994; 1996) identified them as the 'pure loan demand' approach and the 'mixed portfolio-loan demand' approach, respectively. In the former, central banks choose to accommodate loan demand in order to avert crises ('political endogeneity'), while in the latter, it is in the nature of banking systems that credit and thus money are endogenous ('economic endogeneity').

We will define the structuralist approach here to include explicitly the role of liquidity preference as a major influence on the volume of credit created by the banks. This is consistent with the history of the not fully accommmodationist approach to endogenous money, which can be traced back at least as far as Keynes. This broader structuralist approach, further, involves a focus on the structure, not only of the banking sector, but also of the company and household sectors as influencing the demand for credit, and the consequences of credit creation. Further, since these structures change over time, the appropriate theory may also change. Similarly, allowance needs to be made for different national structural characteristics. A particular change of which we take note is the move away from reserve requirements or cash ratios in some major countries (the UK, the USA, Canada and New Zealand). We set out a synthetic account of structural endogeneity in the next section.

The modern literature features a variety of arguments ranging from insistence on fundamental difference between structuralists and horizontalists, to the argument that there is no fundamental difference between the two approaches. We examine these claims in the third section, by discussing structuralism explicitly in relation to horizontalism. In particular we consider how far the differences stem from talking at cross purposes with respect to a particular formal framework. In particular we consider the status of the diagrammatical representation of monetary theory and policy. By entitling his book *Horizontalists and Verticalists*, Moore (1988) had put the focus of debate on the slope of a particular function and on dualist extremes. It was natural, therefore, that alternative viewpoints, such as structuralism, should then express, or be interpreted as expressing, a difference with respect to that slope. Thus the structuralist approach is often identified with an upward-sloping credit supply function. But, as was evident in the debates of the Cambridge capital controversies of the 1960s and the Keynesian–monetarist debates of the 1970s, it is rarely the case that all parties have the same conception of the framework underpinning the disputed curve.

2. The main features of structural endogeneity

When we consider structuralist endogeneity, we find a complex account that refers to the way in which banking structure enables bank deposits to be used as money, which in turn gives the banks freedom to create credit (and thus money), addresses the extent to which the central bank freely facilitates this process, and considers the structural interactions between the banks, their customers and the central bank. Rather than a combination of absolute freedom and absolute constraints, we have a set of mutual interactions in terms of institutional design and behaviour. Much depends, for any account of a real situation, on the current structural framework, and also the current conjuncture, as it affects expectations and actions. It is no wonder that no single curve can capture the essence of structural endogeneity, nor that discussion in terms of a single curve should become mired in confusion. The following is an attempt at some clarification.

The key features of what we have identified above as the post-Keynesian approach to money supply endogeneity can be summarized as follows:

1. The money supply is not fully determined by the monetary authorities.
2. Money comes into being substantially (though not exclusively) through the credit market.

The main additional features of the structuralist approach can be summarized as follows:

3. The authorities do exert an influence on monetary conditions by:
    - setting the interest rate on borrowed reserves
    - discouraging banks' borrowing of reserves ('frown costs')
    - using open market operations to manipulate market rates.
4. The banks also influence monetary conditions by:
    - influencing the rate set by the central bank
    - influencing both loan and deposit rates (in which both oligopolistic market structure and liquidity preference play a large part)
    - innovating to avoid borrowing reserves and raising capital
    - setting the conditions for credit supply.
5. Structural endogeneity helps to explain:
    - the interactions of endogenous money and liquidity preference

- financial instability/financial crises
- monetary developments as endogenous to, and active within, the economic process.
6. These explanations are contingent on the particular structural arrangements in place in particular contexts (of time and place).

The rest of this section will be devoted to explaining the thinking behind this approach, while its differences from the accommodationist approach will be explored further in the following section.

2.1 Structural change in banking

We begin with the last feature (no. 6, above), since this is fundamental: if an explanation is structural, then structure matters, yet structures change. Such change is not generally simply capricious; there is a general logic behind the development of banking structures which Chick (1992; 1993) has explained in her stages of banking development framework. At the heart of this structure is the central role of money in capitalist societies. Banks' special role arises historically from the acceptance of their liabilities as a means of payment and store of value. These liabilities could be banks' own notes, or deposits. It is more convenient to use these, rather than coin, in most payments, and as a store of value. But the issuers must be trusted to honour their liabilities. Only when this trust is established will the use of notes, or the redeposit ratio (where deposits are treated as money), be sufficiently high that banks can feel free to create credit (as a multiple of reserves of coin) (stage two). As soon as this stage is reached, the money supply is affected by credit creation, which in the process creates new money (in the form of notes or deposits). Further, banks learn to increase this capacity by interbank lending of reserves (stage three).

Banks hold reserves, not necessarily to meet regulatory requirements, but to encourage trust in their capacity to honour their liabilities. But in an unregulated environment, banks could (even at an early stage of development) innovate in such a way as to minimize their holdings (Dow and Smithin, 1992). Central banking developed partly in response to the need to promote trust in the banking system as a whole. In most countries this took the form of requiring minimum reserve holdings, but, when adherence to these requirements threatened instability, the lender-of-last-resort facility emerged (stage four). This latter development increased confidence in the banking system as a whole, but substantially reduced the control of the central bank over monetary aggregates; that is, it increased the degree of endogeneity of the money supply. Banks now had the right to borrow reserves as required to back credit increases. Central banks then had to resort to alternative means of attempting to control the money supply, such as direct credit controls.

The success of this system in underpinning the growth of the financial superstructure of non-bank financial intermediaries introduced new problems for the banks. The new competition over share of an expanding market induced structural change within banking in the form of liability management (stage five). Banks innovated in new liabilities to satisfy the demand for liquidity, thus evading central bank controls and at the same time attracting market share. But to do so, they had to offer ever more attractive deposit rates, which in turn pushed up loan rates. Further, the banks' new eagerness to increase their loan portfolios fuelled an increase in deposits and thus money, but also increased their exposure to what proved in many cases to be bad debts.

The authorities' response to this situation was influenced by monetarist theory, which identified this monetary growth as the cause of inflation. New efforts were made to control credit creation by means of capital adequacy ratios as a substitute for reserve requirements. The latter have increasingly been removed, as being ineffectual for controlling deposit growth in the face of the lender-of-last-resort facility (Sellon and Weiner, 1997). This in turn induced further structural change in banking, as banks attempted both to deal with the legacy of bad debts and to minimize the costly and (in the face of bad debts) difficult task of raising capital to back credit creation. This structural change is most associated with securitization as the primary mechanism for reducing capital requirements, but also included a range of mechanisms for profit-making activities off the balance sheet (most notably in derivatives markets, but also in the provision of a range of financial services) (stage six). Capital adequacy ratios have not reduced the endogeneity of credit supply, but rather changed its nature. Now it is substantially in the hands of the stock market how far credit can be expanded.

Continued competition between banks and non-bank financial intermediaries encouraged a process of financial deregulation which opened up new markets, at the same time as banks were expanding their activities beyond those of traditional banking. The result has been a blurring of the distinction between banks and non-bank financial intermediaries (stage seven). This has been reinforced by the application of capital adequacy ratios equally to different types of institution according to the risk profile of their assets. Yet the fact that it is still bank liabilities that are the primary means of payment means that banks still have the distinctive capacity to create credit when they do want to use it. Further, the successful operation of the payments system requires banks to maintain positive balances with the central bank. This is achieved through the repurchase agreements, whose rate the central bank sets.

Of course not all banking systems follow the stages precisely in this way. But the later stages have been experienced sufficiently closely by major western banking systems to help us understand, not only the different aspects of structural endogeneity, but also the way in which this view of monetary systems has evolved. We now consider the other features of structural endogeneity against this backdrop of the changing structure of banking.

2.2   The money supply is not fully determined by the monetary authorities

It is a widely held view that the money supply is endogenous in the sense that it is not fully in the control of the monetary authorities. In neoclassical economics this endogeneity may be limited, as in Tobin's (1963) portfolio theory, to the size of the multiplier, or, as in global monetarism (Frenkel and Johnson, 1976), to the volume of reserves being determined by the balance of payments. Money supply endogeneity can nowadays even be adopted for operational convenience in modelling (Cottrell, 1994), just like money supply exogeneity was previously assumed for convenience in most macroeconomic models until recently, in the face of evidence to the contrary (Dow, 1997b). But in post-Keynesian economics, the endogeneity of the money supply follows more fundamentally from experience of a banking structure where the central bank acts as a lender of last resort and where banks can in any case innovate to create new money assets in order to evade central bank control. (Some degree of endogeneity is also evident throughout banking history, as shown by Chick's framework; see also Wray, 1990.) This has been fully documented in a range of theoretical and empirical studies (going back as far as Keynes's

Treatise on Money, but more recently in the Radcliffe Report: Committee on the Working of the Monetary System, 1959; Wojnilower, 1980; Rousseas, 1986; Moore, 1988).

2.3   Money arises as the counterpart to credit

Money assets are those that have the attributes of money, which allows them to perform money functions. In modern banking systems, the bulk of money consists of bank deposits; with bank innovation the range of deposits performing money functions has increased, requiring revisions to the definition of money. Bank deposits come into being primarily as the counterpart to new credit. They also come into being when banks buy securities. (See Chick and Dow, 2002, for an analysis that addresses these two sources of deposits.) (Some further deposits may also arise from government expenditure if the government banks with the central bank, or from balance of payments surpluses.) Once the new deposits are drawn down, or an overdraft facility exercised (credit normally being granted with a view to expenditure), the new deposits circulate within the banking system. (As loans are paid back, the deposits are extinguished.) It is through this mechanism that monetary aggregates are correlated with the price level. If there is pressure for inflation in the system – endogenous money theorists emphasize particularly cost-push forces for inflation – then credit demand will reflect the need to cover increased wage bills and/or prices. Far from money causing inflation (as in the monetarist model), money comes at the end of the causal process by which inflation occurs (Davidson and Weintraub, 1973).

2.4   Central bank influence on monetary conditions

The tool of monetary policy over which the authorities have most direct control is the rate of interest on the liquidity they are prepared to lend to the banking system. In modern times, this is conventionally the rate at which the central bank takes on repurchase agreements from the banks, the 'repo' rate. Even where there are no reserve requirements as such, banks require liquidity (balances with the central bank) for settling payments. But quantitatively this is now a much smaller amount, reducing the leverage of the central bank. Where there is insufficient liquidity in the interbank market, banks have no other choice but to borrow from the central bank.

In practice, however, the use made of the lender-of-last-resort facility is limited (Moore, 1988: 117–19). It varies from one national regime to another, but there is a recognized phenomenon of central bank discouragement from borrowing reserves, characterized as 'frown costs', to be considered along with the financial borrowing cost. In any case, central banks act in such a way as to enforce monetary policy by routinely entering the money market to create the desired liquidity conditions. Indeed, since it is known that this is their practice, any change in the announced repo rate has force primarily as a signal of the likely pattern of central bank market intervention, rather than as a price as such (Dow and Saville, 1988).

2.5   The banks' influence on monetary conditions

The central bank of course does not set monetary policy in a vacuum, but rather conditions its interest rate decision on market expectations. This is clearly an important feature of inflation targeting, where the market expects the repo rate to be set at such a level as to achieve the target. It is evident (for example from examination of the minutes of the meetings of the UK's Monetary Policy Committee, MPC) that there is a reluctance to confound market expectations in case this should be construed as an inconsistency in policy stance. Thus market rate expectations are included in the *Inflation Report* on which the MPC bases its decisions, and decisions tend to be surprising only at the margin (as in the balance of opinion within the MPC). The market is playing an important role in determining the rate, given the target set for the central bank.

As far as credit creation is concerned, the relevant rate is the loan rate, which is set by the banks themselves. The banks tend to move their prime rate in step with the central bank rate. But for most borrowing, particularly marginal borrowing, there is considerable scope for banks to lean against monetary policy. The difference (or mark-up) between the marginal cost of liquidity (the repo rate) and the actual loan rate charged on loans has been the subject of intensive enquiry within the post-Keynesian literature (see most recently Mariscal and Howells, 2002).[3] The mark-up has two major components. The first reflects the competitive structure of the banking sector: the more oligopolistic it is, the larger the mark-up. Further, market power can vary between different segments of the market, so that small firms in remote regions, for example, may face much higher mark-ups than other borrowers (Dow, 1996a). In market segments where competition is fiercer, mark-ups will be squeezed.

The second component reflects the banks' perception of lender's risk. At any one time, borrowers (or at least categories of borrower) can be arrayed in terms of relative perceived risk, and thus appropriate risk premia. But a key feature of post-Keynesian analysis (which explained the very existence and role of money) is uncertainty, or unquantifiable risk, as a pervasive feature of capitalist societies. Lender's risk cannot be calculated objectively, but rather by rule of thumb. Keynes (1936: 144–5) pointed out that this adds to the mark-up on loan rates. He further pointed out that estimation of such risk is subject to fluctuations, such that '[d]uring a boom the popular estimation of the magnitude of . . . lender's risk is apt to become unusually and imprudently low' (ibid.: 145). The same is true of borrowers' perception of the risk they face.

Minsky (1975; 1982) built on this analysis a theory of financial instability resulting from fluctuations over the cycle in borrowers' and lenders' perception of risk, and the consequent cycle in credit. Credit is thus both endogenous to the cycle, and fuels it. It works in conjunction with the fluctuations in liquidity preference which accompany the cycle, rising at times when confidence in expectations is low (precautionary demand) and when expectations of falls in asset prices are confidently held (speculative demand). Unlike Tobin's (1963) portfolio theory of money demand, these changes in liquidity preference with respect to the rate of interest are not predictable in their force or their timing. During the upturn, liquidity preference is low, as expectations of rising asset prices are confidently held. As reasonable expected returns in productive activity reach a ceiling, activity shifts further towards speculative trading, increasing the financial fragility of the economy, making it more vulnerable to any of a number of events which could trigger a turnaround. Liquidity preference rises, and assets are sold, weakening asset prices and fuelling the move into a downturn, which further encourages liquidity preference to strengthen. High liquidity preference takes the form of an increased demand for liquidity, as against commitment to investment goods, consumer durables and illiquid financial assets. It therefore discourages expenditure (Dow and Dow, 1989). Liquidity preference also discourages bank lending, just when the demand for liquidity for working capital and to meet cash-flow and service debt is increasing. When banks' confidence in their risk assessment is low, or when their expectation of default and of falling values of collateral is high, they will be less willing to extend credit. Banks may then exercise their own liquidity preference. This may take the form of choosing investments over loans. Even facing the possibility of falling securities prices, they may be preferable to loans where there is the possibility of default. While there may be collateral on loans, the timing of realizing its value depends on the timing of the default; securities markets provide much more liquidity. However, banks may take the strategic decision not to seek profits by continuing to expand their asset portfolios, but rather through other, off-balance-sheet activities. For some borrowers, then, the mark-up becomes prohibitive, just when their demand for liquidity is becoming urgent. This credit cycle, further, is reinforced by capital adequacy ratios: capital markets provide banks with the necessary capital when they share the 'imprudently low' assessment of risk, and withhold it when they too perceive lender's risk to be excessive.

Minsky's analysis reinforced the Keynesian view, that monetary policy would be better addressed to prudential measures to stabilize financial markets over the cycle than to attempting to choke off booms, when to do so would simply increase financial instability. This lesson seems to have become embedded in central bank practice, so that it is normal now for central banks to provide liquidity to the markets in times of crisis, rather than to remove it.

When the monetary authorities do try to squeeze the availability of liquidity, the banks have proved to be adept at innovating in such a way as to allow them to expand credit at their chosen pace (Minsky, 1982: ch. 7). This has been a central argument of endogenous money theory. Even if the authorities could control the supply of money by one definition, the banks would innovate to produce another money asset which renders the definition of money redundant. This is the import of Goodhart's Law (Goodhart, 1984). Nevertheless, the authorities can still have a short-run impact in the form of credit crunches, since innovation takes time (Wojnilower, 1980). While reserve requirements were still in force, the focus was on diverting demand to bank liabilities which did not carry reserve requirements. Now that balances for settlement purposes are the pressure point, the form of innovation has changed to focus on issues of payments settlement between banks (Sellon and Weiner, 1997); meeting the requirements of Basel II similarly is a driver for innovation to minimize the need to raise capital.

Bank innovation can also affect the impact of monetary policy even when it has been the result of strategic issues within the sector. Structural market diffusion is by no means complete. Further, the experience of diffusion has not been totally successful. Banks are moving back from the universal banking model, often retaining a full range of services within a holding company, but institutionally separating different functions within the company structure. Thus, while a particular banking organization might be willing to extend credit as much as possible (as long as bank liquidity preference is low), this will tend to apply only to chosen market segments.[4] The extent to which credit creation arises, given a particular monetary policy stance, depends therefore on the strategic plans of the banks.

2.6   *The nature and role of structural endogeneity*

We have now seen how credit, and thus money, arises endogenously from the various decisions taken by the central bank, by the private sector banks, by businesses and by households. Money arose as a social necessity. When bank liabilities assumed the attributes of money, this in turn facilitated credit creation, which in turn allowed investment to proceed ahead of saving. The banks took advantage of their unusual capacity to lend long on the basis of short-term deposits, which followed from the fact that deposits were used for payment and thus the redeposit ratio was high. Central banks historically have been in a position to take the macro view of banking. They have thus evolved a range of practices designed to ensure the prudence of the banking system in order to ensure financial stability, and thus perpetuate the acceptability of bank deposits in payment. Thus the lender-of-last-resort facility arose as one element of the structure of regulation and monitoring of banks (as well as managing the payment system and the foreign exchanges). Central banks were thus able to sustain the confidence in banks' liabilities as money without which the whole financial, and economic, structure would collapse.

We have also seen how liquidity preference and credit creation interact with each other, and with expenditure decisions, over the business cycle to add further force to the cycle and to pose the specific risk of financial crisis as the upturn makes the financial structure more and more fragile. The structural endogeneity theory emphasizes in particular the liquidity preference of the banks themselves, as determining their attitude to credit creation.[5] But this is just one aspect of the banks' active influence on credit, alongside borrowers and the central bank, and thus on the economy. Structural endogeneity thus stands alongside the non-neutrality of money, the other key feature of post-Keynesian monetary theory. Keynes himself was quite clear that banks were not passively located between the central bank and borrowers:

> [I]n general, the banks hold the key position in the transition from a lower to a higher scale of activity . . . The investment market can become congested through shortage of cash. It can never become congested through shortage of saving. This is the most fundamental of my conclusions in this field. (Keynes, 1973: 222)

It was the specific attempts in the 1980s to enforce monetarist ideas in order to reduce inflation which encouraged the various extensions of the endogenous money argument outlined above. The monetary authorities did have an impact, but not the textbook monetarist impact of a neutral reduction in the price level. We saw that raising interest rates did not have a direct effect on monetary aggregates, but rather only eventually had their effect through inducing economic recession as investment, output and employment contracted. The banks innovated extensively to diversify from traditional banking activities in order to minimize the risks posed by the financial instability of the period. The nature of the impact of monetary actions depends on the structure to which they are applied. But that impact in turn spurs on innovations which change the structure.

3.   Structural endogeneity theory and accommodationist theory

This account of endogenous money is shared with the accommodationist or horizontalist approach in terms of the first two features in the list above: that the monetary authorities do not control the money supply and that money arises out of credit creation. But accommodationists focus more on the central bank as setting the repo rate exogenously, with the banks satisfying all demand for credit at that rate grossed up by a mark-up determined by competitive structure. The role for liquidity preference is explicitly denied: 'money has no role to play' (Lavoie, 1984: 791).

The demand for money is conflated with the demand for credit, which is accommodated, removing any potentially constraining influence from liquidity preference. Indeed the expression 'credit-money' is often used to signify that the money came into being through the granting of credit, and that the two need not be distinguished.[6] Indeed there is an explicit argument (for example in Moore, 1988) that overdraft facilities mean that there is no need to hold idle money balances. Yet liquidity preference refers to the desire to keep assets liquid, not necessarily to borrow. In any case, the question remains as to whether all demand for overdraft facilities is accommodated; these facilities are not in fact universally available (Dow, 1996a).

Further, it is argued that there can be no excess supply of money, since any excess will be used to repay loans ('reflux'). But there is no reason why any 'excess' should be at the disposal of borrowers. By conflating money with credit, the mistake is made of conflating the holders of money with the recipients of credit, even though the purpose of the credit is to transfer the resulting deposits to others in exchange for goods, services or assets (Cottrell, 1986).

But the accommodationists' removal of any focus on money, quite apart from the detailed arguments addressed above, has more fundamental consequences for our understanding of money and banking in modern economies. By eliminating liquidity preference, the role of money in capitalist societies also disappears from view. Along with it disappears the reason that banks have the special capacity to create credit and the reason for the lender-of-last-resort facility (see Chick, 2000; Fontana's, 2000, arguments along these lines with respect to the circuitist approach). By conflating money with credit, the role of money as a safe asset to hold, as a substitute for longer-term financial assets and real assets, is lost. Yet this is what underpins the structure of modern banking, with the central bank supplying cash balances to the banks for payments settlement, bank liabilities therefore being trusted as a means of payment, and the superstructure of the rest of the financial system being anchored by bank liabilities.

A further accommodationist argument is that liquidity preference theory puts the focus on stocks, while the endogenous money approach (particularly when expressed in terms of a monetary circuit) focuses on flows. However, the outline of the structuralist approach provided above demonstrates that liquidity preference theory is being used in the analysis of an economic process (over the cycle) where decisions about liquidity are as much about whether to incur debt, or extend bank credit, which alter the size of stocks as about disposition of existing stocks; it is a dynamic interaction of stocks and flows. Further, taking account of developments in financial structure, it must be recognized that a significant portion of credit is created to finance purchases of financial assets; this is an important element in the euphoric set of expectations about returns on speculative assets which fuels financial instability towards the peak of the cycle in Minsky's analysis. Both the accommodationist approach and the circuitist approach tie credit creation into the need to finance production and investment. But the link with production and investment is more tenuous when the finance of financial investment, and the driving forces within financial markets, are considered. Thus, not only are output, employment and investment decisions influenced by the behaviour of the banks as well as the central bank rate, but they are also affected by the behaviour of speculation in financial markets (as Keynes, 1936: ch. 12, explained), and by the effect of developments in these markets in turn on the banking system.

Lavoie (1996) explicitly states that there is a wish among accommodationists to remove from endogenous money theory the neoclassical notion of scarcity, identified with the rate of interest being driven up by a shortage of liquidity as output rises. For structuralists, there may indeed be scarcity of finance, especially for particular groups of borrowers. But the relationship with the rate of interest is not the deterministic one we find in mainstream economics. In other words, the rate of interest is not fully determined by stable and predictable demand and supply functions. Much of the debate has focused on this question of scarcity, as represented by the slope of the credit supply curve. The structural approach is associated with an upward-sloping curve, compared to the horizontal curve of the accommodationists. Such a focus follows Moore's (1988) depiction of his difference from monetarism (and textbook 'Keynesianism') in terms of 'horizontalism and verticalism'. But there is tremendous scope for confusion when trying to represent different accounts of real-world processes in terms of a supply curve. We proceed now to consider carefully what is meant by the different parties.

Lavoie (1996) and Pollin (1991) focus on the slope of the credit supply curve as the critical difference between horizontalists and structuralists. For Lavoie the issue is whether or not interest rates rise as output rises, so that he is assuming that movement along the credit axis corresponds to expanding output. This could be due to non-accommodating behaviour by the central bank, such that the repo rate is raised as output increases. But then he argues that this should more correctly be shown by a shift up in the horizontal credit supply curve. Alternatively it could reflect the non-accommodative behaviour of the banks due to an increase in their liquidity preference. But Lavoie claims that such behaviour is already embedded in norms of risk assessment and does not warrant an upward-sloping supply curve. Again, if risk perception changes it can be handled by shift factors (see further Arestis and Eichner, 1988: 1010).

But, as Minsky's analysis shows, there may be systematic revisions to risk assessment as the economy proceeds through the cycle, so that there is a strong argument that this matter should be kept on the surface as a determinant of credit supply. While Lavoie, like other accommodationists, prefers to keep the issue of risk assessment in the background as a micro issue, Minsky's argument about risk perception over the business cycle is a macro one. As Hodgson (1988: ch. 6) argues, conventions are by definition macro rather than micro phenomena. As far as the credit supply curve is concerned, it depends whether it is static or dynamic. It also depends on the circumstances being depicted: in an upturn, the dynamic credit supply curve may well be downward-sloping, while upward-sloping in the downturn. But of course, over the business cycle, there will be changes also in liquidity preference and in credit demand, which respond to the same changing circumstances as the credit supply curve. Arestis and Howells (1996) suggest a framework of shifting sets of money demand and supply functions, where the points of intersection may well trace out a horizontal relation – but not necessarily. They thus query the meaning of the horizontal money supply curve of the accommodationists, in particular pointing out the scope for confusion between stocks and flows (money generally being analysed as a stock and credit as a flow). Not surprisingly, given the different ways in which credit supply is understood in the different frameworks, there is a fundamental identification problem when it comes to empirical analysis, making it impossible to settle by empirical testing which approach better reflects reality (Palley, 1991).

Let us consider further the distinction between static and dynamic functions in terms of how market diagrams are understood more generally. The debate over factor market diagrams in the Cambridge capital controversies, and over the slopes of the IS and LM curves during the neoclassical synthesis period, revealed different understandings. The mainstream understanding was of curves representing reversible functions, with each point representing one of an infinite array of possibilities, and where only equilibrium positions have meaning. Thus one would talk of the amount of money which would be supplied at different interest rates. The alternative, post-Keynesian, understanding of curves is as representing relations which are not necessarily reversible. Different points along a curve represent movement, either in logical time (where the purpose is to highlight causal relations) or in real time (where the purpose is to replicate real developments over time) (Dow, 1996b: ch. 6). The focus is on process (as in Arestis and Howells's treatment) rather than equilibrium.

I would suggest that the source of the difference between the accommodationist approach and the structural approach is thus fundamental in terms of theoretical framework. Chick and Dow (2002) presented a structural analysis of monetary policy explicitly as 'non-dualist'. The point was to get away from either/or treatments of endogenous money and liquidity preference (as being mutually exclusive) on the one hand, and from static curves, with specific slopes, suppressing a dynamic process, on the other. Drawing on Dow (1997a), this analysis prised apart the credit market and money market to demonstrate the interactions between the different forces at work in each (albeit often responding to similar stimuli, such as a collapse in confidence in expectations). It also, as do Arestis and Howells (1996), probed into the structure of interest rates. The tendency in accommodationist theory to suppress the forces at work behind risk assessment leads to a tendency to suppress differences between rates, and thus the risk premium on loan rates.

We set out this framework here again in order further to explain the structuralist approach. This framework differs from Palley's (1994) four-quadrant framework in that reserves and the bank multiplier are no longer relevant without reserve requirements. What is relevant is the central bank's capacity to influence the marginal cost of funds to the banks, through setting the repo rate, and by operating in the wholesale money market.

Figure 3.1 shows the credit supply curve as a dynamic relation over time, having some positive slope, although this is not necessary to the analysis. The loan rate, i_l, is composed of three items: the marginal cost of funds to the banks, the wholesale rate, i_w, plus a basic mark-up, which is composed of an element reflecting the competitiveness, and thus market power, of the banks, plus a premium to cover for perceived risk. The first item is the rate addressed by the monetary authorities in its attempt to enforce its repo rate, while the third component is subject to fluctuations over the business cycle. To the extent that the principle of increasing risk applies at the macro level in the circumstances under consideration (something which Lavoie, 1996, disputes as a general principle), the curve will have an increasingly positive slope for higher levels of credit. The point at which the curve starts to slope up may be pushed further and further to the right if expectations of default risk are low, but will move left in a downturn. Credit rationing occurs when the curve becomes vertical. But these are changes that occur over time, and need to be analysed in terms of how they also affect other aspects of the framework. The credit demand curve is shown as downward-sloping in a conventional way.

The volume of credit, C_0, established by the intersection of these credit supply and demand curves at point A, automatically determines the supply of money in the money market diagram. This is shown by carrying this total down into the money market diagram as a given total, M_0. The word 'given' is used advisedly; the money stock is exogenous to the money market as a subsystem, but is endogenous to the credit market

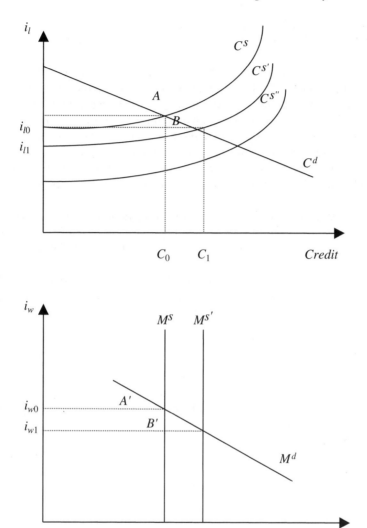

Figure 3.1   Interaction between the credit market and the money market

as a subsystem. The price in the money market is the wholesale rate, i_w. The demand for money is shown as a conventional downward-sloping function. The curve is liable to shifts depending on the state of confidence in expectations of asset prices. In particular, speculative demand may increase if the expectation forms that longer-term asset prices are likely to fall. But further, precautionary demand may increase as asset-holders lose confidence in their ability to predict asset price movements. Both factors are important and require separate modes of enquiry in order for analysts to predict money demand shifts.

Suppose that the demand for money and the stock of money coincide at point A', at the market rate, i_{w0}, which had also determined i_{l0}. Suppose the banks' perception of risk now falls so that credit supply shifts to $C^{s'}$, resulting in an increase in credit to C_1 at point

B and thus in deposits to M_1 at point B'. Other things being equal, the wholesale rate falls to i_{w1}, so that the credit supply curve shifts to $C^{s''}$, further increasing the volume of credit and thus deposits.

As far as monetary policy is concerned, the capacity of the monetary authorities to influence wholesale rates is the key. This can be shown as a direct effect on i_l in the credit market, or on one of the curves in the money market, depending on the mechanism employed. But the scope for influence is not deterministic, either in terms of the rate itself, or in terms of its influence on the credit market. A change in intercept of the credit supply curve may be more than offset in its effect on credit levels by a change in elasticity. Prediction of changes in elasticity requires close enquiry into conventional judgement in financial and product markets using, if necessary, a variety of empirical and analytical methods.

In the first example, the process was seen as starting in the credit market. But the process may also be affected by developments originating in the money market. Suppose the monetary authorities want to tighten monetary conditions by raising the repo rate, and they enforce the new, higher, rate by adding to demand in the money market. This is represented by a shift out in the demand for money function from M^d to $M^{d'}$, as in Figure 3.2. This pushes money market rates up, which in turn pushes up the cost of funds to banks, and thus pushes up the credit supply curve and the lending rate. But then this reduces the supply of deposits, which pushes up money market rates further, and so on, as illustrated in Figure 3.2. There is a range of possibilities here depending on how flat the credit supply curve is, whether there are other factors shifting it, etc. The money market starts at A, but the tightening monetary policy pushes interest rates up from i_{w0} to i_{w1} at B. This pushes up wholesale rates for the banks so that the credit supply curve moves up to $C^{s'}$ and the credit market moves from A' to B'. This reduces the supply of money to $M^{s'}$, which pushes the money market rate up further, and so on.

In practice, in the market process, as key variables change, things are rarely equal. The curves depend crucially on a variety of factors; some, such as competitive structure, are likely to be stable. But others, such as banks' perceived risk, may be stable for a time, but are also liable to periodic adjustment. What at first sight may appear to be an unstable cumulative process will, in practice, over time, adjust as expectations and confidence in those expectations change; the system is self-organizing. But there is a limit to how far two-dimensional diagrams can capture the process. They should only be regarded as an aid to thought.

4.   Conclusion

In line with its name, the structuralist approach focuses on the structural aspects of the financial system and its place in the overall economic structure. It also focuses on processes within that structure, and processes which in turn change that structure. Such an approach cannot deal with its subject matter dualistically. It is at this level that we may most appropriately see the source of differences with accommodationists. The structuralist approach can accommodate liquidity preference along with endogenous money. It sees all parties as influencing outcomes, without any having absolute control over any part of the system, nor any being absolutely constrained. The central bank has significant influence as a major player in markets which takes the macro view, but that influence (even on interest rates) is tempered by the private sector. Borrowers have considerable influence on

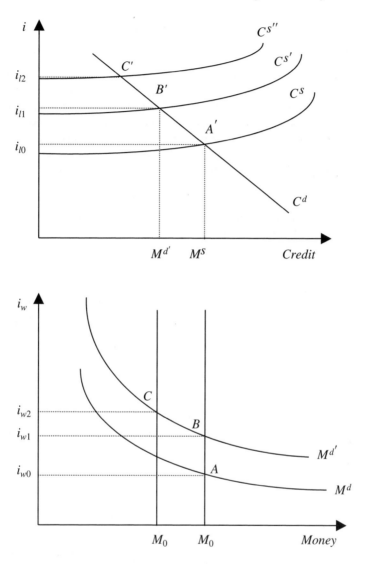

Figure 3.2 Interaction between the credit and money markets with an increase in precautionary demand for money

the volume of credit, but are subject to bank strategy with respect to market segments, and bank liquidity preference and risk perception at a systemic level. There are clearly imbalances of power, between the central bank and the banks, and between the banks and certain market segments among borrowers. We are not talking about the type of neutral interactions of a general equilibrium system. But structuralism allows for analysis of more complex interactions than the accommodationist approach. It is important for the way in which these differences have been discussed in the literature that the structural approach does not lend itself to capture within a single diagram other than as a partial aid to thought. While much accommodationist writing accedes to the more complex picture painted by structuralists, the focus on the slope of a single curve, whose meaning is highly questionable, does their work a disservice.

We have seen that structural endogeneity theory is closely tied in with the other pillar of post-Keynesian monetary theory: the non-neutrality of money. Not only are the interactions between central banks, banks and banks' customers complex, but the interactions with the economy are also complex. We have identified some general principles, governing the emergence of bank deposits as money, and the role of the central banks, for example. But any analysis designed to inform a real situation needs to be expressed in terms of the relevant structural arrangements. As these arrangements evolve, we can expect to see the structural theory of endogenous money also evolve.

Notes

*   This chapter has benefited from the helpful comments and suggestions of Victoria Chick.
1.   The repo rate is the discount rate associated with (normally two-week) repurchase agreements with respect to government securities.
2.   Wray (1990) sets out the historical development of endogeneity theories. See Chick (1973) for an early treatment of the issues.
3.   The matter is further complicated by the fact that the interest rate does not reflect the full cost to the borrower because of joint-costing of related services (Chick and Dow, 2002).
4.   Post-Keynesian analysis is based on the view that markets are in general segmented; this means that gross substitution does not apply:
5.   This view can be found in Keynes (1973: 201–23); see further Dow (1982), Kregel (1984–85), Dow and Dow (1989), Wray (1990).
6.   This is the case also of the circuitist approach (see Chapters 6 and 7 of this volume on circuit theory and Chick, 2000).

References

Arestis, P. and A.S. Eichner (1988), 'The Post-Keynesian and institutionalist theory of money and credit', *Journal of Economic Issues*, **22**(December), 1003–22.

Arestis, P. and P. Howells (1996), 'Theoretical reflections on endogenous money: the problem with "convenience lending"', *Cambridge Journal of Economics*, **20**(5), 539–52.

Chick, V. (1973), *The Theory of Monetary Policy*, Oxford: Parkgate.

Chick, V. (1992), 'The evolution of the banking system and the theory of saving, investment and interest', in P. Arestis and S.C. Dow (eds), *Money, Method and Keynes: Selected Essays of Victoria Chick*, London: Macmillan, 193–205.

Chick, V. (1993), 'The evolution of the banking system and the theory of monetary policy', in S.F. Frowen, *Monetary Theory and Monetary Policy: New Tracks for the 1990s*, London: Macmillan, 79–92.

Chick, V. (2000), 'Money and effective demand', in J. Smithin (ed.), *What is Money?* London: Routledge, 124–38.

Chick, V. and S.C. Dow (2002), 'Monetary policy with endogenous money and liquidity preference: a nondualistic treatment', *Journal of Post Keynesian Economics*, **24**(4), 587–608.

Committee on the Working of the Monetary System (1959), *Report* (Cmnd. 827), London: HMSO.

Cottrell, A. (1986), 'The endogeneity of money and money-income causality', *Scottish Journal of Political Economy*, **33**(1), 2–27.

Cottrell, A. (1994), 'Post-Keynesian monetary economics', *Cambridge Journal of Economics*, **18**(6), 587–606.

Davidson, P. and S. Weintraub (1973), 'Money as cause and effect', *Economic Journal*, **84**(332), 1117–32.

Dow, A.C. and S.C. Dow (1989), 'Endogenous money creation and idle balances', in J. Pheby (ed.), *New Directions in Post Keynesian Economics*, Aldershot, UK and Brookfield, USA: Edward Elgar, 147–64.

Dow, J.C.R. and I. Saville (1988), *A Critique of Monetary Policy*, Oxford: Clarendon.

Dow, S.C. (1982), 'The regional composition of the money multiplier process', *Scottish Journal of Political Economy*, **29**(1), 22–44.

Dow, S.C. (1996a), 'Horizontalism: a critique', *Cambridge Journal of Economics*, **20**(4), 497–508.

Dow, S.C. (1996b), *The Methodology of Macroeconomic Thought*, Cheltenham, UK and Brookfield, USA: Edward Elgar.

Dow, S.C. (1997a), 'Endogenous money', in G.C. Harcourt and P. Riach (eds), *The Second Edition of the General Theory*, London: Routledge, 61–78.

Dow, S.C. (1997b), 'The money supply as a theoretical and policy variable', *Archives of Economic History*, **8**(1–2), 7–36.

Dow, S.C. and J. Smithin (1992), 'Free banking in Scotland, 1695–1845', *Scottish Journal of Political Economy*, **39**(4), 374–90.

Fontana, G. (2000), 'Post Keynesians and circuitists on money and uncertainty: an attempt at generality', *Journal of Post Keynesian Economics*, **23**(1), 27–48.

Frenkel, J.A. and H.G. Johnson (1976), *The Monetary Approach to the Balance of Payments*, Toronto: University of Toronto Press.

Goodhart, C.A.E. (1984), *Monetary Theory and Practice: The UK Experience*, London: Macmillan.

Hewitson, G. (1995), 'Post-Keynesian monetary theory: some issues', *Journal of Economic Surveys*, **9**(3), 285–310.

Hodgson, G. (1988), *Economics and Institutions*, Cambridge: Polity Press.

Kaldor, N. (1982), *The Scourge of Monetarism*, Oxford: Oxford University Press.

Keynes, J.M. (1936), *The General Theory of Employment, Interest and Money*, London: Macmillan.

Keynes, J.M. (1973), *The General Theory and After: Defence and Development. Collected Writings of John Maynard Keynes*, Vol. XIV, London: Macmillan for the Royal Economic Society.

Kregel, J. (1984–85), 'Constraints on the expansion of output and employment: real or monetary?', *Journal of Post Keynesian Economics*, **7**(2), 139–52.

Lavoie, M. (1984), 'The endogenous flow of credit and the Post Keynesian theory of money', *Journal of Economic Issues*, **18**(3), 771–97.

Lavoie, M. (1996), 'Horizontalism, structuralism, liquidity preference and the principle of increasing risk', *Scottish Journal of Political Economy*, **43**(3), 275–300.

Mariscal, I.B.-F. and P. Howells (2002), 'Central banks and market interest rates', *Journal of Post Keynesian Economics*, **24**(4), 568–86.

McCallum, B. (1986), 'On "real" and "sticky price" theories of the business cycle', *Journal of Money, Credit, and Banking*, **18**(4), 397–414.

Minsky, H.P. (1975), *John Maynard Keynes*, London: Macmillan.

Minsky, H.P. (1982), *Inflation, Recession and Economic Policy*, Brighton: Wheatsheaf.

Moore, B.J. (1988), *Horizontalists and Verticalists: The Macroeconomics of Credit Money*, Cambridge: Cambridge University Press.

Palley, T.I. (1991), 'The endogenous money supply: consensus and disagreement', *Journal of Post Keynesian Economics*, **13**(3), 397–403.

Palley, T.I. (1994), 'Competing views of the money supply process: theory and evidence', *Metroeconomica*, **45**(1), 67–88.

Palley, T.I. (1996), *Post Keynesian Economics: Debt, Distribution and the Macro Economy*, London: Macmillan.

Pollin, R. (1991), 'Two theories of money supply endogeneity: some empirical evidence', *Journal of Post Keynesian Economics*, **13**(3), 366–96.

Rousseas, S. (1986), *Post Keynesian Monetary Economics*, Armonk, NY: M.E. Sharpe.

Sellon, G. and S.E. Weiner (1997), 'Monetary policy without reserve requirements: case studies and options for the United States', *Federal Reserve Bank of Kansas City Economic Review*, **82**(2), 5–30.

Tobin, J. (1963), 'Commercial banks as creators of "money"', in D. Carson (ed.), *Banking and Monetary Studies*, Homewood, IL: R.D. Irwin.

Wojnilower, A.M. (1980), 'The central role of credit crunches in recent financial history', *Brookings Papers on Economic Activity*, no. 2.

Wray, R. (1990), *Money and Credit in Capitalist Economies: the Endogenous Money Approach*, Aldershot, UK and Brookfield, USA: Edward Elgar.

4 The endogeneity of money: empirical evidence
Peter Howells

1. Introduction

Any survey of empirical work on the endogeneity of money faces a fundamental problem of where to draw the line. Take the easy case first. We could confine our attention to works that select themselves because their author(s) present them as such. Alternatively, we could use the fact that 'Endogenous money theory is one of the main cornerstones of post-Keynesian economics' (Fontana, 2003, p. 291) to select on the basis of work which has been published in post-Keynesian, or otherwise sympathetic, contexts. Either approach would draw the line in a broadly similar position.

The problem with this approach is that monetary policy is inevitably pragmatic. Policy must confront what *is*, even if macroeconomic textbooks continue with the fiction that central banks target the money *stock* directly (exploiting a mechanical relationship between bank reserves and deposits) and that monetary policy 'shocks' must always work through real-balance effects.[1] By contrast, we know that central banks set the rate of interest and allow reserves and deposits to be demand-determined, because they have been telling us so for many years: 'in the real-world banks extend credit, creating deposits in the process, and look for the reserves later' (Holmes, 1969, p. 73); and, more recently: 'In the United Kingdom, money is endogenous – the Bank supplies base money on demand at its prevailing interest rate and broad money is created by the banking system' (King, 1994, p. 264).[2]

The same message comes from the 'new consensus' view on monetary policy and its recognition of Taylor rules as a more accurate characterization of how central banks actually work than any focus on monetary aggregates. Maybe our line should be drawn to encompass any work that recognizes that the central bank sets the rate of interest and all else is market-determined. Inevitably, this enlarges the field considerably.

Finally, and closely related to the pragmatism of policy research, we should recognize that in the UK at least, even when monetary aggregates *were* of some concern to policy-makers (roughly the period from 1968 to 1985), analysis of the money stock focused upon *changes* (rather than stocks) and explained these changes through the 'flow of funds identity' whereby the flow of *new* money (on the left-hand side) was 'explained' by its credit counterparts (on the right-hand side). This is admitting at the very least that the quantity of money is best seen as being determined by the *supply* of bank credit even if we need to look further for the source of the *demand* for bank credit in order to clinch the argument that the new money is *endogenously* determined. On this view, what passes for some very mainstream empirical work in the 1980s, and even earlier, was also in effect shedding some (unintentional) light on the second link in the endogenous money chain: loans create deposits. Taking this approach draws the boundary still more widely.

Here we take the 'core' of the endogeneity hypothesis to comprise two causal links: loans depend upon economic activity (broadly defined); and those loans create deposits. In section 2, we concentrate on tests of the former and in section 3 we look at the loan–deposit link. In both cases we draw the boundaries fairly widely. In section 4 we look at the empirical work on what we shall call 'secondary' issues such as the accommodationist/structuralist debate, the reconciliation of the demand for credit with the demand for money, and the link between central bank rate and market interest rates. In section 5 we summarize and conclude.

2.   The demand for bank loans

Although the endogeneity of the money supply was recognized years ago (notably by Schumpeter, 1911; Wicksell, 1898) and had powerful supporters in the not so distant past (e.g. Kaldor, 1970; 1982; 1985; Kaldor and Trevithick, 1981; Davidson and Weintraub, 1973), it was Basil Moore who did most to confront the monetarist revival of the 1980s. His book, *Horizontalists and Verticalists* (1988) remains the most substantial theoretical and empirical treatise on the subject, though not now, of course, without its critics.

In that book, Moore set out the core of the endogeneity hypothesis, including the assertion that the demand for credit has its origins in the production decisions of firms. In chapter 9 this proposition is subject to empirical testing. The dependent variable is the flow of new bank lending to US industrial and commercial companies (ICCs) 1965(1)–1979(4). The estimation follows the same approach as that in a paper published in *Economica* in 1985 which had an antecedent in a Bank of England working paper (Moore and Threadgold, 1980). What is remarkable about all three is the theoretical basis which Moore gives for the estimated model. 'It stems from the recognition that the production process takes time, so that production costs are normally incurred *prior* to the receipt of sales proceeds' (Moore and Threadgold, 1985, p. 67). Here we have an explicit test of the hypothesis that the demand for loans (and ultimately the creation of deposits) depends upon the 'state of trade', meaning in this case firms' production plans. If anything happens to increase firms operating costs – an increase in input prices, the decision to increase output, a change in corporate tax rates, *inter alia* – then firms will require more working capital and this will be met by an increase in bank loans.

Bearing in mind the different data sets, the results are remarkably similar in all three cases. Using the preferred equation from the 1980 paper, we have:

$$LDI_t = 131.6 - 0.727\Delta W_t - 1.162\Delta IB_{t-1} - 0.472S_t - 0.932\Delta T_t - 475.4RT - 16.58r$$

where *LDI* is the quarterly flow of new bank lending to ICCs; *W* is the wage bill; *IB* is the import bill; *S* is stock building (additions to inventories); *T* is ICCs' tax bill; *RT* is a variable to capture the effect of 'round tripping' – periods when ICCs could earn more on deposit than the cost of borrowing – and *r* is the real own rate of interest on loans. With the exception of the latter, all variables are in nominal terms. This equation explained about 81 per cent of the flow of new lending to UK ICCs. For the USA the figure was 75 per cent (Moore, 1988, p. 228).[3]

These studies appeared to establish two fundamental precepts of the post-Keynesian view of money supply determination. The first is that it was prior changes in firms' operating conditions (the 'state of trade') that was principally responsible for changes in the flow of new loans (and therefore the rate of deposit creation). The second was that the interest-elasticity of the demand for credit was low. The latter purported to show that the central bank's ability to control credit and money growth was extremely limited. The only instrument at its disposal was a short-term nominal interest rate, and even where changes could be made to have a predictable effect on the *real* rate, this made little difference to the flow of new loans.

It was not only economists with a particular point to make about endogenous money who were anxious to explore the behaviour of bank lending in the late 1970s. Recall the context in the UK, which had introduced the 'Competition and Credit Control' measures in 1971, a package which swept away the long-standing use of administrative controls over money and credit and promised, in future, that the Bank of England would rely solely upon changes in minimum lending rate as its policy instrument. Subsequent events derailed these hopes and saw the interest instrument reinforced by the supplementary special deposit scheme (SSD – the 'corset') intermittently from December 1973. Notice, however, that the SSD scheme was designed in such a way as to penalize banks that allowed 'excess' growth in their interest-bearing eligible liabilities ('IBELS') – roughly speaking their interest-bearing deposits. The purpose of this was to discourage banks bidding for deposits and thus to help drive a wedge between lending and deposit rates. This in turn recognized the point (later publicized by Sprenkle and Miller, 1980) that the demand for both money and credit depended, *inter alia*, on the *spread* between these two rates. As the spread approaches zero the demand for money and credit tends to infinity.

In 1981 the primacy of interest rates as the policy instrument was restated, along with the mechanism whereby it was thought to influence money and credit growth. A rise in rates increases the cost of borrowing and thus slows the rate of deposit creation. If, at the same time, lending rates can be raised *relative to* deposit rates, then so much the better since there is then a secondary effect as agents switch from money to non-money assets and lower the cost of non-bank credit relative to bank loans.

In this environment, it is not surprising that the late 1970s and early 1980s saw a flurry of studies, some of which approached the demand for bank credit as a portfolio decision, rather like studies of the demand for money, wherein the decision to take out a bank loan was considered the equivalent of the purchase of a negative asset, but others certainly recognized the importance of economic activity, in levels and changes.

In the UK, HM Treasury (HMT), the National Institute of Economic and Social Research (NIESR) and the Bank of England all had well-developed models of the demand for bank lending, and their main characteristics were compared by Cuthbertson and Foster (1982).[4] The Bank of England model was essentially similar to the model estimated by Moore and Threadgold (1980) and carried through Moore's subsequent work: the dependent variable was the *flow* of *nominal* lending to ICCs. Firms' costs were important and there was a low elasticity on the real cost of borrowing. By contrast, the HMT model was expressed wholly in real terms (except the interest rate) and sought to explain the *stock* of bank loans while the NIESR model focused, like the Bank of England, on flows, but in *real* terms (but again with nominal interest rates). Only the Bank of England refers explicitly to firms' costs; the NIESR model had the change in manufacturing output as its activity variable while the HMT model had (the level of) real GDP. Given these differences, it is difficult to compare the models, though if we are prepared to treat real GDP as a proxy for firms' output, then all three find that the level or change in firms' output is significant. The Bank model, because it is estimated in nominal terms, in effect adds the cost of producing that output as an important variable. The notable differences arise over interest rates, though again direct comparison is difficult.

The NIESR model differed by treating (nominal) interest rates as a spread (between the return on assets and the cost of borrowing). The results suggested that in the short run bank lending was highly sensitive but from a policy point of view there was the problem of uncertainty regarding the behaviour of the spread in response to a change in the official rate. If, for example, the rate on assets changed more rapidly than banks repriced their loans in response to an increase in the official rate, there would be the perverse outcome that money and credit *expanded*. The HMT model, with a (single) nominal rate on bank lending, also showed a negative elasticity, intermediate between the NIESR and Bank of England/Moore and Threadgold equation. It is clear that by the mid-1980s there was a well-established tradition of explaining the demand for bank lending primarily by reference to the demand from ICCs (rather than a broader range of agents) and that this tradition was accepted in orthodox circles. Furthermore, while the HMT and NIESR approaches differed in several details from that of Moore and Threadgold, these can be exaggerated. For example, if we treat GDP and the volume of firms' output as closely related, then it was widely accepted that both the level and change in *real* bank lending were significantly influenced by ICCs' output plans. If we wanted to explain the behaviour of *nominal* lending, then it was legitimate also to consider firm's costs (at least this seemed to be proven for the *flow* of nominal lending) and thus to support the view that *changes in* the money stock were traceable to firm's production and costs. Any major differences of opinion concerned the role of interest rates, and this was important because of the emerging consensus that a short-term interest rate, set by the central bank, was the only plausible policy instrument.

We turn now to more recent developments regarding the origin of loan demand and look at work that is to some degree critical of the two propositions commonly associated with the endogeneity hypothesis: that it is firms' production plans that are central to the demand for credit and that interest rates have little impact on this demand. We start with the latter.

We have already seen that studies of the demand for credit which otherwise had a number of features in common differed over the role of interest rates. Before going further, we should note not only the obvious – that the distinction between real and nominal, and the possible relevance of *relative* interest rates, opens up the possibility of virtually unlimited formulations for empirical purposes – but also the fact that the post-Keynesian literature on endogenous money has itself generated a good deal of theoretical controversy on what interest rates are 'relevant', much of it associated with the structuralist/accommodationist debate.[5] But the picture is more complex even than this. Not only can one advance different theoretical conceptions of the relevant interest rate and then select from a wide range of different rates for empirical purposes, but when it comes to *real* rates, judgements have to be made about how to model inflation expectations and, in the UK especially, *lending* rates have also to be 'estimated' because of UK banks' reluctance to divulge actual rates on grounds of commercial sensitivity.

The difficulties this can cause were stressed by Hewitson (1997). In the Moore/Threadgold studies the real rate of interest was the real rate charged on bank loans. This was constructed as the official rate set by the central bank plus a 2 per cent mark-up, then adjusted for inflation expectations by using a proxy constructed by the Bank of England. Both steps involve untested assumptions. In the case of the mark-up, one might imagine that profit-maximizing banks having difficulty in funding the demand for loans would increase their lending rates and thus the mark-up. This of course shows why interest rate behaviour is related to the accommodationist/structuralist debate. If the central bank always 'accommodates' fully, why should banks have difficulty in funding new loans? But if one believes that agents, including banks, experience different degrees of liquidity preference in response to different conditions (Bibow, 1998; Dow and Dow, 1995; Dow, 1996; Wray, 1995), then it is quite inappropriate to assume a constant mark-up.

We come back to the point that if the only plausible instrument of policy is an official rate set by the central bank, then the responsiveness of market rates to any change in the official rate is of widespread and urgent interest. Thus studies at the Bank of England include Dale (1993) and Dale and Haldane (1993). The 'stickiness' of market interest rates is also a matter of wider public policy, bearing as it does on the degree of competition in the banking sector and the price that people are paying for financial services and products. Within a post-Keynesian framework, and explicitly concerned with the demand for money and the demand for credit, there is the evidence (for the UK) in Biefang-Frisancho Mariscal and Howells (2002). All of these studies show that there is considerable elasticity in the response of market rates to a change in the official rate. First of all, we need to distinguish a short-run response from the ultimate equilibrium position which may or may not leave relativities unchanged. Even if it does, short run disequilibrium may be quite sufficiently large and long-lasting to have some effect on the demand for different types of credit. We noted above that it is difficult to get explicit data on bank lending rates, especially to ICCs, and therefore tests of bank loan rate behaviour do not feature largely in the studies above. However, there is much evidence that suggests a constant mark-up is at best a simplification. For example, Heffernan (1997) shows that in response to a change in the official rate, the adjustment in the cost of (bank) mortgage loans was only 37 per cent complete after one month, while the adjustment of personal loan rates took much longer. In the UK, we know that many bank loan rates are priced by a mark-up over LIBOR (London Interbank Offer Rate) rather than the official rate itself, though we know little about the mark-up. However, if LIBOR itself shows a varying relationship with the official rate, then we know that assuming a constant mark-up of loan over official rate is unsatisfactory. This was the thinking behind testing the LIBOR–Treasury bill rate (TBR) spread in Biefang-Frisancho Marsical and Howells (2002). Using monthly data from 1986 to 2001 in an unrestricted VAR model, they found a cointegrating relationship between LIBOR and TBR. In the long run, LIBOR is about 0.3 per cent above the official rate. But adjustment of LIBOR to a change in the official rate takes about two months, while adjustment of other (deposit and bond) rates takes much longer. On this evidence, it's clear that in recent years in the UK bank loan rates diverged from the official rate, every time there was a change, for a period of at least two months.

The modelling of inflationary expectations in Moore and Threadgold also involves an untested assumption, namely that expectations are actually formed in the way modelled by the Bank of England's proxy. But more seriously, Hewitson argues, the use of a real rate is anyway inappropriate. It is the cash flow arising from the nominal rate that firms have to meet and, if they expect inflation to be high or low, they will expect the nominal value of their revenues to increase rapidly or slowly. That said, one might still expect firms' demand for credit to be inelastic with respect to the nominal rate since firms face bankruptcy if they cannot meet their (nominal) obligations.

Other criticisms identified by Hewitson included simultaneous equation bias arising from the fact that the central bank's setting of the rate is partly dependent on the behaviour of variables in the loan demand function. Because of the central bank's reaction function, the official interest rate ceases to be exogenous in the statistical sense. Furthermore, estimating in first differences, as Moore and Threadgold had done, meant that their results contained no useful information about long-run relationships.

Bearing these problems in mind, Hewitson set out to test the demand for credit model using Australian data. The tests were carried out for each of four dependent variables, some monthly and some biannual, ending in 1990, since there was no single Australian series which corresponded exactly to the ICC series used in the UK studies. To avoid the weaknesses in the Moore and Threadgold work, her approach differed in two important respects: first, the use of an error correction model in order to avoid the spurious regression problem while establishing useful information about long-run relationships; second, the use of a *nominal* interest rate actually charged on bank lending as more appropriate and also as a means of avoiding the simultaneous equation bias that would result by including the central bank's official rate (plus fixed mark-up).

The estimations were carried out for each of the four variables representing firms' demand for credit. The results, from a Moore and Threadgold point of view, were disappointing. Sometimes the error correction term was insignificant; sometimes the long-run solution derived from the ECM differed from the cointegrating regression from which the ECM was derived; some equations suffered from non-normality of the residuals and, most conspicuously, the wage bill variable was generally insignificant while the rate of interest was sometimes significant, sometimes not. Hewitson's conclusion listed a number of possible explanations for the results, but the fact remained that her results were not supportive of the working capital demand for loans and the low interest elasticity.

The fact that changes in ICCs' working capital requirements may not provide a very satisfactory explanation for variations in the flow of new bank loans does not, of course, mean that they (and the resulting deposits) are not endogenously determined. Endogeneity requires only that the flow of loans is dependent upon other variables within the system. Instead of concentrating upon *firms'* demand for working capital, one might look at a broader-based demand for credit. In this case the explanatory variables might include nominal GDP or total final expenditure. A dramatic move towards a broader-based analysis was offered by Howells and Hussein (1999), who experimented with a measure of total transactions (i.e. including transactions in assets and secondhand goods) as the driving force behind the demand for loans. This was motivated by four factors. The first was a recognition that firms' demand for credit was a diminishing fraction of the total demand, which was shifting increasingly towards households. By 1997, 60 per cent of total bank and building society lending in the UK was going to households, compared with only 20 per cent to ICCs (and 20 per cent to financial firms) (Bank of England, 1997).[6] The second was the performance of the monetary sector model developed by Arestis and Biefang-Frisancho Mariscal (1995). This performed quite well when judged by conventional criteria and it was notable for recognizing three distinct sources of demand for credit: a household demand for credit (excluding for house purchase); a household demand for mortgage finance; and a demand by ICCs. Interestingly, the ICC equation suggested that stockbuilding was a highly significant variable while interest rates were insignificant (broadly supportive of the Moore/Threadgold position). The household demands for credit, however, were influenced by interest rates, specifically by a loan–deposit spread. The model was clearly suggestive of a need to look at broader origins of credit demand.

The third factor was the observation that while the ratio of total transactions to GDP in the UK had been fairly stable, it increased dramatically during the 1980s, rising from 1.9 in 1976 to 3.1 in 1989. This measure of transactions excluded large-value, same-day payments between financial firms. Adding those in produces a rise from a ratio of approximately 20 to 55 over the same period (Howells and Biefang-Frisancho Mariscal, 1992, p. 93). This possibility had been recognized by Keynes in the *Treatise* and by Fisher (1911), both of whom recognized a distinction between 'income' (= GDP) transactions and other or 'financial' transactions (excluded from GDP). While income transactions might be closely related to GDP, transactions in secondhand (real or financial) assets

> need not be, and are not, governed by the volume of current output. The pace at which a circle of financiers, speculators and investors hand round to one another particular pieces of wealth, or title to such, which they are neither producing nor consuming but merely exchanging, bears no definite relation to the rate of current production. The volume of such transactions is subject to very wide and incalculable fluctuations . . . (Keynes, 1971, V, p. 42)

The final factor motivating an interest in total transactions was the notion that the demand for money (and credit) should depend upon expenditure plans, in general, and not just upon spending upon current output. Where the demand for money was concerned, this was already getting some recognition. For example, Anderson (1993) showed that the boom in mortgage refinancing in the USA had led to an increase in the volume and volatility of financial transactions relative to GDP transactions, and that this had measurable effects upon the demand for M1 deposits. More recently, Palley (1995) and Pollin and Schaberg (1998) had demonstrated that money demand estimates in the USA could be improved by recognizing a role for total transactions where the behaviour of the latter is proxied by measures that refer to some part of the property market and to financial activity, two major categories of spending included in *total* transactions but excluded from conventional measures of GDP. Following this, Howells and Hussein (1997) showed that a total transactions series itself gave better results than either GDP or wealth in an otherwise standard money demand equation.

The first attempt to apply a similar reasoning to the demand for credit was in Howells and Biefang-Frisancho Mariscal (1992). Although the paper was ostensibly about the divergent behaviour of transactions and income velocities, it contained the argument that the demand for credit (and thus the resulting supply of deposits) was heavily influenced by total transactions. It was easily shown that transactions velocity had remained relatively constant. It was a rather oblique, or initial, formulation of the idea that loans (and deposits) might be endogenously determined but that we should focus upon total, including speculative and property, spending rather than firms' costs of production.

Howells and Hussein (1999) featured the comparative properties of two estimations, one including GDP and the other including a measure of total transactions as explanatory variables in equations with the flow of real bank lending as the dependent variable. The RHS variables included also a variety of nominal interest rates (on loans, deposits, bonds and on foreign currency) and an inflation term. The estimations were based on quarterly data covering the period 1973(1)–1994(4). Changes in both GDP and total transactions were significant at the 1 per cent level and both models passed the usual diagnostic tests. However, the total transactions model was superior when it came to out-of-sample forecasts. Interestingly, in the light of Moore and Threadgold's earlier work, interest rates (domestic, foreign, simple or as spreads) played no significant part. The present state of knowledge does, therefore, seem to suggest that the flow of bank loans is endogenously determined but it is to be explained by a very wide category of spending (rather than by spending of any one group or any particular category of goods and services). It does also seem as if changes in interest rates have rather limited impact.

3.   Loans and deposits

The second part of the endogeneity hypothesis, namely that the loans supplied in response to the demand for bank credit create corresponding deposits, has attracted less detailed investigation. No doubt this is because it is less controversial as a result of the banks' balance sheet identity. The starting point is the recognition that banks' assets are all, in some form or another, loans. They may be marketable – as commercial or Treasury bills – or non-marketable. Even deposits with the central bank are loans (to the public sector). Given this identity, a change in bank loans must be matched by a change in deposits, and deposits are the dominant part of the money stock. This is widely recognized in the so-called flow of funds (FoF) identity or 'credit counterparts' approach to the analysis of changes in the money stock.

The FoF identity can be written with numerous variations, but in its simplest form it says:

$$\Delta D \equiv \Delta BL_p + \Delta BL_g \tag{4.1}$$

The change in total bank deposits is the counterpart of changes in total bank lending, i.e. to the non-bank public or to government. For a change in the total stock of *money* we must add in any change in notes and coin held by the non-bank public and then we can write:

$$\Delta M \equiv \Delta BL_p + \Delta BL_g + \Delta C_p \tag{4.2}$$

The government's total borrowing needs can be financed in various ways, and the amount of finance provided by banks arises as a residual, providing whatever is required after all other sources of borrowing have been exhausted. Thus:

$$PSBR \equiv \Delta G_p + \Delta C_p - \Delta ext + \Delta BL_g \tag{4.3}$$

The budget deficit, adjusted for sales and purchases of foreign currency, must be financed by selling government debt, or by issuing notes and coin or by borrowing from banks.

The fact that two sides of an identity must balance is not of itself telling us anything about causality. Indeed, as Cuthbertson (1985b, pp. 176–7) shows, it is not difficult to rearrange the terms in (4.3); recall that the monetary base is cash held by the non-bank public plus bank lending to the government in the form of (banks') reserve assets, and then rewrite (4.2) so that a change in the base appears on the RHS. In these circumstances, we are back to the base-multiplier model (albeit written in first differences) which is the framework normally adopted for the analysis of a money stock exogenously determined by the reserve operations of the central bank.

Making out a case that *causality* runs from loans to deposits requires some empirical evidence. But it is worth pausing for a moment to consider whether there is not something about the fact that analysis of monetary changes is carried out through the FoF model which *disposes* researchers to be sympathetic towards the idea of endogeneity. It is a question of the *insights* that we get from arranging an identity in a particular way. For example, if we write out the base-multiplier model in conventional form, the identity (a) highlights stocks (rather than flows) and (b) suggests that these stocks are fixed unless the central bank decides otherwise. In modern jargon, the 'default' setting in the model is a fixed money supply. By contrast, the FoF model focuses on flows and encourages us to think of positive flows as the 'normal' or 'default' case. This is undoubtedly more realistic: central banks, even if they are concerned with monetary aggregates, do not aim at a given stock of money. Their target is the rate of growth and, if they do nothing, in this model, the money supply will continue to expand. It is worth considering that this 'expansion as the norm' makes the FoF model an obvious framework for the analysis of an endogenously determined money stock. Furthermore, the model is also very convenient for tracing the effects of the rate of interest when used as the policy instrument. Its relevance to lending to the non-bank public (ΔBL_p) is obvious and the return on government debt is also relevant to debt sales (ΔG_p). It is easy to see how the FoF equation can be used to analyse issues surrounding an endogenously determined money supply.

Attempts to establish causality empirically are, inevitably, limited to testing for causality in the statistical sense, and this is a good deal more limited than the sense in which we normally use the term. In a statistical context, 'causal' means 'containing information that helps better predict a variable' (Desai, 1981, p. 402).[7]

In *Horizontalists and Verticalists* Moore offered a range of Granger and Sims causality tests on four different measures of (US) money, the monetary base and bank loans. The data were monthly and covered, with some variations, the period 1974–80. In Moore's own words:

> The evidence presented strongly suggests that *unidirectional* causality runs from bank lending to each of the four monetary aggregates. Each monetary aggregate has been shown in turn to cause the monetary base unidirectionally. The single exception is the feedback relationship found to exist between the monetary base and M2. (Moore, 1988, pp. 162–3, emphasis added)

A broadly similar investigation by Thomas Palley (1994), albeit for a longer time period, came to similar results.

In 1998 Howells and Hussein followed up both in a study that took quarterly data from the G7 countries for periods which all ended in 1992 or 1993 and began somewhere between 1957 and 1977. The study tested only for the relationship between bank loans and broad money, and drew on a number of developments in econometric methodology after Moore's 1988 work. For example, the Phillips–Perron (1988) test was used to establish the degree of cointegration between the bank loan and broad money series because of its advantage in allowing for serial correlation and heteroscedasticity. Having established the degree of cointegration, Howells and Hussein then estimated a vector error correction model in which the lagged cointegrating residuals were entered as an explanatory variable and then tested for causality.

The second link in the endogeneity chain was broadly confirmed across the G7: broad money is 'Granger-caused' by loans, whatever the reputation and rhetoric of the central bank (Howells and Hussein, 1998, p. 337). However, what the results also showed was that there were signs of reverse causality (i.e. from deposits to loans) in each of the G7, most convincingly for Germany and Japan. The presence of bidirectional causality was interpreted by Howells and Hussein as providing some evidence for the debate, which we take up in more detail in the next section, about the relationship between the demand for credit and the demand for money. Put briefly at this point, we can see the problem if we just look back at the FoF identity (4.2) above. This says that the change in the quantity of *money* is identical to the sum of *credit* flows. But money and credit are not the same thing, and if we define money, as we do, as a subset of financial assets *held by the non-bank public*, then (4.4) raises the question of what has happened to the demand for money (not to mention the vast literature devoted to its analysis). As Cuthbertson (1985b) says: 'There is an implicit demand for money in the model [i.e. (4.2)] but only *in equilibrium*' (p. 173, emphasis in original). But this raises the question of what sort of mechanism ensures that the flow of new deposits, created by the motives of those who wish to borrow more, will be equal to the wealth that the mass of the population just wants to hold as extra money balances. Hence, evidence from causality tests that there is feedback from deposits to loans suggests that the demand for money *does* matter and is therefore evidence against Moore's position.

Just as the Howells/Hussein results were being published, however, other developments on the econometric front were ensuring that the issue would have to be revisited. In 1997, Caporale and Pittis showed that omission of an important variable can result in invalid inference about the causality structure of a bivariate system (such as that tested by Moore, 1988; 1989; Palley, 1994; and Howells and Hussein, 1998). However, searching for the role of a third variable by estimating a trivariate vector autoregressive model also has its problems. In Caporale and Howells (2001) the investigators followed the suggestion of Toda and Yamamoto (1995), whose method involved augmenting the correct order of the VAR by the maximal order of integration which characterizes the series being used.

The potential of this approach for exploring the question of causality in an endogenous money context is considerable since it enables us to explore the first link in the endogeneity chain at the same time as we investigate the second. In the present case, for example, we might hypothesize that the omitted variable is the wage bill, or import bill or GDP or, as Caporale and Howells (2001) did, the total transactions variable that performed well in Howells and Hussein (1999). This enabled them to investigate simultaneously the causal impact of total transactions on the flow of new loans and the connection between new loans and new deposits. It also enabled them to explore any direct link between transactions and deposits. The study focused solely on the UK, using quarterly data from 1970 to 1998.

The findings confirmed again the loan–deposit link but it also suggested feedback from loans to deposits and, in their interpretation, some role for the demand for money. The novelty in the findings, however, was that while transactions also appeared to cause deposits *directly*, transactions did not appear to cause loans. Although the methods are completely different (a demand for loans equation against causality tests), this latter finding must raise some doubt about the inference drawn in Howells and Hussain (1999), namely, that changes in total spending plans drive changes in bank loans.

So far as the second link in the endogeneity chain is concerned, therefore, the present state of empirical knowledge appears to confirm the hypothesis that loans cause deposits.

The only controversial aspect of these findings concerns bidirectional causality and the possibility of a feedback from deposits to loans. Howells and Hussein (1998) found widespread evidence for this, and it appears again in Caporale and Howells (2001). As we noted above, its relevance to the endogeneity argument is not that it threatens the core in any way, but that it relates to what we called in our introduction one of the secondary questions, namely the question of how the demand for money and the demand for credit interact.

3. Remaining issues
In this section we look at three more issues that have attracted a degree of empirical investigation. Paramount among these, judged by the amount of attention given to it, must be the question of *why* the money supply is endogenous: the accommodationist/structuralist debate.

Before that, however, we shall tidy up two loose ends by looking at two issues on which we have already touched and which are interrelated, namely the reconciliation of the demand for money with the demand for credit, and the behaviour of market interest rates in response to central bank action.

The 'reconciliation problem' has a long history, though it has not always featured explicitly in accounts of endogenous money. A recent survey of the problem, its history and suggested solutions appears in Howells (2001, §5.8).

The problem begins with the fact that the demand for bank loans emanates from one set of agents with their own motives (for them it is an income–expenditure decision) while the demand for money emanates from another set with different motives (for them it is a portfolio decision). So long as this distinction exists, there must be a question of how the flow of new deposits, created by a subset of agents with income–expenditure deficits, is to be matched with the population's desire to arrange their wealth in such a way that they are willing to hold the additional money. And hold it they must (a) in order to satisfy the banks' balance sheet identity in which loans equal deposits and (b) because money is defined exclusively as deposits *held* by the non-bank private sector – in Dennis Robertson's memorable phrase, 'All money which is anywhere, must be somewhere' (Robertson, 1963, p. 350).

The possibility that the endogenous production of deposits could differ (*ex ante*) from the demand for them had been raised in 1986 [1992] by Victoria Chick. In what she described as 'stage 2 banking' it becomes possible for investment to precede saving because firms can borrow from banks whose loans create the new deposits with which to finance the new investment. Chick's immediate concern is how exactly to *describe* the extra deposits as a form of saving. But the reference to the demand for them is obvious:

> though the deposits are willingly held there is no actual decision to save. The deposits represent a passive (and grateful) acceptance of means of payment by workers and traders. Some of it will doubtless be used for consumption, some of it saved . . . [However] while individuals quite happily accepted claims on deposits – acceptability after all is the hallmark of the means of payment – the point on which I wish to insist is that no one actually asks those who subsequently have larger deposits whether the expansion of bank balance sheets was alright with them. (Chick, 1986 [1992], p. 200)

But Chick's target in 1986 was the earlier paper by Kaldor and Trevithick (1981). This had ruled out any problem in connection with the demand for endogenous money on the grounds that there would be an *automatic* application of excess receipts of money to the repayment of overdrafts. Thus the individual actions of borrowers taking out new loans (or extending existing ones) could threaten an 'excess' creation of deposits *ex ante*, but the moment 'excess' deposits were recognized they would be devoted by their holders to repaying existing debt. Thus limiting the deposit-creating process – *ex post* – to only those deposits which people were willing to hold.

Note that 'automatically' is the keyword. It is a reasonable assumption that those with overdrafts who have receipts in excess of payments will use the excess to reduce their debt and this will ('automatically') reduce the quantity of new deposits that are actually created. The problem is – not everyone has an overdraft. Once it is accepted that the first-round recipients of 'new' money may not wish to hold it, then the problems begin. Some *process* must be triggered by agents as they seek to adjust.

The same issue surfaced in the debate between Goodhart (1989; 1991) and Moore (1991) a few years later and again between Howells (1995; 1997) and Moore (1997). Moore's position throughout these exchanges is essentially that an equilibrium demand for money makes no sense in a world of endogenous money. In Moore (1991) this was argued on the grounds that if money exists then there must be uncertainty, and if there is uncertainty then 'general equilibrium' is impossible. This is reinforced by the nature of money, which means that it is always accepted as a means of payment. This, argued Moore, shows that there is a permanent and limitless 'demand' for money.

However, as Goodhart (1991) points out, whatever reservations one may have about *general* equilibrium, this does not entitle one to deny that people have preferences which they will seek to achieve – in this case by swapping money for other assets. And, as Howells (1997) argues, treating 'acceptability in exchange' as equivalent to a 'demand for money' is to distort the meaning of the latter rather dramatically.

Two areas of empirical work have some bearing on this issue. The first, as we have seen, involves causality tests. If, as seems to be the case, there is some evidence that causality runs from deposits to loans as well as from loans to deposits, then it is hard not to interpret this as some sort of evidence that the demand for money plays a role in the ability of the banking system to create deposits by its response to loan demand. As seen above, the balance of evidence from causality tests does suggest that the demand for money is relevant.

The second involves the behaviour of interest rates, which is relevant for two reasons. First, if we accept that there is something in the reconciliation problem, then this is bound to affect relative interest rates. Take as an example an 'excess' rate of deposit expansion. According to Goodhart (and Howells), agents will periodically exchange their excess deposits for other assets. The price of these assets will rise and their yields will fall. If, for convenience, we talk of 'bonds' as the alternative to money, then bond rates will fall relative to money's own rate and also relative to the rate charged on bank loans.

The behaviour of interest rates is relevant also because we recall that the core of the endogeneity thesis involves the proposition that central banks set the rate of interest and thereafter the quantity of loans (and deposits) is demand-determined. Furthermore, central banks are perfectly open in their recognition of an official short-term interest rate as the only feasible instrument of monetary policy. A rise, for example, in the official rate should, it is hoped, reduce the *rate of expansion* of loans and deposits. But there is considerable debate over the elasticity of the demand for bank loans with respect to the rate of interest and at least some evidence that this may be rather low. In other words, in a conventional diagram, the demand for bank loans is steeply sloped and a large change in interest rates causes little movement along the quantity axis. But if we think again about *relative* interest rates, as some of the studies in section 2 do, we can see why the situation may not be so bleak. Look again at the imaginary sequence in the paragraph above: switching between money and bonds causes relative interest rates to change. Now consider the case where the central bank raises the official rate and most interest rates follow roughly in step (quickly at the short end, less directly and more slowly at the long). Suppose now that money's own rate is sticky. We now have a situation where all rates have risen relative to money's own rate. This has widened the bond–deposit spread and agents switch from money to bonds, putting a brake on the rise in bond yields. If loan rates adjust by the amount of the official rate change, then (unrestrained) loan rates rise relative to the (moderated) bond rates and another differential widens. Since the issue of bonds is a partial substitute for bank loans and bonds now offer a (relatively) cheaper form of finance, our steep loan demand curve shifts inward and the effectiveness of the official rate change is enhanced. This mechanism, and the role of relative interest rates more generally, is discussed in more detail in Arestis and Biefang-Frisancho Mariscal (1995), pp. 550–53.

Thus any approach to endogenous money must take interest rates seriously – partly by virtue of the reconciliation problem, partly because it is central to policy decisions in an endogenous money regime. What happens to relative rates is an empirical question. As early as 1984, Goodhart expressed some scepticism about the authorities' ability to engineer the sort of relative rate changes just outlined[8] as he witnessed the effects of liability management leading to competitive (and 'unsticky') deposit rates. This is broadly confirmed in the paper by Biefang-Frisancho Mariscal and Howells (2002) but all the interest studies referred to in section 2 above should be read for the light that they shed on the very complex question of relative interest rates and not just for what they tell us about bank mark-ups.

Finally, we need to consider the evidence that has emerged in the course of the accommodationist/structuralist debate, or, as it is sometimes caricatured, the question of whether there is a horizontal money supply curve. An altogether more useful way of trying to capture the importance of this debate is to say that it is addressing the question of *why* the money supply is endogenous. Is it endogenous because, as the accommodationists (e.g. Kaldor, 1970; Moore, 1988; Lavoie, 1992) hold, the central bank willingly makes available any quantity of additional reserves required by banks to validate their lending? Or is it endogenous because, as the structuralists (e.g. Arestis, 1997; Chick, 1983; Dow, 1997; Pollin, 1991; Sawyer, 1996; Wray, 1990) would have it, banks' own innovative behaviour enables them either to 'create' reserves or to economize on them in such a way that their lending is largely free of any central bank constraint? Fontana (2003) is one of many good summaries of the debate and suggests a diagrammatic representation of the two positions.

The most direct test of these two positions was carried out a few years ago by Pollin (1991). Recall that the accommodationist position assumes that the central bank will always make available the quantity of reserves required by banks in order to support their lending. This may be for political reasons – a desire not to see interest rates rise – or precautionary reasons – a desire to avoid the risk of a banking collapse. If this were the case, Pollin argued, we would expect to see a stable ('stationary') relationship between the volume of bank loans and the volume of reserves. On checking this ratio, for the USA, over six NBER cycles from 1953 to 1988, Pollin found that the mean increased over time and quite rapidly in later periods. From this, and the behaviour of variances, Pollin drew the conclusion that this favoured the structuralist case – banks appeared to have found ways of increasing their lending per unit of reserves, *as if* they were reserve-constrained.

Another test was suggested by the mechanism encouraging banks to innovate on the reserves front, namely the tendency for market interest rates to rise (relative to the official rate) as the reserve shortage took hold and then to fall as successful innovation eased the shortage. In the presence of structural endogeneity, therefore, interest rate determination is not a one-way causal process running from the central bank to market rates: on the contrary, there will be evidence of bidirectional causality. Using Granger–Sims causality tests and looking at 240 observations on a range of interest rates between 1968 and 1988, Pollin found evidence that two-way causality increased with term. Long-term rates showed signs of a complex interaction with federal funds rate, while short-term rates appeared to be more directly and unidirectionally 'caused' by federal funds rate. The earlier evidence that we reported on the behaviour of UK interest rate relativities is not inconsistent with these findings, though the UK tests were not done for this purpose and were not conducted within a causality framework.

Although these tests appear to lend considerable support to the structuralist position, they have not proved definitive. Taking the loan/reserves ratio, for example, one might argue (see Palley, 1991) that one would expect an increase over time since banks are profit-seeking institutions and reserves act as a tax on bank outputs. Thus banks have a continuing incentive to economize on reserves, whatever may be the position of the central bank, and one might imagine that they become more effective in this as innovations take place.

There is also a problem in the interpretation of the apparent two-way causality between the Fed and market interest rates. Recall that the bidirectional causality appears for longer rather than very short rates. How we interpret this should be qualified by how we think the term structure of interest rates is determined. Assume that expectations play some role, i.e. that current long rates embody some expectation of what future short rates will be. In these circumstances, causality tests of the Granger–Sims type will show that the future Fed rate is better explained by including a current long rate than without it.

4. Conclusion

So, after all this effort, what do we know? First, the money supply *is* endogenous. Leaving aside the writers of macroeconomic textbooks, no one doubts this. Central bank governors tell us it is so and we can see for ourselves that central banks set a rate of interest as the sole instrument of policy, usually amidst a great deal of media attention, and all else is market-determined. There is no point in debating this any more.

But questions of detail remain: for example, the question of where precisely within the economic system the demand for loans originates. Traditionally in post-Keynesian economics, and more recently in circuitist theory, the emphasis has been upon firms' working capital needs. This seems misplaced in the light of the evidence (a) that household demand for bank credit is now (in the USA and the UK at least) much larger than firms' borrowing requirements and (b) that estimates of firms' loan demand which focuses narrowly upon the wage, import and tax bills do not perform well. Better results are obtained, even for firms' demand for credit, by including a wider measure of economic activity such as

GDP, and good estimates of the *total* demand for credit (including households) can be obtained by recognizing that the demand for loans originates with the widest variety of spending plans including those involving secondhand assets. None of this undermines the central hypothesis: the demand for loans originates within the economic system.

Second, loans do create deposits. There is ample causality evidence for this. The issue that remains open for further investigation is the significance of the two-way causality. We have seen that this may be some evidence that the demand for money, as well as the demand for loans, plays some part in the money creation process, and this would then give some support to the view that we have to think about how the demand for money and the demand for loans are reconciled. One obvious mechanism is largely through portfolio adjustment and (we have seen) this would be supported by what we have also established about changes in interest rates following a change in the central bank's official rate.

Finally, we can still discuss and investigate the role of the central bank in connection with the supply of reserves. Direct tests of hypotheses associated with the accommodationist and structuralist positions are inconclusive, but could be refined. At the moment, the structuralist position perhaps looks the stronger by virtue of its appeal to evidence about liquidity preference, which indirectly lends it some support. But the case is far from closed. It clearly is the case, widely chronicled in the financial press, that central banks go to great lengths to prevent day-by-day reserve shortages.

Notes

1. Recent examples include Dornbusch et al. (2003), Mankiw (2003), Burda and Wyplosz (2005). Less excusable is Mishkin (2004), which is offered to readers as a specialist guide to money and banking. Reading these texts, one is reminded of Charles Goodhart's denunciation of the base-multiplier model of money supply determination as 'such an incomplete way of describing the process of the determination of the stock of money that it amounts to misinstruction'. Extraordinary as it may seem, Goodhart wrote those words more than 20 years ago (Goodhart, 1984, p. 188).
2. At the time of their remarks, Alan Holmes was former NYFRB senior vice president while Mervyn King was deputy governor of the Bank of England.
3. There was also a study using South African data (see Moore and Smit, 1986), with broadly similar results.
4. Cuthbertson himself went on to develop a more general model of the demand for bank loans by ICCs (Cuthbertson, 1985a) in which the HMT and NIESR (but not the Bank of England) models were nested. Later, with the help of J. Slow (Cuthbertson and Slow, 1990), he estimated an error correction model for bank advances to ICCs in which changes in the wage and import bill variables were correctly signed (i.e. as per Moore and Threadgold) but were insignificant. The interest rate charged on bank loans and paid on short-dated assets were both significant.
5. Examples include Palley (1991; 1994), Pollin (1991); Wray (1992); Hewitson (1995); Dow (1996); Biefang-Frisancho Mariscal and Howells (2002); Fontana (2003).
6. Arestis and Biefang-Frisancho Mariscal (1995, pp. 545–6) date the 'crossover' in relative shares of bank credit going to UK ICCs and households in 1983.
7. See also Dow (1988) for a methodological discussion of concepts such as 'endogeneity' and 'causality' when applied to the money supply.
8. 'It is not that the demand for lending has become less sensitive to changes in relative interest rates. If anything, it has become more so. The problem lies in the increasing inability of the authorities to cause changes in relative rates by changing the level of absolute rates' (Goodhart, 1984, pp. 154–5).

References

Anderson, R.G. (1993), 'The effect of mortgage refinancing on money demand and the monetary aggregates', *Federal Reserve Bank of St Louis Review*, **75**(4), 49–63.
Arestis, P. (1997), 'PKE theoretical aspects of money and finance', in P. Arestis (ed.), *Money, Pricing, Distribution and Monetary Integration*, London: Macmillan, 9–33.
Arestis, P. and Biefang-Frisancho Mariscal, I. (1995), 'The endogenous money stock: empirical observations from the UK', *Journal of Post Keynesian Economics*, **17**(4), 545–59.

Bank of England (1997), *Statistical Abstract* (I), table 10.

Bibow, J. (1998), 'On Keynesian theories of liquidity preference', *The Manchester School*, **66**, 238–73.

Biefang-Frisancho Mariscal, I. and Howells, P.G.A. (2002), 'Central banks and market interest rates', *Journal of Post Keynesian Economics*, **24**, 569–85.

Burda, M. and Wyplosz, C. (2005), *Macroeconomics*, 4th edn, Oxford: Oxford University Press.

Caporale, G.M. and Howells, P.G.A. (2001), 'Money, credit and spending: drawing causal inferences', *Scottish Journal of Political Economy*, **48**(5), 547–57.

Caporale, G.M. and Pittis, N. (1997), 'Causality and forecasting in incomplete systems', *Journal of Forecasting*, **66**, 425–37.

Chick, V. (1983), *Macroeconomics after Keynes: a reconsideration of the General Theory*, Oxford: Philip Allan.

Chick, V. (1986), 'The evolution of the banking system and the theory of saving, investment and interest', *Économies et Sociétés* (Série M P, no. 3); also in P. Arestis and S.C. Dow (eds) (1992), *On Money, Method and Keynes: Selected Essays*, London: Macmillan.

Cuthbertson, K. (1985a), 'Sterling bank lending to UK industrial and commericial companies', *Oxford Bulletin of Economics and Statistics*, **47**(2), 91–118.

Cuthbertson, K. (1985b), *The Supply and Demand for Money*, Oxford: Blackwell.

Cuthbertson, K. and Slow, J. (1990), 'Bank advances and liquid asset holdings of UK industrial and commercial companies', mimeo, Department of Economics, University of Newcastle. See also Cuthbertson, K. 'Monetary control: theory, empirics and practicalities', in P. Arestis (ed.), *Money and Banking: Issues for the Twenty-first Century*, London: Macmillan, 1993, 192–219.

Cuthbertson, K. and Foster, N. (1982), 'Bank lending to industrial and commercial companies in three models of the UK economy', *National Institute of Economic Review*, **102**, 63–75.

Dale, S. (1993), 'Effects of changes in official rate upon money market rates since 1987', *Manchester School, Proceedings of the Money, Macroeconomics and Finance Research Group*, 76–94.

Dale, S. and Haldane, A.G. (1993), 'Interest rate control in a model of monetary policy', Working Paper Series No. 17, Bank of England.

Davidson, P. and Weintraub, S. (1973), 'Money as cause and effect', *Economic Journal*, **83**(332), 1117–32.

Desai, M. (1981), *Testing Monetarism*, London: Pinter.

Dornbusch, R., Fischer, S. and Startz, R. (2003), *Macroeconomics*, 9th edn, New York: McGraw-Hill.

Dow, A.C. and Dow, S.C. (1995), 'Endogenous money creation and idle balances', in M. Musella and C. Panico (eds), *The Money Supply in the Economic Process: A Post Keynesian Perspective*, Aldershot, UK and Brookfield, US: Edward Elgar, 473–90.

Dow, S.C. (1988), 'Money supply endogeneity', *Economie Appliquée*, **61**, 19–39.

Dow, S.C. (1996), 'Horizontalism: a critique', *Cambridge Journal of Economics*, **20**, 497–508.

Dow, S.C. (1997), 'Endogenous money', in G.C. Harcourt and P.A. Riach (eds), *A 'Second Edition' of the General Theory*, London: Routledge, 61–78.

Fisher, I. (1911 [1963]), *The Purchasing Power of Money*, New York: Macmillan. Reprinted New York: Augustus Kelley.

Fontana, G. (2003), 'Post Keynesian approaches to endogenous money: a time framework explanation', *Review of Political Economy*, **15**(3), 291–314.

Goodhart, C.A.E. (1984), *Monetary Policy in Theory and Practice*, London: Macmillan.

Goodhart, C.A.E. (1989), 'Has Moore become too horizontal?', *Journal of Post Keynesian Economics*, **12**(1), 29–34.

Goodhart, C.A.E. (1991), 'Is the concept of an equilibrium demand for money meaningful?', *Journal of Post Keynesian Economics*, **14**(1), 134–6.

Heffernan, S. (1997), 'Modelling British interest rate adjustment: an error-correction approach', *Economica*, **64**(254), 291–321.

Hewitson, G. (1995), 'Post Keynesian monetary theory: some issues', *Journal of Post Keynesian Economics*, **9**, 285–310.

Hewitson, G. (1997), 'The Post Keynesian "demand for credit" model', *Australian Economic Papers*, **36**, 127–43.

Holmes, A. (1969), 'Operational constraints on the stabilization of money supply growth', in *Controlling Monetary Aggregates*, Boston, MA: Federal Reserve Bank of Boston, 65–77.

Howells, P.G.A. (1995), 'The demand for endogenous money', *Journal of Post Keynesian Economics*, **18**(1), 89–106.

Howells, P.G.A. (1997), 'The demand for endogenous money: a rejoinder', *Journal of Post Keynesian Economics*, **19**(3), 429–34.

Howells, P.G.A. (2001), 'The endogeneity of money', in P. Arestis and M. Sawyer (eds), *Money, Finance and Capitalist Development*, Cheltenham, UK and Northampton, MA, USA: Edward Elgar, 134–78.

Howells, P.G.A. and Biefang-Frisancho Mariscal, I. (1992), 'An explanation for the recent behaviour of income and transactions velocities in the UK', *Journal of Post Keynesian Economics*, **14**(3), 85–105.

Howells, P.G.A. and Hussein, K.A. (1997), 'The demand for money: total transactions as the scale variable', *Economics Letters*, **55**(3), 371–7.

Howells, P.G.A. and Hussein, K.A. (1998), 'The endogeneity of money: evidence from the G7', *Scottish Journal of Political Economy*, **45**(3), 329–40.

Howells, P.G.A. and Hussein, K.A. (1999), 'The demand for bank loans and the "State of Trade"', *Journal of Post Keynesian Economics*, **21**(3), 441–54.

Kaldor, N. (1970), 'The new monetarism', *Lloyds Bank Review*, **97**, 1–17.

Kaldor, N. and Trevithick, J. (1981), 'A Keynesian perspective on money', *Lloyds Bank Review*, January, **139**, 1–19.

Kaldor, N. (1982), *The Scourge of Monetarism*, Oxford: Oxford University Press.

Kaldor, N. (1985), 'How monetarism failed', *Challenge*, **28**(2), 4–13.

Keynes, J.M. (1971 [1930]), *The Treatise on Money*, Vol. 1. Reprinted as Vol. V of *Collected Writings*, London: Macmillan for the Royal Economic Society.

King, M. (1994), 'The transmission mechanism of monetary policy', *Bank of England Quarterly Bulletin*, August, 261–7.

Lavoie, M. (1992), *Foundations of Post Keynesian Economics*, Aldershot, UK and Brookfield, USA: Edward Elgar.

Mankiw, G. (2003), *Macroeconomics*, 5th edn, New York: Worth.

Mishkin, F.S. (2004), *The Economics of Money, Banking and Financial Markets*, 7th edn, New York: Pearson–Addison-Wesley.

Moore, B.J. (1988), *Horizontalists and Verticalists*, Cambridge: Cambridge University Press.

Moore, B.J. (1989), 'The endogeneity of money', *Review of Political Economy*, **1**(1), 64–93.

Moore, B.J. (1991), 'Has the demand for money been mislaid?', *Journal of Post Keynesian Economics*, **14**(1), 125–33.

Moore, B.J. (1997), 'Reconciliation of the supply and demand for endogenous money', *Journal of Post Keynesian Economics*, **19**(3), 423–8.

Moore, B.J. and Threadgold, A. (1980), *Bank Lending and the Money Supply: the Case of the UK*, Bank of England Discussion Paper no. 10.

Moore, B.J. and Threadgold, A. (1985), 'Corporate bank borrowing in the UK, 1965–81', *Economica*, **52**, 65–78.

Moore, B.J. and Smit, B.W. (1986), 'Wages, money and inflation', *South African Journal of Economics*, **54**(1), 80–93.

Palley, T.I. (1991), 'The endogenous money supply: consensus and disagreement', *Journal of Post Keynesian Economics*, **13**, 397–403.

Palley, T.I. (1994), 'Competing views of the money supply', *Metroeconomica*, **45**, 67–88.

Palley, T.I. (1995), 'The demand for money and non-GDP transactions', *Economic Letters*, **48**, 145–54.

Phillips, P. and Perron, P. (1998), 'Testing for a unit root in time series regression', *Biometrika*, **75**(2), 335–46.

Pollin, R. (1991), 'Two theories of money supply endogeneity: some empirical evidence', *Journal of Post Keynesian Economics*, **13**, 366–96.

Pollin, R. and Schaberg, H. (1998), 'Asset exchanges, financial market trading and the M2 income velocity puzzle', *Journal of Post Keynesian Economics*, **21**(1), 135–62.

Robertson, D.H. (1963), *Lectures on Economic Principles*, London: Fontana.

Sawyer, M.C. (1996), 'Money, finance and interest rates', in P. Arestis (ed.), *Keynes, Money and the Open Economy*, Cheltenham, UK and Brookfield, USA: Edward Elgar, 50–67.

Schumpeter, J.A. (1911), *The Theory of Economic Development*, trans. R. Opie, Cambridge, MA: Harvard University Press.

Sprenkle, C. M. and Miller, M.H. (1980), 'The precautionary demand for narrow and broad money', *Economica*, **47**, 407–21.

Toda, H.Y. and Yamamoto, T. (1995), 'Statistical inference in vector autoregressions with possibly integrated processes', *Journal of Econometrics*, **66**, 225–50.

Wicksell, K. (1936 [1898]), *Interest and Prices: a study of the causes regulating the value of money*, London: Macmillan.

Wray, L.R. (1990), *Money and Credit in Capitalist Economies: the endogenous money approach*, Aldershot, UK and Brookfield, US: Edward Elgar.

Wray, L.R. (1992), 'Commercial banks, the central bank and endogenous money', *Journal of Post Keynesian Economics*, **14**, 282–97.

Wray, L.R. (1995), 'Keynesian monetary theory: liquidity preference or black box horizontalism?', *Journal of Economic Issues*, **29**, 273–83.

5 Chartalism and the tax-driven approach to money
*Pavlina R. Tcherneva**

1. Introduction

Economists, numismatists, sociologists and anthropologists alike have long probed the vexing question 'What is money?' And it seems Keynes's 'Babylonian madness' has infected a new generation of scholars unsettled by the conventional accounts of the origins, nature and role of money.[1] Among them are the advocates of a heterodox approach identified as 'Chartalism', 'neo-Chartalism', 'tax-driven money', 'modern money', or 'money as a creature of the state'.

The Chartalist contribution turns on the recognition that money cannot be appropriately studied in isolation from the powers of the state – be it modern nation-states or ancient governing bodies. It thus offers a view diametrically opposed to that of orthodox theory, where money spontaneously emerges as a medium of exchange from the attempts of enterprising individuals to minimize the transaction costs of barter. The standard story deems money to be neutral – a veil, a simple medium of exchange, which lubricates markets and derives its value from its metallic content.

Chartalism, on the other hand, posits that money (broadly speaking) is a unit of account, designated by a public authority for the codification of social debt obligations. More specifically, in the modern world, this debt relation is between the population and the nation-state in the form of a tax liability. Thus money is a creature of the state and a tax credit for extinguishing this debt. If money is to be considered a veil at all, it is a veil of the historically specific nature of these debt relationships. Therefore, Chartalism insists on a historically grounded and socially embedded analysis of money.

This chapter distinguishes between several broad Chartalist propositions about the origin, nature and role of money, and several specific propositions about money in the modern context. It offers only a cursory examination of the historical record to illuminate the essential characteristics of money emphasized in the Chartalist tradition. Chartalist ideas are not new, although they are most closely associated with the writings of Georg Friedrich Knapp of the German Historical School. Thus the chapter briefly surveys instances in the history of thought which have emphasized the chartal nature of money. The paper then expounds on Chartalism, clarifying aspects of the concepts and drawing out the implications for modern currencies. It concludes with a discussion of the various applications of this approach to policy.

Chartalism: the broad propositions

The historical record suggests an examination of Chartalism according to its broad and specific propositions. The latter address the nature of money in the modern context, and although Chartalism should not be narrowly identified with the modern money approach, the specific propositions are more important for understanding today's economies, modern currencies, and government monetary and fiscal policy.

Very briefly, the broad propositions of Chartalism are:

1. The atomistic view of money emerging as a medium of exchange to minimize trans-action costs of barter among utility-maximizing individuals finds no support in the historical record.
2. The appropriate *context* for the study of money is cultural and institutional, with special emphasis on social and political considerations.
3. Consequently, Chartalists locate the *origins* of money in the public sector, however broadly defined.
4. In its very *nature* money is a social relation of a particular kind – it is a credit–debt relationship.
5. Chartalism offers a stratified view of social debt relationships where definitive money (the liability of the ruling body) sits at the top of the hierarchy.
6. Money *functions*, first and foremost, as an abstract unit of account, which is then used as a means of payment and the settling of debt. Silver, paper, gold or whatever 'thing' serves as a medium of exchange is only the empirical manifestation of what is essentially a state-administered unit of account. Thus the function of money as a medium of exchange is incidental to and contingent on its first two functions as a unit of account and a means of payment.
7. From here, as Ingham aptly put it, money of account is 'logically anterior and historically prior to market exchange' (2004: p. 25).

Neo-Chartalism: the specific propositions
The recent revival of the Chartalist tradition, also dubbed neo-chartalism, tax-driven money, or the modern money approach is particularly concerned with understanding modern currencies. Thus contemporary Chartalists advance several specific propositions about money in the modern world:

1. Modern currencies exist within the context of certain state powers. The two essential powers are:
    (a) the power to levy taxes on its subjects, and
    (b) the power to declare what it will accept in payment of taxes.
2. Thus the state delimits money to be that which will be accepted at government pay offices for extinguishing debt to the state.
3. The purpose of taxation is not to finance government spending but to create demand for the currency – hence the term 'tax-driven money'.
4. Logically, and in practice, government spending comes *prior* to taxation, to provide that which is necessary to pay taxes.
5. In the modern world, states usually have monopoly power over the issue of their currency. States with sovereign currency control (i.e. which do not operate under the restrictions of fixed exchange rates, dollarization, monetary unions or currency boards) do not face any *operational* financial constraints (although they may face political constraints).[2]
6. Nations that issue their own currency have no imperative to borrow or tax to finance spending. While taxes create demand for the currency, borrowing is an *ex ante* interest rate maintenance operation. This leads to dramatically different policy conclusions.

7. As a monopolist over its currency, the state also has the power to set prices, which include both the interest rate and how the currency exchanges for other goods and services.

Neo-Chartalism is appropriately subsumed under the broad Chartalist school of thought. When it is said that 'money is a creature of the state' or that 'taxes drive money', two things are important to keep in mind. First, 'state' refers not just to modern nation-states, but also to any governing authority such as a sovereign government, ancient palace, priest, temple, or a colonial governor. Second, 'tax' denotes not just modern income, estate or other head tax, but also any non-reciprocal obligation to that governing authority – compulsory fines, fees, dues, tribute, taxes and other obligations.

Before detailing the broad and specific propositions of Chartalism, the next two sections take a cursory look at the historical record of the origins of money and the recognition of the chartal nature of money in the history of thought.

2.   History of money
Chartalists insist on a socially embedded and historically grounded study of money. While a conclusive chronicle of its genesis is perhaps impossible to attain, they turn to a historically informed analysis to unearth a more accurate account of the nature, origin and role of money.[3]

Genesis of money
It is a well-established fact that money pre-dated minting by nearly 3000 years. Thus Chartalists aim to correct a common error of conflating the origins of money with the origins of coinage (Innes, 1913: p. 394, Knapp, 1924: p. 1, Hudson, 2003: p. 40).

Very generally, they advance two accounts of money's origins. Grierson (1977), Goodhart (1998) and Wray (2001) posit that money originated in ancient penal systems which instituted compensation schedules of fines, similar to *wergild*, as a means of settling one's debt for inflicted wrongdoing to the injured party. These debts were settled according to a complex system of disbursements, which were eventually centralized into payments to the state for crimes. Subsequently, the public authority added various other fines, dues, fees and taxes to the list of compulsory obligations of the population.

The second account offered by Hudson (2003), and supported by some Assyriologist scholars (ibid.: p. 45, n. 3), traces the origins of money to the Mesopotamian temples and palaces, which developed an elaborate system of internal accounting of credits and debts. These large public institutions played a key role in establishing a general unit of account and store of value (initially for internal record keeping but also for administering prices). Hudson argues that money evolved through public institutions as standardized weight, independently from the practice of injury payments.

These stories are not mutually exclusive. As Ingham speculates, since a system of debts for social transgressions existed in pre-Mesopotamian societies, it is highly likely that 'the calculation of social obligations was transformed into a means of measuring the equivalencies between commodities' (2004: p. 91). Henry's analysis of ancient Egypt (2004) bridges the two accounts. In Egypt, as in Mesopotamia, money emerged from the necessity of the ruling class to maintain accounts of agricultural crops and accumulated surpluses, but it also served as a means of accounting for payment of levies, foreign tribute, and tribal obligations to the kings and priests.[4]

The importance of the historical record is: (1) to delineate the nature of money as a social debt relationship; (2) to stress the role of public institutions in establishing a standard unit of account by codifying accounting schemes and price lists; and (3) to show that in all cases money was a pre-market phenomenon, representing initially an abstract unit of account and means of payment, and only later a generalized medium of exchange.

The chartality of money

The above discussion gives a preliminary indication of the chartal nature of money. History reveals the role of the public authority in establishing a universal equivalent for measuring debts and in determining what 'thing' will be used to correspond to this accounting measure.

As Knapp explains, payments are always measured in units of value (1973 [1924]: pp. 7–8). Money then is chartal because the state makes a 'proclamation . . . that a piece of such and such a description shall be valid as so many units of value' (ibid.: p. 30). And it is beside the point what material will be used to correspond to those units of value. Money is a 'ticket' or 'token' used as a means of payment or measure of value. The means of payment, 'whether coins or warrants' or any 'object made of a worthless material', is a 'sign-bearing object' to which '[state] ordinance gives a use independent of its material' (ibid.: p. 32).

This is what gives Chartalism its name: 'Perhaps the Latin word "Charta" can bear the sense of ticket or token . . . Our means of payment have this token, or Chartal, form' (ibid.). Hereafter, Knapp defines money to always be a 'Chartal means of payment' (ibid.: p. 38).

It is important to distinguish between the 'money of account' and the 'money-thing', i.e., between the abstract unit of account and the physical object that corresponds to it. Keynes explains: 'money-of-account is the *description* or *title* and the money is the *thing* which answers to the description' (Keynes, 1930: pp. 3–4, original emphasis). Orthodox theories fail to differentiate the money of account from the empirical object that serves as money, leading to several irresolvable conundrums of monetary theory (see below).

Finally, 'definitive' money is that which is accepted at state pay offices: 'chartality has developed . . . for the State says that the pieces have such and such an appearance and that their validity is fixed by proclamation' (Knapp, 1973 [1924]: p. 36). Keynes similarly argues that 'the Age of Chartalist or State Money was reached when the State claimed the right to declare what thing should answer as money to the current money-of-account – when it claims the right not only to enforce the dictionary but also to write the dictionary' (Keynes, 1930: p. 5).

From Mesopotamia and Egypt to modern economies, rulers, governors and nation-states have always 'written the dictionary'. Chartalism is thus able to explain why seemingly worthless objects such as tally sticks, clay tablets or paper have been used to serve as money.[5] Governing authorities have not only picked the money of account and declared what 'thing' will answer as money, but they have also used taxation as a vehicle for launching new currencies. This is perhaps nowhere clearer than in the cases of colonial Africa.

> African economies were monetised by imposing taxes and insisting on payment of taxes with the European currency. The experience of paying taxes was not new to Africa. What was new was the requirement that the taxes be paid in European currency. Compulsory payment of taxes in European currency was a critical measure in the monetisation of African economies as well as the spread of wage labour. (Ake, 1981: p. 34)

> *Money* taxes [in Africa] were introduced on numerous items – cattle, land, houses, and the people
> themselves. Money to pay taxes was got by growing cash crops or working on European farms
> or in their mines. (Rodney, 1972: p. 165, original emphasis)

The tax requirement payable in European currency was all that was needed for the colon-
ized tribes to start using the new money. Taxation compelled the community's members to
sell goods and services to the colonizers in return for the currency that would discharge their
tax obligation. Taxation turned out to be a highly effective means of coercing Africans to
enter cash crop production and to offer their labour for sale (see also Forstater, 2005).

Public authorities, like colonial governors, not only 'wrote the dictionary' but also did
so for many millennia. As Keynes pointed out, money has been chartal money for at least
4000 years:

> The State, therefore, comes in first of all as the authority of law which enforces the payment of the
> thing which corresponds to the name or description in the contract. But it comes doubly when, in
> addition, it claims the right to determine and declare *what thing* corresponds to the name, and to
> vary its declaration from time to time – when, that is to say it claims the right to re-edit the dic-
> tionary. This right is claimed by all modern States and has been so claimed for some four thou-
> sand years at least. It is when this stage in the evolution of Money has been reached that Knapp's
> Chartalism – the doctrine that money is peculiarly a creation of the State – is fully realized. . . .
> To-day all civilized money is, beyond the possibility of dispute, Chartalist. (Keynes, 1930: pp. 4–5)

3. Chartal money in the history of thought

Many scholars, both orthodox and heterodox, have dealt with the chartal nature of
money. Wray (1998) and Forstater (2006) have documented these instances in the history
of thought. Their surveys seem to indicate two separate lines of research:

1. The first uses the chartal nature of money to identify its role in the evolution of
    markets (Ingham, Henry), the introduction of new currencies, the spread of central-
    ized governments (Polanyi, Lovejoy), and the emergence of capitalism and wage
    labour (Marx, Ake).
2. The second detects the tax-driven nature of money in its attempts to discover why
    seemingly worthless paper circulates as a medium of exchange (Smith, Say, Mill,
    Wicksteed).

From the first group of scholars, for example, Polanyi clearly rejects the traditional treatment of cowrie shells as 'primitive money' (Forstater, 2006). In studying the introduction
of non-metallic money in Africa, Polanyi observes that cowrie existed alongside metal
currencies, which were already well established in the continent. The cowrie was, in fact,
an example of 'the launching of a currency as an instrument of taxation' (1966: p. 189,
quoted in Forstater, 2006). Polanyi furthermore argues that the emergence of non-
metallic currencies should be correctly regarded 'as a feature in the spread both of *centralized government* and of food markets in the early [African] empires which left its
imprint on the local history of money' (ibid.).

Lovejoy (as Ake and Rodney above) similarly reports that taxation in pre-colonial
Nigeria was used to generate demand for new currencies:

> emirates [of Nigeria] paid their levies in cowries as well, so that the taxation system
> effectively assured that people participated in the market economy and used the currency,

a policy remarkably similar to the one which the later colonial regimes pursued in their efforts to see their own currencies accepted. (Lovejoy, 1974: p. 581, quoted in Forstater, 2006)

Marx also wrote on the tax imperative behind modern money, but his focus was on its role in the rise of capitalism and wage-labour. It is well known that Marx had a commodity theory of money, but he none the less emphasized that money relations obfuscate the underlying social relations of production (Ingham, 2004: p. 61). This, Forstater argues, played a key role in Marx's emphasis on the role of taxation and the state in monetizing primitive economies and accelerating the accumulation of capital (see detailed analysis in Forstater, 2006). The transformation of all taxes into money taxes has led to the transformation of all labour into wage labour, much like the African colonial experience above (Marx, 1857).

The second group of scholars who had contemplated the idea of tax-driven money were those concerned with the value of money and those who attempted to solve the (neo)classical riddle, why certain units of seemingly useless material circulate as medium of exchange while others, of apparent worth, do not.

One need not look further than Adam Smith's *Wealth of Nations* for acknowledgement of the chartal nature of money and the role of taxation.[6]

> A prince, who should enact that a certain proportion of his taxes should be paid in a paper money of a certain kind, might thereby give a certain value to this paper money; even though the term of its final discharge and redemption should depend altogether on the will of the prince. (Smith, 1776: p. 312)

Forstater reports that Say and Mill too recognized that paper had value because it was 'made efficient to discharge the perpetually recurring claims of public taxation' (Say, 1964 [1880]: p. 280, quoted in Forstater, 2006) and because the state had consented 'to receive it in payment of taxes' (Mill, 1848: pp. 542–3, quoted in Forstater, 2006). Mill further added that, if the issuer is the sovereign state, it can arbitrarily fix the quantity and value of paper currency (ibid.). Mill here seems to acknowledge the Chartalist claim that the sovereign state, in effect, 'writes the dictionary' by picking the unit of account and arbitrarily fixing its value. Finally, Wicksteed explicitly acknowledged the role of taxation as a method of creating a perpetual desire for money so that the government could acquire all goods and service necessary for its official and other purposes (Wicksteed, quoted in Forstater, 2006).

While the tax-driven money approach finds some support in the history of economic thought, simple recognition of the tax imperative behind money was not sufficient to draw out the full implications and logical extensions behind the chartality of money. Clearly neoclassical economists struggled to understand the use of paper money, but the tax-driven nature of money simply did not square with the traditional view of money as a veil. Thus, the next section recaps the Chartalist position by means of comparison with the orthodox story or – as Knapp (1973 [1924]) and Goodhart (1998) call it – the Metallist position.

4.   Metallism vs Chartalism

Some of the differences between Metallism and Chartalism (M-theory and C-theory respectively [Goodhart, 1998]) have already surfaced in the previous sections. The traditional story of the origins, nature and role of money is all too familiar. According to M-theory, markets formed first as a result of individuals' inherent disposition for exchange. Over time, money naturally emerged to lubricate these markets by dramatically reducing transaction costs.

M-theory focuses on money as a medium of exchange. Its *value* stems from the intrinsic properties of the commodity that backs it – usually a type of precious metal (and hence the term Metallism). Money owes its *existence* to rational agents who spontaneously pick a commodity for exchange, pressed by the requirements of the double coincidence of wants (Goodhart, 1998: p. 410). Money, therefore, *originates* in the private sector and only exists to facilitate market transactions. Because money has no special properties that endow it with a principal role, monetary analysis takes a backseat to 'real' analysis.

Since orthodox analysis turns on the smooth functioning of private markets, it generally abstracts from the role (or intervention) of government. The absence of any link between state and money also explains why M-theory cannot account for the important and almost universal 'one nation–one currency' relationship (Goodhart, 1998). Metallism struggles to find value in modern fiat money, no longer backed by any commodity of intrinsic worth. For M-theory, paper currency circulates because governments have usurped control over money and because it continues to reduce transaction costs of barter (Goodhart, 1998: p. 417, n. 21).

Chartalists find several problems with the Metallist story. Specifically, they identify two circular arguments, which pertain to the use of money as a medium of exchange, means of payment and store of abstract value. The first deals with money's existence. For M-theory, money is a consequence of rational agents 'holding the most tradeable commodity in a barter economy' (Ingham, 2000: p. 20). In other words: (a) money is universal because rational agents use it; and (b) rational agents use it because it is universal. Attempts to resolve this circularity by concentrating on money's role in reducing transaction costs have been unsatisfactory.

The logical difficulties emerge from the 'identification problem' – benefits from using a particular commodity as medium of exchange can be recognized only *after* that commodity has already been in use. Coins, for example, must be minted and circulated *before* the benefits of reduced transaction cost are recognized. And, as Goodhart notes, the costs of using an unworked precious metal can themselves be quite high (1998: p. 411). Thus the argument that private agents collectively and spontaneously choose a certain commodity for exchange *because* it reduces costs is, at a minimum, tenuous.

The second circular argument pertains to the other functions of money. Orthodox reasoning is that: (a) money is a store of abstract value because it is a means of payment; and (b) it is a means of payment because it is a store of abstract value (Ingham, 2000: p. 21). Essentially, there is no *definitive* property that gives money its special status. In the absence of an unambiguous condition that explains the use of gold, wooden sticks or salt as money, *spontaneous choice* becomes essential to the orthodox story and it must be assumed *a priori*. The result is a 'helicopter drop' theory of money (Cottrell, 1994: p. 590, n. 2).

C-theory does not suffer from the 'identification problem' or the 'spontaneous choice' paradox. It has no difficulty explaining the introduction and circulation of fiat currency or the 'one nation–one currency' regularity. This is because the origin of money is located outside private markets and rests within the complex web of social (debt) relations where the state has a principal role.[7]

The legitimate and sovereign powers of the governing body render money 'a creature of the state' (Lerner, 1947). Its *value* stems from the powers of the money-issuing authority.

There is nothing spontaneous about its existence; rather, it is contingent on what the state has declared to accept in payment of taxes, fees and dues at public offices. Various 'money-things' have dominated private markets because they have been chosen for acceptation at government pay offices for settling of debt. Chartalists avoid circular reasoning by pointing out that money's role as a unit of account *preceded* its role as a means of payment and a medium of exchange. This role was instituted by the state's capacity to denominate price lists and debt contracts into the elected unit of account.

5.   Acceptation: legal tender law or the hierarchy of debt?

Before elaborating on Chartalist theory and its application to policy, one additional clarification is in order. It is commonly believed that the chartal nature of money rests within the power of the state to administer legal tender laws (Schumpeter, 1954: p. 1090). But when Knapp proclaimed that 'money is a creature of law' (1973 [1924]: p. 1), he did *not* propose that 'money is a creature of legal tender law', and in fact he explicitly rejected such an interpretation. Chartalists argue that acceptation depends not on the legal tender status of money but on the stratified order of social debt relationships. The power to delegate taxes and determine how they will be paid explains why state money is the *most acceptable* form of debt.

If money is debt, clearly anyone can issue money (Minsky, 1986: p. 228). Minsky stressed that, as a balance sheet item, money is an asset to the holder and a liability to the issuer. What is important, however, is not the capacity to create debt but the ability to induce someone else to hold it (ibid.). In a sense, debt becomes money only *after* acceptation has occurred (Bell, 2001: p. 151). Different monies have varied degrees of acceptability, which suggests a hierarchical ordering of debts (Minsky, 1986; Wray, 1990; Bell, 2001).

If social debt relationships are organized in a pyramidal fashion, then the least acceptable forms of money are at the bottom of the pyramid, while the most acceptable ones are at the top (see Bell, 2001). Furthermore, each liability is convertible into a higher and more acceptable form of debt. What liability, then, sits at the top of the pyramid?

To settle debts, *all* economic agents except one, the state, are always required to deliver a *third party's* IOU, or something *outside* the credit–debt relationship. Since only the sovereign can deliver its own IOU to settle debts, its promise sits at the top of the pyramid. The only thing the state is 'liable for' is to accept its own IOU at public pay offices (Wray, 2003a: p. 146, n. 9).[8]

This stratified view of social debt relationships provides a preliminary indication of the primacy of state currency. But can agents simply refuse to take the sovereign's money and, therefore, undermine its position in the pyramid? The answer is 'no', because as long as there is someone in the economy who is required to pay taxes denominated in the state's currency, that money will always be accepted.

This indicates that the *emission* of currency is not an essential power of the state. In fact it has a contingent character. The state may very well declare that it will accept payment of taxes in, say, salt, cowries, or wooden sticks. Indeed, such historical examples exist, although generally sovereigns have preferred to use their own stamp or paper or something over which they possess full and unconditional control. The essence of state money lies neither in the ability to create laws, nor in the ability to print money, but in the ability of the government to create *'the promise of last resort'* (Ingham, 2000: p. 29, emphasis added), that is, to levy taxes and declare what will be accepted at pay offices for extinguishing debt to the state. The unit of account that settles tax obligations is delimited by the special authority, which 'does the counting' (ibid.: p. 22).

Knapp himself emphasized this point: 'Nor can legal tender be taken as the test, for in monetary systems there are frequently kinds of money which are not legal tender . . . but the *acceptation* . . . is decisive. State acceptation delimits the monetary systems' (Knapp, 1973 [1924]: p. 95, original emphasis); and Keynes endorsed it: 'Knapp accepts as "Money" – rightly, I think – anything which the State undertakes to accept at its pay-offices, whether or not it is declared legal-tender between citizens' (Keynes, 1930: p. 6, n. 1). Legal code is only a manifestation of state powers. Lack of legal tender laws does not mean that state money is unacceptable – such is the case in the European Union, for example, where no formal legal tender laws exist, yet the euro circulates widely.[9]

What, then, is the purpose of legal tender laws? Davidson provides the answer: legal tender laws determine that which will be 'universally acceptable – *in the eyes of the court* – in the discharge of contractual obligations' (2002: p. 75, emphasis added). Therefore, legal tender laws only ensure that when a dispute is settled by the courts in terms of dollars (for example), dollars must be accepted.

Money is indeed a creature of law – not legal tender law, but law which imposes and enforces non-reciprocal obligations on the population. The 'money-thing' is only the empirical manifestation of the state's choice of the 'money of account' that extinguishes these obligations. This is the nature of the tax-driven money mechanism.

This chapter began by outlining several broad and specific propositions of Chartalism. Thus far, the focus has been primarily on the former. The role of the public authority and taxation was used to decipher the nature of money as a creature of the state and to locate its position in the topmost strata of social debt relations. The contrast with the Metallist story revealed the importance of distinguishing between the 'money-thing' and the 'money of account'. Finally it was shown that the chartality of money stems not from legal tender laws but from the state's ability to create the promise of last resort.

What light, then, does Chartalism shed on money in the modern world and specifically on government fiscal and monetary operations? The remainder of this chapter concentrates on the specific propositions of neo-Chartalism and their applications to policy.

6. Money in the modern world

Neo-Chartalists are particularly concerned with sovereign currencies – those inconvertible into gold or any foreign currency through fixed exchange rates (Mosler, 1997–98; Wray, 2001). Their main point of departure is that most modern economies operate on the basis of high-powered money (HPM) systems. HPM – reserves, coins, federal notes and Treasury cheques – is that which settles tax obligations and sits at the top of the debt pyramid. Accordingly, it is also the money 'into which bank liabilities are converted' and which is used for clearing in the bank community (between banks themselves or between private banks and the central bank) (Wray, 1998: p. 77). Only a proper understanding of how HPM is supplied through the economy and its effect on the monetary system can lay bare the full implications of modern fiscal and monetary policy.

Modern money is state money. Taxation today functions to create demand for state currencies in order for the money-issuing authority to purchase requisite goods and services from the private sector. Taxation, in a sense, is a vehicle for moving resources from the private to the public domain. Government spending in sovereign currency systems is not limited by the ability of the state to 'raise' revenue. In fact, as it will be explained below, sovereign governments face no operational financial constraints.

To fully grasp the logic of sovereign financing, one must make the analytic distinction between the government and non-government sectors. For the private sector, spending is indeed restricted by its capacity to earn revenue or to borrow. This is not the case for the public sector, which 'finances' its expenditures in its own money. This is a reflection of its single supplier (monopoly) status. For example, in the USA, the dollar is not a 'limited resource of the government' (Mosler, 1997–98: p. 169). Rather it is a tax credit to the population, which is confronted with a dollar-denominated tax liability. Thus government spending provides to the population that which is necessary to pay taxes (dollars). The government need not collect taxes in order to spend; rather it is the private sector, which must earn dollars to settle its tax debt. The consolidated government (including the Treasury and the central bank) is never revenue constrained in its own currency.

If the purpose of taxation is to create demand for state money, then logically and operationally, tax collections cannot occur before the government has provided that which it demands for payment of taxes. In other words, spending comes first and taxation follows later. Another way of seeing this causality is to say that government spending 'finances' private sector 'tax payments' and not vice versa. Several other implications follow.

Deficits and surpluses
Government spending supplies high-powered money to the population. If the private sector wishes to hoard some of it – a normal condition of the system – deficits necessarily result as a matter of accounting logic.[10] Furthermore, the government cannot collect more in taxes than it has previously spent; thus balanced budgets are the theoretical minimum that can be achieved. But the private sector's desire to net save ensures that deficits are generated. The market demand for currency, therefore, determines the size of the deficit (Wray, 1998: pp. 77–80).

In a given year, of course, surpluses are possible, but they are always limited by the amount of deficit spending in previous years. If during the accounting period government spending falls short of tax collections, private sector holdings of net financial assets necessarily decline. The implication is that surpluses always reduce private sector net savings, while deficits replenish them. It should also be noted that, when governments run surpluses, they do not 'get' anything because tax collections 'destroy' high-powered money (Mitchell and Mosler, 2005: p. 9). To understand this, a closer look at government spending and taxing operations is necessary.

Government spending and taxation
There is no great mystery behind government spending and taxation. The government spends simply by writing Treasury cheques or by crediting private bank accounts. Conversely, when the Treasury receives a cheque for tax payment, it debits the commercial bank account on which the cheque was drawn. At present, it is not necessary to distinguish between the Federal Reserve and the Treasury when discussing government outlays and receipts. The reason is that when the Treasury writes a cheque drawn on its account at the Fed, it effectively writes a claim on itself. As Bell and Wray (2002–3) note, intergovernmental balance sheet activity is of little consequence, because it has no impact on the reserve level of the banking system as a whole (p. 264). What is important, however,

is that the consolidated actions of the Fed and the Treasury result in an immediate change in the system-wide level of reserves. It is this effect on reserves that matters for understanding policy.

Government fiscal policy is one of two important factors that change the level of reserve balances in the banking system. The other is through Fed open market operations. The Treasury is the main supplier of HPM. When it writes a cheque on its account at the Fed, by accounting necessity, reserve balances in the banking system increase. When it collects tax payments, on the other hand, bank reserves decline. Alternatively, when the Fed buys bonds in the open market, it adds reserves, and when it sells bonds, it drains them. What Chartalism makes clear next is that the effect of fiscal policy on reserve balances can be large and disruptive. Thus, while Treasury operations are discretionary, central bank operations are largely defensive in nature.

High-powered money, borrowing and interest rates
Historically banks have aimed to minimize non-interest-bearing reserve balances. Essentially, reserves in excess of what is necessary to meet daily payment commitments are lent in the overnight market to earn interest. Alternatively, if banks cannot meet reserve requirements, they will borrow reserves in the overnight market. All else equal, these operations do not change the level of reserves in the banking system as a whole. Government spending and taxation, however, do. Any new injection of 'outside money' (HPM) floods the banking system with excess reserves. Banks try to pass the unwanted reserves to other member banks but, in the aggregate of course, these attempts are ineffective and they only depress overnight interest rates. Government spending, therefore, increases system-wide reserves and exerts a downward pressure on interest rates.

Alternatively, the collection of tax revenue reduces high-powered money, i.e. reserves are destroyed. Since required reserve ratios are computed with a lag (*even* in a contemporaneous accounting system [see Wray, 1998: pp. 102–4]), all else equal, tax payments cause a system-wide deficiency of reserves. The reserve effect is the opposite and, as banks scramble to obtain the necessary reserves in the overnight market, the federal funds rate is bid up above its target rate. In sum, discretionary Treasury action directly influences overnight interest rates through its impact on reserves.

The government has devised various ways for mitigating the reserve effect of fiscal policy. The first *modus operandi* is the utilization of tax and loan accounts (T&Ls), which offer only temporary relief to these considerable reserve fluctuations (see Bell, 2000 for detailed analysis). While T&Ls reduce the reserve impact of government spending, the calls on these accounts never match the exact amount of tax collections or government spending. Therefore, there is *always* a flux in reserves in the banking system as a whole that must be offset in order to avoid swings in the overnight interest rate (ibid.).

The second method for dealing with the excess or deficiency in reserve balances is through open market operations. To drain the infusion of excess reserves, the Fed offers bonds for sale in the open market. With this action it effectively provides an interest-bearing alternative to banks' interest-free excess reserves and prevents the overnight interest rate from falling to its logical zero-bid limit.[11] Bond purchases, conversely, add reserves when there is a system-wide reserve deficiency and thus relieve any upward pressure on the overnight rate. Therefore, open market operations are more appropriately viewed, not as borrowing or lending procedures of the government, but as interest rate maintenance operations.

From here, several considerations emerge. First, coordinating activities between the Treasury and the Fed notwithstanding, it is clear that fiscal policy is discretionary and has a significant impact on reserve balances. Second, in an era of positive interest rate policy, the Fed has no choice but to act defensively to offset these reserve fluctuations via open market operations. Thus the Fed largely operates in a non-discretionary manner (Wray, 1998; Fullwiler, 2003).

Both taxation and borrowing deplete reserves. Taxation simply destroys them, while borrowing drains them by exchanging uncompensated private sector assets (excess reserves) with interest-bearing ones (bonds). Taxation and borrowing are not financing operations for the government but they do affect *private* sector nominal wealth. The former simply reduces 'outside money' (i.e. private sector net saving) while the latter exchanges one asset for another, leaving wealth 'intact' (Wray, 2003a: p. 151).

All of the above completely reverses conventional wisdom. Governments do not need the public's money to spend; rather the public needs the government's money to pay taxes. Government spending always creates new money, while taxation always destroys it. Spending and taxing are two independent operations. Taxes are not stockpiled and cannot be respent in order to 'finance' future expenditures. Finally, bond sales are necessary to drain excess reserves generated by fiscal operations in order to maintain a positive interest rate.

The value of the currency and exogenous pricing

Because monetary policy is accommodative and fiscal policy is discretionary, Chartalism assigns the responsibility for maintaining the value of the currency to the latter. It was already shown that taxes impart value to government money. As Innes stressed: 'A dollar of money is a dollar, not because of the material of which it is made, but because of the dollar of tax which is imposed to redeem it' (1914: p. 165). But he also argued that 'the more government money there is in circulation, the poorer we are' (ibid.: p. 161). In other words, if government money in circulation far exceeds the total tax liability, the value of the currency will fall. So it is not only the *requirement* to pay taxes, but also the *difficulty* of obtaining that which is necessary for payment of taxes, that give money its value.

For example, in discussing the experience of American colonies with inconvertible paper money, Smith recognized that excessive issue relative to taxation was the key to why some currencies maintained their value while others did not (for details see Wray, 1998: pp. 21–2). Wray explains: 'it is the acceptance of the paper money in payment of taxes and the restriction of the issue in relation to the total tax liability that gives value to the paper money' (ibid.: p. 23).

This important relationship between leakages and injections of HPM, however, is difficult to gauge. Chartalists argue that, since the currency is a public monopoly, the government has at its disposal a direct way of determining its value. Recall that for Knapp payments with chartal money measure a certain number of units of value. For example, if the state required that to obtain one unit of HPM, a person must supply one hour of labour, then money will be worth exactly that – one hour of labour (Wray, 2003b: p. 104). Thus, as a monopoly issuer of the currency, the state can determine what money will be worth by setting 'unilaterally the terms of exchange that it will offer to those seeking its currency' (Mosler and Forstater, 1999: p. 174).[12]

What this means is that the state as a monopoly supplier of HPM has the power to exogenously set the price at which it will provide HPM, i.e. the price at which it buys assets, goods and services from the private sector. While it is hardly desirable for the state to set the prices of all goods and services it purchases, it none the less has this prerogative. As it will be discussed later, Chartalists recognize that the money monopolist need only set *one* price to anchor the value of its currency.

Lastly, Chartalists point out that it is not necessary to force slack on the economy (as espoused by traditional economists) in order to maintain the purchasing power of the currency. Rather full employment policies, if properly implemented, can do the job (Wray, 2003a: p. 106).

Unemployment

Once again, government deficit spending necessarily results in increased private sector holdings of net financial assets. If the non-government sector chronically desires to save more than it invests, the result will be a widening demand gap (Wray, 1998: p. 83). This demand gap cannot be filled by other private sector agents, because in order for some people to increase their holdings of net savings, others must reduce theirs. In the aggregate, an increase in the desire to net save can only be accommodated by an increase in government deficit spending. Mosler explains:

> Unemployment occurs when, in aggregate, the private sector wants to work and earn the monetary unit of account, but does not want to spend all it would earn (if fully employed) on the current products of industry . . . Involuntary unemployment is evidence that the desired holding of net financial assets of the private sector exceeds the actual [net savings] allowed by government fiscal policy. (Mosler, 1997–98: pp. 176–7)

Similarly, Wray concludes that 'unemployment is *de facto* evidence that the government's deficit is too low to provide the level of net saving desired'. In a sense unemployment keeps the value of the currency, because it is a reflection of a position where the 'government has kept the supply of fiat money too scarce' (1998: p. 84).

For Chartalists it is not necessary to use unemployment to fight inflation. Rather they advance a full employment policy in which the state exogenously sets one important price in the economy, which in turn serves as stabilization anchor for all other prices (ibid.: pp. 3–10). This proposal rests on the recognition that the state does not face operational financial constraints, that unemployment is a result of restricting the issue of the currency, and that the state can exercise exogenous pricing.

But before explaining this proposal, it is important to point out that Chartalist propositions are not *necessarily* tied to any particular policy prescription; they are simply a way of understanding the state's powers and liabilities and its financing and pricing options.

The above implications of Chartalism outline the essential causal government powers regardless of whether they are exercised or not. Many governments willingly restrict the issue of the currency by balancing budgets. This in no way indicates that they actually face operational financial constraints. These are self-imposed, perhaps subject to political or ideological constraints. Governments furthermore do not explicitly employ their prerogative to set prices, even though they can. The value of the currency fluctuates, but this does not mean that states cannot devise a mechanism that serves as an anchor for the currency's value. Chartalism simply delivers the important implications of sovereign currency control that illuminate policy choices.

7.   Policy extensions

After disclosing the nature of government finance, Chartalists argue that governments *can* and *should* implement 'functional finance'. The latter was proposed by the late Abba Lerner, who vigorously objected to any conventional ideas about what constitutes 'sound' finance.

Functional finance can be subsumed under the Chartalist approach, because it appropriately recognizes money as a creature of the state and attributes two important policy roles to government. Lerner (1947) argued that the state, by virtue of its discretionary power to create and destroy money, has the obligation to keep its spending at a rate that maintains (1) the value of the currency and (2) the full employment level of demand for current output.

For the government to achieve its two main objectives, Lerner proposed two principles of functional finance, which inform decisions on the requisite amount of government spending and the manner of financing it. More specifically, the first principle provides that total government spending should be 'neither greater nor less than that rate which at the current prices would buy all the goods that it is possible to produce' (1943: p. 39). Spending below this level results in unemployment, while spending above it causes inflation. The goal is to keep spending always at the 'right' level in order to ensure full employment and price stability. The second principle states that government spending should be 'financed' through the issue of new currency. This second 'law' of functional finance is based on Lerner's recognition that taxation does not finance spending but instead reduces private sector money hoards (ibid.: pp. 40–41).

Functional finance can be implemented in any country in which the government provides the domestic currency (Wray, 2003a: p. 145). Two policies, virtually identical in design, that embrace the functional finance approach are the employer of last resort (ELR) (Mosler, 1997–98; Wray, 1998) and the buffer stock employment model (Mitchell, 1998). These policy prescriptions aim to stabilize the value of the currency by simultaneously eliminating unemployment. The proposals are motivated by the recognition that sovereign states have no operational financial constraints, can discretionarily set one important price in the economy, and can provide an infinitely elastic demand for labour.

Chartalists have advocated such employment programmes based on the work of Hyman Minsky and Abba Lerner and which recall the New Deal experience in the USA. The employer of last resort (to use Minsky's terminology) is very simply a government programme that offers a job at a fixed wage/benefits package to anyone who has not found employment in the private sector but is ready, willing and able to work.

The ELR is proposed as a universal programme without any means tests, thereby providing an infinitely elastic demand for labour by definition. It eliminates unemployment by offering a job to anyone who wants one. Through the ELR, the government sets only the price of public sector labour, allowing all other prices to be determined in the market (Mosler, 1997–98: p. 175). So long as the ELR wage is fixed, it will provide a sufficiently stable benchmark for the value of the currency (Wray, 1998: p. 131). As explained above, the value of the currency is determined by what one must do to obtain it, and with ELR in place, it is clear exactly what that is: the value of the currency is equal to one hour of ELR work at the going ELR wage.

Furthermore, it is argued that ELR enhances price stability because of its buffer stock mechanism (Mitchell, 1998). In a nutshell, when recessions hit, jobless workers find employment in the public sector at the ELR wage. Total government spending rises to relieve deflationary pressures. Alternatively, when the economy heats up and non-government demand for labour increases, ELR workers are hired into private sector jobs at a premium over the ELR wage. Government spending automatically contracts, relieving the inflationary pressures in the economy. Thus, public sector employment acts as a buffer stock that shrinks and expands counter-cyclically. This buffer stock mechanism ensures that government spending is (as Lerner instructed) always at the 'right' level.

This proposal innovatively suggests that full employment can anchor the value of the currency (quite contrary to the conventional belief that unemployment is necessary to curb inflation). The ELR programme utilizes the logical extensions of chartal money to achieve the two goals of government – the elimination of unemployment and the stabilization of prices.

Space does not permit a detailed discussion of this proposal; what is important is to emphasize its chartal institutional features. The ELR/buffer stock approach recognizes that:

1. The government is the only institution that can divorce 'the offer of labour from the profitability of hiring workers' (Minsky, 1986: p. 308) and can thus provide an infinitely elastic demand for labour, without concerns about financing.
2. The government can formulate an anchor for the value of its currency by exogenously fixing the wage of ELR workers.
3. The government can utilize a buffer stock mechanism to ensure that spending is always at the right level – neither more, nor less.
4. The responsibility for full employment and price stability rests with the Treasury, not the Fed. 'Sound finance' assumes a whole new meaning: it is that which secures full employment and price stability.

Chartalists stress that such an employment programme is a policy option only for countries with sovereign control over their currencies. It is not a viable proposal for nations that have dollarized or operate under currency boards or other fixed exchange rate regimes. This is because the important link between the money-issuing authority and the fiscal agent has been severed, thereby drastically reducing the range of available stabilization policy options. Goodhart has pointed out that, similarly, the present institutional design of the European Monetary Union exhibits an 'unprecedented divorce between the main monetary and fiscal authorities' (1998: p. 410). Kregel (1999) has advanced an innovative proposal to correct for this institutional flaw and allow the EMU to implement an ELR-type of programme. He recommends that the European Central Bank act as the fiscal agent for the Euro-zone as a whole and implement functional finance to secure high employment and price stability.

Chartalist analysis can equally be applied to the study of contemporary domestic issues, such as the provision of universal retirement, healthcare and education. The present debate on the social security 'crisis' in the USA, for example, and virtually the entire rhetoric on government budgeting, rest on fictitious beliefs concerning fiscal spending limitations. Chartalism insists that focus on non-existent problems disables adequate policy responses to pressing issues such as economic growth, development, and currency and price stability. Only after we abstract from conjured obstacles to fiscal policy can we begin to address problems relating to the provision of adequate healthcare and education, viable employment opportunities, and requisite goods and services for the ageing population.

8.   Conclusion

This chapter began with the broad and specific propositions of Chartalism. These constructively illuminate the tax-driven nature of money and the sovereign powers of modern states. While Chartalism is not wedded to a single policy proposal, it logically identifies functional finance as a viable tool for economic stabilization. Chartal insights can be applied to many different areas, from understanding various currency regimes to such issues as social security and unemployment. Chartalism is especially suited for studying contemporary monetary and fiscal policy.

In closing, it is appropriate to recall Lerner's cogent observation that 'The problem of money cannot be separated from the problems of economics generally just as the problems of economics cannot be separated from the larger problems of human prosperity, peace, and survival' (1947: p. 317).

Lerner further cautioned that in sovereign currency regimes 'Functional Finance will work no matter who pulls the levers [and that] those who do not use Functional Finance, . . . will stand no chance in the long run against others who will' (1943: p. 51). Chartalism is capable of contributing constructively to the public debate about viable policy actions in the public's interest.

Notes

* Helpful comments by Mathew Forstater, John Henry and Warren Mosler are gratefully acknowledged.
1. In a paper of the same title, Ingham recounts what Keynes referred to as his 'Babylonian madness'. In a letter to Lydia Lopokova, Keynes wrote that, endeavouring to locate the true origins of money in ancient Near East civilizations, he 'became absorbed to the point of frenzy' (Ingham, 2000: p. 16, n. 3).
2. Chartalism is not limited to floating exchange rate systems – 'even a gold standard can be a Chartalist system' (Wray, 2001: p. 1). The choice of exchange rate regime has various implications for state spending power, but it does not mean that the state has lost the ability to levy a tax on its subjects and declare how this tax will be paid.
3. A detailed analysis of the history of money is beyond the scope of this chapter. Interested readers are directed to Chapter 1 by Tymoigne and Wray in the present volume.
4. Henry further adds that money cannot exist without power and authority. Societies based on hospitality and exchange simply had no use for it, while in a stratified society the ruling class is compelled to devise standard units of account, which measure not only the economic surplus collected in the form of taxes, but also the royal gifts and religious dues that were imposed on the underlying population (2004: p. 90).
5. The case of Egypt is particularly interesting because the official unit of account, called the *deben*, had no relation to any specific object. It was an abstract weight measure equaling 92 grams, whereby various 'things' – wheat, copper, or silver – equivalent to 92 g, and multiples thereof, served as money (Henry, 2004: p. 92).
6. For a detailed discussion of Smith's position, see Wray (1998): pp. 19–23 and Wray (2000): pp. 47–9.
7. This does not mean that the private sector cannot or has not created money (Goodhart, 1998: p. 418). The point is that the explanations of money's origins, which rest on the role of the state, are empirically more compelling.
8. For example, to be accepted, household or firm IOUs must at least be convertible into deposits (bank money) or cash (state money). Likewise, bank deposits must necessarily be convertible into reserves or cash (state high-powered money) to be accepted. State money is always at the end of the convertibility chain.
9. Note also that a violation of the 'one nation–one currency' regularity does not mean that the state has lost the power to tax and declare what will extinguish tax obligations. In the case of currency boards, for example, the state has *willingly* abandoned sovereign control over its own currency in favour of a foreign monetary unit but, as long as the domestic currency is demanded for payment of taxes, it will circulate. In

fully dollarized countries, the state has *chosen* to declare that all debts are payable in dollars (even if it does not have sovereign control over the issue of dollars). In all of the above cases, the state has nevertheless exercised its prerogative to determine what will serve as 'definitive' money.

10. Godley (1999) has demonstrated that, by accounting necessity, public sector deficits equal private sector surpluses (including those of firms, households and foreigners).
11. For technical discussion of Fed operations, see Fullwiler (2003, 2005).
12. Wray notes: 'If the state simply handed HPM on request, its value would be close to zero as anyone could meet her tax liability simply by requesting HPM' (2003b: p. 104).

References

Ake, C. (1981), *A Political Economy of Africa*, Essex, UK: Longman Press.
Bell, S. (2000), 'Do taxes and bonds finance government spending?', *Journal of Economic Issues*, **34**(3): 603–20.
Bell, S. (2001), 'The role of the state and the hierarchy of money', *Cambridge Journal of Economics*, **25**, 149–63.
Bell, S. and Wray, L.R. (2002–3), 'Fiscal effects on reserves and the independence of the Fed', *Journal of Post Keynesian Economics*, **25**(2): 263–72.
Cottrell, A. (1994), 'Post-Keynesian monetary economics', *Cambridge Journal of Economics*, **18**, 587–605.
Davidson, P. (2002), *Financial Markets, Money and the Real World*, Cheltenham, UK and Northampton, MA, USA: Edward Elgar.
Forstater, M. (2005), 'Taxation and primitive accumulation: the case of colonial Africa', *Research in Political Economy*, **22**, 51–64.
Forstater, M. (2006), 'Tax-driven money: Additional evidence from the history of thought, economic history, and economic policy', in M. Setterfield (ed.), *Complexity, Endogenous Money, and Exogenous Interest Rates*, Cheltenham, UK and Northampton, MA, USA: Edward Elgar.
Fullwiler, S.T. (2003), 'Timeliness and the Fed's daily tactics', *Journal of Economic Issues*, **37**(4): 851–80.
Fullwiler, S.T. (2005), 'Paying interest on reserve balances: it's more significant than you think', *Journal of Economic Issues*, **39**(2): 543–9.
Godley, W. (1999), 'Seven unsustainable processes', *Special Report*, Levy Economics Institute.
Goodhart, C.A.E. (1998), 'The two concepts of money: Implications for the analysis of optimal currency areas', *European Journal of Political Economy*, **14**: 407–32, reprinted in S. Bell and E. Nell (eds), *The State, the Market and the Euro*, Cheltenham, UK and Northampton, MA, USA: Edward Elgar, 2003, pp. 1–25.
Grierson, P. (1997), *The Origins of Money*, London: Athlone Press.
Henry J.F. (2004), 'The social origins of money: The case of Egypt', in L.R. Wray (ed.), *Credit and State Theories of Money*, Cheltenham, UK and Northampton, MA, USA: Edward Elgar, pp. 79–98.
Hudson, M. (2003), 'The creditary/monetary debate in historical perspective', in S. Bell and E. Nell (eds), *The State, the Market and the Euro*, Cheltenham, UK and Northampton, MA, USA: Edward Elgar, pp. 39–76.
Innes, A.M. (1913), 'What is money?', *Banking Law Journal*, May: 377–408.
Innes, A.M. (1914), 'The credit theory of money', *Banking Law Journal*, January–December **31**: 151–68.
Ingham, G. (2000), 'Babylonian madness: on the historical and sociological origins of money', in J. Smithin (ed.), *What is Money?*, London: Routledge, pp. 16–41.
Ingham, G. (2004), *The Nature of Money*, Cambridge: Polity Press.
Keynes, J.M. (1930), *A Treatise on Money*, London: Macmillan.
Knapp, G.F. (1973 [1924]), *The State Theory of Money*, Clifton, NY: Augustus M. Kelley.
Kregel, J. (1999), 'Price stability and full employment as complements in a new Europe', in P. Davidson and J. Kregel (eds), *Full Employment and Price Stability in a Global Economy*, Cheltenham, UK and Northampton, MA, USA: Edward Elgar, pp. 178–94.
Lerner, A.P. (1943), 'Functional finance and the federal debt', *Social Research*, **10**: 38–57.
Lerner, A.P. (1947), 'Money as a creature of the state', *The American Economic Review*, **37**: 312–17.
Lovejoy, Paul, E. (1974), 'Interregional monetary flows in the precolonial trade of Nigeria', *Journal of African History*, **XV**(4): 563–85.
Marx, K. (1973 [1857]), *Grundrisse: Foundations of the Critique of Political Economy*, New York: Vintage.
Mill, John Stuart (1848), *Principles of Political Economy*, London: J.W. Parker.
Minsky, H. (1986), *Stabilizing an Unstable Economy*, New Haven, CT: Yale University Press.
Mitchell, W. (1998), 'The buffer stock employment model', *Journal of Economic Issues*, **32**(2): 547–55.
Mitchell, W. and Mosler, W. (2005), 'Essential elements of a modern monetary economy with applications to social security privatisation and the intergenerational debate', CofFEE Working Paper 05-01, Newcastle, Australia: Centre of Full Employment and Equity, February.
Mosler, W. (1997–98), 'Full employment and price stability', *Journal of Post Keynesian Economics*, **20**(2): 167–82.
Mosler, W. and Forstater, M. (1999), 'General framework for the analysis of currencies and commodities', in P. Davidson and J. Kregel (eds), *Full Employment and Price Stability in a Global Economy*, Cheltenham, UK and Northampton, MA, USA: Edward Elgar, pp. 166–77.

Polanyi, K. (1966), *Dahomey and the Slave Trade: An Analysis of an Archaic Economy*, Seattle, WA: University of Washington Press.

Rodney, Walter (1972), *How Europe Underdeveloped Africa*, Washington, DC: Howard University Press.

Say, Jean-Baptiste (1964 [1880]), *A Treatise on Political Economy*, 4th edn, New York: A.M. Kelley.

Schumpeter, J.A. (1954), *History of Economic Analysis*, Oxford: Oxford University Press.

Smith, A. (1937 [1776]), *The Wealth of Nations*, the Cannan edition, New York: The Modern Library.

Wray, R.L. (1990), *Money and Credit in Capitalist Economies: The Endogenous Money Approach*, Aldershot, UK and Brookfield, USA: Edward Elgar.

Wray, L.R. (1998), *Understanding Modern Money: The Key to Full Employment and Price Stability*, Cheltenham, UK and Lyme, USA: Edward Elgar.

Wray, L.R. (2000), 'Modern money', in J. Smithin (ed.), *What is Money?*, London: Routledge, pp. 42–66.

Wray, L.R. (2001), 'Understanding modern money: Clarifications and extensions', *CofFEE Conference Proceedings*, Newcastle, Australia: Centre of Full Employment and Equity, December, http://e1.newcastle.edu.au/coffee/pubs/workshops/12_2001/wray.pdf.

Wray, L.R. (2003a), 'Functional finance and US government budget surpluses', in E. Nell and M. Forstater (eds), *Reinventing Functional Finance*, Cheltenham, UK and Northampton, MA, USA: Edward Elgar, pp. 141–59.

Wray, L.R. (2003b), 'The Neo-Chartalist approach to money', in S. Bell and E. Nell (eds), *The State, the Market and the Euro*, Cheltenham, UK and Northampton, MA, USA: Edward Elgar, pp. 89–110.

6 French circuit theory
Claude Gnos

Introduction

The concept of the circuit was first used in economics by the Physiocrats of eighteenth-century France. They viewed production as a cycle beginning with advances, that is, capital expenditure, and ending when the goods that had been produced were sold. To that extent, the late twentieth-century revival of the circuit concept, notably by Bernard Schmitt (1960; 1966; 1984), Jacques Le Bourva (1962), Alain Barrère (1979; 1990a; 1990b) and Alain Parguez (1975), was a salute to a French tradition. This is not the whole story, though. Circuitist thinking, although usually unsung, has underpinned many approaches to economics from Marx to Keynes by way of Wicksell,[1] Schumpeter, Kalecki and J. Robinson.[2] Indeed, today's French circuit school owes much to Keynes, to whom Schmitt, Barrère and Parguez all referred extensively. And it is Keynes's heterodoxy, as opposed to the conventional neoclassical view of Keynes's economics, that was their source of inspiration. Hence the affinities of French circuitists with post-Keynesians (for a detailed review of common ground and differences, see Deleplace and Nell, 1996; Arena, 1996; Rochon, 1999a). Circuit theory also counts an Italian branch which emerged in the 1980s on Graziani's (1989; 2003) initiative and which explicitly focuses on Keynes's monetary theory of production (cf. Fontana and Realfonzo, 2005). French and Italian circuitist approaches have also inspired post-Keynesians outside Europe, especially in Canada (Lavoie, 1984; Rochon, 1999a; 1999b and Seccareccia, 1996). This affinity between circuit theory and Keynes's heterodoxy and now post-Keynesian theory will be a recurrent theme in this chapter. It should help readers familiar with post-Keynesian literature to grasp the significance of the circuit approach and help also to confirm its veracity.

The second section explains the general significance of the circuit, particularly as opposed to neoclassical economics, and as the underpinning of Keynes's principle of effective demand. The third section deals with the monetary theory behind the circuit approach, which is clearly akin to the theory of endogenous money but also provides new insights. The fourth section looks at how the circuit is involved in economic policy issues. The fifth section will conclude.

The general significance of the circuit

Circuitists see the economy, meaning the present-day monetary economies of production, as being based on an asymmetrical (hierarchical) relationship between firms (or entrepreneurs) and workers. Firms employ workers and pay them money wages. In spending their money wages, workers gain access to a fraction of the output, the size of that fraction varying according to the price they pay for goods in markets. Symmetrically, firms earn profits formed by the surplus of the price received for the goods sold over the wage-bill the firms paid out, allowing them and their backers to appropriate the complementary part of the output.

First, it will be seen that the features outlined here set circuit theory apart from the neo-classical view inherited from Smith (1776) by which the economy is composed of indi-vidual agents who simultaneously supply their productive services on a first set of markets and create demand on a second set for the goods produced. To be clear, circuitists do not of course deny the existence of markets and the correlated role of supply and demand in determining wages and prices. What they refute, by reference to Keynes's notion of the entrepreneur economy, is the idea that market transactions may ultimately be seen as mere exchanges of productive services and goods for one another, with the terms of trade sup-posedly being determined through adjustments taking place in interdependent markets in conformity with the agents' preferences. Second, it will be confirmed that the circuitist approach, as its proponents argue, implicitly underpins Keynes's principle of effective demand to which circuitists therefore subscribe.

A representation of the economy in sharp contrast to the neoclassical view
To help readers to appraise this first point, it is first worth recalling that Walras (1926), after elaborating on the determination of exchanges of commodities for one another, encapsulated production in his theory of exchange. To that end, he had to deal with labour, or what he termed the productive services of workers, land and capital, on equal terms.[3] The prices paid for these services, he went on to explain, make up the production cost of the goods the entrepreneur eventually sells:

> [the entrepreneur] leases land from land-owners on payment of a rent, hires the personal facul-ties of workers on payment of wages, borrows capital from capitalists on payment of interest charges and, finally, having applied certain productive services to the raw materials, sells the resulting product on his own account. (p. 227)

In solving what he termed 'the equations of production', Walras came to the conclusion that markets are in equilibrium when supply equals demand for each product and service, and when 'the selling prices of the products [are] equal to the costs of the services employed in making them' (pp. 253–4). Here the entrepreneur, wearing his entrepreneur's hat (as a person he also is a factor of production like other workers), is a mere intermediary between the market for productive services (including the productive services of the entrepreneur) and the market for manufactured goods. The volume of output and its distribution are determined by the interplay of supply and demand in markets depending on the productivity of each factor and on individual preferences.

In arguing against Walras's representation of things, circuitists underscore the distinc-tion Keynes made (Keynes, 1933a; 1933b) between a 'real-wage or co-operative economy' and 'a money-wage or entrepreneur economy'. In the former, which Keynes also termed the 'real exchange economy', 'the factors of production are rewarded by dividing up in agreed proportions the actual output of their co-operative efforts' (Keynes, 1933b, p. 77). This, he emphasized, was the case presupposed by the classical economists wherein the determination of employment is linked to the interplay of supply and demand in the labour market, with supply and demand 'depending upon the expected amount of [workers'] reward in terms of output in general' (p. 76). The 'money-wage or entrepreneur economy' is original in that entrepreneurs (or firms) play the crucial role. They are the ones who decide on the volume of employment in relation to the money proceeds they expect from the sale of their output. This case, Keynes argued, was clearly separate from the former:

> In a real-wage and co-operative economy there is no obstacle in the way of the employment of an additional unit of labour if this unit will add to the social product output expected to have an exchange-value equal to 10 bushels of wheat, which is sufficient to balance the disutility of the additional employment. . . . But in a money-wage or entrepreneur economy the criterion is different. Production will only take place if the expenditure of £100 in hiring factors of production will yield an output which is expected to sell for at least £100. (Keynes, 1933b, p. 78)

As he put it, especially with reference to Marx's famous formula $M–C–M'$ by which the investment of funds amounts to the transformation of a given sum of money into goods (commodities) and then back into an increased sum of money,

> [a]n entrepreneur is interested, not in the amount of product, but in the amount of money which will fall to his share. He will increase his output if by doing so he expects to increase his money profit, even though this profit represents a smaller quantity of product than before. (Keynes, 1933b, p. 82)

> [t]he firm is dealing throughout in terms of sums of money. It has no object in the world except to end up with more money than it started with. That is the essential characteristic of an entrepreneur economy. (Ibid., p. 89)

These various points speak volumes. Circuitists clearly opt for a representation that, as Keynes emphasized, contrasts sharply with the neoclassical paradigm of general equilibrium. To complete the picture, it ought to be pointed out that circuitists have adopted Keynes's principle of effective demand which, they argue, is based on the circuit (cf. Barrère, 1990a; Poulon, 1982), although Keynes was silent about any affiliation. Let us now consider this principle as it will help in the further presentation of French circuit theory.

A foundation for Keynes's principle of effective demand
In support of their argument that the circuit underpins Keynes's principle of effective demand, circuitists first observe that Keynes constructed the principle of effective demand in line with his conception of the entrepreneur economy outlined in his 1933 writings, that is, on the successive spending and proceeds of sales entrepreneurs are to incur for a given volume of employment. As Keynes put it, 'entrepreneurs endeavour to fix the amount of employment at the level at which they expect to maximize the excess of the proceeds over the factor cost' (pp. 24–5). Second, circuitists emphasize that, although he is not fully explicit on this issue, Keynes on this occasion outlined a theory of distribution wherein profits are a redistributed share of wages, which is transferred from purchasers to firms (cf. Gnos, 1998). And the fact is that while factor cost (which amounts to wages since Keynes considered labour as the sole factor of production – more on this below), which forms factors' income,[4] is paid by entrepreneurs, profit, that is entrepreneurs' income, is derived from the surplus, paid by consumers, of prices over factor cost. This feature of Keynes's approach to employment determination confirms the divergence between the entrepreneur economy he argued for and the real-wage economy vaunted by neoclassical economists. The money paid on wages is not the simple transitory and neutral medium in the exchange of the services of labour for goods that neoclassical economics claims it is.[5]

As for money profits, they are in no way paid in the so-called productive services market but on the contrary are formed in the goods market.

It is fair to say that circuitists, in their analysis of the production process and the determination of employment, do not claim to be original relative to Keynes and his post-Keynesian followers. The hallmark of circuitists is their interest in the underpinnings of the Keynesian representation of the monetary economy of production, which derives from their concern to deepen our understanding of the real world. In this respect, a crucial issue may be raised here.

In the *General Theory*, Keynes proposed, in dealing with the theory of employment and the economic system as a whole, 'to make use of only two fundamental units of quantity, namely, quantities of money-value and quantities of employment' (pp. 41–3). This proposal puzzled his interpreters, notably Hicks (1975), and tended to be ignored. Circuitists on the contrary revived it. Their rejection of the neoclassical theory of a real-exchange economy meant they could abandon Walras's tripartite distinction between the productive services of labour, capital and land, and endorse Keynes's proposal that

> [i]t is preferable to regard labour, including, of course, the personal services of the entrepreneur and his assistants, as the sole factor of production, operating in a given environment of technique, natural resources, capital equipment and effective demand. This partly explains why we have been able to take the unit of labour as the sole physical unit which we require in our economic system, apart from units of money and of time. (Keynes, 1936, pp. 213–14)

In truth, this is neither, as the quotation may suggest, a question of theorist's preferences, nor a denial of the actual role that capital and land play in the production process. It is rather a matter of logic given the monetary and financial characteristics of the entrepreneur economy. Let us consider this point further.

Walras, who abstracted from money, held that capital was real; it belonged to capitalists and firms hired its productive services. But Walras's view becomes untenable when the monetary and financial dimension of capital is taken into account. Entrepreneurs do not hire the supposed services of capital goods but borrow money incomes saved by their recipients (who may be implicitly firms' owners when retained earnings are invested) and spend them on capital goods. In this way, entrepreneurs (firms) invest money incomes in the purchase of means of production (equipment and intermediary goods), and their problem then, when selling the goods produced in the market, just as the principle of effective demand puts it, is to recoup their expenses, that is to say their production costs, and obtain a net yield (profit) that will allow them to pay interest and dividends on the funds invested. Therefore the remuneration of capital is not formed in a specific market that is somehow pre-existent to the goods markets and supposedly represents a payment for the productive services provided by capital.

Unlike capital, labour is in no way a good that is produced. Just as Walras argued, labour is therefore purchased in a specific market, separate from any goods markets. The reference to Walras here is subject to a qualification, however. In real or material terms, one may argue that entrepreneurs buy the productive services of labour. But in monetary and financial terms, which prevail in the entrepreneur economy, the argument is different. Firms simply buy a quantity of labour from which they expect to obtain a given yield in the goods market. In this regard, although labour is not bought in goods markets, it is to be treated on the same footing as capital equipment. However, labour diverges from capital in that, when paying for capital goods, entrepreneurs spend existing incomes, while they form new incomes when paying for labour. Hence labour may be considered as the sole factor of production, that is, in modern terminology, of value added.

The foregoing considerations also help us to conceive of the role of land. Like labour, land is to be purchased in a specific market, separate from the goods markets, but unlike wages, rent is not the price paid for land. When buying land, firms make a payment that defines an investment, just as when they pay for capital goods. Rent, then, is akin to interest and dividends; it remunerates the funds invested in land and is a redistributed share of profits. Of course, firms may rent land instead of buying it. This means that someone else made the investment instead of them, and they have to pay rent to the landowners out of their profits.

All in all, analysis confirms that it is possible, as circuitists claim, to focus on the successive formation and spending of wages while accepting Keynes's proposals on the choice of units and the definition of the factors of production. To make this conclusion clear, suppose that firms pay, in the current period, wage-bills amounting to £1000 to produce output that will be sold for £1200 in the market (we abstract from the cost of capital equipment or 'user cost' in Keynes's terminology, and from the purchase of intermediary goods, which are also paid for by consumers out of their incomes when they buy the goods produced). May we argue that £1000 is a relevant yardstick for the current output? To answer affirmatively, we have just to insist that all incomes apart from wages are derived from profits, which are incomes transferred from consumers to firms when prices exceed factor cost. This means that the extra £200 is not additional to the wage-bill paid by firms, but is part of that wage-bill. This argument may be more easily understood by thinking of value added taxes, which increase the price of goods in the markets, thus allowing the government to capture part of consumers' income. No one would conclude that levying taxes actually increases the value added in the economy.

Some commentators, including circuitists, have wondered how wages amounting to £1000 can pay for goods sold for £1200 (for comments see notably Renaud, 2000, and Rochon, 2005). This difficulty arises from a methodological error, however. Sale proceeds amounting to £1200 do not result, as commentators seem to assume, from a single transaction but from a series of transactions over time, with individual production processes overlapping each other. Firms, then, have no difficulty in making profits out of wages provided wage-earners and their dependants are prepared to buy goods at prices exceeding production costs. Moreover, profits are themselves spent on goods, and so contribute to the recording of a £1200 aggregate price. With reference to the difficulty they perceive, some circuitists (cf. Parguez, 1996) have endorsed Kalecki's principle that workers spend the money they earn whereas entrepreneurs earn the money they spend. This argument is to be considered with a critical eye. Entrepreneurs may certainly spend their profits in advance thanks to bank credit, as the authors usually argued, but this still begs the question of how profits are actually formed.

To hammer our point home, suppose now that the goods produced are sold for £900. How is this to be analysed? Firms actually make a loss: they spend £1000 and recoup £900 only. Keynes examined such a case in his *Treatise on Money* (1930, pp. 159–60). He explained that the incomes that consumers do not spend on goods (£100 in our example) define savings that firms have to borrow either directly or indirectly through banks to make good their losses. He concluded 'that the increased saving has not increased in the least the aggregate wealth of the community; it has simply caused a transfer of wealth from the pockets of the entrepreneurs into the pockets of the general public' (p. 159). We thus have confirmation that the notion of profit (firms' losses are negative profits) as a transfer of wealth or income is not at all alien to Keynes. This also confirms that the wage-bill is an adequate yardstick for the value of output: it is the sum of money income that, from a macroeconomic point of view, will necessarily be spent on the purchase of the goods produced. Namely, £900 is paid by consumers, and the remaining £100 is met by firms. Of course, as mentioned earlier, this conclusion does not refute the existence of markets and the correlated role of supply and demand in determining prices. It claims that the interplay of supply and demand in markets is not the ultimate characteristic of a monetary economy of production, and is subject to a macroeconomic constraint based on the asymmetrical relationship of firms with their employees and the correlated circular flow of the wages, those wages being formed when firms invest money in the production of goods and being eventually spent on the goods produced.

The monetary conditions of the circuit
The preceding section focused on the asymmetrical relationship between firms and workers which underpins the circuit. A further characteristic now has to be accounted for, namely the pre-eminent role of money in the working of the circuit. First, we shall observe that this is another point of convergence between post-Keynesians and circuitists, with both schools sharing the endogenous view of money. However, circuitists insist on the accounting nature of money and aim to supplement the endogenous view of money with an in-depth examination of the connection between money and the real and financial relationships binding firms and the workers they employ. Second, still with a view to helping readers to grasp the circuitist approach, it will be shown that, despite appearances, the circuit is not an oversimplified model in the face of the diversity of monetary transactions.

Circuit theory as a component of the endogenous money approach
The circuitists' espousal of the endogenous money thesis stems directly from their rejection of the classical real-exchange economy. In the classical view, money is a commodity that is involved in the exchange of one good for another. Even paper and bank monies are to be considered as goods (albeit immaterial ones), the quantity of which is exogenously determined. This is so because the idea of exchange is tied in with the assumption that there are goods out there to be exchanged for one another. The involvement of money in exchanges does not alter this assumption. Circuit theory, with its focus on the production process that is initiated by investment (advances) and is fully completed only after a lapse of time, entails a different conception of money. Money allows firms to buy capital goods and labour before the output of their productive activity is available to them. Money, circuitists argue, is an instrument of credit. In support of their argument they refer to actual practice, where money is no more than entries in bank accounts, recording borrowers' liabilities and lenders' assets. Their approach to money is clearly akin to the post-Keynesian view that money creation is credit-driven. In the words of Arestis, the circuit school is 'a strong component of the endogenous money thesis' (1996, p. 113).

In the post-Keynesian literature, the endogeneity of money has more often than not been linked to the behaviour of banks which may be more or less receptive to the demand for money. This is not the whole story, however. In his pioneering work, Moore (1988) showed that endogeneity is fundamentally bound up with the nature of money, while opposing credit money to commodity money:

> Because commodity money is a material thing rather than a financial claim, it is an asset to its holder but a liability to no one. Thus, the quantity of commodity money in existence denotes nothing about the outstanding volume of credit. . . . Since the supply of credit money is furnished by the extension of credit, the supply schedule is no longer independent of demand . . . the stock of bank money is completely determined by borrowers' demand for credit. (pp. 13–14)

Indeed, we may be certain that the nature of money is a prevalent issue: even if central banks and the banking system were to systematically refuse to accommodate the demand for credit, the endogenous money thesis would still hold since credit money cannot exist unless it is borrowed by someone. Moore's argument is powerful: credit money cannot exist as an asset to depositors if it is not simultaneously a liability for banks and ultimately for bank borrowers; hence the decisive role of the demand for credit.

Circuitists share Moore's view of the endogeneity of money. In *Monnaie, salaires et profits*, Schmitt insisted back in 1966 on the novel features of modern money, which is created by banks in response to demand for credit, and consists in bank liabilities which are IOUs, that is, claims to money.[6] Schmitt developed his views in several publications in the 1960–70s, and gave rise to what has become the common circuitist view that banks issue debts upon themselves *ex nihilo* which they lend to economic agents, especially firms, who spend them on goods and labour. Eventually, the argument goes, borrowers recover the money they spent, out of their own takings, and are thus able to reimburse their bank loans. As Parguez and Seccareccia put it,

> [i]n the initial phase when banks grant credit, they issue new debts upon themselves which they lend to non-bank agents. . . . The second phase of the monetary circuit is the period during which non-bank agents spend the money they have borrowed to acquire real resources, which are generally labour and produced commodities. Sellers of labour services or commodities acquire the quantity of money which has been created in the first phase. . . . In the third and last stage of the monetary circuit, the initial holders of bank debts seek to recover them in the reflux process out of their receipts generated by their initial expenditure. They can now replenish their deposits and pay back their loans. (Parguez and Seccareccia, 2000, p. 104)

However, Schmitt deepened his analysis, and came to the conclusion that the definition of money may involve some further subtleties (Schmitt, 1984). He made his point with reference to bookkeeping, observing that, strictly speaking, banks do not issue liabilities which they lend to firms. They actually debit and credit accounts with purely nominal units of money, and so build up assets and liabilities which simultaneously tie the banks themselves and their borrowers and depositors. This refinement is not just hair-splitting; it has crucial implications for understanding the role of banks, the definition of money and the nature of the circuit.

On the common circuitist view, banks' liabilities are the counterpart to the produced goods and labour that borrowers (firms) acquire. They are literally exchanged for goods and labour. Then, sellers of goods and labour are presumably paid in full-blown money: credit is on the assets side of banks' books but not on the liabilities side. As Parguez and Seccareccia put it, 'it would be wrong to conceive holders of bank liability as bank creditors' (Parguez and Seccareccia, 2000, pp. 105–6). With reference to bookkeeping Schmitt (1984) points out a double flaw in this view.

First, the double-entry principle does not allow banks to extend credit to borrowers without gaining an equivalent credit from depositors. This is an argument Keynes made in the *General Theory*[7] and that on the post-Keynesian side has been confirmed by Moore (Moore, 1988). As a consequence, banks' liabilities, that is, deposits, are the source of bank financing, and match the credit they grant to borrowers. Depositors are creditors of banks and ultimately the creditors of bank borrowers. Banks (as Moore also emphasizes) are thus one type of financial intermediary; they are not the actual source of the credit granted to borrowers. Money creation has to be seen for what it really is: bookkeeping entries – debits and credits that banks record in their books in nominal units of account, and that resolve into banks' assets and liabilities denoting (indirect) financial relations between borrowers and depositors. Bank money is therefore a dual entity, and not one and the same thing as considered in monetary flows (payments) and stocks (assets).

The second point, which is closely related to the first, concerns the nature of the circuit. The common circuitist view in a sense maintains the (neo)classical approach by which economic transactions are exchanges achieved by means of a peculiar good or asset that is deemed to be money. The rigorous reference to bookkeeping delivers a more original view, so much so that Schmitt came to distance himself from other circuitists. In his contribution to this volume, Rossi (Chapter 8) presents in great detail the theory of money emission that Schmitt then further developed. There is no doubt, however, that the paradigm of the circuit remains central to Schmitt's approach. And so it is legitimate in this chapter to adopt Schmitt's later findings on the nature and the role of money as part of this presentation of circuit theory. The objective is to present this theory in what I believe is its most coherent and relevant form. The nature of the circuit may then be specified in the following way.

The payment of wages, which comes down to crediting workers' bank accounts with mere units of account, defines assets that link workers (depositors) and firms (borrowers) through banks. There is no string of transmissions of deposits that the banks would issue on themselves, and then lend to firms which, in turn, would transfer them to workers. What then is the meaning of the financial relationship between firms and workers? The answer results from the asymmetrical relationship connecting firms and workers, and underpinning the circuit. Firms pay for labour having in view the output which that employment will generate and which they will subsequently sell at a profit, while workers work having in view the share of output which will fall to them. The output is thus the object of the commitment of both firms and workers in the production process, and also of the financial relationships that are generated by this process. We may surmise that if production were an instantaneous process, firms would pay workers at once, in kind (assuming that the nature of the goods produced would suit workers' needs). But when time is taken into consideration, it can be seen that firms have to postpone delivering the goods being produced to workers, and so require credit from their workers. Monetary payments, which banks may effectively make by means of units of account because the object of the monetary transactions is nothing other than the real goods produced, ratify the firms' commitment to deliver goods to their workers later on. Simultaneously, workers temporarily save their income in the form of bank deposits, and thereby grant credit to firms. Furthermore, the homogeneity and convertibility of bank monies allow the development of a complex network of transactions allowing every worker and his dependants to buy whichever goods best meet their needs, regardless of the particular goods the worker actually produced. The accounting nature of bank money, and the financial relationships monetary payments establish, allow distribution phenomena that would be impossible under the (neo)classical assumption that economic transactions are exchanges. Exchanges confront equally valued quantities of goods and currency (whether value is considered as 'absolute' or 'relative'), and distribution cannot be conceived of unless one distinguishes, as Walras did, as many factors of production as there are income categories. Not so in the circuit view. As shown above, the distribution of the output is dependent on the excess of prices over the wage-bill paid by firms.

A representation of the deep relationships underpinning actual monetary economies of production

Our methodology, here, will consist in showing that the various monetary transactions taking place in the economy may accurately be thought of as parts of either the flux or reflux of monetary wages constituting the circuit. Let us successively consider the financing of firms' outlays on wages and capital goods and the financing of households' spending.

According to the foregoing presentation of circuit theory, firms ask banks for credit in order to pay wages. The formation of deposits ensues to the benefit of workers while firms become simultaneously indebted to banks. All in all, banks create money at firms' demand. This consists for the banks in crediting and debiting accounts, and, by the same token, they act as financial intermediaries between firms and workers. The transaction is recorded on banks' balance sheets as shown in Table 6.1.

This is a simplified presentation. In practice, firms may also pay wage-bills out of existing deposits derived from borrowing savings on the financial markets or from profits earned previously. Should circuit theory be considered as a theory that applies only in overdraft economies, which is what France and Italy were at the time the theory originated (cf. Lavoie, 2005, p. 257)? No, in fact, there is no question that the theory is universally true. Let us distinguish between firm F1 which, in paying its wage-bills, generated the incomes (wages and the ensuing profits) that are borrowed by a second firm, F2. To pay F2's wage-bill, the banks debit F2's account and credit its workers' accounts. The banks' role ends there, but the circuit analysis still holds. What actually occurs is a threefold financial operation: (1) Income-holders lend deposits to F2 on the financial markets, which simply means that they convert their savings from liquid into illiquid assets (from deposits into F2's liabilities); they clearly do not part with their savings. (2) The conversion of income-holders' savings from liquid to illiquid assets does not involve, in macroeconomic terms, the spending of savings. This is so because the corresponding output has not yet been sold, to wit, F1 is still indebted to the banks (Table 6.2).[8] Hence income-holders are still, but this is only implicit in the financial operations actually recorded either in the

Table 6.1   Entries resulting from the payment of wages from banks' loans

	Banks	
Assets	Liabilities	
Loans to firms	£w	Deposits of workers	£w

Table 6.2   Entries resulting from firm F2 paying wages from deposits borrowed on the financial markets

		Banks	
Assets		Liabilities	
Loan to firms F1	£x	Deposits of F2 workers	£x

banks' books or in the financial markets, lending the output corresponding to their saved incomes to F1. (3) F2's workers are credited with deposits (Table 6.2), to which there corresponds a new output and which, as explained above, they currently save and lend to firm F2 (F2 holds the output that is being produced until wages are spent). It should be noted that when paying wages out of their own profits, firms do not spend their profits either; they merely immobilise them, and the above analysis applies.

Throughout this chapter, we have emphasized the reference circuitists make to Keynes's heterodoxy. Here is another opportunity to emphasize Keynes's legacy, in noting that the point we are examining corresponds precisely to Keynes's analysis of the finance motive (1937a; 1937b; 1937c). To start production, Keynes argues, firms have to secure finance that may be provided by banks (notably in the form of overdraft facilities) or by the market (Keynes, 1937a, pp. 208–9). Such finance, which amounts to 'a provision of cash', he continues, 'does not absorb or exhaust any resources', but generates new net saving when invested in a new production: 'Each new net investment has new net saving attached to it' (ibid., p. 209). We have just confirmed that, when paying wages, firms do not spend pre-existing savings, whatever the origin of the cash they spend, whether loans are granted by banks issuing money or income-holders who part with their cash. The payment of wages actually generates savings corresponding to the investment made by firms in new production. The reference to Keynes's writings on the finance motive provides us with an opportunity to pursue the analysis of money and the role of banks. So far, we have emphasized that bank deposits are the materialization of financial relationships between borrowers and depositors in which banks are go-betweens. Nevertheless, depositors are in the first place in direct relation with banks: depositors hold claims on banks, not on borrowers. This is what the notion of cash brings out. Banks are not only financial intermediaries; they are also, so to say, monetary intermediaries in that they make payments by crediting and debiting accounts. In this respect, deposits define cash, that is the ability for depositors to ask banks to make payments on their behalf. This is what firms obtain in the first instance when borrowing from banks or from deposit-holders on the financial markets.

Let us now consider firms' outlays on capital goods. Like wage-bill payments, these outlays may, in practice, be financed from bank loans (money creation) or from deposits obtained in the financial markets. The second case is the easier to consider. It means that firms spend incomes on the purchase of goods, just as income-holders usually do, and will have to reimburse lenders later on, out of their profits. The first case is trickier. It seems to contradict circuit theory, by which incomes (wages) are successively formed and spent, and banks are mere financial intermediaries. Banks seemingly finance the purchase of goods *ex nihilo*, without any need to transfer pre-existing (saved) incomes to borrowers. However, the contradiction is only apparent.

Table 6.3 Entries resulting from the funding of firm F2's purchases of capital goods from bank loans

Banks			
Assets		Liabilities	
Loan to firm F2	£y	Deposits of F1's workers	£y

Table 6.4 The effect of households' spending from current incomes

Banks			
Assets		Liabilities	
Loans to firms	£w−x	Deposits of households H1	£w−x

The production of the capital goods we are considering has given rise to workers' deposits with banks. To simplify, we may suppose that firm F1 that produced these latter goods had borrowed from banks to pay its workers' wages. Suppose now that firm F2 borrows from banks to pay for the capital goods produced. New deposits are credited to the benefit of F1. As a consequence, F1 can repay its bank loans, and finally (Table 6.3) only two entries remain alive in the banks' books: the debt of F2 which borrowed from the banks in order to buy the capital goods, and the asset (deposits) of F1's workers, who produced these goods and are saving their wages.

What Table 6.3 shows, then, in conformity with the findings of circuit theory, is that, although it borrowed money from the banks, which created supplementary deposits to that end, F2 did not spend resources that banks somehow created *ex nihilo*, but existing incomes saved and lent, through banks, by F1's workers. The latter are now, through the banks, creditors of F2.

Let us turn now to the financing of households' expenses. According to circuit theory, households spend the incomes earned by wage-earners and partially redistributed out of firms' profits. Income spending then allows firms to refund their bank loans. In Table 6.4, we suppose that in a first step households H1 spend £x out of deposits amounting to £w. There therefore remains £w−x deposits, with the corresponding £w−x loans to firms that have not yet been repaid.

Obviously, households also resort to bank loans. For an example, Arestis and Howells (1999) observe that 'the greater part of loan demand in the UK depends upon the decisions of households rather than firms' (p. 117). What happens then? To dispel suspicion, suppose that households H2 ask banks for credit and obtain a £z loan which they spend on goods, so allowing firms to repay their loans up to this amount. In the banks' books the situation is then as shown in Table 6.5.

This means that up to £z, H1's deposits cover equivalent loans to households H2. Implicitly, that is, through banks, H1 grants credit to H2: the latter has spent the income of the former, which it will have to pay back later on, out of its own income. This confirms our overall argument. Whichever way monetary transactions are funded, they are

Table 6.5   The effect of households' spending from bank loans

	Banks		
Assets		Liabilities	
Loans to firms	£$w-z$	Deposits of households H1	£w
Loans to households H2	£z		

part of the same scheme, that is, the circuit of money wages which are successively formed and spent, and may be redistributed and lent. It can also be seen that money creation in monetary payments by banks may have different meanings depending on whether that money (that is, cash as defined above) is granted to firms or households, and spent on goods or labour. This is so because, as circuitists argue, entries in banks' books have meaning with reference to the output that is produced and then bought by income-holders in the sequence of the flux and reflux of money wages.

Economic policy
Economic policy is no doubt one of the reasons for the existence of any economic theory in the first place, and circuitists do not challenge this. Given their proximity to Keynes's theory, they are much involved in examining the employment issue. However, in espousing the endogenous money thesis they also endorse the post-Keynesian rejection of neo-quantitativist monetary policies (see Parguez, 2001). In keeping with the presentation of circuit theory above, the focus here is on the relevance of circuit theory with respect to Keynes's method of analysis of the emblematic case of unemployment. First, we show that circuit theory underscores the originality of Keynes's theory of unemployment. Second, we develop some further considerations on circuitists' approach to economic policy with reference to present-day unemployment in Europe.

Circuit theory emphasizing the originality of Keynes's theory of unemployment
Keynes attributed unemployment to a demand deficiency due to excessive savings and recommended that the state should substitute itself for individual income-holders in spending the income available. In doing so he sought to refute the (neo)classical argument that involuntary unemployment is unlikely to occur except when wage and price rigidities impede the adjustment of supply and demand in markets. As he warned in the preface to the *General Theory*, to understand his claim, readers should 'escape from habitual modes of thought and expression' (1936, p. viii). He also warned that it would not be easy to escape entrenched ways of thinking, which unfortunately proved to be the case. Indeed, it is commonly argued, especially in the current writings of the 'New Keynesians' (cf. Ball et al., 1991), that Keynesian unemployment is due to some exogenous fall or 'shock' in demand which, given price and wage rigidity, deviates output and employment from their equilibrium values. On this interpretation, Keynes was original in establishing a model in which quantities instead of prices are supposed to adjust. In this view, examining why demand may be deficient is not at issue.[9] Policy recommendations then focus on the ways and means of establishing wage and price flexibility. Along with post-Keynesian writers (see notably Rotheim, 1998), circuitists seek

to restore Keynes's original message. To that end, they claim that circuit theory helps to characterise Keynes's analysis as a coherent argument and to challenge the (neo)classical analysis (cf. Gnos, 2004; 2005).

In what is Keynes's message original? As a first step, we may refer to the asymmetrical role in which Keynes casts entrepreneurs, which circuit theory emphasizes. Employment is not determined by the interplay of supply and demand in markets, but unilaterally by entrepreneurs who make a decision with reference to the demand they expect for their output. This is where Keynes himself, and many post-Keynesians after him, introduced the role of uncertainty. Depending on psychological factors, entrepreneurs may feel more or less confident with regard to their forthcoming proceeds from sales, and so increase or reduce employment. On this view, economic policy should aim at sustaining confidence and reducing uncertainty, notably in establishing stable institutions that will exercise control over the environment of economic activity. Even investment by the state, which Keynes viewed primarily as a means to sustain demand, is then to be considered as a way of sustaining entrepreneurs' confidence; long-term investment programmes are particularly useful in promoting stability in entrepreneurs' expectations. Fontana (2000) commented that, contrary to post-Keynesians, circuitists do not expand on the context of uncertainty in which entrepreneurs decide on the level of activity of firms. This is, in fact, essentially a difference of focus, not a denial; and circuitists are fully able to support post-Keynesian recommendations in the field.

As a second step, we of course have to consider demand deficiency *per se*. Again, emphasis may be placed onto the role of uncertainty. This is what Davidson (2002) does when explaining that uncertainty exacerbates households' liquidity preference and so deters them from spending their cash on goods. Keynes, for his part, emphasized what he termed a fundamental psychological rule that households spend a smaller part of their income in proportion as it grows (1936, pp. 96–7); hence the famous notion of households' decreasing marginal propensity to consume. Whatever the cause of demand deficiency may be, however, it should be noted that the reference to the circuit is necessary to the argument. This is so because Keynes does not simply argue that demand is insufficient, as New Keynesians currently do, but that saving exceeds investment. He logically means, in this way, that households earn incomes that they do not spend in full, which would not be a drawback if entrepreneurs were to borrow the incomes saved and spend them on capital goods (pp. 27–34). Keynes's argument is puzzling, however. As mentioned earlier, he also insists on the necessary equality of saving and investment. This sounds like a contradiction, and much intrigued his contemporaries and followers. Circuit theory confirms this equality, which results from the payment of wages (cf. above). It also states that all the wages earned by workers, and partially redistributed in profits and their subdivisions, are spent on goods. Also, nevertheless, while making clear the theory of distribution underlying the principle of effective demand, it is in a position to conceive of the possibility of an excess of saving over investment as defined by Keynes. What the excess of saving entails is firms' losses: firms are committed to bearing the cost of the unsold goods (it turns out that part of their initial investment on wages was sunk without hope of recovery), which is of course a situation they try to avoid by reducing their scale of production if they are expecting deficient demand.

In opposition to neoclassical economists, who advocate wage and price flexibility, Keynes insists that '[t]he essential character of [his] argument is precisely the same whether or not money-wages, etc., are liable to change' (Keynes, 1936, p. 27). He further explains, in chapter 19 of the *General Theory*, that the classical argument that, in any given industry, a reduction in money-wages would boost sales by cutting production costs and hence the price of output, rests on the questionable assumption 'that the reduction in money-wages will leave demand unaffected'. This amounts to unduly transposing a microeconomic argument into the realm of macroeconomics (pp. 257–9). Circuit theory undoubtedly supports Keynes's viewpoint in highlighting the methodology of the principle of effective demand. Demand is fuelled by wages. To cut wages is to diminish demand in the same proportion. By the way, Keynes is quite explicit on this: 'if the wage-unit changes, the expenditure on consumption corresponding to a given level of employment will, like prices, change in the same proportion' (p. 92). To be fair, Keynes does acknowledge that under certain circumstances production may be stimulated by a reduction in money-wages, but in coming to this conclusion he has to make certain assumptions with respect to the propensity to consume, which confirms that methodology is at issue:[10] 'A reduction in money-wages is quite capable in certain circumstances of affording a stimulus to output, as the classical theory supposes. My difference from this theory is primarily a difference of analysis' (p. 257). The divergence of Keynes's theory from the classical framework could hardly be made more explicit. The attempt by the 'Keynesians', whether 'old' or 'new', to reduce Keynes's originality to price and wage rigidity is all the more surprising, and needs anyway to be dismissed.

Circuit theory and unemployment in Europe today
A possible cause of present-day unemployment, especially in Europe, is probably not to be found in excessive saving due to the psychology of income-holders. If investment is deficient, however, leaving aside any discussion of restrictive fiscal policies (cf. Parguez, 2000), it is mainly because of production costs, essentially of wages that are notoriously higher in Western European countries that in Eastern Europe, in South East Asia or in China. These lower production costs prompt Western companies to relocate their plants, as the current debate about 'delocalization' illustrates. A twofold vicious circle has been generated.

On the one hand, in response to firms' complaints, governments are promoting supply-side policies that translate into wage-deflation and so cause demand to fall even further. For example, while in France, from the early 1960s to the early 1980s, the share of wages (including insurance contributions paid by employers and which benefit wage-earners and their families) rose from 60 per cent to nearly 68 per cent in value added, it fell dramatically to 59 per cent in the late 1980s, that is, within a very few years. It then further dipped to the 57.9 per cent figure recorded in 2000, and now (2004) stands at about 58 per cent.[11] This change is clearly the outcome of the restrictive pay policies implemented since 1983. A similar pattern is found in other Western European countries, especially in Italy and Germany.[12] By the way, it is interesting to observe that, in France for instance, the authorities recurrently refer to stagnation in households' consumption to explain low growth and unemployment. This means that, although they advocate and apply supply-oriented policies, governments in practice acknowledge the role of demand. They do not, then, of course, recommend wage rises; they instead promote easier borrowing or favour intergenerational transfers of wealth, considering that younger people will spend more than their elders.

On the other hand, imports from low-cost countries, in allowing households to buy goods at attractive prices, favour wage deflation, which means that Western European wage-earners are less and less able to buy goods produced in their domestic economies.

However, from a practical point of view, how could entrepreneurs sustain competition in today's globalized economy if policies favouring wage stability not to mention wage expansion were adopted in Western Europe? As said, wages in France have been falling since 1983. This policy came in after the first phase of Mitterrand's presidency, which was characterized by demand-side policies that failed because consumers preferred cheap imports to more expensive goods produced in the domestic economy. This unsuccessful policy sounded like a final, failed attempt to implement Keynesian policies. Circuitists note that Keynes did not, however, leave us at a loss for a solution. Challenging the classical argument that a reduction in money-wages would stimulate demand by lowering production costs and hence the price of output, Keynes made clear that his conclusion in favour of wage stability applies 'provided that equilibrium with the rest of the world can be secured by means of fluctuating exchanges' (Keynes, 1936, p. 271). Schmitt took this point into account when expanding on Keynes's proposals for an International Clearing Union (Keynes, 1941; 1942) to advocate a world monetary reform (Schmitt, 1973) and when criticizing the official project for a single European currency compared with the advantages of retaining the domestic currencies and introducing a common currency in the international payments of European countries alone (Schmitt, 1988). Of course, these considerations are to be compared, on the post-Keynesian side, to Davidson's (1991; 2002) own proposal for a reform of the world's money. A methodological feature of Keynes's heterodoxy endorsed by circuitists and post-Keynesians alike consists in tying in money and real variables, and also in considering the structural organization of the economy. It is not surprising, then, that these features may be simultaneously summoned up in the search for solutions to economic problems. In this same vein, Schmitt (1984; 1996) has developed an analysis, in the framework of his theory of money emission, which explores the possible causes of demand deficiency and connects unemployment and inflation (see Rossi, Chapter 8, this volume). All in all, Keynes and his circuitist and post-Keynesian interpreters' view of unemployment and its cure is part of a global view of the way the world in which we live works and the way it should be ordered.

Conclusion
This presentation of circuit theory has focused on the reference circuitists make to Keynes's heterodoxy. It has been a means to emphasize the affinity of circuit theory with post-Keynesian theory, and so to help readers more familiar with the latter to grasp the significance of the circuit and its place in heterodox economics. It has also been a means to figure out a pre-eminent feature of circuit theory, its proponents' conviction that Keynes provided economic theory with a sustainable original scheme, in stark contrast with the neoclassical 'real exchange economy', the foundations of which need to be clarified and extended in order to clear up misunderstandings such as those that allowed orthodox theorists to consider Keynes's theory as a special case of their own representation. It is this need that induced a handful of French economists, pre-eminently Schmitt, Barrère, Le Bourva and Parguez, to make a point of reviving the time-honoured conception of the circuit which they suspected underpinned Keynes's heterodoxy. This was not an easy task, as is obvious from some of the characteristics of their analysis as presented above, especially the question of money, its definition and its role. But, as we hope to have convinced readers, this was (is) the price to be paid in order to better grasp the ins and outs of Keynes's theoretical revolution and, more importantly, of the real world in which

we live, and its plagues such as unemployment. Needless to say, despite Kregel's encouragements that 'the circuit approach has [indeed] done much to reawaken interest in Keynes's monetary theory of production and to extend it in new directions' (Kregel, 1987, p. 11),[13] much remains to be done in this field.

Notes

1. See Graziani (2003).
2. On Robinson and the circuit, see Gnos and Rochon (2003) and Rochon (2004).
3. 'The elementary factors of production are three in number. In listing these factors, most authors employ the terms: land, labour and capital. But these terms are not sufficiently rigorous to serve as a foundation for rational deduction. Labour is the service of human faculties or of persons. We must rank labour, therefore, not with land and capital, but with land-services ['rente'] rendered by land, and with capital-services ['profit'] rendered by capital-goods' (Walras, 1926, p. 212).
4. 'The factor cost is, of course, the same thing, looked at from the point of view of entrepreneur, as what the factors of production regard as their income' (Keynes, 1936, p. 23).
5. So much so that Walras claimed 'we can abstract from money in circulation' (1926, p. 220).
6. As Schumpeter (1954, p. 321) once put it, 'you cannot ride on a claim to a horse, but you can pay with a claim to money'.
7. 'The prevalence of the idea that saving and investment, taken in their straightforward sense, can differ from one another, is to be explained, I think, by an optical illusion due to regarding an individual depositor's relation to this bank as being a one-sided transaction, instead of seeing it as the two-sided transaction which it actually is. It is supposed that a depositor and his bank can somehow contrive between them to perform an operation by which savings can disappear into the banking system so that they are lost to investment, or, contrariwise, that the banking system can make it possible for investment to occur, to which no saving corresponds' (Keynes, 1936, p. 81n).
8. When income-holders lend their savings to firms which spend them on capital goods, the situation is different. Income-holders certainly convert their savings from liquid to illiquid assets, but from a macroeconomic viewpoint the corresponding incomes are spent: the output which is, say, the real content of the incomes, is bought by borrowers. The latter will reimburse the loan later out of their own incomes.
9. As Stiglitz (1993) points out, New Keynesians are not actually interested in examining why demand may be deficient.
10. For a more comprehensive discussion of this point, see Gnos (2003b and 2004).
11. Source: Timbeau (2002) and INSEE (2005).
12. As regards Germany, see Hein and Truger (2005).
13. Kregel is quoted here from Arena (1996), p. 427.

References

Arena, R. (1996), 'Investment decisions in circuit and Post Keynesian approaches: a comparison', in G. Deleplace and E. Nell (eds), *Money in Motion: the Post Keynesian and Circulation Approaches*, London and New York: Macmillan and St Martin's Press, pp. 417–33.

Arestis, P. (1996), 'Post-Keynesian economics: towards coherence', *Cambridge Journal of Economics*, **20**, pp. 111–35.

Arestis, P. and P. Howells (1999), 'The supply of credit money and the demand for deposits: a reply', *Cambridge Journal of Economics*, **23**(1), pp. 115–19.

Ball, L., Mankiw, G. and Romer, D. (1991), 'The New-Keynesian economics and the output–inflation trade-off', in G. Mankiw and D. Romer (eds), *New Keynesian Economics*, vol. 1, Cambridge, MA: MIT Press, pp. 147–211.

Barrère, A. (1979), *Déséquilibres économiques et contre-révolution keynésienne*, Paris: Economica.

Barrère, A. (1990a), 'Signification générale du circuit: une interprétation', *Économies et Sociétés*, série Monnaie et Production, **2**(6), pp. 9–34.

Barrère, A. (1990b), *Macroéconomie keynésienne: le projet économique de John Maynard Keynes*, Paris: Dunod.

Davidson, P. (1991), 'What international payments scheme would Keynes have suggested for the twenty-first century?', in P. Davidson and J.A. Kregel (eds), *Economic Problems of the 1990s: Europe, the Developing Countries and the United States*, Aldershot, UK and Brookfield, US: Edward Elgar, pp. 85–104.

Davidson, P. (2002), *Financial Markets, Money and the Real World*, Cheltenham, UK and Northampton, MA, USA: Edward Elgar.

Deleplace, G. and E. Nell (1996), 'Introduction: monetary circulation and effective demand', in G. Deleplace and E. Nell, *Money in Motion: the Post Keynesian and Circulation Approaches*, London and New York: Macmillan and St Martin's Press, pp. 3–41.

Fontana, G. (2000), 'Post Keynesians and Circuitists on money and uncertainty: an attempt at generality', *Journal of Post Keynesian Economics*, **23**(1), pp. 27–48.

Fontana G. and R. Realfonzo (eds) (2005), *The Monetary Theory of Production*, New York: Palgrave Macmillan.

Gnos, C. (1998), 'The Keynesian identity of income and output', in A. Jolink and P. Fontaine (eds), *Historical Perspectives on Macroeconomics: 60 Years After the General Theory*, London: Routledge, pp. 40–48.

Gnos, C. (2003a), 'Circuit theory as an explanation of the complex real world', in L.-P. Rochon and Rossi (eds), *Studies in Modern Theories of Money*, London: Routledge, pp. 322–38.

Gnos, C. (2003b), 'The employment issue: Post Keynesian economics challenging New Keynesian economics', in E. Hein, A. Heise and A. Truger (eds), *Neu Keynesianismus; Der neue wirtschaftspolitische Mainstream?*, Marburg: Metropolis, pp. 117–33.

Gnos, C. (2004), 'Analysing and fighting recession with reference to Keynes', in L.R. Wray and M. Forstater (eds), *Contemporary Post Keynesian Analysis*, Cheltenham, UK and Northampton, MA, USA: Edward Elgar, pp. 301–9.

Gnos, C. (2005), 'Circuit theory and the employment issue', in G. Fontana and R. Realfonzo (eds), *The Monetary Theory of Production*, New York: Palgrave Macmillan, pp. 173–83.

Gnos, C. and Rochon L.-P. (2003), 'Joan Robinson and Keynes: finance, relative prices and the monetary circuit', *Review of Political Economy*, **15**(4), pp. 483–91.

Graziani, A. (1989), *The Theory of the Monetary Circuit*, Thames Papers in Political Economy.

Graziani, A. (2003), *The Monetary Theory of Production*, Cambridge: Cambridge University Press.

Hein, E. and A. Truger (2005), 'What ever happened to Germany? Is the decline of the former European key currency country caused by structural sclerosis or by macroeconomic mismanagement?', *International Review of Applied Economics*, **19**(1), pp. 3–28.

Hicks, J. (1975), *The Crisis in Keynesian Economics*, Oxford: Basil Blackwell.

Institut National des Etudes Statistiques (2005), *Tableaux de l'économie française*, Paris: INSEE.

Keynes, J.M. (1930), *The Treatise on Money*, in D. Moggridge (ed.) (1971), *The Collected Writings of John Maynard Keynes*, Vol. V, London: The Macmillan Press.

Keynes, J.M. (1933a), 'A monetary theory of production', in D. Moggridge (ed.) (1973), *The Collected Writings of John Maynard Keynes*, Vol. XIII, London: The Macmillan Press, pp. 408–11.

Keynes, J.M. (1933b), 'The distinction between a co-operative economy and an entrepreneur economy', in D. Moggridge (ed.) (1973), *The Collected Writings of John Maynard Keynes*, Vol. XXIX, London: The Macmillan Press, pp. 76–106.

Keynes, J.M. (1936), *The General Theory of Employment, Interest and Money*, in D. Moggridge (ed.) (1971), *The Collected Writings of John Maynard Keynes*, Vol. VII, London: The Macmillan Press.

Keynes, J.M. (1937a), 'Ex post and ex ante', in *The General Theory and After*, Part II, *Defence and Development*, in D. Moggridge (ed.) (1973), *The Collected Writings of John Maynard Keynes*, Vol. XIV, London: The Macmillan Press.

Keynes, J.M. (1937b), 'Alternative theories of the rate of interest', *The Economic Journal*, June 1937, in *The General Theory and After*, Part II, *Defence and Development*, in D. Moggridge (ed.) (1973), *The Collected Writings of John Maynard Keynes*, Vol. XIV, London: The Macmillan Press.

Keynes, J.M. (1937c), 'The "ex ante" theory of the rate of interest', *The Economic Journal*, December 1937, in *The General Theory and After*, Part II, *Defence and Development*, in D. Moggridge (ed.) (1973), *The Collected Writings of John Maynard Keynes*, Vol. XIV, London: The Macmillan Press.

Keynes, J.M. (1941), 'Proposals for an international currency union', in D. Moggridge (ed.) (1980), *The Collected Writings of John Maynard Keynes*, Vol. XXV, London: The Macmillan Press, pp. 42–61.

Keynes, J.M. (1942), 'Proposals for an international clearing union', in D. Moggridge (ed.) (1980), *The Collected Writings of John Maynard Keynes*, Vol. XXV, London: The Macmillan Press, pp. 168–96.

Kregel, J.A. (1987), 'Shylock and Hamlet, or are there bulls and bears in the circuit?', *Économies et Sociétés*, **9**.

Lavoie, M. (1984), 'Un modèle post-Keynésien d'économie monétaire fondé sur la théorie du circuit', *Économies et Sociétés*, **59**(1), pp. 233–58.

Lavoie, M. (1987), 'Monnaie et production: une synthèse de la théorie du circuit', *Économies et Sociétés*, **21**, pp. 65–111.

Lavoie, M. (2005), 'Lessons from asset-based financial systems with zero-reserve requirements', in G. Fontana and R. Realfonzo (eds), *The Monetary Theory of Production*, New York: Palgrave Macmillan, pp. 257–68.

Le Bourva, J. (1962), 'Création de la monnaie et multiplicateur du crédit', *Revue Economique*, **13**(1), pp. 29–56.

Moore, B.J. (1988), *Horizontalists and Verticalists: The Macroeconomics of Credit Money*, New York: Cambridge University Press.

Parguez, A. (1975), *Monnaie et macroéconomie*, Paris: Economica.

Parguez, A. (1996), 'Beyond scarcity: a reappraisal of the theory of the monetary circuit', in G. Deleplace and E. Nell (eds), *Money in Motion: the Post Keynesian and Circulation Approaches*, London and New York: Macmillan and St Martin's Press, pp. 155–99.

Parguez, A. (2001), 'Money without scarcity: from the horizontalist revolution to the theory of the monetary circuit', in L.-P. Rochon and M. Vernengo (eds), *Credit, Interest Rates and the Open Economy*, Cheltenham, UK and Northampton, MA, USA: Edward Elgar, pp. 69–103.

Parguez, A. and M. Seccareccia (2000), 'The credit theory of money: the monetary circuit approach', in J. Smithin (ed.), *What is Money?*, London and New York: Routledge, pp. 101–23.

Poulon, F. (1982), *Macroéconomie approfondie, Equilibre, Déséquilibre, Circuit*, Paris: Cujas.

Renaud, J.-F. (2000), 'The problem of the monetary realization of profits in a Post Keynesian sequential financing model: two solutions of the Kaleckian option', *Review of Political Economy*, **12**(3), pp. 285–303.

Rochon, L.-P. (1999a), *Credit, Money and Production: An Alternative Post-Keynesian Approach*, Cheltenham, UK and Northampton, MA, USA: Edward Elgar.

Rochon, L.-P. (1999b), 'The creation and circulation of endogenous money: a circuit dynamic approach', *Journal of Economic Issues*, **33**(1), pp. 1–21.

Rochon, L.-P. (2004), 'Joan Robinson on credit, money and production: a forgotten contribution', in W. Gibson (ed.), *Joan Robinson's Economics: A Centennial Celebration*, Cheltenham, UK and Northampton, MA, USA: Edward Elgar, pp. 267–82.

Rochon, L.-P. (2005), 'The existence of monetary profits within the monetary circuit', in G. Fontana and R. Realfonzo (eds), *The Monetary Theory of Production*, Basingstoke and New York: Palgrave Macmillan, pp. 125–38.

Rotheim, R.J. (1998), 'New Keynesian macroeconomics and markets', in R.J. Rotheim (ed.), *New Keynesian Economics/Post Keynesian Alternatives*, London: Routledge, pp. 51–70.

Schmitt, B. (1960), *La formation du pouvoir d'achat*, Paris: Sirey.

Schmitt, B. (1966), *Monnaie, salaries et profits*, Paris: Presses Universitaires de France.

Schmitt, B. (1972), *Macroeconomic Theory. A Fundamental Revision*, Albeuve (Switzerland): Castella.

Schmitt, B. (1973), *New Proposals for World Monetary Reform*, Albeuve (Switzerland): Castella.

Schmitt, B. (1984), *Inflation, chômage et malformation du capital*, Albeuve (Switzerland), Castella and Paris: Economica.

Schmitt, B. (1988), *L'Ecu est les souverainetés nationales en Europe*, Paris: Dunod.

Schmitt, B. (1996), 'Unemployment: is there a principal cause?', in A. Cencini and M. Baranzini (eds), *Inflation and Unemployment. Contributions to a new macroeconomic approach*, London and New York: Routledge, pp. 75–105.

Schumpeter, J.A. (1954), *History of Economic Analysis*, New York: Oxford University Press.

Seccareccia, M. (1996), 'Post Keynesian fundism and monetary circulation', in G. Deleplace and E. Nell (eds), *Money in Motion: the Post Keynesian and Circulation Approaches*, London and New York: Macmillan and St Martin's Press, pp. 400–416.

Smith, A. (1976), *An Inquiry into the Nature and Causes of the Wealth of Nations*, in *The Glasgow Edition of the Works and Correspondence of Adam Smith*, Vol. 2, Oxford: Oxford University Press.

Stiglitz, J.E. (1993), *Economics*, New York: W.W. Norton.

Timbeau, X. (2002), 'Le partage de la valeur ajoutée en France', *Revue de l'OFCE*, **80**, pp. 63–85.

Walras, L. (1926), *Eléments d'Economie Politique Pure*, in W. Jaffé (ed.) (1954), *Elements of Pure Economics*, London: George Allen and Unwin.

7 The Italian circuitist approach
Riccardo Realfonzo

1. Introduction

The Italian circuitist approach (hereafter: ICA) is part of the broad and heterogeneous course of heterodox economics literature. It is an approach linked with Augusto Graziani's work on the subject since the early 1980s, and with publications by the authors who have developed his analysis in various directions (Riccardo Bellofiore, Marcello Messori, Riccardo Realfonzo; but also Biagio Bossone, Emiliano Brancaccio, Giuseppe Fontana, Guglielmo Forges Davanzati, Alberto Zazzaro and others). It is not only in Italy that circuit theory is widespread. In fact, during the second half of the 1900s a growing number of increasingly systematic studies were devoted to it by scholars from France (Alain Parguez, Bernard Schmitt, François Poulon; but also Claude Gnos, Elie Sadigh), Canada (Marc Lavoie, Mario Seccareccia, Louis-Philippe Rochon), Britain (Wynne Godley, Francis Cripps) and Switzerland (Alvaro Cencini, Sergio Rossi). The growing interest aroused by the ICA, and in general by monetary circuit theory, is witnessed by countless conferences and seminars exploring the possible avenues of comparison with the other heterodox approaches, mainly post-Keynesian and Sraffian (see Deleplace and Nell, 1996 and Fontana and Realfonzo, 2005; but also Rochon and Rossi, 2003 and Brancaccio, 2005).

In this chapter I will try to provide a simplified exposition of the contributions by the Italian school of the monetary circuit and an overall interpretation.

2. Main 'sources' and arguments of the ICA

The ICA has drawn sustenance from some great works from the history of economic thought, belonging to traditions which are different in many respects but which share the idea that the economic process must be described as a circular sequence of monetary flows. It is for this reason that the $M–C–M'$ capital cycle described by Karl Marx in *Das Kapital* has always been recognized as the starting point of circuit theory. Marx's influence on circuit theory, and in general on macroeconomics in the tradition of the monetary theory of production, has been underlined repeatedly by the supporters of the ICA. In Graziani's vision, scholars such as Wicksell, Schumpeter and Keynes made up a veritable 'underground Marxist genre' (Graziani, 1982). It is no coincidence that ICA literature has put forward a re-reading of Marx's theory of money and value. According to this macroeconomic approach to Marx, money is essentially the means of commanding over living labour in production. In the view of some Italian scholars, the Marxian labour theory of value can be set out in terms of the monetary circuit model (Bellofiore, 1989; 1997; Bellofiore and Realfonzo, 2003).

The other main reference points for the ICA are represented by the pure credit model theorized by Knut Wicksell in *Interest and Prices* (ch. 9, sect. B) and by the theory of economic dynamics contained in Schumpeter's *Theory of Economic Development*.[1] But the overriding source of inspiration of the monetary circuit approach is undoubtedly found in the works of John Maynard Keynes; not only the *General Theory* but also *Treatise on Money* and some other writings that preceded and followed the *General Theory* dealing with the 'monetary theory of production' (see in particular Keynes, 1933). The ICA gives a 'continuist' interpretation of Keynes's work, sustaining the complementary nature of the *Treatise* and *The General Theory* (Forges Davanzati and Realfonzo, 2005a; Realfonzo, 1998).[2]

With reference to the Italian tradition, the authors who cleared the way for studies on the monetary circuit were Antonio de Viti de Marco (1898), Marco Fanno (1993 [1931]; 1947; 1992 [1932–34]), Luigi Lugli (1939) and Paolo Sylos Labini (1948).[3] However, it is only with the contributions of the last 30 years that the ICA has acquired the continuity and homogeneity typical of any consolidated line of research. Graziani and the other proponents of the monetary circuit theory worked both towards the historical–theoretical reconstruction and towards a more profound analysis. Their work gave rise to a debate between supporters and critics which is still under way.

The ICA rejects the methodological individualism typical of the neoclassical tradition, and, in line with the socio-historical method of analysis associated with the classical, Marxian and Keynesian traditions, assumes a triangular structure of agents (banks, firms, workers). It proposes a sequential model in which the economic process is described by means of a flow of money into the economic circuit. The ICA emphasizes the profoundly conflicting monetary nature of capitalist economies. The most significant conclusions maintained by the Italian studies on the monetary circuit are as follows:

(a)   money is a pure symbol, the result of a bank loan; money supply is endogenous;
(b)   the volume of production and employment depends on the expected level of aggregate demand;
(c)   income distribution essentially depends on the relative market power of the macroeconomic agents and on their access to bank finance;
(d)   the role of the money market (that of supplying firms with initial finance) is distinguished from the role of the financial market (that of trying to contrast the household's propensity for liquidity by supplying firms with final finance).

3.   The monetary circuit

The Italian literature on the monetary circuit sprang from a simple description of the sequence of the phases of the circuit put forward by Graziani (1984; 1989; 1994; 2004a).[4] Let us consider a closed economy with no state sector, in which there are three macro agents operating: banks, firms and workers. Banks have the task of financing the production process through the creation of money, and of selecting business plans; firms, through access to credit, buy factors of production and direct the production process, making decisions on the quantity and quality of output; workers supply labour services. The working of the economy is described as a sequential process, characterized by successive phases whose links form a circuit of money. A clear understanding of the circuit theory can be obtained from Figure 7.1.

The phases in the circuit are:

1.   Banks grant (totally or in part) the financing requested by firms, creating money (opening of the circuit).

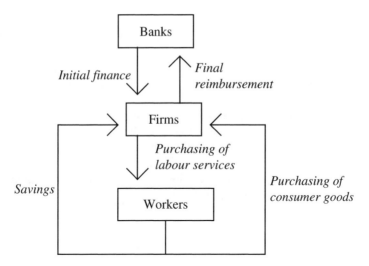

Figure 7.1   The circuit theory

2. Once financing has been obtained, firms buy inputs. Considering firms in the aggregate, their only expenditure coincides with the total wage bill; at this point money passes from firms to workers.
3. Once labour services have been purchased, firms carry out production; in the simplest case, firms produce homogeneous goods.
4. At the end of the production process, firms put the goods on the market. It can be envisaged that firms set the sale price following a *mark-up* principle. Supposing workers have a propensity to consume equal to one, firms recover the entire wage bill and maintain ownership of a proportion (corresponding to the mark-up) of the goods produced. If the propensity to consume is less than one, once the workers have purchased consumer goods they must make a further choice about how to use their savings, either hoarding (increase in cash reserves) or investing (purchase of shares). If all the money savings are invested in shares on the financial market, firms manage to recover the whole wage bill.
5. Once goods and shares have been sold, firms repay the banks (closure of the circuit).

In the following sections we will examine specific aspects of monetary circuit theory.

4.   Theory of money
In the area of monetary theory the ICA reaches the following conclusions:

(a) in the capitalist economy money is necessarily a pure symbol, a bank liability, with no intrinsic value and no necessary relation with an exogenous money base;
(b) the injection of money into the economic circuit takes place when there is a demand for financing: the money supply is demand-driven;
(c) there may be a stock of money with the agents at the closure of the circuit if there is a demand for cash reserves;
(d) from the above it is deduced that money supply is fully endogenous.

In order to understand the arguments set out above, we need to go back to the triangular definition of the structure of agents and to the representation of the working of the monetary circuit. As has been pointed out, in order for there to be production, firms must buy labour-power but, as production has not yet taken place, no goods exist to pay for it; the real wage is necessarily paid in arrears. Thus there are two possibilities (Graziani, 1994):

(1)   firms do not make any advance payment to workers and, at the end of the production process, share with them the goods produced. But in this case, as Robertson (1926) recalled, the theory would lead to a model of the economy with the double features of a 'barter economy' (money has no significant function) and of a 'cooperative economy' (agents take production decisions together and share the final product);
(2)   firms pay money wages in advance.

It is evident that a consistent model of a monetary economy requires the second option. At this point there are again two possible choices:

(a)   firms pay workers with promises of payment (promissory notes);
(b)   firms resort to the banks, which create money.

The possibility of firms paying workers with promissory notes must be rejected. Let us see why. Firms' promissory notes are either final means of payment or merely promises to pay. Let us assume that firms pay for labour-power by issuing liabilities which are accepted by workers as final means of payment. In such a situation, firms enjoy 'rights of seigniorage'. Indeed, in exchange for a paper instrument of no value issued by themselves they obtain labour-power and are released from any subsequent payment. The possibility that liabilities issued by firms give rise to final payments can be discarded if one is looking for a model in which all parties possess equal rights and there are no seignorial powers. Alternatively, it could be supposed that workers are paid by means of liabilities issued by firms and that these liabilities do not give rise to final payments. In this case the liabilities are, in effect, mere promises to pay, i.e. certificates of credit. With this formulation we arrive at a *credit economy model*, whose substance is no different from that of a barter economy. Indeed, if firms initially pay their workers with mere promissory notes, they will subsequently have to extinguish their debt by transferring goods directly. In this way, barter is merely postponed.

Therefore, if one wants to describe the functioning of a system characterized by a triangular structure of agents, i.e. a system which includes a labour market and, at the same time, one wants to exclude a barter model, the only possible means of payment consists of liabilities issued by the banking system.

What has just been said does not mean that, from the point of view of the ICA, money has always been a pure sign. In this regard, the logical reconstruction of the history of money and banking can follow two possible approaches: an 'evolutionary approach' and an 'institutional approach' (Realfonzo, 2001).

The 'evolutionary approach' considers it possible that in pre-capitalistic forms of the economy money had a commodity nature. In this respect the neoclassical description of the evolution of the payment system from pure barter to the introduction of a commodity money is considered correct for the initial stages of the development. At the same time, the idea that, initially, banks were nothing more than pure financial intermediaries is also confirmed. However, according to this heterodox 'evolutionary approach', the neoclassical description proves to be valid for the pre-capitalist stages alone. In fact, with the advent of capitalism, money took on the nature of a pure symbol and banks became creators of money. A similar approach has recently been developed by Chick (1986) and in Italy it was put forward by de Viti de Marco (1898).

According to the 'institutional approach', money has never possessed a commodity nature and banks have never acted as pure financial intermediaries. Money is defined as a social institution; it may have a 'commodity vehicle' (a 'material support'); however, this has nothing to do with the nature of money. Within the 'institutional approach', money can be alternatively described either as the result of a social convention or as the outcome of a state imposition. In the Italian debate the article by Heinsohn and Steiger (1983) has had a certain influence. According to the two authors, money has always been a pure symbol: it was created as a result of the uncertainty that followed the introduction of the system of private property and the consequent 'abolition of collective security provided by tribal and feudal estate' (ibid., p. 14).[5] But a certain influence has also been exerted by the other branch of the institutionalist approach, which holds that 'credit money could not exist without the State . . . all credit-driven money is by its very nature a fiat money irrespective of whether it takes the form of commercial bank or central bank liability' (Parguez and Seccareccia, 1999).

In any case the two approaches agree that in capitalist economies, given the triangular structure of operators (banks, firms, workers), money is necessarily a book-keeping entry in the bank's balance sheets: it is pure credit.

5. The bank as creator of money

Let us suppose that in order to finance their production, firms resort to bank credit (Graziani, 1987; 2003b). Banks register the credit granted to firms on the credit side of their balance sheets, and the amount of the deposits created in favour of firms on the debit side. Subsequently, firms use the deposits to pay their workers. At this point, banks transfer ownership of the deposits to workers, cancelling those of the entrepreneurs. In this new situation, firms remain indebted to the banks, the workers are the banks' creditors, while bank balance sheets report the credits granted to firms on the asset side and debts to workers as a liability. Bank deposits have acted as *final means of payment* for firms, inasmuch as they have effectively freed themselves of any debt relationship with workers. In an economy without barter, the only possible money is the bank promissory note: even though it is not a commodity, only this promissory note can release firms from all the debts owed to their workers. In this sense, the means of payment 'assumes the form of a triangular transaction'. It is therefore clear that the theorists of the monetary circuit define the bank as the agent that has the function of creating money. This expression refers to the capacity of ordinary credit institutions (commercial banks) to transform non-monetary activity, like simple promises to pay, into activities that are money, in other words that are accepted by the community as a final means of payment. In the monetary economy money is therefore embodied in entries in banks' balance sheets. Naturally every act of creating money is registered in a double entry in the balance sheet (on one side the issue of money is entered as a bank liability, on the other it is entered as a credit towards the lender). In this sense it is clear that from the point of view of the economy as a whole money does not represent wealth; the exact opposite is however true from the point of view of the individual possessor of money.[6]

It should be stressed that in their examination of the money supply, the circuit theorists invert the mainstream approach (Realfonzo, 1998; Zazzaro, 1995). The mainstream, in fact, envisages first the definition of the concept of money base (legal tender issued by the central bank), then the construction of the multiplier of bank deposits, and lastly the definition of the supply (effective and potential) of money. In other words the mainstream confirms the old saw that 'deposits make loans'.

The circuit theorists reverse the traditional approach following Schumpeter's argument that the functioning of the accounting system in a capitalist society emerges with great clarity if one begins with the study of the 'fundamental theoretical case', which is, basically, the Wicksellian model of pure credit (a 'pure accounting system') where all payments take place by means of entries in bank balance sheets (the 'fundamental concept of the theory of money'). In other words the circuit theorists show that even without legal tender, the system could theoretically work since bank money is accepted through the confidence that agents have in the bank.

It follows that the logic of the multiplier of bank deposits is completely rejected. Ordinary credit institutions do not multiply anything; they create money ('loans make deposits'). Obviously this is not to deny that a specific monetary set-up where bank money is by law tied to a money that commercial banks cannot create can tend to place a cap on the expansion of bank credits. But in this regard some circuit theorists express doubt. Ultimately, this concerns 'the limit to the credit which the bank can grant . . . cannot be fixed, either rationally or practically . . . [it] depends on the forecast . . . of the amount of future compensations' (de Viti de Marco, 1934, p. 51). As can be seen, the Italian monetary circuit authors adopt positions near to (but not coinciding with) the horizontalist ones expressed by Moore (1988).

6.   Demand for money and the endogenous nature of the money supply

Having clarified the banking system's capacity to create money theoretically with no limits, the Italian authors show that the size of the monetary flows involving the circuit and of the stocks of cash reserves found at the closure of the circuit (in equilibrium) depend (essentially) on the demand for money. Following Keynes's teaching, monetary circuit theory distinguishes between the demand for money to finance production (which Keynes called 'finance motive') and the demand for cash reserves (dependent on the famous transactions, precautionary and speculative motives) (Graziani, 1987; 1994; 1996; Messori, 1991).

The finance motive explains the creation of money and its injection into the economy. As has already been pointed out, in order for production of goods to take place, firms have to obtain bank financing. They will therefore apply to the banks, which will grant financing to the firms considered credit-worthy, by opening a deposit in their favour. In this way money is injected into the economy, enabling business to purchase raw materials and labour. Supposing for the sake of simplicity that the banks accept all the requests for financing (absence of rationing), the size of the monetary flows (i.e. the quantity of money which, at any given period, flows into the economy) depends on the firms' demand for finance.

The demand for cash reserves leads to the formation of money stocks which are present at the closure of the circuit. Let us just suppose that the agents have a zero propensity to liquidity. This would mean that once firms have paid wages, production has been completed, and wages have been spent on consumer goods and in the financial market, firms would come back into possession of the whole amount of initial financing and would therefore be able to repay the bank. In this way, money initially injected into the circuit would flow back to the banks (destruction of money). This would mean that at the end of the circuit there would be no stock of money reserves. In a stationary economy (and disregarding the question of interest payments) it can be imagined that in the following period the amount of money flowing into the circuit (and in the end flowing back to the banks) is constant. Let us now suppose that the propensity to liquidity becomes positive: agents will not spend all the money that enters their coffers and will keep some cash reserves. In this case the 'final finance', namely the income of firms as a whole from the sale of goods and shares, is lower than the 'initial finance'. This simply means that at the closure of the circuit a certain amount of money remains 'idle' in the agents' reserves. From what has been observed above, it can be deduced that both money flows and the formation of money stocks depend essentially on the demand for money.

However, one needs to note several aspects that do not escape the attention of the Italian interpreters of the monetary circuit. First, it seems evident that there is a relation between the size of money flows and the formation of money reserves. All other conditions being equal, the more money flows into the circuit, the higher the money incomes will be and the more cash reserves will be formed. On the other hand, all conditions still being equal, an increase in the propensity to liquidity leads to a reduction in the money flowing back to the banks. It is also clear that in the case of a closed economy with no state sector, the formation of cash reserves must correspond to a situation of firms' indebtedness towards the banks and/or of firm bankruptcy.

Second, it should be underlined that the hypothesis that the banking system fulfils all the requests for financing is hardly credible (Forges Davanzati and Realfonzo, 2005a). It is far more realistic to assume that the banks assess credit-worthiness and therefore do not accept all the applications for financing (rationing of bank credit). This simple observation leads the Italian monetary circuit scholars to clarify the meaning of the thesis that money supply is demand-driven. It is true that the size of the circuit's money flows and the size of the money stocks depend respectively on the demand for money for financial purposes and on the demand for money as a store of value. However, money flows and stocks are affected by the behaviour of the bankers: if there is bank credit rationing, these flows and funds are just a fraction of the potential demand for money.

In conclusion, in the vision of the theorists of the circuit, the functions of demand for money and the function of money supply are interdependent (see Graziani, 1989; 1994; Realfonzo, 1998, chs 2 and 6).

7. Equilibrium, disequilibrium, the closure of the circuit

The Italian authors of the monetary circuit show that this approach is able to explain the reproduction of the monetary economy in equilibrium as well as disequilibrium. Circuit theorists point out that as long as agents consider money exclusively in its function as a means of payment, the circuit closes in equilibrium (Graziani, 1984). Let us suppose in fact that each agent, whether businessperson or worker, immediately spends the money that enters their possession by purchasing goods or services. In that case all the money injected initially into the economy will flow back to the firms and from them to the banks (destruction of money). In this respect the circuit school refers to the teachings of Keynes's *Treatise on Money*. In this case the circuit closes in equilibrium.

However, equilibrium is only one of the two possible ways in which the circuit can close. In this regard the monetary circuit theorists return to the teaching of *The General Theory*. They maintain that because of its structural features, the capitalist economy is characterized by the presence of systemic uncertainty (Fontana, 2000; Fontana and Gerrard, 2002; Graziani, 1994). And for this reason it is impossible to ignore that money functions as a store of value to give a form of insurance against uncertainty. Agents' attitude to money therefore depends on the widespread expectations in the economy. When negative expectations spread, agents start to use money increasingly as a store of value and less as a means of payment. Money reserves grow and this rules out the possibility that money can flow back to the banks and therefore that the circuit can close in equilibrium. A crisis occurs when negative expectations spread. It takes the form of an interruption of the monetary circuit due to the accumulation of cash reserves and leads to a drop in production and in employment.

From these comments it emerges clearly that the Italian school of the monetary circuit is putting forward a 'continuist' interpretation of Keynes (Forges Davanzati and Realfonzo, 2005a). In other words it sees *The Treatise on Money* and *The General Theory* as two consistent and complementary works. The ICA theorists intend to create a macroeconomic model that keeps Keynes's two works together: a single coherent theory capable of demonstrating the conditions of equilibrium and the causes of disequilibrium of a monetary economy in which money is a means of payment and a store of value.

At this point it may be useful to examine the concept of equilibrium and of the closure of the monetary circuit in greater depth. These are in fact issues that have generated a debate among the scholars (Messori, 1985; Graziani, 1994; Messori and Zazzaro, 2004; 2005), the conclusions of which can be summed up as follows.

Let us consider the simplest monetary circuit schema, with assumptions of a closed economy and no state sector. Let us suppose the agents decide to keep their cash reserves constant. In this case money injected into the circuit at the beginning of the period will flow back to the banks. But it is clear that firms as a whole will not be able to repay the money interest to banks and they will remain indebted to them. There is an even worse situation for firms if the agents decide to increase their money reserves. If this happens, firms will owe not only the interest but also part of the capital. On the other hand, it is clear that firms will be able to repay the initial financing and the related total interest only in the following cases:

(a)   there is a reduction of the cash reserves and the consequent expenditure on goods, services and shares is sufficient to assure the firms an income equal to the size of the initial financing plus the relative interest;

(b)   supposing there is a foreign sector and assuming a foreign surplus that is sufficient to assure the firms an income equal to the size of the initial financing plus interest;

(c)   supposing there is a state sector and assuming a public deficit that is sufficient to assure the firms an income equal to the size of the initial financing plus relative interest.

If a state sector is considered in the model, and a deficit expenditure (for example, the payment of pensions) financed by money issued by the central bank is assumed, it is of relevance that public expenditure acts as a new source of finance for firms: it will increase the 'final finance' (the amount of money spent in order to buy goods and securities). It is interesting to point out – at least with reference to the share of state expenditure that increases firms' returns in the goods market – that this is free finance for firms: it is not a consequence of a firm's debt towards commercial banks but of a state debt towards the central bank. It is worth stressing that the increase in inflow of money into circulation due to state deficit spending could give firms a chance to reimburse (the totality or a share of) bank interest in money terms.

The three cases above show that, according to the ICA, it is theoretically possible for the circuit to close with the destruction of the money initially injected into the economy and with the payment of money interest to banks by firms. However, if one looks closely, case (a) implies an explanation of the formation of money reserves in the previous periods and this necessarily leads to the presence either of firms' debts or of firms' bankruptcy inherited from the past; alternatively, case (a) above can be explained with the foreign surplus or with the public deficit in the previous periods and this therefore refers essentially to cases (b) and (c). Cases (b) and (c) are significant. In this respect it should however be underlined that the reproduction of the monetary economy in a steady-state equilibrium would imply either a permanent surplus in the foreign balance of payments or a continuous growth of the public debt (Graziani, 1994).

Let us now return to the basic case (closed economy without a state sector, constant cash reserves), since it will enable us to pinpoint one of the typical features of the monetary economy according to the ICA. In the basic schema of the monetary circuit, firms repay the initial financing but cannot reimburse interest to banks in money terms: they can just repay interest in kind or postpone the payment. From this the exponents of the monetary circuit draw the conclusion that the concept of equilibrium of a monetary economy envisages the presence of 'a *normal* level of firms' debt to banks' (Graziani, 1994). The debt level is 'normal' if it is judged sustainable by the banks that agree to continue financing firms in spite of existing debt. Obviously, in the monetary economy the whole amount of firms' debt to banks tends to grow (suffice it to think of the simple mechanism of compound interest). This is a growth that may be considered normal by banks and therefore perfectly compatible with the reproduction of the system.

8. Money market and financial market

The ICA makes a sharp distinction between the nature and functions of the money market and those of the financial market (Graziani, 1984; 1994). In the money market banks and firms bargain. The aim of the bargaining is the initial finance as well as the interest rate. As has been pointed out, the money market is the 'place' where banks select firms and where the overall monetary financing is decided. The financial market logically comes into operation at a later moment in the economic process. When households have received their money income and they have subdivided it into savings and consumption, they can decide to use part of their savings for the purchase of shares in the financial market. From the households' point of view, therefore, the financial market is the 'place' where they try to use their savings in a remunerative way. From the point of view of firms as a whole, the financial market plays the role of recuperating the liquidity not collected through the sale of goods and services. In the financial market, therefore, those who operate are households and firms.

In view of the above, it becomes clear that according to the ICA there is a sort of hierarchy between the money market and the financial market: the financial market could not even operate if money had not been previously created and injected into the circuit through the money market. As a result, while it is possible for a single firm to finance itself exclusively through the financial market, it is impossible for firms as a whole. This conclusion is valid unless there are such levels of public deficit spending and/or of surplus in the balance of payments that enough money flows into the financial market through the workers' decisions to buy shares.

The interest rate that is formed in the financial market is the price firms have to pay to collect money savings. In this regard, circuit theorists underline the difference between the interest rate that is formed in the money market and the interest rate that is formed in the financial market. Mainly, the scholars of the ICA underline the difference between the debt contracted by firms to banks (strong agents, able to exert real influence on the running of firms) and the debt contracted with households (who in contrast are substantially incapable of influencing firms). On this point, although shares are formally a slice of the ownership of firms, Graziani talks about firms' 'figurative debt' towards the households (Graziani, 1984; 1994).

9.   Production, employment, distribution

The ICA follows the Keynesian approach in maintaining that the volume of production is autonomously fixed by firms, based on the expected level of aggregate demand. Naturally, production decisions taken by firms may or may not be supported by banks. If there is credit rationing by banks, firms are unable to translate their production plans into real production processes. To make the matter more complicated, it can be shown that the production decisions taken by firms are also influenced by the possibility of equity rationing. One conclusion drawn by theorists of the circuit is that the financial structure of firms is not neutral with respect to production decisions.

Let us consider the simplest case of a closed economy without a public sector. Supposing that Ye is the expected level of aggregate demand for the period in question, firms will fix the level of production Ys of the single good produced so as to satisfy the demand:

$$Ys = Ye.$$

If π is the average labour productivity, the level of employment desired by firms will be established as follows:

$$Ys/\pi = N.$$

The employment level depends on firms' production decisions and therefore on the expected aggregate demand. The labour market is thus described as the place where any shortage in aggregate demand is dumped (generating involuntary unemployment). If w is the average money wage agreed in bargaining with workers, then wN will be the total money wage bill and this will correspond to the total demand for financing F that firms as a whole will make of the banking system:

$$F = wN.$$

If banks totally fulfil the firms' request for financing, employment N and production Ys will be realized. Once production has occurred, firms, which operate in non-perfectly competitive markets, will use the mark-up principle to set the price of the single good produced, applying the margin q to the cost of production:

$$p = (w/\pi)(1 + q).$$

The level of q depends on market power (degree of monopoly) and this in turn can be made to depend on the industrial concentration ratio (Forges Davanzati and Realfonzo, 2005a). The greater the firms' market power, the higher the *price/production costs* ratio will be.

Once the price is fixed, the distribution of income is clearly also fixed. The ratio of wages to total product $W/Y = wN/p\pi N$ and the ratio of profits to total product $P/Y = 1 - W/Y$ will be:

$$W/Y = 1/(1 + q);$$
$$P/Y = q/(1 + q).$$

These are, as one can see, the very well-known results reached by Kalecki (1971). Clearly, then, the ICA develops a theory of distribution of a post-Keynesian type, influenced primarily by the works of Kalecki and Keynes.

Naturally, given the mark-up, the higher the level of production (and therefore the expenditure on inputs), the higher the firm's real profit. So the higher the expected aggregate demand, the higher the level of production and the higher the absolute values of total profits and of real money wages. It is understandable why the advocates of the ICA repeat Kalecki's old thesis that whereas wage-earners can spend as much as they have earned, firms as a whole earn as much as they have spent. This means that the more businesses as a whole spend on inputs (and therefore the more financing is granted by banks), the higher production and therefore profits will be.[7]

A peculiar contribution by the ICA to the theory of distribution concerns the question of wage bargaining and particularly the relation between the bargained real wage, the actual real wage and the labour productivity (Forges Davanzati and Realfonzo, 2000; 2004).[8] On this point it is very useful to refer to the sequential nature of the economy described by the ICA.

In the ICA model, as in Keynes's original work, in the labour market bargaining concerns only money wages. In fact, the price level (and therefore the real wage) is known only at a later phase, when workers spend their money wage in the goods market. This obviously does not mean that, at the time when they bargain for their money wage, workers have no expectations about the price level, but their expectations will not necessarily be confirmed by the market. Consequently, there may be a difference between the *ex ante* real wage (expected by workers) and the *ex post* real wage (the actual real wage). If workers' expectations about the price level are confirmed, the expected real wage coincides with the actual real wage.[9]

Let us suppose that firms fix a price higher than the expected price. As a result, there would be a decrease in the real wage below the expected level. According to the ICA, workers cannot oppose the decrease in the real wage by wage bargaining. In fact, they only negotiate the money wage with firms. Let us assume that workers later demand an increase in the money wage that re-establishes, at the new level of prices, the expected real wage. As we know, banks have no constraints in granting firms credit and it can be supposed that they agree to the businesses' requests for expansion of credit. Consequently the amount of financing will grow and, with it, money wages. Nevertheless, if firms do not reduce q, in the market for goods the price will increase again and workers will find their expectations dashed once more. This means that an increase in prices, an increase in money wages, a further increase in prices and so on may in principle be repeated *ad infinitum*.[10]

From this point of view, the only effective reaction by the workers is a reduction of labour productivity in the production process. To understand this conclusion, let us suppose for the sake of simplicity that workers have adaptive expectations about price levels and a propensity to consume equal to 1; and that the banks fulfil the firms' requests for financing. Let us then make the following specific hypotheses about the labour market: the higher the expected real wage, the higher the labour productivity;[11] the agreed real wage grows with the growth of employment. Let us use q to indicate the mark-up that firms can set, given the industrial concentration ratio. On this hypothesis it is possible to show that the conclusions reached are those illustrated in Figure 7.2 (Forges Davanzati and Realfonzo, 2000).

In Figure 7.2, the line w/p^e indicates the expected real wage which is, by assumption, positively dependent on the level of employment. The lines π and w/p respectively indicate the relationship between productivity and employment (*via* the expected real wage) and between the actual real wage and employment for the mark-up q. The line Ns indicates the total number of workers available in the economy. In the lower panel, production functions are represented. The technical production function, $Q = \pi N$, shows the maximum output that can be obtained for any level of employment (given the technology) assuming that workers display full cooperative behaviour. The endogenous production function – $Q = \pi[w/p^e]N$ – shows the relationship between employment and the level of output produced for each value of labour intensity. In this analysis the *endogenous production function* is the relevant production function: actual production depends on labour productivity and output is lower than or (in the case of fully cooperative behaviour) equal to the maximum level technologically feasible. Note that there is stability of prices and wages (*monetary equilibrium*) in correspondence to the employment level E^*, when the expected real wage is equal to the effective real wage.

In the case of Figure 7.2, firms will maximize profits by employing all the workers (Ns) and the expected real wage will be greater than the actual real wage. Workers will react by demanding increases in money wages; firms will grant these increases and will apply to the banks for greater financing; the banks will grant the loans, production will be carried out and prices will again be higher than the workers expected and the real wage will therefore be lower than they expected. In this way a cumulative process of wage and price rises is triggered, which could in theory continue *ad infinitum*.

At this point it can be supposed that workers will reduce their productivity in the consequent production period when the actual real wage is lower than the expected real wage. This is the *workers' reaction function*; it works when the actual real wage is lower than the expected real wage.[12] In this case, if we assume that firms are not 'hit and run' but have an interest in continuing to operate in the economy in the future, then they must respect workers' expectations about real wages. In fact, a price level higher than that expected by workers would determine a reduction in labour productivity, output, and consequently

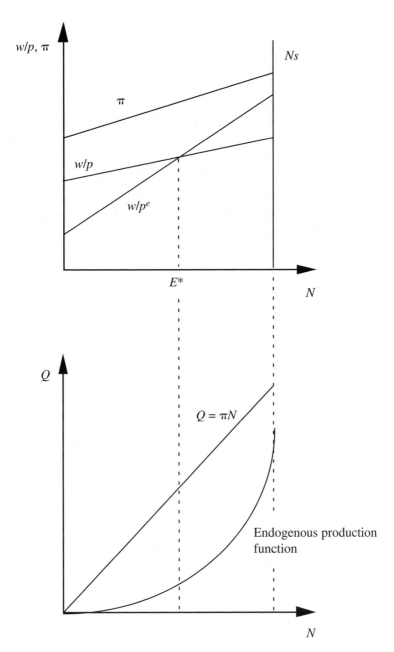

Figure 7.2   Actual and expected real wage, productivity and the endogenous production function

profits in the ensuing periods of production. When a workers' reaction function is taken into consideration, the equilibrium employment necessarily corresponds to the 'monetary equilibrium' (in correspondence with E^*), for the simple reason that firms are forced to respect workers' expectations. Therefore, workers' reaction allows inflationary pushes to be avoided.

Another significant conclusion of the ICA is that deregulation of the labour market does not increase employment (Forges Davanzati and Realfonzo, 2004). A model exploring the effects of labour relationship deregulation on employment has been put forward. Two basic assumptions have been superimposed on the standard Keynesian theoretical framework: (a) deregulation increases uncertainty and therefore reduces the propensity to consume; and (b) it works as a discipline device, in that – due to the credibility of the threat of dismissal – there is an increase in worker effort, and thus in labour productivity. The overall effect of labour market deregulation is the reduction in equilibrium employment, due both to the fall of aggregate demand and to the increase in labour productivity.[13]

10.   Concluding remarks

The ICA reaches conclusions that radically differ from those of the orthodox neoclassical theory. The starting point of the ICA is the idea that in capitalist economies power is not fairly distributed among macroeconomic agents; the consequence is that only the entrepreneurs have access to bank finance. The availability of money-capital is the means to impose the firm's decisions concerning production, employment and distribution. The capitalist process is described as the working of the sequential process of an intrinsically monetary economy. In capitalist economies there is systemic uncertainty and for this reason firms' decisions on both the level of production and employment are essentially determined by the expected level of the aggregate demand.

Notes

1. For an interpretation of the twentieth-century debate on money and banking from a circuitist point of view see Realfonzo (1998).
2. On this topic see also Fontana (2003).
3. De Viti de Marco maintained a theory of the development stages of the banking system and showed that banks are creators of money; according to de Viti de Marco, money supply is demand driven. The most famous works by Fanno (1993 [1931]; 1947; 1992 [1932–4]) are inspired by Wicksell's pure credit model. They centre around a description of the process of a sequential monetary economy and the analysis of the permanent tendency towards disequilibrium between savings and investment. Considerably less well known are the theoretical contributions by the banker Lugli (1939). This author takes up the version of the evolution of the payment system proposed by de Viti de Marco and L.A. Hahn, maintaining the need to develop a model of monetary economy to set against the neoclassical model of a barter economy. The essay by Sylos Labini (1948) is an early work in which the author clearly feels the influence of Schumpeter. In particular, he develops the Schumpeterian approach to the theory of interest and to bank credit as the means to remove inputs from their previous uses.
4. For other general descriptions of the monetary circuit see Messori (1988), Bellofiore and Seccareccia (1999); Bossone (2001); Figuera (2001); Realfonzo (1998; 2003).
5. Heinsohn and Steiger (1983) advance a 'witness theory' of the origin of banks (see also Wray, 1990, ch. 1).
6. 'Nobody who has ever lost a sixpence through a crack in the floor will dispute this. But it is by no means obvious that the world as a whole would be impoverished in the same degree' (Robertson, 1926, p. 31).
7. In a model with two types of goods – consumer goods (wage goods) and investment goods – decisions about the composition of production determine the distribution of income. The higher the demand for and production of investment goods, the higher the profits for firms.
8. For an interpretation of the working of the labour market in a monetary economy of production from a Marxian point of view see Bellofiore and Realfonzo (1997); and Bellofiore et al., 2000.

9. In a model with two types of goods (consumer goods and investment goods) this happens when voluntary saving equals investments. When investments exceed voluntary savings there is a positive gap between the expected real wage and the actual real wage which gives rise to forced saving.
10. For this reason, even if workers could impose a cost-of-living escalator agreement, this would not affect the real wage since the *ex-post* money wage increase can always be annulled by a further growth in prices.
11. It is assumed that workers can choose the level of labour productivity in an interval going from fully cooperative behaviour to fully conflictual behaviour (Forges Davanzati and Realfonzo, 2000).
12. The workers' reaction function can be written as: $\pi_{t+1} = \phi \{[\pi_t/(1+q)]^e - \pi_t/(1+q)\}$; with $\phi' < 0$ and $\pi_{t+1} < \pi_t$.
13. However, it has also been argued that deregulation may improve entrepreneurs' expectations and, thus, may increase investment and aggregate demand, acting as a counterbalancing effect.

References

Bellofiore, R. (1989), 'A monetary labor theory of value', *Review of Radical Political Economics*, **21**(1–2), 1–26.
Bellofiore, R. (ed.) (1997), 'Marxian theory: the Italian debate', special issue of the *International Journal of Political Economy*, **27**(2).
Bellofiore, R. and Realfonzo, R. (1997), 'Finance and the labor theory of value: toward a macroeconomic theory of distribution from a monetary perspective', *International Journal of Political Economy*, **27**(2), 97–118.
Bellofiore, R. and Realfonzo, R. (2003), 'Money as finance and money as universal equivalent: re-reading Marxian monetary theory', in L.-P. Rochon and S. Rossi (eds), *Modern Theories of Money: The Nature and Role of Money in Capitalist Economies*, Cheltenham, UK and Northampton, MA, USA: Edward Elgar, 198–218.
Bellofiore, R. and Seccareccia, M. (1999), 'Monetary circuit', in P.A. O'Hara (ed.), *Encyclopedia of Political Economy*, London and New York: Routledge, 753–6.
Bellofiore, R., Forges Davanzati, G. and Realfonzo, R. (2000), 'Marx inside the circuit. Discipline device, wage bargaining and unemployment in a sequential monetary economy', *Review of Political Economy*, **12**(1), 403–17.
Bossone, B. (2001), 'Circuit theory of banking and finance', *Journal of Banking and Finance*, **25**(5), 857–90.
Brancaccio, E. (2005), 'Un modello di teoria monetaria della produzione capitalistica. Un'alternativa "classico-circuitista" al paradigma neoclassico della scarsità', *Il pensiero economico italiano*, **13**(1), 91–122.
Chick, V. (1986), 'The evolution of the banking system and the theory of saving, investment and interest', *Économies et Sociétés*, **20**(8–9), 111–26.
Deleplace, G. and Nell, E. (eds) (1996), *Money in Motion: The Post Keynesian and Circulation Approaches*, London and New York: Macmillan and St Martin's Press.
de Viti de Marco, A. (1898), *La funzione della banca*, Rendiconti della Reale Accademia dei Lincei, V, vol. VII; 2nd edn 1934, 3rd edn 1936.
Fanno, M. (1947), *La teoria delle fluttuazioni economiche*, Padua: CEDAM.
Fanno, M. (1992) [1932–4], *Teoria del credito e della circolazione*, Naples: ESI.
Fanno, M. (1993) [1931], 'Production cycles, credit cycles and industrial fluctuations', *Structural Change and Economic Dynamics*, **4**(2), 403–37.
Figuera, S. (2001), *Theorie Monetaire dans l'economie Capitalista*, Paris: L'Harmattan.
Fontana, G. (2000), 'Post Keynesians and Circuitists on money and uncertainty: an attempt at generality', *Journal of Post Keynesian Economics*, **23**(1), 27–48.
Fontana, G. (2003), 'Keynes's *A Treatise on Money*', in J. King (ed.), *Elgar Companion to Post Keynesian Economics*, Cheltenham, UK and Northampton, MA, USA: 237–41.
Fontana, G. and Gerrard, B. (2002), 'The monetary context of economic behaviour', *Review of Social Economy*, **60**(2), 243–62.
Fontana, G. and Realfonzo, R. (eds) (2005), *The Monetary Theory of Production. Tradition and Perspectives*, Basingstoke: Palgrave Macmillan.
Forges Davanzati, G. and Realfonzo, R. (2000), 'Wages, labour productivity and unemployment in a model of the monetary theory of production', *Èconomie appliquée*, **4**, 117–38.
Forges Davanzati, G. and Realfonzo, R. (2004), 'Labour market deregulation and unemployment in a monetary economy', in R. Arena and N. Salvadori (eds), *Money, Credit and the Role of the State*, Aldershot: Ashgate, 65–74.
Forges Davanzati, G. and Realfonzo, R. (2005a), 'Bank mergers, monopoly power and unemployment. A Post Keynesian-*Circuitiste* approach', in G. Fontana and R. Realfonzo (eds), *The Monetary Theory of Production. Tradition and Perspectives*, Basingstoke: Palgrave Macmillan, 155–71.
Forges Davanzati, G. and Realfonzo, R. (2005b), 'Towards a "continuist" interpretation of Keynes: Labour market deregulation in a monetary economy', mimeo.
Graziani, A. (1982) 'L'analisi marxista e la struttura del capitalismo moderno', in *Storia del marxismo*, Vol. 4, Turin: Einaudi.
Graziani, A. (1984), 'Moneta senza crisi', *Studi economici*, **39**(24), 3–37.

Graziani, A. (1987), 'Keynes's finance motive', *Économies et Sociétés* (Série Monnaie et Production, 4), **21**(9), 23–42.

Graziani, A. (1989), *The Theory of Monetary Circuit*, Thames Papers in Political Economy, London.

Graziani, A. (1994), *La teoria monetaria della produzione*, Arezzo: Banca Popolare dell'Etruria e del Lazio/Studi e ricerche.

Graziani, A. (1996), 'Money as purchasing power and money as a stock of wealth in Keynesian economic thought', in G. Deleplace and E. Nell (eds), *Money in Motion: The Post Keynesian and Circulation Approaches*, London and New York: Macmillan and St Martin's Press, 139–54.

Graziani, A. (2003a), *The Monetary Theory of Production*, Cambridge: Cambridge University Press.

Graziani A. (2003b), 'Finance motive', in J.E. King (ed.), *Elgar Companion to Post Keynesian Economics*, Cheltenham, UK and Northampton, MA, USA: Edward Elgar, 142–5.

Heinsohn, G. and Steiger, O. (1983), 'Private property, debts and interest or: the origin of money and the rise and fall of monetary economies', *Studi economici*, **21**, 3–56.

Kalecki, M. (1971), *Selected Essays on the Dynamics of the Capitalist Economy*, Cambridge: Cambridge University Press.

Keynes, J.M. (1930), *A Treatise on Money*; reprinted in J.M. Keynes, *Collected Writings*, Vols V and VI, London: Macmillan, 1971.

Keynes, J.M. (1933), 'The monetary theory of production'; reprinted in J.M. Keynes, *Collected Writings*, Vol. XIII, London: Macmillan, 1973, 408–11.

Keynes, J.M. (1936), *The General Theory of Employment, Interest and Money*; reprinted in J.M. Keynes, *Collected Writings*, Vol. VII, London: Macmillan, 1973.

Lugli, L. (1939), *Economia monetaria ed economia creditizia*, Milan: Giuffré.

Marx, K. (1976), *Capital*, London: Penguin.

Messori, M. (1985), 'Le circuit de la monnaie. Acquis et problèmes non résolus', in R. Arena and A. Graziani (eds), *Production, circulation et monnaie*, Paris : Presses Universitaires de France.

Messori, M. (1991), 'Keynes' *General Theory* and the endogenous money supply', *Économie Appliquée*, **44**(1), 125–32.

Messori, M. and Zazzaro, A. (2004), 'Monetary profits within the circuit ponzi finance or *mors tua, vita mea?*', Quaderni di ricerca, 200, Università Politecnica delle Marche.

Messori, M. and Zazzaro, A. (2005), 'Single period analysis: financial markets, firms' failures and closure of the monetary circuit', in G. Fontana and R. Realfonzo (eds), *The Monetary Theory of Production. Tradition and Perspectives*, Basingstoke: Palgrave Macmillan, 111–23.

Moore, B. (1988), *Horizontalists and Verticalists. The Macroeconomics of Credit Money*, Cambridge: Cambridge University Press.

Parguez, A. and M. Seccareccia (1999), 'A credit theory of money: the monetary circuit approach', in J. Smithin (ed.), *What is Money?*, London: Routledge.

Realfonzo, R. (1998), *Money and Banking: Theory and Debate (1900–1940)*, Cheltenham, UK and Lyme, USA: Edward Elgar.

Realfonzo, R. (2001), 'Bank creation of money and endogenous money supply as the outcome of the evolution of the banking system: Antonio de Viti de Marco's contribution', in L.-P. Rochon and M. Vernengo (eds), *Credit, Interest Rates and the Open Economy. Essays in the Horizontalist Tradition*, Cheltenham, UK and Northampton, MA, USA: Edward Elgar, 193–212.

Realfonzo, R. (2003), 'Circuit theory', in J. King (ed.), *Elgar Companion to Post-Keynesian Economics*, Cheltenham, UK and Northampton, MA, USA: Edward Elgar, 60–64.

Robertson, D.H. (1926), *Banking Policy and the Price Level*, London: King.

Rochon, L.-P. and Rossi, S. (eds) (2003), *Modern Theories of Money: The Nature and Role of Money in Capitalist Economies*, Cheltenham, UK and Northampton, MA, USA: Edward Elgar.

Schumpeter, J.A. (1959) [1912], *The Theory of Economic Development*, Cambridge, MA: Harvard University Press.

Schumpeter, J.A. (1970), *Das Wesen des Geldes*, Göttingen: Vandenhoeck & Ruprecht.

Sylos Labini, P. (1948), 'Saggio dell'interesse e reddito sociale', *Rendiconti della classe di scienze morali, storiche e filologiche*, Accademia Nazionale dei Lincei, **3**(11–12), 426–53.

Wicksell, K. (1962) [1898], *Interest and Prices*, New York: Augustus Kelley.

Wray, L.R. (1990), *Money and Credit in Capitalist Economies. The Endogenous Approach*, Aldershot, UK and Brookfield, US: Edward Elgar.

Zazzaro, A. (1995), 'La specificità delle banche. Teorie a confronto da una prospettiva schumpeteriana', *Studi economici*, **50**(55), 113–51.

8   The theory of money emissions
*Sergio Rossi**

Introduction

The theory of money emissions is a paradigm of monetary macroeconomics that in the late 1950s emerged in France (Dijon) and Switzerland (Fribourg) under the lead of Bernard Schmitt, who gave rise to the École de Dijon et Fribourg, later on also labelled as the 'quantum theory' of money and production.[1] Today, its most prominent scholars, besides Schmitt himself, are Alvaro Cencini and Claude Gnos. This school of economic thought inspired the French–Italian theory of the monetary circuit – now also known as monetary theory of production – which was born in France in the 1960s and has since spread out to Canada. Indeed, the founding fathers of the monetary circuit approach recognized, in their early writings on this subject matter, that their research work had been inspired by Schmitt's (see Parguez, 1975; Graziani, 1990). Graziani (1994, p. 13, our translation) goes so far as to acknowledge that Schmitt 'is the author who has developed most rigorously both the theoretical and the terminological principles of the doctrine of the circuit, and has adhered to them with steadfast consistency'.[2] Also, Le Bourva (1962) – who is often referred to as the forerunner of the modern theory of the monetary circuit in the French speaking domain, or even as a forerunner of the post-Keynesian theory of endogenous money *à la* Kaldor–Moore (Lavoie, 1992, p. 436) – explicitly refers to Schmitt (1960) when he adopts the terminology introduced by the latter author to express the monetary circuit in a wage (or entrepreneur) economy, in Keynes's sense. Over the years, however, the theory of money emissions and the theory of the monetary circuit have evolved differently from each other. This is so much so that, in the early 1990s, Schmitt came to reject the label 'circuit theory' to define his own school of monetary thinking. As Graziani (1994, pp. 13–14) points out, the reason for this rejection may be ascribed to the rather loose conceptual ground on which, according to Schmitt, the modern theory of the monetary circuit is based (see Gnos and Rasera, 1985). Indeed, the theory of money emissions argued by the Dijon–Fribourg school and the theory of the monetary circuit argued by a number of scholars in the post-Keynesian tradition 'have many differences and very few similarities, although their focus is the same, namely, the working of our monetary economies of production' (Rochon and Rossi, 2003, p. xxxvi). In particular, the theory of money emissions considers the essential role of the circuit of wages in the macroeconomy, as in circuit theory, but has a different conception of money as such, which modifies circuit analysis fully and radically. In fact, the theory of money emissions may be considered as an analytical sophistication of the modern theory of the monetary circuit. While the latter theory considers money's purchasing power as *given*, and studies its circulation in the macroeconomy over time and between different categories of agents, the theory of money emissions *explains* the formation of money's purchasing power (see Schmitt, 1960).

The next section introduces the new analysis of money proposed by the Schmitt school, and presents an investigation of a monetary economy of production in such a theoretical framework. The third section investigates the process of capital accumulation, showing how the theory of money emissions explains inflation and unemployment with respect to the monetary–structural anomalies of fixed capital accumulation in modern economic systems. The fourth section moves the analysis into the arena of international monetary economics. It addresses the exchange rate issue in light of the theory of money emissions, and summarizes the analysis by the Schmitt school of monetary unions, focusing in particular on European monetary integration. The last section concludes.

A new analysis of money and production
A new analysis of money
The theory of money emissions – hereafter TME – sets off from a new analysis of money, which it conceives of as a purely numerical thing, namely, a double-entry record in a bank's bookkeeping for the settlement of economic transactions. These payments refer to all sorts of transactions that may be observed between any two agents in modern capitalist economies of production and exchange. The starting point of the analysis is book-entry money, and in particular the relationship between banks' double-entry bookkeeping and money's emission. In this perspective, money's emission, and nature, can be understood by analysing payments. Indeed, as Schmitt (1996, p. 88) argues, '[m]oney and payments are one and the same thing', because, in his view, the emission of money occurs *within* payments, while money balances (bank deposits) exist *between* payments. In fact, banks keep books in which they record all debt obligations for further reference and settlement. Now, any payment involves three parties, namely, a payer, a payee and a banker (Parguez and Seccareccia, 2000, p. 101). If the payment were simply a 'dyadic' exchange, that is, a 'bipolar' operation between the exchanging agents, in which the payer handed over to the payee an acknowledgement of debt that the payer himself fabricates (say, a piece of paper), then this payment would not be final but merely promised. As Graziani (2003, p. 60) points out, '[i]f a simple promise of payment could perform the role of final payment, buyers would be endowed with a seigniorage privilege, namely with a right of withdrawing goods from the market without giving anything in exchange'. In reality nobody can finally pay by surrendering a promise to pay. Payment finality is crucial for market exchanges: it applies to all kinds of markets, and makes sure that 'a seller of a good, or service, or another asset, receives something of equal value from the purchaser, which leaves the seller with no further claim on the buyer' (Goodhart, 1989, p. 26). This is the peculiar role of money, which is therefore essentially a means of final payment.

When a (final) payment occurs, the banking system intervenes to provide the contracting (non-bank) agents with the number of money units necessary to measure the object of the transaction economically and to issue the means of settling debt between these agents. In short, money is a unit of account as well as a means of payment. It is the unit of measure of the physical (be it material or immaterial) object exchanged between two non-bank agents: without money, no numerical standard would be available to measure the value of those objects that agents exchange. Further, money is also the means for the contracting parties to finally settle their debt obligations. The point to be stressed here is that money is indeed the means, not the object, of the payment. Banks themselves cannot provide the 'content' of payments: this is the result of production, that is to say, the effort accomplished by workers in a monetary economy of production. What banks can do independently of production is to write in their books a mere 'bipolar', or 'dyadic', operation: for instance, client I may be entered on the liabilities side of a bank's balance sheet for any

Table 8.1   Loans and deposits resulting from opening a line of credit

Bank			
Assets		Liabilities	
Loan to client I	$+£x$	Deposit of client I	$+£x$

Table 8.2   Loans and deposits resulting from a payment order

Bank			
Assets		Liabilities	
Loan to client I	$+£x$	Deposit of client II	$+£x$

given amount only in so far as the same client is simultaneously entered, and for the same amount, on the assets side of the same balance sheet (Table 8.1).

As Table 8.1 shows, before production is taken into account, a bank can only give rise to an asset–liability relation with the same non-bank agent, here in the person of client I. In particular, the bank issues a unit of account – which is of a purely numerical nature – for both the agent's debt and the same agent's credit to the bank. The bank is thus simultaneously a debtor to client I – who is the recipient of an emission of a number of (x) money units – and a creditor of the same client, who owes this number of (x) money units to the bank issuing it in a blank operation. Now, this operation, devoid of substance as it is, is not deprived of meaning as far as monetary analysis is concerned. In fact, such an operation, which is indeed an off-balance-sheet record that banks never book, depicts the credit line that a bank may open to one of its (creditworthy) clients, before any amount is actually drawn on it. As well noted by Graziani (1990, p. 11), 'no one would borrow money from a bank before a payment comes due . . . since there would be no point in borrowing money and paying interest on it while keeping it idle'. The circular flow between the bank and its client I is indeed pointless, unless a payment has to be made in favour of another agent, say, client II. 'Money therefore *only comes into existence the moment a payment is made*. At that moment, in one and the same act, money is created, the borrower becomes a debtor to the bank and the agent receiving a payment becomes the creditor of the same bank' (p. 11). As a result, the off-balance-sheet operation virtually recorded in Table 8.1 has to be replaced by the double-entry shown in Table 8.2.

Starting from tabula rasa, to rule out the temptation to explain the birth of a bank deposit by having recourse to a pre-existent, yet unexplained deposit, it clearly appears that the bank owns a claim against client I that is balanced by an equivalent claim that client II owns against the bank – which is thus a mere go-between between non-bank agents: the position of client I offsets the position of client II. The claim owned by client II, in the form of a bank deposit, defines his credit against the issuing bank. This, however, does not mean that the bank *lends* the money that it issues for an amount of x units. The emission of money must indeed not be mixed up with a credit operation that the issuing bank may undertake in favour of the economy: the bank is neither a creditor nor a debtor of the economy when it issues money, because it is simultaneously debited *and* credited with the number of (*x*) money units that it issues. Money is therefore an 'asset–liability' (Schmitt, 1975a, p. 13): it is notably issued for every payment, which is recorded on both sides of a bank's balance sheet, therefore affecting at one and the same instant the payer's as well as the payee's accounting position. It takes no more than an instant to enter a payment in a bank's ledger: like the two faces of a same coin, any entry on the liabilities side of a balance sheet cannot be made, and exist in point of fact, independently of the corresponding entry on the assets side of it (and vice versa).

Strictly speaking, then, money never leaves the bank issuing it. The payment order that the payer (say, client I) addresses to the bank in favour of the payee, client II, is carried out by this bank through a simple double-entry in its books, by means of which money can be viewed as a flow from and to its source (money hoarding is impossible). The instantaneous reflux of money to its point of origin, namely, the very bank issuing it, is not an equilibrium condition at all, but a logical and essential law of bank money (Cencini, 1995, p. 18). The principle of double-entry bookkeeping imposes this fact, which is stronger than any form of behaviour. Therefore, the circuit of money *proprio sensu* has no positive duration in time: it lasts an instant, because it takes an instant to record a payment in a bank's ledger. The question immediately arises as to the value of money, particularly when the latter is defined as a numerical standard whose 'life cycle' is instantaneous and thus, some might be led to claim, deprived of any usefulness in the real world of economics. To answer this question, the new analysis of money calls for a new analysis of production, because it is through the association of money and production that a double entry in the books of the banking system testifies exchange-value. In fact, the sense and the full originality of the TME cannot be appraised if the analysis is not based, from the beginning, on production.

A new analysis of production
The TME explains how money is introduced into real-world economies through production: it is the payment of firms' production costs that allows for the association of money (essentially an incorporeal or purely numerical form) and produced output. As Lavoie (1984, p. 774) argued in this regard, '[m]oney is introduced into the economy through the productive activities of the firms, as these activities generate income. There can be no money without production.'

In the TME, the payment of production costs is defined as an emission in which money and output are one and the same thing, that is to say, income. In particular, since the only production costs for the set of firms are due to labour, namely, wages (intra-firms' purchases cancel out), the Schmitt school argues that

> [t]hrough the payment of wages, money and output meet, fusing in a unique object called 'income'. By putting money and output together, money acquires a real content [hence value], and output is given a monetary form. In other words, money measures (numerically) goods, and goods define the real content of money. (Cencini, 1995, p. 15)

All produced goods and services need to be measured in economic terms, because as physical entities they form 'a non-homogeneous complex which cannot be measured' (Keynes, 1936, p. 38). Hence, in order to measure production exactly and objectively, human beings need to resort to an incorporeal standard, to wit, money, which gives its numerical homogeneity to any physically produced output (see Rossi, 2001, pp. 122–7).

Now, elaboration on the unit of measure in economics leads the Schmitt school to put forward a new interpretation of Keynes's (1936, p. 41) concept of the wage unit, which Schmitt defines as the measurement unit in economics, 'because monetary wages define the equivalence of form and substance, that is, of the product and the number of units of money paid out in wages' (Schmitt, 1986, p. 118). The measurement of output is therefore equivalent to the determination of national income, on the ground of Keynes's (1930, p. 123) definition, 'to mean identically the same thing by the three expressions: (1) *the community's money-income*; (2) *the earnings of the factors of production*; and (3) *the cost of production*' – a threefold definition that clearly completes Keynes's statement defining 'the Purchasing Power of Money [as] the power of money to buy the goods and services on the purchase of which for purposes of consumption a given community of individuals expend their money income' (p. 54).

Based on Keynes's (1930, p. 134) view that 'human effort', that is, production, and 'human consumption are the ultimate matters from which alone economic transactions are capable of deriving any significance', the Schmitt school puts forward an investigation of the production–consumption process in which production is not a function of time, but an instantaneous event – in economic, though not in physical, terms – that 'quantises' time: 'in economics, production is an instantaneous event relating to a finite and indivisible period of time (a quantum of time) and its result, the product, is nothing other than this quantum. . . . In particular, the payment of wages is an instantaneous event which, defining a positive income formation, refers to a finite period of time [namely, the period over which wages accrue on a contractual basis]' (Cencini, 2001, pp. 116–17). If the payment of current wages occurs once per calendar month, then each month is defined as a finite and indivisible period of time, and the corresponding income is formed as a net magnitude for the national economy as a whole. Indeed, what workers earn is not lost by firms, which, in this framework, have no pre-existent deposits at their disposal with which they may pay the current wage bill. Further, as Cencini (2001, pp. 124–5) shows, even when firms use a pre-existent bank deposit to pay out wages, thus activating a wage fund (that is, a circulating capital), the emission of money occurs, in any way, as if it started from tabula rasa. Indeed, the distinction between money (a numerical form) and bank deposits (a liquid store of value) reveals that any wage payments, even those carried out in practice with a circulating capital, need an asset–liability emission in order to be finalized (Table 8.3). In bookkeeping terms, national income formation can thus be depicted as a result of the payment of wages for the relevant production period.

Entered on the assets side of the banks' balance sheet, firms are indebted for the exact amount earned by their workers and deposited on the liabilities side. From an analytical viewpoint, it is output itself that is entered on the banks' assets side. Thus, the payment of wages establishes a

Table 8.3   The formation of national income as a bank deposit

Bank			
Assets		Liabilities	
Loan to firms	+ £x	Deposit of workers	+ £x

close relationship (an identity) between income – earned by workers – and output – the very object of firms' debt. (Cencini, 2001, p. 117)

Following the classical approach to macroeconomics, the TME conceives of a monetary economy of production as composed by firms and workers (that is, wage-earners) in an environment where banks provide them with money. This analytical approach shows that firms have a debt (to banks) in so far as they obtain in exchange on the labour market a stock of output to be sold on the market for produced goods. For their part, wage-earners obtain on the labour market their own product in the form of money wages (bank deposits). This represents an absolute exchange, whereby an object (output) is transformed from a physical into an economic thing, which defines a net magnitude for the whole economy, namely, national output first owned by wage-earners (see Rossi, 2003).

When firms ask banks to pay out wages to workers, the payment occurs indeed in a triangular operation that gives rise to a money income (first owned by wage-earners, in the form of deposits in the banking system) that is new, and net, for the whole economy. Labour is not a commodity, but the factor of produced goods and services. Hence payment of labour costs does not require the expenditure of a pre-existent bank deposit, which the set of firms may own. Wage-earners produce real goods and services as a result of their efforts, and their wages are the result of an emission on which both firms and banks concur, together: firms decide and organize production activities, while banks 'monetize' them, the banking system providing the unit of account and means of payment needed to measure output objectively as well as to settle the firms' debt towards their workers.

> The payment of wages is an emission: this means that . . . workers receive *their own product*, in money. This transaction does not merely define an equivalence but an identity: every worker gets a sum of money that, because of it being issued in the payment of wages, identifies itself with the real product of this same worker. Within the same transaction, the firm gives and receives the same object, which shows that the exchange is indeed absolute. (Schmitt, 1984, p. 347, our translation)

Income is thus the result of banking and production activities working together for the production, circulation, and final consumption of goods and services. In this approach, '[i]ncome is no longer conceived of as a flow of expenditure through time, but as a result of a constantly renewed process of creation at each phase of production of goods and services' (Baranzini and Cencini, 2001, p. viii). Income defines an exchange-value that exists in the form of a bank deposit, which is the result of a loan that banks grant to firms to finance production, and that can be paid back when firms have been able to sell output on the goods market. From a macroeconomic point of view, then, the measure of national income must necessarily be the same, numerically, when it is taken in the flow of total production and when it is taken in the flow of total consumption. As Keynes (1930, p. 134) argued, income can indeed be divided '(1) into the parts which have been *earned* by the production of consumption-goods and of investment-goods respectively, and (2) into the parts which are *expended* on consumption-goods and on savings respectively'. On this ground, the Dijon–Fribourg school considers Keynes's (1936) fundamental identities between income and output, and between saving and investment, as the building blocks of modern macroeconomics, so much so that they are consistent with the principle of effective demand (see Gnos, 1998).

Elaboration of this analysis leads Schmitt to put forward a new interpretation of Keynes's (1936, p. 25) principle of effective demand. In Schmitt's view (1986, p. 117), 'effective demand is defined as a two-way flux, firms "giving" and "receiving" the same product', which is also a restatement of the principle of absolute exchange illustrated by the payment of wages. This means, however, that national income formation (total supply) and income final expenditure (total demand) are two identical magnitudes, a statement that for some critics of the Schmitt school means that the latter view is framed in a Say's Law, full-employment economy (see Lavoie, 1987, p. 87). In fact, Schmitt (1975a, p. 19, our translation) puts forward this interpretation of Say's Law: 'every purchase is financed by a sale and every sale finances a purchase' on labour, product, and financial markets considered altogether and simultaneously. Even though financial markets are in some way different from the market for produced goods and services,

> it cannot be denied that a single transaction can involve them simultaneously. The final purchase of a commodity, for example, implies the selling of a deposit certificate by the buyer of the real good, who thereby becomes a seller on the financial market *and* a buyer on the commodity market. This is so because income is formed as a bank deposit and may be spent by its owner only if the latter is prepared to part with his entitlement to it. (Cencini, 2001, p. 79)

This new interpretation of Say's Law, which Cencini (2001, p. 56) labels as 'the law of the logical identity of sales and purchases', is verified also when transactions occur on the financial market only – the agent buying securities being simultaneously a seller of claims on an equivalent bank deposit – as well as when transactions occur on the labour market – the agent selling productive services being simultaneously a purchaser of a bank deposit.

Once this law is taken into account, it becomes evident that the emission of money through banks' bookkeeping for the payment of production costs, and the ensuing income–output identity, are a fact that does not depend on full-employment equilibrium. The identity between total demand (income) and total supply (output) is indeed not at all inconsistent with the possibility that total demand can be above or below the level of total supply. In fact, the monetary macroeconomic analysis developed by the Schmitt school considers unemployment situations. To be sure, the TME is deeply involved in the analysis of the macroeconomic causes of unemployment, which hampers all those capitalist economies suffering from an overaccumulation of capital. This is indeed an issue closely linked to the functional distribution of income, to which we now turn to investigate both of them in light of the TME.

Functional income distribution and capital accumulation

In the TME, '[o]nce the measure of output is determined, the next step is to tackle the problem of capital accumulation, which plays a crucial role in the explanation of pathological states of our economic systems, such as inflation and unemployment' (Baranzini and Cencini, 2001, p. x). As capital accumulation depends on the investment of profit by capitalists, or firms in the two-category approach adopted by the Schmitt school, the way profits are formed in the economy as a whole must be explained first.

The process of functional income distribution

According to the TME, the formation of national income gives rise to a sum of bank deposits first in the possession of wage-earners. The total amount of newly formed bank

Table 8.4   The expenditure of workers' deposit on the product market

Bank		
Assets	Liabilities	
	Deposit of workers	−£x
	Deposit of firms	+£x

deposits is the economic definition of newly produced output. This does not mean, however, that wage-earners or, more generally speaking, original income-holders can obtain the whole produced output by spending the total amount of the newly formed bank deposits. In fact, firms can and do obtain their income share, namely, profit, by marking up prices on the market for produced goods and services. To illustrate how firms as a whole earn a profit, which is thus an income that wage-earners are forced to abandon on the product market when they dispose of their deposits, let us consider here the expenditure of the whole sum of bank deposits in the possession of workers (see Table 8.3).

In order to start a process of capital accumulation, any economic system, be it advanced, emerging, developing, or in transition, has to form a profit that is net in the economy as a whole. This profit must be in the form of a bank deposit, in order for firms to finance investment and hence raise the capital stock in the whole economy. Both the analysis of profit formation and that of capital accumulation may therefore proceed by an investigation of banks' bookkeeping: any transaction implies a payment, and any payment can be traced in a bank's ledger according to the TME.

Let us thus assume that wage-earners, as original income-holders, decide to spend their bank deposits in full, and for the purchase of saleable output. This output, as we noted in the previous section, is measured by the number of money units issued by the banking sector when paying out the corresponding wages. For expositional ease, we may subsume the latter sector under a single bank (see Rossi, 2005a, for elaboration of a multi-bank framework and the necessary intervention of a central bank). If so, then the expenditure of the workers' income for an amount of x units in the consumption goods market, in which firms may mark up retail prices, gives rise to a distribution of income between firms and workers. Let us first consider the book-entry result of the expenditure of the workers' deposit in purchasing output on the goods market (Table 8.4).

Workers spend the deposit they originally owned, and in doing so transform a monetary into a real magnitude: deposit-holders dispose of their deposit and obtain the output originally related to it (or an equivalent output, if we consider the thousands of real goods and services produced over a year by modern capitalist economies). As a result, firms can recover on the product market the funds they need to reimburse the bank loan they obtained for the corresponding payment of wages (see Table 8.3).

Now, if analysis were stopped here, profit would not exist, or, at least, it would not be explained by this analysis, so much so that in the theory of the monetary circuit the explanation of aggregate profits is a conundrum that indeed has no solution: 'once the principal has been repaid to banks, the possibility that firms as a whole can realise their profits in money terms or can pay interest owed to banks in money terms is ruled out' (Zazzaro, 2003, p. 233). The TME, however, offers a way out of this impasse. The explanation of profits at

Table 8.5   The formation of profit as a bank deposit

	Bank	
Assets	Liabilities	
	Deposit of workers	$-£(x-y)$
	Deposit of workers	$-£y$
	Deposit of firms	$+£(x-y)$
	Deposit of firms	$+£y$

the macroeconomic level is based on firms' marking up the production costs of those goods that wage-earners purchase (that is, wage or consumption goods). Suppose that, in the numerical example depicted in Table 8.4, the costs of producing those wage goods that firms sell at a retail price of $£x$ are equal to $£x-y$ (with $0<y<x$). In this case, which is indeed the general case in the real world, firms obtain a bank deposit of $£x$ and give in exchange an output whose costs of production are only a fraction of the deposit they obtain on the goods market. As a result, owing to the mark-up in retail prices, a transfer of income to the benefit of firms at the expense of original income-holders (wage-earners) occurs for a part of produced output. This part, namely profit, is both monetary and real: the corresponding bank deposit ($£y$) is a financial claim on a real stock of yet unsold goods that are deposited with firms. Wage-earners obtain less in real terms than they would be entitled to obtain according to their remuneration on the factor market, at the time when wages were paid out by banks: there is a stock of yet unsold goods – a 'forced saving', as it were – which define the real aspect of the monetary profit recorded as a bank deposit (Table 8.5).

With respect to Table 8.4, if we separate, just analytically, the expenditure of the workers' deposit ($£x$) into two parts, as we do in Table 8.5, the first part covering the production costs of sold output ($£x-y$), while the second part represents the firms' profit ($£y$), we notice that firms as a whole obtain a deposit ($£x$) that more than covers the production costs of output sold. So firms can reimburse the corresponding bank loan ($£x-y$) and decide what to do with the residual, that is, their gross profit (before the payment of taxes, bank interests, dividends and so on), represented by a bank deposit of $£y$.

In short, firms own an amount of bank deposits ($£y$) that are the alter ego of a stock of as-yet-unsold output, and have to decide how to spend these deposits. If we ignore here all sorts of tax payments, firms have a number of alternative uses for which the bank deposits they have gained can be spent. Firms may in particular (i) distribute interests and/or dividends to the firms' share- and/or stock-holders, or (ii) invest this sum in the production process for a new output, to be defined.

In the first case it is the stock- and/or share-holders' community that is the recipient of the firms' monetary profit, in the form of a bank deposit of $£y$. Whether these income-holders spend this deposit directly, by purchasing the as-yet-unsold goods, or indirectly, via financial market operations that, in the end, will result in a final purchase of these same goods, the monetary and real forms of profit go hand in hand in both cases: both are consumed, or more precisely destroyed, as macroeconomic magnitudes as soon as the relevant income-holders spend the corresponding amount of bank deposits ($£y$) on the market for produced goods and services.

In the second case analysis is slightly more complex, because it involves a twofold operation whose result is both an income formation and an income expenditure at the macroeconomic level. An expenditure by firms on the factor market is an income-generating operation, for it gives rise to a bank deposit as a result of the workers' remuneration. This operation, when carried out with a pre-existent deposit that firms may have earned as profit, can also define, however, a purchase by the firms of the very product of the workers so remunerated. The decision to invest a profit in the production process being instrumental for the dynamics of capital accumulation, it is this alternative expenditure of the firms' profit that we need to investigate further here, positively as well as normatively.

The process of capital accumulation
The monetary profit and a corresponding stock of as-yet-unsold output are the two faces of a circulating capital that can be used to diverting some of those workers previously employed in producing consumption goods towards the production of capital goods. The investment of profit for a new production transforms a circulating capital into a fixed capital in the economy. As was argued by Hicks (1974, p. 309), fixed capital is both a fund and a physical capital: '[i]f it is capital in the volume sense that is being measured, capital is physical goods; but in the value sense capital is not physical goods. It is a sum of values which may conveniently be described as a Fund'. Schmitt (1984, pp. 165–75) expands on this twofold nature of fixed capital, arguing that any production of capital goods requires the investment of an equivalent amount of current income – which is saved by the economy as a whole – including that part of money income that its original holders have definitively transferred to firms as net profit of the latter. Now, '[w]hat is new in the analysis of capital accumulation propounded by the quantum theory of money and production is the role played by the structure of the monetary system of payments' (Baranzini and Cencini, 2001, p. xvi). In particular, the process of capital accumulation in a monetary production economy may occur either in an orderly or in a disorderly way, the latter being defined as a pathology of modern capitalist economies, giving rise to inflation as well as unemployment.

According to Schmitt (1984), the process of capital accumulation occurs in a pathological way today, since it is recorded by banks' bookkeeping in a still-unrefined, unstructured way. In particular, those transactions representing capital accumulation are not at all distinguished from income flows in book-entry terms by modern banking. In the words of Baranzini and Cencini (2001, p. xvi), this means that

> although invested by firms, profits are still available in the form of loanable bank deposits. Logically, the part of profits invested in the production of fixed capital goods should no longer be available on the financial market. Invested profits – which define a macroeconomic saving – are transformed into fixed capital, and it is in this form that they should be registered by banks. What is definitively saved by society as a whole should not be lent to anybody. Yet, contrary to logic, this is what happens today, since invested profits reappear as renewed income deposits. We are thus confronted with a *duplication*, the same income – the profit spent in the production of means of production – being still available to feed another expenditure on the commodity market.

Now, this is a pathological duplication that has far-reaching consequences in terms of inflationary and deflationary pressures. As Cencini (1996, p. 59) argues, '[t]he problem with the actual structure of domestic payments is that the formation of fixed capital does not lead to the capitalisation of profits [in the banks' bookkeeping system of accounts]'. It is because invested profits are not withdrawn from financial circulation that they are still available as 'loanable funds', which banks will lend out to the non-bank public. However, let us stress that it is not the investment of firms' profit, and the accumulation of capital, that are an issue *per se*. The problem in this regard is the way in which these operations are actually recorded in the banks' double-entry bookkeeping structure. To date, the expenditure of profit on the factor market (productively) consumes this profit, but not the corresponding deposit, which remains thus available in the financial system and therefore may be spent on the market for produced goods and services. This raises a macroeconomic problem, namely, inflation, because a capital is definitively fixed into the capital goods newly produced by the investment of profit, while the corresponding bank deposit continues to exist and may thus exert an inflationary pressure on the product market.

This, however, is not the end of the story. If analysis stopped here, the inflationary gap would not exist. There is indeed a stock of as-yet-unsold goods – as a result of the formation of the firms' profit – that corresponds to the bank deposit spent by firms on the labour market. In other words, the sum of bank deposits earned by workers in the investment-goods sector gives, to these workers, the power to purchase those wage goods forcedly saved by wage-earners in the period when profit is formed. The investment of profit is indeed the conversion of a stock of wage goods into new capital goods fixed within firms (Schmitt, 1984, p. 166). Deprived of the power to purchase these newly produced goods, however, those workers having produced them are remunerated with a bank deposit ($£y$) that has the necessary and sufficient purchasing power over the stock of as-yet-unsold (consumption) goods resulting from the mark-up mechanism noted above. As Schmitt (ibid., p. 190, our translation) puts it, 'the money units issued in the investment of profit find ultimately a "body", that is, the wage goods saved within the process by which monetary profit is formed'. Hence, although the investment of profits 'empties' the newly formed bank deposits of their real 'content', namely, new capital goods, this does not affect the relation between money and output, to wit, between total demand and total supply in the economy as a whole.

The inflationary gap in the money–output relationship appears only when the production of new replacement goods (fixed capital amortization) is taken into account. Including an income-destroying expenditure into an income-generating expenditure – as is the payment of current wages in the investment-goods sector with a pre-existent bank deposit (to wit, profits) – leads to monetary disorder 'as soon as instrumental goods are being used and new capital (amortization) goods are produced to repair the loss due to wear and tear' (Cencini, 2001, p. 203). When amortization is taken into account, the newly formed income – paid out in the form of bank deposits to the wage-earners in the investment-goods sector – has no real 'content' as such, neither directly nor 'by substitution'. This is so, because, in this case, not only does the payment of current wages with a pre-existent deposit withdraw the newly produced output from this deposit, but it also makes it impossible to 'fill the gap' – thus preserving the money–output relationship – with a stock of previously 'saved-up' wage goods. In this case, no saved-up goods exist. Hence this bank deposit is bound to be spent for the purchase of the available goods, adding therefore to the agents' demand for wage goods and leading to the formation of an extra profit in this sector, a profit that firms may then invest to obtain new capital goods that further increase the fixed capital accumulated in the economy. When this occurs, however, fixed capital increases more and more, leading to a fall in the rate of profit. To avoid overaccumulation of capital – which makes its remuneration no longer profitable – firms will therefore invest part of their monetary profits into a new production of wage goods. When this happens, however, total supply is increased, but with no equivalent increase in total demand: in the present structure of banks' bookkeeping, an expenditure that concerns the investment of profit gives rise to a bank deposit that is 'emptied' of its original 'content', that is, the newly produced goods and services. This deposit has no purchasing power of its own. It thus represents a purely nominal income:

> when the banks' bookkeeping structure is such that financial and capital departments are not kept separate, investment leads to the replacement of a real income with a purely nominal one. When this occurs at a relatively early stage of the process of capital accumulation, the nominal increase entails inflation only. Yet, if it occurs at a later stage, when production of fixed capital goods is partially replaced by production of wage goods, the nominal increase is unable to match the rise in real supply. The purchase of new consumption goods requires a positive purchasing power, which a purely nominal income does not have. Deflation results therefore from the pathological process of capital accumulation having reached a level where fixed capital can no longer grow at the same pace as before. (Baranzini and Cencini, 2001, p. xviii)

Now, both inflation and deflation – the latter leading to involuntary unemployment – can be eradicated from modern capitalist economies by introducing into the banks' bookkeeping structure a threefold distinction between money, income and fixed capital (Schmitt, 1984, pp. 301–32). This can be done by developing the banking structure of our payment systems so as to organize all sorts of payments within three accounting departments, namely, the monetary, financial and fixed capital departments. 'Whereas the first two departments are needed to account for the logical distinction between money and income, the third is required to avoid profits already invested in the production of capital goods still being available on the financial market' (Cencini, 2001, p. 204).

When the shortcomings in the bookkeeping structure of our system of domestic payments are solved according to the ontological distinction between money, income and fixed capital, the investment of profits will take place in a structurally sound banking system, within which the sum of bank deposits that firms invest in any new production processes will be transferred from the financial to the fixed capital department, so as no longer to be available for financial circulation. As a result, the payment of wages – which is recorded in the financial department, the only department existing today in the banks' bookkeeping – will no longer occur out of a pre-existent deposit in the same bookkeeping. This will give rise to the necessary and sufficient purchasing power to leave the relation between total demand and total supply, hence the money–output relation, unaltered and sound. 'From then on, capital accumulation will take place according to the logical nature of bank money and the threefold distinction between money as such, income and capital' (Cencini, 2001, p. 205; see also Rossi, 2001, pp. 169–84).

International monetary issues and European monetary union

Monetary macroeconomics not only concerns domestic phenomena and issues, but also has some international bearing, which involves the world as a whole in terms of development and growth. In this framework, the TME deals with a number of problems, among which we find the exchange rate issue, that is, the instability of today's international monetary and financial architecture (the post-Bretton Woods regime), and the European Monetary Union (EMU), with its deflationary bias and the problematic integration of the new member countries of the European Union (EU) into the single currency area.

The international monetary and financial architecture

The current world monetary regime for international payments is the result of the Bretton Woods agreement (1944), which gave rise to the so-called key-currency (or dollar) standard. In short, today, all international settlements take place using a few local currencies (the yen, the euro and the US dollar), in what is thus an asymmetrical architecture, to say the least. 'No true system of international clearing exists, and no international standard has yet replaced the US dollar' (Baranzini and Cencini, 2001, p. xix). In this framework, the problem is analogous to the one observed in domestic monetary analysis, and indeed concerns the emission of international money. The key questions that were at stake at the Bretton Woods conference in 1944 still need to be answered by academics and policy makers today. Can a national currency play the role of international money essentially? Does the world economy need an international standard? Which institution should issue it, and how? What is the link between money and credit at the international level? What kind of reform do the Bretton Woods institutions need in this respect?

The TME is well developed in this regard. It shows, in particular, following Rueff (1979), that a key-currency country subjects its money to a process of duplication when it pays in local money for its net imports of goods and services. Duplication of the bank deposits owned by the rest of the world, then, creates an international, speculative capital that is crucial for explaining the observed, yet unpredictable, volatility on foreign exchange markets. The argument runs as follows. Suppose that a key-currency country, A, has to pay for its net commercial imports a given amount of money A (say, x) to the rest of the world, R. In this case, in today's regime, country A transfers to R a financial claim on A's deposits in its banking system. As a matter of fact, the deposits themselves are still entirely recorded in A's banking system, in which they had been formed by the local monetary economy of production. These same bank deposits, however, are also recorded – in duplicate – in the banking system of the rest of the world, R, which is indeed a net commercial exporter in this stylized example and, as such, is paid with an amount of money A (x) that it enters – as foreign exchange reserves – on the assets side of its banking system's balance sheet. These bank deposits recorded in R have no real 'content' whatsoever. Deprived of any link with production activities, which would give a real object to them, these claims (a financial capital) circulate erratically, thus subjecting the foreign exchange market to erratic fluctuations that hamper the development of our capitalist economies, be they advanced, emerging, developing, or in transition. In short, the present regime of international payments – which lacks an international standard *proprio sensu* – transforms national currencies from means into objects of payment, a transformation that is pathological.

> As soon as currencies are transformed into objects of trade, their exchange rates vary according to their sales and purchases, and speculation arises with a view to making capital gains from these variations. It is not surprising, thus, that this kind of speculation becomes the main cause of exchange rate fluctuations, which, in turn, become the main incentive to speculation. (Baranzini and Cencini, 2001, p. xxi)

Now, the required structural reform of the international monetary and financial architecture should carry out and then put to practical use the plan proposed by Keynes at the Bretton Woods conference. Advocated by Schmitt (1973), this plan consists in issuing a truly international bank money, say bancor, so as to comply with the instantaneous circular use of money as a means of payment at the international level. This new, international money must be issued by an international central bank, that is, the central bank of national central banks, every time a payment involves a country or a currency area for the final settlement of cross-border transactions. In the above stylized example, this means that the proposed international settlement institution – which can be set up by a structural–monetary reform of today's international financial institutions, such as the International Monetary Fund – would issue the means of final payment by which country A can finally pay R for its net imports of goods and services, by an exchange in which country A is simultaneously a net exporter of securities to R. In this framework, 'the law of the logical identity of sales and purchases' (Cencini, 2001, p. 56) applies in a way similar to domestic payments. The emission of bancor by the new world bank has the task to vehiculate real goods and services from R to A, and securities from A to R, leaving thus the exchange rate between money A (MA) and money R (MR) unaffected by foreign trade. In particular, x units of MA are supplied (against z bancor) in the payment of country A's trade deficit, at the same instant as x units of MA are demanded (against z bancor) in payment of those securities sold by country A to R. Similarly, y units of MR are demanded (against z bancor) in payment of R's trade surplus, at the same instant as y units of MR are supplied (against z bancor) in payment of those securities bought by R. Each currency being simultaneously supplied and demanded against the same amount of bancor, its exchange rate is never affected by international transactions – be they on product or financial markets. Hence, speculation cannot alter exchange rates in such a system.

> Through absolute exchange, goods and services sold by R would become the content of money A, while the securities exported by A would take the form of money R. The new system of international settlements would thus guarantee the real payment of each transaction through the circular use of a currency – the new world money – which would never be transformed into a final good. (Baranzini and Cencini, 2001, p. xxii)

Provided that the proposed new international settlement agent respects all the principles of sound banking, as well as international best practices in that field, the international monetary reform propounded by the Schmitt school will dispose of the famous 'incompatible triad' *à la* Mundell, and thus allow for full international capital mobility, monetary policy autonomy, as well as stable – though not fixed – exchange rates (see Rossi, 2006).

Now, if a world monetary reform along the lines just sketched out here appears utopian for political reasons, its fundamental architecture can be easily established at a regional level – for instance, at the European level in connection with the enlargement of the EU – so as to implement a new world monetary order on regional grounds, without *ipso facto* abolishing national currencies and the room for manoeuvre they offer to any domestic policy makers. The Schmitt school has always been very critical of the various plans for monetary union that have been proposed by a number of European officials and academics (see, in this respect, Schmitt, 1975b; 1977; 1988).

European monetary integration

Any monetary union, as the EMU, elicits free capital movements between its member countries. As far as a national currency exists, its book-entry nature prevents it from 'fleeing' from the issuing country to another. As the TME shows, 'it is impossible for the whole sum of bank deposits formed in a given country to be transferred to another country' (Baranzini and Cencini, 2001, p. xxiii). By contrast, there are no barriers to protect any country in a monetary union from capital inflows as well as outflows that may disrupt the national economy, say, in case of asymmetric shocks hitting only a part of the multinational currency area. This provides a strong argument in favour of macroeconomic convergence, nominal as well as real, among those countries wishing to adopt a single currency, such as the euro, and therefore relinquish their monetary sovereignty – particularly an independent monetary policy that can help attain domestic economic policy goals. Now, within the whole euro area, all capital is free to move from one region to another, where profitability might be higher and therefore attract capital. If capital moves, however, there is a risk that labour market conditions may change drastically, and dramatically in those monetary union countries experiencing capital outflows. This may increase unemployment in the latter countries, and also adds some upward pressures on prices in those member countries into which capital is flowing. This is aggravated by the fact that the monetary policy strategy of the European Central Bank has a strong deflationary bias on production activities, hence on growth and employment, in the whole euro area (see Rossi, 2004a, for elaboration on this point).

The May 2004 enlargement of the EU raises some further problems in an economic policy perspective. The absence of real convergence between many new EU countries and the rest of the EU might pose a problem for the former countries if they adopt the euro at the end of the nominal convergence process enshrined in the EU Treaty. In particular, adopting the single currency will dispose of the 'barrier' that impedes any capital flight from those countries still having their own currency. This means that if the new EU countries stick to their local currencies, they will not suffer from those capital outflows that are bound to occur if they join the single currency area, on account of the higher profitability of investing capital in some other part of Euroland. To be true, as the new EU countries have fully liberalized their capital account transactions, as is required by the EU Treaty under the label of the *acquis communautaire*, they might attract speculative as well as direct investment flows from abroad, particularly if they adopt an exchange rate regime that stimulates costless one-way bets by speculators (see Rossi, 2004b). As many financial crises that occurred in the 1990s showed, however, these financial flows can be reversed abruptly, with dramatic effects, particularly strong in emerging and transition economies where a social security system does not exist to counteract output and employment losses. This indeed is a problem that could be accentuated if the new EU countries were to join the EMU, abandoning their currencies and thereby the monetary room for manoeuvre the latter offer to limit the negative outcome of a crisis.

In this respect, the Schmitt school calls for the creation of a European clearing institution that would integrate the new EU countries monetarily (in so far as these countries wished it), without any of the drawbacks that a full participation in the EMU implies. To this end, and to avoid the destabilizing effects on production activities generated by foreign exchange volatility and speculation, the creation and workings of a European clearing institution that provides for the final settlement of cross-border transactions is enough, but instrumental, for transforming the present system of relative exchanges between new EU countries, as well as between them and the rest of the world, into a system of absolute exchanges. Once again, the exchange rate problem could be disposed of, without abandoning national monetary sovereignties, if the monetary and financial architecture of the European settlement system were reformed structurally. As Baranzini and Cencini (2001, p. xxv) argue, this means that 'exchange rate stability may be reached without replacing national currencies with a unique European currency'.

Conclusion

The TME is a fundamental breakthrough in monetary macroeconomics. Starting from a new analysis of money, which the Schmitt school conceives of as an asset–liability that banks issue each time a payment is made, the scholars working in this tradition study the macroeconomic and monetary causes of some major anomalies, or pathologies, of modern capitalist economies of production and exchange, national as well as international. As the TME shows, production and consumption are two emissions of the same quantum of time, created by production and destroyed by consumption. Schmitt shows that inflation as well as deflation can be explained by referring to the monetary anomalies of the current structure of banks' bookkeeping, with an analytical approach characterized by Keynes's identities as well as by a new interpretation of Say's Law – which indeed is the law of the logical identity between sales and purchases of each agent, considered within any period of time. New solutions are thereby drawn for those macroeconomic disturbances that are still severing the development of our monetary economies of production and exchange. At the domestic level, a monetary–structural reform of the banks' book-entry system of accounts is called for by Schmitt's school, to eradicate those inflationary and deflationary pressures that this school notes in the process of fixed capital accumulation, resulting from the investment of firms' profit. At the international level, a monetary–structural reform of the world monetary regime based on the key-currency (or dollar) standard is also called for by the Schmitt school, to eventually dispose of the current financial instability as well as exchange rate volatility that both hamper economic development and growth of capitalist systems – be they advanced, emerging, developing, or in transition. The solution proposed by Schmitt consists in setting up an international settlement institution to be in charge of the final payment of all cross-border transactions via the emission of a truly international money, as distinct and separate from national currencies, which thus stop being objects of trade – and speculation – in foreign exchange markets.

Notes

* The author is grateful to Alvaro Cencini, Claude Gnos, Malcolm Sawyer and Bernard Schmitt for their comments. The usual disclaimer applies.
1. See in particular Schmitt (1960; 1972; 1975a; 1984).
2. Graziani (1990, p. 32, fn. 7) also maintains that 'Schmitt is the author who has gone more deeply into the analysis of banking activity'.

References

Baranzini, M. and A. Cencini (2001), 'Foreword', in S. Rossi, *Money and Inflation: A New Macroeconomic Analysis*, Cheltenham, UK and Northampton, MA, USA: Edward Elgar, viii–xli (reprinted 2003).

Cencini, A. (1995), *Monetary Theory, National and International*, London and New York: Routledge (revised paperback edition 1997).

Cencini, A. (1996), 'Inflation and deflation: the two faces of the same reality', in A. Cencini and M. Baranzini (eds), *Inflation and Unemployment: Contributions to a New Macroeconomic Approach*, London and New York: Routledge, 17–60.

Cencini, A. (2001), *Monetary Macroeconomics: A New Approach*, London and New York: Routledge.

Gnos, C. (1998), 'The Keynesian identity of income and output', in P. Fontaine and A. Jolink (eds), *Historical Perspective on Macroeconomics: Sixty Years After the General Theory*, London and New York: Routledge, 40–48.

Gnos, C. and J.-B. Rasera (1985), 'Circuit et circulation: une fausse analogie', *Cahiers de la Revue d'économie politique*, special issue, 41–57.

Goodhart, C.A.E. (1989), *Money, Information and Uncertainty*, Basingstoke and London: Macmillan, 2nd edn (first published 1975).

Graziani, A. (1990), 'The theory of the monetary circuit', *Économies et Sociétés* (Série Monnaie et Production, 7), **24**(6), 7–36.

Graziani, A. (1994), *La teoria monetaria della produzione*, Arezzo: Banca Popolare dell'Etruria e del Lazio.

Graziani, A. (2003), *The Monetary Theory of Production*, Cambridge: Cambridge University Press.

Hicks, J.R. (1974), 'Capital controversies: ancient and modern', *American Economic Review*, **64**(2), 307–16.

Keynes, J.M. (1930/1971), *A Treatise on Money* (Vol. I *The Pure Theory of Money*), London: Macmillan. Reprinted in *The Collected Writings of John Maynard Keynes*, Vol. V, London and Basingstoke: Macmillan.

Keynes, J.M. (1936/1973), *The General Theory of Employment, Interest and Money*, London: Macmillan. Reprinted in *The Collected Writings of John Maynard Keynes*, Vol. VII, London and Basingstoke: Macmillan.

Lavoie, M. (1984), 'The endogenous flow of credit and the Post Keynesian theory of money', *Journal of Economic Issues*, **18**(3), 771–97.

Lavoie, M. (1987), 'Monnaie et production: une synthèse de la théorie du circuit', *Économies et Sociétés* (Série Monnaie et Production, 4), **21**(9), 65–101.

Lavoie, M. (1992), 'Jacques Le Bourva's theory of endogenous credit-money', *Review of Political Economy*, **4**(4), 436–46.

Le Bourva, J. (1962), 'Création de la monnaie et multiplicateur du crédit', *Revue économique*, **13**(1), 29–56.

Parguez, A. (1975), *Monnaie et macroéconomie: théorie de la monnaie en déséquilibre*, Paris: Economica.

Parguez, A. and M. Seccareccia (2000), 'The credit theory of money: the monetary circuit approach', in J. Smithin (ed.), *What is Money?*, London and New York: Routledge, 101–23.

Rochon, L.-P. and S. Rossi (eds) (2003), *Modern Theories of Money: The Nature and Role of Money in Capitalist Economies*, Cheltenham, UK and Northampton, MA, USA: Edward Elgar.

Rossi, S. (2001), *Money and Inflation: A New Macroeconomic Analysis*, Cheltenham, UK and Northampton, MA, USA: Edward Elgar (reprinted 2003).

Rossi, S. (2003), 'Money and banking in a monetary theory of production', in L.-P. Rochon and S. Rossi (eds), *Modern Theories of Money: The Nature and Role of Money in Capitalist Economies*, Cheltenham, UK and Northampton, MA, USA: Edward Elgar, 339–59.

Rossi, S. (2004a), 'Inflation targeting and sacrifice ratios: the case of the European Central Bank', *International Journal of Political Economy*, **34**(2), 69–85.

Rossi, S. (2004b), 'Monetary integration strategies and perspectives of new EU countries', *International Review of Applied Economics*, **18**(4), 443–69.

Rossi, S. (2005), 'Central banking in a monetary theory of production: the economics of payment finality from a circular-flow perspective', in G. Fontana and R. Realfonzo (eds), *The Monetary Theory of Production: Tradition and Perspectives*, Basingstoke: Palgrave Macmillan, 139–51.

Rossi, S. (2006), 'The monetary-policy relevance of an international settlement institution: the Keynes plan 60 years later', in A. Giacomin and M.C. Marcuzzo (eds), *Money and Markets: A Doctrinal Approach*, London and New York: Routledge, forthcoming.

Rueff, J. (1979), *Oeuvres complètes*, Paris: Plon.

Schmitt, B. (1960), *La formation du pouvoir d'achat: l'investissement de la monnaie*, Paris: Sirey.

Schmitt, B. (1972), *Macroeconomic Theory, a Fundamental Revision*, Albeuve: Castella.

Schmitt, B. (1973), *New Proposals for World Monetary Reform*, Albeuve: Castella.

Schmitt, B. (1975a), *Théorie unitaire de la monnaie, nationale et internationale*, Albeuve: Castella.

Schmitt, B. (1975b), *Génération de la monnaie des monnaies européennes*, Albeuve: Castella.

Schmitt, B. (1977), *La monnaie européenne*, Paris: Presses Universitaires de France.

Schmitt, B. (1984), *Inflation, chômage et malformations du capital: macroéconomie quantique*, Paris and Albeuve: Economica and Castella.

Schmitt, B. (1986), 'The process of formation of economics in relation to other sciences', in M. Baranzini and R. Scazzieri (eds), *Foundations of Economics: Structures of Inquiry and Economic Theory*, Oxford and New York: Basil Blackwell and St Martin's Press, 103–32.

Schmitt, B. (1988), *L'ÉCU et les souverainetés nationales en Europe*, Paris: Dunod.
Schmitt, B. (1996), 'Unemployment: is there a principal cause?', in A. Cencini and M. Baranzini (eds), *Inflation and Unemployment: Contributions to a New Macroeconomic Approach*, London and New York: Routledge, 75–105.
Zazzaro, A. (2003), 'How heterodox is the heterodoxy of monetary circuit theory? The nature of money and the microeconomics of the circuit', in L.-P. Rochon and S. Rossi (eds), *Modern Theories of Money: The Nature and Role of Money in Capitalist Economies*, Cheltenham, UK and Northampton, MA, USA: Edward Elgar, 218–45.

9   Keynes and money
Paul Davidson

Introduction

John Maynard Keynes was probably the most important and famous economist of the twentieth century. Keynes was primarily a specialist in monetary theory. The words money, monetary, currency appear in the title of all Keynes's major books on economic theory. His conceptualization of money, however, differs significantly from that of classical economic theory, while the latter has dominated mainstream economists' thought from the eighteenth century to today. The purpose of this chapter is to explain why Keynes's conceptualization of money is revolutionary.

'Money', Nobel laureate John R. Hicks (1967, p. 1) declared, 'is defined by its functions . . . money is what money does'. While economists have spilled more printers' ink over the topic of money than any other, confusion over the meaning and nature of money continues to plague the economics profession. A clear, unambiguous taxonomy is essential for good scientific inquiry. All useful classification schemes in science require the scientist to categorize entities by their essential functions and properties. For example, even though a whale looks like a fish, swims like a fish, and will die (like a fish) if it is out of water too long, biologists classify whales as mammals not fish because whales suckle their young. Even though the uninstructed person may think a whale is more similar to a fish than to his/her own mammalian self, biologists classify whales according to an essential property and not to similarity in looks.

If a successful scientific taxonomy is to be developed in economics, therefore, money should be defined by its essential functions and properties. Most of the disputes among various schools of thought on the role of money in an economic system are due to differing conceptualizations of the functions and properties of money and its relations to the passage of time.

Time is a device that prevents all things from happening at once. The production process requires the passage of a significant amount of calendar time. Even consumption, especially of durables, may necessitate the passage of time. In all orthodox mainstream theories (i.e., monetarism, general equilibrium theory, neo-Walrasian theory, rational expectations theory, neoclassical synthesis Keynesianism, new classical economics, and New Keynesianism), on the other hand, historical time is treated as if it is irrelevant. All of these theories are explicitly or implicitly based on an Arrow–Debreu–Walrasian general equilibrium analytical framework where all contractual agreements for the production and exchange of goods and services from today until the end of time are assumed to be agreed upon in the initial instant of the economic system.

A general equilibrium analysis is the equivalent of the 'Big Bang' in astrophysics – an event thought to have occurred at the creation of the universe that sent the planets, solar systems and other heavenly bodies into a predetermined time path that can never be altered. The 'Big Bang' general equilibrium analysis that is the foundation of all mainstream theories requires the assumption that money is neutral, i.e., money does not affect all real production, consumption and employment decisions, at least in the long run.

In all these mainstream theories, present and future equilibrium economic activities are logically determined and paid for, *at the initial instant*, when spot and forward contracts covering all economic events until the end of calendar time are agreed upon by all parties to the contracts. Consequently these theories assume either that future events can be known to all economic decision makers with perfect certainty or at least that all future events can be reliably statistically predicted based on calculating probability distributions drawn from existing market data. These calculated probability distributions are assumed to govern all past, present and future economic events.[1] Accordingly, money need never be held as a security blanket to protect individuals against unforeseen and unforeseeable events.

The sole function of money in classical theory systems is as a numeraire, that is, a yardstick by which to measure the relative prices (and therefore scarcities) of the various goods that are produced. In the long run, real output, employment and economic growth are solely determined by the exogenous factors of technology and preferences. Money cannot affect long-run real outcomes. In the short run some classical-based theories where money wages and/or prices are assumed not to be freely flexibly (e.g., monetarism, New Keynesianism), money is permitted to have a transient effect on employment and real output. Nevertheless, in the long run, money is assumed to be neutral. Say's Law prevails, so that supply creates its own demand, and there must be an automatic market mechanism that ensures the full employment of available resources in the most efficient manner possible, given the exogenously determined preferences of the residents of the economy and the technological properties of production.

Addressing *The General Theory* chiefly to his 'fellow economists', Keynes (1936, p. v) insisted that such classical theories were irrelevant to understanding real-world economic problems. He wrote (ibid., p. 3):

> the postulates of the classical theory are applicable to a special case only and not to the general case . . . Moreover, the characteristics of the special case assumed by the classical theory happen not to be those of the economic society in which we actually live, with the result that its teaching is misleading and disastrous if we attempt to apply it to the facts of experience.

Keynes (ibid., p. 26) believed that he could *logically* demonstrate why 'Say's Law . . . is not the true law relating the aggregate demand and supply functions' in either the short run or the long run, even if, hypothetically, all money wages and prices are flexible. Keynes's message was that, until we get our theory to accurately mirror and apply to the 'facts of experience', and especially the role of money and liquidity, there is little hope of getting our policies right. Unfortunately, since Keynes's revolutionary theory was aborted in the 1940s by leading American economists who called themselves neoclassical synthesis Keynesians, Keynes's message was forgotten. Consequently this message is just as relevant today as it was in 1936.

Keynes (1936, p. 16) compared those economists whose theoretical logic was grounded in the neutral money axiom and Say's Law to Euclidean geometers living in a non-Euclidean world,

> who discovering that in experience straight lines apparently parallel often meet, rebuke the lines for not keeping straight – as the only remedy for the unfortunate collisions which are taking

place. Yet, in truth, there is no remedy except to throw over the axiom of parallels and to work out a non-Euclidean geometry. Something similar is required today in economics.

To throw over an axiom is to reject what the faithful believe are 'universal truths'. Keynes's revolution in economic theory was truly a revolt against orthodox theory since it aimed at rejecting some basic mainstream axioms to provide a logical foundation for a non-Say's Law model applicable to the real world in which we happen to live. Unfortunately, since Keynes, orthodox economists, seduced by a technical methodology which promised precision and unique results at the expense of applicability and accuracy, have reintroduced more sophisticated forms of the 'special case' classical axioms that Keynes rejected. Consequently Keynes's revolution against classical theory was almost immediately shunted on to a wrong track as more obtuse versions of classical theory became the keystone of modern mainstream macroeconomic theory. Neoclassical synthesis Keynesians,[2] monetarists, the new classical economists, as well as the New Keynesians, have reconstructed macrotheory by reintroducing the restrictive classical axioms that Keynes struggled to overthrow.

Keynes's revolution against classical theory requires the analyst to recognize that a monetary economy operates quite differently from a non-monetary system, so that, in the short as well as the long run, money is never neutral. Spot and forward money contracts and the civil law of contracts are human institutions created to organize production and exchange transactions that will be operative over an uncertain (not statistically predictable) future. A spot contract is one that specifies that delivery and payment are to be made on the spot; that is, the moment after the spot contract is agreed upon by the contracting parties, delivery and payment are required. A forward contract, on the other hand, is one that specifies the future date(s) for delivery of goods and/or services by the seller and money payment by the buyer. Accordingly, in all real-world legal contracts a calendar time date is specified when the buyer must meet his/her contractual obligation (liability) with the delivery of money to the seller, who must deliver the 'goods' at a specified date. An economy that utilizes spot *and* forward money contracts to organize production and exchange activities is called an entrepreneurial economy.

In the world of experience, that thing that the state declares will legally discharge any contractual obligation under the civil law of contracts is *money*. In an entrepreneurial economic system the concept of money requires two concomitant features and two necessary properties. A necessary characteristic of money in an entrepreneurial economy was spelled out by Keynes as early as the very beginning of his *Treatise on Money* (1930, p. 3): 'Money [is] that by delivery of which debt-contracts and price-contracts are *discharged*, and in the shape of which a store of General Purchasing Power is held.' In other words, that thing that we call money has two specific functions: (1) money is the *means of contractual settlement* and (2) money is *a store of value*, i.e., a vehicle for moving purchasing power over time – a time machine.

This time-machine function is known as *liquidity*. The possession of liquidity means that the person has sufficient money (or other liquid assets that can be readily resold for money in an orderly, organized market) to meet all his/her contractual obligations as they come due. In a world of uncertainty, a decision maker cannot know what spot and forward contracts either already entered into or entered into in the future will either (1) be defaulted by the buyer when the decision maker is the seller, or (2) will come due, for which there will be a need for money to discharge these contractual obligations when the decision maker is the buyer. Accordingly, the more uncertainty the decision maker feels about future economic events, the more money he/she will desire to hold to meet such unforeseen contingencies.

This characteristic of liquidity can be possessed in various degrees by some, but not all, durables. Since any durable besides money can*not* (by definition) settle a contract, then for durables other than money to be a liquidity time machine they must be resaleable in well-organized, orderly spot markets for that thing (money) that the civil law of contracts declares can discharge a contractual liability. Money therefore is the liquid asset *par excellence*, for it can always settle any contractual obligation as long as the residents of the economy are law abiding and recognize the civil law of contracts.

The degree of liquidity of any durable asset other than money depends on its prompt and easy resaleability in well-organized and orderly spot markets. For any market to be organized and orderly there must be a *market maker*, i.e., an institution that stands ready to:

(a)   sell the asset whenever those who want to buy (the bulls) are overwhelming those who want to sell (the bears), or

(b)   buy when the bears are overpowering the bulls.

By making the market, the market maker assures all market participants that, no matter what happens, the market price of the asset in terms of money will change over time in an orderly manner upwards or downwards.

A *fully liquid asset* is defined as any durable other than money where the participants 'know' that the market price in terms of monetary units will not change for the foreseeable future. For a durable to be a fully liquid asset there must be a market maker who can guarantee that the price of the asset will not change over time even if circumstances change. An example of a fully liquid asset is a foreign currency whose value in terms of domestic currency is fixed by the central bank of the nation. (As long as the central bank has sufficient foreign reserves, it can, if it wishes, guarantee a fixed exchange rate.)

A *liquid asset* is a durable asset readily resaleable in an organized market, but the market maker does not guarantee an unchanging market price. The market maker only guarantees that the market price will change, *in an orderly manner*, given the explicit, known rules under which the market maker operates. For any liquid asset the next moment's market price is never known with certainty. What is known is that the next moment's price will not differ in a disorderly way from this moment's price – as long as the market maker has a sufficient stock of the asset and liquidity to back up his/her assurance of an orderly market.[3]

An *illiquid asset* is a durable that cannot be readily resaleable at any price. Illiquid assets do not have organized, orderly resale markets. There is no market maker who is willing to organize an orderly spot market for the asset.

According to Keynes (1936, ch. 17), all liquid assets have certain necessary properties. These essential properties are: (1) the elasticity of production of money and all other liquid assets is approximately zero, and (2) the elasticity of substitution between liquid assets and the products of industry is zero. (These elasticity properties will be discussed below.)

What are the classical axioms that Keynes overthrew?

There are three fundamental restrictive classical axioms that Keynes rejected in developing his revolutionary logical analysis of an entrepreneurial economy. These classical axioms are (1) *the axiom of neutral money* where money does not affect real outcomes, (2) *the axiom of an ergodic economic world* where the future can always be reliably predicted, and (3) *the axiom of gross substitution* where everything is a substitute for everything else. Keynes believed that the characteristics of a real-world entrepreneurial economic system could be modelled only by overthrowing these fundamental axioms that are the foundation of all mainstream theories.

Removal of these three axioms permits an analysis of an economic system where (1) money matters in the long and short run; that is, money is never neutral; it affects real decision making.[4] (2) The economic system is moving through calendar time from an irrevocable past to an uncertain, not reliably predictable (non-ergodic), future. In uncertain, non-ergodic circumstances, decision-making agents 'know' that the future cannot be reliably predicted in any probability sense (see Davidson, 1982–83). (3) Forward contracts in money terms are a human institution developed to efficiently organize time-consuming production and exchange processes. The money-wage contract is the most ubiquitous of these contracts. Modern production economies are therefore organized on a money-wage contract-based system. (4) Unemployment, rather than full employment, is a common *laissez-faire* situation in a market-oriented, monetary production economy.

Only the monetarists and the new classical theorists (like Ricardo before them)

> offer us the supreme intellectual achievement, unattainable by weaker spirits, of adopting a hypothetical world remote from experience as though it was the world of experience and then living in it consistently. With most of . . . [the neoclassical synthesis Old and New Keynesians] common sense cannot help breaking in – with injury to their logical consistency. (Keynes, 1936, pp. 192–3)

Spending, constrained demand, Say's Law and gross substitution

Keynes's *General Theory* is developed via an aggregate supply–aggregate demand function analysis which can be used to illustrate the difference between Say's Law and Keynes's analytical structure (Keynes, 1936, pp. 25–6).

The process of production takes time from inception to completion. Entrepreneurs must hire workers and order raw materials before the product can be finished and sold to the buyer. For entrepreneurs to hire workers and order raw materials they must have some expectation of possible sales revenues at a future date when the product is fabricated and available for sale. The aggregate supply function (Z) relates entrepreneurs' expected sales proceeds with the level of employment (N) entrepreneurs will hire today for any volume of expected sales receipts in the future. In Figure 9.1a this aggregate supply (Z) function is drawn as upward-sloping, indicating that the higher entrepreneurs' sales expectations, the more workers they will hire. The aggregate demand function relates buyers' desired expenditure flows for any given level of employment. In Figure 9.1b, the aggregate demand (D) function is drawn as upward-sloping, indicating that the greater the level of employment hire, the more income households will earn and therefore the more buyers will spend on goods and services.

The aggregate supply and demand functions can be brought together in a single quadrant to provide the equilibrium employment solution. In Figure 9.2a the aggregate supply

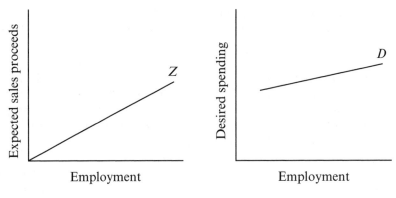

Figure 9.1a   *Figure 9.1b*

(Z) and aggregate demand (D) functions are drawn as they would be developed in a Say's Law world where supply creates its own demand. In a Say's Law world (as explained below and as shown in Figure 9.2a), the aggregate supply and demand functions are coincident throughout their entire length. Thus, if at any point of time the actual employment level is N_1^a, actual demand is constrained to point G. Any coordinated expansion in hiring by entrepreneurs to provide additional output (say to point H in Figure 9.2a) will (by definition of Say's Law) increase actual demand concomitantly to point H and full employment (N_f^a) could be established. In a Say's Law world there is no obstacle to full employment.

In Figure 9.2b, on the other hand, the aggregate demand and supply functions are distinguishable functions which intersect at a single point, the point of *effective demand* (E); and in a manner consistent with Keynes's theory (1936, p. 25) the equilibrium level of employment is N_1^b. At the full employment level (N_f^b in Figure 9.2b) there is a deficiency in effective demand equal to the vertical distance $\overline{JK}$. Accordingly, if entrepreneurs hire N_f^b, when they bring the product to market they will find aggregate demand is less than their sales receipts expectations. Hence these disappointing sales will force entrepreneurs to recognize that the output produced by hiring the full employment N_f^b number of workers cannot be profitably sold. Entrepreneurs will reduce their hiring of workers until N_1^b workers are hired. At that point sales (and therefore) profit expectations will be met and there is no reason for entrepreneurs to change their hiring decisions unless their expectations of buyers demand change.

As defined by Keynes, Say's Law requires that the aggregate supply curve coincide with the aggregate demand curve over its entire length so that supply can create its own demand. Accordingly, *effective demand*, 'instead of having a unique equilibrium value, is an infinite range of values, all equally admissible' (Keynes, 1936, p. 26). If, therefore, Say's Law prevails, then the economy is in neutral equilibrium where actual demand is *constrained* only by actual income (supply). In other words, Say's Law requires that aggregate demand is a *constrained demand function* (in the terminology of Clower, 1965, or Barro and Grossman, 1976); and a 'short-side of the market rationing' rule limits employment opportunities. This short-side rule is specifically adopted by Malinvaud (1977, pp. 12–35) to 'explain' Keynesian unemployment. It has also been used by many self-claimed 'Keynesians' to explain what their logical unconstrained model cannot.[5]

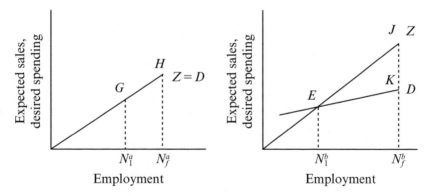

Figure 9.2a Say's Law   *Figure 9.2b Keynes's theory*

In the Clower neoclassical synthesis version of the Keynesian system, which has been labelled the dual decision hypothesis with a coordination failure, purchasing decisions are always equal to, and constrained by, *actual* income. The economy is in neutral equilibrium at any level of actual income. There is no obstacle to full employment except that entrepreneurs do not receive a market signal that they would be able profitably to sell the full employment output if only they coordinated and marched together to the full employment hiring level. Unemployment is solely due to a 'coordination failure' of the market system to signal entrepreneurs that if they only hired the full employment level of workers, actual income would equal *notional* (full employment) *income* and the spending decisions by income-earners would be equal to, and constrained by, the full employment budget line and all markets would clear.[6] Hence, in contrast to Keynes (1936, p. 301), these 'Keynesians' argue that if only entrepreneurs hired all workers, there would never be an insufficiency of aggregate demand.

Those who believe that a short-side rule or constrained demand function limits employment opportunities, if they follow their logic and not their common sense, should have supported former President Reagan's proposal for solving the unemployment problem. In a conference with reporters in the spring of 1983 (when the USA was just beginning to recover from the largest unemployment rate that it had experienced since the Great Depression of the 1930s), President Reagan suggested that unemployment could be ended if each business firm in the nation immediately hired one more worker. Since there were more firms than unemployed workers in the economy at this time, this Reagan solution was obviously statistically accurate. Unless, however, the employment of these additional workers created a demand for the additional output produced at a profitable price (additional supply creating *pari passu* additional demand), it would not be in the self-interest of the existing firms to hire all the additional workers necessary to achieve full employment.

Nevertheless, neoclassical Keynesians, who believe in the so-called constrained demand function, should have applauded Reagan's clarion call for firms to coordinate increased hiring. If each firm does hire an additional worker so that full employment is (at least momentarily) achieved, then, in this constrained demand analysis, actual income flows earned would be equal to notional income and therefore aggregate demand would not be constrained short of full employment and the economy could reach the point *H* in Figure 9.2a. There is no coordination failure – and no short-side rule limits job opportunities.

In a Keynesian world of entrepreneurial decision making, on the other hand, involuntary unemployment is due to an insufficiency or lack of effective demand (at full employment), as shown by the vertical distance JK in Figure 9.2b. The sales of the additional output produced by private sector entrepreneurs hiring workers above the N_1^b level in Figure 9.2 cannot be profitable.

Keynes would never have endorsed Reagan's Say's Law solution to the unemployment problem. In a closed economy context, Keynes held that *neither* of the two private sector components of the aggregate demand function (D_1 and D_2, i.e., aggregate consumption expenditures and investment spending) are necessarily constrained by actual currently earned income, although D_1 spending may be related to income earned! To put it bluntly and in its most irritating – thought-provoking – form, the underlying axioms of Keynes's revolutionary theory of effective demand requires that *the demand for goods produced by labour need never be constrained by actual earned income. Spending is only constrained by liquidity and/or timidity considerations.* Thus the budget constraint, in a Keynesian model, need never limit either individual spending or aggregate spending at less then full employment.

In the real world, planned spending need never be equal to, or even constrained by, actual income as long as (a) agents who earn income by either selling their labour or goods produced by labour in the private sector are not required to spend all of their earned income on goods produced by labour, and/or (b) agents who plan to spend on currently producible goods are not required to earn income (previously or concurrently) with their exercise of this demand (where by demand we mean want *plus the ability to pay*).

Hahn (1977, p. 31) has put point (a) as meaning that Say's Law is done away with and involuntary unemployment can occur whenever there are 'resting places for savings in other than reproducible assets' so that all income earned by engaging in the production of goods is not, in the short or long run, spent on assets producible by labour. For savings to find such ultimate resting places, the axiom of gross substitution must be thrown over.

This gross substitution axiom is the backbone of mainstream economics; it is the assumption that any good is a substitute for any other good. The gross substitution axiom assumes that if the demand for good x goes up, its relative price will rise, inducing demand to spill over to the now relatively cheaper substitute good y. For an economist to deny this 'universal truth' of gross substitutability between objects of demand is revolutionary heresy – and as in the days of the Inquisition, the modern-day College of Cardinals of mainstream economics destroys all non-believers, if not by burning them at the stake, then by banishing them from the mainstream professional journals. Yet in Keynes's (1936, ch. 17) analysis 'The Essential Properties of Interest and Money' require that:

1. The elasticity of production of liquid assets including money is approximately zero. This means that private entrepreneurs cannot produce more of these assets by hiring more workers if the demand for liquid assets increases. In other words, liquid assets are not producible by private entrepreneurs' hiring of additional workers; this means that money (and other liquid assets) does not grow on trees.
2. The elasticity of substitution between all liquid assets, including money (which are not reproducible by labour in the private sector) and producibles (in the private sector), is zero or negligible. Accordingly, when the price of money increases, people will not substitute the purchase of the products of industry for their demand for money for liquidity (savings) purposes.

These two elasticity properties that Keynes believed are *essential* to the concepts of money and liquidity mean that a basic axiom of Keynes's logical framework is that non-producible assets that can be used to store savings are not gross substitutes for producible assets in savers' portfolios. If this elasticity of substitution between liquid assets and the products of industry is significantly different from zero (if the gross substitution axiom is ubiquitously true[7]), then even if savers attempt to use non-reproducible assets for storing their increments of wealth, this increase in demand will increase the price of non-producibles. This relative price rise in non-producibles will, under the gross substitution axiom, induce savers to substitute reproducible durables for non-producibles in their wealth holdings and therefore non-producibles will not be, in Hahn's terminology, 'ultimate resting places for savings'. The gross substitution axiom therefore restores Say's Law and denies the logical possibility of involuntary unemployment.

In *Debate With His Critics*, Friedman (1974, pp. 146–8) could correctly attack Tobin and other neoclassical Keynesians for logical inconsistencies involving 'differences in the range of assets considered' as possible gross substitutes in savings portfolios. For Friedman (1974, p. 29) the total spectrum of assets eligible for savings includes 'houses, automobiles, let alone furniture, household appliances, clothes and so on'. (After all, in his *permanent income hypothesis*, Friedman deliberately defines savings so as to include the purchase of producible durable goods.) Thus Friedman, in his logical world remote from reality, can 'prove' that savings do not create unemployment; for the Samuelsons, Tobins and Solows of the world, their common sense, if not their logic, tells them better. To overthrow the axiom of gross substitution in an intertemporal context is truly heretical. It changes the entire perspective of what is meant by 'rational' or 'optimal' savings, of why people save or what they save. Hicks (1979, pp. 76–7, n. 7) noted that all Keynes needed to say was that income was divided between current consumption and a vague provision for the uncertain future. The mathematical assumption that 'planned expenditures at specified different dates in the future have independent utilities [and are gross substitutes] . . . I find quite unacceptable . . . the normal condition is that there is strong complementarity between them [consumption plans in successive periods]'. Indeed Danziger et al. (1982–83) showed that the facts regarding consumption spending by the elderly are incompatible with the notion of intertemporal gross substitution of consumption plans which underlie both life cycle models and overlapping generation models currently so popular in mainstream macroeconomic theory.

In the absence of the axiom of gross substitution, income effects (e.g., the Keynesian multiplier) predominate and can swamp any hypothetical neoclassical substitution effects induced by relative price changes. Consequently, relative price changes via a flexible pricing mechanism will not be the cure-all 'snake-oil' medicine usually recommended by many neoclassical doctors for the unfortunate economic maladies that are occurring in the real world.

Investment spending, liquidity and the neutral money axiom

Agents who plan to buy the products of industry in the current period are not required to earn income currently or previously to their exercise of spending in today's market. This implies that spending for what Keynes (1936, p. 24) called D_2 (the demand for fixed and working capital goods[8]) spending on the products of industry reproducible by labour in the private sector is *not* constrained by either today's actual income or endowments. For

Keynes, given animal spirits and not timidity on the part of entrepreneurs, D_2 is constrained solely by the *monetary*, and not the real, *expected return on liquid assets* (ibid., ch. 17). As long as the expected monetary return on working and fixed capital exceeds the monetary rate of interest, it pays to borrow from the money-creating banking system to purchase newly produced capital goods. Accordingly, the rate of interest, which is strictly a monetary phenomenon in Keynes, rules the roost in terms of determining how much D_2 spending occurs in any period.

Keynes (1936, p. 142) believed that the 'real rate of interest' concept, developed by Irving Fisher, was a logical confusion. In a monetary economy moving through calendar time towards an uncertain (statistically unpredictable) future there is no such thing as a forward-looking real rate of interest. Moreover, money has an impact on the real sector in both the short and long run. Thus, money is a real phenomenon.

This is just the reverse of what classical theory and modern mainstream theory teaches students of economics. In orthodox macrotheory the rate of interest is a real (technologically determined) factor, while money (at least in the long run) does not affect the real output flow. This reversal of the importance of the significance of money and interest rates for real and monetary phenomena between orthodox and Keynes's theory is the result of Keynes's rejection of a second neoclassical universal truth – the axiom of neutral money.

For the D_2 component of aggregate demand not to be constrained by actual income, agents must have the ability to finance investment by borrowing from a banking system which can create money in response to an increase in the demand for loans. Such money creation is therefore inevitably tied to the creation of money (debt) contracts. This financing mechanism involves the heresy of overthrowing the neutral money axiom. Hahn (1983, p. 44) describes this axiom as one where

> The objectives of agents that determine their actions and plans do not depend on any nominal magnitudes. Agents care only about 'real' things such as goods . . . leisure and effort. We know this as the axiom of the absence of money illusion, which it seems impossible to abandon in any sensible sense.

This axiom implies that money is a veil, so that all economic decisions are made on the basis of real phenomena and relative prices alone. Money does not matter! But in the world we live in, money does matter, for: (1) money provides a liquid security blanket for those fearing an uncertain future where some contractual commitment can come due and cannot be met out of the expected cash flow in the future period; and (2) money can be created and lent to borrowers that the bankers deem creditworthy. These borrowers can then purchase goods and services from these borrowed (unearned) funds. To reject the neutral money axiom, therefore, does not require assuming that agents suffer from a money illusion. It only means that 'money is not neutral'; money matters in both the short run and the long run, or as Keynes (1973, p. 408) put it:

> The theory which I desiderate would deal . . . with an economy in which money plays a part of its own and affects motives and decisions, and is, in short, one of the operative factors in the situation, so that the course of events cannot be predicted in either the long period or in the short, without a knowledge of the behaviour of money between the first state and the last. And it is this which we ought to mean when we speak of a monetary economy.

Can anything be more revolutionary? In this passage from an article entitled 'The Monetary Theory of Production' (and I emphasize the word *Monetary*) Keynes specifically rejects the neutral money axiom! The only objective for a firm is to end the production process (which takes time) by liquidating its working capital in order to end up with more money than it started with (Keynes, 1979, p. 82).

This can be easily illustrated. Suppose during the next great depression a firm has a production process gestation period of one year. At the beginning of the year it hires workers, buys materials, and so on, on forward money contracts for the entire production process and thereby has, except for acts of God, controlled its costs of production. Suppose that, during the year, the relevant price index falls by 10 per cent but the price at which the firm expected to sell its product at the end of the gestation period falls by only 5 per cent. In relative real terms the firm is better off; but in the real world the firm is really worse off as the market sales revenue falls by 5 per cent, but its money costs of production (which were fixed at the initial instant of hiring labour and ordering raw materials) are fixed by money contract.

Suppose we change the hypothesis to indicate a 50 per cent fall in the price index and a 45 per cent decline in the sale price of the firm's product. The firm still has a 5 per cent improvement in real terms, but in all likelihood if this occurs the firm will soon have to file for bankruptcy. (Of course a good classical economist would respond that the firm will not go bankrupt if it can recontract its labour hiring and raw material order contracts without penalty – but such recontracts without penalties are not a characteristic of the world we live in.)

If on the other hand we had assumed that the CPI goes up by 10 per cent (or 50 per cent) while the firm's product price went up by 5 per cent (or 45 per cent), although the firm's real position has deteriorated, its real-world position is better. As long as money contracts are used to efficiently plan the production process, production decisions will be affected by nominal values and money is a real phenomenon!

Once we admit that money is a real phenomenon, that money matters, then the traditional neutral money axiom must be rejected. Hahn should realize this, since Arrow and Hahn have demonstrated that:

> The terms in which contracts are made matter. In particular, if money is the goods in terms of which contracts are made, then the prices of goods in terms of money are of special significance. This is not the case if we consider an economy without a past or future. . . . *If a serious monetary theory* comes to be written, the fact that contracts are made in terms of money will be of considerable importance. (Arrow and Hahn, 1971, pp. 356–7, italics added)

Moreover, Arrow and Hahn demonstrate (ibid., p. 361) that, if contracts are made in terms of money (so that money affects real decisions) in an economy moving along in calendar time with a past and a future, then *all existence theorems of a general equilibrium solution are jeopardized*. The existence of money contracts – a characteristic of the world in which Keynes lived and in which we still do – implies that there need never exist, in the long run or the short run, any rational expectations equilibrium or general equilibrium market-clearing price vector. The general equilibrium analysis is, therefore, inapplicable to a world where agents engage in production and exchange by the use of money contracts.

The pervasive ergodic axiom – precision vs accuracy

Most mainstream economists suffer from the pervasive form of envy which we may call the 'Economist's Disease'; that is, these economists want to be considered as first-class scientists dealing with a 'hard science' rather than be seen as 'second-class' citizens of the scientific community who deal with the non-precise 'social' and 'political' sciences. These economists, mistaking precision (rather than accuracy) as the hallmark of 'true' science, prefer to be precise rather than accurate.

Precision conveys 'sharpness to minute detail'. Accuracy, on the other hand, means 'care to obtain conformity with fact or truth'. For example, if you phone the plumber to fix an emergency breakdown in your plumbing system and he responds by indicating he will be there in exactly 12 minutes, he is being precise, but not exercising care to obtain conformity with fact or truth. If he says he will be there before the day is over, he is being accurate, if not necessarily precise.

Most economists, unfortunately, prefer to be precisely wrong rather than roughly right or accurate. The ergodic axiom permits economists to act 'as if' they were dealing with a 'hard' science where data are homogeneous with respect to time.

In order to predict the magnitude of future events, one should draw a sample from a future statistical universe. Since that is impossible, most hard scientists presume that they are studying ergodic stochastic processes. In an ergodic world, observations of a time-series realization (i.e. historical data) are useful information regarding the probability distribution of the stochastic process which generated that realization. If the process is ergodic, then using past-time series (or cross-sectional) data that are used to calculate probability distributions is equivalent to drawing the data from the future. In essence, past observations also provide information about the probability distribution over a universe of realizations which exist at any point of time such as today or tomorrow. Then the data drawn from past observations also provide useful information regarding the future probability distribution of events. Hence, by scientifically studying the past, as generated by an ergodic situation, present and future events can be reliably forecasted in terms of statistical probabilities calculated from past observations.

Keynes (1936, ch. 12) rejected this view that past information from economic time-series realizations provides reliable, useful data which permit stochastic predictions of the economic future. In a world where observations are drawn from a non-ergodic stochastic environment, past data cannot provide any reliable information about future probability distributions. Agents in a non-ergodic environment 'know' they cannot reliably know future outcomes. In an economy operating in a non-ergodic environment, therefore – our economic world – liquidity matters, money is never neutral, and neither Say's Law nor Walras's Law is relevant. In such a world, Keynes's revolutionary logical analysis is relevant.

Conclusions

Mainstream economic theory has not followed Keynes's revolutionary logical analysis to develop what Arrow and Hahn have called a 'serious monetary theory' in which contracts are made in terms of money in an economy moving from an irrevocable past to an uncertain, non-ergodic future. At the very beginning of his *Treatise on Money*, Keynes (1930, p. 3) reminded the reader that, in a modern economy, money exists only because there are contracts, and therefore money is intimately related to the existence of money contracts.

In his writings Keynes explicitly made assumptions that are incompatible with (a) the gross substitution axiom, (b) the neutral money axiom and (c) the ergodic axiom. Unfortunately, the early popularizers and professional interpreters of Keynes's analysis, such as Paul Samuelson, either did not read what Keynes wrote, or did not comprehend Keynes's revolutionary logic requiring the overthrow of these fundamental mainstream axioms. Nevertheless, Keynes's policy prescriptions made a great deal of common sense. Hence Keynes won the policy battles of the first three decades after the publication of *The General Theory*, even though 'Keynesians' had erected a 'neoclassical synthesis' microfoundation to Keynes's macroeconomics which could not logically support Keynes's general theory case.

From a logical standpoint the neoclassical synthesis Keynesians had created a Keynesian Cheshire Cat – a grin without a body. Thus Friedman and the rational expectations, new classical theorists were able to destroy the rickety neoclassical Keynesian scaffolding and replace it with a technologically advanced, logically consistent, but irrelevant and inaccurate theory.

Almost seven decades after publication of Keynes's *General Theory*, it is surprising how few in the economics profession are willing or able to defend the logical basis of Keynes's analysis. It is almost as if many believed that, as Clower (1965, p. 120) indicated, 'the *General Theory* is theoretical nonsense' unless Keynes believed in the constrained demand function, dual decision hypothesis. Yet we have shown above that this constrained demand function analysis implies Say's Law. Hence, if Clower was correct in his claim that Keynes had the dual decision hypothesis at the back of his mind, then Keynes was a theoretical charlatan in claiming that his analysis eliminated Say's Law. Of course, it is Clower and the other neoclassical synthesis Keynesians who maintain axioms rejected by Keynes who are in error in trying to apply Keynes's label to their logical system.

At the Royal Economic Society's centennial celebration of Keynes's birth in July 1983, the detractors of Keynes on the programme far exceeded those who were attempting to honour Keynes's accomplishments and build on his legacy. Some, such as Professors Samuelson and Solow, proudly labelled themselves as 'reconstructed Keynesians' to differentiate their theory from the 'unreconstructed' Keynesians of Cambridge, England. As Samuelson put it, a reconstructed Keynesian was one who found the Keynesian structure imperfect and had therefore to reconstruct it.

This 'reconstructed Keynesian' appellation is, however, a misnomer when applied to the neoclassical synthesis Keynesian approach of Samuelson and Solow. These mainstream American 'Keynesian' models never began with the same logical foundations and axioms as Keynes's model. Hence these Keynesians cannot, and will not, reconstruct Keynes until they throw over the neoclassical axioms rejected by Keynes.

The 'unreconstructed' Keynesians – or post-Keynesians as I would call them – recognize that there may be many flaws in the Keynes superstructure and that time has brought forth new and different pressing problems. Post-Keynesians may not have worked out all the answers, but at least they recognize that Keynes started with a logically different theoretical system – a system that accurately reflects the characteristics of the real economic world: those of Wall Street and the corporate boardroom, rather than those of Robinson Crusoe or the medieval fair.

Post-Keynesians recognize that their logical model is neither fully developed, nor as neat and precise, as the mainstream model. After all, the number of person-hours put into developing the orthodox model exceeds those invested in the post-Keynesian analysis several million-fold. Nevertheless, post-Keynesians believe that it is better to develop a model which emphasizes the special characteristics of the economic world in which we live than to continually refine and polish a beautifully precise, but irrelevant, model. Moreover, when one is dealing with human activity and institutions, one may be, in the nature of things, outside the realm of the formally precise. For Keynes, as well as for post-Keynesians, the guiding motto is 'it is better to be roughly right than precisely wrong!'

After the revolution comes evolution. Post-Keynesians are trying to build on the logical foundations of Keynes's real-world analysis to resolve modern-day economic problems. They invite all who possess open minds to undertake the further evolution of Keynes's logical heresy and to explore a Keynesian (non-Euclidean) world where the axioms of ergodicity, of gross substitution, and neutral money are not universal truths applicable to all economic decision-making processes.

Unlike Samuelson's 'reconstructed Keynesians,' post-Keynesians do not believe that a regression to pre-Keynesian (Euclidean) axioms represents progress, no matter how much technological garb these postulates are wrapped in. Only in the world of Doublespeak can a regressive analytical structure be considered an advance!

Notes

1. This assumption is called the ergodic axiom.
2. For example, Samuelson, Solow and Tobin.
3. In organized security markets, when the market maker appears to be running out of liquidity, there is usually an institutional stand-by 'circuit breaker' that closes the market until the market maker can obtain sufficient liquidity to reopen it. During the period when the market is shut down, the asset can be considered illiquid.
4. Despite Friedman's use of the motto 'money matters', he remains faithful to the neutral money axiom and therefore assumes that the quantity of money cannot affect the long-run real outcome of his system. In his own description of his logical framework, Friedman (1974, p. 27) states: 'changes in the quantity of money as such *in the long run* have a negligible effect on real income so that nonmonetary forces are "all that matter" for changes in real income over decades and money "does not matter" . . . I regard the description of our position as "money is all that matters for changes in *nominal income* and for *short-run* changes in real income"as an exaggeration but one that gives the right flavor to our conclusions'.
5. These economists, however, have the difficulty that their logic is based on Say's Law, but their common sense tells them that unemployment is a problem which the system cannot solve without direct government interference. Thus they turned to *ad hoc* modifications of their neoclassical model – a short-side rule or a constrained demand function – to abrogate Say's Law and achieve a non-Walrasian equilibrium, at least in the short run.
6. Since, in this neoclassical world, engaging in a production process is assumed distasteful, it would seem axiomatic that no agents would contribute to production unless they planned to spend all their income on producible goods. Consequently, full employment hiring decisions should always bring forth sufficient demand to buy all the products of industry.

   This belief also underlies the rational expectations hypothesis via Lucas's aggregate supply analysis. Lucas believes there is no way of explaining real-world unemployment patterns except via an analysis of intertemporal substitutability of labour by optimizing households (see Lucas, 1983, p. 4). In order for households to achieve utility maximization solely in terms of the four arguments of Lucas's utility function – (1) today's consumption, (2) today's labour supply, (3) tomorrow's consumption, (4) tomorrow's labour supply – Lucas must assume that the intertemporal marginal propensity to spend on producible goods is unity. Say's Law therefore prevails by assumption. Unemployed workers are optimizing by preferring leisure today with rational expectations that they will get more real income per unit of effort tomorrow when they go back to work. Hence today's unemployed are not suffering any loss in permanent real welfare, i.e., the colliding lines that we observe are not really colliding it is all apparently an optical illusion.

   If, on the other hand, you believe, as Keynes did and post-Keynesians do, that today's unemployed know they are suffering a permanent loss in real well-being, then you must throw off the classical axioms of gross substitution *and* the axiom of reals, and enter the world of Keynes's non-Euclidean economics! In such a world, the desire to possess liquidity – liquid assets not producible by labour – is also an argument in any labour (factor owner) supply function.

7. Empirical work by Benjamin Friedman (1993) has demonstrated that the facts do not justify assuming gross substitutability among all assets in savers' portfolios.
8. Or even consumer durables.

References

Arrow, K.J. and Hahn, F.H. (1971), *General Competitive Analysis*, San Francisco: Holden-Day.

Barro, R.J. and Grossman, H.J. (1976), *Money, Employment and Inflation*, Cambridge: Cambridge University Press.

Clower, R.W. (1965), 'The Keynesian counterrevolution: a theoretical appraisal', in F.H. Hahn and F.P.R. Brechling (eds), *The Theory of Interest Rates*, London: Macmillan.

Danziger, S., Van der Gaag, J., Smolensky, E. and Taussig, M.K. (1982–83), 'The life cycle hypothesis and consumption behavior of the elderly', *Journal of Post Keynesian Economics*, **5**, 208–27.

Davidson, P. (1982–83), 'Rational expectations: a fallacious foundation for studying crucial decision making processes', *Journal of Post Keynesian Economics*, **5**, 182–98.

Friedman, B. (1993), 'The substitutability of debt and equity securities', National Bureau of Economic Research working paper 1130, May.

Friedman, M. (1974), 'A theoretical framework for monetary analysis', in R.J. Gordon (ed.), *Milton Friedman's Monetary Framework: A Debate with his Critics*, Chicago: Chicago University Press, Ch. 1.

Hahn, F.H. (1977), 'Keynesian economics and general equilibrium theory', in G.C. Harcourt (ed.), *Microfoundations of Macroeconomics*, London: Macmillan, pp. 14–49.

Hahn, F.H. (1983), *Money and Inflation*, Cambridge, MA: MIT Press.

Hicks, J.R. (1967), *Critical Essays in Monetary Theory*, London: Clarendon Press.

Hicks, J.R. (1979), *Causality in Economics*, New York: Basic Books.

Keynes, J.M. (1930), *A Treatise on Money*, Vol. I, London: Macmillan.

Keynes, J.M. (1936), *The General Theory of Employment, Interest and Money*, New York: Harcourt, Brace.

Keynes, J.M. (1973), 'A monetary theory of production', in D. Moggridge (ed.), *The Collected Writings of John Maynard Keynes*, Vol. 13, London: Macmillan.

Keynes, J.M. (1979), *The Collected Writings of John Maynard Keynes*, Vol. 29, edited by D. Moggridge, London: Macmillan.

Lucas, R.E. (1983), *Studies in Business Cycle Theory*, Cambridge, MA: MIT Press.

Malinvaud, E. (1977), *The Theory of Unemployment Reconsidered*, Oxford: Blackwell.

10 Minsky on financial instability

Elisabetta De Antoni

1. Introduction

In *Money, Interest and Prices* (1956), Patinkin showed that the market mechanism produces a coherent – if not optimal – result. In this way the neoclassical synthesis came to maturity, reabsorbing the Keynesian revolution and restoring a trust in the market mechanisms that new classical macroeconomics and real business cycle theory would later reaffirm. From his first writings (again in the mid-1950s) and all his life, Minsky questioned the omnipotence of the market. According to Minsky, the synthesis succeeded in incorporating *The General Theory* into neoclassical theory since it had amputated the most innovative and revolutionary aspects of Keynes's thought. In Minsky's 1975 rereading, a Keynes without uncertainty (as interpreted by the synthesis) is like a Hamlet without its Prince (p. 57). Uncertainty mainly hits financial markets and the expected returns on capital assets. Instead of the Smithian paradigm of the 'village fair', Keynes adopted the paradigm of 'Wall Street' (p. 58). Subjective evaluations ruling financial markets and expected returns on real assets are changeable and consequently investment is volatile. The equilibrium continuously changes with the passing of time and the system never succeeds in reaching it. 'Keynesian economics . . . is the economics of permanent disequilibrium' (p. 68). Starting from these presuppositions, Minsky resolved to 'recover the revolutionary thrust of *The General Theory*' (p. v). To this end, he focused on financial relations in an advanced capitalist economy, on investments under conditions of uncertainty, on the destabilizing processes and the instability characterizing advanced capitalistic economies. The following five sections will examine these developments of Minsky's thought, together with its recent applications to the real world. As we shall see, Minsky's economics is endogenously unstable, tending in sequence to an expansion, to a speculative boom and to a financial crisis followed by a debt deflation and a deep depression. It is a vibrant economy whose fundamental instability is upward. This, however, raises the question (examined in section 7) of the relationship between the economics of Minsky and the economics of Keynes. The problem is relevant since Minsky is generally considered to be one of the main post-Keynesian economists. The conclusions are summarized in section 8.

2. Finance and the key role of the relationship between debt commitments and profits

The basic criticism made by Minsky against the neoclassical synthesis is that it neglected financial relationships, precisely those in which instability lurks.

> In today's standard economic theory, an abstract non-financial economy is analyzed. Theorems about this abstract economy are assumed to be essentially valid for economies with complex financial and monetary institutions and usages. This logical jump is an act of faith . . . Modern orthodox economics is not and cannot be a basis for a serious approach to economic policy. (Minsky, 1986, p. 173)

From the beginning, Minsky places finance at the centre of his analysis. Advanced capitalist economies presuppose large and expensive long-term investments that are debt financed. The underlying assumption is that investments generate profits greater than debt commitments. In a world dominated by uncertainty, this assumption is not necessarily confirmed by facts. Thus the solidity of the financial system cannot be taken for granted. More generally, the coherence of a financially advanced economic system requires not only the clearing of all individual markets. It also requires that investments actually generate profits greater than debt commitments (Minsky, 1986, p. 141).

The relationship between debt commitments and profits is central to Minsky's analysis. To start with, it allowed him to attack the dominant theory in the following three directions.

1. Minsky rejected the neoclassical dichotomy – which had been brought back as a long-run equilibrium relationship by the neoclassical synthesis – between monetary and real sectors and between the determination of absolute prices (in the monetary sector) and relative prices (in the real sector). From Minsky's viewpoint, monetary and real sectors are intimately connected since investments are financed by indebtedness. Analogously, absolute prices are as important as relative ones: through their mark-up component, they have to generate sufficient profits to allow the fulfilment of firms' debt commitments.

2. Minsky questioned the efficacy of the price mechanism. According to Patinkin, unemployment implies a fall in money wages and prices that – by increasing real money balances – stimulates consumption and aggregate demand, thus driving the system to the full employment equilibrium. Minsky objected that, in a world with inside business debt, the price mechanism might work in a direction opposite to the one envisaged by Patinkin. As in Fisher (1933), price deflation increases the real value of debts and therefore depresses aggregate demand. Above all, in so far as wage and price deflation is associated with a fall in profits, it reduces firms' ability to fulfil inherited debt commitments. In this way it jeopardizes the robustness of the financial system, with possible depressing effects on long-term expectations and investments. In line with the experience of 1929–33 and the 'true' thought of Keynes, the fall in prices might thus accentuate unemployment instead of reabsorbing it (Minsky, 1975; 1978; 1986).

3. Minsky pointed out that financial stability cannot be taken for granted by assumption as it is in the neoclassical synthesis (and in the subsequent new classical macroeconomics). In his opinion: 'Significant incoherence occurs because market processes do not assure that effective demand always will be sufficient to yield profit flows large enough to enable "bankers" and "businessmen" to fulfill their commitments on debts . . .' (Minsky, 1980, p. 26).

The contraposition between debt commitments and profits is also the basis for the well-known distinction (Minsky, 1986, pp. 206–7) between hedge, speculative and ultraspeculative (or Ponzi) finance, which Minsky used to measure the degree of financial stability. In the case of hedge units, creditors and debtors foresee that realized and expected cash receipts are more than sufficient to meet all debt commitments now and in the future. On the contrary, in the case of non-hedge units, creditors and debtors foresee that the debt commitments exceed the realized and/or expected cash receipts for one or more initial periods. They foresee, however, that a future bonanza will reverse this relationship in subsequent periods. Non-hedge units in their turn can be divided into speculative and ultraspeculative (or Ponzi) units. In the case of speculative units, the expectation is that initially cash receipts will allow the fulfilment of interest payments but not the loan repayments. *Ceteris paribus*, speculative units are thus bound to initially roll over their debt. In the case of ultraspeculative or Ponzi units, the expectation is that initially cash receipts will be unable to meet both the loan repayments and the interest payments. *Ceteris paribus*, the indebtedness of these units is therefore destined to grow with the passing of time.

According to Minsky, the distinction between the three kinds of units can be traced to the synchronization between assets and liabilities. From this point of view, the hedge units are those funding the purchase of their long-term assets with long-term liabilities such as shares or long-term (fixed-interest rate) bonds.[1] On the other hand, non-hedge units are those funding their long-term assets with short-term indebtedness. While their debt commitments are concentrated in the initial phase of the life of their investment projects, their expected returns are concentrated in the final phase. As a consequence, these units initially plan to roll over (speculative) or even to increase (Ponzi) their indebtedness. The result is that, while hedge units are vulnerable only to the possibility that realized cash receipts turn out to be less than expected, speculative and ultraspeculative (or Ponzi) units – that have to borrow in order to fulfil their debt commitments – are also vulnerable to the availability and the cost of credit.

The mixture of hedge, speculative and Ponzi units present in the economy then becomes a measure of the robustness of the financial system. Let us take the example of a table: the less vulnerable to shocks, the more robust it is (Vercelli, 2001). The same holds for financial systems: a financial system is robust if dominated by hedge units and fragile if dominated by speculative and Ponzi units. In the first case, it is vulnerable only to real shocks; in the second case it is also vulnerable to financial shocks. Given the common practice of financing long-term positions with short-term indebtedness, firms, financial institutions and the government can be currently classified as speculative units. We thus live in a regime of financial fragility. In addition, any possible fall in profits or credit tightening is bound to reduce the hedge units and/or to increase the speculative and ultraspeculative units, thus raising the degree of financial fragility.

The relationship between debt commitments and profits is central to Minsky's theory (Minsky, 1975, p. 86). Given the limits of collective and individual rationality, in Minsky's world the recent experience is the main guide to the future. The ease with which payment commitments have been met in the recent past determines the confidence in the future fulfilment of debt commitments. This triggers an important deviation amplifying mechanism: 'A history of success will tend to diminish the margins of safety that business and bankers require and will thus tend to be associated with increased investment; a history of failure will do the opposite' (Minsky, 1986, p. 187).

3.   Minsky's 'financial' theory of investment
As we have seen, Minsky questions the Patinkin thesis according to which the system spontaneously tends to a long-run general equilibrium. As if this were not enough, however, he also rejects the less ambitious concept of short-run equilibrium. As a consequence of the volatility of expectations, this is a constantly changing equilibrium that the system can reach only by chance and for an instant (Minsky, 1975, p. 86). With this,

Minsky totally rejects the 'crutch' represented by the concept of equilibrium. Instead of speaking of equilibrium or disequilibrium, Minsky (1986, p. 176) – just like Joan Robinson (1971) – prefers to refer to states of tranquillity hiding within themselves disruptive forces destined to gain strength with the passing of time. In his view, 'instability is determined by mechanisms within the system, not outside it; our economy is not unstable because it is shocked by oil, wars or monetary surprises, but because of its nature' (Minsky, 1986, p. 172).[2]

Minsky's theory, as the theory that Minsky attributes to Keynes, is at the same time 'an investment theory of the business cycle and a financial theory of investment' (Minsky, 1978, p. 30). From the first point of view, it is a theory that identifies investment as the first cause of income fluctuations (Minsky, 1986, p. 171). According to Minsky, the role of consumption is minor and mainly consists in its multiplicative effects. As far as investment determination is concerned, Minsky claims that the basic characteristic of a capitalist economy is the existence of two prices: the (more volatile and uncertain) price of capital assets and the price of current production. Belonging to both categories, investment has the function of aligning the two prices. By so doing, however, it attracts uncertainty, passing it on to the rest of the economy.[3]

In Figure 10.1, the two prices at the basis of Minsky's analysis are shown by the broken lines, which appear to be similar to those in Tobin's q theory of investment.[4] The broken horizontal line Pk gives at the same time the price of capital assets – equal to the present value PV of expected profits Πe – and the demand price for investment goods. Capital assets are valuable since they are a source of expected profits which – depending on the scarcity of capital and therefore on expected demand instead of on the marginal productivity of capital – are prone to a high uncertainty. The price of capital assets is equal to the present value of these expected profits; by analogy, it also represents the demand price for investment goods. The rising broken curve Pi gives the supply price of investment goods, similar to the price of current production. It is composed of the technologically determined cost (which, given the productive capacity, from a certain point curves upwards) plus the interest on the short-run financing required by the production of investment

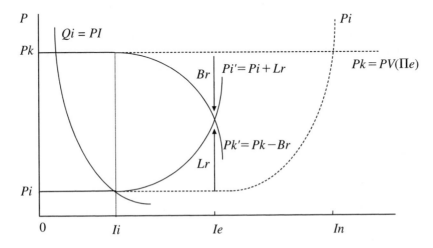

Figure 10.1   The determination of investment

goods plus the mark-up. The intersection between the broken demand price horizontal line Pk and the broken supply price curve Pi determines the level In of investments in Figure 10.1. This level could be defined as 'notional' since – up to now – firms do not yet know if and how it can be funded.

Having identified the profitable opportunities for investment (In in Figure 10.1) whose present value $Pk = PV(\Pi e)$ is higher than the cost Pi, firms have to establish how to finance the purchase of new machinery. To this end, first they have to foresee the internal funds (gross profits minus taxes and debt commitments) they will be able to accumulate during the gestation period 'between the decision to invest and the completion of investment' (Minsky, 1986, p. 185). The difference between the value of profitable investments and the expected internal funds will give the extent of external funds (loans, bonds or equities financing) demanded by firms at the moment of purchase. The supply of funds aligns itself to the demand of funds.

The above-mentioned financial considerations are represented by the solid lines in Figure 10.1. The equilateral hyperbola $Qi = PI$ gives the combinations of P and I compatible with the internal funds Qi that the firms foresee accumulating during the gestation period of investment. The intersection of the equilateral hyperbola Qi and the supply price curve Pi gives the level of investment – Ii in Figure 10.1 – that can be financed with the expected internal funds. For investment levels greater than Ii, firms will have to resort to indebtedness. Indebtedness in its turn involves the risk – a borrower's risk (Br) for firms and a lender's risk (Lr) for their financiers – that expectations go wrong and that, once installed, investment generates profits less than debt commitments. *Ceteris paribus*, this risk increases with debt commitments and therefore with indebtedness.

For investment levels greater than the one that can be internally funded, i.e. greater than Ii in Figure 10.1, the curve of the demand price for and the curve of the supply price of investment goods have to be adjusted for the increasing risks related to indebtedness. The result is again represented by the solid lines in Figure 10.1. The borrower's risk-adjusted demand price curve, shown as $Pk' = Pk - Br$ in Figure 10.1, is obtained by subtracting the borrower's risk Br from the original demand price Pk. To quote Minsky: 'Borrower's risk shows up in a declining demand price for capital assets. It is not reflected in any financing charges; it mirrors the view that increased exposure to default will be worthwhile only if there is a compensating potential capital gain' (see Minsky, 1986, p. 190). The risk-adjusted supply price curve, shown as $Pi' = Pi + Lr$ in Figure 10.1, is obtained by adding the lender's risk Lr to the original supply price Pi. To quote Minsky again:

> The supply schedule of investment goods rises after some output. However, lender's risk imparts a rising thrust to the supply conditions for capital assets independent of technological-supply conditions. This rising thrust takes a concrete form in the financing conditions that bankers set. In loan and bond contracts, lender's risk is expressed in higher stated interest rates, in terms to maturity, and in covenants and codicils. (Minsky, 1986, p. 192)

The intersection between the solid line of the borrower's risk-adjusted demand price Pk' and the solid line of the lender's risk-adjusted supply price Pi' determines the effective level of investments, Ie in Figure 10.1. The excess of effective investments Ie over internally financed investments Ii shows the level of indebtedness. The gap between the original demand price $Pk = PV(\Pi e)$ and the original supply price Pi, corresponding to Ie, gives the safety margins required by firms and their financiers in the face of the risks related to indebtedness.[5] Together with the capitalization factor[6] used to calculate the original demand price $Pk = PV(\Pi e)$, these safety margins are the channel through which uncertainty about the future fulfilment of debt commitments influences investment decisions.

In order to analyse the implications of the preceding analysis, let us see what happens if the rate of interest increases. The initial situation is represented by the solid lines in Figure 10.2. Following Minsky (1986, p. 195), the long-term rate of interest is used to actualize expected profits; it therefore negatively affects the original demand price for investment $Pk = PV(\Pi e)$. The short-run rate of interest represents a cost for the producers of investment goods and thus positively affects the original supply price of investment goods. In the presence of a general increase in the level of interest rates, the original (and consequently the adjusted) demand price for capital assets thus falls as long as long-term interest rates increase, while the original (and consequently the adjusted) supply price of investment output rises as short-term interest rates rise. As shown by the shift from the solid to the broken lines in Figure 10.2, the over-all effect of an increase in interest rates is a fall in effective investments from $Ie0$ to $Ie1$.[7] Minsky's analysis thus confirms the traditional negative relationship between investments and the rate of interest. Its novelty is that this relationship remains in the background. As we shall see, dominating the scene are expectations and the degree of confidence placed on them.

The role of the determinants of investment that are different from interest rates – given, respectively, by profit expectations (Qi, Πe) and by uncertainty about the future fulfilment of debt commitments (Br, Lr) – is summarized in Figure 10.3, which shows the case of an unexpected increase in realized profits. The initial situation is again represented by the solid lines. To start with, following Minsky (1986, pp. 193–4), the increase in profits gives rise to an increase in the available internal funds Qi, thus causing a rightward shift of the equilateral hyperbola $Qi = PI$, of the level of internally financed investments Ii, and of the borrower's and lender's risks starting from Ii. As shown by point $0'$, the result is an internally funded increase in effective investments (from $Ie0$ to $Ie0'$). This, however, is not

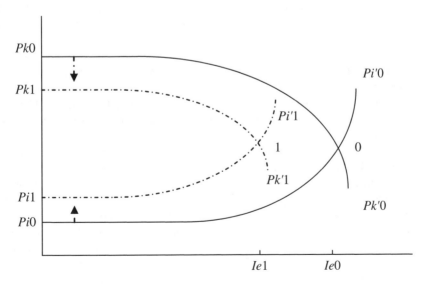

Figure 10.2   The effect on investments of an increase in interest rates

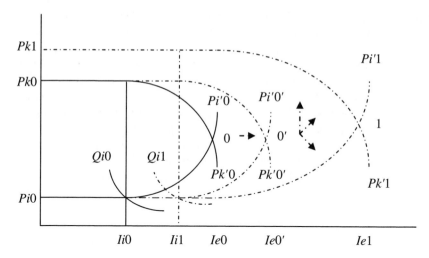

Figure 10.3   The effects on investments of an unexpected increase in profits

yet the end of the story. By increasing profits expected after the installation of the invest-ment goods Πe, the rise in current profits has two further effects. First, it increases the original demand price for investment goods $Pk = PV(\Pi e)$. Second, it increases the confi-dence in the future fulfilment of debt commitments, thus reducing the borrower's and lender's risks.[8] In both cases, the result is a further increase in effective investment (from *Ie0′* to *Ie1* in Figure 10.3) that this time is financed by indebtedness. *Implicitly*, Minsky is thus assuming that the unexpected rise in current profits is perceived as permanent. If it were not so, according to his analysis, current profits would not have any effect on exter-nally financed investments in Figure 10.3.

Minsky's theory is a 'financial' theory of investment under conditions of uncertainty, a theory inspired by Keynes (Minsky, 1972) that focuses on the ways in which investment is financed and on the perceived risks connected to indebtedness. Its main implications emerge form Figure 10.3. An increase in expected profits gives rise to an increase in both internally and externally financed investments. In its turn, the higher indebtedness is asso-ciated to lower safety margins. Economic growth thus leads to a more fragile financial system. The just-mentioned implications, however, are anything but granted. They are the result of the particular role assigned to profits and of the particular shapes assigned to the *Pk* and *Pi* curves.

To start with, it is worthwhile recalling that the equilateral hyperbola *Qi* in Figure 10.3 refers to expected internal funds and therefore profits.[9] Since expected internal funds are given by assumption, higher investments inevitably require higher indebtedness. In his subsequent works, Minsky recognizes that investments are a source of profits and thus of internal funds. In some passages (Minsky, 1975, p. 114; 1986, pp. 193–4; 1980), he then tries to incorporate this phenomenon in his investment function. First, he assumes that – once realized – effective investments *Ie1* cause an unexpected increase in internal funds analogous to the one shown by the rightward shift of the equilateral hyperbola from *Qi0* to *Qi1* in Figure 10.3. By so doing, he *implicitly* assumes that investments can only partially self-finance themselves. In addition, Minsky *implicitly* assumes that the increase

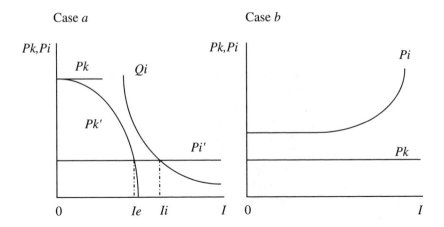

Figure 10.4   The situations after a crisis

in profits is perceived as permanent. This increase thus raises both profit expectations and confidence, stimulating externally financed investments from *Ie*0′ to *Ie*1 in Figure 10.3.[10] The whole aforementioned procedure does not seem fully convincing; the same obviously holds for Minsky's conclusions.

Turning to the shapes of the functions, let us imagine that the adjusted demand price curve *Pk*′ is downward sloping from the beginning and/or that the adjusted supply price curve *Pi*′ is upward sloping from the beginning. In such a case, the effective level of investments (*Ie*) determined by the intersection between the two curves might turn out to be less than the level that can be internally financed (*Ii*). Internal funds would be used not only to finance investments, but also to reduce indebtedness or to accumulate financial assets. Above all, the increase in profits would not cause any rise in investments and might be used to reduce indebtedness, instead of stimulating it. Indeed, Minsky takes into account the case (case *a* in Figure 10.4) of an adjusted demand price curve downward sloping from the beginning which gives rise to effective investments *Ie* smaller than the level that can be internally financed *Ii* (1975, p. 127).[11] Minsky also takes into account the case (case *b* in Figure 10.4) of 'present value reversal', in which the original demand price falls below the original supply price and consequently firms have no profitable opportunity to invest (ibid., 1986, p. 195). In Minsky's opinion, however, these are exceptional cases characterizing the situations after a crisis (1975, p. 115; 1986, p. 195). Under normal conditions, the investment function is the one described above.

Which are, then, the 'normal conditions' that Minsky has in mind? As we have seen, Minsky refers (i) to a horizontal original supply price curve *Pi* and (ii) to an original demand price curve *Pk* placed above the *Pi* curve and again horizontal. Minsky is thus referring, respectively, to an economy with unutilized resources and profitable investment opportunities, in which firms and their financiers expect with certainty that any increase in output will find its own demand.[12] Under these circumstances, firms use all their profits and borrow in order to invest. Investment is limited by the safety margins required to offset the risks connected to indebtedness, not by the insufficient profitability of investments or by the risk of negative yields. Any increase in profits is not merely reinvested.

Being perceived as permanent, it improves expectations and confidence, thus stimulating indebtedness and externally financed investments. To sum up, what Minsky seems to consider as normal is a vibrant and euphoric economy with unutilized resources.

4. The interdependence between investments and profits and the related deviation-amplifying processes

Minsky conjectured the financial instability hypothesis from the beginning (Minsky, 1957). To justify it analytically, he first introduced his investment theory with the related relationship from profits to investments (Minsky, 1972). Then he added the relationship from investments to profits (1975, p. 114). The resulting interdependence (Minsky, 1980, 1986) became the 'keystone' of the deviation-amplifying processes underlying Minsky's financial instability hypothesis. Making reference to a vibrant and euphoric economy, Minsky's writings generally dwell longer on the expansionary phase of the cycle. Following Minsky, Figure 10.5 thus assumes an initial increase in investments.

Let us consider the initial link (from investments to profits) in Figure 10.5. In his works, Minsky adopts a conception *à la* Levy–Kaleki–Kaldor, according to which income distribution mirrors the level and composition of aggregate demand rather than input productivity. In clearing the goods market, income fluctuations align profits to the sum of investments, government budget, net exports and capitalists' consumption net of workers' savings.[13] The initial increase in investment thus generates an equal increase in profits in Figure 10.5.[14] Profits, however, in their turn affect investments. According to the investment function, the increase in realized profits has three effects: (i) it raises profits expected during the gestation period of investment, thus increasing expected internal funds (Qi); (ii) it raises profits expected after the investments are installed and used in production (Πe), thus increasing the original demand price of investments $Pk = PV(\Pi e)$; and (iii) it raises the confidence (*Conf*) in future profits exceeding debt commitments, thus reducing the borrower's and lender's risks. As shown in Figure 10.5, the three effects imply a second increase in investment, which is financed partly internally (Ii) and partly by indebtedness (*Iind*). This new increase in investments brings us back to the starting point in Figure 10.5, giving rise to further increases in profits and investments. As shown by the solid arrows in Figure 10.5, the interdependence between investments and profits thus becomes the basis of an upward spiral involving all the variables concerned.

The aforementioned deviation-amplifying mechanisms are fuelled (or strengthened) by their repercussions on the money market. This brings us to the broken arrows in Figure 10.5. The first upward-sloping broken arrow refers to the supply side of the money market. In Minsky's view, money is endogenously created and influences the demand for

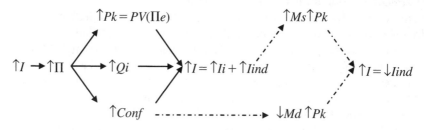

Figure 10.5   The deviation-amplifying processes

non-monetary assets, rather than for goods. In so far as the increase in indebtedness implies an increase in bank credit, it also implies an increase in money supply *Ms*. The result is an increase in the price of capital assets *Pk* which, according to Minsky's investment function, determines a new (this time externally financed) increase of investments on the extreme right of Figure 10.5.

The horizontal broken arrow in Figure 10.5 refers to the demand side of the money market. As a premise, Minsky (1986) denies that the main characteristic of money lies in having a fixed price (the prices of goods and assets on which its purchasing power depends are variable) or in being the medium of exchange (in socialist countries money was the medium of exchange but did not have any special role in the economy). According to Minsky, the main characteristic of money is that it allows the fulfilment of the payment commitments connected to indebtedness and productive activity. Money is mainly demanded since it offers 'insurance services' against bankruptcy (p. 180). The value of these insurance services depends on the confidence in the future. In Figure 10.5, the greater confidence due to the rise in profits thus determines a portfolio reallocation from money to non-monetary assets that increases capital asset prices. The result is a new increase in externally financed investments on the extreme right of Figure 10.5. This increase brings us back to the starting point in the figure, where the aforementioned deviation-amplifying mechanisms start again.[15]

To sum up, if we consider Figure 10.5 as a whole, the initial increase in investments triggers an upward spiral that involves all the variables concerned (with the only exception being the demand for money, which falls). According to this spiral, growth is associated not only with increasing indebtedness but also with an increasing confidence, i.e. with decreasing safety margins. With the passing of time, the financial system becomes more and more fragile. Sooner or later, a growing economy will become prone to financial crises. As we have seen, however, this conclusion presupposes a vibrant and euphoric economy in which profits are not only reinvested but are also perceived as permanent, thus stimulating indebtedness and confidence.

5.   Minsky's financial instability hypothesis

In 1936 Jacob Viner proposed the rigidity-based interpretation of Keynes destined to become dominant thanks to the neoclassical synthesis. In 1937, Keynes rejected that interpretation, pointing out that *The General Theory* was a theory of the fluctuations in production and employment originating from financial markets. Minsky traced his financial instability hypothesis to the reply of Keynes to Viner (Minsky, 1977). Such a hypothesis found its most mature formulation in his 1986 volume, *Stabilizing an Unstable Economy*.

The starting point of Minsky's financial instability hypothesis is that 'Stability – or tranquillity – is destabilising' (Minsky, 1975, p. 127; 1978, p. 37), and that 'the fundamental instability is upward' (1975, p. 165; 1986, pp. 119–20). A period of tranquillity (in which the financial system is robust and there are no relevant shocks, so that profits are systematically greater than debt commitments) increases the confidence of firms and financial intermediaries, thus reducing both the value placed upon liquidity and the borrowers' and lenders' risks. This means, respectively, that the price of capital assets increases and that the desired safety margins decrease. According to Minsky's investment function, the result is an increase in investment financed by indebtedness (1986, p. 183). This increase, in its turn, triggers the deviation-amplifying mechanisms described in the previous section. In this way, the expansion turns into a boom financed by indebtedness.

At this point, Minsky focuses on two drawbacks of the boom. The first refers to the general euphoria. The increasing confidence implies decreasing safety margins. Firms' debt commitments increase more rapidly than profits, ending by rising above them. Indebtedness not only grows fast, but increasingly takes the shape of short-term debt, which requires the repayment of principal at a faster pace than the cash generated by the underlying operation permits. Given the expectation of a future bonanza, firms start financing by indebtedness not only the principal (speculative financing) but also interest payments (ultraspeculative or Ponzi finance). The fulfilment of debt commitments is no longer based on profits but, respectively, on the rolling over or the increase in indebtedness. From being initially robust, the financial system becomes fragile. Turning to the second drawback, we observe that the persistence of the boom inevitably ends up creating either bottlenecks in the financial system or inflationary pressures, pushing the central bank in a deflationary direction. In both cases, the result is an increase in the rate of interest.[16]

The rise in the interest rate does not just end the boom, turning the investment–profit–investment chain into a downward spiral. In a now fragile financial system, it sets off the financial crisis: firms are no longer able to fulfil their debt commitments in the normal way, i.e. by profits or indebtedness (Minsky, 1982b). The unexpected increase in the cost of funds is associated with the unexpected fall in (the yet insufficient) profits. The fulfilment of inherited debt commitments would thus require an increase in indebtedness. This solution, however, is neither desirable nor possible since the confidence underlying indebtedness fades away. Given this situation, the primary aim of firms (shared by their financiers) becomes to fulfil inherited debt commitments and to reduce indebtedness rather than finance new investments. The only way to reach the new target is by the sale of assets, which after the boom are mainly illiquid assets. This, however, implies a fall in the price of the assets which, by reducing the net wealth of firms and financial intermediaries, reinforces the need to squeeze indebtedness by selling assets. Assets prices fall precipitously. The fall of capital asset prices strengthens the fall of investments and profits, and vice versa. The crisis thus turns into a debt deflation, which in Minsky's framework is an asset price as well as a profit deflation (Minsky, 1992). The progressive fall in profits and asset prices will end by making the fulfilment of debt commitments impossible. The consequence will be a wave of bankruptcies, which in its turn will end in a deep depression.

Destruction, however, is creative. Only hedge units (able to fulfil their debt commitments by profits) survive. Under these circumstances, a phase of tranquillity will suffice to reactivate the sequence just described. According to Minsky's financial instability hypothesis, the system will again experience an expansion, a speculative boom, a financial crisis and a debt deflation, along with a deep depression. Turning to the real world, Minsky finds confirmation of his analysis. The financial instability of the American economy, which he had previously denounced (Minsky, 1963), surfaced in the mid-1960s, giving rise to the crises of 1966, 1970, 1974–75, 1979 and 1982 (Minsky, 1986). Financial instability had, however, also characterized the periods preceding the two world wars. This confirms that financial crises are systemic and not idiosyncratic (Minsky, 1991). Looking ahead, Minsky wonders whether 'It' can happen again (Minsky, 1982a). 'It' is the Great Depression, and Minsky's answer is affirmative.

Given the tendency of capitalist economies to financial crises, followed by debt deflations and deep depressions, the issue of the efficacy of economic policies acquires a crucial
role. From this point of view, Minsky does not place much faith in monetary policy:
'Monetary policy to constrain undue expansion and inflation operates by way of disrupting financial markets and asset values. Monetary policy to induce expansion operates
by interest rates and the availability of credit, which do not yield increased investment if
current and anticipated profits are low' (1986, pp. 303–4). Instead of aiming to control
the money supply or the behaviour of the economy, the central bank should focus on its
function as lender of last resort. By enabling the financing of financial institutions and by
sustaining asset prices (as well as by carefully regulating the financial system), the central
bank might prevent financial crisis, so removing the threat of debt deflations and deep
depressions.

In fact, Minsky assigns to fiscal policy the task of promoting full employment and stabilizing the economy. As he puts it, 'Fiscal policies are more powerful economic control
weapons than monetary manipulations' (1986, p. 304). According to Minsky, the role of
fiscal policy is not only to underpin demand and to drive the system to full employment,
so offsetting the essential failure of a capitalist market economy to provide sufficient
aggregate demand. Through fiscal stabilizers, 'big government' can protect the robustness
of the financial system by supporting profits and by issuing government bonds during
recessions. Finally, big government has the function to reduce inequality and insecurity
and to promote a high-performance path to competitiveness (as an alternative to the low-
wage path). This requires not only incentives for private investment but also public investment in education and training, science and technology, and infrastructure.

According to Minsky (1982a, p. xi), 'The most significant economic event of the era
since World War II is something that has not happened: there has not been a deep and
long-lasting depression.' In Minsky's view, the merit of this success goes to the lending of
last resort by the central bank and to the presence of a big government. We must thus
proceed in this direction, since 'laissez-faire is a prescription for economic disaster'
(Minsky and Whalen, 1996, p. 161).

6. The applications of Minsky's financial instability hypothesis to the real world

Minsky's analysis has been recently utilized to interpret important instability episodes,
which are obviously related to situations of upward instability. As we have seen, during
his life, Minsky himself saw a confirmation of his analysis in the numerous financial crises
experienced by the American economy. Some authors extend Minsky's preoccupations
with the financial stability of the USA to the present. Together with other economists of
the Levy Economics Institute, Godley et al. (2004) focus on the financial imbalances currently characterizing the American economy. Given the heavy indebtedness of the private
sector and the large government and external deficits, the maintenance of satisfactory
growth in the medium term will require a consistent devaluation of the dollar. This will
be coupled with a fall in the domestic absorption of goods and services, which will impart
a deflationary impulse to the rest of the world.

Sawyer (2001) criticizes the European single currency from a Minskyan perspective.
Minsky's approach would have implied rather different policy arrangements for the
European monetary union. The primary task assigned to the European Central Bank would
have been financial (rather than price) stability. The importance of lender-of-last-resort

interventions in aborting and containing debt deflations (and therefore the thrust towards deep depressions) would have been recognized instead of being ignored. The role of fiscal policy in ensuring financial stability and in supporting the economy would have been recognized, instead of subordinating fiscal to monetary policy in controlling inflation. The scope of fiscal policy would have been expanded through the institution of a European federal budget instead of being limited through the introduction of constraints on national government budgets. The deflationary impacts of fiscal constraints that led to the recent loosening of the Growth and Stability Pact would have been recognized in advance of their taking place.

Minsky's financial instability theory was mainly developed in the context of a closed economy. Its extension to the open economy, however, gave rise to stimulating interpretations of the crisis that took place in Southeast Asia in 1997–98. According to Arestis and Glickman (2002), the possibility of borrowing abroad fuels both the upward instability and the tendency towards financial fragility of open, liberalized, developing economies. In the absence of capital controls – and especially if interest rates are low in the major financial centres – liquid funds will switch into these economies, reinforcing their upward instability. Through the increase in domestic deposits and in domestic security prices, capital inflow will also stimulate both the availability of credit and the propensity to borrow, strengthening the tendency to a higher indebtedness. In addition, units which borrow abroad will have to fulfil their debt commitments in foreign currency and thus will also become vulnerable to movements in the exchange rate. The increase in indebtedness, together with the denomination in foreign currency of part of it, will stimulate the tendency towards financial fragility. The economy will thus become prone (i) to a crisis that is domestic in origin but impacts on its external situation (a '*d to e*' crisis), (ii) to a crisis that is external in origin but impacts on its domestic situation (an '*e to d*' crisis), and (iii) to deviation-amplifying interactions between (i) and (ii).

The '*d to e*' crisis is essentially the one described in section 5. Once more, however, the openness of the economy accentuates the problems. When the crisis evolves into a debt deflation and a big depression, a flight towards liquidity will ensue. Some investors will seek to diversify the now larger liquidity by shifting into other currencies. Others will act in anticipation of behaviour of this kind. The domestic currency will be sold heavily, and this will trigger an exchange rate crisis. The devaluation will increase the difficulties of the units with debt commitments in foreign currency and cash receipts in domestic currency, thus intensifying the crisis.

The opening of the economy introduces also the possibility of an '*e to d*' crisis. Capital inflow sustains the domestic exchange rate and thus worsens the current account. As the ratio between foreign indebtedness and foreign reserves grows, speculators may begin to doubt the ability of the state to support the currency and move, possibly on a massive scale, against the currency concerned. As a consequence of the devaluation, units with debt commitments in foreign currency and cash receipts in domestic currency will experience more difficulties in fulfilling their debt commitments. Capital outflow will imply a decrease in domestic deposits as well as the sale of domestic assets and thus the fall in their prices. As a consequence, the rolling over of domestic debts will also become more difficult. The devaluation can thus trigger a financial crisis. Under the pressures emanating from the international financial system, during both the '*d to e*' and the '*e to d*' crises, the central bank will raise interest rates in order to bolster the exchange rate. In an open economy, monetary policy thus ends up accentuating the debt-deflation processes instead of mitigating them as Minsky suggested.

According to Arestis and Glickman (2002), the crisis experienced in Southeast Asia in 1997–98 is an '*e to d*' crisis. Its distinctiveness is that the crisis experienced by the various countries coincided with the spread of financial liberalization processes. Financial liberalization sweeps away the rules and conventions which previously governed the financial system, speeding up the process by which debt ratios rise. It also weakens the barrier of financial conservatism which, in Minsky's view, acts to contain speculative behaviours. From a Minskyan perspective, the connection between liberalization, financial instability and financial crises is thus perfectly understandable. As Minsky claimed, controls on domestic financial systems and on capital movements preserve the stability of the financial system.

Kregel (2001) also offers a Minskyan interpretation of the Asian financial crisis. Both directly and through its effects on the exchange rates, a rise in foreign interest rates increases the debt commitments in the indebted developing countries. Whether this greater fragility turns into instability and crises will depend on the willingness of foreign banks to extend foreign currency lending. If foreign banks are unwilling to do so, the 'normal functioning' of the financial system will be compromised. The result will be a Minskyan debt-deflation process. Firms and banks will try to liquidate their stocks of goods and assets in order to fulfil their debt commitments and reduce their debts. The consequent fall in the price of their products, in the price of their assets and in the value of the domestic currency, however, will further diminish their ability to fulfil debt commitments and to reduce debts.

Mistaking the crisis for a traditional balance of payments crisis, the IMF required a reduction in government expenditure and tight monetary targets. This, however, was the opposite of what was required from the point of view of stopping a Minskyan debt-deflation crisis. A slowdown in domestic demand could only reduce the cash receipts of firms, while the increase in interest rates could only increase their financing costs. A more reasonable response would have been to attempt to slow down the withdrawal of foreign lending and to ease the conditions of payment. At the same time, expansionary monetary and fiscal policies should have been adopted in order to reinforce the financial system and hinder debt deflation.

Arestis (2001) compares the Southeast Asia crises of 1997–98 with the crises of the period 1977–96. All these crises have some features in common. They were preceded by a process of financial deregulation that prompted a climate of euphoria and speculation. However, those of 1997–98 were currency speculative-induced crises while those of 1977–96 were balance of payments speculative-induced crises. The crisis of 1997–98 was triggered by the devaluation caused by the reversal of capital flow due to the rise of the ratio between foreign indebtedness and foreign reserves. The origin of the crises of the period 1977–96 was, instead, the balance of payments deficit due to an unsustainable speculative consumption boom. In any case, both kinds of crises are perfectly understandable from a Minskyan perspective.

The frequency and the enormous costs of financial crises point to the need for a reform of the international financial system. The massive increase in the volume of foreign exchange transactions over recent years, relative to the volume of international trade, implies that the financial transactions influenced by differential interest rates and by expected exchange rate movements have grown relative to transactions related to international trade. According to Sawyer (2001), this is not unconnected with the higher volatility of exchange rates observed in the post-Bretton Woods era. In the presence of foreign indebtedness, the exchange rate volatility can threaten the calculations of either the lender or the borrower, thus increasing financial instability. On this basis, Sawyer (2001) suggests (i) measures to reduce international financial flows not related to trade or to foreign direct investment, for instance the introduction of a Tobin tax, (ii) the regulation of global financial institutions, (iii) the institution of an international lender of last resort, and (iv) the international coordination of domestic and exchange rate policies.

7.   Minsky as an interpreter of Keynes

Many objections can be raised about Minsky's financial instability hypothesis. Between the lines, sometimes Minsky seems conscious of them. This might be why he prefers to speak of a financial instability 'hypothesis' rather than of a financial instability 'theory'. Objections aside, an interesting question is: what is the relationship between Minsky and Keynes?

Minsky is generally classified as one of the main exponents of the post-Keynesian School (see King, 2002 and the following debate in the *Journal of post-Keynesian Economics*). Minsky himself presented his vision as an authentic interpretation/a legitimate extension of Keynes's thought. In Minsky's rereading, Keynes lived through the experience of the Great Depression. He thus dwelt upon the particular case of an economy which, as a consequence of a financial crisis followed by a debt deflation, fell into a deep depression. Under these circumstances, the demand price for investment falls below the supply price, resulting in a collapse in investments and thus in profits. Pessimism gives rise to a perfectly elastic demand for money: it is the liquidity trap according to which money loses the ability to influence the interest rate. The only way out is represented by government expenditure.

According to Minsky, however, Keynes considered the Great Depression as only an extreme case. Although he did not develop it, Keynes had in mind a cyclical perspective:

> The evidence that it is legitimate to interpret *The General Theory* as dealing with an economy that is cyclical by reason of its essential institutions is spread throughout the volume. References to cyclical phenomena occur not only in chapter 22 of *The General Theory*, 'Notes on the Trade Cycle', which explicitly deals with business cycles, and in the rebuttal to Viner in *The Quarterly Journal of Economics* of February 1937, but throughout his book. When *The General Theory* is read from the perspective that the subject matter is a sophisticated capitalist economy, whose past and whose future entail business cycles, the ratifying references for an interpretation within a cyclical context are everywhere evident. (Minsky, 1975, p. 58)

From a cyclical perspective, recessions can be traced back to the preceding boom. Quoting Minsky:

> In some important sense, what was lost from the insights of the 1920s and 1930s is more significant than what has been retained . . . The spectacular panics, debt deflations, and deep depressions that historically followed a speculative boom as well the recovery from depressions are of lesser importance in the analysis of instability than the developments over a period characterized by sustained growth that lead to the emergence of fragile and unstable financial structures. (Minsky, 1986, p. 173)

We thus come to the main point: Minsky's fundamental instability is upward (1975, p. 165; 1980, p. 518). The aim of Minsky was to bring back Keynes's theory to its cyclical perspective (Minsky, 1975, pp. 79–80). With his financial instability hypothesis, however, Minsky introduced an upward instability which seems to be totally foreign to Keynes's thought. What are, then, the relationships between Minsky and Keynes? Undoubtedly, the basic vision of the two authors is the same. Let us think for instance about the relevance attributed to uncertainty and accumulation, about the refusal of the assumption of individual and collective rationality, about the crucial role assigned to institutions and about the attention paid to the socio-political dimension. According to the present rereading, however, Minsky and Keynes refer to different realities. Minsky looks at a vibrant economy with upward instability, naturally inclined to overinvestment and overindebtedness. Keynes looks at a depressed economy, tending to chronic underinvestment and thus to high and long-lasting unemployment.

Taking into account the analogies and the differences, the two authors might be considered as two faces of the same coin, two faces that look, however, in opposite directions. From this perspective, Minsky might be considered as an author who has extended the economics of Keynes to a vibrant and euphoric economy, making it even more general and modern, and influencing a whole generation of Keynesian economists. If Keynes had observed the US economy of the last 15 years, he too might have started to worry about upward instability. On the other hand, Minsky's upward instability seems totally foreign to today's European economies.

8. Conclusions

In Minsky's rereading, a Keynes without uncertainty is like a Hamlet without its Prince. Uncertainty mainly hits financial markets and the expected returns on capital assets. Minsky thus focused on financial relations in an advanced capitalist economy, on investment under conditions of uncertainty and on the cyclical nature of the economic process. By so doing, he became one of the main exponents of the post-Keynesian School.

Our presentation of Minsky's thought shows, however, that there are important differences between Minsky and Keynes. Minsky looks at a vibrant economy with upward instability, naturally inclined to overinvestment and overindebtedness. Keynes looks at a depressed economy tending to chronic underinvestment and to high and long-lasting unemployment. The two authors might, however, be considered as two faces of the same coin, two faces that look in opposite directions. From this perspective Minsky might be considered as an author who has extended the economics of Keynes, making it even more general and modern.

Notes

1. Minsky does not specify the clause of fixed interest rates. In the absence of this clause, however, his reasoning would give rise to the ambiguity described in Arestis and Glickman (2002). A hedge unit with long-term variable interest rate indebtedness would remain vulnerable to the conditions prevailing in the financial markets. Thus, contrarily to what follows, the incidence of hedge units would not mirror the stability of the financial system intended as invulnerability to financial shocks.
2. On this important aspect, see Vercelli (2001). According to Vercelli, Keynes referred to a short-run unemployment equilibrium destined to fluctuate whenever current views about the future change. Minsky had in mind a system whose structure and whose dynamic behaviour endogenously change with the passing of time.
3. On this, see Kregel (1992).
4. On this, see for instance Tobin and Brainard (1977).

5. If realized profits turn out to be less than those expected, safety margins will increase firms' capacity to meet debt commitments. They consequently increase the robustness of the financial system, intended as its capacity to absorb the shocks under conditions of normal functioning (i.e. without implying the sale of assets). If realized profits turn out to be equal to or greater than expected ones, safety margins will represent a compensation to firms and their financiers in the face of the respective risks.

6. To quote Minsky (1986, p. 183), 'As sketched in the previous section, the quantity of money, the value placed upon liquidity, and the income and liquidity characteristics of the various capital and financial assets lead to the set of prices of capital and financial assets.' As we shall see, according to Minsky the value placed on liquidity is positively related to the level of uncertainty.

7. In Figure 10.2, the level of investments Ii (from which borrower's and lender's risks start) that can be financed by the given internal funds Qi falls if the original supply price Pi increases. This is why, in the shift from the solid to the broken lines, the bifurcation between the original and the adjusted curves moves leftwards.

8. Obviously, the fall in the lender's risk (Lr) turns into a decrease in the lenders' risk-adjusted supply price (Pi') only if the financing contract allows the lender to modify the terms of the financing (see Minsky, 1986, p. 194).

9. For this important aspect, see Lavoie and Seccareccia (2001).

10. Quoting Minsky: 'If the actual cash flows . . . exceed the anticipated cash flows . . ., then the amount of external financing actually required will be smaller than expected. When this occurs, the balance sheet with the newly acquired capital assets will be less encumbered by debt than originally anticipated. Such a better-than-anticipated balance sheet means that both the firms and its bankers view the investing units as having unused borrowing power, and the financing conditions for subsequent investments will be more favorable' (Minsky, 1986, pp. 193–4).

11. Minsky refers this case to an individual firm characterized by a high sensitivity of borrower's risk to investments. However, how can investments imply a borrower's risk if they do not require any borrowing?

12. Keeping returns and costs as given, let us assume that firms have in mind a given expected demand for their products. Under these circumstances, the increase in investments might imply (i) the expectation of an excess supply of goods and thus of falling good prices and of falling investment yields, and (ii) an increasing 'economic' risk that the excess supply might remain unsold giving rise to losses. The expectation of decreasing yields would imply an original demand price curve Pk – and thus also an adjusted demand price curve Pk' – decreasing from the beginning. The appearance of the economic risk of investment projects would accentuate the downward slope of the adjusted demand price curve Pk'. For investment levels greater than Ii, it would also increase the lender's risk and thus the upward slope of the adjusted supply price curve Pi'.

13. Aggregate saving S is the sum of workers' saving (Sw) and capitalists' saving (Sc), equal to the difference between capitalist profits (Π) and capitalist consumption (Cc). This means that $S = Sw + (\Pi - Cc)$. By substituting into the goods market equilibrium condition, $I + DF + NX = S$, and rearranging, we get: $\Pi = I + DF + NX + Cc - Sw$. Profits Π are therefore determined by investments I, government deficit DF, net exports NX plus capitalists' consumption Cc net of workers' saving Sw.

14. Minsky (1986, p. 153), however, carefully underlines that – since profit has to cover overheads and ancillary expenses, financial commitments and so on – the remaining internal funds Qi are less than the investment. The implication is that, even if investment generates an equal amount of profits, it is not able to finance itself and thus needs indebtedness.

15. Minsky adds that the increase in the price of capital assets fuels expectations of capital gains that stimulate the demand for capital assets, giving rise to further increases in their price. By raising the net worth of firms and financial intermediaries, the increase in the price of capital assets also stimulates both the propensity to borrow and the availability of credit, thus strengthening the tendency to increase indebtedness.

16. Quoting the author: 'However, the internal workings of the banking mechanism or central bank action to constrain inflation will result in the supply of finance being less than infinitely elastic leading to a rapid increase in short-term interest rates' (see Minsky, 1978, p. 45). The reference to the central bank, however, is not clear since Minsky assumes an edogenous money supply.

References

Arestis, P. (2001), 'Recent banking and financial crises: Minsky versus the financial liberalizations', in Bellofiore, R. and Ferri, P. (eds), *Financial Keynesianism and Market Instability: the Economic Legacy of Hyman Minsky*, Vol. 1, Cheltenham, UK and Northampton, MA, USA: Edward Elgar, 159–79.

Arestis, P. and Glickman, M. (2002), 'Financial crisis in Southeast Asia: dispelling illusion the Minskyan way', *Cambridge Journal of Economics*, **26**(2), 237–60.

Fisher, I. (1933), 'The debt-deflation theory of great depressions', *Econometrica*, **1**(4), 337–57.

Godley, W., Izurieta, A. and Zezza, G. (2004), 'Prospects and policies for the U.S. economy: why net exports must now be the motor for U.S. growth', *Strategic Analysis – Prospects and Policies for the U.S. Economy*, Levy Economics Institute of Bard College, Annandale-on-Hudson, NY.

Keynes, J.M. (1936), *The General Theory of Employment, Interest and Money*, London: Macmillan.

Keynes, J.M. (1937), 'The general theory of employment', *The Quarterly Journal of Economics*, **51**(2), 209–23.

King, J.E. (2002), *A History of Post-Keynesian Economics since 1936*, Cheltenham, UK and Northampton, MA, USA: Edward Elgar.

Kregel, J. (1992), 'Minsky's "two price" theory of financial instability and monetary policy: discounting versus open market intervention', in Fazzari, S. and Papadimitriou, D.B. (eds), *Financial Conditions and Macroeconomic Performance: Essays in Houor of Hyman P. Minsky*, Armoule, NY and London: M.E. Sharpe, 85–103.

Kregel, J. (2001), 'Yes, "it" did happen again – the Minsky crisis in Asia', in Bellofiore, R. and Ferri, P. (eds), *Financial Keynesianism and Market Instability: the Economic Legacy of Hyman Minsky*, Vol. 1, Cheltenham, UK and Northampton, MA, USA: Edward Elgar, 194–213.

Lavoie, M. and Seccareccia, M. (2001), 'Minsky's financial fragility hypothesis: a missing macroeconomic link?', in Bellofiore, R. and Ferri, P. (eds), *Financial Fragility and Investment in the Capitalist Economy: the Economic Legacy of Hyman Minsky*, Vol. 2, Cheltenham, UK and Northampton, MA, USA: Edward Elgar, 76–99.

Minsky, H.P. (1957), 'Monetary systems and accelerator models', *The American Economic Review*, **XLVII**(6), 859–83.

Minsky, H.P. (1963), 'Can "It" happen again?', in Carson, D. (ed.), *Banking and Monetary Studies*, Homewood, IL: R.D. Irwin, 101–11.

Minsky, H.P. (1972), 'An exposition of a Keynesian theory of investment', in Szego, G.P. and Shell, S. (eds), *Mathematical Methods in Investment and Finance*, Amsterdam: North-Holland, 207–33.

Minsky, H.P. (1975), *John Maynard Keynes*, New York: Columbia University Press.

Minsky, H.P. (1977), 'The financial instability hypothesis: an interpretation of Keynes and an alternative to standard theory', *Nebraska Journal of Economics and Business*, **16**(Winter), 5–16.

Minsky, H.P. (1978), 'The financial instability hypothesis: a restatement', Thames Papers in Political Economy, North East London Polytechnic. Reprinted in Arestis, P. and Skouras, T. (eds) (1985), *Post Keynesian Economic Theory*, Armonk, NY: M.E. Sharpe, 24–55.

Minsky, H.P. (1980), 'Capitalist financial processes and the instability of capitalism', *Journal of Economic Issues*, **XIV**(2), 505–22.

Minsky, H.P. (1982a), *Can 'It' Happen Again? Essays on Instability and Finance*, Armonk, NY: M.E. Sharpe.

Minsky, H.P. (1982b), 'Debt deflation processes in today's institutional environment', *Banca Nazionale del Lavoro – Quarterly Review*, **143**(December), 375–95.

Minsky, H.P. (1986), *Stabilizing an Unstable Economy*, New Haven, CT: Yale University Press.

Minsky, H.P. (1991), 'Financial crises: Systemic or idiosyncratic?', Working Paper No. 51, Levy Economics Institute of Bard College, Annandale-on-Hudson, NY.

Minsky, H.P. (1992), 'Debt deflation processes in today's institutional environment', *Banca Nazionale del Lavoro – Quarterly Review*, **35**(December), 265–77.

Minsky, H.P. and Whalen, C.J. (1996), 'Economic insecurity and the institutional prerequisites for successful capitalism', *Journal of Post Keynesian Economics*, **19**(2), 155–71.

Patinkin, D. (1956), *Money, Interest and Prices: an Integration of Monetary and Value Theory*, Evanston, IL: Row Peterson.

Robinson, J. (1971), *Economic Heresies*, London: Macmillan.

Sawyer, M. (2001), 'Minsky's analysis, the European single currency and the global financial system', in Bellofiore, R. and Ferri, P. (eds), *Financial Keynesianism and Market Instability the Economic Legacy of Hyman Minsky*, Vol. 2, Cheltenham, UK and Northampton, MA, USA: Edward Elgar, 179–93.

Tobin, J. and Brainard, W. (1977), 'Asset markets and the cost of capital', in Belassa, B. and Nelson, R. (eds), *Private Values and Public Policy; Essays in Honor of William Fellner*, New York: North Holland Publishing Company, 235–63.

Vercelli, A. (2001), 'Minsky, Keynes and the structural instability of a sophisticated monetary economy', in Bellofiore, R. and Ferri, P. (eds), *Financial Fragility and Investment in the Capitalist Econmy: the Economic Legacy of Hyman Minsky*, Vol. 1, Cheltenham, UK and Northampton, MA, USA: Edward Elgar, 33–53.

11 Kalecki on money and finance
Malcolm Sawyer

1. Introduction

Expenditure has to be financed and planned increases in expenditure require additional finance if the plans are to come to fruition. Any analysis of the role of aggregate demand in the determination of the level of economic activity requires consideration to be paid to the question of the financing of expenditure. Kalecki's analysis of the role of aggregate demand was set in a business cycle framework in which fluctuations in investment were the major generator of fluctuations in economic activity.

Kalecki's analysis (and models based on his work, which are given the epithet Kaleckian) often appears to be in real terms and to be undertaken without explicit reference to money. For example, models such as Dutt (1987) and Sawyer (1994), which are described as Kaleckian, make no explicit reference to money. The treatment of investment may seem also to be an example in that the emphasis in the decision to invest is placed on factors such as profitability and capacity utilization. However, the assumption is clearly made that credit is available to finance the expenditure. In this form, money and credit are treated in an accommodationist fashion; that is, the amount of credit and money follows the demand for credit. But Kalecki also recognized that any expansion could be aborted if banks did not provide the requisite loans and credit (or raised the price of loans in the face of the increased demand for loans sufficient to choke off the increased demand).

In one sense, money could be viewed as neutral in that the factors influencing the level of economic activity, prices and wages and so on are real factors, and the amount of money serves to validate the effects of those real factors. However, banks have the power to not meet the demand for loans, and to determine which firms have access to credit and which do not, and that ensures that the manner in which money is created through the loans process determines the future course of the economy.

In this chapter on Kalecki's monetary analysis, we begin by a lengthy discussion of the relationship between investment and credit creation, and the implications of that for the nature and role of money. This seeks to establish that Kalecki adopted an essentially endogenous money approach and was fully aware of the financing requirements of investment. The following two sections consider the real balance (Pigou) effect and the Keynes effect as mechanisms viewed as generating higher levels of demand and a return to full employment as prices fell. Kalecki dismissed both of these mechanisms. In a rather brief paper, Kalecki enunciated 'the principle of increasing risk' whereby the limitations on a firm's capacity to borrow come from the rising degree of risk (of default) as the amount of the borrowing rose (relative to their profits and size). Section 5 reviews the implications of the 'principle of increasing risk'. Interest rates were seen by Kalecki as not determined by the interaction of savings and investment, and, like Keynes, he viewed interest rates as what may be termed a monetary phenomenon. Section 6 outlines his approach to the determination of interest rates. Monetary policy is the subject of section 7, and section 8 argues that Kalecki considered different types of money (e.g. narrow money, broad money) as fulfilling different functions.

2. Credit money and investment

In his writings in the 1930s, in which Kalecki advanced the crucial role of investment in the expansion of the level of economic activity, he clearly saw the key role of the extension of credit in the financing of that expansion. The main focus of that analysis was on investment decisions, and not on the extension of credit by banks, which was viewed as generally permissive. The working assumption was made in the early writings that 'the financing of additional investment is effected by the so-called creation of purchasing power. The demand for bank credit increases, and these are granted by the banks' (Kalecki, *CW* I, p. 190).[1] This corresponds to the notion that banks are willing to meet the demand for loans at the prevailing rate of interest on loans as set by the banks. However, whether this working assumption held depends on decisions made by the banks. The banks could respond to an increased demand for loans by raising the corresponding rate of interest.

> [T]he possibility of stimulating the business upswing is based on the assumption that the banking system, especially the central bank, will be able to expand credits without such a considerable increase in the rate of interest. If the banking system reacted so inflexibly to every increase in the demand for credit, then no boom would be possible on account of a new invention, nor any automatic upswing in the business cycle. . . . Investments would cease to be the channel through which additional purchasing power, unquestionably the *primus movens* of the business upswing, flows into the economy. (Ibid., p. 489)

In a similar vein, he argued that

> if this rate [of interest on loans] were to increase sufficiently fast for the influence of the increase in gross profitability to be fully offset, an upswing would prove impossible. There is thus a close connection between the phenomenon of the business cycle and the response of the banking system to the increase in demand for money in circulation, at a rate of interest which is not prohibitive to the rise in investment. (Ibid., p. 473)

The expansion of demand then requires that sufficient finance is provided, and banks have it in their hands to cut off any increase in demand if they are not prepared to meet the demand for loans.

Kalecki acknowledged the link between the cycle and money creation. He asked:

> how can capitalists invest more than remains from their current profits after spending part of them for personal consumption? This is made possible by the banking system in various forms of credit inflation. Hence, . . . without credit inflation there would be no fluctuations in investment activity. *Business fluctuations are strictly connected with credit inflation* . . . A similar type of inflation is the financing of investments from bank deposits, a process usually not classified as inflation but one which perhaps has the greatest importance in the inflationary financing of investments during an upswing in the business cycle. (*CW* I, pp. 148 and 149; emphasis in original)

Kalecki defined inflation in terms of 'the creation of purchasing power not based on a contribution to current social income' (ibid., p. 148).

The granting of bank loans enables the investment and other forms of expenditure to proceed, and there is a subsequent creation of bank deposits and money. But how far the money thereby created remains in existence depends of the extent of reflux (though Kalecki did not use that terminology) whereby the initial expansion of loans circulates as deposits, and then some, if not all, of those deposits are used to repay loans.

> Disregarding the technical side of the money market, e.g. the variable demand for means of payment, we may say that these outlays are 'financing themselves'. Imagine, for instance, that some capitalists withdraw during a year a certain amount from their savings deposits, or borrow the amount at the central bank, in order to invest it in the construction of some additional equipment. In the course of the same year that amount will be received by other capitalists in the form of profits (since according to our assumptions, workers do not save), and again put into a bank as a savings deposit or used to pay off a debt to the central bank. Thus the circle will close itself. (Ibid., p. 472)

On the financing of demand, Kalecki began by analysing the case where balance sheet value of assets and liabilities remains constant during business cycle. He divided the liabilities of the consolidated balance sheet of banks into:

> (i) 'unattached' deposits, i.e. deposits without a specific designation; (ii) investment reserves, i.e. funds used for the immediate financing of the production of capital goods; and (iii) money in circulation, i.e. cash balances and banknotes in circulation'. (Ibid., p. 93)

When enterprises plan to increase investment, they conceptually shift funds from the 'unattached' deposits to the investment reserves. When I (investment orders) are greater than A (production of investment goods), then there is a net flow from (i) to (ii), which is taken to be typical of a cyclical upswing. When I is less than A, typical of the downswing, then the net flow will be in the reverse direction. The funds held as 'investment reserves' could be viewed as those fulfilling the 'finance motive', to use the terminology of Keynes (1937).

Kalecki then proceeded by dropping the assumption of constant balance sheet value.

> In reality, the increased demand for investment reserves and money in circulation is met not only by a change of unattached deposits to deposits of specific designation but also by an expansion of the credit operations of banks, i.e. by credit inflation in the strict sense, when the assets and liabilities of banks increase. In other words, the increase of credits is matched on the side of assets by an increase in investment reserves, and on the side of liabilities by an increase of money in circulation. (*CW* I, p. 95)

However, there can be some lasting expansion in the stock of money following an expansion of loan because of an increased transactions demand for money. Kalecki noted that there is 'an increased demand for money in circulation [in the upswing of the business cycle] in connection with the rise in production and prices' (ibid., p. 93). Hence the transactions demand to hold money increases. However, the transactions demand for money is influenced by relevant rates of interest.

> Fluctuations in the demand for investment reserves and money in circulation are tightly linked with changes in the rate of interest. For a partial conversion of unattached deposits into 'attached' accounts to take place, the spread between the 'credit' rate (the discount rate, interest on stocks and bonds, etc.) and the bank rate on deposits must increase. Only then will it pay owners of unattached deposits to invest in stocks and bonds, thereby providing funds for conversion to attached accounts. This greater spread between the credit rate and the bank rate

on deposits is also required to stimulate the expansion of banks' credit operations, i.e. for credit inflation in the strict sense. (Ibid., pp. 96–7)

It is relevant to note that Kalecki envisaged that the relationship between the different rates of interest could change, and in particular that there is not a constant mark-up by banks as between, for example, the interest rate on loans and that on deposits.

The expansion of the banks' balance sheets was seen by Kalecki to be driven by an increase in loans. This is a significant element in the endogenous money approach in that loans are seen to drive deposits, rather than the reverse causation. Kalecki argued that the volume of bank deposits would be determined by the volume of bank loans, provided that interest rates adjusted so that the public were willing to hold that volume of bank deposits.

> It has been frequently maintained that bank deposits are fully determined by bank credits; and, in particular, that the movement of deposits in wartime depends on the amount of government borrowing from the banks. The statement is correct, but subject to the condition that the short-term rate of interest is allowed to vary. If, for instance, banks buy more bills while the total volume of business transactions is unchanged, bank deposits will rise but the short-term rate of interest must fall. If the short-term rate of interest is unchanged . . . current accounts will increase more or less proportionately with the volume of transactions. (Kalecki, *CW* VII, p. 159)

A footnote adds the caveat that 'provided there is no change in the habits of cash holding and there is no considerable shift between accounts of high and low velocity'. A significant aspect of this analysis is that the structure of interest rates is seen to change as the balance sheets change.

This line of argument fits in well with the endogenous money approach in that the expansion of deposits is initiated by an expansion of loans, but those deposits only remain in existence if there is an increased demand for them, and that generally requires an increase in the demand for money and that may require a change in relevant interest rates.

An increase in investment and subsequent increase in output brings about a greater transactions demand, and loans tend to increase (cf. Kalecki, *CW* I, pp. 293–4).[2] Then 'banks are obliged to sell bills and bonds in order to expand their credits' (ibid., p. 294). The sale of bills increases the discount rate: Kalecki envisaged the central bank supplying cash by buying bills and bonds on the market (ibid., p. 293). He indicated that the interest rate on deposit accounts usually rose in line with the discount rate, and hence there would be little incentive for the time deposit holders to switch to bills. Current accounts (roughly now M1) bore a zero rate of interest at the time Kalecki was writing, and the holders of such accounts would then have an incentive to switch into bills: the transactions demand for that money declines. For the sale of bonds, Kalecki thought the effect on the interest rate on bonds would be rather less than the effect on the discount rate. However, he then argued that 'it is plausible that a deposit-owner . . . may be induced to buy bonds even though the rate on deposits has increased much more than the yield of bonds' (ibid., p. 296).

Here Kalecki viewed the central bank discount rate as rather market determined, and not exogenous (in the sense of uninfluenced by events in the financial or other markets). This discount rate would vary in response to the demand for bills by the banks. The discount rate forms the base for the determination of other interest rates. An increased demand for loans can be seen to lead to changes in relative interest rates (e.g. as between loans and deposits) and to changes in the absolute level of interest rates. It could be anticipated that it is relative rates which influence portfolio decisions and the absolute rate which influences investment decisions (though note Kalecki's scepticism on the effects of interest rates on investment).

The credit expansion by a single bank is constrained by the activities of other banks.

> An individual bank cannot carry out such operations without restraint, but must moderate the rate of its credit inflation in line with the rate of this inflation in other banks, for otherwise its settlements with other banks, to which its cheques go, will be unfavourable for it, and balancing processes will set in. Its rate of credit inflation will be checked, and that of other banks will be raised. The effects of credit inflation of private banks are exactly the same as the inflationary effects of the central bank. (*CW* I, pp. 150–51)

Kalecki's analysis of money largely concerned money as a medium of exchange rather than as a store of wealth. He distinguished between narrow money and broad money (other than narrow money), with most discussion concerning the former, and the demand for the latter being related to wealth and a spectrum of interest rates. Money is credit money, and the creation of credit money is generally required if the economy is to expand. But the amount of money that remains in existence depends upon the demand to hold that money.

3.   The real balance effect

The real balance or Pigou effect has played a major role in macroeconomic debates for more than six decades. This effect postulates that the real level of aggregate demand depends on the real value of the stock of money. With a given nominal stock of money, as prices fall the real value of the money stock rises, thereby, it is argued, stimulating aggregate demand. The simple argument was that in conditions of unemployment and excess capacity, prices would in general fall, thereby raising the real value of money (and any financial assets with a price fixed in nominal terms). The rising real value of money would have a wealth effect in stimulating spending and raising aggregate demand. This would continue until full employment was restored.

In the debates following the publication of *The General Theory* (Keynes, 1936), particularly as undertaken in the IS–LM framework, the operation of the real balance or Pigou effect was viewed as providing a market mechanism by which full employment would be eventually restored. In the IS–LM curve approach, a lower price level (given the money stock) would lead to a higher real supply of money, thereby shifting the LM curve outwards, and would through the real balance effect shift the IS curve in a reflationary direction. Overall, the effects of lower prices would be to raise demand, and this is then reflected in the aggregate demand (AD) curve providing a negative relationship between price level and output. The particular significance of this line of argument was that it appeared to provide a market mechanism (through declining prices) whereby full employment would be restored. It was, however, recognized that this might be a slow process and the same effect could be achieved through increasing the money supply directly.

In more recent developments, much of the so-called New Keynesian literature on aggregate demand is based on representing demand as depending on the real value of the stock of money, and hence real demand varies as the price level changes (bringing about a change in the real value of the money stock). For example, in their book on unemployment, Layard et al. (1991) portray aggregate demand as depending on, *inter alia*, the real stock of money. In a similar vein many models in the New Keynesian approach model aggregate demand in terms of the real stock of money.

It was acknowledged that the empirical significance of the real balance effect may be small as it depends on the wealth effects of a high real money stock on consumer expenditure. But what Kalecki showed, and which is now well evident in the endogenous money approach, was that the theoretical arguments are invalid. Simply put, the endogenous money approach invalidates the real balance effect on the grounds that money does not constitute net worth, so that a decline in the price level has no systematic effect on real wealth. It is well known that credit money does not constitute net worth since whilst a deposit is an asset for the individual, it constitutes a liability for the bank. Further, the banks' balance sheets are composed of assets and liabilities generally denominated in nominal terms, and hence the real net wealth of the banks is not changed through variations in the price level. Further, the endogenous money approach invalidates the LM curve argument given above in which the demand for money was viewed as adjusting to the (real) stock of money. With endogenous money, the adjustment is the reverse in that the stock of money adjusts to the demand for money.

A brief two-page paper by Kalecki (1944) (reprinted as Kalecki, *CW* I, pp. 342–3) was a major attack on the real balance (Pigou) effect on the level of effective demand. This paper should have driven the use of the Pigou effect out of macroeconomic analysis, but it did not. In that paper, Kalecki made the two major points against the reliance on falling prices to restore full employment. First, he argued that an

> increase in the real value of the stock of money does not mean a rise in the total real value of possession if all the money (cash and deposits) is 'backed' by credits to persons and firms, i.e. if all the assets of the banking system consist of such credits. For in this case, to the gain for money-holders there corresponds an equal loss for the bank debtors. The total real value of possessions increases only to the extent to which money is backed by gold.

A footnote adds 'Or government securities. The classics and Prof. Pigou do not, however, postulate the existence of national debt as an essential feature of capitalist economy.' It could have been added that government securities involve assets (the prospect of future income) and liabilities (the prospect of future taxes to pay the interest on bonds) and to that degree do not constitute net worth for the private sector. Kalecki also pointed out that when gold forms a small part of national wealth, the fall in wage rates and prices necessary to restore aggregate demand to the full employment level would be enormous.

The second point arises from the observation that loans and deposits are the two sides of the banks' balance sheets (and also of the public's balance sheet). A fall in the general level of prices raises the value of bank deposits (but thereby increases the real value of the liabilities of the banks), but it also raises the real value of loans. Whilst banks benefit from the higher value of loans (which are an asset for them), the firms are now faced with higher real debt. The fall in prices also means a fall in the nominal income level, making it more difficult to service the debt. The falls in the general level of prices would increase the real value of debts and 'would consequently lead to wholesale bankruptcy and a confidence crisis' (*CW* I, p. 343).

4.   The Keynes effect

The so-called 'Keynes effect' was another mechanism through which it was perceived that aggregate demand could be stimulated through lower prices. The lower prices would mean that the real value of the stock of money would increase. But the demand for money would decline in line with the decline in prices. In real terms, the supply of money has increased and the demand for money remained unchanged; in nominal terms, the supply of money remains unchanged and the demand for money falls. In the approach of Keynes, the interest rate is seen as set by the interaction of the demand for and supply of money. In this context, this would lead to a fall in the rate of interest (which would raise the demand for money to bring it more closely in line with the supply of money).

Kalecki dismissed the significance of the 'Keynes effect'. He argued that if wages and prices decline, then

> the value of output must diminish and the demand for cash for transactions fall off. Thus the rate of interest tends to decline, and this encourages investment so that we have yet another possible way for a wage cut to raise employment. This argument, though theoretically quite correct is, however, without practical importance. The increase in the demand for cash in general affects only slightly the long-term rate of interest, which is the most important rate in the determination of the level of investment. Thus it seems quite justifiable to neglect this channel through which a wage reduction could influence the level of employment. (*CW* I, p. 283)

In a similar vein, in a book review published in 1937 (reprinted as *CW* VII, pp. 314–5), Kalecki considered a case where there was a very substantial reduction in all prices and wages. He then argued that

> the demand for cash for transactions declines, the rate of interest falls off, and this may encourage investment activity, and thus increase effective demand. This is, however, a complicated process not at all equivalent to an increase in 'the purchasing power of money' proportionate to the fall in costs and prices. And its result may be slight indeed, for the fall in the long-term rate of interest is likely to be small. (Ibid., p. 314)

5.   Principle of increasing risk and finance

The discussion above on investment made clear the significance of the terms on which banks were willing to supply credit to firms. For investment to proceed, credit had to be available. In a more general setting, Kalecki in effect summarized the conditions governing the borrowing by enterprises, whether in the form of loans, bonds or equity, in the phrase the 'principle of increasing risk'.

This principle can be simply stated. The more a company wishes to borrow (relative to its profits and to its own wealth), the greater is the perceived risk (on the part of the potential lender and of the borrower) that the company will not be able to repay the loan (interest and principal). The lender will charge a risk premium to cover the greater risk exposure, and hence the cost of borrowing will rise with the volume of borrowing. But the higher cost would raise the risk of default and at some point the cost of borrowing may become prohibitive. Kalecki (1937; *CW* I, pp. 285–93), in his paper on the principle of increasing risk, does not explicitly mention banks and their lending but is rather concerned with the cost of finance facing the individual firm where 'the entrepreneur is not cautious enough in his investment activity, the creditor who imposes on his calculation the burden of increasing risk, charging the successive portions of credits above a certain amount with a rising rate of interest' (ibid., p. 288). In a later paper Kalecki stated that 'a firm considering expansion must face the fact that, given the amount of entrepreneurial capital, the risk increases with the amount invested' (1954; *CW* II, p. 278). However, in this version of 1954 he did not translate that increased risk into increased loan charges (ibid., pp. 277–81).

There appears to be a conflict between the principle of increasing risk (as applied to bank loans) and the working assumption that Kalecki made, as indicated above, to the effect when 'the demand for bank credit increases . . . these are granted by the banks' (*CW* I, p. 190). However, in Kalecki's approach, the granting of loans at the prevailing rate of interest is a condition for the full expansion of planned investment to take place and, as other quotes given above indicate, the banks could abort any expansion if they raised interest rates on loans substantially rather than meeting the increased demand for loans. But there is clearly a conflict between the principle of increasing risk and the ready availability of loans at the prevailing rate of interest (on loans) which has been generally assumed in much of the endogenous money supply literature, especially by those of a horizontalist persuasion (e.g. Moore, 1988; Lavoie, 1992; 1996; see also Arestis, 1996 for some discussion).

A number of comments on the relationship between the principle of increasing risk and the shape and slope of the supply of loans curve can be made. First, Kalecki viewed the 'principle of increasing risk' and the rising cost of finance as significant factors limiting the expansion of the individual firm. He dismissed the significance of diseconomies of large scale and the limitations of the size of the market as constraints on the expansion of the firm (*CW* II, p. 277). He continued by arguing that there is a factor

> of decisive importance in limiting the size of the firm: the amount of entrepreneurial capital, i.e. the amount of capital owned by the firm. The access of a firm to the capital market, or in other words the amount of rentier capital it may hope to obtain, is determined to a large extent by the amount of its entrepreneurial capital. . . . It follows . . . that the expansion of the firm depends on its accumulation of capital out of current profits. This will enable the firm to undertake new investment without encountering the obstacles of the limited capital market or 'increasing risk'. Not only can savings out of current profits be directly invested in the business, but this increase in the firm's capital will make it possible to contract new loans. (Ibid., pp. 277–8)

It may then be concluded that Kalecki saw the operation of the 'principle of increasing risk' as a significant feature of a capitalist economy, and not a peripheral one. This would suggest that an analysis of a market capitalist economy which draws on the work of Kalecki should retain the 'principle of increasing risk' as a component.

Second, most enterprises (the more 'cautious' ones, following the terminology in the quote from Kalecki given above) may be far below the borrowing levels at which the 'principle of increasing risk' would have a major effect on the cost and availability of borrowing. In such a case, most enterprises may be observed to face approximately constant costs of borrowing since they would find it too costly to stray into the scale of borrowing, relative to profits and own wealth, where the costs rise sharply. 'Many firms will not use to the full the potentialities of the capital market because of the "increasing risk" involved in expansion' (*CW* II, p. 278), though it should be noted that this arises from firms' own perceptions of the risks faced.

Kalecki argued that 'it would be impossible for a firm to borrow capital above a certain level determined by the amount of its entrepreneurial capital' (ibid., p. 277); further, 'that firms below a certain size have no access whatever to the capital market' (ibid., p. 278). Hence the loans schedule facing many enterprises will have a final vertical section, and for other enterprises the loan schedule may in effect be non-existent.

Third, over the course of the business cycle, an enterprise's ability to borrow from banks can be seen to depend on two sets of factors. On the one hand, there is the balance between loan repayment commitments and its profit flow. The loan repayment commitments would depend, *inter alia*, on its past borrowing and the extent to which it has been able to repay loans based on borrowing from households in the form of bonds, equity etc. On the other hand, the banks' willingness to lend may vary as their 'liquidity preference' and general optimism and pessimism vary. It is then a complex matter to say how the volume of borrowing in the form of loans and the relationship between loans and interest rates will vary during the course of the business cycle. There is no general prediction that can be made as to the co-movements of loans, the stock of money and interest rates over the course of the cycle.

The 'principle of increasing risk' applies at the level of the firm, and it is seen as operating to limit the growth of the firm. For the firm, its own stream of profits is a significant influence on its ability to borrow. In the macroeconomic approach of Kalecki, the volume of aggregate profits is determined by the level of aggregate investment. This is derived (taking the simple case of a closed private economy) from the equality between savings (S) and investment (I), and from the assumption that savings arise from profits and that savings out of wages are negligible. Savings are then equal to $s\,P$ (where s is propensity to save out of profits) in turn equal to I (investment): hence $P = I/s$. At the aggregate level, Kalecki was clear that causation ran from the investment spending decisions to the volume of savings (and thereby to profits).

> We have shown that the spending of the capitalists 'forces' a capitalist income which is equal to this spending. As the spending of the capitalists consists of their consumption and investment, and the income of the capitalists of their consumption and saving, it can also be said that the investment 'forces' saving to an amount which is equal to the amount of their investment. (*CW* I, p. 532)

Thus it is not possible to proceed immediately to the aggregate level by the summation of the individual level since the borrowing of a firm depends on its investment plans, and the collective realization of those investment plans determines profits, which in turn influence the ability of enterprises to borrow.

It is argued here that the 'principle of increasing risk' would support the construction of an upward-sloping supply of credit (loans) by the banks' schedule facing an individual firm. It has, though, already been suggested that firms may seek to ensure that they typically do not borrow so much as to put them into a position where the cost of borrowing which they face rises rapidly. But it is also argued that this tells us nothing about the supply of money (bank deposits) schedule.

6.   Interest rate determination

The idea that the interest rate adjusts to ensure equality between savings and investment at full employment (expressed in, for example, the loanable funds approach) has been central to much non-Keynesian economics. A major element of the contributions of Kalecki and of Keynes was to see savings and investment as brought into equality through variations in the level of economic activity. Under the loanable funds approach, the interest rate equates the demand for and supply of loans, but those in turn are related with investment (demand for loans) and savings (the basis of the supply of loans). In effect, Kalecki's arguments concerning the rate of interest can be divided into two parts. First, if the rate of interest is not determined by loanable funds, how is it determined, or, in the case of Kalecki, how are the various interest rates determined? Second, what impact does the rate of interest have on demand? The first of these questions is examined in this section, and the second in the next section on monetary policy.

The rate of interest can be seen as a monetary, rather than a real, phenomenon. Kalecki wrote that

> the rate of interest cannot be determined by the demand for and supply of capital because investment automatically brings into existence an equal amount of savings. Thus, investment 'finances itself' whatever the level of the rate of interest. The rate of interest is, therefore, the result of the interplay of other factors. (*CW* II, p. 262)

In a similar vein, Keynes argued that

> the rate of interest at any time, being the reward for parting with liquidity, is a measure of the unwillingness of those who possess money to part with their liquid control over it. The rate of interest is . . . the 'price' which equilibrates the desire to hold wealth in the form of cash with the available quantity of cash. (Keynes, 1936, p. 167)

An important aspect of any Kaleckian analysis of interest rates must be the influence of monetary and financial factors on interest rates, rather than any notion of the demand for and supply of loanable funds determining interest rates.

Kalecki did not envisage that the interest rate was determined by the interaction of savings and investment (equivalently the loanable funds approach). Instead, he argued

> that the short-term rate is determined by the value of transactions and the supply of money by banks; and that the long-term rate is determined by anticipations of the short-term rate based on past experience, and estimates of the risk involved in the possible depreciation of long-term assets. (*CW* II, p. 262)

The determination of the short-term rate of interest was seen by Kalecki as arising from the transactions demand for money, interacting with the stock of money. The notation used is that M is the stock of money, which consists of current bank accounts and notes (i.e. close to M1 in present parlance), and T is total turnover. The short-term interest rate 'is the remuneration for forgoing the convenience of holding cash in its pure form' (though 'money' would be a better term here than 'cash'). It should be noted that Kalecki implicitly assumed that the rate of interest on holding money was zero, which would be an assumption in line with the prevailing practice at the time Kalecki was writing (and for many years after) that banks did not pay interest on current accounts.[3]

> When holding money is compared with holding short bills, the only difference is that the bill is not directly usable for settling transactions and that it yields interest. When holding money and holding a bond is compared, however, the risk of a fall in the price of the bond has also to be taken into consideration. (*CW* II, p. 263)

He concluded

> that the velocity of circulation V is an increasing function of the short-term rate of interest ρ or: $T/M = V(\rho)$. It follows directly from this equation that given the function V the short-term rate of interest, ρ, is determined by the [nominal] value of transactions, T, and the supply of money, M, which, in turn, is determined by banking policy. (Ibid.)

Kalecki's discussion of the equality of transactions demand for money and the stock of money is characteristically laconic, but can be elaborated as follows. The banks can vary their portfolios of assets and liabilities and in doing so influence the structure and general level of interest rates and the stock of money. However, the level of interest rates and the (nominal) level of economic activity also influence the non-bank sector's willingness to hold money. Further, 'banking policy' will influence the supply of money, where I would argue that the term should be read to include the lending policies of commercial banks as well as the setting of the discount rate by the central bank. Indeed, Kalecki's later discussion in the paper from which the quote above was taken implies the former rather than the latter.

Kalecki described the determination of the stock of money in the following way:

> The process by which banks increase the supply of money deserves to be considered in some detail. For the sake of simplicity, let us assume that bank deposits consist only of current accounts. Imagine that banks decide to reduce their cash ratio (i.e. the ratio of the amount of notes and accounts in the central bank to deposits) and buy bills. The price of bills will rise, and thus the short-term rate of interest will fall to that level at which the public will be prepared to add to their current accounts the amount which the banks expend on bills. (*CW* II, p. 267)

The stock of money and the short-term interest rate (on bills) are thus viewed as determined by the interaction of the willingness of banks to supply money and of the public to hold (demand) money.

The long-term rate of interest (on bonds) is linked with the short-term rate of interest (on bills) based on substitution between the corresponding financial assets. The precise mechanism is not of central importance here but it can be readily summarized by the following: 'In order to establish a connection between the short-term and the long-term rate of interest, we shall examine the problem of substitution between a representative short-term asset, say a bill of exchange, and a representative long-term asset, say a consol' (*CW* II, p. 268). He derived the following relationship:

$$ r = \frac{\rho_e}{1 + \dfrac{g}{r_{\max}}} + \frac{g - \varepsilon}{1 + \dfrac{g}{r_{\max}}} $$

where r is long-term interest rate, ρ_e is expected rate of interest on bills (averaged over the holding period of bonds), $r_{\max}$ the yield corresponding to the minimum 'plausible' price that bonds could reach at the end of the expected holding period, g is a parameter relating the expected gain on bonds to the minimum 'plausible' price and ε reflects the uncertainties in the rate of return on bills and the recurrent purchase costs.

It is readily apparent that Kalecki's approach to the determination of the short-term and long-term rates of interest is one based on monetary factors. There is no mention of loanable funds or of the equality between savings and investment, which is much as expected given the quotes with which we began the chapter. There is also the general notion that relative interest rates are influenced by substitution between different financial assets.

7.   Monetary policy

Kalecki wrote rather little on monetary policy, and, when he did, saw monetary policy in terms of open market operations and variations in the rate of interest. However, his discussions suggest severe doubts about the effectiveness of monetary policy as a means of stimulating the level of aggregate demand. The doubts stem from a combination of the view that long-term interest rates were seen as relevant for many investment decisions but that the movements in the long-term rates of interest were rather small. 'The relative stability of the long-term rate of interest is generally known. . . . It seems unlikely that changes in the long-term rate of interest of the order of those noticed . . . can influence investment activity' (*CW* I, pp. 296–7).[4] This leads him to dismiss those theories of the business cycle which suggest that the end of a boom derives from an increase in the rate of interest. 'For the rate of interest can stop the boom only by hampering investment, and it is chiefly the long-term rate which matters in investment activity' (ibid., p. 298). It would also be the case that a substantial fall in the rate of interest would be necessary to have a significant effect on investment (cf. ibid., p. 403).

Kalecki also argued that 'it has . . . long been indicated that it is not at all certain whether consumption is really encouraged or discouraged by a higher rate of interest' (ibid., p. 262). Further, increases in wealth (notably stock market values), generated by declines in the level of interest rates, would have little effect on consumer expenditure by capitalists. 'The effect would be significant, most probably, only if the fall in the rate of interest were considerable, which would require open-market operations on a very large scale' (ibid., p. 403).

Two significant points arise from Kalecki's brief comments on monetary policy. First, monetary policy can have relatively little impact on the level of aggregate demand, and in part this arises from the notion that long-term interest rates may influence spending decisions but themselves vary little. Second, in so far as monetary policy can influence spending, it does so through effects on investment. It could then be added, though Kalecki himself did not, that monetary policy would then influence the real side of the economy (through investment and thereby capacity) and the classical dichotomy is thereby undermined.

8.   Different types of money

In the Keynesian framework, the familiar distinction is drawn between the transactions motive and the speculative (portfolio) motive for holding money (recognizing that there was also a now largely forgotten precautionary motive and the finance motive), where the former is related to the level of nominal income and the latter to the level of wealth. However, the resulting two (or three) demands for money fuse into a single demand function which is then often estimated with the demand for money as a function of income, rates of interest etc. This has been summarized in the following terms:

> The distinction between the demand for transactions and precautionary balances, determined chiefly by the level of income, and that for speculative balances, determined by the rate of interest, is often referred to as the distinction between the demand for *active* and *idle* balances. Since all money is at each moment being held by someone, this terminology is not too helpful empirically, and we do not use it in this book. (Laidler, 1985, p. 51)

In the approach of Kalecki there is a recognition of a transactions-related demand and a portfolio (wealth-related) demand for money, but each of the demands is related to a different definition of money. This contrasts with the approach of Keynes, in which the various motives for holding money (transactions, precautionary, speculative) are, in effect, fused to give an overall demand for money.

The transactions demand for money is a demand for money used as a medium of exchange, which is satisfied by a narrow definition of money. The general tone of Kalecki's discussion suggests that he was concerned with money as a medium of exchange rather than as a means of final payment, though the distinction is not one to which Kalecki gave any attention. The portfolio demand for money is a demand for money as a store of wealth, which is generally linked with a broader definition of money and excluding those forms of money which yield a zero or negligible rate of interest. The notation used here is that M0 refers to base money (coins, notes and reserves with the central bank), M1 refers to those liabilities of the banking system whose transfer is a generally accepted medium of exchange (but not here notes and coins), M2/1 refers to broad money M2 minus M1 and is those liabilities of the banking system which have a fixed nominal value but which are not directly transferable. Banks are defined here as those institutions some of whose liabilities are generally accepted as medium of exchange. Other financial institutions may accept deposits with a fixed nominal value and could be counted part of a broad money stock, but here we confine M2 to the liabilities of the banks.

In Kalecki's approach, the demand for M0 is linked to wages as a transaction demand, but this reflects the situation in the 1940s when most workers did not have access to a bank account. In 'Wage bill and cash circulation' (*CW* VII, pp. 38–44), Kalecki correlates wage bill with the circulation of coins and notes. 'This correlation may then be used as the basis of an extrapolated estimate of the current wage bill' (p. 38). The demand for M0 by the public is clearly seen as a transactions demand.

The demand for M1 is also a transactions demand, as discussed above. In particular, Kalecki argued that 'if the short-term rate of interest is unchanged . . . current accounts [i.e. M1] will increase more or less proportionately with the volume of transactions' (ibid., p. 159), which can be read as saying that the demand for M1 is the transactions demand. Hence (and in light of the discussion in the previous section) the demand for M1 can be taken as a function of the volume of transactions and of the short-term rate of interest.

There is little discussion by Kalecki of the nature of the demand for broad money. He did, however, remark that

> the rise in deposit accounts [i.e. M2/1] depends on the rate of accumulation of liquid reserves of the public and the relative attractiveness of deposit accounts as compared with other relevant assets. The 'lending power' of the banks is then limited by these determinants of the movement of deposits [in current accounts and in deposit accounts]. (*CW* VII, p. 159)

In a similar vein, he argued that

> savings are 'invested' in deposits either because more of them are needed as cash balances for transactions, or because this type of reserves seems for various reasons more attractive than the holding of bonds. In the first case deposits accumulating on current accounts are 'tied up' in settling transactions (chiefly by firms) and are not available for spending on consumption. The second case, the accumulation of deposits mainly on deposit account, does not differ fundamentally from investment in long-term securities. It is sometimes said that it is easier to liquidate

deposits than bonds and to use the proceeds for consumption. This, however, is relevant only when actual dissaving takes place: as long as consumption is below current income the form in which past savings are held is of no importance. And even in the case of dissavings the obstacles in parting with a bond as compared with withdrawing a deposit seem to have been rather exaggerated. (Ibid., pp. 84–5)

However, he does not indicate why or how there is this exaggeration.

In the specific context of the UK in the period 1938–42, Kalecki reported that current account deposits (M1) rose rapidly (almost doubling in four years) whilst deposit accounts (M2/1) were almost static. He then remarked that

there is no reason to expect a similar pace in the movement of current and deposit accounts, for . . . with a given short-term rate of interest current accounts increase more or less proportionately with the volume of transactions while the rise in deposit accounts depends on the rate of accumulation of liquid reserves and the attractiveness of deposit accounts as compared with other relevant assets. (Ibid., p. 162)

Thus it can be concluded that the demand for M2/1 is a portfolio demand related to the wealth of the public and to the spectrum of interest rates including the rate on deposit accounts (and it would be expected that the demand for M2/1 would be positively related to the deposit account rate of interest, though the demand for M1 would be negatively related to that interest rate).

It can first be noted that if the identification of M1 with a transactions demand and M2/1 with a portfolio demand is correct, then it follows that if there is concern over the relationship between the demand for money and the level of nominal income, then M1 is the relevant definition of money. It is not a matter of saying that the relevant definition of money for the purposes of monetary policy and demand management is that for which there is a stable demand, but rather that which is the generally accepted medium of exchange. But in the approach of Kalecki, the view is that the nominal volume of transactions determines the demand for money, rather than the stock of money determining the nominal volume of transactions.

Second, in so far as the stocks of M1 and M2/1 are demand driven, they can readily evolve in quite different ways over time, simply because the former is transactions driven whilst the latter is wealth (portfolio) driven. If the income to wealth ratio is stable, then it could be that the evolution of M1 and M2/1 follow similar paths as the demand for each of them evolves in similar ways.

Third, the linkage between M1 and M2/1 arises because of the ready transferability by individuals from M2/1 deposits to M1 deposits, in part because those different types of deposits are held with the same financial institution and in part because the relative price of the two types of deposits is fixed at 1 since both have a nominal price of unity. There are some costs (monetary, time etc.) of making the transfer between current accounts and deposit accounts, as there are with other transfers between financial assets, though no price uncertainty. In the event that a bank was indifferent between M1 deposits and M2/1 deposits (and hence, e.g., held the same reserve ratio for M1 and for M2/1), then it could be argued that the potential purchasing power in the economy at a particular time was measured by M2 (including M1), a point discussed further below.

When the stock of money is viewed as essentially demand determined, then it is immediately apparent that the time paths of different definitions of money will typically diverge in so far as the factors influencing the demand for the different definitions of money are also different.

Fourth, Kalecki noted, albeit in a footnote in one of his early papers, that the shift between different types of money would have implications for the reserves of the banking system. 'This increase in circulation contains, *inter alia*, an increase in the cash reserves of banks in connection with the shift of certain sums from time to demand deposits . . . which also takes place on account of an increase in turnover' (*CW* I, p. 150, n. 2). Banks then hold different reserve ratios against time deposits than against demand deposits, with less reserves held against time deposits. Then if the public shift from holding time deposits into demand deposits, there would be effects on the banks, which now have less reserves than they would wish. Banks would take measures to secure more reserves (from the central bank) and may change the relative composition of interest rates.

9.   Conclusions

Kalecki's discussion of money and finance was typically terse and scattered over a range of papers, and he did not give a systematic presentation of his analysis of money. We can, though, seek to summarize the main aspects of Kalecki's analysis, and we would argue that there are six key features. These are:

1. Loans have to be provided by the banking system to enterprises if their planned investment decisions are to come to fruition, thereby generating an immediate increase in the stock of money.
2. The stock of money depends on the willingness of the non-bank public to hold (demand) money.
3. The stock of money also depends on the decisions and actions of the banking system.
4. Loans are provided subject to the principle of increasing risk.
5. A change in the demand for loans generates a change in the balance sheet of banks, with consequent effects on the structure of interest rates.
6. A distinction must be drawn between money as a medium of exchange and money as a store of value, with different moneys serving those purposes.

Notes

1. Quotations from Kalecki are all taken from his *Collected Works*, indicated by *CW*, followed by the appropriate volume number.
2. In the discussion to which reference is made in the text, Kalecki used the term 'advances' for what we have termed 'loans', and 'a loan' to signify bonds when he wrote about the floatation of loans (cf. *CW* I, p. 293).
3. British terminology is followed here, hence current accounts equate with demand deposits and deposit accounts with time deposits.
4. This was written at a time when changes in short-term interest rates tended to be limited and the argument may not apply now, when central banks vary short-term interest rates frequently.

References

Arestis, P. (1996), 'Kalecki's role in post Keynesian economics: an overview', in J.E. King (ed.), *An Alternative Macroeconomic Theory: the Kaleckian Model and Post-Keynesian Economics*, Boston, MA: Kluwer, pp. 11–34.

Dutt, A.K. (1987), 'Competition, monopoly power and the uniform rate of profit', *Review of Radical Political Economics*, **19**, 55–72.

Kalecki, M. (1990), *Capitalism: Business Cycles and Full Employment. Collected Works of Michal Kalecki*, Vol. I (edited by J. Osiatynski), Oxford: Clarendon Press (*CW* I).

Kalecki, M. (1991), *Capitalism: Economic Dynamics. Collected Works of Michal Kalecki*. Vol. II (edited by J. Osiatynski), Oxford: Clarendon Press (*CW* II).

Kalecki, M. (1997), *Studies in Applied Economics 1940–1967 Miscellanea, Collected Works of Michal Kalecki*, Vol. VII (edited by J. Osiatynski), Oxford: Clarendon Press (*CW* VII).

Keynes, J.M. (1936), *The General Theory of Employment, Interest and Money*, London: Macmillan.

Keynes, J.M. (1937), 'The ex-ante theory of the rate of interest', *Economic Journal*, **47**, 663–9.

Laidler, D. (1985), *The Demand for Money: Theories, Evidence and Problems*, New York: Harper & Row.

Lavoie, M. (1992), *Foundation of Post-Keynesian Economic Analysis*, Aldershot, UK and Brookfield, US: Edward Elgar.

Lavoie, M. (1996), 'Horizontalism, structuralism, liquidity preference and the principle of increasing risk', *Scottish Journal of Political Economy*, **43**(3), 275–300.

Layard, R., Jackman, R. and Nickell, S. (1991), *Unemployment: Macroeconomic Performance and the Labour Market*, Oxford: Oxford University Press.

Moore, B. (1988), *Horizontalists and Verticalists: the Macroeconomics of Credit Money*, Cambridge: Cambridge University Press.

Sawyer, M. (1994), 'Prices, capacity utilisation and employment in the Post Keynesian traditions', in A.K. Dutt (ed.), *New Directions in Analytical Political Economy*, Aldershot, UK and Brookfield, US: Edward Elgar.

12 Karl Marx's theory of money and credit
Suzanne de Brunhoff and Duncan K. Foley

From the point of view of later heterodox economics, three features of Marx's theory are particularly important: (1) Marx sees the function of measure of value rather than as medium of circulation as the primary property of money; (2) he treats the quantity of circulating money as endogenous, and the prices of commodities as exogenous, in contrast to the quantity of money theory of prices; (3) he refutes 'Say's Law', the view that because every sale is a purchase there cannot be an excess or deficiency of money demand for commodities in the aggregate. Marx presents a theory of commodity money, where a produced commodity (typically gold) functions as money. This perspective allows him to resolve all the outstanding monetary issues of his time, but raises the question of how to adapt his theory to monetary systems based on the credit of the state, which is not convertible into a money commodity such as gold.

Marx situates his theory of money in the context of his broader theory of the capitalist mode of production. He sees money as inherent in the commodity as a unity of use-value and exchange-value. While the commodity form, and with it money, appear in civilized societies such as the ancient empires of the Mediterranean, the Middle East, and Asia before capitalism develops, it is only with the full flowering of capitalism as a mode of production that the commodity and money reach their full development, deeply entwined with the class divisions of capitalism.

Although Marx found in the classical political economists, Adam Smith and David Ricardo, a theory of labour-value which he adopted in a modified form, his conception of money is his own, perhaps his chief original contribution to economic theory. 'Even Adam Smith and Ricardo, the best representatives of the school, treat the form of value as a thing of no importance, as having no connexion with the inherent value of commodities' (*Capital* I, i, p. 81).

Marx developed his mature theory of money in the course of his extensive study of capitalist society that culminated in *Capital*. The seeds of the full theory appear in the *Grundrisse*, which has a major 'Chapter on Money'. Marx elaborated his ideas on money in his *Contribution to the Critique of Political Economy*. He reformulated these basic ideas, with some significant changes of emphasis and language, in the first three chapters of Volume I of *Capital*. Marx also wrote extensively on the theory of credit, interest, and 'fictitious capital' in notebooks created before the publication of the first volume of *Capital* (1867) but published only after Marx's death under Friedrich Engels's editorship as Volume III of *Capital*. Marx investigated the function of money-capital in the circuit of capital in manuscripts largely written after the publication of the first volume of *Capital*, and published as Volume II. These texts are the primary sources for our understanding of Marx's theory of money and credit. The interested reader will find Arnon (1984), Bellofiore (1998), de Brunhoff (1976), Foley (1983, 2005), Itoh and Lapavitsas (1998), and Rubin (1972) useful secondary sources.

Marx's conception of money breaks with the various forms of the quantity of money theory of prices that were dominant at the time. Although the modern form of the quantity theory, culminating in the monetarism of Milton Friedman, has been very influential since the Second World War, Marx's critique of the quantity theory has not been discussed in comparable depth by contemporary economists. It is therefore important to understand Marx's ideas, to develop them as a critique of the dominant orthodoxy, and to open the way to a theory of money that can address contemporary monetary institutions. Although monetary turmoil is permanent, notably in the rate of exchange between the dollar and other foreign currencies, and alternating fears of inflation and deflation in money prices of commodities, the economic status of money and its relation to movements of the 'real' economy, production, employment and distribution, remain obscure. Let us look at what clarification Marx's ideas can bring to these issues.

1.   Money as the 'general equivalent' and the circulation of commodities
In the first three chapters of *Capital*, on the origin of the general equivalent form of value in the exchange of commodities, Marx shows how money is endogenous to commodity circulation. The different forms and functions of money are introduced as premises of the transformation of money into capital.

Marx develops a qualitative theory of money, which is deeply rooted in the notion of labour-value. Money is brought into being by the social division of labour among individual producers of use-values transformed into exchange-values. Commodity exchange, which has nothing in common with the simple barter of goods, introduces specific constraints on the expenditure of labour crystallized in products bought and sold in markets. The socialization of individual labour in the market imposes a social norm on individual producers, that of the average labour time expended in the production of a commodity which has the same use-value. In Marx's view the exchange of produced commodities as equivalents fundamentally reflects their common origin as products of human labour.

In its simplest form commodity exchange equates products with different use-values and produced by different forms of concrete labour. Marx represents this aspect of commodity exchange as the *elementary form of value*: for example, one pound of iron is equivalent to 20 yards of linen as exchange-value. Here the iron is related to the linen as an equivalent in exchange, and the linen expresses the exchange-value of the iron. Marx says the iron takes on the *relative form* of value and the linen the *equivalent form*. (Since exchange in this sense is symmetric, we could alternatively, but not simultaneously, say that 20 yards of linen are equivalent to one pound of iron, putting the linen in the relative position and the iron in the equivalent position.)

Because commodity exchange tends to spread across more and more use-values, the elementary form of value gives rise to the *extended form*, in which the pound of iron is successively seen as equivalent to 20 yards of linen, one coat, a table, and so on through all other commodities. In the extended form of value all of the possible equivalents of the iron (or any other particular commodity) successively take on the function of equivalent to express its exchange-value. The extended form of value, however, tends to transform itself by a *gestalt* figure-ground reversal to the *general form of value*, in which one commodity (say iron) takes on the role of equivalent for all the other commodities. Twenty yards of linen, one coat, a table and so on are all equivalent to one pound of iron, which thus becomes the *general equivalent*. (The general equivalent appears in orthodox economics as the purely formal concept of numéraire, a particular commodity chosen arbitrarily to express the relative price of other commodities.)

Marx sees the emergence of a general equivalent as the fundamental form of money. But for him the choice of a general equivalent is not just a matter of a formal designation of one commodity as numéraire in analytical terms, but is a real historical process through which a society comes to recognize one commodity as a *socially accepted general equivalent* in the day-to-day practice of commodity exchange. The emergence of a socially accepted general equivalent (a money commodity) is fundamentally a spontaneous, decentralized process, like the formation of exchange-value itself.

The emergence of money as a socially accepted general equivalent for other commodities in circulation is thus inherent in the practice of commodity exchange. Money is a commodity produced by labour, but whose use-value acquires a particular social status. This is the case with gold and silver when they become circulating money for domestic and foreign transactions. Their monetary role sanctions and reinforces the constraints placed by the social commodity division of labour on individual producers/exchangers. It is in this way that the use-values of goods which have become commodities to be sold on the market acquire an exchange-value.

In the process money plays many roles and takes diverse forms. Starting as the measure of the labour of producers of exchange-values in one country or between countries on international markets, it becomes the general hallmark of what can be sold and bought as a use-value made social by the market. Whatever is not produced as a commodity by the social division of labour, like the air we breathe, appears as a natural gift without exchange-value, whose use-value cannot be commercialized. Marx's central idea is that in commodity circulation 'commodities enter with a price and money with a value'. This determination is simultaneous and reciprocal.

This is the foundation of Marx's radical critique of the quantity of money theory of prices.

> The erroneous notion that . . . prices that are determined by the quantity of the circulating medium, and that the latter depends on the quantity of the precious metal in a country, . . . was based . . . on the absurd hypothesis that commodities are without a price and money without a value when they enter into circulation. (*Capital* I, pp. 123–4)

Marx develops his own theory of the functions and forms of money: as measure of value and standard of price, means of circulation, object of hoarding. Commodity exchange, distinct from the barter of products, brings with it certain specific social relations, which give birth to a 'fetishism' of the commodity and of money which Marx wants to dispel.

The money commodity: measure of value and standard of price
Money's function as a measure of value of commodities is inherent in its determination as a socially accepted general equivalent. In this way, gold, for example, comes to be generally recognized as the representative of pure exchange-value, the expression of abstract social labour time. The price which each commodity brings to the marketplace (whether or not it can actually realize it in sale) is expressed as a certain quantity of the money commodity. In any short period market prices of commodities can fluctuate apparently at random, but commodity production and specifically capitalist commodity production introduces fundamental regulating principles that result in long-period stabilization of

commodity prices. These regulating principles are expressed through the competition of capitalist producers, and tend to make the long-period prices of commodities adjust so that the rate of profit on capital, suitably adjusted for risk and other relevant contingencies, is equalized across the production of different commodities. This same process regulates the value of gold as the money commodity, since it is produced under capitalist relations of production, so that the profit rate in gold production cannot permanently diverge from the average profit rate in the capitalist system as a whole.

While the equalization of the rate of profit gives the value of the money commodity and the money prices of other commodities stability in the long period, the even longer-term forces of technical change ensure that the long-period prices of commodities themselves will continually fluctuate. The money commodity is a measure of value at any point in time, but not an invariable standard of value, which is an impossibility in the chaotic conditions of capitalist production.

The emergence of a money commodity as a socially accepted general equivalent and measure of the value of other commodities creates the need for the standardization of the money commodity in terms of purity and weight. '[Money] is the measure of value inasmuch as it is the socially recognized incarnation of human labour. It is the standard of price inasmuch as it is a fixed weight of metal' (*Capital* I, p. 96). According to Marx, money as measure of value becomes the standard of price according to the specific institutions of each country. The national state determines the relation between gold and national money, 'currency' circulating inside a country. This, as unit of account, represents a quantity of gold into which it is convertible. The minting of gold is a special public function. 'Coining, like the establishment of a standard of price, is the business of the state' (ibid., p. 124). Thus the ingots brought to the Mint are transformed into pieces of money containing an amount of gold that conforms to the official standard. From 1791 to 1933, for example, the US dollar was defined as one-twentieth of an ounce of gold of a certain purity and, except for the suspension of convertibility of the dollar into gold during and immediately after the crisis of the Civil War, representatives of gold money such as banknotes were convertible into gold at this price. In 1933 the US dollar was devalued to one thirty-fifth part of an ounce of gold, and this was the price at which foreign states could sell a part of their dollar reserves to the American Treasury until the suspension of convertibility of the dollar in 1971. But in that period gold was already demonetized in domestic and international circulation, an issue to which we shall return below.

The state institutions which intervene to define a domestic standard of price do not thereby create money nor determine the amount of money which circulates, despite the claims of the monetarists. Money is endogenous to the circulation of commodities, and it is in response to its fundamental character that institutions develop to manage it. Gold can be replaced by various substitutes, such as notes issued by the state, or private immaterial symbols – banknotes, certificates of indebtedness, etc. – providing that they are all defined in terms of and convertible into the gold money of which they are representatives.

Marx does not endorse Ricardo's search (1817) for 'an invariable standard of prices' that is 'a commodity invariable in its value' and shows that none can exist. The gold commodity itself has a fluctuating labour-value. In introducing a distinction between the exchange-value of gold, which varies over time, and the gold standard of price, fixed by the state, Marx has resolved Ricardo's question by modifying it, through his analysis of the different social forms of the general equivalent commodity.

The theory of money as a socially accepted general equivalent introduced by Marx has been the subject of numerous critiques. The chief of these concerns the determination of the value of money and the value of commodities. In addition, some also question the meaning of the use of money in pre-capitalist modes of production. Marx refers to Greek antiquity, and writes that Aristotle discovered the concept of the money-form. But he argues that Greek philosophy could not conceptualize the general equivalent because of 'the absence of any concept of value' (*Capital* I, i, p. 59). Plato, who conceived the division of labour as a division of social classes, speaks of money 'from the standpoint of use-value alone' (*Capital* I, ii, pp. 365–6). Real monetary practice thus developed for a long time before the theoretical comprehension of money and commodity circulation. As we have seen, even the discovery of labour-value by the classical political economists, fundamental as it was, did not lead them to the concept of money which Marx has.

Money as means of circulation of commodities
The second function of money is that of means of circulation in the chain: sale of commodities–money–purchase of commodities (*C–M–C* in Marx's notation). In Marx's view the role of money as a means of circulation follows from its emergence as a socially accepted general equivalent and measure of value. The money commodity is present conceptually in every exchange of commodities because it expresses the exchange-value of each commodity.

Marx understands clearly that the relation between the quantity of money in circulation and the value of transactions it can mediate depends on the *velocity of circulation*, that is, the number of commodity transactions on average each unit of commodity money participates in over a given period of time. Marx uses the equation of exchange, which relates the quantity of money in circulation, M, to the velocity of circulation, V, the average price of commodities, P, and the quantity of commodities bought and sold in a period, as $MV = PQ$, to determine the quantity of money in circulation M, since velocity and the quantity of commodities in circulation are determined by historical factors and the development of capitalist and financial institutions, and the prices of commodities in terms of money, as we have seen, are determined by relative costs of production. In modern terminology, Marx views the quantity of money in active circulation as endogenous, thereby sharply and fundamentally departing from the orthodox approach of the quantity of money theory of prices.

From this point of view it is evident that while the money-commodity must be present conceptually in every transaction to express the exchange-value of a commodity, it need not be materially present in order to circulate commodities. Various representatives of the money-commodity, such as nominally valued coins which do not contain a full weight of the money commodity, currency issued by the state (but convertible into the money commodity at the standard of price), private banknotes, or evidence of debt such as bills of exchange, can take the place of the money-commodity as means of circulation.

It thus appears that commodity circulation by means of a money commodity has the capacity to perpetuate itself indefinitely. Marx has eliminated the quantity theory concept of an excess or shortage of money which would push the prices of commodities up (inflation) or down (deflation), except, to be sure, in the case of absurd measures put in place by misadvised governments. Normally movements of prices arise from changes in the technical conditions of production of commodities, including the money commodity, so that to explain inflation or deflation it is necessary to examine the real underlying conditions of commodity production.

But commodity circulation has its own disequilibria, which are not correctable by political interventions. Marx here attacks 'the Law of Markets' formulated by J.-B. Say, according to which since every sale implies a purchase there must be a general equilibrium of commodity transactions.

> Nothing can be more childish than the dogma that because every sale is a purchase, and every purchase a sale, the circulation of commodities necessarily implies an equilibrium of sales and purchases. . . . But no one is forthwith bound to purchase because he has just sold. Circulation bursts through all restrictions as to time, place and individuals. (*Capital* I, pp. 113–14)

Commodity circulation, in so far as it reflects the social division of labour among individuals, is not the direct socialization of use-values exchanged as exchange-values against money. It necessarily involves certain disequilibria – excess supply and demand of particular commodities – and certain crises. There is no quantitative self-regulating principle in the circulation *C–M–C*. This point is, however, not developed here, since the study of crises is addressed in relation to the analysis of the capitalist mode of production.

The study of the monetary form to this point allows us to reject two conceptions which are constantly utilized in contemporary monetary theory, the quantity of money theory of prices, and Say's Law of Markets, according to which supply creates its own demand and the equilibrium of aggregate supply and demand is guaranteed.

Money as store of value
Marx introduces a third function of money in the last section of his chapter on the monetary circulation of commodities: *hoarding*. This is a component of the demand for money which the quantity theory cannot comprehend, even when it invokes the velocity of circulation of money, V, in the familiar equation of exchange, $MV = PQ$. In the twentieth century, J.M. Keynes (1936) introduced 'liquidity' as the specific character of money and as the basis of a demand for that good which can above all influence the investment of wealthy (unproductive) 'rentiers' who hold financial assets. Still, Keynes's heterodox theory of money differs in important ways from Marx's analysis of the general equivalent and the introduction of hoarding. Keynes sees money and its value as social conventions, not in Marx's terms as arising directly from the nature of commodity production. While Keynes's concept of *liquidity preference* has some parallels to Marx's theory of hoarding, his notion that the interest rate mediates the holding of money reserves has no echo in Marx's discussion.

In hoarding, 'commodities are sold not for the purpose of buying others, but in order to replace their commodity form by their money form'. Money becomes in itself an object of desire, able to be appropriated and conserved individually. 'Thus social power becomes the private power of private persons' (*Capital* I, p. 132). The instability of the value of gold makes no difference. 'In its qualitative aspect, money has no bounds to its efficiency, i.e., it is the universal representation of universal wealth, because it is convertible into any other commodity' (ibid., p. 133). For Marx, hoarding is not a component of economic saving, but a fetishized form of demand for money which Molière's miser Harpagon expresses in caricature.

Nevertheless, hoarding has a monetary function in a metallic circulation, which entails the need for reserves of gold. The quantity of money required for circulation varies according to the rise and fall of commodity production. Hoarding allows the formation of reserves which can be introduced into circulation or withdrawn from it. As we shall see, the formation of monetary hoards also provides the historical origin of money-capital, one of the preconditions for the development of the capitalist mode of production.

Hoarding calls into existence specialized monetary institutions capable of accumulating and releasing gold reserves, banks, with their strong-rooms. The role of banks is not completely investigated at this point in Marx's exposition.

Money as means of payment

Instead, Marx introduces a new function of money, as *means of payment*, arising from credit transactions that require monetary settlement at a point in time after the sale of the commodity. These credit transactions interrupt the movement of exchanges between commodities sold for money which serve for the purchase of another commodity, and figured above in *C–M–C*. 'The means of payment enter the circulation but only after the commodity has left it . . . The seller's commodity circulates, and realizes its price, but only in the form of a legal claim upon money' (*Capital* I, p. 136).

In addition, the certificates of debt can themselves circulate. The question here is not of loans made for the lender's profit, but of a *credit system* where promises to pay circulate, giving rise to intermediaries that specialize in credit transactions. This system develops spontaneously, as an autonomous mechanism, where money takes the form of unit of account. Public finance depends on the credit system just as much as private producers. Nevertheless, the monetary constraint asserts itself brutally in times of crises of production or commerce when it appears as an urgent need for 'hard cash' to clear the books. Marx indicated later that these monetary crises can appear even in non-capitalist modes of production, and are distinct from those whose fulcrum is money-capital incarnated by the central bank, the stock exchange and the money market.

World money

The end of section 3 of the chapter on money in *Capital* I is entitled 'Universal Money'. Here Marx explains the function of gold in international trade and finance. In relation to the market exchange among the different countries of the world, gold serves primarily to clear external accounts, which national currencies cannot accomplish. Thus international trade presupposes an incessant movement of flows of gold of constantly changing size. Marx assumes here that the gold standard is a universal monetary regime, which implies a world market among developed capitalist countries which have to finance their balances of payments. The gold market and the rates of exchange of national currencies with respect to each other are mentioned, but without detailed analysis. On this question there are only notes published by Engels as the third volume of *Capital* after Marx's death.

Marx's theory of money

Marx broke with all the ideas of the quantity theory, whether they refer to the determining role in the level of money prices of the quantity of gold or of notes in circulation. These ideas stem, according to Marx, from a misunderstanding of the nature and the specific roles of the money form in all commodity circulation. States can regulate the socially accepted general equivalent in their own territory, and in international trade, through the establishment and maintenance of a standard of price, but their issue of notes and their monetary policies rest on the base of money and the price form. Marx also breaks with the ideas of J.-B. Say, according to which commodity exchanges are forcibly equilibrated because every sale presupposes a purchase – which eliminates the problem of crises and the role that various types of money play in them.

The heterodox conception of money presented by Marx serves also to introduce the concept of *capital*. On the one hand, it is impossible to have capital without money. This means that capital cannot be merely a collection of goods having a use-value as means of production, in the hands of particular economic agents, entrepreneurial capitalists. Thus, no money, no capital. But on the other hand the social commodity and money relation cannot itself bring into being the capitalist social relation, which presupposes the production of surplus value and the transformation of circulation $C–M–C$ into $M–C–M'$. In this sense, money does not explain capital. It is a necessary, but not sufficient condition.

2. The transformation of money into capital

We have seen that hoarding meets the need for private and national reserves of money. The ownership of money is not the result of theft, as Proudhon would have it, which is not to say that the private appropriation of money and of the means of production is merely 'the fruit of labour and of saving'. But after the violence of *primitive accumulation* (which we discuss in detail below) in the capitalist mode of production, the accumulation of capital rests on a mechanism of exploitation of wage labour which conforms to legal and moral norms. This is the process explained by the analysis of the transformation of money into capital, in the section of the first volume of *Capital*, which follows the analysis of commodities and money. The monetary heterodoxy championed by Marx is thus related to a heterodox conception of capital.

We review briefly here Marx's analysis of capital accumulation, with special attention to the concepts of credit and money-capital. For Marx's theory of capitalist social relations, 'the circulation of commodities is the starting point of capital' (*Capital* I, ii, p. 147). The capitalist mode of production developed from the beginning of the sixteenth century, with 'the capital of merchant and usurer' as its sources of *money-capital*. The activity of these agents transforms the schema of circulation commodities–money–commodities into another form, money–commodities–money + profit, or $M–C–M'$, which is no longer an exchange of equivalents. How can we explain $M–M'$, which seems to violate the law of value?

Marx comments at length on the phenomenon of credit in the ancient form of usury, condemned by Aristotle, and later by Luther. Even if the usurer, for whom 'money begets money', has not disappeared, he is an antique in the context of modern capitalism. As for the merchant who makes a profit by selling dear and buying cheap, he makes a purely speculative profit at the expense of consumers, and does not represent any increase in the value of commodities in circulation. The activity of the usurer and the merchant is a source of accumulation of money-capital for themselves, but not an increase in the commodity values in circulation. 'It is impossible for capital to produced by circulation, and it is equally impossible for it to originate apart from circulation' (*Capital* I, ii, p. 165).

Marx resolves this 'contradiction' by introducing the market for waged labour-power, the only commodity whose employment by capital can create a value larger than that of the wage goods which guarantee its reproduction. The money wage which allows access to these goods embodies a certain number of hours of labour time, fewer than those the worker labours for capital. The unpaid labour time is appropriated as surplus value by the capitalist employer who has means of production and money. Neither theft nor violence are required: the purchase/sale of labour-power takes place legally, according to a contract between free agents. Labour-power is paid at its value according to the standards of living of the time. To explain the mechanism of exploitation of workers by capital, however, Marx needs to modify the theory of value of the classical political economists, and to use his heterodox conception of money. The 'mystery' of commodity circulation evaporates when this circulation includes the commodity labour-power. This circulation is then written as $M–C–C'–M' = M + m$, where C represents waged labour-power and means of production which produce a commodity, C', whose value is larger than its costs of production, and incorporates a surplus value which becomes profit, m, on the capital invested.

On the historical level it is primitive accumulation which describes the actual conditions of formation of the capitalist mode of production. The three principal conditions are the following: the formation of a proletariat whose members are constrained to sell their labour-power to live; the rise of international trade, of colonization, and of the pillage of the resources of countries that have them, mainly gold, spices and other items in scarce supply in Europe; and the growth of the public debt of European states to the benefit of creditors and official collectors of taxes. These processes started in the fourteenth and fifteenth centuries, though Marx concentrates on what happened in England in the sixteenth and seventeenth centuries as the paradigmatic case for the expropriation of small peasant proprietors, the suppression of common lands, and the system of enclosures for the benefit of large landowners. These expropriations and expulsions threw the landless labourers onto the roads, just at the time when the first manufacturers required workers. Marx tells this story as a historic drama, in which the state plays its part through law and repression.

The accumulation of gold and wealth in countries that underwent colonization gives a considerable boost to European merchant capital. Pillage, violence against indigenous peoples, repressed revolts, conflicts among the fleets of competing powers – are all aspects of the violence of the primitive accumulation of capital. As for the public debt, which was in large part incurred to finance national fleets and armies, it facilitated the enrichment of creditors of the states and the emergence of financiers who amassed considerable amounts of money-capital. This violent history is not to be read in the origin of the general equivalent presented at the beginning of volume I of *Capital*, nor in the story of merchants' or usurers' capital. Once the capitalist mode of production establishes its own laws to conform to its own requirements, they appear to be natural and eternal. But other contradictions then appear, according to Marx, which involve especially the role of money-capital and new forms of money.

Money, money-capital and capitalist finance

The circuit of capital begins with a sum of money-capital, M. But there is no guarantee that the industrial capitalist entrepreneur who intends to set the circuit in motion himself actually already has a money-capital sufficient to his project. The industrial capitalist may assemble the necessary money-capital by borrowing from one or many holders of money reserves, either directly, or through the intermediation of a bank or other financial institution. In its abstract form, the contract between the financial capitalist who owns the money reserves and the industrial capitalist who intends to use them to finance actual production is easy to understand: the financial capitalist lets the industrial capitalist use the money for a fixed term in exchange for its repayment together with a part of the surplus value appropriated from production.

Competition for funds among industrial capitalists, however, leads to a standardization of the loan contract. Since the financial capitalist is indifferent to the specific use the industrial capitalist will make of his money, all industrial capitalists will have to offer the same terms (allowing for risk or other relevant contingencies) to financial capitalists. The financial capitalist will demand a payment of surplus value proportional to the loan, whether or not the industrial capitalist actually manages to make a profit on the project or not, and this proportion, the interest rate, will be the same for all loans made at any moment. This form of loan contract obscures the source of interest as a part of surplus value, and makes it seem that interest is inherent in the money reserve itself. Thus, as capitalist production develops, owners of money reserves, come to think of earning the current market interest rate (which will vary according to the riskiness and maturity of the loan) as the inherent power of money. An industrial capitalist who uses his own money reserves to finance part or all of his production comes to see the foregone interest he could have received by lending his money to someone else as an *opportunity cost*, and will implicitly charge himself interest on his own funds. The industrial capitalist comes to think of his own profit as the surplus value he can appropriate from production in excess of the market interest rate, his *profit of enterprise*. Thus the emergence of a market rate of interest and the instinctive habit of charging it on available money reserves, either explicitly or implicitly, becomes an unquestioned axiom of capitalist social life. Its corollary is the *discounting* of future financial or other benefits to mimic the effects of compound interest, even when there is no actual money loan involved at all.

In Marx's view there is no systematic law or tendency governing the relation between the interest rate and the gross rate of profit (the ratio of the total surplus value to the capital invested in industrial capitalist production). The relative bargaining power of financial and industrial capital constantly shifts depending on the state of the business cycle, the organization of financial institutions, the intervention of the state, and other contingencies. At any moment there is a well-defined structure of interest rates for loans of varying maturity and risk, but over time it inevitably changes.

Thus capital splits into financial capital and industrial capital. The first receives surplus value in the form of interest and the second in the form of profit of enterprise. This distinction corresponds to different capitalist functions, discharged by different agents. This division obscures the unity of capital, which rests on surplus value. Marx wants to show what is behind this distinction of two forms of capital, and what illusions it promotes concerning the capitalist revenues of financiers and entrepreneurs. The opposition between the real economy of production and finance linked to money is a constant problem for economic analysis. Marx presents it as the expression of the bifurcation of the process of capital accumulation in modern societies into two parts, specialized either in the accumulation and management of money-capital, or of capitalist production.

Thus money dematerializes, as the credit system substitutes for the monetary system and becomes an agent of accumulation of capital. The credit system specific to capitalism has a two-fold character. On the one hand it grafts itself on to commodity circulation, as Marx explained at the beginning of *Capital*, and we have reviewed above. On the other hand metallic money is replaced in circulation by certificates of debt among the multiple agents of the system which facilitates the mobility of money-capital. Marx expands on this point in volume II of *Capital*, which deals with 'The process of Circulation of Capital' (1885). 'The so-called credit economy is merely a form of a money economy' (ibid., p. 110). But it is as necessary to capitalism as the development of the means of transport of commodities from one geographical point to another. It is above all in the texts of Marx assembled by Engels for the publication of volume III of *Capital* (1894) that one finds numerous notes describing the credit system. 'Credit money springs directly from the function of money as a means of payment. Certificates of the debts owing for the purchase of commodities circulate for the purpose of transferring those debts to others' (*Capital* III, pp. 139–40). This first aspect of the credit system presupposes the formation of reserves of money, as we have indicated above. A supplementary clarification bears on this point:

> The transformation of money into a means of payment makes it necessary to accumulate money against the date fixed for the payment of the debt. While hoarding, as a distinct means of acquiring riches, vanishes with the progress of the civil society, the functions of reserves grows with this progress. (Ibid., p. 142)

These reserves, which especially guarantee the convertibility of banknotes, are 'the pivot of the entire credit system. The central bank is the pivot of the credit system. And the metal reserve in turn is the pivot of the bank' (ibid., pp. 572–3). According to Marx, this requirement is admitted as much by Tooke, advocate of the Banking Principle, as by Overstone, whose conception of money revives the quantity theory.

The credit system peculiar to capitalism thus has indelible monetary roots: a unit of account which presupposes a monetary standard, reserves of gold centralized in the central bank of the country. These serve also to settle the international balance of payments. In times of commercial or industrial crisis, the demand for 'hard cash' upsets the network of credits/debts, and the credit system regresses to a monetary system. It is therefore inseparable from capitalist accumulation and the business cycle. This is its specific function, as Marx explains many times from different points of view: as a condition for the centralization and concentration of productive capital; as money-capital commanding through the rate of interest a part of capitalist profit; but also as the origin of illusions about money being able by itself to ensure its own accumulation; and as the foundation of banking and finance.

Concentration and centralization of capital through credit

In volume I of *Capital*, Marx introduced the idea that the credit system is, along with competition, an indispensable agent for the accumulation of productive capital at the social level. This accumulation, an expanded reproduction, presupposes a *concentration* of means of production through the funds required by numerous capitalist owners for investment and the payment of wages. Thus a mechanism of *centralization* is at work, through which large enterprises form themselves by means of mergers and acquisitions. Here the credit system plays a decisive role, in various ways: from access to bank credit to the financing of corporations.

> The world would be without railways if it had had to wait until accumulation had got far enough for individual capitals to be adequate for the construction of a railway. Centralization, on the contrary, accomplished this . . . by means of joint-stock companies. (*Capital* I, p. 628)

This change of scale also facilitates technical progress.

This form of 'socialization' of capital through the credit system has on occasion given rise to reformist fantasies among Marxist authors such as Hilferding (1910), and among the Soviet economists who worked on Russian development after the 1917 revolution. In this way of thinking, the centralizing economic effects of the credit system have been disconnected from what Marx would call the monetary system. Then it is possible to believe that a state can evade the constraints inherent in the employment of private money-capital by nationalizing banks, and allocating credit in the service of a central investment programme. After the Second World War, France, in its effort to reconstruct its capitalist economy, nationalized large private commercial banks, and large enterprises in the energy and transport sectors. Later, in the 1980s, a resurgence of domestic and international capital brought the reprivatization of the banking sector, and postwar French 'indicative planning' lapsed into disuse. These episodes show that the indispensable centralizing role of the credit system is not in reality a viable path to the 'socialization' of capital.

Marx insisted on this point, in opposition to the illusions of the Saint-Simonian socialists, who called for credit at a low or zero rate of interest as a way to favour the real accumulation of means of production and the creation of an abundance of products. But the credit system is always two-edged. As centralizer of investment funds, 'the credit system possesses indeed the form of universal book-keeping and distribution of means of production on a social scale, but solely the form' (*Capital* III, p. 608). If this system can none the less serve in the transition from one mode of production to another, which would not be capitalist, this presupposes, Marx argues, not only the abolition of private property but also that of commodity production (ibid., p. 607). Even 'free credit' is not a way to get out of the commodity relations of capitalism.

The hope that reform of credit and the provision of cheap credit can resolve the class contradictions of the capitalist mode of production reappears in every period of capitalist development. In the current period, for example, the vogue to provide cooperative 'micro-credit' to the poor peasants of the Third World is an expression of this tendency.

Financial and industrial capital

Marx devoted many pages to the analysis of money-capital as the source of the credit system special to capitalism. Since money-capital plays a key role in the development of capitalist production, the remuneration of those who are its owners through a rate of interest has its origin as a part of the profit of production arising from surplus value: the rate of interest is a deduction from the profit of the entrepreneur to pay the owner of money-capital who has provided the funds underwriting the activities of the productive enterprise. This practice corresponds to a difference between two sorts of capitalist business, which take different forms: 'The capital splits into capital property outside the production process, and yielding interest to capital itself, and capital in the production process which yields a profit of enterprise through its function' (*Capital* III, p. 375).

The division between finance and production, which results in qualitatively different capital incomes, reflects the individual experience of capitalists. 'But to apply it to the total capital of society is of course preposterous' (ibid., p. 376). Individual specialization characterizes the whole structure of the capitalist accumulation system. This in turn rests on the appropriation of surplus value from the exploitation of wage labour, which, however, is obscured by emergence of different forms of income, for example, interest and profit of enterprise.

Just as the actual organization of production, and supervision and discipline of workers, becomes the province of specialists in 'human resource management', finance becomes the function of specialized salaried managers.

> Stock companies in general – developed with the credit system – have an increasing tendency to separate this work of management as a function from the management of capital, be itself owned or borrowed . . . A numerous class of . . . managers [are paid as] skilled workers. . . . (Ibid., pp. 388–9)

These financial specialists secure the functioning of the credit system which is indispensable to the accumulation of capital. But their status is ambiguous, as is that of financiers, who form

> a new financial aristocracy, a new variety of parasites, in the shape of promoters, speculators, and simply nominal directors, a whole system of swindling and cheating by means of corporation promotion, stocks, insurance and stock speculation. (Ibid., pp. 440–41)

As in the case of the possessors of money-capital, the origin of their incomes in the surplus value appropriated in capitalist production is obscured by the form these incomes take, which in this case appears to reflect specialized financial skills (ibid., p. 882).

Finance and 'fictitious capital'

Money-capital does not directly put in motion a productive process from which a capitalist profit arises, but none the less participates in surplus value. As we have seen, the rate of interest appears as an income inherent in money-capital, which that capital creates as a value in itself, as if it were productive of surplus value. Understanding the rate of interest is the key to the grasping the phenomenon of *capitalization* of streams of revenue into sums of money even if these streams of revenue do not arise as part of capitalist surplus value. Money appears to

> increase by itself as the growing is to trees . . . Every periodic income is capitalized by calculating it on the basis of the average rate of interest as an income which would be realized by capital borrowed at the rate of interest . . . All connection with the actual process of expansion of capital is thus completely lost. (*Capital* III, p. 466)

Marx calls the wealth that arises from this process of capitalization *fictitious capital*, which develops from these collective illusions about the source of financial revenues.

This is the case with the public debt, which generates a stream of revenue in the form of interest, but does not represent any sort of real or monetary capital invested in capitalist production. The expenditures of the state, when they exceed tax revenues, give rise to debt. The creditors of the state, who receive a part of the annual tax revenue, have 'a claim on the State's revenue' and not on a capital, but the value of their state bonds is indistinguishable to them from the value of their corporate bonds or stocks.

Banks and other financial institutions
Marx takes English banks, and their relation to the Bank of England, as his paradigmatic model of the development of financial institutions because he thought the English system had developed most completely both on the domestic and international level.

> [W]ith the development of large-scale industry, money-capital, so far as it appears on the market, is not represented by some individual capitalist . . . but assumed the nature of a centralized, organized mass, which, quite different from actual production, is subject to the control of banking, i.e., the representative of social capital. (*Capital* III, p. 368)

The banks become '*the general manager of money-capital*'. The banking system central-izes 'money savings and temporary idle money of all classes deposited with them. Small amounts, each in itself incapable of acting in the capacity of money-capital, merge together into large masses, and thus form a money power' (ibid., p. 403). Their banknotes serve as money in place of metal coin. Understanding this function, however, does not prevent Marx from criticizing the 'bankocracy' and its parasitic character in relation to the activities of industrial producers and merchants.

The Bank of England played a central role in this system. It was a national institution, allied with the state, although it was in Marx's time the private property of its stockhold-ers. Its role was to centralize the gold reserves of the country to support commerce and international finance. A second responsibility of the Bank of England concerned what we call today monetary policy: this was 'the regulation of the market rate of interest' through the manipulation of the Bank rate, which was (and remains to this day) the guiding rate for domestic bank credit and had powerful effects on international flows of capital. The ability of the Bank of England to attract short-term international capital by raising the Bank rate reflected the quasi-monopoly status of England in the functioning of inter-national markets.

When he describes 'the primitive accumulation of capital' (*Capital* I, pp. 755–6), Marx shows that the Bank of England was not the first national bank, but that it had become the most important. From its founding in 1694 it took on many public functions: execut-ing the payments of the British government and managing the growing public debt; strik-ing the coins put into circulation; issuing banknotes. Little by little the Bank of England became the centre of gravity of the national and the international credit system.

This centralized management of the credit system, however, could not avert domestic crises or their spread on the international level. These crises are related to the business cycle, but can develop in a relatively autonomous manner. But crises do not destroy the capitalist credit system. 'Credit, likewise a social form of wealth, grows out of money and takes its place. It is faith in the social character of production' (*Capital* III, 1894, p. 574). This con-fidence is shaken during cyclical crises, but it recovers with the recovery of business.

Engels, the editor of Marx's texts, is much more pessimistic in 1894 both about crises and the dominant role of England in the world capitalist economy. A new globalization in the last decades of the nineteenth century, which Marx did not live to see, changed the game.

> The colossal expansion of transport and communication – ocean liners, railways, electrical teleg-raphy, the Suez canal has made a real world-market a fact. The former monopoly of England in industry has been challenged by a number of competing industrial nations. (*Capital* III, p. 489, n. 8)

Further, at the national level the formation of cartels and trusts, and the rise of protectionism (except in England) set the stage for an international industrial war, and of a general crisis much deeper than the episode of 1867 on which Marx frequently commented. Must Marx's analyses be modified as capitalism changes its form?

Marx and contemporary monetary theory

Now that we have reviewed Marx's analysis of money and finance, it makes sense to discuss the heterodox character of Marx's theory in relation to other approaches to monetary theory.

Monetary economics, including the heterodox tradition, has abandoned Marx's practice of relating the value of money to the labour-value of a money-commodity. This seems to be a reaction to the decline of the gold standard as a system of international money and the demonetization of gold in all contemporary capitalist societies. Gold has been replaced as money by state debt, which serves as a national unit of account and a means of circulation. No economic agent can escape using money. According to the monetarists, while the sovereign state can issue money acceptable by everyone in commodity circulation internal to a country, it has to respect certain rigorous quantitative norms to avoid inflation and deflation, and to maintain the external valuation of its currency.

Many of the fundamental insights of Marx's theory remain relevant and indispensable to understanding contemporary monetary issues. Money still serves as the socially accepted general equivalent through which commodities can express their underlying exchange-value. The mechanism of the exploitation of labour through the commoditization of labour-power works just as well with a state-credit monetary system as it does with a commodity-money system. Money still crystallizes the exchange-value of commodities of widely differing use-values and in this way equalizes the products of diverse concrete labours.

The inability of monetarism to stabilize a definition of money under which the demand for money (and hence velocity) is a stable function underlines important insights of Marx. One is his insistence that the equation of exchange is proximately a determinant of the quantity of money in circulation, not of the price level. Marx's approach directs our thinking to understanding what the mechanisms are that provide the circulating medium necessary to realize the prices of produced commodities. In modern capitalist economies this mechanism is the banking system, which can flexibly expand and contract credit to meet the needs of circulation. Marx's approach is highly compatible with the practice of contemporary central banks, which supply reserves endogenously to the banking system to maintain a target interest rate. Marx's recognition of the ease with which various forms of symbolic and credit money can take the place of 'hard cash' in the circulation of commodities is also relevant to the problem of defining 'money' operationally. There is a wide spectrum of close substitutes for cash as means of circulation of commodities, and even as means of payment. In these respects Marx's theory provides a rich and flexible mode of comprehending contemporary monetary institutions.

Marx's insistence that monetary phenomena are, far from being purely technical aspects of an efficient allocation of resources, deeply entwined with the class contradictions of capitalism also retains its freshness and importance. With the abandonment of the gold standard and a universal adoption of managed state-credit monetary systems in the capitalist world, money and monetary policy has become an important terrain of class struggle. The degree to which central banks will accommodate, for example, wage pressures from workers, greatly influences the distribution of income between wages and surplus value. An accommodative monetary policy will allow workers to seek substantial wage gains in a context of low unemployment and hence low risk of job loss. We have seen this drama play out in the USA and other advanced capitalist countries in the 1970s, which was a period of substantial inflation, but also substantial working-class gains in the distribution of income. In reaction to this pattern, central banks have adopted policies of 'inflation targeting', raising interest rates to moderate the pace of capital accumulation and reduce the growth of the demand for labour when inflationary wage pressures appear. From a Marxian point of view this policy might more appropriately be called 'surplus-value targeting', since its effects have included stabilization and rolling back of the distributional gains of the working class through a greatly heightened insecurity of employment. The emergence of this pattern of monetary policy also had far-reaching consequences for the relations between financial and industrial capitalists, since it required raising interest rates sharply, and thus diverting a larger proportion of surplus value as interest income.

Monetary and financial issues also play an enormous role in the regulation of the contradictions of world capitalism and the relations between advanced capitalist countries and the rest of the world. Less-developed countries have access to world capital markets in periods of financial crisis primarily through the mediation of international financial institutions, particularly the International Monetary Fund and the World Bank. These institutions have emerged as agents of enforcement of the policies of liberalized trade, investment, and financial flows favoured by the advanced capitalist countries. The political economy of developing countries is increasingly shaped by the imperative of maintaining their access to world capital markets, managing the turbulence of short-term capital flows in the context of liberalized trade and investment policies, and regulating their internal class contradictions through restrictive demand policies.

In the absence of a single world money issued by a supranational institution, which was the utopian reform proposed by Keynes in the 1940s, a hierarchy of moneys and the domination of one among them in international transactions has persisted. This was the situation of the English pound sterling under the gold standard before 1914, and of the US dollar after the Second World War and the end of the gold standard. Despite the massive external debt of the USA, the dollar is still, at the beginning of the twenty-first century, the principal unit of account and means of payment for international transactions. The American dollar has the largest share in the bundle of four great currencies which serve as the basic standard for the International Monetary Fund: the dollar, the euro, the Japanese yen and the pound sterling.

In contrast to the 1930s, during which the great international economic and political crisis gave birth to several monetary confrontations – devaluations of currencies, exchange controls – at the turn of the twenty-first century it appears that a hierarchical consensus has managed to overcome the problems the dollar experienced in the 1970s. The crises of 1997–98, involving East Asian currencies and the Russian rouble, have been contained under the leadership of the USA.

Nevertheless this monetary consensus has not eliminated clashes between the great currencies, particularly between the dollar and the euro. These conflicts can become destabilizing when they reflect a hegemonic rivalry between great powers, in a context where each great state seeks to deflect to the others its own stresses and crises. The history of money and of monetary policy takes its place among the channels through which capitalism spreads across the whole world, and the harshness of the primitive accumulation of money-capital Marx describes recurs regularly in our modern civilized world.

References

Arnon, Arie (1984), 'Marx's theory of money – the formative years', *History of Political Economy*, **16**, 311–26.
Bellofiore, Ricardo (1998) (ed.), *Marxian Economics A Reappraisal*, Volume I, London: Macmillan.
de Brunhoff, Suzanne (1976), *Marx on Money*, New York: Urizen.
Foley, Duncan K. (1983), 'Money and effective demand in Marx's scheme of expanded reproduction', in Padma Desai (ed.), *Marxism, Central Planning and the Soviet Economy, Essays in Honor of Alexander Erlich*, Cambridge, MA: MIT Press, pp. 19–32.
Foley, Duncan K. (2005), 'Marx's theory of money in historical perspective', in Fred Moseley (ed.), *Marx's Theory of Money: Modern Appraisals*, London: Palgrave Macmillan, pp. 36–49.
Hilferding, Rudolf (ed.) ([1910] 1981), *Finance Capital: A Study of the Latest Phase of Capitalist Development*, trans. Morris Watnick and Sam Gordon, London: Routledge; Boston: Kegan Paul.
Itoh, Makoto and Costas Lapavitsas (1998), *Political Economy of Money and Finance*, London: Palgrave Macmillan.
Keynes, John Maynard (1936), *The General Theory of Employment, Interest, and Money*, London: Macmillan.
Marx, Karl (1967), *Capital*, Volumes I (1867), II (1885), III (1894), New York: International Publishers.
Marx, Karl (1970), *A Contribution to the Critique of Political Economy* (1859), New York: International Publishers.
Marx, Karl (1973), *Grundrisse: Foundations of the Critique of Political Economy (Rough Draft)*, New York: Pelican, 1973.
Ricardo, David ([1817] 1951), *On the Principles of Political Economy and Taxation*, Cambridge: Cambridge University Press.
Rubin, I.I. (1972), *Essays on Marx's Theory of Value*, Chicago: Black and Red.

13 The transmission mechanism of monetary policy: a critical review

Greg Hannsgen[*]

Recently, many economists have credited the late-1990s economic boom in the USA to the easy money policies of the Federal Reserve. On the other hand, it has been observed that very low interest rates have had very little effect in improving the chronically weak Japanese economy. With those observations in mind, it would clearly be useful to have some theory of how money, monetary policy and interest rates affect the economy. Most analyses of the way in which monetary policy affects GDP and its components (the monetary transmission mechanism) assume that the central bank dictates the exact amount of money circulating at any given time. Post-Keynesian and other heterodox authors, in propounding the theory of endogenous money, argue instead that the central bank cannot control the money supply. Is there a theory of how money affects the economy when it is endogenous (Arestis and Sawyer, 2004; forthcoming)?

Since endogeneity implies that the amount of money in the economy adjusts to the demand for money, endogenous money theorists cannot base their theories on the notion that too much or too little money is in circulation. This amount is not subject to manipulation by policy. Instead, the effects of monetary policy must arise because policy affects interest rates. Since endogenous money theorists emphasize that money originates when credit is issued by banks, post-Keynesian monetary thinkers emphasize the effects of interest rates on credit. Moreover, heterodox economists are most interested in the effects of money on real variables, such as GDP, rather than inflation. They believe money can affect prices and inflation, but they argue that these effects are indirect and of secondary importance to cost increases.

Numerous alternative means exist to explain the transmission mechanism, and many of them will be described in this chapter. First, because investment has historically been one of the most volatile components of output, many theories concentrate on the effects of interest rates on fixed investment and inventories. Specifically, interest rates affect the price of money in the financial markets, and firms will not undertake an investment project if it yields a return less than this price. Second, cash flow is actually a much more important source of investment funds than borrowing; it will be shown that cash flow can either weaken the case for the centrality of interest rates or complement it. Third, and closely related to the second point, interest rates are an important cost for the firm; as such they affect prices and the distribution of income among 'factors of production'. Fourth, consumer borrowing can contribute greatly to the demand for goods and services, and such borrowing may be at least somewhat sensitive to the interest rate. Fifth, interest rate levels can affect international flows of capital, which in turn has the potential to change exchange rates. Since exchange rates are extremely important variables in their own right, they should be taken into consideration in analysing the transmission mechanism. Sixth, borrowed money can be used to purchase financial assets, not just capital goods. Hence, changes in the cost of borrowing may affect the markets for bonds and stocks, which in turn affect real output.

The chapter closes with a consideration of the term structure and risk premia of interest rates. This topic is very important for the monetary transmission mechanism because few of the effects of monetary policy listed above depend directly upon the short-term interest rates controlled by central banks. Rather, they depend on the rates available on commercial paper and bonds, mortgages, and so on. It is not always the case that the central bank can move these rates as it wishes. The chapter will discuss mainly Keynes's ideas on this issue, because, as is often the case, Keynes identified the key issues at stake, and future work will build from his.

The phenomenon to be explained: the potency of monetary policy

Before beginning with a taxonomy of interest rate effects, it is useful to consider the bottom line: do changes in interest rate (somehow) influence the level of economic activity? Figure 13.1 shows an 'impulse response function' from a vector autoregression with three monthly variables (for the USA): the federal funds rate, industrial production (a measure of economic output), and the consumer price index (in that order). The latter two variables are used in log form and 24 lags of all variables are included in each equation.[1] The impulse response function shows how output and prices react to a random shock to the interest rate, in this case a shock of one standard deviation, or about 50 basis points, in magnitude. The paths are surrounded by vertical bars of two standard deviations in height. The graph shows a statistically significant fall in output and a rise in prices in response to the hypothetical interest rate shock. The effect on output is greatest at a time horizon of approximately 24 months. These findings have been partially replicated using data from ten of the economies that now form the euro area: a positive shock to the base interest rate leads to a temporary fall in output that peaks at three to six quarters after the shock (Mojon and Peersman, 2003). While recent evidence suggests that the

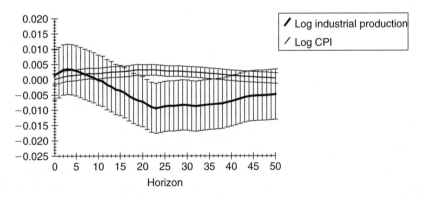

Source: Economagic.com and author's computations. Data: monthly, August 1954 to June 2002. Figure shows impulse response of the logs of industrial production and the consumer price index (CPI) to a one-standard-deviation shock in the federal funds rate (FFR). Regression equations included 24 lags of all variables. Identified using Cholesky scheme, with the variables ordered as follows: FFR, industrial production, CPI.

Figure 13.1   Impulse responses to one standard error (SE) shock in the equation for FFR (1954–2002)

impact of monetary policy may be weakening (Kuttner and Mosser, 2002, p. 15), these data indicate that it does have significant effects over a fairly long period of time. It remains to be seen how and why these effects happen.

Business and the cost of funds: some theories and their limitations

Basil Moore (1988), one of the first and most effective proponents of the theory of endogenous money, sees the transmission mechanism as operating through the equalization of various rates of return (see also Keynes, 1936; Rogers, 1989). Indeed, this is the primary alternative theory of the monetary transmission mechanism. If the real rate of interest is less than the rate of return on investment, businesses will increase their investments until the two returns are equal. Alternatively, firms use the nominal interest rate to determine the net present value of potential investment projects. An increase in the expected stream of returns or a fall in the interest rate increases the net present value of investment projects. What is important here is the *ex ante* (predicted) real rates of return (Moore, 1988, p. 258). Firms can only estimate the rate of inflation; hence they do not know the *ex post* (actual) real rate of interest. Similarly, firms can only guess at the returns their investments might yield (Keynes, 1936, ch. 12). The nominal interest rate is exogenously fixed, so it is the profit rate that adjusts to the interest rate, rather than vice versa. Thus, by wielding its policymaking authority, the central bank can affect the *ex ante* real interest rate, and so strongly influence investment.

This view can be represented by an equation showing the net present value (*NPV*) of a particular project

$$NPV = -C + Q_1/(1+r) + Q_2/(1+r)^2 + Q_3/(1+r)^3 + \ldots + Q_N/(1+r)^N$$

where *C* is the cost of the project (assumed to be incurred entirely in period 0), the Q_is are the returns to the investment in each of the subsequent periods (1 through *N*), and *r* is the discount rate (presumably the rate at which funds can be borrowed on the bond market). As the interest rate *r* rises, the net present value of each available project will fall. At any given time, a certain number of projects will have a positive *NPV*, and the firm will undertake those projects. In this view, the central bank can cause private investment to increase by lowering interest rates, which will cause more projects to have a positive *NPV*.

It cannot be emphasized enough that the Q_is in the equation above are merely estimates of uncertain quantities. They are profits, which depend not only on the physical productivity of a new plant or other investment, but also on the firm's ability to sell the product a number of years into the future. In fact, it was in his chapter on investment that Keynes emphasized most the importance of fundamental uncertainty (Keynes, 1936, ch. 12). This notion contrasts with the neoclassical notion of risk (but often referred to as uncertainty). In a neoclassical general equilibrium setting, for example, all agents know that particular 'states of the world' will obtain with known probabilities. For example, the probability of rain tomorrow might be 50 percent. The agent can prepare for any eventuality by purchasing commodities that are contingent on certain states of affairs, for example, one umbrella in the event of rain.

The type of uncertainty contemplated in Keynes's theory was very different:

> The game of roulette is not subject, in this sense, to uncertainty; nor is the prospect of a victory bond being drawn. Or, again, the expectation of life is only slightly uncertain. Even the weather

is only moderately uncertain. The sense in which I am using the term is that in which the prospect of a European war is uncertain, or the price of copper and the rate of interest twenty years hence, or the obsolescence of a new invention, or the position of private wealth owners in the social system in 1970. About these matters there is no scientific basis on which to form any calculable probability whatever. We simply do not know. (1936, p. 113)

Davidson (1982–83; 1991; 2002) has modernized Keynes's argument, using the statistical concept of nonergodicity (Hamilton, 1994, pp. 45–7). Ergodicity is a feature of certain stochastic processes. All nonstationary processes (those whose moments, such as autocorrelations, are not the same at every date) are nonergodic in this sense. During the 1980s much empirical work was done on the stationarity of important economic time series variables. The debate has not been fully settled, but there is much evidence that most common variables are nonstationary.

For nonergodic variables, sample moments (averages, variances, etc.) do not converge on their true values over time. The implication is that future realizations of random variables, such as the profits of a particular firm, cannot be predicted based on prior empirical observations. Any given historical situation is unique, and statistical techniques cannot uncover how the unique situation will evolve from now on. Hence firms cannot form any 'rational expectations' of the Q_is, nor are the Q_is connected with any objective, observable data.

Nonergodicity applies to stochastic processes. Another type of process is deterministic, but also has interesting implications for the type of expectations that appear in investment demand equations. Consider how the complex behavior might affect the calculation of the Q_is. One form of complex (or chaotic) behavior is 'sensitive dependence on the initial conditions'. This means that we suppose hypothetically that the economy is in one of two certain states at date 1. These two states (say, levels of GDP and other variables) may initially be very close together. But the state of the two economies later, say at date 100, may be very far apart.

If the world is chaotic (and many systems in the physical world indeed are), then it may be impossible to accurately determine the Q_is in time 10 based on the data in time 1. Any small error in measuring the initial state of the world could result in large prediction errors. Past observations may say that if the world is in state s in time 1, then it will be in state s' at date 10. But these past observations will be of little use if we observe that the world is in a slightly different state (call it s^*) in date 1. For then, the date 10 observation can be $s^{*\prime}$, a situation far away from s' (Gandolfo, 1997, pp. 503–5). Once again, the implication is that expectations of future profits, and hence *NPV*s and investment, follow no natural law that can be observationally detected.

Thus, in the view of Moore and some other heterodox thinkers, the role of the interest rate is to act as a discount rate, or opportunity cost of funds, to be used in calculating the *ex ante NPV* of potential investment projects. This approach is consistent with much of the *General Theory*. But Keynes also argued at times that the true opportunity cost of investment funds was set, not on the market for bonds or other interest-bearing assets, but on the stock market.

Keynes argued as follows:

The daily revaluations of the stock exchange, though they are primarily made to facilitate transfers of old investments between one individual and another, inevitably exert a decisive influence on the rate of current investment. For there is no sense in building up a new enterprise at a greater cost than that at which a similar existing enterprise can be purchased: whilst there is an induce-ment to spend on a new project what may seem an extravagant sum, if it can be floated off on the Stock Exchange at an immediate profit. (1936, p. 151)

In concrete terms, the argument would run as follows. Suppose that a firm operating one textile mill is valued on the stock market at a total capitalization of $100 million. Then, a second firm wishing to expand its output would be foolish to invest $200 million in building a new mill. Hence an important determinant of investment is the ratio, Q (no subscript), of the market capitalization of the relevant type of firm to the cost of pur-chasing new capital equipment on the market for capital goods. If the ratio is greater than one, a firm wishing to expand its capacity will prefer to build a new factory, purchase new software, etc., rather taking over an existing firm. If Q is less than one, the firm will take over a rival instead. Q can be defined as (Palley, 2001):

$$P_E E / K P_K$$

where P_E is the price of the firm's stock, E is the number of outstanding shares, K is the number of capital goods, and P_K is the price of capital goods. (The credit market is sim-plified away.) If markets are rational, they will value the firm's equity at the expected dis-counted value of future profits, $NPV + C$. Moreover, KP_K, the replacement value of the firm's capital goods, will be equal to C, where C is the aggregate price of all ongoing investment projects. Putting these relationships together,

$$Q = P_E E / K P_K = (NPV + C)/C$$

Q theory then says that firms should undertake investments for which $Q > 1$. Introducing this condition leads to

$$NPV > 0.$$

This view of the determinants of investment does not leave out the role of interest rates. In fact, Q will be determined in part by the ruling rate of interest. If an investor can earn a return of 10 percent on government bonds, then the value of Q must allow for at least a 10 percent return on stocks. The rate of interest enters the expression for Q in the NPV term.

One advantage of Q theory over the Keynesian theories described above is that the latter did not peg investment to any observable variables. This raises the possibility of *ad hoc* explanations such as: the economy is in a recession, so it must be that the state of expectation was poor. The very uncertain basis for Keynesian expectations makes it difficult to test the theory or come up with determinate results (Eatwell and Milgate, 1983, p. 13). On the other hand, Q is observable. We can test Q theory by observing the effect of Q on investment, and, hence, on output and employment.

Next, this chapter will present some criticisms of Keynes's theories, starting with Q theory, and then moving to problems with cost of capital-based theories in general. The progenitors of Q theory always recognized empirical problems. Specifically, the number that is relevant is 'marginal' Q, or the Q of a new investment, not the Q of an entire business. Clearly, in deciding whether to build a new factory, a business will consider the likely profitability of *that* investment, not previous ones. So, observed stock market values are not the appropriate numerator of Q. It is difficult to find any empirically verifiable metric of marginal Q. This fact reduces the appeal of Q, as opposed to a theory that bases investment purely on the (unobservable) subjective expectations of businesses.

Efforts to empirically test Q theory using actual stock indexes have not been successful. It is interesting to note that the ratio of takeover activity to investment tends to be at its highest when stock market valuations, and hence Q, are highest (Medlen, 2003). This observation suggests that takeover activity is not a matter of bargain hunting when markets are undervalued, but of a general bullishness affecting both merging firms and other stock purchasers. Real investment does not always benefit from stock market bullishness. This suggests that merger activity and stock market valuation are part of the same phenomenon, with real investment determined by other forces.

It is also important to recognize that Q relies upon strong assumptions about the motivation of managers and the rationality of stock market investors. A moment ago, it was assumed that both managers and firms have identical and correct expectations about future revenues. This rendered the $Q > 1$ and $NPV > 0$ conditions identical. This sort of assumption is what has led some critics of the theory to argue that it conflates the interests and knowledge of managers with stockholders and assumes that the latter are completely rational (Crotty, 1990; 1992). It is easy to drop the assumption of perfect foresight of the Qs by replacing them with (possibly irrational) expectations based on partial information. It then seems likely that the expected Q_is of the managers of a firm will differ from those of the stock markets. Then the Q and NPV criteria will give diverging signals regarding the desirability of new investment. Firms may be interested in making investments whose Q is less than unity.

Another problem with Q is that managers may set goals that are independent of stock market valuations. For example, managers may maximize sales growth, with profitability considerations acting as a mere constraint (Palley, 2001). They may have a different discount rate than financial markets. This observation is simply an example of a principal–agent problem, which arises because shareholders' and managers' interests are not identical (Crotty, 1990; 1992; Palley, 2001).

Keynes saw a role for the 'animal spirits' of 'entrepreneurs', not just those of stock market investors. He states that small businesses, before the predominance of public corporations, 'embarked on business as a way of life, not really relying on a precise calculation of prospective profit' (1936, p. 150). Even now, Keynes believed, 'Enterprise only pretends to itself be mainly actuated by the statements in its own prospectus, however candid and sincere. Only a little more than an expedition to the South Pole, is it based on an exact calculation of benefits to come' (p. 161).

There are thus two possible explanations of the rate of investment that depend on what Keynes dubbed 'the state of expectation'. First, the entrepreneurs invest when they are confident of the profitability of investment. Second, and alternatively, entrepreneurs make their choices with an eye on the stock market valuations of their firms. These market values are in turn determined by the state of expectation *of the stockholders*. The question then becomes whether entrepreneurs, when animal spirits move them, have the ability to initiate new investments. It will be argued below that large corporations, at least, have access to internal funds, which will enable them to make their own decisions, based upon their own estimates of the Q_is in their own NPV calculations.

It must be emphasized that the Keynesian theory as portrayed above, even if fully accepted, is not as favorable as sometimes thought to the view that interest rates have an important influence on business investment. Keynes emphasized the importance of expectations of profits in determining the Q_is above. These were largely conventional, with little basis in definite fact, and they could change very rapidly. This suggests the possibility that movements of the Q_is (expected revenues) are so wide that they swamp any reasonable changes in the rate of interest r.

In considering this possibility, Keynes says that interest rates 'exercise, at any rate, in normal circumstances, a great, though not a decisive, influence on the rate of investment. Only experience, however, can show how far management of the rate of interest is capable of continuously stimulating the appropriate level of investment' (Keynes, 1936, p. 164). He then states the case more strongly: 'It seems likely that the fluctuations in the market estimation of the marginal efficiency of different types of capital will be too great to be offset by any practicable changes in the rate of interest.' In other words, the Fed may move interest rates in a range between 2 and 8 percent, but estimates of the profitability of investment may range between negative 20 percent and 20 percent.[2] If the expected rate of return of an investment, because of a weak state of confidence, falls to negative 20 percent, the central bank will not be able to cause that investment to be made, even if it lowers interest rates to the bottom of its range. Expectations of rates of return and NPVs are likely to have a wide range, because of the fact emphasized above that they have no rational basis.

Another difficulty with the NPV and Q theories of investment is that they rest on an inverse relationship between the amount of investment or capital on the one hand, and the interest rate on the other (Rogers, 1989, ch. 2; Eatwell and Milgate, 1983; Garegnani, 1983). One can see this if one watches the present value of all projects as the rate of discount rises. As the rate rises, fewer and fewer investment projects will meet the positive NPV condition. So, there will be less demand for investment funds. One can thus map the total demand for investment funds against the interest rate. Some authors reject this relationship for two reasons: (1) (the analytical reason) the inverse relationship does not have any foundation in logic, since the cost of capital represented by any given set of machines, factories, etc. is itself a function of the interest rate; and (2) (the pragmatic reason) the relationship in question guarantees the existence of a full-employment rate of interest. If (2) is true, and if the economist can posit some mechanism whereby the interest rate automatically falls in times of recession, he or she can argue that the private economy will spontaneously achieve full employment without government intervention (Garegnani, 1983, p. 55). The first point is thought by some to be an implication of the outcome of the famous Cambridge capital controversy. Not all of the critics of neoclassical capital theory who were active in the controversy agree that it implies that NPV theories of the type used in some Keynesian macroeconomics are invalid or logically flawed (Robinson, 1983).

Several additional problems arise in connection with *all* cost-based theories of business investment, such as Moore's and Q theory. Both of these theories are 'price' theories, in that they make investment a function of the cost of external funds (either bond issues, bank loans, or equity issues). It is important to keep external funds in perspective. In 2003, capital expenditures by nonfarm, nonfinancial corporations amounted to $764.9 billion.

This figure stands against $797.7 billion in US internal funds, a rough measure of the retained earnings of corporations available for investment projects. So, corporations need not have borrowed any net funds to pay for capital expenditures (the majority of which went toward fixed investment, which includes new structures, software and equipment). And indeed, they raised only a net $97.5 billion via bond and equity issues, new short-term commercial paper, and other capital market instruments combined (Federal Reserve Board, 2004, Z1 release, table F102).

Cross-sectional data from Europe indicate a similar situation (Chatelain et al., 2003 and author's calculations). The mean ratio of cash flow to investment for Italian firms was 1.37, for French firms 2.70, for Spanish firms, 1.99, and for German firms, 1.57. These data accounted for firms employing at least 19 percent of the workforce in all four countries.

Many firms are not even on the market for borrowed funds. Only about 8 percent of the thousands of firms in the US Compustat data set raise money through commercial paper programs (Carpenter et al., 1994, p. 83). An additional 12 percent of these firms raise money in the bond markets but not via commercial paper. Many firms do not have bond ratings and must raise any external funds through private placements.

There are many reasons why firms use mainly their profits to finance investment. One key fact is that there is often a wide spread between the bid and ask prices for finance (Eichner, 1991). That is, firms must pay more for loans than they can earn in financial investments. One reason for this sort of spread is that high agency and transactions costs push the cost of capital to firms much higher than the return on risk-free assets. Agency costs include the costs of monitoring and enforcing debt contracts and setting aside funds to cover default risks. Agency costs would theoretically be highest for small firms whose financial situations are not tracked by bond-rating agencies, Wall Street firms and the business press. Indeed, data show that the smallest industrial firms rely most on internal finance (Fazzari et al., 1988, p. 147). On the other hand, in oligopolistic industries, leading firms generally possess sufficient pricing power to raise needed funds. So those firms who may most need external funds often cannot obtain them, and vice versa.

John Kenneth Galbraith interestingly traces the use of internal funds to a need by corporations to reduce uncertainty:

> Control of the supply of savings is strategic for industrial planning. Capital use is large. No form of market uncertainty is so serious as that involving the terms and conditions on which capital is obtained. Apart from the normal disadvantages of an uncertain price, there is the danger that, under some circumstances, supply will not be forthcoming at an acceptable price. This will be the precise moment when misfortune or miscalculation has made the need more urgent. And unlike the suppliers of raw materials or labor, the supplier of funds has traditionally been conceded some degree of power. The provision of credit carries with it to know, and even to suggest, how it is used. This dilutes the authority of the planning unit [corporation]. All of these dangers and difficulties are avoided if the firm has a secure source of capital from its own earnings. (1985 [1967], p. 36)

The more conventional argument, involving agency costs, has been fashionable for some time in neoclassical circles, but arguably has post-Keynesian roots. Kalecki argued for the 'principle of increasing risk', which has a resemblance to some more modern theories (1968, chs 8 and 9). In Kalecki's view, firms tended to try to limit their reliance on outside sources of finance. One reason is that even publicly traded companies were not 'brother-hoods of shareholders'. Insiders tend to have a grip on most companies, and the use of stock issues to raise money can potentially dilute their interest. Any use of borrowing can lead to a possibility of bankruptcy, which would lead to a loss of control to creditors. Short of bankruptcy, high interest costs can increase the possibility of capital losses in the event profits are not sufficient to pay financing costs. These sorts of risks to insiders (which Kalecki referred to as borrower's risk) increase as the extent of external finance increases.

All of this led Kalecki to posit that investment was a function of entrepreneurial capital or the gross savings (retained earnings) of firms. Not only could retained earnings be directly used to finance investment, but they also could be used as evidence of creditworthiness. This sort of reasoning is consistent with a more modern body of literature on the 'broad credit channel' (see, for example, Bernanke and Gertler, 1995; Bernanke et al., 1999). Proponents of this theory argue that not only cash flow, but also other measures of financial health, are critical for a firm's ability to attract capital and loans. Such measures may be sensitive to changes in monetary policy, since the latter can affect the value of collateral assets, etc. The so-called 'narrow credit channel' depends upon the ability of the central bank to reduce banks' access to loanable funds. The fact that 'purchased funds' are now readily available, in the form of large certificates of deposits etc., to banks in need of cash is now being recognized by many neoclassical authors, and the narrow channel has fallen out of favor (Romer and Romer, 1990; see Moore, 1988 and Wray, 1990 for heterodox accounts).[3]

The emphasis on increasing risk was combined with more conventional theories in the work of several post-Keynesians, including Hyman P. Minksy (1975; 1986). Minsky's theory was known as a 'two-price' theory, and the ratio of the two prices resembled Q in some respects. However, Minsky added some twists that made his theory both more realistic and more robust to critiques such as Kalecki's.

The first price in Minsky's theory was the supply price of capital goods. The second was the demand price. Both of these prices were represented in the 'two-price diagram' as schedules of prices for all potential levels of investment. As shown in Figure 13.2, the supply price of capital rises with increasing investment (P_I). There are two reasons for this.

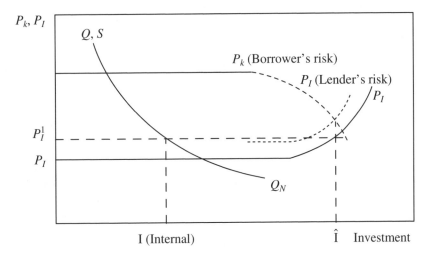

Source: Rae Ann Moore, based on Minsky (1986, p. 191).

Figure 13.2 The two-price diagram

First, costs of production of investment goods rose with increased output, just as in any Marshallian supply curve. Second, lender's risk was added to the costs of capital ('P_I lender's risk' in the graph). This was reflected in 'higher stated interest rates, in terms to maturity, and in covenants and codicils. Covenants and codicils might restrict dividends, limit further borrowings, and constrain the sale of assets; they might also require the maintenance of some minimum stated net worth.' All of these restrictive terms reflect concern by the lender that it is incurring increasing risk as it extends greater and greater amounts of credit. The terms reflect conventional margins of safety, such as maximum debt–equity ratios. These margins can change over time, for example, when lenders become more complacent after a long period of prosperity.

The demand price for investment ('P_K borrower's risk') also reflected the importance of margins of safety. As in Kalecki's argument, higher levels of investment increased risk not only to lenders but also to those who directly controlled the investing company. This increasing borrower's risk implies that the demand price for capital schedule slopes downward, which is also shown in Figure 13.2. A third line (Q_N) indicates the flow of internal funds. This schedule is a hyperbola because it represents constant nominal revenues, which are the product of the (price and quantity) variables on both axes. It is only the amount of funding to the right of that curve's intersection with the supply-price curve that must be financed externally.

The level of investment is given by the intersection of the P_K (borrower's risk) and P_I (lender's risk). This point is determined by many factors: the conventional margins of safety of firms and financiers, the uncertain expectations as to the profitability of a given venture, the availability of internal funds, and other factors. One could see it as a Q theory with an additional emphasis on conditions of finance, or a Kaleckian theory with an increased weight on the psychology of market participants.

The importance of so many nonprice factors would lead one to suspect that empirical studies would indicate a low elasticity of investment to interest rates. One recent study of user cost elasticities in the USA found, in its 'preferred parsimonious specification', that none of its user-cost elasticity estimates differed by more than two standard deviations from -0.25 (Chirinko et al., 1999, p. 69). The long-run user-cost elasticities found in one recent study were -0.663 in Germany, -0.106 in France, -0.111 in Italy, and -0.259 in Spain (Chatelain et al., 2003). Bernanke and Gertler (1995) describe similar data and observe that

[i]n general, empirical studies of supposedly 'interest sensitive' components of aggregate spending have in fact had great difficulty in identifying a quantitatively important effect of the neoclassical cost-of-capital variable. (p. 27)

There are two further considerations. First, user cost has many components and is affected by depreciation and other variables. Hence the elasticity of user cost with respect to the interest rate is often fairly small; even if user cost is an important determinant of investment, interest rate policy may not be a good way to reduce user cost. The second point is that the elasticities above change in the presence of a cash flow variable to -0.521, -0.027, -0.204 and -0.278, respectively. This leads one to expect that interest rate changes may exert their influence partly through their effect on cash flow, a statistically significant variable in its own right. Chirinko et al. note the same phenomenon and apply the term 'income effect' in contrast to the substitution effect between inputs from standard economic theory.

This line of reasoning implies that the lack of a traditional 'interest rate channel' does not imply that interest rates do not matter for firms. Davidson has emphasized the importance of cash flow commitments in an uncertain world (2002, p. 78). Agents use forward contracts, denominated in money terms, to help reduce the uncertainty they face about the terms of future transactions. Hence the possession of adequate cash reserves and cash flows is essential in a capitalist economy.

> In an entrepreneurial system where it is always possible that unforeseeable events may make it difficult to meet one's future contractual obligations, a primary consideration in the plans of all participants in the system is that before they put their plans into operation they need to possess sufficient liquidity to meet their existing and planned future contractual liabilities as well as to have ample liquidity to meet emergency future contractual agreements. (Ibid., p. 74)

Davidson emphasizes the importance of money in criticizing general equilibrium theory. In that sort of theory, all payments for the rest of time are settled in a single period, eliding the problem that Davidson sees as so crucial. 'Logically consistent mainstream theory emasculates the importance of money, cash inflows, cash outflows and liquidity from any historical time setting. There are never any cash-flow problems in the model.' On the other hand,

> In the real world, payments and receipts are contractually generated in the form of money in a sequential time setting as buyers and sellers engage in spot and forward markets . . . Liquidity is a fundamental recurring problem whenever people organize most of their income receipt and payment activities on a forward money contractual basis. For real-world enterprises and households, the balancing of their checkbook inflows and outflows to maintain liquidity is the most serious economic problem they face every day of their lives. (Ibid., p. 78)

The importance of money contracts is what makes money nonneutral in the long run (Davidson, 1991, p. 9).

One important forward contract denominated in money is the debt taken on by the firm to finance the purchase of some form of capital good. An increase in debt allows a firm to make more discretionary purchases. But each loan adds to a legacy of past debt, requiring cash interest payments. Minsky emphasizes the cash flow aspects of the acquisition of capital assets (1986, ch. 8). The role of interest payments in cash flow calculations can be shown with a simple equation (Eichner, 1991, p. 472; notation slightly changed):

$$E = F + \Delta D - DS$$

where E is the amount of funds available to the firm to make discretionary expenditures such as investments, F is the amount of internal funds, or cash flow, ΔD is the change in the firm's debt, or the amount it borrows during a given period, and DS is the firm's debt service costs on previously incurred debt. Now, additional loans affect E in two ways. First, they temporarily add to funds currently available, through an increase in the ΔD term. Second, they permanently add to the DS term. If funds are borrowed in the form of perpetuities that pay a given amount of interest every period forever, then the change in DS for a given ΔD is simply $r \cdot \Delta D$, where r is the interest rate on the loan. While the funds newly raised help the firm make purchases in the period in which they are obtained, they add to the firm's debt service costs forever, which compromises future cash flow. Less cash flow is available for discretionary purchases in the long term.

This leads to an important possible avenue for the interest rate to affect investment, even when conventional channels of influence are not operative. Given that the *DS* term in the equation is proportional to the interest rate, any increase in rates translates into a reduction in available cash flow (Chirinko et al., 1999). And, as we have argued, cash flow is perhaps a more important determinant of investment than cost-of-capital variables.

Minsky, like Davidson, puts a strong emphasis on the cash flow aspects of finance. He divided firms into hedge, speculative, and Ponzi units (1975; 1986). A hedge unit has adequate cash flow to pay both the interest and principal on its loans. A speculative unit cannot meet commitments to repay principal out of ongoing cash flows. Therefore, it must borrow money to repay the principal of its outstanding loans. Finally, a Ponzi unit must borrow money to pay both interest and principal. In terms of the equation above, for a Ponzi unit, F is less than DS, so that ΔD is used to offset DS. When a large number of firms become Ponzi units, the economy reaches a state of what Minsky called 'financial fragility'. In particular, the economy would be vulnerable to increases in interest rates. In fact, note that any firm that finances long-term projects with short-term borrowing is a Ponzi firm by Minsky's definition.

A closely related means of monetary transmission could be dubbed the cost-push channel (Barth and Ramey, 2001; Taylor, 2004, pp. 89–90; Hannsgen, 2004). Interest rates, the argument goes, are a component of costs: when they rise, they have the same effect as any other increase in costs. The resulting inflationary effect has been used to explain the long-observed positive correlation between interest rates and prices or inflation. (See Figure 13.1 for a variant on this finding.) Thomas Tooke, the first to note the correlation (later known as Gibson's paradox), stated the point in this way:

> Suppose, then, that the reduced rate is general, and the loans of such length of time as to admit of being extensively acted upon by the different dealers of commodities . . . [Then] the diminished cost of production hence arising would, by the competition of the producers, inevitably cause a fall of prices of all the articles into the cost of which the interest of money entered as an ingredient. (1844, quoted in Garegnani, 1983, p. 78)

Our concern is with effects on output, rather than prices. In a theory in which prices are determined by costs, interest rate hikes can lead not only to price increases, but also to changes in the distribution of income between those who earn interest and those who have few investments (Sraffa, 1960; Pivetti, 2001). They can also raise the relative prices of goods in which interest payments are an especially important 'ingredient'. Such changes in distribution and pricing could clearly, by affecting the demand for commodities, lead to changes in the composition and amount of output.

Some other important effects of policy: household spending, exchange rates and speculation

All of the possible channels of monetary policy transmission examined so far involve the business sector. But it is no secret that consumers have been borrowing at a furious rate in the USA; surely low interest rates can affect their spending. Net household borrowing climbed rapidly during the 1990s and early 2000s, reaching roughly 12 percent of GDP in 2002, led by a boom in home mortgage refinancing (Shaikh et al., 2003, p. 5). This development was clearly related to the downward trend in consumer rates that began in the early 1980s (ibid.). But for many less well-off consumers, interest rates are primarily driven by the markups charged by banks and other lending institutions to compensate for the risk of default, rather than by the cost of funds (Palley, 2002, p. 22). It is hard to imagine that monetary policy alone could ever cause a repeat of the ten-percentage-point fall in mortgage rates that took place from 1982 to 2003. Moreover, borrowing is often driven by constraints, rather than its relative price. On the one hand, many consumers are limited by the amount banks are willing to provide them. On the other hand, these same consumers may be in such dire straits that they feel they have to take advantage of loans they can obtain at any rate. This leads to the observation that in 1998, households with incomes under $50 000 had a debt–income ratio of 2.98, while those with incomes above that figure had a ratio of 1.40 (Palley, 2002, p. 21). Households so deeply in debt as the former group may not be very responsive to slight changes in interest rates. As with corporate business, it may be those households who least need credit that are most able to obtain it.

Particularly in small open economies, the most important effect of interest rates may, naturally enough, involve cross-border transactions. Since the 1960s, the world's capital markets have been opened. As a result, changes in interest rates can cause shifts in the capital account. Now that foreigners can invest in domestic securities and currency, they may respond to an incremental increase in the domestic interest rate by first buying domestic currency and then converting it into domestic financial investments. Such purchases are thought to increase the value of the home currency, which of course can impact imports and exports.

In the exogenous-money world, inflows of foreign capital can cause domestic inflation, similarly to any other increase in the money supply. But post-Keynesians have different ideas about the role of capital flows (Lavoie, 2001; Godley and Lavoie, 2004). Post-Keynesians have always downplayed the influence of increases in the money supply. If a firm has too much money, it generally purchases an interest-bearing asset, such as a government bond. The central bank is happy to sell the bond, because it wishes to keep the rate of interest on bonds constant, and a purchase by a private individual would otherwise have a tendency to lower the return. Hence there is no 'excess' money sloshing around, causing trouble. One could substitute for the word bond in the last few sentences the words 'certificate of deposit', 'Treasury bill', or 'commercial paper'.

Heterodox thinkers believe that a similar process occurs when capital flows into a country (Lavoie, 2001). Following a domestic interest rate rise, foreign investors may purchase domestic securities from domestic nationals. These sellers then deposit their foreign funds in a bank, exchanging them for domestic currency or bank deposits. The bank then presumably sells the foreign exchange to the central bank in return for reserve deposits. But the process does not stop there. Unless the county's demand for currency has for some reason risen, the bank will want to exchange its new reserves for earning assets, such as government bonds. (They will have already granted loans to all creditworthy borrowers.) Once again, the central bank is happy to oblige by selling a bond; if it does not, the price of bonds will be bid up above target. Finally, the money supply is at the same demand-determined level. The central bank holds more foreign reserves; if it should attempt to sell them, the domestic currency would appreciate. However, there is nothing automatic or inevitable about such an attempt.

An example is the recent building up of huge stocks of foreign reserves by several East Asian central banks. Eventually, these reserves may be sold off in an abrupt manner, causing a crisis. But for now, no spontaneous adjustments of the exchange rate will take place. For some theorists holding views of this sort, the exchange rate is very similar to the interest rate or stock prices in Keynes's thought, in that all three are set largely by convention and mass psychology (Vernengo, 2001). The situation of a country losing reserves is not symmetric to that of the country absorbing reserves, but most nations hold sufficient foreign reserves to 'buy back' all their currency and central bank deposits (Obstfeld and Rogoff, 1995, p. 78).

Nonetheless, capital flows often have an impact on exchange rates. The main neoclassical theory of the impact of interest rates on exchange rates, the so-called uncovered interest parity condition, finds little empirical support. But for relatively large countries, interest rate moves can be used roughly to set an appropriate exchange rate. As Wicksell put it,

> A country which maintains sufficiently high its borrower's and lender's rates of interest need never fear that its notes will depreciate. In theory, indeed, it should much rather be possible for such a country to raise its currency to any height . . . irrespective of anything that is taking place abroad in the monetary sphere. (Wicksell, quoted in Vernengo, 2001, p. 262)

Arestis and Sawyer (forthcoming) note that recent empirical work supports this view more strongly than studies using older data. But domestic interest rates are forced into exact equality with foreign rates only when the liabilities of all countries are perfectly substitutable in the eyes of investors. The ongoing 'home bias' in financial investment (a preference to invest in the domestic country's assets, all other things equal) is but one piece of evidence for a partial lack of substitutability.

Once exchange rates are affected, the impact on an economy can be large. Summarizing results of their own, which are in accord with those of other researchers, Godley et al. (2004, p. 3) estimate that the effect on the balance of trade of a 10 percent devaluation would be about 1 percent of GDP, assuming GDP were held constant.

Interest rates can also have an important impact on the economy through their influence on asset prices. If interest rates are in the neighborhood of 2 percent, as they recently were in the USA, it makes sense for those with access to borrowed funds to purchase assets that offer a greater return. Clearly, one variant of this phenomenon is the purchase of stock 'on margin', or with borrowed funds. Another option is to borrow funds to buy real estate that is expected to appreciate. A cycle can develop in which credit is used to buy assets, which rise in value. The increases in the value of the assets can then be leveraged for further asset purchases. If many investors are playing the same game, an asset bubble may develop. One might dub this form of monetary transmission the 'speculation channel'.

The uncertain link between policy-determined and long-term rates

So far, the effect of the interest rate has been examined from many angles. But this chapter has neglected the issue of *which* interest rate is the relevant one. If short-term rates are the most important for investment, the Fed has great power. For while firms wishing to purchase capital goods do not borrow on the reserves market (which is closed to non-dealers in the USA), all short-term rates fairly closely track open market rates (in the USA, the federal funds rate, or FFR). Rates at a maturity of up to about six months follow open market rates because of the possibility of arbitrage.

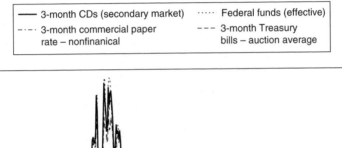

Figure 13.3 Various short-term interest rates (US)

It is important to realize that in an endogenous-money world, it is always the other interest rates that adjust to the FFR, rather than vice versa. The FFR in an endogenous-money world (all real economies) is targeted by the central bank. So, an incipient change in the FFR is always nipped in the bud by the central bank, unless the bank wishes to change deliberately the FFR. So, if the FFR should start to rise above (fall below) the central bank's target, the Fed purchases (sells) securities, causing a return to target. This means that all short rates are forced to adjust to the open market rate, as set by the central bank.

Figure 13.3 shows the relationship between various short-term interest rates. This chart shows just how pervasive the arbitrage is in short-term credit markets. It is clear that to control the FFR is to control the entire range of short-term interest rates.

Short-term interest rates are probably not as important as long-term ones for influencing the rate of investment and other components of demand. Almost by definition, the relevant rate for investment decisions is the long-term one. Fixed investment pays off over a long term, and firms are probably reluctant to finance a long-term project with short-term borrowing, simply because of the risk of interest rate increases. (Inventories and working capital are more closely related to short-term rates.) Keynes himself noted this point:

> Where . . . [as in the USA, 1933–34] open-market operations have been limited to the purchase of very short-dated securities, the effect [of open market operations] may . . . be mainly confined to the very short-term rate of interest and have but little reaction on the much more important long-term rates of interest. (1936, p. 197)

Clearly, long-term interest rates are subject to the same kind of arbitrage seen in the case of different short-term rates. If an investor expects the short-term rate to stay at

2 percent with 100 percent certainty, then he or she can with confidence invest in a long-term bond yielding 3 percent. But over the longer term, the fundamentals of bond value, including the short-term rate, are likely to change. Therefore, in contrast to investors in short-run instruments such as commercial paper, bond investors must be wary of capital loss. There are many reasons why capital loss might occur, but Keynes emphasized capital loss due to a rise in yields, which move in the opposite direction of bond values. The intuition of such capital losses is as follows: (1) a bond promises to pay a certain amount of money at some future date(s); (2) if, at some point after the investor has purchased the bond, the interest rate rises, then the price of future money payments will fall and (3) hence, the value of the original bond falls.

Keynes used a formula to show how the prospects of a capital loss might affect the actual rate of return of a fixed-income investment such as a bond. The change in the return of the security (including capital loss), R, due to a change in the short-term interest rate could be relatively large (Taylor, 2004, p. 140).

Keynes presents an example:

> If . . . the rate of interest is already as low as 2 percent, the running yield will only offset a rise in it of as little as 0.04 percent per annum. This, indeed, is perhaps the chief obstacle to a fall in the rate of interest to a very low level . . . [A] long-term rate of interest of (say) 2 percent leaves more to fear than to hope, and offers, at the same time, a running yield which is only sufficient to offset a very small measure of fear. (1936, p. 202)

The point is that the interest payments earned on a bond can be very low compared to the loss an investor can incur in the event of a capital loss due to a rise in rates. Moreover, the effect of a capital loss is magnified when interest rates are already low.

Now, capital losses on bonds are, in Keynes's eyes, just as uncertain as capital losses in stocks. Like the values of stocks, as pointed out above, bond values are based on a very fragile set of expectations. These expectations are in normal times governed by convention. But since the convention has little firm basis in fact, it is subject to rapid changes in response to minor changes in 'fundamentals'. This leads Keynes to state that 'It is evident . . . that the rate of interest is a highly psychological phenomenon' (ibid., p. 202) or alternatively that 'the rate of interest is a highly conventional, rather than a highly psychological, phenomenon' (p. 203).

Keynes was especially concerned with the case in which the interest rate was stuck at a level *above* that which was consistent with full employment: 'The long-term rate may be more recalcitrant (than the short-term one) when once it has fallen to a level which, on the basis of past experience and present expectations of future monetary policy, is considered "unsafe" by representative opinion' (p. 203). A given rate of interest may be particularly recalcitrant if it is thought to be 'natural' or based on fundamentals, rather than convention (p. 204). However, it is possible for the central bank to change the psychology of the markets: 'precisely because it is not rooted in secure knowledge, it will not be always unduly resistant to a modest measure of persistence and consistency of purpose by the monetary authority' (p. 204).

The fear-of-capital-loss theory of interest rate rigidity has some drawbacks. It rests on the notion that an expected 'safe' rate of interest exists in the minds of investors, and that fears of capital loss set in once yields fall to that rate. But neo-Ricardian Keynesians such as Garegnani (1983) find this story unsatisfactory:

The position of the speculative demand for money schedule, and hence the rate of interest, thus comes to depend on expectations about the future course of the latter. However, in the absence of their ulterior explanation, these expectations introduce a serious element of indeterminacy into the theory. (p. 53)

This is the same objection some economists raise against the animal spirits theory of investment determination: whatever data are observed, they can be justified *ad hoc* as the result of some vaguely specified psychological factors. More to the point, the fear-of-capital-loss theory of long-term interest rates depends upon the existence of a 'safe interest rate' below which concerns over capital losses predominate. To argue that this rate stays at a certain level for a prolonged period of time (long enough to cause a recession), one must assert that the 'safe interest rate' remains stable even in the face of continuing data showing that capital losses are not in fact occurring. It seems more likely that the perceived safe rate would eventually fall in line with the actual rate (Garegnani, 1983, p. 53). Then, no obstacle would exist to the achievement of any rate of interest; on the other hand, some other theory of the long-term rate would have to be found to replace Keynes's.

Concluding remarks

This chapter shows that a plethora of explanations exist of the monetary transmission mechanism. In fact, several important theories have been left out. As the empirical results presented early in the chapter show, interest rates do indeed have some impact on output. But empirics and theory alike caution us not to assume that monetary policy is all-powerful. It is possible that, given the uncertainty of the effects described here, the best use of monetary policy may be as a stabilizing tool, rather than as a gas pedal to maneuver the economy away from recession and excessive inflation. Then, the interest rate could be kept at a low level, as it was with some success in the USA immediately after the Second World War. If a gun is extremely imprecise and erratic, it may be best not to fire it at all. Rapid changes in interest rates may or may not affect fixed investment in the direction desired by policymakers. But it is known that the speculative channel does the most mischief when rates vary dramatically over time.

Notes

* The author wishes to thank the editors for incisive comments that greatly improved the chapter.
1. For a justification of the use of the federal funds rate as a monetary policy variable, see Bernanke and Blinder (1992). For general explications of this type of monetary VAR and further results, see Christiano et al. (1999), Leeper et al. (1996), and Bernanke and Mihov (1998).
2. For a statement of a similar view, put in a slightly different way, see Arestis and Sawyer (forthcoming). Arestis and Sawyer argue that the 'equilibrium', or full employment, interest rate may be below a zero nominal level.
3. Some authors who, to their credit, recognize this point fail to realize that it also vitiates the notion that the Fed can control the *liabilities* of banks. Since banks create assets and liabilities simultaneously, this view is difficult to accept. When the Fed buys reserves, depositors may have to be induced to exchange 'reservable' deposits (such as checking accounts) for assets such as certificates of deposit for which reserves are not required. But various types of bank liabilities are very close substitutes and can readily be exchanged for one another as necessary. Kuttner and Mosser (2002, p. 19) also point out that, for various reasons, reserve requirements are no longer a binding constraint on the amount of reserves held for most banks.

References

Arestis, Philip and Malcolm Sawyer (2004), 'Can monetary policy affect the real economy?', *European Review of Economics and Finance*, **3**(3), 9–32.

Arestis, Philip and Malcolm Sawyer (forthcoming), 'The role and nature of monetary policy when money is endogenous', *Cambridge Journal of Economics*.

Barth, III, M.J. and V.A. Ramey (2001), 'The cost channel of monetary transmission', *NBER Macroeconomics Annual*, 199–240.

Bernanke, Ben S. and Alan Blinder (1992), 'The federal funds rate and the channels of monetary transmission', *American Economic Review*, **82**, 901–21.

Bernanke, Ben S. and Mark Gertler (1995), 'Inside the black box: the credit channel of monetary transmission', *Journal of Economic Perspectives*, **9**, 27–48.

Bernanke, Ben S. and Ilian Mihov (1998), 'Measuring monetary policy', *Quarterly Journal of Economics*, **113**, 869–902.

Bernanke, Ben S., Mark Gertler and Simon Gilchrist (1999), 'The financial accelerator in a quantitative business cycle framework', in J. Taylor and M. Woodford (eds), *Handbook of Macroeconomics*, Vol. 1C, Oxford, UK: Elsevier, 1341–93.

Carpenter, Robert E., Steven M. Fazzari and Bruce C. Petersen (1994), 'Inventory investment, internal-finance fluctuations, and the business cycle', *Brookings Papers on Economic Activity*, 75–122.

Chatelain, J.B., A. Generale, I. Hernando, P. Vermeulen and U. von Kalckreuth (2003), 'Firm investment and monetary policy transmission in the euro area', in I. Angeloni, A. Kashyap and B. Mojon (eds), *Monetary Policy Transmission in the Euro Area*, Cambridge, UK: Cambridge University Press, 133–61.

Chirinko, Robert S., Steven M. Fazzari and Andrew P. Meyer (1999), 'How responsive is business capital formation to its user cost? An exploration with micro data', *Journal of Public Economics*, **74**, 53–80.

Christiano, Lawrence J., Martin Eichenbaum and Charles Evans (1999), 'Monetary policy shocks: what have we learned and to what end', in *Handbook of Macroeconomics*, Vol. 1A, Oxford: Elsevier Science, 65–148.

Crotty, James R. (1990), 'Owner–manager conflict and financial theories of investment instability: a critical assessment of Keynes, Tobin, and Minsky', *Journal of Post Keynesian Economics*, **12**, 519–36.

Crotty, James R. (1992), 'Neoclassical and Keynesian approaches to the theory of investment', *Journal of Post Keynesian Economics*, **14**, 483–95.

Davidson, Paul (1978), *Money and the Real World*, London: Macmillan.

Davidson, Paul (1982–83), 'Rational expectations: a fallacious foundation for studying crucial decision-making processes', *Journal of Post Keynesian Economics*, **5**, 182–98.

Davidson, Paul (1991), 'Is probability theory relevant for uncertainty? A post Keynesian perspective', *Journal of Economic Perspectives*, **5**, 129–43.

Davidson, Paul (2002), *Financial Markets, Money and the Real World*, Cheltenham, UK and Northampton, MA, USA: Edward Elgar.

Eatwell, J. and M. Milgate (1983), 'Introduction', in J. Eatwell and M. Milgate (eds), *Keynes's Economics and the Theory of Value and Distribution*, Oxford: Oxford University Press, 1–17.

Eichner, Alfred S. (1991), *The Macrodynamics of Advanced Market Economies*, Armonk, NY: M.E. Sharpe.

Fazzari, Steven M., R. Glenn Hubbard and Bruce C. Petersen (1988), 'Financing constraints and corporate investment', *Brookings Papers on Economic Activity*, 141–95.

Federal Reserve Board of Governors (2004), Flow of Funds of the United States.

Galbraith, John Kenneth (1985 [1967]), *The New Industrial State*, 4th edn, New York: New American Library.

Gandolfo, Giancarlo (1997), *Economic Dynamics*, study edn, Berlin: Springer.

Garegnani, P. (1983), 'Notes on consumption, investment and effective demand', in John Eatwell and Murray Milgate (eds), *Keynes's Economics and the Theory of Value and Distribution*, Oxford: Oxford University Press, 21–69.

Godley, Wynne, Alex Izurieta and Gennaro Zezza (2004), *Prospects and Policies for the U.S. Economy: Why Net Exports Must Now Be the Motor for U.S. Growth*, Strategic Analysis, Annandale-on-Hudson, NY: The Levy Economics Institute and Cambridge Endowment for Research in Finance.

Godley, Wynne and Marc Lavoie (2004), 'Simple open economy macro with comprehensive accounting – a radical alternative to the Mundell Fleming model', Working Paper No. 15, Cambridge, UK: Cambridge Endowment for Research in Finance.

Hamilton, James D. (1994), *Time Series Analysis*, Princeton, NJ: Princeton University Press.

Hannsgen, Greg (2004), 'Gibson's paradox, monetary policy, and the emergence of cycles', Working Paper No. 411, Annandale-on-Hudson, NY: The Levy Economics Institute.

Kalecki, Michal (1968), *Theory of Economic Dynamics: An Essay on Cyclical and Long-Run Changes in Capitalist Economy*, New York: Modern Reader Paperbacks.

Keynes, John Maynard (1936), *The General Theory of Employment, Interest and Money*, New York: Harcourt, Brace and Co.

Kuttner, Kenneth N. and Patricia Mosser (2002), 'The monetary transmission mechanism: some answers and further questions', *Federal Reserve Bank of New York Economic Policy Review*, **8**: 15–26.

Lavoie, Marc (2001), 'The reflux mechanism and the open economy', in Louis-Philippe Rochon and Matias Vernengo (eds), *Credit, Interest Rates, and the Open Economy*, Cheltenham, UK and Northampton, MA, USA: Edward Elgar, 215–42.

Leeper, Eric M., Christopher A. Sims and Tao Zha (1996), 'What does monetary policy do?', *Brookings Papers on Economic Activity*, 1–79.

Medlen, Craig (2003), 'The trouble with Q', *Journal of Post Keynesian Economics*, **25**, 693–8.

Minsky, Hyman P. (1975), *John Maynard Keynes*, New York: Columbia University Press.

Minsky, Hyman P. (1986), *Stabilizing an Unstable Economy*, New Haven, CT: Yale University Press.

Mojon, B. and G. Peersman (2003), 'A VAR description of the effects of monetary policy in the individual countries of the euro area', in I. Angeloni, A. Kashyap and B. Mojon (eds), *Monetary Policy Transmission in the Euro Area*, Cambridge, UK: Cambridge University Press, 56–74.

Moore, Basil (1988), *Horizontalists and Verticalists: The Macroeconomics of Credit Money*, Cambridge, UK: Cambridge University Press.

Obstfeld, Maurice and Kenneth Rogoff (1995), 'The mirage of fixed exchange rates', *Journal of Economic Perspectives*, **9**, 73–96.

Palley, Thomas I. (2001), 'The stock market and investment: another look at the micro-foundations of q theory', *Cambridge Journal of Economics*, **25**, 657–67.

Palley, Thomas I. (2002), 'Economic contradictions coming home to roost? Does the U.S. economy face a long-term aggregate demand generation problem?', *Journal of Post Keynesian Economics*, **25**, 9–32.

Pivetti, Massimo (2001), 'Money endogeneity and monetary non-neutrality: a Sraffian perspective', in Louis-Philippe Rochon and Matias Vernengo (eds), *Credit, Interest Rates and the Open Economy*, Cheltenham, UK and Northampton, MA, USA: Edward Elgar, 104–19.

Robinson, Joan (1983), 'Garegnani on effective demand', in John Eatwell and Murray Milgate (eds), *Keynes's Economics and the Theory of Value and Distribution*, Oxford: Oxford University Press, 70–71.

Rogers, Colin (1989), *Money, Interest and Capital: A Study in the Foundations of Monetary Theory*, Cambridge, UK: Cambridge University Press.

Romer, Christina D. and David H. Romer (1990), 'New evidence on the monetary transmission mechanism', *Brookings Papers on Economic Activity*, 149–213.

Shaikh, Anwar M., Dimitri B. Papadimitriou, Claudio H. Dos Santos and Gennaro Zezza (2003), *Deficits, Debts, and Growth: A Reprieve But Not a Pardon*, Strategic Analysis, Annandale-on-Hudson, NY: The Levy Economics Institute.

Sraffa, Piero (1960), *Production of Commodities by Means of Commodities*, Cambridge, UK: Cambridge University Press.

Taylor, Lance (2004), *Reconstructing Macroeconomics: Structuralist Proposals and Critiques of the Mainstream*, Cambridge, MA: Harvard University Press.

Vernengo, Matias (2001), 'Foreign exchange, interest and prices: the conventional exchange rate', in Louis-Philippe Rochon and Matias Vernengo (eds), *Credit, Interest Rates and the Open Economy*, Cheltenham, UK and Northampton, MA, USA: Edward Elgar, 256–70.

Wray, L. Randall (1990), *Money and Credit in Capitalist Economies: The Endogenous Money Approach*, Aldershot, UK and Brookfield, US: Edward Elgar.

14 Monetary policy
James Forder

The Phillips curve and Friedman's proposal

It is difficult not to be struck by the high proportion of economists who assent to the doctrine of the neutrality of money. Just as notable, perhaps, although much less often noted, is the degree of agreement on a picture of how – as a result of what came to be called 'the monetarist counter-revolution' – that consensus emerged. This picture is not only routinely presented in textbooks, but can also be found to underlie numerous policy statements, to motivate institutional design, and even to be assumed in political memoirs. And indeed, in certain important respects, it might be more important in shaping today's policymaking environment than the doctrine of 'the classical dichotomy' itself.

In the form in which they have been accepted, these things were most clearly popularized in Friedman's (1977) Nobel Lecture. He attributed the deterioration in performance before then to a mistaken belief among policymakers that there existed an exploitable tradeoff between inflation and unemployment in the manner superficially suggested by the work of Phillips (1958). Friedman's view was that as policymakers acted on this idea and raised inflation, unemployment fell temporarily, but only so long as the inflation was unanticipated or its effects misunderstood by wage bargainers. In the longer term, unemployment would return to its 'natural rate', but with inflation at a higher level. From there policymakers could still lower unemployment, but only with even greater inflation so that the additional part of that inflation would once again be 'a surprise'. The data underlying the original Phillips curve, he suggested, were misleading because they came from a period of price stability. And, he said, what was required for analytical purposes was to replace the Phillips curve with what became known as its 'expectations-augmented' version.

Whether this is a fair characterization of policymaking intentions in the Keynesian era must be open to considerable doubt. It is, in the first place, hard to find advocates of a policy of exploiting the Phillips curve in the way he describes. Certainly there are those who thought demand management could lower unemployment. But they do not tend to suggest that this would be desirable even if it raised inflation above its optimum. And it is also true that there were those like Tobin (1972) who suggested that market imperfections are such that a small positive rate of inflation will improve their performance. But those arguments are about the optimal rate of inflation rather than being primarily about demand management, and in any case do not depend on mistaken expectations, so Friedman's argument is not effective against them. These authors are not proposing, then, to act on a theory like that of Lipsey (1960) which sees Phillips's relation as arising from an increased pressure of demand raising both unemployment and inflation. And Lipsey himself, as well as others engaged in estimating the Phillips curve, like Samuelson and Solow (1960), specifically say that the relationship should not be presumed to be independent of policy actions taken in the light of it. Furthermore, when the Phillips curve was at the centre of policy debate it was usually not because policymakers were interested in how high they might raise inflation, but because it provided an estimate of what would be required to stop it – indeed this was the aspect stressed by Phillips himself. No tendency to rising levels of inflation arises from policy based on that idea.

None of this is to deny that it would have been common ground that, if policy pushed unemployment too low, wages and hence prices would start to rise. Keynes would not have doubted that, and the problem was also noted perfectly clearly in the White Paper *Employment Policy* of 1944. The issue for the most part was how low unemployment could be pushed without causing inflation and what countermeasures outside the realm of demand management itself could be used to control prices. The 'Phillips curve' played little role in that.

One might well say, of course, that more lasting interest is to be found in Friedman's theory than in his interpretation of intellectual history. In that area the existence of the natural rate of unemployment is the central contention. The importance of this idea arises in large part from the fact that his conception of the natural rate made it not just an equilibrium, but a stable equilibrium, so that absent disturbing forces unemployment will always move towards it. A central consequence of this is that the hypothesis was a fundamental challenge to Keynes's idea – adopted much more strongly by some of his followers – that the unmanaged capitalist system might deliver permanently high unemployment.

The theory that Friedman advanced supporting his contention also has the important effect of making equilibrium unemployment voluntary. This comes through more clearly in Friedman (1968) – his Presidential Address to the American Economic Association – than in the Nobel Lecture. His argument was that an increase in inflation initially appears to employers as an increase in demand for their product and they respond by raising their wage offer to attract extra workers. The previously unemployed workers, also not realizing that a general inflation is under way, perceive this offer as an increase in real wages and accept it. If the workers were better informed so that they realized all prices were rising, they would realize that real wages were no higher, and remain unemployed. In due course, when the true position becomes apparent, Friedman supposed, the extra workers would again opt for unemployment and the temporary increase in output would be reversed. The crucial consideration is that, given full information, neither the workers nor their employers would wish to see the increase in employment that the policy brings. That is why it lasts only as long as the misperception does. But equally, since no one truly benefits from it, this policy would not be desirable even if its effects were permanent.

These considerations obviously make the basic case against policy activism, but in addition the doctrine of the natural rate is essential to the view – also famously and powerfully adopted by Friedman – that the rate of inflation is determined by the growth of the supply of money. Friedman's argument arose directly from the 'Quantity Theory' by which the quantity of money multiplied by its velocity of circulation is equal to the price index multiplied by the number of transactions made. But it is only because variations in employment, and hence the number of transactions, are presumed to be transitory that changes in the money supply can be presumed to affect prices rather than quantities. This still leaves the question of what determines the velocity of circulation of money, but Friedman (1956) had argued that this was reasonably predictable and the consequence was that control of the supply of money could always be made to deliver the desired rate of inflation over a reasonable time-period.

There was then one other key component of Friedman's outlook on which he laid great stress. That was his advocacy of policy 'rules' over discretion, and in particular his advocacy of a fixed rate of growth of the supply of money.

This argument had two major strands – one of general application which applied to any country, and one that, as it was originally put by Friedman, was more particular to the USA. The first was that although there might be a case in principle for activist policy arising from the fact that temporary, exogenous disturbances might drive the economy from its equilibrium, it was not feasible to act on this. The reason is that it is too difficult: although market outcomes may be far from perfect, and there is certainly some variability in activity and inflation, so that a business cycle will always be detectable, attempts by policymakers to improve on these outcomes are likely, on average, to be damaging. Policy tools are blunt instruments because there are 'long and variable lags' in their operation and they have to be used in ignorance of the precise condition of the economy and of contemporaneous developments. And furthermore, suggested Friedman, if policymakers adopt the attitude that it is their job to intervene in market outcomes, they are very likely to try to achieve too much, and this is all the more likely to result in damaging policy. Certainly, British experience of policymakers making numerous minor adjustments to policy in a quest for very low levels of unemployment, together with the sharp reversals that followed whenever the balance of payments deteriorated sufficiently, did nothing to suggest that he was wrong to suppose that a more steady and if necessary less ambitious policy would have worked better. Thus, said Friedman, the best course of action was to rely on the equilibrating forces of the market, imperfect as they may be, and on the stability of the demand for money, imperfect as it too may be, rather than seek a better approximation to perfection through 'fine-tuning' policy to the perceived circumstances of the day.

The second argument, advanced by Friedman (1962), suggested that rules could be a device for controlling what would otherwise be the arbitrary power of central bankers. By the time of Friedman (1982) he clearly felt that the Federal Reserve, because it lacked an 'electoral bottom line', had permitted excessive inflation. Consequently it would be desirable for Congress to bind the Federal Reserve to a legislated money-growth rule. Here, the point of the 'rule' was not that it was in contrast to fine-tuning, but rather that it limited the ability of policymakers to pursue their private advantage.

Theoretical doubts

A number of objections to the monetarist outlook were raised. At the most practical level, the politics of the proposal were questioned. For example, Goldthorpe (1978) found the origins of inflation in social conflict and thought this more likely to be exacerbated than reduced by tight money. In the most extreme versions of this idea it was felt there would be a danger to Western political systems, and there was certainly a suggestion that monetarist policy might be unimplementable in a democracy if it resulted, even temporarily, in high unemployment.

Another prominent doubt concerned the natural rate of unemployment. Merely to assume that its existence arises from wage flexibility certainly will not do. Whether wages are flexible is one question, and the view that they are not, and particularly that they are not downwardly flexible, clearly has much to recommend it. Considerable theoretical efforts, including by Keynes (1936), have gone into proposing rational reasons why this would be so, with Alchian (1970) and Okun (1981) making important contributions even before the business of rationalizing price-stickiness became the *raison d'être* of much 'New Keynesian' theorizing.

Although a sufficient degree of wage-stickiness makes a case for policy activism, it is unfortunate that the point has come to obscure a more fundamental Keynesian argument. That is that even if wages are (or were caused to be) fully flexible, that would not deliver full employment. The reason can be seen as follows. Unless there is to be a matching increase in sales, it is futile to hope for an increase in output. Therefore, a fall in wages can result in a fall in unemployment only to the extent that it increases sales. Falling wages are clearly not conducive to greater consumption by wage-earners; and nor are the circumstances in which their consumption falls likely to encourage extra investment. Even if profits rise, capital-owners are unlikely to increase their consumption sufficiently to raise employment. At fixed exchange rates, falling wages and prices might increase exports, but that helps neither the country with a floating exchange rate nor anybody else in the circumstances where unemployment is more or less worldwide.

There are numerous ways in which one might hope to rebut this view, and much of Keynes (1936), chapter 19 is concerned with considering them. Many details might be questioned, but whatever the final resolution, it is clear that the simple extrapolation from a single employer to the whole economy will not do. No one doubts that if wages paid by a firm fall, other things equal, it can reduce its price, sell more and hence be led to hire more workers. But when wages across the economy fall, it is not true that other things are equal – quite the opposite: they are crucially unequal since many of those to whom the firm seeks to sell its product are earning lower wages.

Although he gives it little attention, Friedman (1968) does respond to this point. He does so by invoking the 'Pigou effect'. If wages fall, costs fall, and hence prices fall. As this happens, individuals' cash holdings rise in value and this is an increase in their wealth which will, in due course, lead to their purchasing more. That is the required rise in demand. As a matter of theory, this response is inadequate, as Tobin (1980, ch. 1), for example, demonstrates. The most important point there is that as prices fall, the real value of debt rises, and whilst the volume of funds lent is equal to that borrowed, it is likely to be the borrowers, seeking to avoid bankruptcy, rather than the lenders, enjoying an increased value of interest payments, who adjust their behaviour most markedly. The effort to honour debt commitments in nominal terms must therefore be expected to reduce demand, worsening, not improving, the employment situation. A further point that is less often noted is that there is a curious empirical inadequacy in the invocation of Pigou. It is a matter of empirical fact that, in the postwar period, wages did not fall. Therefore, whatever it was that maintained high employment in that period cannot have been the Pigou effect. That should have, but did not, direct monetarists' attention on to other explanations – with the operation of policy being a likely candidate.

More sophisticated criticisms of the classical dichotomy are available, with that of Tobin (1965) being a widely noted one. He takes up the Keynesian point that money is not just a device for transactions, but also a store of value. The rate of return on money is therefore a relevant consideration in agents' portfolio-balance decisions. If it is lowered – through inflation – they will hold other assets, including capital equipment. The capital intensity of an economy can therefore be affected by monetary policy. And if that is true, it must be that employment and growth might be affected too.

Another question was how 'money' should be defined. The monetarist argument required that there be a definition of money which both made it readily controllable by the authorities and causally connected to the price level in a reasonably predictable way. In policy implementation this combination made for considerable difficulty. If money is given a narrow definition such as 'notes and coins', it is reasonable to suppose that a determined policymaker can at least limit its growth. But on the other hand it is not reasonable to suppose that private agents would then be unable to find other means to carry on their transactions – by, for example, writing cheques against bank loans credited to their accounts. Giving money a wider definition – including, say, a range of bank deposits – puts the determination of its supply substantially in the hands of the banking sector and so brings into question the extent to which policymakers will be able to control it. In quantity theory terms, one could say that the first option – giving money a narrow definition – makes the stability of its velocity irrelevant, since substitutes are always available; on the other hand, the broad definition opens the door to the possibility that the direction of causation runs from inflation, and the inducement this gives the banks to make larger loans, to increases in the supply of money. Kaldor (1970) was viciously critical of monetarist proposals for this kind of reason, among others, and Dow and Saville (1990) were later to trace many of the practical difficulties of monetarism in Britain to precisely this problem.

The methodological aspects of monetarist attempts to confirm their central claims also came into question. Hendry (1980) noted that simply relying on the fact that over long periods money growth preceded price level increases could hardly support anything substantial in the light of the fact that better results could be had using cumulative rainfall to 'explain' the prices. When more sophisticated arguments were made, such as the attempt of Friedman and Schwartz (1982) to demonstrate monetarist propositions from British data, they encountered more sophisticated, albeit less impish, rebuttals, including notably that of Hendry and Ericsson (1991).

And finally, there was the question of what was to be said about fiscal policy. The simple claim that inflation could be controlled by monetary policy, on the face of it, leaves fiscal policy free for other purposes. But on the other hand, the doctrine of the natural rate entails that fiscal policy cannot affect employment either – and the presentation from the Nobel Lecture would almost force one to believe that an attempt to exploit the Phillips curve by fiscal means would result in inflation whatever its effect on the money supply. Perhaps all that needs to be said is that the wider political project that sailed under the flag of 'monetarism' in the 1970s and 1980s certainly sought a reduction in government borrowing and expenditure, and that this may well have influenced the Thatcher government's initial choice of a broad definitions of money – sterling M3 – as the measure to be targeted. On this definition the budget deficit is one of the determinants of the supply of money, so that fiscal conservatism became a necessity for monetary control.

The implementation of monetarism

Until the election of Thatcher in 1979, monetary policy in the UK was only intermittently accorded a significant role in economic management. In the immediate postwar period, under Dalton's 'cheap money' policy it was used to stabilize long-term interest rates. That soon became infeasible. A brief attempt to control demand with monetary policy in the 1950s culminated in the creation of the Radcliffe Committee and its report of 1959 suggesting monetary policy had little power there. Thereafter, interest rate decisions were taken mainly by reference to the management of sterling and the regulation of the volume of credit was achieved by direct controls on bank lending.

In 1971 an approach called 'Competition and Credit Control' was adopted by the Conservative government with the intention of moving from quantitative to interest rate control of money growth. In the event, the experiment was short-lived. Among the reasons for this were probably inadequacies of design and monetary data collection, but it was also apparent that the shift of regime itself and the resultant liberalization of banking practice led to changes of behaviour which made for unexpected difficulties in interpreting the data. Most importantly, however, when unemployment reached one million at the beginning of 1972, the Heath government's 'u-turn' made a counter-inflationary interest rate policy impracticable in the light of the sharply expansionary fiscal and exchange rate policies. So the approach was abandoned and quantitative controls reintroduced in 1973.

Money supply targets also featured in the Labour government's response – heavily guided by the IMF – to the sterling crisis of 1976. Whether this was anything more than cosmetic was always doubtful, and Chancellor of the Exchequer Healey (1989, p. 434) himself claimed to have set the 'targets' by relabelling the pre-existing money growth 'forecasts'.

But the arrival of the Thatcher government saw the advent of much the most whole-hearted monetarism. In particular this government adopted Friedman's case for monetary targets, but with a small additional rationale which was later to assume great importance. It comes from a mild ramification of the theory of the expectations-augmented Phillips curve. Friedman had explained the increase in expected inflation – commonsensically – by reference to the fact that actual inflation had been observed to rise. That was not to be interpreted as the last word on expectations formation and it came to be believed that an announced plan to reduce inflation might lead expectations in the appropriate direction in advance of the actual stabilization of prices. On the theory of the expectations-augmented Phillips curve this would then permit disinflation with reduced cost in terms of unemployment – or, in the limiting case, no cost at all.

This argument in itself makes a case for pre-announced targets, and therefore a further case for what might loosely be called a 'rule' of policy, but the Thatcher Conservatives were also most conscious of the fact that – perhaps because of the previous record of their party in office – such announcements might well be treated with a large degree of scepticism. A consequence was that their 'targets', and in particular those of the Medium Term Financial Strategy, took on the role of being a promise as well as an announcement – a commitment as well as a forecast.

In the event, the targets still tended to be missed. One can always argue – as monetarist theorists sometimes did – that this was due to a lack of the will to meet them. But that lack of will was not apparent in many of the other actions of the Thatcher government, and in particular there seemed to be no deficiency of willingness to tolerate high unemployment – whereas the Heath government panicked when unemployment reached one million; the Thatcher government saw it rise to three, still asserting the overriding importance of sound money. Indeed, it won an election in 1983 arguing this line. One can also argue that it would have been inappropriate to meet the targets either because the figures were distorted by financial liberalization, or because of the disinflationary impact of the unexpected strength of sterling. Both of these views have merit. But the first – and particularly bearing in mind that the same excuse had already been used in 1971 – must call into doubt the value of the policy. Financial change is a constant feature of capitalist economies. If that fact renders the demand for money unpredictable, then that would seem to be a vindication of one of the long-standing objections to monetary targeting. And the second point similarly suggests a weakness of the theory since it amounts to an admission that the money supply is not the determinant of inflation over the relevant time-period. In either case policy seemed not to be guided by its stated rationale. As a result, the policy was slowly abandoned. First target ranges were adjusted; then the measure of money changed and multiple measures used simultaneously. Gradually, the exchange rate grew in importance and in due course supplanted monetary targeting altogether.

As to the role of targets in improving forecastability and reducing the costs of disinflation, there is something of a paradox. In the first place, it is difficult to see that the announcement of targets had any effect on expected inflation. Since the monetary targets were not met, one might say that this outcome is consistent with some insight on the part of the wage-bargainers. But on the other hand, what must not escape attention is that despite all the intellectual failings of the policy, despite its incomplete implementation, and despite the apparent refutation of some of its essential elements, inflation still fell. Indeed, after an initial rise, it fell faster than had been forecast. Those who had felt that the point of announcing targets was to improve economic efficiency by allowing the private sector to plan effectively should have found in this outcome another defeat, but the overwhelming view was that of the pragmatically minded, who saw the quick defeat of inflation as a greater victory than had been anticipated.

Hysteresis and the 'non-accelerating inflation rate of unemployment'

Nevertheless, this success came at a price that should be seen as embodying the greatest failure of Friedman's theory. That price is not only the sharp rise in unemployment that the monetary contraction brought, but the fact that when inflation was controlled, unemployment did not fall. After such a dramatic change in policy and outcomes, expectations of inflation should not lag far behind reality, and once they catch up, unemployment must return to its 'natural rate'. But by no stretch of the imagination was this promise fulfilled in Britain or, for the most part, in continental Europe.

What is more, when, in 1986, unemployment did start to fall at a significant pace, that did not prove sustainable. The 1980s ended with inflation again a problem and yet even then unemployment remained above the level it had been at the start of the experiment; above the level that had induced Heath's u-turn; and indeed, at the top of the inflationary boom in 1990, unemployment was higher than at any time – boom or recession – in British postwar history up to the election of Thatcher. A more categorical refutation of Friedman's optimistic view of the self-regulating economy and the 'natural rate' of unemployment is hard to envisage. What could one say about the location of the 'expectations-augmented Phillips curve', and how it came to be there, in 1990?

It must be said, however, that the case is no better for the old-style demand-managers. A Keynesian would certainly have said that, contrary to Friedman, unemployment would not fall without a stimulus to demand. But as events unfolded, there was a stimulus to demand – originating in the private sector. The difficulty is that if one judges by inflation, the Keynesian criticism to be laid against the government was that it allowed the boom to run too far when demand should have been restrained. And yet despite this, unemployment did not return even to the level of the worst recessions of the 1970s.

One response is that the 1980s saw a deterioration in supply-side efficiency. The first difficulty with this is that, in fact, the Thatcher period saw what are usually regarded as dramatic supply-side improvements. The privatization programme, the reduction of the real value of benefits and of marginal tax rates, greater regulation of trade unions, and the decline of their membership, are all considerations which point to a lower level of the 'natural rate' of unemployment.

A further concern arises from the fact that by Friedman's theory, unemployment at the natural rate is voluntary. The doctrine is that the unemployed can work at the going wage if they so wish. That is why there is no need for the government to increase demand to 'create jobs'. This was not an argument Friedman made about a theoretical case where there were no imperfections of the labour market – on the contrary, he specifically defined the natural rate in the light of those imperfections. The relevance of these imperfections is that, by raising the non-wage costs of employing people, they lower the wage that an employer will be able to pay. The worker may then decline employment, but their being unemployed is voluntary. It is true that the regulation has prevented a beneficial trade, since if the firm could avoid the costs of the regulation it would be willing to pay a wage the worker would accept. But that does not change the fact that the reason people are unemployed is that – according to this theory – they choose to be. The issue, obviously, is whether it is even remotely plausible that those who remained unemployed in Britain in the boom of 1990, and even more, those who have endured the unemployment in the euro area since then, have done so voluntarily. And even if one were to prefer a more sophisticated version of the natural rate theory where a degree of involuntary unemployment is possible, there would still be no apparent explanation of why the number of involuntarily unemployed should have increased so dramatically.

A better explanation of developments is in terms of unemployment hysteresis. The suggestion is that the level of unemployment at which inflation begins to rise depends, among other things, on the history of unemployment itself. Many reasons for hysteresis-effects have been suggested, such as the deskilling of the long-term unemployed, and the power of 'insider' groups to raise wages without regard to the interests of the unemployed. Layard, et al. (1991) offered a detailed account of the development of European unemployment making much use of this idea, and the rate of unemployment at which inflation is stable became know initially as 'the non-accelerating inflation rate of unemployment', and then later, as estimation difficulties mounted, as 'the time-varying NAIRU'.

One notable aspect of such treatments is that they move away from the presumption that unemployment is, in a straightforward way, voluntary. And the more serious treatments offered specific insight into the labour market policies which might reduce the NAIRU. Another important implication is that in so far as widespread long-term unemployment causes a deterioration of the labour market, policymakers would be advised to avoid long and deep recessions. That insight may have come too late for British policymakers of the 1980s, but the European policymakers of the 1990s would have benefited by paying more attention.

This point also raises a doubt as to whether models incorporating hysteresis should be regarded as exhibiting money neutrality. One view is that the 'unemployment equilibrium' is determined by supply-side factors and these are real factors, not monetary ones. The list of such factors may have been expanded by work such as Layard et al.'s, but supply-side they remain. Certainly it is not suggested that there is any exploitable Phillips curve. On the other hand, to the extent that monetary policy affects the length and depth of a recession, it might affect the development of those supply-side factors and thereby play a longer-term role, and demand-side policy is then instrumental in determining supply-side outcomes.

As things developed, it became fairly common for the expression 'NAIRU' to be used as if it were merely another name for the natural rate of unemployment, so that the implication is that the full battery of Friedmanite presumptions is being made. But, curiously, practice sometimes seems to be based on something rather different. Although early attempts to estimate the NAIRU sought to understand its microeconomic determinants, later ones – impressed by its 'time-varying' qualities – often treat the exercise as being merely one of estimating the level of unemployment that will, for the time being, be consistent with inflation stability. The presumption would seem to be that policymakers should use demand policy to move unemployment to the level required to achieve their desired change in inflation. That is already a far cry from Friedman's self-balancing world. Yet some policymakers seem to ignore even this. Perhaps most notably, the Greenspan Federal Reserve did not think that policy must tighten as unemployment falls towards the estimated NAIRU. And as a result they have been rewarded by lower estimates of what the NAIRU 'really is'. One must suspect either that the determinants of the NAIRU are so volatile as to make its value as an equilibrium concept negligible, or that the remnants of Friedman's theory underlying it are defective and it would be better to dispense with the concept of equilibrium unemployment altogether. Perhaps, for example, there is no universal tendency for inflation to rise if unemployment falls only slowly, even to very low levels.

Rational expectations and the theory of credibility

As these weakness in the monetarist foundations were becoming apparent, further theoretical effort was being brought to bear on the combination of rational expectations and monetarist theory. The assumption of rational expectations has been formulated in various ways, but the most succinct is that it is the assumption that economic agents know the true model of the economy, including the probability distributions of any random variables. The key consequence is that any forecasting errors that agents make will themselves be random.

In the application of this idea to monetary policy Sargent and Wallace (1975) achieved some renown for making what is, in retrospect, rather an obvious point. That is that if, as Friedman claimed, deviations of unemployment from the natural rate occur only when labour market expectations are incorrect, and if they can never be systematically incorrect, then there can be no systematic deviations from the natural rate. Consequently macroeconomic policy can have no systematic effects.

This conclusion is evidently Friedmanite in reinforcing the case against activist policy, but it gives a firmer rationale to the case against fine-tuning. That is that such policy can never be effective, not because of the limitations of policymaking, but because of the great understanding of private agents. One might try to resurrect it by appealing to something like the policymaker's superior information about the state of the economy, but no such device will lead to more than a feeble case for intervention since, for example in this particular case, the possibility exists of simply making the information available to the public.

For the most part, although the rational expectations revolution generated a great deal of excitement among theorists, it had relatively little effect on monetary policymaking. The exception to its lack of influence, however, is the development of Sargent and Wallace's analysis in a particular direction first of all by Kydland and Prescott (1977), and more influentially still by Barro and Gordon (1983).

Sargent and Wallace had gone as far as saying that any anticipated monetary policy would result in an outcome at the natural rate of unemployment and a rate of inflation determined by monetary policy. One could say that in the Sargent and Wallace analysis there was an infinite number of equilibria – all with unemployment at its natural rate but each characterized by a different rate of inflation and expected inflation. Those authors seemed to presume that once this was understood the policymaker would select the best of those equilibria by setting policy to achieve optimal inflation.

Barro and Gordon made a number of further assumptions and then argued, in effect, that Sargent and Wallace's analysis was incomplete because its conception of equilibrium was inadequate and that the proper analysis would require the policymaker to deliver the rate of inflation which the private sector would anticipate in light of the fact that positive inflation surprises could, in the manner of Friedman, reduce unemployment. In this connection they emphasized that although in Friedman's model equilibrium unemployment was voluntary, there was still a social benefit in 'fooling' some of the unemployed into work because of the market imperfections that drive employment below the socially optimal level. As a result, said Barro and Gordon, wage-bargainers would not set wages in the expectation of zero inflation because if they did, the opportunity would exist for the policymaker to deliver some positive rate of inflation, thereby temporarily lowering unemployment. The only true equilibrium, then, was where wages were set on the expectation of a rate of inflation that was just high enough so that, afterwards, the policymaker would have no incentive – for fear of extreme inflation – actually to set it any higher. The unfortunate outcome of all this optimizing behaviour was that inflation would be suboptimally high while unemployment remained at the natural rate. In principle the policymaker could still achieve price stability, but only by setting inflation lower than had been expected and thereby generating unemployment above the natural rate. But that policy was, on the assumptions made, worse than achieving natural rate unemployment at positive inflation.

The cleverness – as distinct, of course, from the utility – of this argument is hard to overstate. Most importantly, it is clever because it generates suboptimal outcomes out of perfectly rational and insightful behaviour, and furthermore – a point greatly neglected in the later literature – does it while assuming that the policymaker is in every way perfectly public-spirited. Friedman had explained the continuous inflation in the USA by the misfeasance of the Federal Reserve, but Kydland and Prescott, and then Barro and Gordon, on the contrary made it the outcome of the fact that the private sector understood the central bank to be doing everything it could in the public interest.

Barro and Gordon, and subsequently a number of other authors, then went on to consider solutions to this problem. A large number of often abstruse proposals can be categorized into those that depend on 'commitment' and those that depend on 'reputation'. The idea of the former is that some means might be found of determining policy in advance so that the private sector could be assured of what would be done before making their wage bargains, and thus price stability achieved without unemployment. An obvious difficulty with this is that it is hard to devise a truly plausible mechanism of commitment. And if one could be devised, there would be the issue of exactly what commitment was to be made, since if the commitment is truly unbreakable, it had better be a commitment to the right thing. The British experience of the early 1980s, and particularly the moderate monetarists' excuses for departing from the targets of the Medium Term Financial Strategy (MTFS), are just one reminder that this is no trivial problem.

The idea of solving Barro and Gordon's problem by 'reputation' was that a policymaker who consistently behaved in what might seem the irrational way of achieving low inflation despite its unemployment consequences would eventually persuade the wage-bargainers that this policy would continue and they would then expect low inflation. The policymaker would have displayed a lack of concern for unemployment and so the technical possibility of reducing it by inflation would cease to affect the minds of the private sector. This approach to the problem, which is due to Backus and Driffill (1985), is perhaps most noteworthy for its apparent implication that firmness and an unwavering pursuit of price stability are essential to economic wellbeing. It thereby seems to legitimize what would otherwise be an attitude of great distain to the plight of the unemployed.

Another consequence of the development of this theory was to bring yet further complication to the debate over rules and discretion. The view adopted by some authors was that the adoption of a 'rule' could in itself be a form of commitment. It might seem that this was what was behind the idea that the announcement of targets could help to make a policy of disinflation credible, and thereby less painful. But for Barro and Gordon, the reason credibility was lacking was that once wages were set, the keeping of the promise would be socially undesirable. That is why simply adopting a target, which could later be abandoned, would be ineffective in their model. The concern motivating the adoption of the 'targets' of the MTFS was much more mundane – namely that after a long period of inflation something exceptional would be required to break the habits of thought it engendered. In that case, without the encumbrances of the theory of rational expectations, a break with the past through the adoption of a new policy stance might, perhaps, be helpful.

But in contrast to Friedman, the case for rules that arose from the credibility literature was not merely that they were guidelines for those wise enough to know their own limitations, nor were they announcements helping to steer the private sector expectations in the right direction, nor were they the means of controlling self-interested central bankers. Rather they were what was required to prevent the policymakers' good intentions from harming the public.

As British policy developed, it is possible to see some influence of the theory of credibility even at a relatively early stage. This is apparent particularly in Chancellor Lawson's views on the benefits of membership of the Exchange Rate Mechanism (ERM) of the European Monetary System. One version of the idea that this could improve credibility was formalized by Giavazzi and Pagano (1988), although other possibilities were discussed in less rigorous ways slightly earlier. An aspect of these ideas was that an announcement of a commitment to an exchange rate target could be more credibility-enhancing than a monetary target because the costs of missing it would involve a higher degree of public embarrassment. The danger of such embarrassment would induce the policymaker to take the measures necessary to avoid this outcome. And the public belief that this would be done would in turn support the expectation of inflation being controlled. It is presumably an idea something like this that explains the determination with which the maintenance of a rather obviously overvalued, and recession-inducing, exchange rate was said to be an essential of good policy even during the election of 1992.

Fairly quickly, however, it proved no easier to meet an exchange rate target in defiance of economic fundamentals than it had been to meet money supply targets. A few apologists for the plan tried to explain this failure as the consequence of the German unification, which resulted in high interest rates there, and consequently in all those countries trying to fix their exchange rates to the Deutschmark, but that undermined the proposition that it was ever desirable to make a commitment to the peg in the first place – policy surely cannot be improved by making an 'unbreakable' commitment to pursuing a policy that is undesirable. And the European recessions brought by the ERM, one would have thought, amply demonstrated this.

In any case, on the theory derived from Barro and Gordon, such a gross breach of a commitment as departure from the ERM should have had a shattering effect on credibility and therefore raised wage settlements immediately. When this did not happen, it would have been a convenient moment to bury rational expectations and the theory of credibility in their family crypt, alongside money supply targets, the stability of velocity, and the natural rate of unemployment. But, alas, this was not to happen – or at least not ostensibly.

Inflation targets

After the catastrophe of the Exchange Rate Mechanism there was an almost immediate adoption of an 'inflation target'. One reason, no doubt, was that after so much had been said to the effect that the exchange rate was sacrosanct, and that the 'credibility' of policy depended on it, something further had to be said to prevent policy seeming completely directionless. And one might say that if the government was to be guided by the supposed lesson of the Phillips curve years – that policy affects only nominal variables – there was not much else left to target.

It would be possible to extract a different view from the experience of New Zealand, where inflation targets had been adopted in 1990. There, the 'Policy Targets Agreements' took the form of a contract whereby the Governor of the Central Bank was appointed on the promise that he would deliver a specified inflation rate, and face possible dismissal otherwise. That at least brings attention on one of the points where it is badly needed – namely the point that central bankers need to be controlled and constrained. And one might go as far as to say that in New Zealand, the enhancement of the accountability of monetary policymakers was not merely something that was achieved by explicit inflation targeting, but was in fact its principal object. But whilst arrangements in some countries pay a certain amount of attention to the issue of democratic accountability, it cannot be truly said of any but New Zealand that enhancing it was very much of the motive for adopting the regime.

In many minds it seems that the best rationale for inflation targets is simply that if inflation is the thing about which policymakers actually care, then it makes sense to target it directly. It remains, of course, far from clear that policymakers should wish to target inflation in all circumstances – it is not as if the monetarism of the early 1980s or the EMS and 'credibility' version of the early 1990s came up to their advocates' expectations in terms of delivering price stability quickly or easily. And if there are high and lasting costs of disinflation, it cannot be obvious that achieving it is always a priority. Indeed, the better designed inflation-targeting regimes pay some heed to this point by incorporating 'escape clauses' permitting governments to suspend the target. The political feasibility of actually invoking these rules must be doubted – particularly while lip-service must be paid to 'credibility' – but the existence of the legal possibility is not to be deprecated.

A further issue is whether central bank control of interest rates is an appropriate means of targeting inflation. It is not clear that quantitative controls can be effectively operated, but on the other hand interest rate control is far from having proven its worth in targeting either the money supply or the exchange rate. It is hard to see why the control of inflation with that tool would be any easier.

A considerable effort has, as a result, gone into considering the paths by which interest rates affect inflation. The Bank of England (1999) gave a revealing account of the wide variety of channels that might exist. In most cases it is ultimately the effect of interest rate changes on demand which is presumed to affect prices. For example, the Bank emphasizes such things as the effect of interest rates on the inducement to save; asset prices; and changes in disposable income after mortgage payments. All of these things, as the Bank says, plainly affect demand, and hence are relevant to the control of inflation although precise quantifications are difficult.

It is strange that this line of thinking does not seem to encourage the advocates of inflation targeting to think of using fiscal policy for the purpose. To advocate an authentic monetarism, where everything turns on the control of the supply of money, is one thing. But once it is admitted that proper monetary analysis involves tracing out all the ways that changes in interest rates affect demand and hence – presumptively – inflation, what can possibly be the reason for neglecting other things which also affect demand? So, for example, changes in taxes must be a more reliable tool than changes in mortgage rates. For one thing, the government controls taxes directly; for another, many people do not have a mortgage, but most pay tax. And government expenditure is itself actually a component of demand. How can its manipulation be less important than an uncertain relationship between central bank interest rates and household saving?

A distinct channel emphasized by the Bank depends on the effect of exchange rate changes. Interest rate increases tend to raise the value of the currency. As well as presumably lowering demand for exports, this directly lowers the domestic currency price of goods priced in world markets, and that has an immediate effect on the domestic price index. This leg of the Bank's argument is really no more satisfactory than the first. For one thing, as is apparent, interest rate control of the exchange rate is no easy matter. Further, there is the issue of how many goods are truly internationally priced. There are, after all, good reasons for sellers to seek to maintain selling-currency price stability.

Even leaving this aside, there is a question as to the rationale of an inflation-targeting policy that is pursued by exchange rate control. The justification for emphasizing the control of inflation is found in the dangers of nominal volatility. But exchange rate volatility must also be damaging. It would be easy to fall into the trap of supposing that if all countries achieve price stability, exchange rate stability will follow. Indeed this might seem to be an extra benefit of the stable-price policy. But if the facts are – as this piece of the Bank's reasoning might suggest – that price stability is only achieved by inducing volatility of the exchange rate, something has clearly gone wrong.

One might, then, have expected the advocates of inflation targeting to propose to pursue their goal substantially by fiscal means. But with a few exceptions, including the rather convenient case of the younger Bush's tax cuts, fiscal policy is treated purely as a matter of 'good housekeeping' with, therefore, no role in demand management. And even when the European 'Growth and Stability Pact' proved unimplementable, the mainstream view was that larger deficits should be allowed in recessions because they are unavoidable, not because they might be useful.

But the detailed attention that has been given to identifying the various ways in which changes in interest rates might affect inflation points to another curiosity of the development of thinking. That is the way in which the apparently commonsense view that if policymakers care about inflation they should target it ignores Friedman's warning against over-ambitious attempts at fine-tuning. Inflation targets themselves are precisely defined, so that, apparently, it is necessary for heated debate to occur over changes in interest rates as small as 0.25 per cent. And in trying to put its analysis of the transmission mechanism to use, the Bank of England, as can be seen from a selection of its Inflation Reports, presumes itself capable of processing information on – among other things – exchange rates, household borrowing, non-financial corporate borrowing, consumption, investment, inventories, labour costs, commodity costs, import costs, capital flows, and house prices, and – lo and behold, even monetary aggregates – in order to make these minuscule policy adjustments. We could hardly be further from heeding Friedman's warning against the pretensions of discretionary management. One consequence is that to describe the policy of inflation targeting as 'following a rule' could be most misleading.

Central bank independence
It is difficult to say what the primary stimulus towards central bank independence was. In retrospect it is astonishing how little discussion of it there was in the 1970s and the early 1980s. The publication of Alesina (1988) certainly brought the issue to prominence, although on the question of central bank independence he did little more than republicize work of Parkin and Bade which had previously been justly ridiculed. The coincidence of this with the establishing of the Delors Committee and the beginning of moves towards what became the European Monetary Union is certainly important. If monetary union was to occur, and there was clearly a great political impetus towards it in certain quarters, it was necessary to satisfy German opinion that the Bundesbank was not being given up for something that would be controlled by French or Italian politicians, or German ones, for that matter. The example of the creation of the European Central Bank itself probably enhanced the standing of the idea of central bank independence, and as it happens, developments in New Zealand which also led to what was called an 'independent' central bank provided another, almost simultaneous, example of this kind of reform.

It is nevertheless surprising how much support the idea attracted. In the first place, it is clearly a way of institutionally embedding the view that monetary policy holds the key to economic success, and the view that price stability is its proper objective. But neither of these ideas had a distinguished record in the preceding period. Monetary control had been conspicuously inadequate in the pursuit of both money supply and exchange rate targets, and the control of inflation had been achieved only at great cost. And the idea of hysteresis clearly suggested that the single-minded pursuit of price stability was not the appropriate goal of policy at all times in any case.

Furthermore, there are a number of little-noted and surprising weaknesses in the case for independence. In the first place, the so-called evidence presented by Alesina and others purported to show only that countries where the letter of the law made for central bank independence experienced low inflation. The manner in which this idea was lapped up by a great number of economists is astonishing. Almost all of them would normally scoff at the idea that formal rules can be relied on to determine behaviour without the need to enquire as to what incentives and what constraints might prevail.

Second, it is a very peculiar doctrine that the way one causes agents to make policy in a principal's interest is to make them free from reproach or censure. And yet the emphasis often put on the value of 'complete' independence, or the desirability of 'constitutional rank' for independence-granting statues, or simply the presumption that it is desirable that the ECB's independence be embedded, as it is, in international treaty, all rest on the that view. And it does nothing to diminish one's concern that an error has been made that the most voluble source of comment to the effect that none of this matters because of course central bankers will always act in the public interest is central bankers themselves.

The theory of credibility is widely advanced as providing some case for independence, but this too involves either muddle or trickery. Barro and Gordon were quite clear, and quite right, to emphasize that the insight of their model was that the problem of credibility arose when the policymaker was acting in the public interest. And indeed it is quite obvious that the policymaker they had in mind was an independent central bank. Therefore the creation of 'independence' cannot possibly be a solution to their problem. One suspects that a more powerful stimulus in support of independence is the fear of the 'political business cycle', more or less of the sort given mathematical shape by Nordhaus (1975). On his account, the exploitability of the Phillips curve in the short run and the presumption that the rise in inflation this brings comes after the fall in unemployment create an incentive to elected policymakers to produce a boom at an appropriate time before an election, and then present the fall in unemployment as the outcome of their skill and a reason to re-elect them. This theory, however, lacks systematic evidence in its support and one only has to remember the Conservative victories of 1983 and 1992 for its plausibility to be greatly damaged.

Nordhaus's theory is, obviously, nothing to do with the theory of credibility since, apart from anything else, it very much requires the voters not to understand what is being done to them – a far cry from the precise understanding of policy motives that generates Barro and Gordon's problem. Nevertheless, the number of otherwise highly distinguished economists who have in some way confounded the credibility problem and the political business cycle is a wonder to behold.

Modern policymaking and the monetarist revolution
The most striking thing about the 'monetarist counter-revolution' is surely the list of things it did not revolutionize: none of Friedman's central theoretical claims is now broadly accepted by professional economists. The ECB alone among major central banks concerns itself much with money supply targets and it is subject to constant criticism for it. The demise of money targeting is of course no wonder, since all the confidence put by Friedman and his followers in the constancy of money demand, or 'the stability of velocity', has proven as ill founded as even the most vituperative of monetarism's early critics suggested it would.

The doctrine of the natural rate has also been shattered. First it was simply refuted by the experience of countries where unemployment did not fall after policy-induced recessions succeeded in controlling inflation. Then the various theories of hysteresis offered a string of reasons – on the supply side – why it should not be expected to. And in due course, even the idea that there exists any stable equilibrium of the labour market was quietly abandoned and demand management returned to the central position in determining employment.

Even the idea that policy should be rule-governed has, in Friedman's sense of a rule, been cast off. It is clearly not the case that any simple procedure is expected to yield good policy. Nor do today's central bankers act in consciousness of the dangers of over-ambition. The idea that an inflation target serves as a 'rule' may, perhaps, owe something to the idea of credibility, but it is certainly not a simple, technical operation of the kind that Friedman held money targeting to be. And what empirical data support the theory of credibility is entirely mysterious. As to Friedman's idea that central bankers need to be constrained because they should not be presumed to act in the public interest, that has not just been abandoned, but all but expunged from the collective memory of economists.

And as to what policy actually seeks to achieve, one could almost say not that we are back at a point before Friedman's Presidential Address, but that we are back in 1957, before the Phillips curve. Policy, at least in the UK and the USA, seeks the lowest level of unemployment compatible with stable prices and does it with demand management. Some policymakers see more inflationary dangers than others, but there is no particular level of unemployment known to be achievable or unachievable, and, beyond the thought that as unemployment goes 'too low' inflation will rise, the outlook identifies no particular villain as the cause of inflation.

A few key, and perhaps lasting, developments can be attributed to the monetarist counter-revolution. Perhaps most importantly it was shown that inflation could be controlled in a modern democracy. The rise of central bank independence, and the power shift it brings, is obviously in some part the historical consequence of monetarism. Incomes policies have clearly been discarded, although so has the reason for discarding them – namely that money growth determines inflation. This too owes something to the same historical episode, and it too involves a change in power relations.

It is clear that the standing of monetary policy has been elevated and that of fiscal policy diminished, but it is hard to detect any rationale for this since demand management's furtive rehabilitation. Inflation targets are clearly not a monetarist policy, but equally clearly they owe a great deal to that line of thinking. In the light of the difficulties of the surrounding theory and the lessons that could have been learned from experience, it may be better not to attempt a strict rationalization of these developments but simply to note that the views in question are both furthered by and conducive to a variety of neo-liberal presumptions.

Indeed, one might pursue this line of thinking a little further and suggest that a crucial ingredient in the environment of policymaking is that the rhetoric of policy plainly avers the classical dichotomy. Monetary forces, it is said, cannot affect real values. What that really means in the context of an ever-changing NAIRU is hard to say, although perhaps not as hard as it is to find any evidence for the proposition. And since most of the better policymakers are showing no sign of targeting any particular level of employment, it is not clear that it is believed in any case. But perhaps rhetoric matters too, and this piece remains ostensibly at the centre of almost all discussion and contributes to defining the intellectual environment in which policy is made.

One might wonder how it is that these elements of our sub-monetarist intellectual culture attract so much support even when so much else that should be essential to the case for them has been abandoned. But it is worth remembering that there is one part of Friedman's argument which is still very widely accepted. It is made explicit – to offer only one of many similar cases – in Blanchard (1997), it was an essential aspect of the intellectual genesis of the Maastricht Treaty, it is clearly presumed by Balls and O'Donnell (2002), and actually explained by Lawson (1992) as motivating his policy. This crucial part of Friedman's argument is his account of the failure of the supposed attempt to exploit the Phillips curve and of its resultant collapse in inflationary chaos. What is still believed, then, from among Friedman's teachings, while so much else has been forgotten, is that there was once a Dark Age where policymakers welcomed inflation and believed that it cured their problems; when they thought the Phillips curve was their greatest discovery; and above all it is believed that the first requirement of policy is that it never return to that place. That imagined history is part of the explanation of why we now have independent central banks, the pretence of monetary rules, and so much emphasis on the elusive NAIRU. So perhaps, after all, it is not the content of his theory, but rather his superficial but rhetorically brilliant intellectual history, which is the lasting legacy of Friedman's monetarist revolution.

References

Alchian, Armen A. (1970), 'Information costs, pricing, and resource unemployment', in E.S. Phelps (ed.), *Microeconomic Foundations of Employment and Inflation Theory*, London: Macmillan: 27–52.

Alesina, Alberto (1988), 'Macroeconomics and politics', *NBER Macroeconomics Annual*: 13–52.

Backus, David and John Driffill (1985), 'Inflation and reputation', *American Economic Review*, **75**(3): 530–38.

Balls, Ed and Gus O'Donnell (eds) (2002), *Reforming Britain's Economic and Financial Policy*, Basingstoke: Palgrave.

Bank of England (1999), 'The transmission mechanism of monetary policy', *Bank of England Quarterly Bulletin*, **39**(2): 161–71.

Barro, Robert and David Gordon (1983), 'A positive theory of monetary policy in a natural rate model', *Journal of Political Economy*, **91**(4): 589–610.

Blanchard, Olivier (1997), *Macroeconomics*, Upper Saddle River, NJ: Prentice Hall.

Dow, J.C.R. and I.D. Saville (1990), *A Critique of Monetary Policy*, Oxford: Oxford University Press.

Friedman, Milton (1956), 'The Quantity Theory of money – a restatement', in M. Friedman (ed.), *Studies in the Quantity Theory of Money*, Chicago: University of Chicago Press: 3–21.

Friedman, Milton (1962), 'Should there be an independent monetary authority?', in L.B. Yeager (ed.), *In Search of a Monetary Constitution*, Cambridge, MA: Harvard University Press: 219–43.

Friedman, Milton (1968), 'The role of monetary policy', *American Economic Review*, **58**(1): 1–17

Friedman, Milton (1977), 'Nobel Lecture: Inflation and unemployment', *Journal of Political Economy*, **85**: 451–72.

Friedman, Milton (1982), 'Monetary policy', *Journal of Money, Credit, and Banking*, **14**(1): 98–118.

Friedman, Milton and Anna Schwartz (1982), *Monetary Trends in the United States and the United Kingdom: Their relation to income, prices, and interest rates, 1867–1975*, Chicago: Chicago University Press.

Giavazzi, Francesco and Marco Pagano (1988), 'The advantage of tying one's hands', *European Economic Review*, **32**: 1055–82.

Goldthorpe, John (1978), 'Problems of political economy after the postwar period', in C. Maier (ed.), *Changing Boundaries of the Political*, Cambridge: Cambridge University Press: 363–408.

Healey, Denis (1989), *The Time of my Life*, London: Penguin.

Hendry, David (1980), 'Econometrics – alchemy or science?', *Economica*, **47**(188): 387–406.

Hendry, David and Neil Ericsson (1991), 'Modeling the demand for narrow money in the United Kingdom and the United States', *European Economic Review*, **35**: 833–86.

Kaldor, Nicholas (1970), 'The new monetarism', *Lloyds Bank Review* (July): 1–17.

Keynes, John M. (1936), *The General Theory of Employment, Interest and Money*, London: Macmillan.

Kydland, Finn and Edward Prescott (1977), 'Rules rather than discretion: the inconsistency of optimal plans', *Journal of Political Economy*, **85**: 473–91.

Lawson, Nigel (1992), *The View from No 11*, London: Transworld Publishers.

Layard, Richard, Stephen Nickell and Richard Jackman (1991), *Unemployment*, Oxford: Oxford University Press.

Lipsey, Richard (1960), 'The relation between unemployment and the rate of change of money wage rates in the United Kingdom, 1982–1957: A further analysis', *Economica*, **27**: 1–31.

Nordhaus, William (1975), 'The political business cycle', *Review of Economic Studies*, **42**: 169–90.

Okun, Arthur M. (1981), *Prices and Quantities*, Oxford: Blackwell.

Phillips, W.H. (1958), 'The relation between unemployment and rate of change of money wage rates in the United Kingdom', *Economica*: 283–99.

Samuelson, Paul A. and Robert Solow (1960), 'Analytical aspects of anti-inflation policy', *American Economic Review*, **50**(2): 177–94.

Sargent, Thomas and Neil Wallace (1975), 'Rational expectations and the theory of economic policy', *Journal of Monetary Economics*, **2**: 76.

Tobin, James (1965), 'Money and economic growth', *Econometrica*, **33**(4): 671–84.

Tobin, James (1972), 'Inflation and unemployment', *American Economic Review*, **62**: 1–18.

Tobin, James (1980), *Asset Accumulation and Economic Activity*, Oxford: Blackwell.

15 Monetary policy in an endogenous money economy
Thomas I. Palley*

1. Constructing a post-Keynesian approach to monetary policy

Monetary theory is a central concern of post-Keynesian (PK) economics, and endogenous money lies at the centre of that concern. However, PK theory has been bogged down in contentious debate surrounding the microeconomic details of the mechanisms of endogenous money. As a result, the macroeconomic and policy consequences of endogenous money have received inadequate attention. This is ironic given that combating the monetarist policy challenge was a major motivation for Kaldor's (1970; 1982) initial formulation of endogenous money.[1]

The PK literature on monetary policy is surprisingly thin. Whereas much has been written on why monetary authorities are compelled to adopt interest rate operating procedures, there is little on how interest rates should be set given the adoption of these procedures.[2] As a result, PK monetary policy has tended to reduce to the prescription that interest rates should be as low as possible – with little guidance as to what that constitutes. This chapter develops a PK framework for monetary policy, at the core of which is the endogeneity of money and finance. It transpires that distinguishing its policy recommendations from those of the mainstream is a subtle exercise. In several instances, despite significant theoretical differences, PK policy recommendations are observationally equivalent to those of the mainstream.

The chapter maintains that the defining 'observable' difference between the mainstream and the suggested PK approach to monetary policy is quantitative regulation of financial intermediary balance sheets. Effective monetary policy requires capacity to attend to both the real economy and financial markets. It therefore confronts two targets, and needs at least two instruments. This is a key difference from current mainstream perspectives (Bernanke, 2002; Bernanke and Gertler, 2000), which maintain that financial market effects work through the funnel of aggregate demand (AD), and all that is therefore needed is a single instrument to control the flow of AD.

The structure of the chapter is as follows. Section 2 examines the mainstream case for interest rate operating procedures, and shows that mainstream analysis can generate a logically coherent case for such procedures. This means that recommendation of interest rate operating procedures is not enough to distinguish mainstream and PK monetary policy analysis. Section 3 then examines the PK case for interest rate operating procedures. Whereas the mainstream justification is constructed in terms of Poole's (1970) IS–LM analysis, the PK justification rests on the theory of endogenous money. Sections 4 and 5 then address the question of how interest rate policy should be set. The mainstream literature on this issue is extensive, and mainstream thinking has evolved from one of non-accelerating inflation rate of unemployment (NAIRU) targeting to inflation targeting. Contrastingly, there is almost no PK literature on this important matter. The chapter therefore breaks new ground by presenting a PK framework for interest rate policy that also rests on inflation targeting. However, once again this entails policy observational equivalence with the mainstream. Sections 6, 7 and 8 then explore why inflation targeting is insufficient, and why it must be supplemented by regulation of financial intermediary balance sheets to guard against the emergence of damaging balance sheet disorders. This need for quantitative regulation distinguishes PK monetary policy from that of the mainstream. Section 9 concludes the chapter. The bottom line is that PK monetary policy has important observational equivalences with mainstream policy recommendations, but behind these equivalences are significant theoretical differences. The major observational policy difference is the identification of need for quantitative financial regulation.

2. The mainstream case for interest rate operating procedures
A core element of the PK approach to monetary policy is an emphasis on interest rate operating procedures. Yet mainstream monetary policy economists also now recommend such an approach, and most central banks have adopted it (Blinder, 1998; Friedman, 2000; Goodhart, 1989). This raises the question of what distinguishes the PK justification of interest rate operating procedures from a mainstream neo-Keynesian or new classical justification.

This section examines the mainstream rationalization of interest rate operating procedures. Paradoxically, within the canonical mainstream IS–LM model, the shift to interest rate operating procedures generates a form of endogenous money supply that can be termed 'central bank endogeneity'.[3] However, it is a conception of endogeneity that is fundamentally different from the PK conception, which is rooted in the credit nature of money.

The shift by central bankers to interest rate operating procedures is fully consistent with the exogenous money models that have historically dominated macroeconomics. This shift can be understood through the literature on instruments, intermediate targets and ultimate targets that was initiated by Poole (1970).[4] The underlying problem confronting the monetary authority is illustrated in Figure 15.1. The monetary authority's ultimate target is the level of real GDP. To hit this ultimate target it must select an intermediate target of the money supply, the nominal interest rate, or inflation.[5] Finally, to hit this intermediate target the monetary authority must choose whether to use the interest rate or the supply of monetary base as its instrument.

In the neo-Keynesian IS–LM model (Poole, 1970) the instrument choice problem is simplified, and it is assumed that the monetary authority can directly control the money supply. This leads to the simple policy recommendation that if the IS is more variable than the LM, the monetary authority should target the money supply. The economic logic is that money supply targeting results in less than full accommodation of IS shocks, whereas

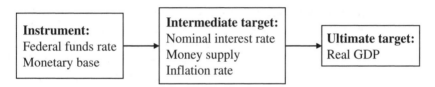

Figure 15.1   The monetary authority's instrument and intermediate target choice problem

interest rate targeting fully accommodates IS shocks. Conversely, if the LM is more variable than the IS, the monetary authority should target the interest rate. Now, the economic logic is that interest rate targeting insulates the real sector against LM (financial sector) shocks, whereas money supply targeting does not.[6]

Analytically, the important implication is that the neo-Keynesian IS–LM model with exogenous money can also explain why central banks adopt interest rate operating procedures. Consequently, the adoption of such procedures is consistent with a non-PK approach to monetary policy. All that is required is that central banks believe that disturbances originate predominantly in the financial sector. And in fact, the shift by central banks to interest rate operating procedures is usually discussed in exactly these terms, as evidenced in the extensive econometric literature on the instability of money demand.[7]

Nor is it the assumption of an exogenous money supply that is critical to Poole's (1970) analysis. Friedman (1975) extended the optimal monetary policy instrument target choice problem to include a distinction between intermediate targets and instruments. In this more refined framework GDP is still the ultimate target, but now there is recognition that the money supply (whether M1, M2 etc.) is largely created by the banking system and the monetary authority only controls the monetary base. This gives rise to an endogenous money supply given by

$$M^s = m(i, y, u_M)H^s = M(i, y, u_M) \quad M_i > 0, M_y > 0 \qquad (15.1)$$

where M^s = money supply, $m(.)$ = money multiplier, i = nominal interest rate, y = real income, u_M = random shock with mean of zero and a finite variance, H^s = supply of monetary base and M_i and M_y represent first derivates of M with respect to i and to y. This particular form of money supply endogeneity can be labelled 'money multiplier–portfolio endogeneity'.[8] Changes in agents' portfolio preferences regarding holding cash, demand deposits and time deposits cause changes in the money multiplier. Within this framework the monetary authority can either target the interest rate, or it can target the money supply using either the interest rate or the monetary base as its instrument. The conclusion remains similar to that of Poole (1970). If the money multiplier is highly variable, thereby making the LM highly variable, the monetary authority should target interest rates. Conversely, if the money multiplier and LM are stable, but the IS is highly variable, the monetary authority should target the monetary base.

The IS–LM model uses a Keynesian aggregate demand closure of the goods market. Sargent and Wallace (1975) extended Poole's (1970) monetary policy instrument choice problem to a rational expectations–new classical macroeconomic framework in which equilibrium GDP (y^*) is supply-side determined. In this case monetary policy cannot impact expected GDP, but it can impact the variance of GDP and it is desirable to minimize that variance. The policy choice problem is identical to that analyzed by Poole (1970). If the IS is highly variable and the LM is not, the monetary authority should target the money supply to minimize temporary deviations from equilibrium. Conversely, if the IS is fixed and the LM is highly variable, the monetary authority should target the interest rate to insulate the real economy and minimize temporary deviations of output. The economic logic remains identical to that of Poole (1970), the only difference being that the monetary authority cannot permanently influence the level of equilibrium output. Thus, even with rational expectations, a new classical supply-side closure to goods markets, and an exogenous money supply, the monetary authority may still choose an interest rate operating procedure. The bottom line is that interest rate based operating procedures are fully consistent with conventional monetary theory. This raises the question of what is different about the PK justification for interest rate operating procedures.

3. The PK case for interest rate operating procedures

The best way to understand the PK approach to interest rate targeting is through the debate over money supply targets. This debate was spurred by the emergence of monetarism in the 1960s as an alternative macroeconomic paradigm. Whereas Keynesians tended to advocate interest rate targeting, monetarists advocated money supply targets.[9] Their argument was that the business cycle was principally driven by money supply fluctuations caused by central banks, and central banks should therefore aim to grow the money supply in steady predictable fashion (Friedman and Schwarz, 1963a; 1963b).

Today, aside from a few diehards at the European Central Bank, most central banks pay little heed to the evolution of money supply aggregates, and interest rates have become the dominant instrument of monetary control. Within the mainstream and central banking community this shift from money supply targeting has been driven by a combination of pragmatic and theoretical considerations. At the pragmatic level, the Thatcher–Volker monetarist experiments of late 1970s and early 1980s made for tremendous interest rate volatility that negatively impacted the business investment environment. In addition, the significance of monetary aggregates became increasingly unclear owing to a progressive breakdown in empirical relations between monetary aggregates, real economic activity and inflation.

At the theoretical level, the mainstream rationalized its abandonment of money supply targeting in terms of the volatility of money demand.[10] Here, the argument was that money demand became increasingly volatile and unpredictable, thereby making monetary targets inappropriate. Such a story fit with Poole's (1970) stochastic IS–LM model in which money demand volatility is best dealt with by targeting interest rates.[11]

However, from a PK standpoint, the above justification for shifting to interest rate targeting represents a case of reaching a correct policy conclusion on the basis of wrong reasoning. Money is an IOU, and the private sector has always been capable of creating IOUs.[12] Moreover, this capacity has been dramatically enhanced by financial innovation and deregulation. Money supply targeting represents an attempt by central banks to control private sector IOU creation through control over either short-term interest rates or the monetary base. However, such targeting is bound to fail since controlling one type of IOU (e.g. M1) merely induces a shift into creation of other types.[13] This process of substitution generates interest rate volatility, and it also causes existing empirical money–output relations to break down.

Viewed from a PK perspective, the logic of monetarism and money supply targets was always flawed, and the financial innovation and deregulation of the last two decades have further exposed the flaws. The non-viability of money supply targets is an inevitable consequence of the endogeneity of finance, a logical necessity rather than a policy choice. Equally important, an endogenous money perspective also provides a clear theoretical explanation of the well-documented breakdown of empirical relationships between monetary aggregates and economic activity. Finally, a PK account of the failure of money supply targeting also explains why money demand became more volatile. Financial innovation and deregulation increase the elasticity of private production of money, enabling the financial system to escape even more easily and quickly quantitative monetary constraints that central banks may try to impose through money supply targets. Money demand must also then change because financial markets clear. However, rather than being causal, the shift in money demand is an equilibrating response to underlying changes in the financial sector's production of liabilities.

In sum, the above analysis shows how different perspectives may agree on the dominance of interest rate operating procedures, but for analytically different reasons. The PK case for interest rate policy is rooted in the endogenous nature of credit money. For new classicals and neo-Keynesians it rests on the volatility of the LM schedule. Paradoxically, within the new classical and neo-Keynesian framework, adoption of interest rate targeting results in a form of endogenous money.

4. How should interest rate policy be guided? The mainstream case for inflation targeting

The recognition that monetary policy should operate through interest rates rather than money supply targets leaves open the question of how interest rates should be set. Whereas the mainstream literature on this subject is extensive, PKs have had little to say formally. This section briefly investigates the mainstream approach to interest rate policy, and then goes on to develop a PK alternative. Once again, despite significant theoretical differences, there turns out to be observational equivalence in policy recommendations.

For much of the last 25 years mainstream monetary policy analysis has focused on targeting the NAIRU. However, recently the NAIRU has receded as a concept for guiding policy, being increasingly replaced by the notion of 'inflation targeting'. As with the retreat from money supply targets, the retreat from NAIRU-based policy has also been driven by pragmatic factors. One problem is that empirical estimates of NAIRU have proven to be extremely volatile (Staiger et al., 1997; Setterfield et al., 1992), thereby undermining the NAIRU's practical usefulness for policy. A second problem is that empirical estimates of the NAIRU tend to track the actual unemployment, thereby risking a 'structural unemployment policy trap' (Palley, 1999a).[14] Such a trap emerges because policymakers are led to misinterpret cyclical jumps in unemployment as jumps in the NAIRU. Lack of a countercyclical policy response can then become self-validating to the extent that prolonged unemployment and demand weakness destroy human, physical and organizational capital, thereby transforming cyclical unemployment into structural unemployment.

The flawed nature of NAIRU as a policy framework has prompted many central bankers – especially in the USA – to quietly abandon it for purposes of guiding interest rate policy. Side by side, mainstream economists have increasingly advocated a new policy framework of inflation targeting. Rather than focusing on labour markets and the unemployment rate, monetary authorities should adopt 'forward looking inflation targets' that are accompanied by 'significant discretion'.[15]

This new policy has been justified in a number of ways. One justification rests on pragmatic empiricism. Here, the argument is that inflation targeting has resulted in good economic outcomes in those countries where central banks have adopted it as their policy framework (Mishkin and Posen, 1997; Bernanke et al., 1999). However, this pragmatic approach leaves open the theoretical explanation regarding why inflation targeting works, and it also leaves open what the target should be.

A second justification is that inflation targeting represents a shift away from 'quantity'-driven policy to 'price'-based policy, with the latter being easier to implement and more efficient. Within the NAIRU framework, inflation can be thought of as a summary statistic of economic conditions. If inflation is increasing, this suggests excess demand conditions; if it is falling, this suggests excess supply conditions. Inflation movements can therefore provide a valuable signal for policy. Viewed in this light, earlier NAIRU-based policy can be thought of taking its cue from quantity signals (i.e. real economic condition), whereas inflation targeting can be thought of as taking its cue from price signals.

A third justification is in terms of information and institutions. This justification derives from the game-theoretic 'rules versus discretion' approach to policy initiated by Kydland and Prescott (1977), and applied to monetary policy by Barro and Gordon (1983). The game-theoretic approach persists with a NAIRU construction of the real economy whereby monetary policy cannot systematically impact the equilibrium rate of unemployment, but in addition it represents monetary policy in terms of a non-cooperative game between an opportunistic monetary authority and the general public.[16] In this non-cooperative game-theoretic framework monetary policy can still impact welfare and real outcomes if (1) it increases the variability of inflation, or (2) inflation enters as a negative argument in agents' utility functions. Given these conditions, the rules approach suggests adoption of transparent, credible monetary institutions and policy arrangements that serve to bind the monetary authority and discourage it from adopting high, variable and uncertain inflation. Inflation targeting can be viewed as such a policy arrangement, and hence the calls for transparent accountable inflation targeting (Posen, 2002).

Before turning to a PK approach to interest rate policy, it is worth pointing out some internal logical consistency flaws in the mainstream's inflation targeting model. The first and most critical flaw is that the mainstream approach to inflation targeting is rationalized in terms of a macroeconomic framework that is based on the idea of NAIRU. Whereas mainstream policymakers have largely rejected NAIRU for purposes of guiding monetary policy, mainstream theoretical analysis remains attached to NAIRU as a theoretical concept. This attachment has important consequences since it means that mainstream models can provide no theoretical guidance as to what the inflation target should be. Analytically, inflation is irrelevant in NAIRU models as expected inflation has no real effects. Instead, what matters is the 'change' in the rate of inflation. Consequently, policy makers should ignore inflation and focus on the change in inflation, which is the true signal as to whether there is excess demand or supply.

Finally, if there are disutility costs to inflation, the mainsteam model suggests that the long-run inflation target should be zero inflation (i.e. price stability). However, in practice central banks and academic advocates of inflation targeting have emphasized a 'low level' of inflation as their target. Thus the mainstream monetary policy community has settled on low inflation targeting as the framework for guiding interest rate policy, yet it is unable to justify this policy recommendation in terms of its own theoretical framework. This suggests that either their policy recommendation is wrong or their framework is wrong.

5.   A PK approach to inflation targeting: the minimum unemployment rate of inflation (MURI)

Although the mainstream has discarded the NAIRU as a policy target, the new policy of inflation targeting is still situated within a NAIRU-based macroeconomic model. For PKs, this is highly problematic since NAIRU is a supply-side theory of macroeconomics in which the level of unemployment depends on the institutions and operation of labour markets. This is fundamentally at odds with the PK macroeconomics, which emphasizes AD considerations.

This leaves open the question of what should guide PK interest rate policy. One possibility is full employment. However, this raises the question of what is full employment. Indeed, NAIRU can itself be argued to be a particular definition of full employment. A second possibility is that interest rate policy should aim at minimizing the potential output gap. However, application of Okun's law reveals that potential output is just the GDP equivalent of full employment or NAIRU. A third possibility is that interest rate policy should be targeted on potential output growth. However, this carries the risk that if the economy is initially below full employment, targeting the potential growth rate will result in a permanent future of less than full employment since the economy only grows fast enough to absorb new entrants to the labour force and does not absorb currently unemployed resources.

This section argues that there is a PK justification for inflation targeting. Thus, just as it was possible to justify interest rate operating procedures within both a new classical and PK macroeconomic framework, so too inflation targeting can be similarly justified.

Traditional Keynesian Phillips curve theory argues for the existence of a permanent policy-exploitable trade-off between inflation and unemployment. This trade-off allows policymakers to buy lasting reductions in the unemployment rate at the cost of higher inflation. However, within the Keynesian model the issue of what constitutes the optimal inflation rate is left hanging on policymaker preferences.[17] Recently, Akerlof et al. (2000) have suggested that the Phillips curve may be backward bending if workers have near-rationality about inflation that leads them to ignore it at low levels. Their model and reasoning is similar to that of Rowthorn (1977), who argues for a backward-bending Phillips curve because workers ignore very low inflation. Palley (2003) provides a different explanation of the backward-bending Phillips curve that has PK microeconomic wage-setting foundations.[18] In this model workers in depressed industries and firms are willing to accept inflation-induced real wage reductions to increase employment, but they do so only as long as the reductions are not too severe. Once inflation rises above a threshold level, workers resist real wage reduction, causing inflation to lose its labour market grease effect. The backward-bending Phillips curve is shown in Figure 15.2, and it generates a minimum unemployment rate of inflation (MURI) denoted by P^*, which is associated with an unemployment rate of U^*. From a PK perspective, the monetary authority should set the MURI as its inflation target, and interest rate policy should be managed to hit this target.

It is worth comparing the difference between a MURI approach to inflation targeting and a NAIRU approach. In the NAIRU framework inflation is an outcome 'summary statistic' that describes the state of economic balance. If inflation is increasing, this indicates that the economy is over-heating (below the NAIRU), and the monetary authority should tighten. The reverse holds if inflation is falling. Contrastingly, in a MURI framework inflation is an 'adjustment mechanism (grease)' that facilitates labour market adjustment.

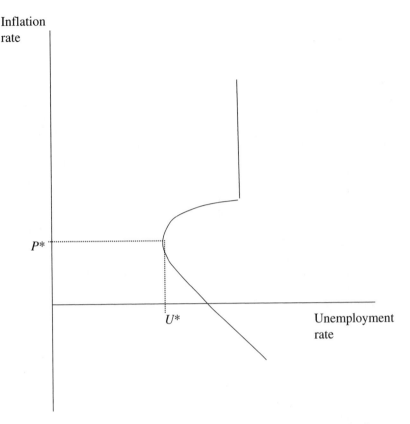

*Figure 15.2   The backward-bending Phillips curve showing the minimum inflation
rate of unemployment (MURI)*

If inflation is below the MURI, an increase in inflation will lower the equilibrium unemployment rate. If it is above, it will raise it. Inflation is therefore an adjustment mechanism
that can be calibrated optimally to minimize unemployment.

Just as the NAIRU is an unobservable concept, so too is the MURI. My own hunch is
that within the USA the MURI lies in a 2–5 percent range, which should serve as the range
for guiding inflation targeting.[19] Such targeting should be forward looking, and capable of
adjusting to temporary supply-side shocks. This is where discretion enters. The target
should also be public and credible, and all of the arguments discussed above for a transparent credible inflation targeting regime continue to apply in principle within a MURI
framework. Monetary policy should avoid creating inflation uncertainty which only generates additional risk premia in financial markets. A last advantage of the MURI is that it
steers clear of the deflation trap and provides an inflation margin that allows for negative
real interest rates should the nominal interest rate ever get pushed to zero (Summers, 1991).

Finally, the MURI model of inflation targeting should be distinguished from conflict or
cost-push inflations. The MURI model applies in situations where the mark-up is in equilibrium, so that income claims are reconciled. In the event of conflict inflation, inflation
targeting stands to validate the claim of the second mover in the wage–price setting game,

and this is usually viewed to be business. Interestingly, post-Keynesians often assume that most inflation is conflict induced, yet the empirical evidence for the USA shows little evidence of this.[20]

6.   Why inflation targeting is insufficient: the problem of asset price and debt bubbles

Thus far the chapter has argued that PK and mainstream monetary policy are observationally equivalent. Both recommend interest rate operating procedures and inflation targeting, albeit for different theoretical reasons. This section argues that PK analysis leads to the conclusion that inflation targeting is an insufficient framework for monetary policy, and must be supplemented by financial intermediary balance sheet regulation that makes for an orderly process of credit creation and allocation. This is a policy recommendation that is observationally distinct from the mainstream.

The reasons for the insufficiency of inflation targets connect with the earlier discussion regarding the failure of monetarist money supply targeting. Such targeting proved unworkable because of the private sector's capacity to circumvent quantitative financial constraints by changing the mix of its financial assets and liabilities. This ability to endogenously create assets and liabilities is also at the root of why inflation targeting is insufficient.

Inflation targeting is an insufficient guide for monetary policy because economies can incur significant balance sheet disorders that build without any immediate effect on inflation. These balance sheet disorders can inflict huge employment and output costs when they ultimately come to be resolved, and hence policy needs to guard against their emergence.[21] Moreover, such disorders are more likely in today's financial markets because innovation and deregulation have increased the elasticity of production of private money. This enables rapid large changes in balance sheets and debt positions, the unsustainability of which only becomes clear later.

The problem for policy is that balance sheet disorders are likely to be overlooked if inflation is the sole target or indicator. However, if interest rate policy is directed toward asset market and balance sheet management, then it is akin to using a policy blunderbuss that inflicts significant collateral damage on the rest of economy. Moreover, there are also significant distributional asymmetries regarding who benefits from asset price bubbles and who bears the cost of higher interest rates.

There are several reasons why the build-up of balance sheet and asset price disorders may have little impact on inflation, thereby rendering inflation indicators an inadequate guide for policy. First, asset prices are not counted as part of inflation measures, and the CPI includes neither equity nor home prices. This can be corrected by adding these prices to the CPI, but it would in turn complicate the process of wage setting and inflation indexation for purposes of real income protection.[22] Second, in a globalized economic environment, increased spending generated by asset price and debt bubbles can be accommodated via the trade deficit. Consequently, there may be no impact on the domestic price level, and instead private agents may incur debts to banks that in turn borrow from foreign lenders. Third, the economic dangers of asset price bubbles may be unrelated to aggregate demand and inflation. For instance, increased asset values may be applied as collateral to incur debt that is used to purchase additional assets, thereby pushing asset prices even higher. In this case, the result may be an unsustainable debt pyramid that pulls down the entire financial transactions system when it crashes. Fourth, the negative spending impacts of asset price bubbles may be compositional rather than aggregate. Thus, asset price bubbles may spur investment booms that are founded on distorted perceptions, and when these investments fail there may be large negative blow-back into the financial system that adversely impacts economic activity.

Moreover, not only does inflation targeting fail to address the problem of emergent balance sheet disorders; it also risks creating policy moral hazard in asset markets. The underlying cause of the moral hazard is that asset prices may rise considerably during periods of expansion without necessarily inducing inflation and a tightening response from the monetary authority. However, once the expansion comes to an end, asset prices stand exposed. At this stage a significant downward correction of asset prices risks negative consequences. First, falling asset prices could freeze markets to the extent that they create negative net equity positions that make it impossible for debt-burdened asset holders to sell. Second, by reducing collateral values, falling asset prices also make it harder to get new loans. Third, falling asset prices make it harder to assess the value of new investment projects, particularly those in areas such as construction. Fourth, falling asset prices may strike at consumer confidence just when maintaining confidence is critical to aggregate demand.

These considerations suggest that the monetary authority will have an interest in actively preventing asset prices from falling. Thus, whereas the monetary authority may pay little heed during the upturn, it steps in to protect values during the downturn. Indeed, this may well have characterized Federal Reserve policy during 2001. *Prima facie*, the mildness of the recession and the relative stability of inflation did not call for as rapid and dramatic interest rate reductions as actually happened, suggesting that the Fed may have been guided by a desire to maintain asset prices and avoid an equity market melt-down.

The Fed was right to pursue this policy, since under the existing system the Fed needs to keep asset prices up in a downturn. However, it is suggestive of the ultimate expression of 'too big to fail', and the moral hazard is clear. Under inflation targeting the Fed may have no cause to actively prevent asset price inflation on the way up, but then find itself compelled to limit asset price declines on the way down. The message to investors is take advantage of this asymmetric policy posture and overweight flex-price asset holdings, which sets the stage for bigger future asset price bubbles.

7.   Asset-based reserve requirements – a solution to the asset and debt bubble problem

The above considerations point to the need for additional policy instruments that enable the monetary authority to target asset markets while leaving interest rates free to target inflation. This need arises because of the endogeneity of finance which is the wellspring of financial instability, and which in turn necessitates balance sheet regulation. This is a uniquely PK concern, and it is here that PK policy becomes observationally distinct.

Asset-based reserve requirements (ABRR) provide an intellectually coherent framework for implementing such regulation. The full details of an ABRR system are described in Palley (2000). The main features of such a system are:

1. financial institutions (FIs) are required to hold reserves against all assets, though some asset categories can be zero-rated;
2. asset reserve requirement ratios are adjustable at the discretion of the central bank; and
3. requirements apply across all financial institutions.

This last condition addresses the fact that earlier business line distinctions have now largely disappeared as a result of deregulation and competitive convergence in financial markets. In this new environment, functional rather than sectoral regulation is needed, with regulation being conducted on the basis of what companies do rather than what they are called. This ensures a level playing field and avoids having regulation confer unfair competitive advantages.

Before going into the merits of ABRR, it is worth exploring how the structure of ABRR compares with other forms of balance sheet regulation. Figure 15.3 describes several different forms of balance sheet regulation. The traditional form of reserve requirements – such as applied to bank deposit accounts – is liability based so that the composition of liabilities determines the level of required reserve holdings. Causation therefore runs from the liabilities side of the balance sheet to the asset side. Collateral requirements, such as margin requirements, are another example of a liabilities-based system with the level of debt determining asset holdings.[23] Risk-based capital standards reverse the direction of causation, and have the composition of assets determine the amount of equity (a liability) that firms must hold. Debt-to-equity requirements are a liability-to-liability form of regulation, and they have the level of debt determining a minimum level of equity holding. Finally, ABRR are a form of asset-to-asset regulation, with the composition of asset determining reserve holdings. In an ABRR system FIs

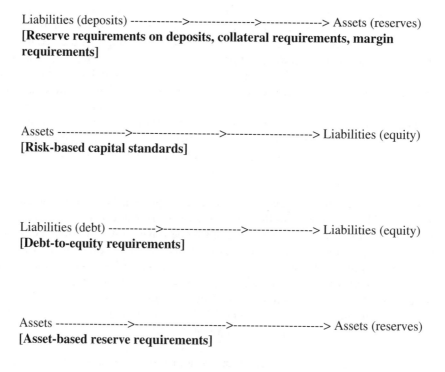

Liabilities (deposits) ------------>---------------->--------------> Assets (reserves)
[Reserve requirements on deposits, collateral requirements, margin requirements]

Assets ---------------->-------------------->--------------------> Liabilities (equity)
[Risk-based capital standards]

Liabilities (debt) ---------->------------------->---------------> Liabilities (equity)
[Debt-to-equity requirements]

Assets ---------------->-------------------->---------------------> Assets (reserves)
[Asset-based reserve requirements]

Note: Arrows represent direction of causation.

Figure 15.3   Different structures of balance sheet regulation

would be obliged to hold liabilities of the central bank as reserves, but in principle qualifying reserve assets could be broadened to include other high-quality liquid assets.

There are several merits to a system of ABRR. First, having the reserve requirement ratio vary by asset category enables the monetary authority to change the relative cost of holding different asset categories by adjusting relative requirements, and this can be done without changing general level of interest rates. For instance, if the monetary authority wants to discourage equity holdings, it can do so by increasing reserve requirements on equity holdings. Likewise, if it wants to discourage commercial mortgage borrowing, it can do so by raising the reserve requirement on new commercial mortgages. In effect, the monetary authority would gain $n-1$ additional policy instruments, where n is the number of asset classes.[24]

A second merit is that ABRR can be used to promote flows of funds to areas deemed to be socially deserving (Pollin, 1993; Thurow, 1972). Thus a lower reserve requirement on a particular asset category, such as community development loans, would increase their relative return and attract more funding.

Third, ABRR have good automatic countercyclical properties. When asset prices and bank lending increase in booms, this will increase the demand for reserves, automatically engendering monetary tightening. Analogously, when asset prices and bank lending fall in slumps, this automatically releases reserves and contributes to monetary expansion. To the extent that modern financial business cycles are driven by expansion and contractions of the asset side of balance sheets, this automatic stabilizer property attaches directly to the most salient part of the financial transmission mechanism.

Fourth, ABRR promises to yield significant seigniorage by increasing the demand for liabilities of the central bank. Fifth, and finally, ABRR promise to strengthen monetary policy open market operations by rebuilding the demand for reserves. Recently, Friedman (1999) has speculated that monetary policy could become irrelevant because of diminished demand for reserves, and because lack of a connection between the demand for reserves and economic activity. ABRR can re-establish a robust and strong link between the demand for reserves and economic activity because expansion of financial asset values and quantities is the central financial component of contemporary economic expansions.

8.   ABRR versus risk-based capital requirements

An alternative system of financial regulation inevitably invites comparison with the current system of risk-based capital standards (RBCS). As noted earlier, a principal difference concerns the way in which balance sheet components link. RBCS rely on an asset-to-liability link, while ABRR work through an asset-to-asset link.

The first advantage of ABRR is that they are a countercyclical automatic stabilizer. In booms, asset prices rise, increasing reserve demands. In slumps, asset prices fall, reducing the demand for reserves. This contrasts with RBCS which are procyclical and a form of automatic destabilizer. Thus the quality of assets tends to improve in booms, freeing up equity capital that is expansionary. Conversely, asset quality tends to deteriorate in downturns so that banks have to find more capital in downturns, which is exactly when it is most difficult to raise capital. This gives FIs an incentive not to make risky loans in recessions, which can contribute to credit crunches. Additionally, ABRR and RCBS have different stabilizing properties regarding asset write-offs, which tend to occur in slumps. Under ABRR, asset write-offs generate an expansionary release of reserves; the reverse holds for asset write-backs, which occur in booms. Contrastingly, under RBCS writing off an asset eliminates equity, and forces banks to find more equity or cut back on risky asset holdings.

A second disadvantage of RBCS is that they are not useful as a tool of discretionary monetary stabilization policy. This is because equity holdings cannot be easily adjusted since equity capital is difficult and costly to raise. A third disadvantage is that RCBS yield no seigniorage benefits, and nor do they improve the efficacy of monetary policy by strengthening the robustness and economic connectedness of the demand for reserves.

In sum, ABRR dominate RBCS as a form of quantitative regulation capable of reining in the increased elasticity of private production of money. The new financial landscape calls for more policy instruments that can support interest rate policy focused on managing the general level of economic activity. ABRR can supply these instruments, providing the monetary authority with specific instruments for dealing with asset and debt bubble problems. These new instruments can of course be supplemented with existing instruments. Thus margin requirements can continue to be used to control equity markets. Finally, capital standards can also have a place to the extent that moral hazard is viewed as the predominant problem. However, such standards are not appropriate as an instrument of business cycle stabilization policy.[25]

9.   Conclusion

This chapter has presented a comprehensive PK framework for monetary policy. This framework involves three elements: (1) interest rate operating procedures, (2) inflation targeting aimed at the MURI, and (3) financial intermediary balance sheet regulation predicated on asset-based reserve requirements. The chapter began by observing that interest rate operating procedures, which are a hallmark of the PK paradigm, are also consistent with an exogenous money paradigm. Next, it turned to the question of how interest rate policy should be managed and argued for inflation targeting based on the MURI. This represents an alternative, more intellectually coherent, argument for inflation targeting than the existing NAIRU-based paradigm. Finally, the chapter argued that inflation targeting is an insufficient basis for monetary policy, and needs to be supplemented by regulation of financial intermediary balance sheets. In this connection, the chapter recommends the adoption of asset-based reserve requirements as an encompassing regulatory framework.

The recommendations of interest rate operating procedures and inflation targeting result in a policy observational equivalence with conventional monetary policy thinking, though in both cases the analytical reasoning is significantly different. The recommendation of balance sheet regulation is unique to PK monetary analysis. The key analytical insight is the endogeneity of money. This makes effective control of the money supply impossible, rendering interest rate targeting the only reliable operating procedure. It also means that the financial system can generate destabilizing balance sheet disorders, and with interest rates targeted on real economic conditions, the monetary authority needs additional policy instruments. Hence the need for asset-based reserve requirements.

Notes

*   This chapter was originally published in *Post Keynesian Principles of Economic Policy*, Gnos, C. and L.-P. Rochon (eds), Cheltenham, UK and Northampton, MA, USA: Edward Elgar, 2005. My thanks to Edward Elgar for permission to reprint material.
1.   Kaldor's thinking on endogenous money can actually be traced back to his 1958 submission to the Radcliffe Committee which investigated the workings of the British monetary system.

2. A recent addition to the PK policy literature is Arestis and Sawyer (2006). They recognize that the monetary authority can only control interest rates. They argue for broadening the objectives of monetary policy to include both inflation and employment conditions, and also argue for use of prudential credit controls. The prudential credit controls recommendation is post-Keynesian in spirit. The broadening of policy objectives to include inflation and unemployment is similar to neo-Keynesian policy economics under which policymakers were advised to select a point on the Phillips curve that maximized social welfare.

3. See Palley (2002a), pp. 159–60.

4. This extensive literature is comprehensively reviewed in Friedman (1990).

5. Choice of inflation as the target of monetary policy is a recent addition to the policy literature. For reasons of space and simplicity it is not addressed in the current chapter. Palley (2002b) explores this issue, and shows that new classical models with a natural rate of unemployment cannot justify inflation targeting. Instead, they can only justify a policy of minimizing the variability of inflation. This is ironic given the mainstream's embrace of low inflation targeting.

6. Under money supply, targeting accommodation is restricted to the interest sensitivity of money, and the willingness of agents to reduce liquidity demands to make space for increased economic activity.

7. The locus classicus for this empirical literature is Goldfeld's (1976) classic paper, 'The case of the missing money'.

8. See Palley (2002a), pp. 161–2.

9. For reviews of this debate see Palley (1993) and De Long (2000).

10. The canonical paper in this line of explanation is Goldfeld (1976).

11. Poole's (1970) paper spawned a cottage industry on the optimal conduct of monetary policy. This literature distinguishes between ultimate targets, intermediate targets and policy instruments. In a sense, it consists of two literatures. The first explores these issues in the context of Keynesian-styled IS–LM models, while the second explores them in the context of new classical macroeconomic models with *ex-ante* labour market clearing and rational expectations. This literature is comprehensively surveyed in Friedman (1990).

12. Wray (1998) emphasizes this feature of money.

13. These shifts are explained by endogenous money supply models in which the choices and lending activities of profit-maximizing banks drive the money supply (Palley, 1987, 1994a).

14. The concept of the NAIRU is reviewed in a symposium in the *Journal of Economic Perspectives*, September–October 1997. Galbraith (1997) is especially critical of the NAIRU as a framework for policy.

15. Mishkin and Posen (1997), Bernanke and Mishkin (1997), and Benanke et al. (1999) represent early proponent presentations for inflation targeting, and have helped put it on the policy front burner.

16. Palley (1998, ch. 7) discusses the political economy of this construction. The mainstream of the economics profession has focused on the distinction between 'control-theoretic' and 'game-theoretic' approaches to monetary policy. At the base of this distinction is the question of whether the monetary authority is 'benevolent' or 'opportunistic'. An alternative political economy approach emphasizes 'class and sectoral differences of interest'. The balance of political power and institutional arrangements then determine whose interests the monetary authority tilts toward. See also Epstein (1992).

17. The standard neo-Keynesian approach to optimal inflation worked via a public policy welfare function in which lower unemployment and inflation rates are both goods, so that policymakers have convex indifference curves in unemployment rate–inflation space. The optimal inflation rate is then determined by the tangent of the policymaker's indifference curve with the Phillips curve. An alternative post-Keynesian approach has inflation–unemployment rate preferences differing by economic class, so that the optimal inflation rate differs by economic class. Which inflation rate prevails depends on the degree of influence of each class over the central bank.

18. These microeconomic foundations are described in Palley (1990).

19. Given the politicized nature of the monetary policy process, there is no guarantee that the monetary authority will target MURI. For instance, financial and industrial capital interests may find their private interests served by a higher unemployment rate and lower inflation rate (Epstein, 1992; Palley, 1998).

20. A comprehensive discussion of the role of second mover advantage in conflict inflation models is contained in Palley (1996, ch. 8), while evidence on the prevalence of wage-led conflict inflation is provided in Palley (1999b).

21. Concerns with balance sheet disorders leads to the debt–deflation hypothesis of Irving Fisher (1933) and the financial instability hypothesis of Hyman Minsky (1982).

22. Boyan et al. (2002) show that including the impact of asset prices on the CPI would raise the rate of inflation by one-quarter percentage point. Since CPI indexation is often used to protect real incomes (as with social security), augmenting the CPI to include asset prices could reward persons twice in that they would benefit from the underlying asset price inflation, and they would then get an income adjustment on top of this. Moreover, this double rewarding would of course be skewed toward the wealthy.

23. It is interesting to compare collateral and conventional liability-based reserve requirements which have banks holding liabilities of the central bank. The latter have the advantage of providing seigniorage, and

central bank liabilities are also absolutely liquid and subject to zero price risk. Contrastingly, collateral can be subject to considerable price fluctuation, which can make collateral requirements highly procyclical. Thus, prices may fall in slumps, obliging agents to ante up more collateral which they may be unable to do. This can then trigger default.

24.   The asset bubble policy problem can be understood in terms of Tinbergen's (1952) targets and instruments framework. Under the current regime the monetary authority has one instrument and two targets (the real economy and financial markets). ABRR will give the monetary authority additional instruments that can be targeted to financial markets, leaving the interest free to target the real economy.

25.   Tobin (1998) has also suggested modernizing the Federal Reserve's balance sheet by allowing it to buy and sell corporate equities and bonds. However, this raises concerns about backdoor nationalization and favoring some companies over others in terms of credit access.

References

Akerlof, G.A., W.T. Dickens and G.L. Perry (2000), 'Near-rational wage and price setting and the long-run Phillips Curve', *Brookings Papers on Economic Activity*, **1**, 1–60.

Arestis, P. and M. Sawyer (2006), 'The nature and role of monetary policy when money is endogenous', *Cambridge Journal of Economics*, forthcoming.

Barro, R.J. and D.B. Gordon (1983), 'A positive theory of monetary policy in a natural rate model', *Journal of Political Economy*, **91**(August), 589–610.

Bernanke, S. Ben (2002), 'Asset price bubbles and monetary policy', remarks before the New York Chapter of the National Association for Business Economics, New York, 15 October.

Bernanke, B.S. and M. Gertler (2000), 'Monetary policy and price volatility', NBER Working Paper 7559, February.

Bernanke, B.S. and F.S. Mishkin (1997), 'Inflation targeting: a new framework for monetary policy?', *Journal of Economic Perspectives*, **11**(2), 97–116.

Bernanke, B.S., T. Laubach, F.S. Mishkin and A.S. Posen (1999), *Inflation Targeting: Lessons from the International Experience*, Princeton: Princeton University Press.

Blinder, A. (1998), *Central Banking in Theory and Practice*, Cambridge, MA: MIT Press.

Boyan, M.F., S.G. Cecchetti and R. O'Sullivan (2002), 'Asset prices in the measurement of inflation', NBER Working Paper 8700, January.

De Long, J.B. (2000), 'The triumph of monetarism?', *The Journal of Economic Perspectives*, **14**(Winter), 83–94.

Epstein, G. (1992), 'A political economy model of comparative central banking', *Review of Radical Political Economics*, **24**, 1–30.

Fisher, I. (1933), 'The debt–deflation theory of great depressions', *Econometrica*, 337–57.

Fontana, G. and A. Palacio-Vera (2002), 'Monetary policy rules: what are we learning?', *Journal of Post Keynesian Economics*, **24**(Summer), 547–68.

Friedman, B. (1975), 'Targets, instruments, and indicators of monetary policy', *Journal of Monetary Economics*, **1**, 443–73.

Friedman, B. (1990), 'Targets and instruments of monetary policy', in B.M. Friedman and F.H. Hahn (eds), *Handbook of Monetary Economics*, Volume 2, New York: North-Holland, pp. 1185–230.

Friedman, B. (1999), 'The future of monetary policy: the central bank as an army with only a signal corps?', *International Finance*, **2**, 321–38.

Friedman, B. (2000), 'The role of interest rates in Federal Reserve policymaking', NBER Working Paper No. 8047.

Friedman, M. and A. Schwartz (1963a), 'Money and business cycles', *Review of Economics and Statistics*, supplement, February, 32–64.

Friedman, M. and A. Schwartz (1963b), *A Monetary History of the United States*, Princeton, NJ: Princeton University Press.

Galbraith, J.K. (1997), 'Test the limit', *Challenge*, **34**(September–October), 66.

Goldfeld, S.M. (1976), 'The case of the missing money', *Brookings Papers on Economic Activity*, **3**, 683–730.

Goodhart, C.A.E. (1989), 'The conduct of monetary policy', *Economic Journal*, **99**, 293–346.

Kaldor, N. (1970), 'The new monetarism', *Lloyds Bank Review*, **97**(July), 1–17.

Kaldor, N. (1982), *The Scourge of Monetarism*, New York: Oxford University Press.

Kydland, F.E. and E.C. Prescott (1977), 'Rules rather than discretion: the inconsistency of optimal plans', *Journal of Political Economy*, **85**, 473–92.

Minsky, H.P. (1982), *Can 'It' Happen Again?*, Armonk, NY: M.E. Sharpe.

Mishkin, F. and A. Posen (1997), 'Inflation targeting: lessons from four countries', *Economic Policy Review*, Federal Reserve Bank of New York, **3**(August), 9–110.

Mishkin, F.S. (2001), 'The transmission mechanism and the role of asset prices in monetary policy', NBER Working Paper 8617, December.

Moore, B.J. (1988), *Horizontalists and Verticalists: the Macroeconomics of Credit Money*, Cambridge: Cambridge University Press.

Palley, T.I. (1987), 'Bank lending, discount window borrowing, and the endogenous money supply: a theoretical framework', *Journal of Post Keynesian Economics*, **10**(2), 282–303.

Palley, T.I. (1990), 'A theory of downward wage rigidity: job commitment costs, replacement costs, and tacit coordination', *Journal of Post Keynesian Economics*, **12**, 466–86.

Palley, T.I. (1993), 'Milton Friedman and the monetarist counter-revolution: a re-appraisal', *Eastern Economic Journal*, **19**(Winter), 71–82.

Palley, T.I. (1994), 'Competing theories of the money supply: theory and evidence', *Metroeconomica*, **45**(1), 67–88.

Palley, T.I. (1996), *Post Keynesian Economics: Debt, Distribution, and the Macro Economy*, London: Macmillan.

Palley, T.I. (1998), *Plenty of Nothing: The Down-sizing of the American Dream and the Case for Structural Keynesianism*, Princeton, NJ: Princeton University Press.

Palley, T.I. (1999a), 'The structural unemployment policy trap: how the NAIRU can mislead policymakers', *New Economy*, **6**(June), 79–83.

Palley, T.I. (1999b), 'The U.S. inflation process: does nominal wage inflation cause price inflation, vice versa, or neither?', *Review of Radical Political Economics*, **31**(September), 12–19.

Palley, T.I. (2000), 'Stabilizing finance: the case for asset based reserve requirements', *Financial Markets and Society*, The Financial Markets Centre, Philomont, VA, August.

Palley, T.I. (2002a), 'Endogenous money: what it is and why it matters', *Metroeconomica*, **53**, 152–80.

Palley, T.I. (2002b), 'Why inflation targeting is not enough: monetary policy in the presence of financial exuberance', paper presented at a conference on Monetary Policy held at the Council on Foreign Relations, New York, July.

Palley, T.I. (2003), 'The backward bending Phillips Curve and the minimum unemployment rate of inflation (MURI): wage adjustment with opportunistic firms', *The Manchester School of Economic and Social Studies*, **71**(1), 35–50.

Pollin, R. (1993), 'Public credit allocation through the Federal Reserve: why it is needed; how it should be done', in Dymski, G.A., G. Epstein and R. Pollin (eds), *Transforming the U.S. Financial System: Equity and Efficiency for the 21st Century*, Armonk, NY: M.E. Sharpe, pp. 321–52.

Poole, W. (1970), 'Optimal choice of monetary policy instruments in a simple stochastic macro model', *Quarterly Journal of Economics*, **84**, 197–216.

Posen, A. (2002), 'Six practical views of central bank transparency', Institute for International Economics, Washington DC, unpublished working paper.

Rowthorn, R.E. (1977), 'Conflict, inflation and money', *Cambridge Journal of Economics*, **1**, 215–39.

Sargent, T.J. and N. Wallace (1975), 'Rational expectations, the optimal monetary instrument, and the optimal money supply rule', *Journal of Political Economy*, **83**, 241–54.

Setterfield, M., D. Gordon and L. Osberg (1992), 'Searching for a will o' the wisp: an empirical study of the NAIRU in Canada', *European Economic Review*, **36**, 119–36.

Staiger, D., J.H. Stock and M.W. Watson (1997), 'The NAIRU, unemployment and monetary policy', *Journal of Economic Perspectives*, **11**, 33–50.

Summers, L. (1991), 'How should long-term monetary policy be determined?', *Journal of Money, Credit, and Banking*, 625–31.

Thurow, L. (1972), 'Proposals for rechanneling funds to meet social priorities', in Federal Reserve Bank of Boston, *Policies for a More Competitive Financial System*, conference proceedings, June, 179–89.

Tinbergen, J. (1952), *On the Theory of Economic Policy*, Amsterdam: North-Holland.

Tobin, J. (1998), 'Monetary policy: recent theory and practice', Cowles Foundation Discussion Paper No. 1187, Yale University.

Wray, L.R. (1998), 'An introduction to a history of money', in *Understanding Modern Money: The Key to Full Employment and Price Stability*, Cheltenham, UK and Lyme, USA: Edward Elgar, pp. 39–73.

16 Central bank and lender of last resort

Michael Knittel, Sybille Sobczak and Peter Spahn

Introduction

The lender of last resort (LLR) is an agent or institution who is active, or is called on for help, in the *credit* market; but the main reason for its prominent status in the history of banking and monetary policy is that its activities are closely intertwined with the preservation of the use and function of *money*. The emergence of money from the banking business linked the microeconomic question of preventing a (banking) firm's bankruptcy with the macroeconomic topic of the stability of the monetary order. Opinions and norms that have been elaborated to guide the proper execution of LLR tasks reflect institutional peculiarities of historical stages in the field of (central) banking. Therefore, 'classical' theories of the LLR have to be studied in order to understand why these findings cannot safely be taken as a cornerstone of a modern approach of the LLR problem.

Designing such an approach is further complicated by the fact that in recent years LLR help was also demanded by, and given to, non-bank financial firms and even to countries which suffered from financial stress or debt overload.[1] In all these cases, the crucial question is how to reconcile two basic economic goals: warding off economy-wide large losses of wealth, production and employment, which might accrue from the downfall of a single, albeit large market agent; and preserving the credibility of the 'constitutional' law of the market system – economic losses should be borne individually – which may be undermined if an insolvent agent is rescued by the intervention of an LLR. Further questions arise as to the organization of LLR facilities in the European Monetary Union.

The basics of the LLR problem

The necessity of LLR services can be derived from the precarious balance sheet structure of commercial banks in a fractional banking system. Liquid reserves (including a negligible quantity of cash) typically fall short of the bulk of deposits (Table 16.1). Extending a bank loan to a non-bank customer implies a creation and exchange of *two* liabilities (cf. Hawtrey, 1923: 9, Hicks, 1989: 55–63): in the long run, when the term of the bill of debt expires, the borrower has to refund high-powered money to the commercial bank. But on the other hand, the bank is a short-run debtor as it is faced with a claim to high-powered

Table 16.1 A commercial bank's balance sheet

Assets	Liabilities
Liquid reserves	Deposits
Illiquid loans	Debt
Tangible assets	Capital

money in the first place, if the customer asks to liquidate his bank account which is granted via the credit contract.

Therefore the bank generally is exposed to a *liquidity problem* that can be relieved by attracting deposits from non-banks; by demanding credit from other banks; by selling assets on the capital markets; or by making use of the central bank's refinancing opportunities. Whereas the first two ways of obtaining cash enlarge the liability side of the bank's balance sheet, the third and fourth imply a change within the items on the asset side, because, in most cases, central banks supply high-powered money by way of discounting or buying bills or bonds.

In normal times, the liquidity management of the commercial bank succeeds in obtaining a sufficient amount of high-powered money which is needed because of the public's regular cash demand and the minimum reserve requirement (cf. Mishkin and Eakins, 2000: ch. 15). Various shocks, however, might trigger a *bank run* where it is impossible to convert all deposits into cash at the same time. The bank is *illiquid* because the stock of liquid reserves, i.e. cash and marketable securities, is smaller than the quantity of those deposits which represent an immediate claim to high-powered money. Commercial banking cannot evade the risk of illiquidity as the stock held as reserve is simultaneously both too large *and* too small:

- It is too large because securities usually bear lower interest compared to loans; this will induce a further expansion of the lending business in 'good times'.
- But each stock of reserves below 100 per cent of deposits is too small because the bank is illiquid in case of a run.

Apart from this basic risk of illiquidity, the bank's balance sheet reveals the *problem of solvency*: acting as an intermediary between borrowers and depositors, the bank holds assets the value of which may vary whereas deposits are nominally fixed in terms of the reserve unit. If a large amount of assets, particularly loans, have to be written off, e.g. because customers default on their debt, the bank's capital might be wiped out. The bank is insolvent in the sense that it is impossible to repay debts and deposits; assets no longer cover liabilities.

Reviewing the list of possible disturbances that might cause a bank run discloses that the problems of illiquidity and insolvency are closely connected.[2] The most obvious case is the spread of rumours indicating that a bank has made 'bad investments'. The presumption of insolvency will immediately bring on the fact of illiquidity, as account holders will try to convert their deposits into cash. Contagion is a related case where bad news about one bank might trigger the suspicion that others suffer from similar problems (e.g. because of heavy engagement in the same industrial sector). A bank run turns into a panic that infests the whole banking sector. Thus, even solvent banks are faced with the illiquidity threat. But there is also the inverse case of a fire-sale insolvency where banks, in order to avert a liquidity problem, sell assets on a massive scale so that their prices collapse, which in turn renders (other) banks insolvent. Therefore firms that are viable under normal market conditions may slip into 'technical' insolvency because of asset price movements which are exogenous to their own behaviour. Finally, events in the field of economics or politics, with no link to the banking sector at all, might lead to a sudden increase of liquidity preference and to a concomitant withdrawal of cash from the banking system.

The emergence of a bank run is a systematic risk in the financial sector which cannot be averted even by following conservative bank behaviour. Cash and liquid assets in an amount sufficient to satisfy a collective desire for liquidity on the part of non-banks do not exist in the banking sector. If depositors' confidence is shaken for whatever reason, a bank run is inescapable, given a sequential-service constraint, i.e. a first-come-first-served rule which governs the distribution of available high-powered money to applicant depositors. 'The run is therefore self-fulfilling and, on *a priori* grounds, may have nothing to do with whether banks are actually sound or unsound' (Moore, 1999: 446). If a market agent finds his bank account blocked, for him it makes no difference whether the reason is illiquidity or insolvency of his bank. What counts is the perception of a loss of his individual wealth.

The induced reduction of spending is one, albeit not the most important, macroeconomic consequence. Banks act as financial intermediaries; therefore the downfall of one banking firm shoots holes in the chain of economy-wide credit relations. Liquidity problems thus are imposed on non-bank agents. Finally, banks economize the use of high-powered money. The transfer of cheques and bank accounts is accepted as a 'payment' because, and as long as, the confidence is sustained that high-powered money can be demanded from the banks at any time.[3] If this confidence is shattered in a banking crisis, the demand for cash, and its volatility, will increase substantially on a macroeconomic level. With commercial banks' deposits included in the definition of money, a banking crisis and the failure of single financial institutions imply a contraction of the money stock. However, the amount of high-powered money remains unaffected; the liquidity crisis is reflected in a shrinking of the money multiplier, indicating a breakdown of trust in financial markets.

Thus there are good reasons why bank runs should be avoided or stopped as fast as possible. A *liquidity crisis* can easily be solved by the central bank by extending the supply of high-powered money. Technically, this LLR policy can be carried out by means of refinancing credits to particular or to all banks, if need be without demanding any collateral, since the essence of a liquidity crisis is a lack of marketable assets on the part of distressed banking firms. There is no concern about possible inflationary consequences of enlarging the money supply because, first, the central bank's action is a short-term response to a short-term problem and, second, people are eager to *hold* money – if they resume spending, the liquidity crisis dissolves.

The assessment of an LLR intervention is more ambiguous if the *insolvency* issue is taken into account. The knowledge that refinancing credits are obtainable in times of financial distress might seduce commercial banks to engage in more profitable, and possibly more risky, loan projects: this is the case of *moral hazard*. 'If the market knows that it is to be supported by a lender of last resort, it will feel less (little? no?) responsibility for the effective functioning of money and capital markets during the next boom' (Kindleberger, 1978: 161). Accordingly, the traditional LLR approach contained the almost unshakeable principle that the essential duty of the central bank did not include distress lending to *any* commercial bank, regardless of the borrowing agent's behaviour and status; insolvent borrowers should not hope to receive ready money (cf. Hawtrey, 1932: 126). Nevertheless, the widespread approval of this principle notwithstanding, the central bank is caught in the conflict of choosing between macro stability (if LLR services are provided) and micro efficiency (if the demand for this service is rejected).

There is no obvious way out of this basic dilemma. Usually, firms can also be deterred from hazardous behaviour by market pressure from their long-run customers. But although depositors in most cases have a long-run relationship with their banking firm, it is the very essence of financial intermediation that 'savers' are not concerned with the decisions of 'investors'. Of course, non-bank agents and commercial bankers could set up contracts which would lessen or even eliminate the prospective losses of depositors in an unregulated liquidity crisis. A 100 per cent reserve system could be adopted where demand liabilities are covered by assets which are not prone to the risk of large price decreases. Or both parties could agree that the option of converting deposits into cash might be suspended during a period of financial strain; the 'last' in the queue of depositors, which otherwise is expected to appear, then has no disadvantage compared to the person who is 'first' in line; this in turn would lessen the probability of the emergence of a queue of nervous bank clients and, thus, a bank run.

However, the predominance of precarious bank balance sheet structures in the real world, if analysed from a neoclassical contract-theory approach, cannot simply be regarded as an institutional inefficiency or a market failure but rather as the outcome of a voluntary choice on the part of individual market agents. An apparently mismatched asset–liability structure might be preferred because it 'provides risk-averse consumers with a risk-sharing arrangement in which they acquire the option of withdrawing funds to meet unforeseen future consumption needs, yet still derive the high rates of return from the maturity transformation process' (Moore, 1999: 447). As a consequence, the contract between the bank and the depositors is incomplete as the latter have no control on the choice of the bank's assets and, accordingly, do not participate in their risk. Although the value and yields of the bank's assets may fluctuate, the depositors' claims to the bank's reserves remain unaffected. Letting depositors share the market risks of the banks' business of acquiring and holding financial assets could relieve this tension. But this poses, first, a practical problem, because individual clients and users of bank notes can hardly assess business practices and solidity of banks. Second, such a reform of banking would at the same time deprive bank deposits of their money functions (cf. Goodhart, 1988: 85–95; Hellwig, 1998).

LLR services in principle can be provided by all (groups of) agents or institutions who are able to collect and make available large sums of liquid assets and/or ready money in a short time; rescue operations typically have to be executed promptly after the incidence of a case of financial stress. But for obvious reasons the LLR task mainly has been assigned to the central bank, because it does not suffer from a liquidity problem; it can bear economic losses more easily; and it might come to a decision much faster compared to some group of market and public agents. It should be emphasized

> that the primary function of the lender of the last resort is not to share default risks among private financial institutions. . . . The job of the lender of last resort is not to preserve individual banks from failure but to preserve the monetary-financial system from being forced into undesirable deflationary pressure by epidemic loss of confidence in its soundness. (Solow, 1982: 247)

The question is whether it is possible to perform the main task, maintaining the public good of financial market stability, without distorting the forces of competition in the banking sector.

The classical doctrine

The name 'LLR' seems to originate with a publication by Sir Francis Baring (1797: 22), who stated that *sound* banks should be allowed to borrow from the central bank, appearing as a 'dernier resort' in times of a crisis. A more profound analysis can be found in the writings of Thornton (1802), which was complemented by the later contribution of Bagehot (1873). A list of 'rules' can be drawn from these classical writers (Meltzer, 1986; Humphrey, 1992). The LLR should:

- be responsible for the stability of the aggregate money supply, not for the survival of individual institutions,
- support the objective of gold convertibility,
- not rescue insolvent banks,
- accommodate creditworthy institutions only,
- charge high (penalty) interest rates in distress lending operations,
- insist upon a provision of good collateral,
- inform the public of its policy in order to further reduce the risk of a panic.

Both Thornton and Bagehot share a macroeconomic, monetary view of the LLR task, which – quite typical for the classical school – strongly objected to any policy intervention motivated by the objective to support unsuccessful market agents and institutions.[4] The risk of contagion, and the need for the central bank to act as an LLR in good time, was well understood.[5] Thornton also saw clearly that an LLR intervention did not bring about a loss of monetary control, let alone risks to price stability. Additional issues of base money would only help to stabilize the money multiplier and prevent the spreading of a financial market disorder. The trend of prices on the goods market would remain unaffected. Besides, price stability was *not* the overriding goal of central banking in the area of the gold standard;[6] the crucial issue was the maintenance of the 'internal' exchange rate, i.e. the gold price.

Backing the national currency by a stock of gold created a specific type of financial market instability. Bank lending to non-banks increased the amount of deposits which represented, finally, a claim to the national reserve. In an unregulated system, commercial banks surely differed in their ranking with respect to their economic soundness. But the high reputation of some banks could easily be exploited by an over-issue of competing banks.[7] The pattern of a financial market crisis then was characterized by the attempt of a double conversion on the part of the public: swapping deposits for notes, and gold for notes. The recommendation to execute LLR policies can be interpreted as a strategy to defend the nation's gold reserve. By extending emergency loans and increasing the note issue a central bank creates even more claims to its gold stock in the first place, but lending freely appears to be the only way to stop an imminent internal and external drain.

Hence, the idea that paper money should be 'backed' by some real or sound asset led bankers and theorists quite naturally to the principle of demanding 'good collateral' in case of distress lending to commercial banks. 'Bank notes emitted without obtaining value in return . . . are [a] great source both of loss and danger to a banking company' (Thornton, 1802: 244). By accepting 'bad bills or bad securities . . . the Bank [of issue] will ultimately lose' (Bagehot, 1873: 97). For Bagehot, the central bank's decision whether to provide distress loans was not based on the business strategy and the balance sheet position of the individual commercial bank but only on the existence of the security. 'Advances should be made on all good banking securities and as largely as the public asks for them' (ibid.; cf. Steiger, 2004; Goodhart, 1999). These statements indicate that the founders of the LLR approach still thought of the central bank as a private company that felt obliged to defend property and profits of its shareholders. Nearly all central banks in the nineteenth century were private institutions; however, the collateral principle has to be reassessed if the LLR becomes a public sector body. This principle might imply an undue restriction of LLR interventions.

Whereas Thornton laid no particular emphasis on the question of how interest rates should support LLR activities (which might be explained by the fact that the law prohibited active interest rate policies at his time), Bagehot can be praised for his innovative views on this issue. His basic principle, 'raise interest rates, but lend freely' (the famous 'Bagehot's Rule'), serves, first, to deter borrowers from central bank credits who are able to obtain money through regular financial market transactions. Second, it tends to alleviate the moral hazard problem as bank managers and owners thus have to tolerate lower profits if the acquisition of liquidity is extremely expensive.[8] Third, higher interest rates would turn capital movements in favour of London so that the Bank of England could handle its own liquidity problem more easily.

Bagehot's more fundamental finding, however, was that rule-based restrictions of the quantity of money in general, if handled strictly, would destabilize the market. A stable money demand can only be preserved if the money supply is flexible in quantitative terms. 'Any notion that money is not to be had, or that it may not to be had at any price, only raises alarm to panic and enhances panic to madness' (Bagehot, 1873: 28). The public may never experience any restriction when switching between deposits and cash. The strict money supply rule, which was the core of the 1844 Peel Act, had to be abolished time and again; often the mere announcement of its suspension sufficed to calm the market (cf. Spahn, 2001: ch. 4). In modern times, Friedman's k per cent rule never has been practised in a literal way, because central bankers had learned that monetary control could only be executed efficiently by means of interest rate policies.

Financial support through macro or micro policies

The assessment of the empirical relevance of the financial instability problem is somewhat mixed. After inspecting the history of banking crises in the last 200 years in many countries, Bordo (1990) came to the conclusion that banking panics were rare events. The establishment of deposit insurance schemes in many countries (1934 in the USA) may have altered the landscape in a substantial way. They helped to prevent bank runs on a large scale because private market agents no longer had to fear wealth losses.[9] These insurance schemes, however, do not provide a perfect 100 per cent protection; so some minimum monitoring on the part of depositors is maintained. Insurance, supervision and the use of LLR facilities (mainly following the classical devices) obviously were quite successful, particularly in the last decades. To some extent, the USA is an exception because the institutional response to the instability problem was delayed. A more recent survey, however, stressed the rising number of banking crises in the last 25 years, often initialized by deregulation and globalization, and amplified by political interference (Rochet, 2003). But, opposing a worried prediction made at the inception of the European Monetary Union (Aglietta, 1999), the European Central Bank (2004) pointed to the strength of the

European banking sector in the latest years which was achieved mainly through the diversification of business fields.

Building on the classical monetary approach, and taking into account the stabilizing effect of deposit insurance schemes, Friedman (1959: 37–8) reopened the debate and argued that there was no longer any place for an LLR in a market economy.

> Even if a bank fails or is reorganized, there is no reason for depositors in other banks to become concerned. Changes in the ratio of deposits to currency still occur as a result of changed preferences. Such changes, however, even if sizeable, tend to be gradual and do not involve runs on individual banks. A liquidity crisis involving such runs on a widespread scale is now almost inconceivable. *The need for rediscounting in order for the Reserve System to serve as a 'lender of last resort' has therefore become obsolete, not because the function has been taken over by someone else but because it no longer needs to be performed.*

Moreover, if the basic concern is the stability of the banking system, and not the survival of any single institute, the necessary liquidity can be supplied via open market policies, which had not been widely used in the classical era. This is the appropriate 'monetary policy' instrument for the macroeconomic purpose, whereas 'banking policy', i.e. direct credit relations between the central bank and single commercial banks, appears to be superfluous. 'Rediscounting is an anachronistic survival of an earlier day and an earlier need. Its original function has disappeared' (Friedman, 1959: 30). The double approach, deposit insurance on the micro level and the provision of a stable money supply on a macro level, was supposed to be an appropriate remedy against the risk that single bank failures might spread via contagion (cf. Brunner and Meltzer, 1988).

Goodfriend and King (1988) support Friedman's view and point to the fact that the money market, where commercial banks trade on short-term paper, has become much broader since the days of Bagehot. Hence creditworthy banks suffering from temporary liquidity shortage could easily obtain funds from other surplus units. Given full information on the banks' assets, private financial institutions will always stand ready to extend loans the amount of which is given by the discounted value of the borrowing bank's assets. If on the other hand a single bank cannot obtain additional funds in the money market, the reason must be found in its insolvency – and again the argument is in line with the classical doctrine.

In the real world, however, information is far from perfect. Potential lenders cannot easily assess the solidity of any borrower's balance sheet position. At least, it turns out to be costly, if sound banks are to be distinguished from dubious ones. Accordingly interbank lending will charge higher interest rates in these cases. But the central bank, if it considers providing distress lending, would face the same difficulty of discerning illiquid from insolvent banks. Because of the prevailing risk the central bank is also forced to charge higher interest rates. Therefore Goodfriend and King see no advantage if the central bank enters the interbank market as a competitor of private institutions. On the contrary, the expectation of its appearance in the money market in times of financial stress might induce banks to run more risky projects. Direct central bank lending and even the accompanying apparatus of regulatory and supervisory activities appear to be redundant.

It is doubtful, however, whether the problems of low information in financial markets can simply be overcome by a mere interest rate premium. Due to asymmetric information, even solvent banks might be excluded from additional borrowing. Surplus units will hesitate to offer funds in the market if they fear that their own future loan demands will not be met. Cautious behaviour might lead to self-fulfilling expectation of liquidity shortage. Again it is obvious that relief can only be provided by the central bank.

The question, then, arises whether interventions of the central bank in the money market should be named LLR activities. Friedman's favoured monetary policy instrument, continuous purchases of long-term securities (executed by trading machine set to the *k*-per cent rule), has not been applied on a large scale. Today central banks prefer a liquidity management which makes use of short-term lending to the banking system. The 'technical' task of providing the economy with an appropriate amount of high-powered money should not interfere with the process of financing and investing on the capital market, and the long-term interest rate should not be distorted by liquidity shocks. Thus practically all central bank activities are performed on the money market. The short-term rate of interest is used as the main policy instrument whereas the quantity of (base) money adjusts endogenously to the needs of banks and non-banks. Taking into account that liquidity preference changes for various reasons, it becomes nearly unworkable to distinguish 'normal' central bank transactions from 'emergency' interventions.[10] Goodhart (1999) therefore suggests that only direct central bank loans to single banking firms should be called an LLR activity.

In opposition to the Friedman school, however, Goodhart (1999: 13–14) does not suggest dispensing with an LLR institution altogether.

> It is unthinkable that any government or central bank would stand idly by and watch the closure of any of its major banks . . ., if the authorities could avoid such events. . . . It is all very well for academic liberals to claim that the best long-term course for the economy would be for the authorities to allow any bank to close its doors, while restricting their assistance to generalised open market operations. Even if the externalities generated by the resultant panic were not so severe as to make this line of action socially wasteful, it would not be politically acceptable, in the sense that a government doing so would suffer extreme unpopularity.

This line of argument appears to be 'non-economic' in that it simply states that political bodies behave according to a different logic compared to economic reasoning. But the political decision in favour of an interventionist rescue operation can be defended on economic grounds by pointing to a possible market failure. Goodhart (1999) holds it to be a myth that 'the market' or some political institution can distinguish between illiquidity and insolvency, at least in the short time span which is available for such a far-reaching decision.[11] The central bank cannot evade making a decision on the rescue of a single banking institution since borrowers who experience any difficulties in the money market ultimately will turn to the monetary authorities. To put it more succinctly: any bank which asks for central bank assistance *necessarily* is located on the indistinct verge between illiquidity and insolvency; banks usually try to circumvent asking for any direct central bank help as long as possible because this entails some loss of reputation.[12] The possibility that a basically solvent, but illiquid bank, is excluded from emergency borrowing because of an incorrect analysis of its economic status entails a potential welfare loss for the economy: 'Extremely valuable and costly-to-replace customer–banking relationships would be lost should the LLR let troubled institutions fall' (Humphrey, 1992: 573).

Goodhart's argument has to be put in perspective as the history of the financial instability problem conveys the impression that banks with a business strategy that is exposed to relatively high risks were seized by contagion effects more often compared to conservative institutes. The latter also succeeded in gaining deposits which were located with imprudent banks in the first place (cf. Moore, 1999). Thus, members of the banking community may be equipped with at least some 'insider' knowledge with respect to the business course and the balance sheet position of their competitors.

But, on the other hand, if general welfare costs of firm closures, beyond the upset of banking panics, are taken into account, the field of consideration is substantially enlarged. It is immediately obvious that insolvent institutions can no longer be excluded from an admission to LLR services on *a priori* grounds. In each case, pros and cons have to be evaluated in a discretionary manner. This represents an economic policy approach that is harshly rejected by those who propagate a more rule-bound decision-making process, but it can be defended by resorting to more or less convincing practical arguments, contingent on the particular case which is under consideration.

The discretionary approach can also be transformed into some kind of rule. The *too-big-to-fail doctrine* simply states that beyond some critical point private agents and institutions have become too 'large' to be allowed to go under in case of any serious internal or external shock, whether caused by mismanagement or not. The necessary adjustment and restructuring processes, individual losses in terms of wealth, income and employment, are said to be too grave to be tolerated. Moreover, again some sort of externality calls for a policy intervention, among which LLR services provided by a central bank have a prominent status: if it is assumed that all banks hold a proportion of assets which are 'subjunctively sound', i.e. which have stable capital value in good times and a low or unstable value in times of market unrest, then the failure of a very large hazardous banking institution will put downward pressure on the prices of 'subjunctively sound' assets held also by solid institutions. The public, anticipating that the latter might be excluded from LLR aid (because their balance sheets now give the impression of insolvency), will start a bank run on these basically solid banks. Therefore central bankers may lay aside classical prescriptions and turn to the simple rule of protecting large financial institutions of whatever type (Moore, 1999).

The too-big-to-fail doctrine came up in the 1980s, in the wake of the Savings & Loans crisis and the bail-out of the Continental Illinois Bank in 1984, when the chief banking regulating agency in the USA testified to Congress that the 11 largest banks were regarded as 'too big to fail'; they should be bailed out so that neither any depositor nor creditor had to fear any loss (Mishkin and Eakins, 2000: 518). This was a remarkable signal to the non-bank sector; any incentive to monitor these banks' investment strategies was eliminated as the new doctrine abolished the limit of $100 000 up to which the Federal Deposit Insurance guaranteed the security of private deposits. It is no surprise that the stock exchange responded with higher share prices of these large banks: financial markets interpreted the quasi-official statement as a credible signal that high-risk, high-profit bank investment strategies would be indirectly supported by monetary policy, even if such a support was not meant to be the immediate aim of a future intervention. Moreover, a too-big-to-fail doctrine violates basic norms of a market society, 'small' agents should not be discriminated compared to 'big' ones, and has adverse effects in the field of competition policies.

The organization of the bail-out of a large US hedge fund, the 'Long-Term Capital Management', in 1998 by the Fed marked a further step in the development of (at least US) LLR practice. A collapse of that firm was expected to bring about a sudden liquidation of a large amount of equities and derivatives which in turn would have destabilized capital and financial markets, accompanied by huge wealth losses on the part of individual and institutional lenders. This was regarded a systemic risk too large to be tolerated. The operation of collecting fresh private capital – no public funds were invested – may be interpreted as an unqualified success.[13] But if even non-bank institutions can hope to receive public and monetary policy support in case of economic predicament, LLR facilities become indistinguishable from market interventions in other fields of the market system where too-big-to-fail has been a 'solid' argument for interventionist policies for long.

Looking for solutions to the moral hazard problem

If the moral hazard problem was to be taken seriously in the case of providing LLR to illiquid but solvent banks, this problem becomes all the more crucial if hazardous firms can hope to be protected from a downfall. But already the introduction of a deposit insurance has added to the moral hazard problem. This reform placed depositors in the same boat with their bankers. Indirectly the former, by means of competitive forces within the banking system, urged the latter to look for more profitable investments the yields of which were distributed in the form of higher interest rates paid on bank deposits. If this implicit agreement should fail, because the bankers' assets and projects turned sour, both parties would apply for LLR assistance.

The LLR can be analysed as a typical insurance problem. If a third party compensates a risk which is embodied in some economic process, it can be expected that more risk will be taken. The form of this market distortion may vary, though. Whereas fire insurance may increase the likelihood that fires break out, on account of lowered care or even of criminal intention, insurance preventing a liquidity crisis will reduce the probability that bank runs will occur. However, the extent of a bank run, and its consequences in the market, are much larger compared to an uninsured regime, if, due to a deliberate decision or to 'technical' failure, it actually occurs.[14] In this context, Solow (1982) makes the very important point that an insurance-induced change of behaviour towards risk as such is not the issue of concern; on the contrary, quite a few economic policy instruments aim to *motivate* private agents to bear more risks, in particular with regard to investing in real assets. Rather, the point is that 'overinvestment' in financial markets might lead to a fragile architecture of complex and obscure creditor–debtor relations of different maturities and qualities, which is apt to collapse if disturbed by even small shocks.[15]

There are a few approaches which can be followed in order to reduce the adverse incentives brought about by the knowledge that LLR services can be expected. 'Bagehot's Rule', i.e. to lend freely, but to charge high interest rates, works on the basis of simple price theory. Through lower profits, the owners of LLR clients are supposed to pay for financial help. In turn, given efficient supervision of managers through shareholders, the former will be urged to cautious investment strategies. According to Goodhart (1999), 'enlightened' classical economists knew that – in spite of the classical norm – insolvent banks could not be sorted out. But Bagehot (1873: 97) allowed that a 'feeble minority' of insolvent firms profited from an insurance mechanism intended to stabilize 'wholesale' financial relations: a price, measured in terms of a deviation from a puristic microeconomic dogma, which the classicals were ready to pay for preserving macroeconomic stability.[16] The decisive element of a Bagehot policy is the clear signal to the market that LLR facilities are available in case of need.

The opposite strategy to restrict moral hazard is the randomization approach. Its logic is to produce a sufficient amount of uncertainty on the part of applicant beneficiaries whether an LLR will step in or not. Assuming rational expectations, the promise of full coverage of all liquidity and solvency risks is not credible anyhow. The knowledge that LLR services might not be provided on a full scale, or can be expected with a probability lower than unity, can work as a self-containing mechanism. According to the *strategy of constructive ambiguity* (Freixas et al., 2003: 23), no central bank should announce in advance in what cases and under which conditions it will stand ready to rescue a troubled institution. Kindleberger (1978: 171–3) had already proposed to enlarge the beneficiaries' uncertainty systematically by sharing the accountability of LLR services between a small number of public institutions. If only *one* institution, e.g. a central bank, is responsible for the decision to rescue a firm or let it go under, the political pressure put on the administrators in charge might be too large to be resisted. If, on the other hand, there are various political institutions which are in charge of the LLR task, each one keeping an eye on this issue from a different point of view, populist demands for bail-outs and other financial rescue operations may be turned down more easily.

However, Kindleberger himself pointed to the time span which is necessary in a multiple-responsibility decision procedure where various political bodies are involved. The process of choosing who will play lifeguard may let the 'failing swimmer drown' (Kindleberger, 1987: 17; cf. Moore, 1999: 458). Sharing a responsibility for some task may also result in a constellation where *no one* feels any strong obligation to strive for the solution to an urgent problem.[17] Thus the strength of the randomization proposal with respect to the moral hazard dilemma characterizes its very weakness as to the financial crisis problem which has to be solved in the first place. Creating uncertainty in the sphere of banking and finance might turn out to be hazardous policy advice, even if the central bank steps in finally. It runs counter to the classical wisdom. 'To lend a great deal, and yet not give the public confidence that you will lend sufficiently and effectually, is the worst of all policies' (Bagehot, 1873: 31–2).

Moreover, the strategy of constructive ambiguity suffers from a time inconsistency problem: one can assume that an LLR activity is clearly welfare improving if market behaviour is not distorted by moral hazard. As a consequence, rational market agents will anticipate that the LLR will intervene whether or not he announces this kind of response or 'strictly' excludes it. Given the expectation that financial help will be provided anyhow, portfolio decisions and investment behaviour of banks may change. The central bank in turn can hardly stay passive in a crisis which now will be heavier because of the accumulated risk-loaded portfolios. The only way out of this predicament would be a strict constitutional rule prohibiting any LLR service – but such a rule again would not be credible given public pressure in economic policy affairs.

Yet another precaution against the attempt to exploit the knowledge that insurance services will be provided in case of need is installed within *clubs* where members observe each other and share a common moral conviction that restrains selfish and 'unfair' behaviour. It may well be the case that the bankers' community represents such a club, at least in the days of Bagehot. This might explain that excessive risk taking (as a market reaction to the establishment of an LLR) was not a major concern in the classical era. A central bank trying 'to find a means of checking moral hazard . . . can take the "English" route of informal controls and inculcation of a club spirit' (Hirsch, 1977: 251; cf. Goodhart,

1988: 69–73). There are a number of caveats against the praise of the club solution to moral hazard: trust developed through the club spirit can be abused by single members; clubs create insiders and outsiders and thus tend to impede the forces and welfare gain of competition (Moore, 1999). Central banks certainly like to control the banking community through implicit or explicit 'gentlemen's agreements', but deregulation and globalization of financial markets has already eroded the traditional, conservative role of a banker. Social and cultural traits in a market society may work as useful preconditions for a proper functioning of market mechanisms, but they cannot be controlled and applied as any technical tool of economic policy.

Finally, the typical response of an insurer to the moral hazard problem is to attempt to control and guide the behaviour of its clients. Therefore, regulation and surveillance were practised in financial markets, in various forms, since the emergence of the two-tiered banking system. Whereas in former times a 'club spirit' informally, at least to some extent, induced a sound bankers' behaviour, state agencies and the law nowadays take a more active part, e.g. by stipulating certain capital adequacy ratios. With a higher ratio, the loss resulting from a depreciation of a bank's assets first falls on the shareholders, before the interests of depositors are threatened. The Free Banking School even demands unlimited liability of commercial banks, which implies that stockholders guarantee the value of deposits by encumbering their personal wealth. This of course would induce private agents to stay away from bank shares (cf. Moore, 1999). Probably it is unwise to go that far; but if an LLR feels compelled to rescue an unsound institution for sake of market stability, surely managers and shareholders should sustain severe losses in income and wealth.

The LLR in the European Monetary Union (EMU)

In the EMU, it seems that some variant of the constructive ambiguity strategy has been established. With a critical undertone, it is named a *destructive ambiguity strategy* (Aglietta, 1999; cf. Goodhart, 2000; Schinasi, 2003): it is not only unclear whether an LLR will intervene or not; moreover, the *identity* of the LLR is in doubt. At least, it is known that the European Central Bank (ECB) is *not* in charge of LLR services. A multiplicity of responsibilities has been created, formally referring to Kindleberger's (1978) suggestion, but probably due to quarrels that accompanied the establishment of European monetary policy institutions; nation states hesitated to transfer too many powers to a supranational body. The ECB surely exerts an almost perfect control of the EMU money market; 'wholesale' liquidity problems therefore can be managed efficiently. But the commitment to a list of securities acceptable as collateral rules out ECB lending to a commercial bank which has no corresponding paper to offer. LLR activities in the narrow sense of the notion and banking supervision are the responsibilities of the national central banks.

The institutional architecture of LLR facilities is far from optimal. Financial market stability in the euro area, as the final aim of an LLR, cannot be split into national segments. The threat of a failure of a large national commercial bank is bound to trigger unrest on the European financial markets. The question how to react, whether a general easing of monetary policy will suffice or firm-specific measures are to be taken, should be answered in a joint decision process at the European level. However, it would be naive to assume that – at least informal – consultations between the ECB and national central banks will not take place in times of an imminent banking crisis. The general imbalance of ever more globalized goods and financial markets, on the one hand, and regulative facilities of national economic policy, on the other hand, has been highlighted for many years. It is not a feature specific to EMU.

The LLR issue in EMU rekindles a controversy that was already debated among classical economists: what are the limitations of LLR capacities of a central bank? There were two answers given in the classical era:

- As central banks in the gold standard were exposed to a liquidity problem, the stock of reserves also formally marked a limit for distress lending and discounting. But Bagehot had forcefully convinced his contemporaries that lending freely at high interest rates was the best remedy for stopping an internal and external drain.
- As central banks were private companies, shareholders would not like to see their capital diminished through some LLR intervention, i.e. if the bank acquires claims which prove to be worthless afterwards; hence the overriding importance attached to the principle that 'good securities' should be offered as collateral.

The second of these limitations is valid in modern times, although central banks were transformed into public institutions. Capital losses now have to be borne by the ministry of finance (being the 'owner' of the central bank) and thus, finally, by the taxpayers. A reform that would establish the ECB as the single euro-area-wide LLR institution would also require an agreement on the terms of a recapitalization of the Bank by contributions of national fiscal authorities, if a large intervention depletes the ECB's initial capital (cf. Goodhart, 1999; Buiter, 2003; Steiger, 2004). The unwillingness of national authorities to consent to such a resolution leaves national central banks in the role of LLRs.

Unfortunately, this is no long-run solution. In former times, French taxpayers may have approved the use of public funds in order to rescue French commercial banks which were active in the French financial market. But do national central banks find sufficient political support to bail out large financial institutions, which may have a national standing leg, but work throughout Europe? Is the free-rider position of other national central banks sustainable, merely to observe the stabilization of euro financial markets? Most probably a banking crisis is needed to overcome the institutional difficulties which presently hinder the establishment of an LLR at the European level.

Notes

1. The issue of the international LLR will not be analysed in this chapter. For an introduction see Fischer (1999).
2. An Australian bulletin of 1893 contains the somewhat ironic statement: 'A solvent bank is an institution which is able to meet its liabilities as long as nobody desires that it should do so, and which can't meet them at any other time. It is built on the principle that everybody can have his money if he doesn't want it, and not otherwise' (quoted from Moore, 1999: 443).
3. The question whether money ought to be defined narrowly or broadly misses the peculiar feature of a two-tier banking system: here single monetary functions, to some extent, are performed by different money assets. Central-bank money alone is a standard of value *and* a means of payment in the sense of an ultimate discharge of contracts. Besides, certain bank deposits, i.e. claims denominated in units of central-bank money ('inside money'), can serve as a means of payment. The transfer of these claims is accepted instead of a definite payment because the promise of these claims being redeemable in central-bank money ('outside money') is taken as credible. The public here assumes that the commercial banks operate under liquidity constraints, regulations and surveillance executed by the central bank. The acceptance of 'inside money' is derived from the reputation of the central-bank money. As and in so far as commercial banks do not issue notes on their own account and name ('Citibank dollar'), they are not able to create money.
4. 'It is by no means intended to imply, that it would become the Bank of England to relieve every distress which the rashness of country banks may bring upon them: the bank, by doing this, might encourage their

improvidence. There seems to be a medium at which a public bank should aim in granting aid to inferior establishments, and which it must often find very difficult to be observed. The relief should neither be so prompt and liberal as to exempt those who misconduct their business from all the natural consequences of their fault, nor so scanty and slow as deeply to involve the general interests. These interests, nevertheless, are sure to be pleaded by every distressed person whose affairs are large, however indifferent or even ruinous may be their state' (Thornton, 1802: 188).

5. 'If any one bank fails, a general run upon the neighbouring ones is apt to take place, which if not checked in the beginning by a pouring into the circulation a large quantity of gold, leads to very extensive mischief' (Thornton, 1802: 180).

6. 'The view . . . of central bank policy as a means of facilitating the achievement and maintenance of reasonable stability in the level of economic activity and of prices was scarcely thought about before 1914, and certainly not accepted, as a formal objective of policy' (Bloomfield, 1959: 24). For a view on Bagehot's 'Lombard Street' from the aspect of macroeconomic stabilization see O'Brien (2001).

7. 'Reputation . . . has a public good element, externalities relating to the reputation of others in the same field, that can easily misused by free riders' (Goodhart, 1988: 64).

8. Goodhart (1999), however, challenges the predominating view that Bagehot really stipulated 'penalty' rates of interest. His reading of 'Lombard Street' leads to the proposition that central bank interest rates should not necessarily exceed contemporaneous market rates (which of course are higher in times of financial stress).

9. 'Deposit insurance is the recognition of the social nature of bank deposits. It transforms a claim on a private debtor into a claim on the banking system as a whole and ultimately on the nation when the scheme is public and benefits explicitly or implicitly from the guarantee of the State. Deposit insurance is what makes money fungible on a contractual basis, the LLR being the ultimate guarantor of fungibility for the part of bank money not covered by deposit insurance. In principle, credible deposit insurance lessens the incentive for bank runs' (Aglietta, 1999: 31).

10. The public *announcement* of easy-money policies when, e.g., a stock market crash threatens to cause financial distress of course helps to avoid any serious contagion effects, even if the practical course of interest policy is hardly different from the intended one.

11. Goodhart draws some support from Bagehot (1873), who – despite the strict classical prohibition of allowing central bank lending to insolvent firms – urged the Bank of England to make its decision, whether to lend or not, dependent on the offered collateral only. 'But this test has really nothing to do with the question of whether . . . the applicant borrower . . . had a capital value below some lower limit' (Goodhart, 1999: 4).

12. 'An individual bank will only go to a central bank for direct LLR assistance when it cannot meet its liquidity needs on the wholesale interbank money market. Almost by definition this must be because it is running out of good security for collateralised loans and other (bank) lenders will not lend to it on an unsecured basis in the quantities required (at acceptable rates). Again almost by definition this latter must be because there is some question about its ultimate solvency. . . . Nowadays illiquidity implies at least the suspicion of insolvency' (Goodhart, 1999: 5).

13. In a similar way, the Bank of England organized a syndicate of established bankers to support the Baring Bank in 1890. However, critics pointed to the fact that in the case of LTCM rescue the Fed intervention actually *prevented* a pure market solution. LTCM managers denied an offer of other private investors, rightly expecting that the group of financiers brought together by the Fed would realize a solution on more favourable terms for LTCM managers and owners (cf. Dowd, 1999; Mishkin and Eakins, 2000: 613; Kho et al., 2000).

14. Solow (1982) draws the analogy to a flood levee, interpreted as a technical insurance device, which surely reduces the future number of floodings, but – as people feel safe and move more closely to the river – if a heavy flood occurs it causes a catastrophe.

15. A banker's adage runs: 'It is not the speed that kills, it is the sudden stop.'

16. Thornton (1802: 186) likewise estimated that the Bank of England's losses due to discounting bills of dubious quality were very small.

17. Often, the group is informally dominated by one agency or person and falls into a state of indecision if for any reason it loses its leader. Alluding to the early 1930s, when the Federal Reserve System lacked a clear response to the swelling bank crises, Friedman and Schwartz (1963: 415–16) concluded that there 'is more than a little element of truth in the jocular description of a committee as a group of people, no one of whom knows what should be done, who jointly decide that nothing can be done'.

References

Aglietta, M. (1999), 'A lender of last resort for Europe', Centre d'Etudes Prospectives et d'Informations Internationales, *Document de Travail*, 99–12, Paris.

Bagehot, W. (1873), *Lombard Street – A Description of the Money Market*, Westport: Hyperion, 1979.

Baring, F. (1797), *Observations on the Establishment of the Bank of England and on the Paper Circulation in the Country*, New York: Kelley, 1967.

Bloomfield, A.I. (1959), *Monetary Policy Under the International Gold Standard, 1880–1914*, New York: Federal Reserve Bank.

Bordo, M.D. (1990), 'The lender of last resort – alternative views and historical experience', *Federal Reserve Bank of Richmond Economic Review*, **76**, 18–29.

Brunner, K. and Meltzer, A.H. (1988), 'Money and credit in the monetary transmission process', *American Economic Review, Papers and Proceedings*, **78**, 446–51.

Buiter, W.H. (2003), 'Two naked emperors? Concerns about the Stability and Growth Pact and second thoughts about central bank independence', *CEPR Discussion Paper*, 4001, London.

Dowd, K. (1999), 'Too big to fail? Long-Term Capital Management and the Federal Reserve', Cato Institute, *Briefing Paper*, 52.

European Central Bank (2004), 'Accounting for the resilience of the EU banking sector since 2000', *Monthly Report*, July, 59–70.

Fischer, S. (1999), 'On the need for an international lender of last resort', *Journal of Economic Perspectives*, **13**(4), 85–104.

Freixas, X. et al. (2003), 'The lender of last resort – a 21st century approach', European Central Bank, *Working Paper*, 298, Frankfurt.

Friedman, M. (1959), *A Program for Monetary Stability*, New York: Fordham University Press, 1970.

Friedman, M. and Schwartz, A.J. (1963), *A Monetary History of the United States, 1867–1960*, Princeton, NJ: Princeton University Press, 1990.

Goodfriend, M. and King, R.A. (1988), 'Financial deregulation, monetary policy and central banking', in Haraf, W.S. and Kushmeider, R.M. (eds), *Restructuring Banking and Financial Services in America*, Washington: American Enterprise Institute.

Goodhart, C.A.E. (1988), *The Evolution of Central Banks*, Cambridge, MA and London: MIT Press.

Goodhart, C.A.E. (1999), 'Myths about the lender of last resort', Financial Markets Group, Special Paper 120, London School of Economics.

Goodhart, C.A.E. (ed.) (2000), *Which Lender of Last Resort for Europe?* A Collection of Papers from the Financial Markets Group of the London School of Economics, London: Central Banking Publications.

Hawtrey, R.G. (1923), *Currency and Credit*, 2nd edn, London et al.: Longmans & Green.

Hawtrey, R.G. (1932), *The Art of Central Banking*, London: Frank Cass & Co., 1970.

Hellwig, M.F. (1998), 'Systemische Risiken im Finanzsektor', in Duwendag, D. (ed.), *Finanzmärkte im Spannungsfeld von Globalisierung, Regulierung und Geldpolitik*, Schriften des Vereins für Socialpolitik, 261, Berlin: Duncker & Humblot, 123–51.

Hicks, J. (1989), *A Market Theory of Money*, Oxford: Clarendon Press.

Hirsch, F. (1977), 'The Bagehot problem', *The Manchester School of Economic and Social Studies*, **45**, 241–57.

Humphrey, T.M. (1992), 'Lender of last resort', in Eatwell, J. et al. (eds), *The New Palgrave Dictionary of Money and Finance*, Basingstoke: Macmillan, 571–4.

Kho, B.-C. et al. (2000), 'U.S. banks, crises, and bailouts – from Mexico to LTCM', *American Economic Review, Papers and Proceedings*, **90**, 28–31.

Kindleberger, C.P. (1978), *Manias, Panics and Crashes*, London: Macmillan, 1981.

Kindleberger, C.P. (1987), '1929 – ten lessons for today', *Challenge*, Anniversary Issue, 15–18.

Meltzer, A. (1986), 'Financial failures and financial policies', in Kaufmann, G.G. and Kormendi, R.C. (eds), *Deregulating Financial Service – Public Policy in Flux*, Cambridge, MA: Ballinger.

Mishkin, F.S. and Eakins, S.G. (2000), *Financial Markets and Institutions*, 3rd edn, Reading et al.: Addison, Wesley, Longman.

Moore, G. (1999), 'Solutions to the moral hazard problem arising from the lender-of-last-resort facility', *Journal of Economic Surveys*, **13**, 443–76.

O'Brien, D.P. (2001), 'Bagehot's *Lombard Street* and macroeconomic stabilisation', *Scottish Journal of Political Economy*, **48**, 425–41.

Rochet, J.-C. (2003), 'Why are there so many banking crises?', *CESifo Economic Studies*, **49**(2), 141–55.

Schinasi, G.J. (2003), 'Responsibility of central banks for stability in financial markets', IMF Working Paper, 03/121.

Solow, R.M. (1982), 'On the lender of last resort', in Kindleberger, C.P. and Laffargue, J. (eds), *Financial Crises*, Cambridge: Cambridge University Press, 237–48.

Spahn, H.-P. (2001), *From Gold to Euro – On Monetary Theory and the History of Currency Systems*, Berlin and Heidelberg: Springer.

Steiger, O. (2004), 'Which lender of last resort for the euro system? A contribution to the theory of central banking', Paper presented at the conference 'Complexity, Endogenous Money and Exogenous Interest Rates', Stellenbosh.

Thornton, H. (1802), *An Enquiry into the Nature and Effects of the Paper Credit of Great Britain*, New York: Kelley, 1965.

17 The theory of interest rates
John Smithin*

Introduction

In discussing the treatment of interest rates in heterodox monetary analysis, there are three key issues that need to be debated/discussed before any other matters can usefully be raised. There are (1) the basic or essential nature of interest, and, specifically, whether or not it is purely a 'monetary phenomenon' as Keynes said, or simply the reflection of some other, supposedly more 'real', economic phenomenon, (2) the distinction between real (in the sense of inflation-adjusted) interest rates and nominal interest rates (in principle, this is an entirely different issue from the first point), and (3), the relationship between interest rates on securities with different terms to maturity, that is between 'short' and 'long' interest rates. The first three sections of this chapter therefore deal with each of these points in turn. There then follows a discussion of alternative theories of interest rate determination. Writers such as Hicks (1989) and Smithin (1994; 2003), for example, have previously claimed that there are fundamentally three such theories, but in this chapter it is now argued that it is more useful to think of *four* alternatives, the fourth (actually the most influential in orthodox circles) being a hybrid of two of the others. Finally, there must be some discussion of the thorny question of the *ethics* of the principle of interest on money, in the context of a capitalist-type economic system.

The nature of interest

Fletcher (1987, 154) highlights an important quote from Keynes to the effect that his (Keynes's) approach to the theory of interest rates simply entails accepting the basic *definition* of interest, that it is 'Nothing more than the inverse proportion between a sum of money and what can be obtained for parting with control over the money in exchange for a debt for a stated period of time.' Further, that 'In stating what it is, I follow the books on arithmetic, and accept the accuracy of what is taught in preparatory schools.' Keynes's attitude is then summed up by the statement: 'The rate of interest is, strictly speaking, a *monetary* phenomenon in the special sense that it is the *own rate* . . . on money itself' (original emphasis). This all seems to be common sense. However, in order to make any use of these simple notions for the purposes of economic theory, it would also be necessary to have a clear understanding of 'money' (i.e. the whole network of accounting and credit relationships that can be included under this rubric) as an important social institution it its own right (Ingham, 1996; 2000; 2004). The monetary system would need to be understood as a set of social arrangements that indeed plays an important role in capitalism, and may actually be a prerequisite for capitalism (Lau and Smithin, 2002), but is relatively autonomous from the 'sphere of production' as such (Ingham, 2004). Such an understanding, however, was not possible within the schemes of thought of either classical or neoclassical economics, and *a fortiori* for their modern descendants in the contemporary mainstream. The reason for this is that the underlying vision or model of economic activity in all of these modes of thought is that of barter exchange. Money plays only a superficial role, as a neutral lubricant of economic activity. It has no independent existence or importance. Therefore the return on money, the rate of interest, can have no independent existence or importance either. It can be seen only as a reflection of certain supposedly more fundamental economic forces, the ubiquitous 'productivity and thrift'.

Clearly, the different views that we are describing correspond closely to Schumpeter's (1954) delineation of two fundamentally different approaches to economics, namely 'real analysis' and 'monetary analysis'. Keynes (1973, 408–11) also distinguished a 'real exchange economy' from a monetary economy. For Keynes a monetary economy is that

> in which money plays a part of its own and affects motives and decisions and is . . . one of the operative factors . . . (and) events cannot be predicted, either in the long period or in the short, without a knowledge of the behaviour of money . . . (e)veryone would . . . agree that it is in a monetary economy in my sense . . . that we actually live.

In other words, the different views on the nature of interest correspond precisely to the different views on the nature of money, and its role in the economy. However, the point is that not everyone *does* agree that it is in a monetary economy in Keynes's sense of the term 'that we actually live'. Humphrey (1993), for example, demonstrates that all the classical and neoclassical economists, without exception, took the opposite view. Their economics was *only* real analysis in Schumpeter's meaning of the term, and as far as interest rates are concerned, they are 'basically determined by productivity and thrift – or more precisely by the marginal productivity of capital and society's rate of time preference' (ibid., 36). As Humphrey shows, this was the view not only of the major classical economists, such as Hume, Smith, Thornton, Ricardo and Mill, but also of the so-called 'neoclassicals', including the likes of Bohm-Bawerk, Marshall, Fisher, Wicksell, Pigou et al. In short, it was an unshakeable orthodoxy for around 200 years from Hume to Keynes. Moreover, after the brief Keynesian interlude, and in the forty years since Friedman (1968), this same opinion has once again become the overwhelming dominant view among mainstream economists (Smithin, 1994; 2003).

What is interesting, however, is that the link between unobservable theoretical concepts such as the marginal productivity of capital and time preference, and the observable interest rate on money, has never been spelt out in any great detail. Keynes (1936, 175) was quick to point this out, saying: 'What is the classical theory of the rate of interest? . . . I find it difficult to state it precisely or to discover an explicit account of it . . .'. Typically, in fact, as Keynes is hinting, there are just a series of *obiter dicta* along the following lines:

> the rate of interest is not . . . derived from the quantity [of money] . . . that depends on another principle; and must proceed from an increase of industry and frugality of arts and commerce. (Hume, quoted by Humphrey, 1993, 37)

> the rate of interest is not regulated by the abundance or scarcity of money, but by the abundance or scarcity of that part of capital not consisting of money. (Ricardo, quoted by Humphrey, 1993, 38)

> It is usually regarded as an axiom in economics . . . that the level of interest on money is not in the last instance determined by a shortage or surplus of money, but by a shortage or surplus of real capital. (Wicksell, quoted by Smithin, 2003, 110)

> I treat the expected real interest rate and output as exogenous with respect to money, because I lack an alternative specification that I regard as theoretically or empirically superior. (Barro, quoted by Smithin, 2003, 111)

But exactly why the interest rate on money should be determined by things that are *not* money usually has to be read between the lines. The sort of argument put forward in the case of a supposed increase in the marginal productivity of physical capital is that this will stimulate an increase in the demand for loans of money, in order to acquire the 'capital', to gain the (presumably also physical) reward. *If* the supply of money is fixed, however, the interest rate on money will therefore rise by the same amount. The key assumption here, obviously, is precisely that the money supply is fixed. In the case of an arbitrary increase in the money supply itself, on the other hand, the argument is that this will simply raise prices, and hence increase the nominal demand for loans by the same amount leaving the real interest rate unchanged (Humphrey, 1993, 36). In this latter case, the implicit assumption is that the supply of *output* is fixed, which Keynes (1936, 179) dismissed as a 'nonsense theory'. Nonsensical or not, it seems clear that the various arguments put forward over the long history of classical and neoclassical economics have been simply those needed to provide some sort of analytical support to a conclusion already predetermined by the basic vision of what an economy is: in particular, that money is not important, and therefore the rate of return on money *cannot* be important in its own right. It must be reflective of other, supposedly more fundamental, forces. The rate of interest is thought of only as a real phenomenon (in this sense) rather than a monetary phenomenon.

Note, however, that the analytical arguments of, for example, Ricardo, and essentially all his followers fall to the ground as soon as is it is recognized that money is endogenous in a credit economy, and that monetary policy really consists of the 'terms on which' (Keynes, 1936, 191) the central bank or monetary authority is willing to accommodate demands for base money: in other words, changes in the interest rate itself, rather than arbitrary changes in a previously fixed money supply. Keynes made precisely this point in the passage just cited from the *General Theory*, which is a model of clarity by the overall standards of this debate. The setting of the interest rate then just boils down to a question of power and politics. Money is something that is needed for the capitalist economy to function, and the price of money is 'negotiated' by a series of institutional, political, and even cultural, maneuvers, of which, ironically, economic theory itself is a major element. It is true that Keynes's own 'monetary' approach to interest rate determination, namely the theory of liquidity preference, promptly tended to confuse matters once again, because of its own internal flaws as pure theory. However, this should not be allowed to deflect attention from the basic point. This is that the first issue to be faced in any discussion of interest rate determination is this basic question of the underlying nature of interest, real or monetary. This, in turn, rests on differing views about the underlying nature of the economy itself and the role of money within it.

It is important also to discuss the exact relationship between interest and profit (the latter, presumably, being indubitably a real economic concept in the sense used above). In the neoclassical economics of 'perfect competition' there was, of course, no such thing as profit, and hence the resort to circumlocutions such as the marginal product of capital. However, their classical predecessors were not so squeamish, and the real return that was held to determine the interest rate was the 'the rate of profits . . . made by the employment of capital' (Ricardo, quoted by Smithin, 2003, 110), or the 'rate of mercantile profit' (Thornton, quoted by Smithin, 2003, 109), or something of the kind. The key point none the less was that this profit was held to determine the interest rate, just as the marginal product of capital was later held to determine interest in neoclassical theory. Therefore a high rate of interest would be always be the *consequence* of high profits. As pointed out by Pivetti (2003), in this respect Marx was in full agreement with the classical economists. In Marxian theory the total amount of profit is basically predetermined beforehand by the theory of surplus value, and the division of this between interest and entrepreneurial profit is then decided (for example, in Vol. III of *Capital*) by a sort of intramural class struggle between financial capitalists and industrial capitalists. The point is, though, that in order for interest to exist, profit would have to exist in the first place, and, in terms of general principle, it would still be true that higher interest rates were associated with higher profits and *vice versa* (Pivetti, 2003, 302). Therefore, in terms of *both* the classical and Marxian theory there is a 'real' theory of interest rates rather than a monetary theory, and profits essentially determine the rate of interest. If, on the other hand (as suggested above), the monetary/financial system is regarded as a relatively independent social institution within the general framework of capitalism, and interest rates are determined first and foremost within this sphere, this would imply rather that interest, wages and entrepreneurial profit each represent *competing* claims on the total of real output in a three-way class struggle. Then, the more commonsense notion that a higher rate of interest would tend to reduce or cut into profits (and for that matter wages as well) would seem to be the more realistic prediction (Davidson, 1996; Smithin, 2005). According to Keynes (1936, 344) the mercantilists (a school despised by the classicals, Marx and the neoclassicals alike) had the right idea on this, where their several opponents did not: 'How easily the mercantilist mind distinguished between interest and the marginal efficiency of capital . . .'. These issues all revolve around the question of whether the interest rate is a real or monetary phenomenon.

Real and nominal interest rates

A further point of confusion is that the distinction made in economics textbooks between *real* and *nominal* interest rates, and usually attributed to Fisher (1896), really should have nothing to do with the above. To avoid misunderstanding, it should immediately be pointed that Irving Fisher himself, as a neoclassical economist, also held that interest was ultimately determined by real forces in the sense of the previous section. Therefore Fisher also subscribed to the same confusion (Tymoigne, 2005). In the context alluded to, however, real should simply mean 'inflation-adjusted', and not refer to any particular theory of how interest rates are determined. This point, however, seems frequently to be missed by both mainstream and heterodox economists alike. In fact, much of the both the classical and neoclassical literature failed even to make the distinction, with the notable exception of Thornton (Humphrey, 1993, 37). As mentioned, Fisher is usually credited with the rediscovery of this notion in the late neoclassical period, but in truth it did not become established at the textbook level until the advent of the more obviously inflationary epoch of the second half of the twentieth century. As far as heterodox economists are concerned, it seems that some writers who have dismissed the idea that there is any such thing as a 'natural' interest rate determined by productivity and thrift, on the grounds outlined above, have also, and by the same token, dismissed the idea that there is any merit in distinguishing the nominal interest rate from the inflation-adjusted real rate for the purposes of economic decision-making. There is, in fact, a fairly well-established tradition in some heterodox circles to the effect that *only* the nominal rate is 'relevant' in a monetary economy (see, for example, Tymoigne, 2005, for a statement and references to the literature). But this conflation of the two ideas can lead to serious problems, in particular in deciding whether or not any particular value of the nominal interest rate actually constitutes a cheap money policy (Smithin, 2003). Given that interest rates are a claim on income, the real rate of interest must be what matters from the point of view of the distribution of real income; and in particular of expected future real income. Also, the level of real interest is important from the point of view of the prospects of preserving the value of financial capital, including, crucially, that held in the form of interest-bearing fixed-nominal value securities (broad money, savings bonds, certificates of deposits, mortgage and other loans, etc.). The existence of such facilities is, in turn, a key strategic variable in capitalism (Lau and Smithin, 2002).

It is true, obviously, that there are ambiguities about the concept of the inflation-adjusted real rate from the statistical point of view. However, these seem only to be of the same order of magnitude as those of most macroeconomic/aggregative or expectational concepts. As usually defined, the real rate is equal to the quoted nominal interest rate minus the *expected* inflation rate. That is:

$$r = i - p^e \tag{17.1}$$

where i is a nominal interest rate, r is the real interest rate, and p^e is the expected rate of inflation. The two problems that immediately arise therefore are, first, that different 'economic agents' can have different expectations, and, second, that the price level itself is only an index number, and it is always possible to dispute whether any particular method of calculating it is correct (either in general, or again across heterogeneous agents). It may reasonably be doubted, however, whether the actual degree of divergence on each of these points in practice is likely to be enough to seriously vitiate the concept of real interest as a theoretical macro variable. That is to say, there seems to be no more difficulty in this respect than in the case of most aggregative concepts. Moreover, and *a fortiori*, if there is to be macroeconomic theorizing at all there is nothing in these arguments to make the alternative, of treating the nominal interest rate in itself as a meaningful concept, a defensible strategy.

Moore (1988, 257–62), among heterodox economists, provides a very clear discussion of the real/nominal issue, and states that 'nominal rates cannot be understood as the sum of some stable real interest rate plus an inflation . . . premium . . . real rates are simply the real value of the nominal rate adjusted for changes in the value of money'. Moreover, Moore goes on to point out that in many cases the real rate in the above sense is actually more variable than the nominal rate. This is simply because the nominal rate is not always adjusted promptly when the inflation rate changes. It seems clear, also, that it will be the variable real rate that will affect economic decision-making in this situation rather than the sticky nominal rate. It is implicit in these observations, of course, that the real interest rate *could* be made more stable (for example, by central bank policy) if the nominal rate were so adjusted. Again, these ideas do militate against the idea that there is any such thing as a 'natural' real rate, but *not* against the notion of a real rate of interest as a definitional concept. The Chicago-trained economist Burstein has similarly distinguished between a natural rate theory of real interest rate determination, and the simple definition of the real interest rate. According to Burstein (1995, 1), there can be both a 'real theory of the real rate of interest' and a 'monetary theory of the real rate of interest'. The former is an accurate description of the classical theory, whereas the latter is what Burstein would attribute to Keynes and others.[1]

The term structure of interest rates

The concept in theoretical finance of the 'term structure of interest rates', which may be illustrated empirically by a graph of the 'yield curve', refers to the relationship between interest rates on debt instruments with different terms to maturity. The annualized yields on instruments with (say) less than one year to run are generically referred to as short rates, and those with several years to run as long rates. Of course we can distinguish between short and long nominal rates, and short and long real rates, exactly as in the previous section.

The distinction between short and long rates impinges on the discussion of the role of interest rates in the economy in two main ways. First, many accounts of how monetary policy affects the economy seem to take it for granted that the activities of the monetary authorities, such as central banks, will have a direct influence mainly at the short end of the market, whereas it is thought that the interest rate that is mainly relevant for economic decision-making (for example, for investment spending) is the long rate. This was certainly true, for example, of the 'neo-Keynesian' model that represented economic orthodoxy in the third quarter of the twentieth century. Such a theory therefore has to provide an adequate account of the 'transmission mechanism', which links short rates to long rates. More to the point, this type of theory can be criticized simply by casting doubt on the existence of such a mechanism, for example, by pointing to situations in which (say) short rates fall, but long rates remain unchanged, or even move in the opposite direction. Counter arguments would have to be along the lines that changes in short rates *per se* also have a significant impact on costs, or, if long rates are indeed the key, that the transmission mechanism will work given time (see below), or finally that there is no reason why monetary policy should not directly operate on the long end (Tily, 2005). There is also, of course, the further (but separate) question of whether changes in interest rates, long or short, once effected, will actually have the impact on the economy attributed to them. This is certainly an issue that has been of concern to several writers in the Keynesian or post-Keynesian tradition, particularly in early contributions dating to the 1950s and 1960s.[2] What is true is that historically high real rates of interest (not necessarily coinciding with high nominal rates), and hence major redistributions of income to rentiers, have been associated with major economic downturns, such as during the depression of the 1930s and the 'Volker experiment' of the 1980s (Lavoie and Seccareccia, 1988).

Second, another type of argument that revolves around the term structure attempts to move the argument about whether or not there is a natural rate of interest away from the short-term money market and locate it in the market for long-term bonds. In other words, even if the short rate of interest can be shown to be influenced by 'monetary factors', it may still be argued that the long rate is the true natural rate, and that ultimately the short rate must conform to this, via the term structure. Humphrey (1993, 42) quotes Pigou to the effect that

> the rate of discount is tied up to the rate of interest . . . on long loans; this rate . . . is determined by the general conditions of demand and supply of real capital; these lie outside the central or any

other bank's control . . . on occasions for a little while a strong central bank could hold its discount rate above or below the rate for long loans . . . attempts to do this for any length of time must lead to a transfer of borrowings between the long and short loan markets, and so defeat itself.

In other words, this argument is not that there is *no* link between long and short rates, but that there is a link and it works the other way round.

Orthodox textbooks on money and banking put forward a number of alternative theories of the relationship between short interest rates and long interest rates with labels such as the 'segmented markets theory', the 'preferred habitat theory', the 'liquidity premium theory' and the 'expectations theory' (Mishkin and Serleitis, 2005, 177–25). Among these, the expectations theory is the one that makes the most sense, and is also the most helpful in understanding the types of situation discussed above, in which the behavior of the long rate does not conform to that of the short rate, or the slope of the yield curve changes. The theory assumes arbitrage between the short and long ends of the market, and hence that the long rate is simply the geometric average of expected future short rates, with some allowance for risk. It would then be readily understandable that an increase or decrease in short rates is not always immediately transmitted to the long end. This would be the case, for example, if the change in short rates is not expected to be permanent, or if it is seen as just a 'blip' against the background of a previously established contrary trend. The message for monetary policy would then be no more than that it may take some time to establish the 'credibility' of any particular policy. As for the slope of the yield curve, the existence of the so-called 'inverted' yield curve (with short rates higher than long rates) clearly corresponds to a situation in which short-term interest rates are currently high, but expected to fall in the future and remain low for some time. A 'normal' yield curve, on the other hand, with a mild upward slope, presumably reflects an expectation that short rates will not change very much in future, together with a risk premium that increases with the length of the time horizon. As for the issue of causality between short and long rates, the expectations theory would seem to rule out the reverse causality between a long-term natural rate and a short-term monetary rate as in the quote from Pigou above. If the short rate is determined by monetary factors, then the long rate must be a 'monetary phenomenon' also, in the sense of being primarily determined by expectations of future monetary conditions.

Alternative theories of interest rate determination

It has often been suggested that there are (fundamentally) three alternative theories of interest rate determination (Hicks, 1989; Smithin, 1994; 2003). These are (1) the 'classical' theory, alluded to above, which argues that the rate of interest is determined by demand and supply in the market for 'real capital' (and fundamentally by productivity and thrift), (2) 'liquidity preference' theory, meaning by this the monetary theory of interest in the specific form given to it by Keynes (1936, 165–74) in the *General Theory*, and (3) the theory that (in recent times) has come to be known as 'horizontalist' theory. This suggests that, given the particular institutions of capitalism, the interest rate is not determined primarily in 'the market', but is a sociopolitical variable, typically administered by the monetary authority in response to a variety of both economic and political pressures. This is also obviously a monetary rather than a real theory (of the real rate of interest).

The classical theory of interest, which Hicks (1989, 74) called 'Marshallian', is usually described as a savings/investment theory. The interest rate is determined by the intersection of the investment and savings functions. The natural rate is the rate consistent both with equilibrium in the capital market and with full employment. By necessity, in this theory it has to be left extremely vague as to what real investment and real saving actually consist of. In the national income accounts these are simply sums of money deflated by a price index, but in theoretical principle the terms supposedly refer to 'real resources' in some sense. According to Wicksell (1898), as quoted by Smithin (2003, 110), for example, 'this natural rate is roughly the real interest of actual business . . . [think] of it as the rate which would be determined by supply and demand if real capital were lent in kind *without the intervention of money*' (emphasis added).

However, even without the intervention of the highly technical capital theory debates of the 1960s, as recently reviewed by Cohen and Harcourt (2003), it is clear that it is difficult to give any intelligible meaning to such a conception. In effect, this is simply a further example of the 'incorrigible confusion'[3] between the idea of interest on money as an expression of a social claim on existing resources, and the properties of the physical world itself, a confusion pervading the entire classical and neoclassical economic literature. Certain writers, such as Coddington (1983) and Kohn (1986), do suggest that the 'loanable funds' theory, put forward by Robertson in the 1930s, was a significant development of the classical interest theory in this respect. The point is that Robertson's approach does at least make it clear that borrowing and lending are actually conducted in money terms rather than 'in kind' (Fletcher, 1987). Coddington (1983, 91, fn. 7) actually goes so far as to criticize Keynes for being 'unable to distinguish' between a savings/investment theory and the loanable funds theory. However, against this it suffices to quote Rogers (1989, 40), who points out that 'It is quite clear . . . that Robertson envisages that the demand and supply of loanable funds – money and financial flows – simply reflects the underlying real forces of productivity and thrift.' In other words, the loanable funds theory was, in reality, just a variation on the overall classical theme.

Meanwhile, according to Keynes's liquidity preference theory the interest rate is determined by the relative demand for a given quantity of money and the existing stock of alternative financial assets, with the generic label of 'bonds'. This is a 'stock' theory rather than a 'flow' theory, as in the case of the savings/investment analysis. An increase in liquidity preference, that is, an increase in the demand for money relative to bonds, would push bond prices down and interest rates up, and *vice versa*. Liquidity preference was Keynes's attempt to break with the natural rate theory and provide a monetary theory of the rate of interest. From the technical point of view, however, there is a problem with the way in which the theory was presented (as opposed to the heuristic value of the concept itself). In order for the theory to work, there must be a relatively fixed supply of money in nominal terms. Otherwise, it would always be possible to argue that the supply of money will simply expand in order to meet changes in the demand for it. This same assumption of a fixed money supply, however, also undermines the theory. In a case with high liquidity preference, for example, there will be deflationary pressure in the economy, which will eventually cause prices to fall. The fall in the aggregate price index then increases the real value of the fixed nominal money supply, ultimately to such an extent as to satisfy the original increase in liquidity preference via this alternative route. This in turn removes the original upward pressure on interest rates. In essence, this is the 'Pigou effect'

(Pigou, 1943), or the 'real balance effect' (Patinkin, 1948), which, as is well known, was quickly seized upon by economic orthodoxy in the decade or so after the publication of the *General Theory* as a main weapon to challenge the theoretical *bona fides* of Keynesian economics. This theoretical problem can only be avoided if the nominal money supply itself is allowed to fall endogenously as, for example, the deflation proceeds. However, in that case there would need to be some alternative explanation of what determines the interest rate, or made it change, in the first place.

In effect, this is what the third interest rate theory, the horizontalist theory, sets out to do. On this view, the interest rate is simply set by some central monetary authority, and the money supply adjusts endogenously as other economic actors both in the real economy and in the various tiers of the 'inverted pyramid' of the financial system make decisions on whether or not to become indebted on those terms. It is implicit that if the monetary authority can set the nominal interest in this manner, it can set the real interest rate also, simply by changing the setting of the nominal policy rate whenever inflation expectations change. The term 'horizontalist' arises because, in a money demand/supply diagram drawn on these assumptions, the money supply function would show up as a horizontal line, rather than the vertical line of classical theory. Clearly, as mentioned above, such a view ultimately rests on a particular vision of the relationships between the constituent parts of the social and economic system of capitalism and, in particular, the role that money, credit and banking play within it. It rests, in other words, on an underlying monetary analysis as defined above. This would include such elements as the idea that a prerequisite for capitalism to exist is that there must be an ultimate or basic asset with the requisite degree of 'moneyness', and also that there is (what conventional economics would call) a distinct 'public good' element to this (Dow and Smithin, 1999), in other words, that there is inevitably a high degree of centralization in the monetary system, and the state is well placed to provide this. The 'chartalist' argument, that state money is base money because of acceptability in the payment of taxes (Wray, 1998), is obviously highly relevant here, and would explain why symmetrically the interest rate set by the state central bank is also the base interest rate. In short, 'the' interest rate is here regarded primarily as a socioeconomic variable, and its main impact is on the distribution of income between rentiers, entrepreneurs and workers, as mediated by the state. It would not be correct to say that the interest rate in this scenario is 'exogenous' to the political economy as whole, as it is presumably influenced by the whole range of both sociopolitical and economic factors that impinge on the decision-making process of the monetary authority (including the influence of orthodox economic theory with its various 'rules' and prescriptions). However, it (the interest rate) is a 'given' from the point of the demand/supply mechanism *per se*, whereas the money supply is definitely endogenous from the standpoint of these same 'markets'.

The simple investment/savings diagram in Figure 17.1 gives some idea of the basic difference between the competing theories of interest rate determination as sketched above. The diagram has the real rate of interest on the vertical axis, and 'real' savings and investment (here treated as sums of money divided by a price index) on the horizontal axis. Putting aside the various conceptual difficulties involved in the construction of these schedules, the classical theory would have a downward-sloping investment function and an upward-sloping savings function. The so-called natural rate of interest, r^N, is given by the intersection of these curves at point 'a' in the figure. It is implicit that the savings function passing through this point represent savings at the 'full employment' level of income.

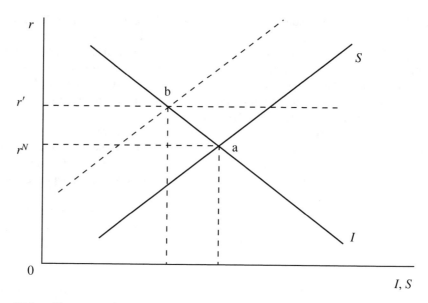

Figure 17.1   Alternative depictions of interest rate determination

On the other hand, both the liquidity preference theory and the sociopolitical horizontalist theory would simply envisage the rate of interest being established at some other level than the natural rate, such as the higher rate r'. We can draw a horizontal line across the page at this point, showing what that rate of interest is. (This is another twist to the meaning of the term 'horizontalist'). If the interest rate can be held at the (in this case) higher level, the only way that equilibrium can be restored is for income to fall, thus shifting the saving function back and to the left. If so, it would be fair to say that the higher interest rate actually *leads to* lower income, lower investment and lower savings. The criticism of the liquidity preference theory with *exogenous* money would be that in fact the interest rate *cannot* be held at r' in those circumstances, due to the real balance effect. The latter tends to increase income once more, and in the diagram will restore the saving function to its original position. In the horizontal theory, however, the money supply itself will be falling,[4] and the final resting place is at point 'b', with lower income and a permanently higher interest rate.

It should be noted, incidentally, that this type of analysis categorically refutes the suggestion, which has been made by a number of authors over the years, including Coddington (1983, 74–5) for example, that if somehow 'properly specified', both a monetary theory of interest and a productivity/thrift theory must lead to the same ultimate conclusion; and that, therefore, continued debate on the issue is 'pointless and depressing' (Patinkin, as quoted by Coddington, 1983, 77). Such transparent attempts to foreclose the discussion are based entirely on a Walrasian-type of analysis, as in Hicks (1946) or Patinkin (1956), with binding budget constraints, a fixed supply of money, given resources and so on. These conditions do not apply in the analysis conducted above. And, obviously, a situation with high interest and low income as at point 'b' is not the 'same as', or equivalent to, a situation with lower interest and higher output at 'a'. There is indeed an *observational* equivalence problem in that investment equals savings in both situations, and the situation could be partially retrieved by advocates of a natural rate simply by asserting that all that has happened in the move from 'a' to 'b' is that the natural rate has risen. This, however, is the same kind of argument as the (actually fairly frequent)[5] assertion that the natural rate of *unemployment* has risen (or fallen) whenever the actual unemployment has risen (or fallen). It could only be sustained by ignoring the whole of the specific causal sequence as set out above. In reality, there would be a whole series of alternative settings of the interest rate, each of which would be associated with an alternative outcome for income and output. Recognizing this, the very concept of a unique natural rate would become untenable. According to Keynes (1936, 191), 'to every banking policy there corresponds a different long-period level of employment; so that there are a number of different positions of long-period equilibrium corresponding to different conceivable interest policies on the part of the monetary authority'.

As mentioned, the horizontal theory is associated in particular with the views of the post-Keynesian school (Kaldor, 1986; Moore, 1988; Lavoie, 1992).[6] However, during the 1990s there was something of an intramural dispute within the post-Keynesian camp, between the horizontalists, also known as 'accommodationists' in the terminology of Pollin (1991), and another group of post-Keynesians known as the 'structuralists' (see, for example, Pollin, 1991; Wray, 1992; Dow, 1996; Palley, 1996; Chick and Dow, 2002). Although there were several different issues that arose and were debated within the confines of this dispute (Lavoie, 1996; Rochon, 1999; Wray, 2004),[7] the main complaint raised against the horizontalist interpretation of a monetary theory of interest rates was actually the extent to which this neglects the issue of liquidity preference (now interpreted as a general principle rather than in the specific version offered by Keynes). The type of argument that can be made is that even if the base interest rate is dictated by the fiat of the monetary authority, other rates in the system, including bank lending rates, must tend to (say) rise as economic activity (say) increases due to liquidity preference considerations. What is thought to occur is that banks and other economic entities will take increasingly illiquid (and hence risky) positions as the boom proceeds. Hence interest rates will rise to reflect this increasing 'financial fragility'. The same process, in the limit, could ultimately provoke a financial crisis *à la* Minksy (1986).

At one time, Wray (1992) argued that this structuralist theory might well be counted as a 'fourth' theory of interest rate determination to stand alongside the other three. On this interpretation, the differences are that this fourth theory would have both endogenous money and endogenous interest rates, whereas the horizontalist theory has endogenous money but an exogenous interest rate, Keynesian liquidity preference theory attempts to combine exogenous money with endogenous interest rates, and the orthodox or classical theory has both exogenous money and exogenous interest rates (the interest rate in that case being exogenous to the monetary system). This position, moreover, is obviously an entirely reasonable one when expressed in such terms. In this chapter, however, we none the less take a contrary position that on other grounds, or viewed from a different angle, the horizontalist and structuralist views are just different versions of the *same* underlying monetary theory of interest rates (see also Fontana, 2003). Rather, we will count the Wicksell-type theories, postulating the existence of *two different types* of interest rate in the economy (a monetary rate and a natural rate), as the fourth main category among types of theories of interest rate determination.

From the point of view of pure theoretical principle one problem with structuralist arguments about illiquid positions, desired ratios of liquid to non-liquid assets, financial fragility etc. is that if money truly is endogenous, meaning in practice that credit is always freely attainable at a given interest rate, then such things cease to have any meaning. It will always be possible to acquire the funds to satisfy any current demands for payment, and there can be no difficulty in the banks 'mov[ing] forward in step', as Keynes (1930, 23) said in the *Treatise on Money*. Recall also that Keynes (1973, 80) wrote to Hicks about the IS–LM model in the following terms:

> it is important to insist . . . that an increase in the inducement to invest *need* not raise the rate of interest. I should agree that unless monetary policy is appropriate it is quite likely to. In this respect I consider that the main difference between the classicals and myself lies in the fact that they regard the rate of interest as a non-monetary phenomenon, so that an increase in the inducement to invest would raise the rate of interest irrespective of monetary policy . . . (Original emphasis)

None the less, and as a practical matter we can refer to our previous discussion of the term structure of interest rates to realize that for both banks and firms investing in longer-term projects, what is also required for them to feel safe with an 'illiquid position' is not only that the central bank is currently accommodating demands for credit creation at a particular interest rate, but also that it will go on doing so in each and every period in the future. Therefore, it is quite easy to envisage situations when there is no such confidence, or simply general uncertainty about what will happen in the future, and hence in which financial fragility, concomitant rises in interest rates, and ultimately financial crisis are all plausible scenarios. By the same token, however, we can also imagine alternative scenarios in which the central bank does establish credibility by pursuing a consistent policy over a succession of short periods, or by directly operating on the long end of the market to manipulate expectations (Tily, 2005). In these circumstances, given sufficient political will, and a correct understanding of the financial system, the authorities are able to enforce their views on the general level of interest rates.[8] In short, both the horizontalists and structuralists have a point, with the implication that the basic or underlying theory of what ultimately determines interest rates is not essentially different (Fontana, 2003). It is more a question of application to different circumstances and different sets of expectations, as well as to differing degrees of resolution and awareness on the part of the 'monetary authorities'.

Alternatively, from the point of view adopted in this chapter, the sort of theory found in Thornton (1802) and Wicksell (1898) can legitimately be counted as a distinct theoretical approach. This was also, incidentally, the view of Mints (1945), writing some 60 years ago. This type of theory, moreover, has renewed relevance at the current time, because the contemporary orthodox approach to 'interest rate operating procedures' (Smithin, 2004) has obviously Wicksellian roots (Taylor, 1993; 2000; Romer, 2000; Goodhart, 2002). Why can the Wicksellian approach be regarded as a different theory from each of the others? The point is that in the classical theory, for example, it was assumed that the interest rate on money was simply a reflection of the natural rate. The argument was that the money rate must literally conform to the natural rate. Only one interest rate was actually observable, but the natural rate could directly be inferred from that. Similarly, in the various types of liquidity preference theory, and in horizontalist theory, there is again only *one* interest rate. There is no natural rate. That concept is simply discarded, and the interest rate that exists in the market is taken to reflect monetary forces only. The difference in

Wicksellian-type theory is the presumed coexistence of two different concepts of the rate of interest at the same time. It is an uneasy, and arguably ultimately untenable, hybrid of the classical theory and the horizontalist theory. (As mentioned, this does not prevent it from being, once again, the current orthodoxy.) The idea is that the interest rates observed in the marketplace may indeed be determined by monetary factors (again primarily by the monopoly power of the central bank). Wicksell, in fact, called the rate set by the banking system the 'market rate'. At the same time, however, there remains a commitment to the idea of a natural rate determined by non-monetary factors. Even though this cannot be observed (or even defined satisfactorily), it is supposed to exist 'off stage', so to speak, and assert its influence behind the scenes. The driving idea behind recommendations for monetary policy comes to be that the purpose of policy is to make the observed market rate conform to the unobservable natural rate, and that if it does not, there will 'be trouble'. If the market rate is set below the putative natural rate, for example, there will be inflation, and if it is set above the natural rate there will be deflation. This is Wicksell's 'cumulative process'. There would therefore logically be two possible explanations of episodes of deflation or inflation. Either the natural rate changes, and the market (policy) rate does not keep up, or the market rate arbitrarily changes when there has been no change in the natural rate.

The Wicksell-type theory is obviously more realistic than the classical theory in that it recognizes the influence of 'money' over interest rates, but the flaw remains in its continued reliance on what can now be seen as the somewhat mystical, and definitely non-observable, natural rate concept, deriving again from the supposedly more fundamental forces that the neoclassical economist believes to dominate the social world. However, once we depart from the idea that the money interest rate is *actually* a reflection of these forces, as in the classical theory, there seems to be no real warrant for any continued belief in its existence. A Wicksellian might argue that the actual appearance of either deflation or inflation is in itself proof that the money rate does not conform to the natural rate, but this requires that the mere proposal or advocacy of a particular theory of inflation be regarded as empirical proof of the same theory. The Wicksellian provenance of the current orthodox theory of monetary policy is easily seen by considering a version of the famous 'Taylor rule' (after Taylor, 1993), such as:

$$r = r_0 + \alpha(p - p^*) + \beta(y - y^*), \quad 0 < \alpha, \beta < 1 \tag{17.2}$$

Here r is the real policy rate set by the central bank, p is the inflation rate, y is the level of output, p^* is the inflation target that the monetary authorities have set themselves, α and β are weights applied to the different policy objectives, and y^* corresponds to the 'natural' or equilibrium level of output, a concept as dubious as that of the natural rate of interest itself. As is well known, the Taylor rule prescribes that the central bank should increase the policy interest rate in real terms whenever the actual inflation rate rises above the inflation target, and *also* (in a kind of pre-emptive strike) if the actual level of output rises above the presumed natural rate. The intercept term in the Taylor rule is usually interpreted precisely as the natural rate of interest or 'equilibrium rate' of interest (Lewis and Mizen, 2000). In other words, it is supposed to have nothing to do with money as such, and is therefore also a benchmark to be aimed at. Now, *if* the inflation target is achieved *and* also the actual level of output is equal to the natural level, then the real policy rate will be equal to the supposed equilibrium rate, in a sort of Wicksellian ideal. That is:

$$r = r_0 \tag{17.3}$$

However, this is illusory because, in fact, in the class of economic models currently in use by central banks and research institutes under the rubric of the 'new consensus', and starting with an arbitrary value of r_0, it is not actually possible to hit the inflation target unless the intercept term itself is changed in response to other parameters in the system (Arestis and Sawyer, 2002). The intercept term itself therefore turns out to be an artifact of monetary policy, and is not a non-monetary natural rate. Within the confines of the model, and assuming an inflation target of zero, it may indeed be possible to define a natural rate as a certain value of the actual interest rate consistent with zero inflation, given current parameters (which would be one part of the Wicksellian formula). However, it is not possible to identify a natural rate in any of the other senses of 'monetary equilibrium' (Laidler, 1999, 55–7), and certainly not as a non-monetary natural rate reflecting 'the rate which would be determined by supply and demand if real capital were lent in kind without the intervention of money'.

Is there a 'fair' rate of interest?

If it is admitted that the interest rate is essentially a socially constructed variable, and can in fact be the target of policy, this immediately raises the question as to what that policy should be, and therefore what the level of interest should be. This question would be inadmissible from the point of view of classical and neoclassical economists, of course. Whatever the level of the interest rate happens to be, it would be interpreted simply as the fair market-determined rate of return to 'capital'. On an alternative understanding of the functioning of capitalism, however, profit, not interest, is the reward for enterprise, and wages are the reward for labor. What then would be the role of the rate of interest in this alternative scheme? Its role, in fact, is ultimately to preserve or enhance the value of accumulated financial capital, which in turn includes past profits and wages not yet spent. Note that in the endogenous money environment, it is not really correct to say that the level of the interest rate represents the return to the suppliers of credit. The banks actually make their profits on the *spread* between lending rates and deposit rates, and, in essence, this is another (special) form of entrepreneurial profit. The basic role of interest, rather, is to preserve or enhance the values of existing sums of money. A strong case can therefore be made on ethical grounds that the optimal value of the *real* rate of interest for rentiers is actually zero. The real value of existing sums of money, representing past effort in the form of work and enterprise, would be preserved, but there would be no increase in their value arising from the mere possession of money. Further accumulation would only be possible by contributing further work or enterprise, or assuming further risk. This state of affairs would not, however, really constitute the 'euthanasia of the rentier' (Keynes, 1936), as it is not the nominal interest rate that is set at zero but the real rate. Accumulated financial capital at least retains its original real value.[9]

As suggested elsewhere (Smithin, 2004), a more reasonable 'practical' stance than a zero real interest rate, in terms of actual politics, might be to suggest that the real interest rate target should be 'low but still positive' (Smithin, 1994; 1996). This is for two main reasons.

First, that if capitalism is to persist as a social order, the 'social contract' must include the financial interests as well as non-financial business and labor. Second, that as (ironically) with the orthodox zero inflation policy, 'zero' is too precarious a target and gives no leeway for mistakes in the downward direction. In other words, the suggestion is that as a practical policy matter the target for the real rate of interest should probably be a small positive constant. What is being suggested is, in fact, an 'incomes policy' of a sort, except that it is an incomes policy for rentiers rather than for labor or entrepreneurs.

Both the suggestion of a theoretical norm of zero for the real interest rate and of the practical norm of a small positive constant are different from the alternative concept of the 'fair interest rate' originally due to Pasinetti (1981), and discussed in some detail by Lavoie and Seccarreccia (1988; 1999). This fair rate would set the real interest rate equal to 'the rate of increase in the productivity of the total amount of labor . . . required to produce consumption goods and increase productive capacity' (Lavoie and Seccarreccia, 1999, 544). In short, the idea is that the real interest rate, for fairness, should equal the rate of growth of 'total factor productivity', as this is expressed in the conventional economic jargon. The difference between this proposal and the idea that real interest must be held constant really turns only on value judgements as to what constitutes 'fairness' in this particular context. Ironically, it involves many of the same issues that arise in the debates between the adherents of the 'productivity norm' versus 'zero inflation' in the orthodox literature on the costs of inflation (Smithin, 1994; 2003). The 'fair' interest rate basically allows the possessors of existing financial capital a share in the rewards from current increases in productivity. On the other hand a zero, or low constant, real interest rate simply preserves (or slightly enhances) the original purchasing power of accumulated financial capital. However, if accumulated financial capital is conceived of as representing the proceeds of *past* productive activity, whereas the essential contribution to ongoing production is that of the entrepreneurs plus workers (who in turn, of course, will themselves accumulate financial capital if their efforts succeed), this is arguably the more 'fair', in terms of preserving the balance between the past, present and future.

Conclusion
A realistic or useful heterodox theory of interest rates must simultaneously reject two familiar notions from the orthodox economic literature. These are, first, the idea that the supply of money can be treated as an exogenous variable, and, second, that there exists some non-monetary 'natural rate' of interest which is beyond the reach of either the monetary authorities or the changing expectations of actors in the financial markets. Examples have been given above of alternative approaches which relaxed one assumption or another, but, because they did not firmly reject both, none the less failed to provide a convincing alternative to what has usually been the orthodox theory.

In a world in which money (or 'financial resources') can be created endogenously through the banking system, so that their supply is not fixed, the interest rate on money becomes essentially a politically determined variable (in the contemporary institutional framework, a variable manipulated by the central bank), rather than a reflection of purely economic forces. Observed economic phenomena, such as changes in the interest rates themselves, changes in inflation rates, changes in economic growth, episodes of financial crisis, etc. are more likely to be the outcome of shifts in the balance of power between different social groups, and also changes in expectations and 'ideas' (Keynes, 1936, 364), than the expression of any intrinsic scarcity or abundance of finance as a result of 'saving'.

Notes

*   The author would like to thank Guiseppe Fontana, Scott Fullwiler, Marc Lavoie, Eric Tymoigne and other participants at the Annual Meetings of the Eastern Economic Association, New York, 2005, for helpful comments and suggestions that have improved this chapter.
1.   In all Burstein's writings there is a remarkably clear recognition that orthodox monetary theory stands or falls on the issue of whether or not such a thing as a natural rate of interest exists. However, he took a very strong position that the natural rate *is* a meaningful concept.
2.   In this respect, of course, the views of some 'Keynesians' were the opposite to those of Keynes (Hirai, 1997; 1998a; 1998b; 1999).
3.   This is a term characteristically used by Keynes to describe the monetary theory of his opponent, Robertson, on similar sorts of issues (Fletcher, 2000, 375).
4.   Cf. Keynes's 'banana parable' in the *Treatise on Money* (1930, 158–60).
5.   See, for example, the criticisms of this practice by Solow (1998) and Stiglitz (2002).
6.   An early article by Lavoie (1984) summarizes most of the essentials of this viewpoint.
7.   Reference should also be made to the article from the 1980s by Dow and Dow (1989), which prefigures most of the issues that came up in these debates.
8.   As Keynes himself certainly thought possible and advocated (Hirai, 1997; 1998a; 1998b; 1999).
9.   Even in Keynes (1936, ch. 16) it is clear that what is envisioned is that the value of accumulated financial capital should not grow, not that it should be entirely wiped out. The reference to 'Pope's father' and his 'chest of guineas' in that chapter suffices to establish the point.

References

Arestis, P. and M. Sawyer (2002), 'The Bank of England macroeconomic model: its nature and implications', *Journal of Post Keynesian Economics*, **24**, 529–45.
Burstein, M.L. (1995), 'Classical macroeconomics for the next century', manuscript, York University, Toronto.
Chick, V. and S.C. Dow (2002), 'Monetary policy with endogenous money and liquidity preference: a non-dualistic treatment', *Journal of Post Keynesian Economics*, **24**(4), 587–608.
Coddington, A. (1983), *Keynesian Economics: The Search for First Principles*, London: George Allen & Unwin.
Cohen, A. and G.C. Harcourt (2003), 'Whatever happened to the Cambridge capital controversies?', *Journal of Economic Perspectives*, **17**(1), 199–214.
Davidson P. (1996), 'In defence of Post Keynesian economics: a reply to Mongiovi', in S. Pressman (ed.), *Interactions in Political Economy: Malvern after Ten Years*, London: Routledge.
Dow, A.C. and S.C. Dow (1989), 'Endogenous money creation and idle balances', in J. Pheby (ed.), *New Directions in Post Keynesian Economics*, Aldershot, UK and Brookfield, US: Edward Elgar.
Dow, S.C. (1996), 'Horizontalism: a critique', *Cambridge Journal of Economics*, **20**, 497–508.
Dow, S.C. and J. Smithin (1999), 'The structure of financial markets and the "first principles" of monetary economics', *Scottish Journal of Political Economy*, **46**, 72–90.
Fisher, I. (1896), *Appreciation and Interest*, New York: American Economic Association.
Fletcher, G.A. (1987), *The Keynesian Revolution and its Critics: Issues of Theory and Policy for the Monetary Production Economy*, London: Macmillan.
Fletcher, G.A. (2000), *Dennis Robertson: The Man and his Work*, Cheltenham, UK and Northampton, MA, USA: Edward Elgar.
Fontana, G. (2003), 'Post Keynesian approaches to endogenous money: a time framework explanation', *Review of Political Economy*, **15**(3), 291–314.
Friedman, M. (1968), 'The role of monetary policy', *American Economic Review*, **58**, 1–17.
Goodhart, C.A.E. (2002), 'The endogeneity of money', in P. Arestis, M. Desai and S.C. Dow (eds), *Money, Macroeconomics and Keynes: Essays in Honour of Victoria Chick*, London: Routledge, 14–24.
Hicks, J.R. (1946), *Value and Capital: An Inquiry Into Some Fundamental Principles of Economic Theory*, 2nd edn, Oxford: Clarendon Press.
Hicks, J.R. (1989), *A Market Theory of Money*, Oxford: Clarendon Press.
Hirai, T. (1997), 'A study of Keynes's economics (I) – from a *Treatise on Money* to the *General Theory*', *Sophia Economic Review*, **43**(1), 67–136.
Hirai, T. (1998a), 'A study of Keynes's economics (II) – from a *Treatise on Money* to the *General Theory*', *Sophia Economic Review*, **43**(2), 13–121.
Hirai, T. (1998b), 'A study of Keynes's economics (III) – from a *Treatise on Money* to the *General Theory*', *Sophia Economic Review*, **44**(1), 35–127.

Hirai, T. (1999), 'A study of Keynes's economics (IV) – from a *Treatise on Money* to the *General Theory*', *Sophia Economic Review*, **44**(2), 25–115.

Humphrey, T.M. (1993), *Money, Banking and Inflation: Essays in the History of Monetary Thought*, Aldershot, UK and Brookfield, US: Edward Elgar.

Ingham, G. (1996), 'Money is a social relation', *Review of Social Economy*, **54**, 243–75.

Ingham, G. (2000), 'Babylonian madness', in J. Smithin (ed.), *What is Money?* London: Routledge, 16–41.

Ingham, G. (2004), *The Nature of Money*, Cambridge: Polity Press.

Kaldor, N. (1986), *The Scourge of Monetarism*, 2nd edn, Oxford: Oxford University Press.

Keynes, J.M. (1930), *A Treatise on Money* (2 vols), London: Macmillan.

Keynes, J.M. (1936), *The General Theory of Employment Interest and Money*, London: Macmillan.

Keynes, J.M. (1973), *The Collected Writings of J.M. Keynes*, Vol. XIV, *The General Theory and After, Part II, Defence and Development*, D. Moggridge (ed.), London: Macmillan.

Kohn, M.G. (1986), 'Monetary analysis, the equilibrium method and Keynes's *General Theory*', *Journal of Political Economy*, **94**, 1191–224.

Laidler, D. (1999), *Fabricating the Keynesian Revolution: Studies in the Inter-War Literature on Money, the Cycle and Unemployment*, Cambridge: Cambridge University Press.

Lau, J.Y.F. and J. Smithin (2002), 'The role of money in capitalism', *International Journal of Political Economy*, **32**(3), 5–22.

Lavoie, M. (1984), 'The endogenous credit flow and the Post Keynesian theory of money', *Journal of Economic Issues*, **18**(3), 233–58.

Lavoie, M. (1992), *Foundations of Post-Keynesian Economic Analysis*, Aldershot, UK and Brookfield, US: Edward Elgar.

Lavoie, M. (1996), 'Horizontalism, structuralism, liquidity preference, and the principle of increasing risk', *Scottish Journal of Political Economy*, **43**, 275–300.

Lavoie, M. and M. Seccareccia (1988), 'Money, interest and rentiers: the twilight of rentier capitalism in Keynes's *Capital Theory*', in O.F. Hamouda and J. Smithin (eds), *Keynes and Public Policy after Fifty Years*, Aldershot, UK and Brookfield, US: Edward Elgar, 145–58.

Lavoie, M. and M. Seccareccia (1999), 'Interest rate: fair', in P. O'Hara (ed.), *Encylopedia of Political Economy*, vol. 1, London: Routledge, 543–5.

Lewis, M.K. and P.D. Mizen (2000), *Monetary Economics*, Oxford: Oxford University Press.

Minsky, H.P. (1986), *Stabilizing an Unstable Economy*, New Haven, CT: Yale University Press.

Mints, L.W. (1945), *A History of Banking Theory in Great Britain and the United States*, Chicago, IL: University of Chicago Press.

Mishkin, F.S. and A. Serletis (2005), *The Economics of Money, Banking and Financial Markets*, 2nd Canadian edn, Toronto: Pearson Education Canada.

Moore, B.M. (1988), *Horizontalists and Verticalists: The Macroeconomics of Credit Money*, Cambridge, Cambridge University Press.

Palley, T. (1996), *Post Keynesian Economics: Debt, Distribution and the Macro Economy*, London: Macmillan.

Pasinetti, L. (1981), *Structural Change and Economic Growth*, Cambridge: Cambridge University Press.

Patinkin, D. (1948), 'Price flexibility and full employment', *American Economic Review*, **38** (September), 543–64.

Patinkin, D. (1956), *Money, Interest and Prices*, Evanston, IL: Row Peterson.

Pigou, A.C. (1943), 'The classical stationary state', *Economic Journal*, **53**, 343–51.

Pivetti, M. (2003), 'Rate of interest', in *The Elgar Companion to Post Keynesian Economics*, edited by J.E. King, Cheltenham, UK and Northampton, MA, USA: Edward Elgar, 299–303.

Pollin, R. (1991), 'Two theories of money supply endogeneity: some empirical evidence', *Journal of Post Keynesian Economics*, **13**, 366–96.

Robertson, D. (1940), *Essays in Monetary Theory*, London: P.S. King & Son.

Rochon, L.-P. (1999), *Credit, Money and Production*, Cheltenham, UK and Northampton, MA, USA: Edward Elgar.

Rogers, C. (1989), *Money, Interest and Capital: A Study in the Foundations of Monetary Theory*, Cambridge: Cambridge University Press.

Romer, D. (2000), 'Keynesian macroeconomics without the LM curve', *Journal of Economic Perspectives*, **14**(2), 149–70.

Schumpeter, J.A. (1954 [1994]), *History of Economic Analysis*, New York: Oxford University Press.

Smithin, J. (1994), *Controversies in Monetary Economics: Ideas, Issues and Policy*, Aldershot, UK and Brookfield, USA: Edward Elgar.

Smithin, J. (1996), *Macroeconomic Policy and the Future of Capitalism: The Revenge of the Rentiers and the Threat to Prosperity*, Aldershot, UK and Brookfield, USA: Edward Elgar.

Smithin, J. (2003), *Controversies in Monetary Economics*, revised edn, Cheltenham, UK and Northampton, MA, USA: Edward Elgar.

Smithin, J. (2004), 'Interest rate operating procedures and income distribution', in M. Lavoie and M. Seccareccia (eds), *Central Banking in the Modern World: Alternative Perspectives*, Cheltenham, UK and Northampton, MA, USA: Edward Elgar, 57–69.

Smithin, J. (2005), 'The real rate of interest, the business cycle, economic growth, and inflation: an alternative theoretical perspective', *Journal of Economic Asymmetries*, **2**(2), December, 1–19.

Solow, R. (1998), 'How cautious must the Fed be?', in B. Friedman (ed.), *Inflation, Unemployment and Monetary Policy*, Cambridge, MA: MIT Press, 1–28.

Stiglitz, J.E. (2002), *Globalization and Its Discontents*, London: Penguin.

Taylor, J.B. (1993), 'Discretion versus policy rules in practice', *Carnegie-Rochester Conference Series on Public Policy*, **39**, 195–214.

Taylor, J.B. (2000), 'Teaching modern macroeconomics at the principles level', *American Economic Review*, **90**, 90–94.

Thornton, H. (1802 [1962]), *An Inquiry into the Nature and Effects of the Paper Credit of Great Britain*, New York: Augustus M. Kelley.

Tily, G. (2005), 'Keynes's theory of liquidity preference and his debt management and monetary policies', manuscript, University College London.

Tymoigne, E. (2005), 'Fisher's theory of interest rate and the notion of the real rate of interest: their relevance for today's economics', presented at the annual meetings of the Eastern Economic Association, New York, February.

Wicksell, K. (1898 [1965]), *Interest and Prices: A Study of the Causes Regulating the Value of Money*, New York: Augustus M. Kelley.

Wray, L.R. (1992), 'Alternative approaches to money and interest rates', *Journal of Economic Issues*, **26**, 1–33.

Wray, L.R. (1998), *Understanding Modern Money: The Key to Full Employment and Price Stability*, Cheltenham, UK and Lyme, USA: Edward Elgar.

Wray, L.R. (2004), 'When are interest rates exogenous?', Working Paper no. 30, Center for Full Employment and Price Stability, University of Missouri at Kansas City, January.

18 The role of banks in the context of economic development with reference to South Korea and India

*Santonu Basu**

Introduction

Banks provide a number of financial services to all modern economies and three are most important, namely offering deposit facilities to savers, intermediating between lenders and borrowers and providing a payment mechanism. These services play not only an important role in the functioning of modern economies but are also crucial for economic development. Banks as deposit-taking institutions not only offer an opportunity to very small savers to convert their savings in the form of financial assets by offering loans to borrowers, but also provide borrowers with an opportunity to invest these funds profitably. It is these investments in various projects that ultimately enable the economy to prosper.

Banks create long-term loans from a very large number of short-term deposits. To do so they use the law of large numbers, which suggests that, while an individual's withdrawal patterns are not predictable, when it is applied to a very large number of depositors, withdrawal patterns are predictable. These loans are transferred in the form of deposits and used as a means of payment. Thus in a peculiar sense banks play a coordinating role between various economic agents via these three services. The crucial point to note here is that it is the bank's ability to create credit or loans which is central not only to the functioning of the economy but also in the context of development. Therefore, development or the growth of the banking sector is crucial in the context of economic development. In the case of developed countries, observation reveals that the process of industrialization increased the demand for credit, which in turn provided the incentive for the banking sector to grow. Banks willingly met this demand, as the borrowers' profits were sufficient to meet the banks' repayment rate, thus meaning that bankers can make a profit from meeting such demand. Furthermore, borrowers' demand for loans was adequately backed by their growing assets. Consequently, government intervention was neither necessary for the growth of the banking sector nor, for that matter, for the growth of the industrial sector. Government only intervened when the excesses of the banking sector either brought a financial crisis or threatened to break down the payment mechanism. It is this observation which gave the impression to the school of liberalization that government intervention retards the growth of the financial sector, which in turn slows the process of industrialization. But what the school overlooked is the economic environment that is necessary for the growth of the banking sector, where two factors play a crucial role, namely the demand for credit and the backing up of this demand by the growing assets of the borrowers. Both of these factors very much depend upon the growth of the industrial sector, which was lacking in the case of developing countries in the early days of independence. While it is true that for the industrial sector to grow there is a need to develop the banking sector, experience also reveals that the growth of the banking sector very much depends upon the growth of the industrial sector. Thus the paramount question that remains to be investigated is how should developing countries proceed? This is the subject matter of this chapter and will be investigated with reference to South Korea and India.

In the first section, we investigate the state of the economy at the initial stage and the opportunity to make profits from engaging in further financial intermediation. In the second section, we investigate if it is possible for private banks, or what is commonly referred to as the market, to take the initiative to finance the process of development with some assistance from the government, or if direct intervention will be required. Having established that intervention will be required, in the third section, we investigate what went wrong with the intervention. This will be followed by the conclusion.

The state of the economy and the banking sector

At the time India and South Korea received their independence, their economies were described as being in a backward state, with high poverty, low education, high mortality rates, and so on. Around 80 per cent of the population was deriving a living from agriculture, where the land was overcrowded. In short, there was little or no remaining surplus that could be extracted from agriculture to reinvest in industrial development. It was recognized that in their current state they could not escape from these problems; nor was there any internal mechanism to indicate that this state was likely to change by itself in the near future. Yet in order to address these problems, it would be essential to transform these economies from their backward state to an advanced industrial state. This involves changing the structure of the economy from one state to another, where the principal aim was to improve the economic well-being of every member of society.

Changing the structure of the economy is an extremely complicated issue, some of the technical aspects of these problems have already been investigated by Nurkse (1953), Rosenstein-Rodan (1943) and Scitovsky (1954). It was recognised from Kuznets's (1955) work that the process of development requires a higher accumulation of capital. But there was a problem in the process of capital accumulation, arising from both the supply side as well as the demand side. The supply-side problem arose from the low per capita income, which itself restrained the generation of sufficient savings required to increase the stocks of reproducible capital (Nurkse, 1953). The demand problem in capital formation also arose from the low per capita income, where the greater proportion of income went on necessities, leaving little to spend on industrial products. Consequently, the demand for industrial products remained low, thereby discouraging private investors from investing in such industries. This problem was further complicated by the fact that the production process in modern industries represents complex sets of interdependent relationships among firms. In this situation, if the coordination among firms is to be propelled by the price-guided system, then investment in a firm may give rise to pecuniary external economies, and consequently its private profitability will understate its social desirability (Rosenstein-Rodan, 1943; Scitovsky, 1954). This possibility of externalities arising from the intertemporal dependence among firms presented a serious impediment to the growth of developing countries.

These problems particularly arise in interdependent industries, where, in the absence of simultaneous growth, one industry may not adjust to the growth in another industry due to difficulties in achieving economies of scale. The fact that these problems are particularly acute for developing countries principally arises not only from the deficiency in overall demand, but also from the extreme unequal distribution of income and wealth, which causes difficulty in capturing the right pattern of demand. The central problem in interdependent industries is whether a complementary decision will be made or not. This has a direct bearing on the future market, and whether the product will be sold. In other words, investment decisions involve some risk and uncertainty, where uncertainty principally arises from the fact that in these conditions investors are unable to approximate the future demand.

To ease the difficulty, the country either has to address the problem that arises from the deficiency in overall demand, which means investing in agriculture, or else must search for an external market. Thus the difference between the two approaches from the point of view of addressing the problem of deficiency in demand is profound, and has not received adequate attention: while the former requires the development of its own market, the latter involves searching for an external market. Given the complexities of the problem, financing development has to be carried out by banks. This is mainly because banks are the main vehicles for mobilizing savings and allocating these savings in the form of credit. Banks' principal task is now not only to make a greater effort to increase the mobilization of savings but also to allocate these savings in the form of credit in such a manner that at one end of the spectrum it allows the country to overcome the problem of deficiency in overall demand and at the other end it allows the country to overcome the problem that arises from externalities, which is an impediment to growth in the interdependent industries.

Given the magnitude of the task that was expected from the banks at this time, it was not recognized that the banking sector operates in the presence of uncertainty. This uncertainty principally arises from the fact that the advancement and the repayment of loans do not take place simultaneously; repayment takes place some time in the future. This means that a time gap enters into the loan equation, which in turn introduces the possibility that the borrower may not be able to repay the loan. This possibility emerges either due to changes in the borrower's own financial circumstances or the borrower may be an impostor. The lender cannot ascertain either of these in advance, and consequently asks for collateral or some form of security as an alternative means to recoup the loan should the borrower default. This alternative means of recouping the loan should the borrower's ability or willingness to pay change is referred to as the credit standard (Basu, 2002; 2003).

The principal task of banks is to raise deposits by offering interest, to re-lend these deposits to borrowers in the form of credit at a higher interest rate, and to make a profit from the difference between the loan rate and the deposit rate. Any borrower who can meet a bank's credit standard requirements and promises to pay the interest rate will receive a loan. Should the borrower have difficulties in meeting his/her obligations, the bank will resort to the credit standard. As long as these borrowers agree to repay the principal plus the interest rate and meet the banks' collateral requirements, banks will not refuse loans. Banks as profit-seeking organizations are neither concerned with whether these borrowers are likely to use their loanable funds for productive or unproductive purposes, nor with whether the project for which the borrowers seek a loan produces any social return or not.

The above argument suggests that there is a need to change the banks' mode of operation in order to make them conform to the requirements of the development process. This effectively means that bankers would now be required to concentrate more on assessing the merits of the borrowers' projects, not only in terms of their expected private rates of return but also in terms of their social rates of return, and not just on investigating borrowers' creditworthiness.

Banks that were operating in the early stage of independence in developing countries mostly engaged in advancing loans for trade-oriented activities and meeting working capital requirements. In most cases, the size of their operation was small, mainly advancing short-term loans comprising of smaller-sized loans, and their survival depended upon short-term returns. However, the process of development requires large long-term loans. These bankers have neither the capital nor the necessary skill required to assess the merits of projects, which involve large long-term loans. These problems are further compounded by the fact that the greater proportion of the money market was in the hands of the informal credit market.

Thus the first problem of the government was how to bring the informal credit market under the control of the formal credit market, so that a greater proportion of savings could be brought into the orbit of the formal market. One option is to open a number of branch facilities not only in the metropolitan area but also outside it. But the problem is that opening branch facilities, especially outside the metropolitan area, is costly, and a private bank whose main motivation is to make a profit and whose survival also depends upon profit is unlikely to participate in such a venture. In addition to this, banks may not have sufficient capital to open additional branch facilities. The other option is to raise the interest rate on deposits, partly to induce savers to move away from the informal sector and partly to transfer that portion of the savings that was kept in the form of unproductive assets into financial assets. But this process also requires banks to raise the interest rate on loans. The problems for banks here are twofold: first, where to find borrowers who are not only willing to pay such high interest rates, but who will also be able to meet the banks' higher credit standard, which will rise as a result of high interest rates; second, even if banks find such borrowers, these borrowers may not agree to undertake projects whose expected rates of return are not known to them but which comply with the objectives of development. Thus, whichever option one may decide to take, there remains a serious difficulty in raising the mobilization of savings without the banks having to sacrifice some profit, at least in the early stage of development.

Given the complex issues involved in the development process, the South Korean government adopted an export-led growth policy after a brief experiment with import substitution policy, while the Indian government adopted an import substitution policy. The export-led growth policy allowed South Korea to avoid the problems that arise from internal demand deficiency, while the import substitution policy did not permit India to overlook the problems that arise from internal demand deficiency. The problem for the South Korean government was to provide information about export opportunities to would-be participatory firms and induce these firms to participate in these ventures. The problem for the Indian government was that it had to address the uncertainty that arises from the internal demand deficiency. This meant that the latter government had to simultaneously address the issue of poverty and the issue of industrialization. This added to the complexity of the problems, which were twofold. First, the government had to directly address how to reduce the level of poverty, so that the standard of living could be raised to a level which could adequately address the problem of demand deficiency. Second, it had to plan for industrialization in a manner that could take care of the problem of externalities. This meant that the nation's scarce resources would be divided into two parts, one of which would be spent directly on addressing the issue of poverty and the other on industrialization.

The South Korean government recognized that private banks are unlikely to participate in the promotion of export ventures and industry development programmes in their infancy because their markets are not established. In other words, whatever potential profit opportunities these markets may offer, the future viability of these industries was not known to the banks. Furthermore, would-be participating firms in these markets often had neither an established track record as successful operators in these industries nor sufficient assets to offer as collateral to banks in order to obtain loans. As the government was the principal initiator of these programmes, it could not ask the participating privately owned firms to comply with the banks' credit standard requirements, especially when the firms themselves did not have sufficient information about these markets, a reason for which the government established trading companies.[1]

The Indian government's problem was more complex. As it adopted the import substitution policy, this meant that it had to develop an intermediate goods sector that would provide the inputs, including capital goods, required for the final output sector and minimize the likelihood of the emergence of externalities. But this development had to be undertaken in the presence of uncertain growth in the demand for goods from the final output sector. In order to ensure a steady growth in the demand for final goods, the government had to develop the agricultural sector. Thus, given the complexities of the problem, the Indian government's task was to induce banks to finance the development of a set of industries, whose growth very much depended upon the growth of other sets of industries, and in order to ensure the growth of the latter sets of industries it also had to finance the development of agriculture. This involved the development of an extremely sophisticated coordination mechanism between all the participatory sectors of the economy. The financial sector's role is to provide the principal means of coordination, i.e. via credit. Furthermore, this credit has to be allocated in such a manner that it does not bring any undue default on loan repayments from any sector of the economy arising from a coordination failure, as the cost of the default has to be borne by the banking sector.

As around 80 per cent of the population's livelihood directly or indirectly depended on agriculture, the government had to organize loans for this section of the community, mainly to improve their living conditions. This meant that the government had to induce banks to open branch facilities in the rural areas. In addition to this, loans had to be organized for artisans and small businesses. This added further complications. Owing to its inability to access any formal loan market facility, this sector formed an alternative loan market, the operational characteristics of which were not well known to the government.[2] Fragmented information that was available at the time only revealed its exploitative operational characteristics.[3] Thus it was necessary for the government to organize bank loan facilities to this sector, so that these borrowers could escape from the grip of exploitative interest rates. But the government faced two critical problems. The first was that these poor borrowers do not have tangible assets that are readily acceptable to the banks as collateral, and thus the problem was how to meet the banks' credit standard. The second problem was that as the size of these loans on these occasions would be small, the administrative cost per unit of loan would be high compared with larger loans. Thus, given the interest rate, these loans would be less profitable than their larger counterparts.

Given the scenario described above, the paramount question that needed to be investigated regarding the private banks, whose main objective is to maximize profit, was how the government could induce them to offer loans to these borrowers.

Thus the problem for both countries was that while the role of banks in the context of development could be readily recognized, for the banks there was hardly any incentive to participate in the development programme. This is simply because participation in such a programme means that banks would not only have to sacrifice profit at least in the early stage of development, but it would make the banking sector extremely fragile, with no guarantee that this fragility would be likely to change in the future. This may suggest that private banks are unlikely to play any active role of their own accord, as has been observed in some developed countries, and some form of persuasion or intervention would be required to engage them in the reconstruction of any nation, at least in the early stage of development.

Market persuasion vs intervention
In 1961 the South Korean government nationalized its major banks, while the Indian government initially chose to follow the path of persuasion. South Korea used the interest rate as an appropriate vehicle for the mobilization of savings. The interest rate on time deposits was raised from 15 to 30 per cent in 1965, and although this rate gradually declined, it remained above 20 per cent up to 1971.[4] As a result of this high rate on deposits, the M2/GNP ratio rose from less than 9 per cent to a little over 33 per cent between 1964 and 1971.[5] This rapid growth of the formal financial sector was largely the result of high deposit rates, which induced asset holders to shift a portion of their funds from the informal financial market to banks. In other words, higher rates allowed the government to bring part of the savings that were kept in alternative forms under the umbrella of nationalized banks. This higher rate also helped to increase the capital inflow, especially from Japan. Needless to say, this higher rate of mobilization was made at the cost of banks, as the rates on time deposits remained higher than those on non-preferential loans between 1965 and 1968, implying that the banks were running at a loss, independent of the performance of the project for which the banks advanced loans.[6]

The Indian government mainly used the extension of branch facilities as a vehicle to mobilize savings. Given the smaller size of operation of these banks, it was recognized that individual banks will not have sufficient resources of their own to open branch facilities outside the metropolitan area. Consequently, banks were encouraged by the Reserve Bank of India (RBI) to merge with other banks, and as a result the total number of banks decreased from 605 to 85 between 1950 and 1969. The number of bank branches increased from 4151 to 8262, and GDS (gross domestic savings) as a percentage of GDP rose from 10.2 to 15.7 per cent during the same period (Krishnaswamy et al., 1987). But the government faced a significant difficulty in inducing private banks to open their branch facilities outside the metropolitan area. Banks that open branch facilities in the rural area are mostly government-sponsored banks such as cooperatives, land mortgage banks and the State Bank of India (SBI).[7] In fact, in 1969 only 22.2 per cent of the banks' total branch facilities were located in rural areas.

The banks' performance, however, both in terms of the extension of branch facilities outside the metropolitan areas as well as in terms of the mobilization of savings, was impressive following the nationalization of banks in 1969. Between 1969 and 1985, branch numbers increased from 8262 to 48 930. By 1985, 57.5 per cent of the branches were operating in the rural area and a further 19.5 per cent in the semi-urban area. GDS as a percentage of GDP rose from 15.7 to 24 per cent between 1969 and 1985. By 1980, over 92 per cent of total deposits came under the control of public sector banks. By the middle of 1985, commercial bank deposits amounted to Rs 764 billion, which was 67 per cent more than at the end of 1981 (Krishnaswamy et al., 1987), and these deposits rose to Rs 2012 billion by 1991, which is almost three times higher than what it was in 1985 (RBI, 1991). Needless to say, as most of these deposits were small in size, the administrative cost per unit of deposit would be expected to be high, thereby increasing the operating costs of banks. Thus, although both countries were successful in mobilizing savings, in the process banks initially had either to incur a loss or sacrifice profit.

In terms of the allocation of loans, South Korea did not have any problems, and this is largely because the government nationalized private banks, which in turn allowed them to control the allocation of loans. However, despite having control over the allocation of loans, it neither introduced a quota system nor imposed restrictions on the allocation of loans; rather it introduced an incentive mechanism to attract market participants to join in the government development programme. Accordingly, the government divided the loan portfolio into two groups. Export and infant industries formed one group and received a preferential loan rate of 6 per cent, and this rate remained below 10 per cent up to 1980. The rest of the economy formed another group and received loans at a non-preferential rate. This rate rose from 16.9 per cent to 26 per cent between 1964 and 1965 and remained roughly around 24.4 per cent between 1966 and 1970. By 1971 the rate had come down to 17 per cent, and remained on average between 17 to 18 per cent up to 1980.[8] The principal aim of the differential interest rate policy is to reduce the net return of those projects that are not accepted by the government. Thus the government, instead of directly imposing restrictions on advancing loans to those activities that were not consistent with government policy, rather created a disincentive for entrepreneurs to engage in such projects. At the same time, the government offered loans at a lower interest rate for the export and infant industry sectors, with the aim to increase the expected net return of these projects, so that their entrepreneurial skills and capital could be attracted to join the government in their development programme. As there was hardly any difference in the deposit rate and interest rate on non-preferential loans, this suggests that profit from loan portfolios was not the concern of the government, and nor did the government attempt to subsidize preferential loans by charging high interest rates on non-preferential loans. In short, the government used differential interest rates to induce market participants to join the government-directed development programme and, therefore, this policy could be considered as an important vehicle to change the state of the economy from a backward to an advanced industrial state. As the number of firms started to join the government-directed development programme, so too did South Korea's growth rate start to increase at a rapid rate. In fact, South Korea enjoyed an unprecedented growth rate for three decades, starting from 6 per cent in the mid-1960s, reaching 8 per cent in the 1980s and continuing to grow at the same rate until the early 1990s. But in the process the banking sector became fragile, leading to the financial crisis in 1997.

However, the Indian experience was very disappointing for many years. It was not only confronted with problems in allocating loans for socially more productive areas of the economy, but also faced difficulties in improving smaller and marginal borrowers' access to the loan market. Initially, it was thought that much of the banks' credit could be channelled into socially more productive areas of the economy via the Reserve Bank of India's (RBI) regulations and incentives. The remainder of the credit facilities could then be provided via the development of financial corporations and government-sponsored banks, such as the Industrial Finance Corporation (IFC), Industrial Development Bank of India (IDBI), cooperative banks and land mortgage banks, and, to provide assistance to small-scale enterprises, similar institutions were developed.

Both the IFC and IDBI were originally established in order to organize large long-term loans that were required for the industrial sector's development. IFC and IDBI's clients in general were large borrowers, and no significant problem was reported or observed in relation to their ability either to raise large long-term loans or to meet large working capital requirements from the banks. But the problem appeared in the government's effort to divert credit to the rural area and small-scale enterprises; the RBI's regulations and incentives largely remained ineffective. It was noted that much of the banks' credit was still being received by private traders, especially wholesale traders and large entrepreneurs. Wholesale traders used this credit for the purchase of food grains, edible oils, oil seeds, raw cotton, sugar etc., with the expectation that they would make a windfall gain from future changes in the prices of these items. In the case of industry, the banks' finance mainly went to maintain inventories and left the entrepreneurs to use their own retained earnings or to seek loans from other financial institutions to finance their fixed investments. In other words, the nature of banks' operations still remained unaltered and mainly short-term.

Consequently, the RBI introduced various selective credit controls, such as regulations against loans for the purchase of food grains, edible oils, oil seeds, raw cotton, sugar etc., in anticipation that this might force banks to divert their credit facilities from the wholesale traders. In addition, it also introduced an upper limit on the size of the loan that otherwise might have been obtained by any individual borrower as a working capital loan, known as the Credit Authorization Scheme (CAS), which was introduced in 1965. This scheme stated that any private individual wishing to borrow Rs 10 million and over required official approval from the RBI.[9] At the same time, in order to improve the access of small-scale enterprises, agriculture and export-oriented activities to the banks' credit, the RBI offered various incentives, including a scheme for guaranteeing bank credit to small-scale sectors, with specific incentives to promote particular types of advances. For example, to promote engineering exports, it provided loans with an interest rate of 4.5 per cent, with the agreement that the banks' lending rates on those loans should not exceed 6 per cent per annum, which was considerably below the commercial rate. Extensive lending support was also provided by the RBI in the form of contributions to the Agricultural Refinance Corporation. Despite these measures, credit still went to those who had larger assets, and the government remained unsuccessful in improving smaller and marginal borrowers' access to the loan market. While the share of credit favouring industry rose from 34 to 67.5 per cent, bank credit to the agricultural sector rose from merely 1.1 to 2 per cent of the total credit between 1951 and 1968 (Gupta, 1988). But to address poverty, the agricultural sector required a much higher share of the total credit and this requirement was further increased by the mid-1960s.

By the mid-1960s the Indian government had adopted the High Yielding Variety Programme (HYVP), with the anticipation that this programme would simultaneously solve India's two most critical problems, food and poverty. Instead, this programme caused a rapid escalation of poverty in the rural area. This was largely because the programme was expensive and, as a result, whatever credit that was available to agriculture was now concentrated in areas where the farmers adopted this programme, and these happened to be relatively well-off farmers, and with increasing access to credit they went for mechanization in agriculture.[10] Combined with the impact of these factors was the declining share of credit to small farmers and the displacement of labourers from the land as a result of mechanization, which caused poverty to escalate in the rural area. The government recognized that in order to stabilize the level of poverty and subsequently to reduce it there was a need to inject a substantial amount of credit not only to the rural area but also among the poor in general. The government finally came to terms with the fact that private banks were unlikely to participate in such a venture.

The Indian experience provides us with a unique example as to why it is so difficult for private banks to assist in the development programme. This is mainly for two reasons. First, in the early days of independence, the financial sector was not developed, meaning they neither had the non-banking financial intermediaries (NBFI) nor a well-developed stock market; banks were the only player in such markets. Consequently, they used to enjoy monopoly power over all borrowers irrespective of their size of operation and, as a result, they never had to take any known credit risk that developed countries' counterparts quite frequently had to take, especially when operating in the large borrowers' market. As a result, bankers were neither trained in how to offer a credit-risk-adjusted interest rate nor knew how to manage it. But to cooperate with the government they had to undertake a substantial amount of credit risk for reasons already explained. Furthermore, in most cases banks knew that they would not be able to charge credit-risk-adjusted interest rates, since many entrepreneurs would be reluctant to borrow under such conditions, as entrepreneurs themselves do not know the expected return from these projects. In the case of agriculture, as the loans are supposed to be allocated for the purpose of reducing poverty, the issue of credit-risk-adjusted interest rates does not arise. In other words, these loans would be offering a low profit to banks, thereby offering a lower incentive to participate in such projects.

This problem was further complicated by the fact that the banks themselves did not have knowledge in relation to these projects' past performances, whether in agriculture or in industry, and from the bankers' point of view, being involved in such projects meant that they had to carry a high liquidity risk, arising from the short-term nature of deposits (with a smaller deposit base) and a long-term commitment to investment, whose approximate level of financial return at regular intervals is not known to banks. In this situation, if a bank had to take a higher credit risk, then the bank could not avoid liquidity risk arising from the possibility of an irregular financial flow, where the return from the entrepreneurs' equity might not be sufficient to meet the shortfall arising in meeting the regular debt repayment. This problem particularly arises from the fact that banks are required to relax their credit standard requirements. Therefore, from the banks' point of view, participating in the government development programme means that they cannot avoid liquidity risk, while their survival depends upon liquidity. Consequently, despite various attempts made by the government, we observe that banks' advancement policy essentially remained short-term. As a response, in 1969 India nationalized its major commercial banks.

Having established a firm control over banks, in 1972 the government adopted a number of poverty alleviation and employment generation schemes known as the *Garibi Hatao* programme. In order to combat poverty, it selected certain sectors of the economy, referred to as 'priority sectors' (which included agriculture and allied activities, small-scale industry, retail trade, transport operations, professionals and craftsmen/women) and decided that commercial banks must assist these sectors by facilitating cheap loans. In short, 'priority sectors' primarily comprised small businesses and agriculture. It was thought that the improvement in access to a cheaper loan facility by small business might generate higher employment, which itself would take care of part of the poverty. The remainder of the poverty was to be directly addressed by loan assistance schemes to the poor, as a result of which they could set up their own businesses, or at least would have reduced their dependence on private moneylenders for loans at a higher interest rate. This in turn could allow them to retain much of their own surplus. This meant that part of the aim of this programme was that commercial bank loans must reach the tiniest units of the economy. Accordingly, the government declared that by March 1979, 'priority sectors' as a whole must receive 33 per cent of the total bank credit. A little less than 50 per cent of this was allocated to the agricultural sector, amounting to 16 per cent of the total credit, with the instruction that small and marginal farmers should receive one and a half times the advances. This limit was subsequently raised to 40 per cent of the total credit, with the instruction that 1 per cent of the advances must be allocated for the extreme poor at an interest rate of 4 per cent. The remainder of the sector would receive loans at an interest rate ranging from 10.5 to 14.5 per cent, as opposed to the commercial rate of 19.5 per cent. Furthermore, collateral requirements for these loans were reduced.

By 1975 the government was able to stabilize the rise in poverty and from 1979 onwards poverty started to decline for the first time. Throughout the 1980s the rates of growth in agricultural and industrial output were much higher than in any previous era.[11] For the first time India recognized that by default it had created a sizeable middle class, emerging from the lopsided or asymmetrical benefit flowing from the success of the HYVP and the 'priority sectors' and the size of this class continued to increase.[12] This, in turn, combined with positive discrimination in securing places in higher education and government jobs for the schedule caste and tribes, ultimately allowed India to enlarge the size of its market, reaching almost one-third of the population. But in the process the banking sector became fragile, carrying the cost of a number of non-performing loans and India too recognized that it could not continue with its current method of financing.

Needless to say, both of these countries were successful in using their intervention policy, i.e. South Korea was able to achieve a high growth rate via promotion of the export sector, while India, although it took a long time, was able to achieve it via enlargement of the size of its own market, but in the process adversely affected its own banking sector. This obviously raises the question as to why the process of development adversely affected the banking sector, which plays such an important role.

Where did it go wrong?
It will be argued that the adverse impact upon the banking sector principally emerged from the fact that South Korea overlooked or underestimated the importance of the credit standard, while India underestimated the importance of the credit-risk-adjusted interest rate; furthermore, India for some peculiar reason did not close down the non-profit-making firms.

However, as the problem emerged in both countries for very different reasons, it may be interesting to investigate why South Korea overlooked the importance of the credit standard, while India underestimated the importance of credit risk.

The information in the last section indicates that from the very beginning neither government was much concerned about the profitability of the banks: while South Korea was mainly concerned about growth, India on the other hand was more concerned about the enlargement of the market. Consequently, neither of them gave much attention to the question of whether the process of funding the development projects would expose banks' loan capital to a very high level of credit risk. Yet both countries' problems principally emerged from ignorance of this factor. The issue of credit risk principally arises from the fact that in the early days of independence most of the entrepreneurs from developing countries had neither adequate capital nor sufficient assets to meet the banks' credit standard in order to obtain the size of loan required to undertake the projects that their respective governments wanted. In this situation, banks had to take a very high level of credit risk, which effectively meant that they became the principal investors. In short, banks' share of loan capital in the total investment often exceeded the entrepreneurs' share of investment, and this introduced the possibility that in the event of a project failure, or if the return from the project was not sufficient to maintain the debt obligation, the return from the entrepreneurs' equity might not be sufficient to meet this shortfall. This means that from the outset of the implementation of the development programmes banks had to carry a relatively high degree of fragility compared to banks from other developed countries and, therefore, the question is how in the process of development would one try to reduce this fragility over time.

In order to investigate this issue it is first necessary to examine the composition of firms' investment funds, i.e. the combination of internal (i.e. entrepreneurial equity) and external funds (i.e. loanable funds) at the initial stage, which will give us some indication of whether, if the project performs adversely, the return from the internal funds will be sufficient to meet the shortfall in the debt repayment rates. This will enable us to ascertain the extent of the fragility of the banking sector in terms of whether it is high or low. For example, in the case of South Korea, firms' internal funds initially constituted 47.7 per cent while external funds constituted 52.3 per cent in 1963–64 (Amsden and Euh, 1993), while in the case of India these figures were 60.1 per cent and 39.9 per cent respectively (Singh, 1995). Although both of these figures are quite high, compared to say the average UK corporation's long-term debt of 26.6 per cent of the total investment (Cobham and Subramanium, 1998), it is reasonable to assume that if the project performed adversely, any shortfall in the repayment could be recouped from the return on the equity finance. Furthermore, if the project fails, then the bank can sell all the company's assets including the entrepreneur's share, to recoup the principal. The above composition of the investment suggests that although South Korea has taken more risk than India, in both cases the entrepreneurs' share is sufficient to protect the banks' capital from unforeseen adverse future events, at least in the initial period. The question therefore that needs to be investigated is how did the problem emerge?

South Korea's problem emerged from its very success. As the economy grew, so did its ability to service the contractual debt commitment, all things being equal. This steady flow of return on loans in turn not only increased firms' credit ratings, but perhaps more importantly it may have increased the confidence of the policy makers. As a result, when the lenders' willingness to offer larger loans to these firms increased, policy makers perhaps overlooked the fact that the process could over-expose the banks' capital. With the increasing access to credit, investors (i.e. borrowers) also did not feel the necessity to rely on internal funds to any great extent for growth, and as a result their share of internal funds in relation to total funds shrank. This in turn caused the debt/equity ratio to rise with the growth of the firm, thereby causing the debt service ratio to rise, which in turn, in the absence of an appropriate credit standard, exposed banks' capital to very high levels of credit risk. For example, as the share of exports rose from 5 to 7 per cent in the mid-1960s to over 20 per cent of GNP by the 1970s (Cole and Park, 1983), the firms' share of internal funds in relation to total funds shrank from 47.7 per cent during 1963–65 to 25.4 per cent during 1966–71, while the share of external funds rose from 52.3 per cent to 74.6 per cent (Amsden and Euh, 1993). During the same period, i.e. between 1963 and 1971, the debt/equity ratio rose from 92 to 328 per cent and the debt service ratio as a percentage of merchandise exports rose from 5.20 to 28.34 per cent (Amsden, 1989). The problem is that if export earnings fall and, as a result, the rate of return from the total investment falls below the repayment rate on the debt commitment, the rate of return from the internal funds may not be sufficient to meet the shortfall. Firms then have to borrow in order to meet their debt commitments. In the case of South Korea, as the large bulk of its debt was held in foreign currency, and this debt rose from US$206 million to US$2.922 billion, and the ratio of foreign debt/GNP rose from 7 per cent to 30 per cent between 1965 and 1971 (Amsden, 1989), this meant that these debts had to be paid in foreign currency. If South Korea's central bank could not organize a rescue package for the troubled firms, it might have to seek a rescue package from a *de facto* central bank should it wish to avoid any major financial crisis. South Korea confronted this problem in 1972.

As the economy grew, the cost of production increased, and exporting firms started to face increasing difficulty in meeting the ever-rising export target. This problem was further aggravated by the growing resistance from two of its main markets, namely Japan and the USA, to importing certain products, such as textiles, which in turn further slowed down the growth in export earnings. The return from the equity (i.e. internal funds), which constituted only 25 per cent of the total investment, was not sufficient to meet the shortfall. By 1971, the number of bankrupt firms receiving foreign loans rose to 200 (Cho, 1989). As the government stood as guarantor for all foreign loans, it could not afford to default on them.

In 1972 the government invalidated all loan agreements between the firms and informal credit lenders, and offered lenders the option of transferring loans into shares in the borrowing firms. This desperate measure may have allowed indebted firms to meet their overseas debt obligations, but at the cost of the informal credit market and of banks.

It appears that the government ignored the problem of credit risk and chose to continue with its old method of financing. By the early 1980s, the economy faced the same problem again as it slowed down, mainly as a result of a collapse of foreign markets in construction, shipping and shipbuilding. The GNP turned negative for the first time since the Korean War. Firms started to face difficulties in maintaining the debt commitment from their own returns, and started to borrow in order to meet the shortfall. As a result, their share of internal funds shrank from an average of 21.1 per cent during 1975–79 to 16.4 per cent by 1980, while their share of external funds rose from 78.9 per cent to 83.6 per cent (Choong-Hwan, 1990). The debt/equity ratio rose from around 370 per cent during the late 1970s to 466 per cent by 1980, and Korea's external debt as a percentage of GNP rose from 32 per cent to 48 per cent between 1979 and 1981 (Amsden, 1989). By 1982, a growing number of highly indebted firms found it difficult to service their debts. Thus the problem in 1971 repeated itself, that is, the problem of over-investment recurred.

Following the crisis, the government decided to abstain from further credit-directed programmes and abolished the preferential lending rates. In addition, NBFI were deregulated and corporations were allowed to issue bonds with a guarantee by commercial banks. The government privatized the commercial banks, but in the presence of large non-performing loans, could not abstain from maintaining control over the banking sector, as the restructuring of the industrial sector required government supervision of credit allocation. The government maintained its control over the interest rate and the credit allocation of the banking sector, which was lifted in 1991, along with its control over the foreign capital inflow. Although the external share as opposed to the internal share of the total investment improved from its early 1980s position, it still remained very high. For example, between 1987 and 1991, the share of external capital funds constituted 73.6 per cent, while the internal share constituted merely 26.4 per cent, of the total investment (Amsden and Euh, 1993). Thus the banking sector remained over-exposed. By 1994, banks had to increase their allocated funds in order to make provision for non-performing loans, but it appears that inadequate attempts were made to reduce the debt/equity ratio, especially for Chaebol. For example, even in 1996 the average debt to equity ratio for the top 30 Chaebol was 898 per cent. This means that these firms borrowed an average of $8.98 against each dollar they owned, and the greater proportion of the loans either came directly from the banks, or was raised via issuing corporate bonds, which were also guaranteed by the banks. Fourteen of these 30 Chaebol were making negative profits in 1996, while for those who were making a positive profit, this remained marginal compared with the total assets, including loans, that were invested (Lee, 1997). Thus it was no wonder that as soon as the economy slowed down it led to a banking crisis.[13]

Although India had taken a more conservative approach at the initial stage, compared to South Korea, for financing its large economic units, it could not maintain that position because the size of the market remained very modest for some time. This was largely because the government was unable to make any appreciable inroads in improving a sizeable portion of the population's livelihood. As a result, effective demand remained quite low even in the mid-1970s. Consequently, many firms, especially the large ones, were unable to capture a sufficient share of the market that was necessary to achieve economies of scale. In short, these firms were running at a loss. The government neither allowed these loss-making firms to close down nor encouraged them to search for an export market. It did not encourage the latter course because it thought that these firms might not be able to capture a sufficient share of the export market (Chakrabarty, 1987). This opinion might have been influenced by the fact that the world was then in the middle of the cold war, and India was not particularly an ally of the Western world, nor was its economic policy following the route of the Western world, and therefore it could not expect to receive the same treatment as that received by South Korea. Instead the government used its 1948 Industrial Labour Dispute Act to protect these firms. This Act states that no large economic units are allowed to close down or to retrench workers on economic grounds without central government permission. The moral justification for this Act is to protect workers' rights. In reality, this Act allowed loss-making firms to continue to survive with government subsidies, which effectively meant that the banks were refinancing these firms. In short, in the absence of provisions for the non-performing loans, banks were carrying the cost of these losses.

The above problem was further aggravated by the way the government used the banks to finance the anti-poverty programme known as the *Garibi Hatao*. The government allocated 40 per cent of the total credit to this programme. In order to ensure that the poor borrowers' access to the loan market was not restricted by the banks' credit standard requirements, collateral requirements were reduced. Thus the government decided to take on the credit risk on smaller loans. But in order to offer cheaper loans to these borrowers, it appears that the government decided not to make any adjustment for the credit risk in the calculation of the interest rate. In other words, no provision was made for the non-performing loans, which constituted 40 per cent of the total loans. This further added to the problems of the banks. If a small fraction of the loan performed adversely, it would have a direct impact upon the banks, and indeed this is what happened. By 1991, 4.7 million loans were advanced to this sector, of which 233 441 were declared sick, meaning that the net loss from these loans exceeded the net worth of these firms (RBI, 1991). In terms of percentages, it only constituted 4.8 per cent of the total loans that were advanced to the priority sector, and altogether, the total bad to doubtful debts amounted to Rs 125.86 billion, constituting only 10.25 per cent of the total loans that were advanced (RBI, 1991). In terms of percentages, this figure was not high enough to cause any major problem for the banks. Thus it appears that the banks made no provision for the non-performing loans, so that banks had to carry their cost. This problem was further aggravated by the presence of weak bankruptcy laws which prevented banks from recouping the principal by selling the collateral. The above experience highlights the fact that in the absence of a credit-risk-adjusted interest rate, if a small fraction of the loan performs adversely, it can put a great strain on the banks. Consequently, the government realized that it could not continue with such a method of finance; it too had to undertake capital market reform.

Conclusion

The analysis that has been presented here suggests that banks play a very important role in financing the process of development. But whether the banks will be playing an active role or requiring government assistance very much depends upon the state of the economic environment. By economic environment we mean whether there exists an opportunity to make a profit by engaging in the process of development. Our analysis suggests that this opportunity at least in the early stage of development was absent, while the risk was very high in terms of credit risk and liquidity risk. Both of these risks arise from the relaxation in the credit standard requirements needed in the early stage of development. Consequently government intervention was necessary in order to absorb these risks.

It is not clear whether the government of both countries understood this; rather it appears that both governments assumed that the banks' reluctance to participate in the development process principally emerged from the low profitability. Consequently, intervention entirely concentrated on the establishment of firm control over the allocation of credit. But the government overlooked the fact that having control over the allocation of loans does not give any control over their repayment. Without the latter, banks cannot survive; hence the importance of the credit standard emerges in order to ensure that the fate of the banks' loanable funds should not be tied to the borrowers' projects. As neither government realized the importance of this issue, both continued their agenda by exposing banks' loan capital. In the case of South Korea the problem only emerged when the economy slowed down, so concentration was focused on the growth rate, without realizing that it further exposed banks' loan capital. India's problem did not emerge from the slowing down in the growth of the economy. In fact, although India's growth rate remained low up until 1980, it never slowed down in any adverse way, and after then it started to increase at a rapid rate. Its problem principally came from the fact that it had not offered a credit-risk-adjusted interest rate, and consequently there remained a very small margin between the deposit rate and the interest rate on loans, suggesting that if a small fraction of the loan functions adversely, banks will be in trouble, and this problem was further magnified by the presence of weak bankruptcy laws. Consequently, both countries had to undertake capital market reform. Needless to say, in both countries, banks' finance played a very important role in the context of development.

Notes

* I would like to thank P. Arestis, M. Hughes and M. Sawyer for their comments on this chapter; I alone am responsible for any remaining errors.
1. For a comprehensive discussion of South Korean industrial policy see Westphal (1990) and Lall (1994).
2. See Karkal (1967) and Basu (1997 and 2002) for more on this issue.
3. See Bagchi (1992), Chandra (1977), Chandavarkar (1965), Singh (1959), Reserve Bank of India (1977), Bhaduri (1973; 1977), Bardhan and Rudra (1978), Rudra (1992), Basu (1983; 1984) and Roth (1979), where the discussion exclusively concentrates on the rural poor.
4. See Amsden (1989) and Cho (1989).
5. See Cole and Park (1983). See also Cho (1989) and Kim (1991) on the above issue. Amsden (1989) pointed out that household savings as a percentage of GDP increased from 0.18 per cent in 1965 to 4.15 per cent in 1966, but declined in the following year. From then onwards no systematic relationship can be observed between interest rate and saving behaviour, suggesting that higher rates perhaps mainly helped to transfer savings that were previously held in an unproductive form.
6. See Cole and Park (1983) for more on this issue.
7. For example, in 1956 the SBI and its associates were directed to open 400 branch facilities in the rural and semi-urban areas in the next five years (RBI, 1969).
8. See Cho (1989), Amsden (1989) and Amsden and Euh (1993).
9. These schemes are similar to licensing scheme arrangements, which subsequently were claimed to have brought corruption to the Indian economic system. See Bhagwati and Desai (1970) for further details on these issues.
10. See Basu (1982) and Rudra (1969) for more on this issue.
11. For example, the growth rate in agriculture was 3.5 per cent in the 1980s compared to 1.8 per cent in the 1970s; similarly, the industrial growth rate in the 1980s was 7.15 per cent compared to 4 per cent in the 1970s. See Basu and Mallick (2004) for further details on this subject.
12. By 'lopsided' or 'asymmetrical benefit' we mean that although the central aim of this programme was to benefit the poor, in reality, a greater proportion of this credit (i.e. 95 per cent) was received by those whose assets' value ranged from Rs 100 000 to 1 million, who constituted 34 per cent of the priority sectors' population, and did not comprise the poor, but the lower- to middle-class population. Only 5 per cent of the credit was received by those whose assets' value was less than Rs 100 000, comprising 66 per cent of the priority sectors' population. See Basu (2002), RBI (1979, vol. 2, tables 1–2), and RBI (1987a; 1987b) for more details on this issue.
13. In fact, the South Korean growth rate came down from 8 per cent to 4 per cent just before the crisis (Arestis and Glickman, 2002).

References

Amsden, A.H. (1989), *Asia's Next Giant: South Korea and Late Industrialisation*, New York: Oxford University Press.
Amsden, A.H. and Euh Yoon-Dae (1993), 'South Korea's financial reforms: good-bye financial repression (maybe), hello new institutional restraints', *World Development*, **21**, 379–90.
Arestis, P. and M. Glickman (2002), 'Financial crisis in South East Asia: dispelling illusion the Minskyan way', *Cambridge Journal of Economics*, **26**, 237–60.
Bagchi, A. (1992), 'Land tax, property rights and peasant insecurity in colonial India', *Journal of Peasant Studies*, **20**, 1–49.

Bardhan, P. and A. Rudra (1978), 'Interlinkage of land, labour and credit relations: an analysis of village survey data in East India', *Economic and Political Weekly*, **13**, February.

Basu, K. (1983), 'The emergence of isolation and interlinkage in rural markets', *Oxford Economic Papers*, **35**, 262–80.

Basu, K. (1984), *The Less Developed Economy: A Critique of Contemporary Theory*, Oxford: Basil Blackwell.

Basu, S. (1982), *An Analysis of the High Yielding Variety Programme in India*, MEc Dissertation, Sydney: University of Sydney.

Basu, S. (1997), 'Why institutional credit agencies are reluctant to lend to the rural poor: a theoretical analysis of the Indian rural credit market', *World Development*, **25**, 267–80.

Basu, S. (2002), *Financial Liberalisation and Intervention: A New Analysis of Credit Rationing*, Cheltenham, UK and Northampton, MA, USA: Edward Elgar.

Basu, S. (2003), 'Why do banks fail?', *International Review of Applied Economics*, **17**, 231–48.

Basu, S. and S. Mallick (2004), 'Why does financial liberalisation lead to credit being switched in favour of unproductive assets? The Indian experience', mimeo.

Bhaduri, A. (1973), 'A study in agricultural backwardness under semi-feudalism', *Economic Journal*, **83**, 120–37.

Bhaduri, A. (1977), 'On the formation of usurious interest rates in backward agriculture', *Cambridge Journal of Economics*, **1**, 34–52.

Bhagwati, J.N. and P. Desai (1970), *India, Planning for Industrialisation*, Oxford: Oxford University Press.

Chakrabarty, S. (1987), *Development Planning: The Indian Experience*, Oxford: Oxford University Press.

Chandavarkar, A. (1965), 'The premium for risk as a determinant of interest rates in underdeveloped rural areas: a comment', *Quarterly Journal of Economics*, **79**, 322–5.

Chandra, B. (1977), *Rise and Growth of Economic Nationalism in India*, New Delhi: People's Publishing House.

Cho, Y. Je (1989), 'Finance and development: The Korean approach', *Oxford Review of Economic Policy*, **5**, 88–102.

Choong-Hwan, R. (1990), 'Korean corporate financing', *Monthly Review*, Korean Exchange Bank, **24**(April), 3–13.

Cobham, D. and Subramanium, R. (1998), 'Corporate finance in developing countries: new evidence for India', *World Development*, **26**, 1033–47.

Cole, D. and Y.C. Park (1983), *Financial Development in Korea, 1945–1978*, Cambridge, MA: Harvard University Press.

Gupta, S.B. (1988), *Monetary Economics: Institutions, Theory and Policy*, New Delhi: S. Chand and Co.

Karkal, G.L. (1967), *Unorganised Money Markets in India*, Bombay: Lalvani Publishing House.

Kim, K.S. (1991), 'The interest-rate reform of 1965 and domestic savings', in Lee-Jay Cho and Kim Yoon Hyung (eds), *Economic Development in the Republic of Korea: A Policy Perspective*, An East–West Centre Book, Honolulu, HI: The University of Hawaii Press.

Krishnaswamy, K.S., K. Krisnamurty and P.D. Sharma (1987), *Improving Domestic Resource Mobilisation through Financial Development: India*, Manila: Asian Development Bank.

Kuznets, S. (1955), 'Towards a theory of economic growth', in R. Levachman (ed.), *National Policy for Economic Welfare at Home and Abroad*, New York: Doubleday and Co, 12–85.

Lall, S. (1994), 'The East Asian miracle: Does the bell toll for industrial strategy?', *World Development*, **22**, 645–54.

Lee, S.J. (1997), 'Financial crisis in Korea', mimeo, Yale University, New Haven, CT.

Nuskse, R. (1953), *Problems of Capital Formation in Under-developed Countries*, Oxford: Oxford University Press.

Reserve Bank of India (1969), *Reports of the All-India Rural Credit Review Committee*, Bombay: RBI.

Reserve Bank of India (1977), *Indebtedness of Rural Households and the Availability of Institutional Finance (All India Debt and Investment Survey, 1971–72)*, Bombay: RBI.

Reserve Bank of India (1979), *Report of the Working Group to Review the System of Cash Credit*, Bombay: RBI.

Reserve Bank of India (1987a), *All-India Debt and Investment Survey 1981–82 (Assets and Liabilities of Households as on 30th of June 1981)*, Bombay: RBI.

Reserve Bank of India (1987b), *All-India Debt and Investment Survey 1981–82 (Statistical Tables Relating to Capital Expenditure and Capital Formation of Households during the year ended 30th of June 1982)*, Bombay: RBI.

Reserve Bank of India (1991), *Banking Statistics*, www.rbi.org.in.

Rosenstein-Rodan, P.N. (1943), 'Problem of industrialisation in Eastern and South-Eastern Europe', *Economic Journal*, **53**, 202–11.

Roth, H.D. (1979), 'Money lenders' management of loan agreement: report on a case study in Dhanbad', *Economic and Political Weekly*, 14 July.

Rudra, A. (1969), 'Big farmers of Punjab – second instalment of results', *Economic and Political Weekly*, **4**(52).

Rudra, A. (1992), *Political Economy of Indian Agriculture*, Calcutta: K.P. Bagchi and Co.

Scitovsky, T. (1954), 'Two concepts of external economies', *Journal of Political Economy*, **62**, 143–51.

Singh, A. (1995), *Corporate Financial Patterns in Industrialising Economies: A Comparative International Study*, IFC Technical Paper No. 2, Washington, DC: World Bank.

Singh, M.M. (1959), 'Monetary policy and economic expansion', *The Indian Economic Review*, **4**, 45–56.

Westphal, L. (1990), 'Industrial policy in an export-propelled economy: lessons from South Korea's experience', *Journal of Economic Perspectives*, **4**, 41–59.

19 Credit rationing
Roy J. Rotheim

Introduction

The purpose of this chapter is to assess and elaborate on the literature that has developed among New Keynesian economists[1] addressing the topic of *credit rationing*, and then to reflect on the nature of the resulting theory and policy from a post-Keynesian perspective. The phrase credit rationing emerged in the early New Keynesian literature (see Hodgman, 1960; Stiglitz and Weiss, 1971; Jaffe and Russell, 1976) to identify the possibility that an equilibrium might occur in the credit market but where some individuals would be unable to borrow funds even though they were willing to pay this equilibrium rate.[2] So while there is an excess demand for funds in the market for liquidity at the current rate of interest, there are no internal forces that would cause that excess demand to be mitigated. The existence of credit rationing provides, according to New Keynesian economists, a 'rigorous' theoretical foundation for explaining credit market failure and what they call the 'credit channel view' of monetary policy. These writers find such 'market failures' to have consequences both for individual borrowers and lenders, and for policy makers. Market failures that lead to credit rationing cause changes in the money stock to have real economic implications; the classical dichotomy is violated and monetary policy may not have its desired results of regulating inflation.

The focus of post-Keynesians is first and foremost methodologically different from the New Keynesian view. The post-Keynesian perspective depicts an open system approach, Keynes's theory of effective demand, in which the markets for capital and ancillary markets are not valid modes by which to consider the demand for and access to credit as well as the consequences those factors might have on the economy as a whole. One might say that conditions of credit 'restriction' are a more appropriate phrase than credit 'rationing' (Rochon, 1999). Instead of separate markets for goods and money (or credit), the starting point and the questions posed by post-Keynesians are characterized by the role of money and finance as it relates to the production of goods and services – Keynes's 'monetary theory of production'. It is not that money has real consequences, as in the New Keynesian view, but rather that monetary and real factors are part and parcel of the same more generalized processes. The relevant mode of discourse is not limited to the impacts that changes in the money stock might have, but rather in what way changes in effective demand cause changes in the money stock to occur endogenously. Not ruled out, however, is the effect that the restraint of high-powered money by central banks might have on the ability of banks to lend, and thus on economic activity. But this question, where the change in high-powered money reflects some exogenous shock to the system, is taken from a more open perspective in post-Keynesian thought, where the central bank may be acting either by accommodation or by some autonomous intervention. Consistent with their neoclassical roots, New Keynesians' methodology expects decisions to hire inputs and produce output to be denominated in real terms. They find, anomalously, that the relevant rate of interest is the nominal, not the real, rate of interest. They have no explanation for this phenomenon. Such a result, however, falls squarely into the heart of the post-Keynesian perspective, through the monetary theory of production and the theory of effective demand.

Through this and other observations, one sees a confluence between the two approaches as some New Keynesians have broached and explored questions and directions that lead them precariously away from what are the neoclassical foundations of their paradigmatic approach (see, especially, Blinder, 1987; Greenwald and Stiglitz, 1993; Stiglitz and Greenwald, 2003). While interesting in their own right, these insights hang in mid-air without the support of an underlying mechanism to give them context, meaning, and therefore enduring analytical or policy direction, things that post-Keynesian economics has striven to achieve.

This chapter will unfold in two broad parts. The first section will address the nature and implications of the New Keynesian approach to the question of credit rationing. Then I shall assess this New Keynesian view from an alternative post-Keynesian perspective focusing on the methodological issues implied by the two approaches, indicating that the interesting insights emergent from recent New Keynesian literature are not sustainable without a coherent theoretical framework, one that transcends their decisively neoclassical roots.

Credit rationing in a New Keynesian framework

Stiglitz and Greenwald (2003) assert that the issue of credit rationing requires a new paradigmatic framework for economic theory. This new paradigm suggests a revival of the loanable funds theory of the rate of interest in which the focus changes from money as an exclusive medium of exchange to that of an instrument of credit for those who wish to engage in productive activities. The analytical framework switches from an understanding of the money creation process on the liability side of the balance sheet to the portfolio decision of banks on the asset side of the balance sheet and interfirm lending. In this framework, the rate of interest should not be thought of as determined in the money market by the demand and supply of money, but rather it should be considered in terms of those factors that define and determine the supply and demand for credit – the rate of interest is no longer a market-clearing price, but a reflection of the portfolio decisions of banks and non-bank lenders in light of informational discrepancies. Contemporary research on this credit view of the rate of interest reflects a new institutional approach in light of the discipline's appreciation of the importance of the economics of information and the way that informational asymmetries between lenders and borrowers can cause failures in the market for loanable funds (see Stiglitz, 2000 and 2002).

This new paradigmatic approach looks at 'the ways in which credit is different from other commodities, the central role of information in the provision of credit, and the institutions – banks and firms – which obtain that information and bear the risk associated with the provision of credit' (Stiglitz and Greenwald, 2003, p. 151). These imperfections and other asymmetries lead to inhibitions on banks and other financial institutions in their ability to provide credit smoothly to the economy. Attention lies, therefore, in matters of the subsequent consequences of the supply side of the loanable funds market. The expressive mode of discourse held by those who espouse the credit view remains a microfoundation for conceptualizing an economy in the aggregate (see Dow, 1996). As such, they consider the 'market' for credit in the economy filtered through the lenses of a relationship between principal (a bank) and agent (borrowers at this bank, presumably to purchase real capital assets) (see Dymski, 1998).

Probably the most radical assertion emanating from this perspective is the idea that the standard model of supply and demand, in which it is solely prices that clear markets, may be 'model specific . . . [it] is not a general property of markets . . .' (Stiglitz and Weiss, 1981, p. 409). It would only be the case, however, if it were assumed 'that prices have neither sorting nor incentive effects' (ibid.). While the traditional supply and demand analysis has been generalized under this New Keynesian framework, it is still not evident that the macroeconomic theories and policies that emerge from this framework, which rely on some form of microfoundation, can exist apart from some statements about the relationship between independent supply and demand curves at both the micro and macro levels.

Credit rationing – microeconomics

The initial work on the New Keynesian view of credit rationing identifies the capital market itself, and whether fluctuations in the rate of interest have the effect of clearing that market (Hodgman, 1960; Jaffe and Russell, 1976; Stiglitz and Weiss, 1981). These authors acknowledged that this mechanism should work smoothly in a world of perfect and costless information: everyone who desires credit at the going rate of interest should have those demands satisfied. They observe, however, that there is an unsatisfied group of those who demand credit at the going rate of interest (who are indistinguishable from those who receive loans), and that there do not appear to be any incentives for lenders to raise the rate of interest to satisfy that excess demand.

There are two factors influencing the decision to supply loanable funds by banks, namely the interest payment banks will receive on the loan and their estimate of the probability that the loan will be repaid. Information on the latter is assumed to be asymmetric: the borrowers know the risk of the investment paying off and therefore the likelihood that they will be in a position to repay the loan; the banks, however, do not possess this information. The argument is that the riskiness of the pool of borrows may be affected by the interest rate itself as the probability of repayment varies within the pool of borrowers. This heightened perception by lenders can be attributable to two factors. The first is *adverse selection*. As interest rates rise in response to increased demands for loanable funds, banks perceive those who remain in the market to be worse risks: 'they are willing to borrow at high interest rates because they perceive their probability of repaying the loan to be low' (Stiglitz and Weiss, 1981, p. 393).[3]

The second is an *incentive effect*, in that higher rates of interest will provide borrowing firms with the incentive to prefer riskier projects. As such, they may reach a point where the higher interest payments accruing to banks will be offset exactly by the greater perceived loss in revenue on account of the asymmetric information about the likelihood of firms repaying their debt, coupled with the assumptions about firm behaviour as interest rates rise. This point is indicated by interest rate $\check{r}^*$ in Figure 19.1 (taken from Stiglitz and Weiss, 1981, p. 394). Given the quantity of reserves held by banks, they would not be willing to lend at higher rates of interest – even if there were a margin of firms who would be willing to borrow at those higher rates – because their expected returns adjusted by their perceived possibility of the loans not being repaid would be lower than at interest rate $\check{r}^*$. The credit market would be in equilibrium at that rate, although the market would not have cleared, implying that credit has been rationed.

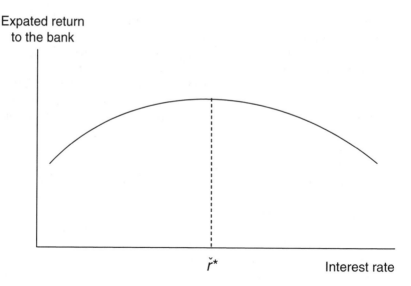

Figure 19.1   Expected returns and interest rates

The basic analytics of their argument can be explained by means of Figure 19.2. The schedule *LS* reflects the willingness of banks to lend funds to borrowers assuming that there are no perceived adverse selection or incentive effects: both lenders and borrowers operate under the same informational framework. Banks would then be willing to extend more credit as interest rates rose because they would know the true probabilities of repayment by borrowers. Interest rates could then serve as that rationing device that generates both equilibrium and market clearing. The demand for loans is reflected in the schedule D_1; then there would be credit market equilibrium where the quantity of loans demanded would be satisfied by banks at L_1 with interest rate $\check{r}_1$. If the demand for loans were to increase to D_2, then the interest rate would rise to $\check{r}_2$ to clear the credit market at L_2. A similar process would occur were loan demand to increase again from D_2 to D_3 (with interest rates rising to clear the market at $\check{r}_3$).

Instead of the traditional loan supply schedule *LS*, let us suppose that banks perceive there to be adverse selection and incentive effects if interest rates were to increase, represented by the loan supply curve *LS**, a reflection of the expected return to the bank schedule in Figure 19.1. Let us begin at interest rate $\check{r}^*$, where the competitive equilibrium reflects a demand for loans D_2 equal to bank loans at L^*. Suppose that the demand for loans increases from D_2 to D_3, such that the quantity of loans demanded at L^D_3 exceeds the quantity of credit banks would be willing to extend, L^*_1, at that rate of interest $\check{r}^*$. Unlike the situation where information was the same for both lender and borrower, if information were asymmetric, then the perceived adverse selection and incentive effects would compel banks not to increase their interest rates above $\check{r}^*$. Here, the *rational* equilibrium in the market for loans/credit occurs at interest rate $\check{r}^*$, where there are unsatisfied borrowers by the amount of $L^D_3 - L^*_1$, the amount by which credit has been rationed (shown by the bold line in Figure 19.2).

A willingness on the part of borrowers to offer greater collateral on loans will not persuade lenders to make available more funds. These offers would not allay the fears of

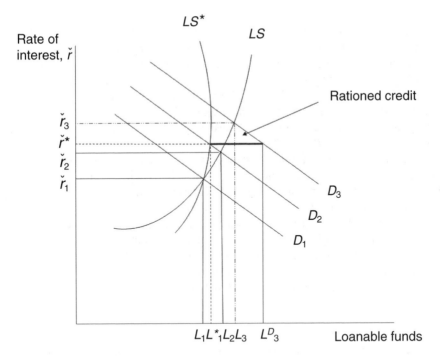

Figure 19.2   Rationed credit

lenders with regard to the possibility of imminent bankruptcy on account of their view of the adverse selection and incentive effects that might occur: '[I]ncreasing the collateral requirements of lenders (beyond some point) may decrease the returns to the bank, by either decreasing the average degree of risk aversion of the pool of borrowers; or in a multiperiod model inducing individual investors to undertake riskier projects' (Stiglitz and Weiss, 1981, p. 394). Consequently, neither the offer of higher interest rates nor greater collateral by borrowers will move lenders to increase the amount of loans they make; credit rationing remains a viable impediment to higher-level credit market equilibrium.

From these microeconomic foundations of credit rationing, these results can now be used to give insights into the macroeconomic implications of the role of credit in an economy in which information is imperfect and where interdependencies and rigidities are the rational consequences of such imperfections. This New Keynesian approach 'identifies incomplete contracts, and, in particular, imperfect indexing, as central market failures, and it attempts both to explain the causes and consequences of these market failures' (Greenwald and Stiglitz, 1993, p. 25). The key issue here is that New Keynesians believe that there must be a microfoundation for any macroeconomic theory and policy. This relationship conveys an important methodological perspective, one that will be addressed later in this chapter.

Credit rationing – macroeconomics
The macroeconomic consequences of credit rationing from a New Keynesian perspective centre on the question as to how monetary policy operates relative to traditional

monetarist and what they call 'Keynesian' conclusions. The monetarist approach is obvious and needs no explanation (see Friedman, 1970). What they mean by 'Keynesian economics' is limited to the 'neoclassical synthesis', the hydraulic mechanism whereby changes in the supply of money affect interest rates, which, in turn, cause investment to rise or fall commensurately. In no way does it reflect what Keynes himself had to say about this relationship, although they do have a better handle on Keynes when they observe that he understood the destabilizing effects that wage and price fluctuations would have on the economy and that wage and price stickiness might contribute to greater stability (see Stiglitz and Greenwald, 2003, p. 26).

Built upon the microeconomic construction of credit rationing, the New Keynesian credit view of monetary policy holds that it is not changes in the stock of money *per se* and the resultant effect that it might have on interest rates that explain fluctuations in production, investment and therefore economic activity. Instead it is 'the terms at which credit is made available *to the private sector* and the *quantity* of credit' that indicate whether monetary policy is or is not effective (Stiglitz and Greenwald, 2003, p. 154). Their analysis addresses two sectors: the banks, which are the suppliers of funds; and corporations, which require funds for their operating expenses and investment. Each sector is assumed to be responsive to conditions of risk aversion and potential impacts of credit constraints and real insolvency:

1. banks' willingness to allocate credit is based on their assessment of the possibility of bankruptcy among potential borrowers under different economic circumstances;[4] and
2. production and investment in the economy will be affected as much if not more by the availability of credit (loanable funds) on corporate balance sheets, than the quantity of money in existence.

Monetary policy more than likely will have real consequences; the classical dichotomy may not be a relevant guide to the efficacy of monetary policy, at least in the short period. With the strong presence of credit rationing it is also not clear what might be the algorithm between changes in the money stock and changes in interest rates, prices, or output, again, at least in the short period.

Stiglitz and Weiss (1992) provide a simple framework that clarifies a more general macroeconomic perspective on monetary policy, where questions of credit availability are more salient than those pertaining to changes in the money supply itself. Let M equal the money supply ('high-powered money') and A the amount of available credit. There are two salient linkages: one between the amount of money and the amount of available credit; the other between the amount of available credit and investment, I. These links are reflected in the following equations:

$$A = aM$$
$$I = Ab$$

Including these equations into the typical national income identity, with a consumption function equal to $C = mY$, yields:

$$Y = \frac{abM + G}{1 - m}$$

This translates into:

$$\Delta Y = \frac{1}{1-m}(ab\Delta M) + \frac{1}{1-m}\Delta G$$

This framework allows them to assess the macroeconomic consequences of changes in monetary policy and/or government spending. And while there are clearly demand and supply issues at stake here, most New Keynesian writers lay greater focus on the supply-side consequences of public policies. Therefore the essence of the New Keynesian message is that one cannot know the impact of a change in monetary policy on nominal income until the magnitude of the two relationships is revealed: between net infusions (or extractions) of high-powered money and available credit (a); and between the availability of credit and subsequent production and investment (b). The coefficient (a) reflects not only the amount of credit offered by banks but also the credit made available among firms. The key point here is that the traditional intermediate targets of monetary policy – interest rates or money supply – are not good barometers of the true impact of the policies themselves (see Stiglitz and Weiss, 1992). Consider a few examples suggested by this New Keynesian approach that would seemingly confirm their view of the importance of credit rationing when considering the effects of monetary policy.

Suppose there is an open market sale of government securities by the monetary authorities (a reduction in high-powered money in the banking system). Begin with the demand for loanable funds (L^D_1) equal to the supply of loanable funds at interest rate, $\check{r}_1$, where the interest rate is the only rationing device (Figure 19.3). Under these circumstances there would be a leftward shift in the supply of loanable funds schedule from LS_1 to LS_2. The contractionary monetary policy would cause the nominal rate of interest to rise from $\check{r}_1$ to $\check{r}_2$, where there would be a reduction in the quantity (equal to the supply) of loans demanded from L^D_1 to L^D_2. The monetarist (and new classical) perspective predicts that the fall in the stock of money would cause a proportionate fall in absolute prices such that the real demand (and supply) of money would not be affected. Then, there would be no effect of this contractionary monetary policy on real sector output or employment.

The so-called 'Keynesian' solution predicts that the higher rate of interest would cause a reduction in investment (and durable consumption) demand; a reduction in the quantity demanded for loanable funds would be prompted by an interest-elastic demand for investment. The New Keynesian 'paradigm' based on the economics of asymmetric information accepts neither the monetarist or 'Keynesian' explanations, asserting instead that it is the availability of funds to potential borrowers, affected primarily by rationed credit, that determines the extent of changes in output (and the price level). This latter perspective is seen in the following elaboration on the previous example (still exhibited in Figure 19.3).

Suppose, instead, that the perception of risk of default by borrowers is a viable component affecting the loan decision of banks. The operative supply schedules for funds would then be $LS_1{}^*$ and $LS_2{}^*$, before and after the contraction in bank reserves, respectively. Before the monetary contraction the amount of credit rationed by banks at the maximum 'rationally determined' interest rate $\check{r}_1{}^*$ is $L^{*D}_1 - L^*_1$. After the contractionary monetary policy (shown as a leftward shift in the adjusted supply of loanable funds schedule from $LS_1{}^*$ and $LS_2{}^*$) the rate of interest would rise from $\check{r}_1{}^*$ to $\check{r}_2{}^*$,

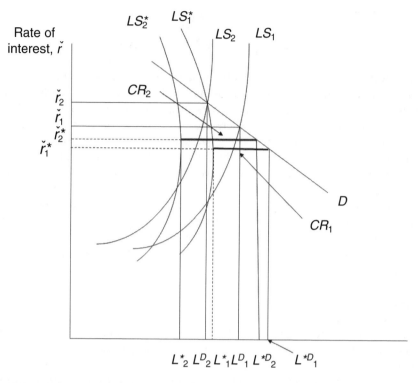

Figure 19.3   Contractionary monetary policy

an increase significantly smaller than what would have occurred had there been no adverse selection and incentive effects $(\check{r}_2{}^* - \check{r}_1{}^*) < (\check{r}_2 - \check{r}_1)$. Even though the interest rate increase in the adjusted case is less than that in the first instance, the amount of credit extended falls to a level lower than what it would have been had the rate of interest served as the only rationing device $(0L^*_2 < 0L^{*D}_2)$. The amount of credit rationed after the contractionary monetary policy has increased from $L^{*D}_1 - L^*_1$ to $L^{*D}_2 - L^*_2$ (indicated by the bold lines in the figure). Now it may be possible that this lower supply of funds (occurring on account of an increase in rationed credit) coupled with a smaller increase in nominal interest rates could cause the price level to fall by a greater amount than in the competitive case. Then, the rising real rates of interest and therefore lower output and employment – the monetarist argument regarding the ineffectiveness of monetary policy – would no longer retain validity once credit rationing was permitted into the model (the explanation for this full effect will be revealed below when the liquidity needs of firms enters the model). Blinder and Stiglitz sum up this argument:

Thus, tight money can depress real economic activity. Note also that, because of credit rationing, all this may happen with little increase in interest rates. So the effectiveness of monetary policy in this model does not rely on large interest elasticities, which often cannot be found empirically. (1983, p. 300)

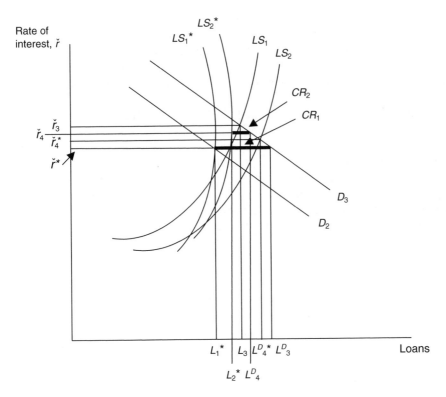

Figure 19.4   Expansionary monetary policy

Suppose, on the other hand, that the central bank increases its purchases of government securities on the open market. Assuming that banks perceive no incentive and adverse selection effects, we see in Figure 19.4 (based on the framework laid out in Figure 19.2) that an increase in the availability of reserves to banks ($LS_2 - LS_1$) would cause the interest rate to fall from $\check{r}_3$ to $\check{r}_4{}^*$. If these effects were perceived by banks to be significant then the increase in the supply of bank reserves (now $LS_2{}^* - LS_1{}^*$) might under some circumstances cause banks to take a more sanguine view of borrowers' abilities to repay their loans. Then, the supply of loanable funds schedule might shift upward as well as outward, meaning that banks' interest rate threshold might actually *rise* for each level of the demand for credit. The increased supply of loanable funds to banks might persuade them to *increase* their interest rates. Banks will now lend out $L_2{}^*$ at an interest rate $\check{r}_4$, which is *higher* than the previous interest rate $\check{r}^*$. One explanation for the *increase* in interest rates with an increase in the supply of bank reserves is that banks might feel that the subsequent increase in economic activity caused by the expansionary monetary policy would reduce the likelihood of bankruptcy among borrowers who do not have access to other sources of finance, and who might be better credit risks. More creditworthy firms would remain in the market even though interest rates are higher (they would be willing to pay those higher rates because the range of expected returns from production and investment would now have increased). Banks would then be free to charge higher interest rates for all borrowers, including those who were excluded previously on account of the credit rationing that occurred before the expansionary monetary policy (CR_1). We see that this changed perception on the part of banks has caused them to ration less credit than before $(CR_2 < CR_1)$, when they could increase interest rates, despite the increase in the amount of funds available for lending.

One could just as easily have envisioned a situation where an expansionary monetary policy could have reduced interest rates *and* increased the amount of credit that was rationed. Here banks might have felt that the expanded monetary policy responding to a declining economy would not have the desired effects on employment and output, and therefore profitability of borrowers and their ability to repay their loans. In this case the perception of lenders regarding adverse selection and incentive effects might worsen, causing them to *lower* interest rates and increase the amount of credit rationed – fewer loans would be made to those firms that banks felt were more likely to repay their loans.

Summing up the argument to this point, New Keynesian theorists hold:

> [I]n a rationing equilibrium, to the extent that monetary policy succeeds in shifting the supply of funds, it will affect the level of investment not through the interest-rate mechanism but rather through the availability of credit. (Stiglitz and Weiss, 1981, p. 405)

> I do not wish to deny . . . that investment depends on interest rates. But interest-rate channels have been well understood for decades, and . . . interest elasticities do not seem large enough to explain the deep recessions that are apparently caused by central bank policy. There must be something else. (Blinder, 1987, pp. 327–8)

The second topic of discussion within this so-called new paradigm of credit is an informational framework that considers the consequences of credit rationing on the balance sheets of firms that require finance to maintain their operations and invest in new plant and equipment. New Keynesians recognize that the balance sheets of producers might be affected by changes in monetary policy, especially with a contractionary monetary policy. While recognizing that there are demand-side effects associated with changes in monetary policy, New Keynesian writers feel that it is the supply-side effects of access to finance and the real wealth of firms that have been minimized by traditional monetary theorists. These supply-side effects may be more significant when considering changes in real activity than those on the demand side. Restrictions on credit brought about by monetary restraint could have strategically complementary effects in the markets for goods and money which create circumstances that affect all firms' balance sheets and therefore output and employment. This analysis has been coined *effective supply failures* by Alan Blinder (1987), where questions of access to finance and the consequences of financial insolvency and possible bankruptcy become salient within this macroeconomic framework. Thus, according to Blinder, 'Firms may have a desired or "notional" supply based on relative prices, expectations, and other variables. But they may need credit to produce the goods. If the required credit is unavailable, there may be a "failure of effective supply" in which firms fail to produce as much as they can sell' (1987, p. 328).

At the heart of this analysis is the point that it is not money, but credit and its availability that provide a better explanation regarding the linkage between monetary policy and changes in prices and output. Thus the credit view of monetary policy recognizes the indeterminacy of the linkages between changes in high-powered money and subsequent changes in economic activity. The reasons for this indeterminacy stem from the direct effect that changes in bank credit have on firm activity (production and investment) but also on the indirect effect that this rationed bank credit has on the supply and demand for credit between and among firms. This latter credit effect is not reflected in changes in the money supply since interfirm extensions of credit are not monetized by the banking system.

Within the context of firm liquidity positions, Stiglitz and Greenwald observe that there are significant 'distortion' effects with monetary policy affecting credit allocation that make problematic the total reliance on monetary policy in terms of stabilizing the economy:

> To be sure, any price change has distributional as well as allocative effects. But given how credit (capital) is allocated, the distributional effects should be given more weight, especially since the distributional impacts can have such allocative consequences. (Stiglitz and Greenwald, 2003, p. 197)

They identify three factors by which such distortionary factors may exacerbate the effects of monetary policy: the impact of rationed bank credit on small versus large firms; the extent to which the financing of inventories becomes problematic; and the widespread existence of intra-firm lending. Let us look at the first and the third.

Blinder and Stiglitz (1983) argue that the real effects of a monetary contraction might be minimal if there are good substitutes for loans, i.e., non-money loans. Large corporations are prone to selling more commercial paper should their working capital loans dry up at banks. However, while large corporations may have ready access to finance beyond the banking system, such may not be the case for small and intermediate size firms which do not have the capability of issuing commercial paper, especially without offering those debt instruments at higher rates of interest (see Hodgman, 1960; Blinder and Stiglitz, 1983; Greenwald and Stiglitz, 1993; Stiglitz and Greenwald, 2003; see also Dow, 1996). Wasmer and Weil suggest that macroeconomic fluctuations are exacerbated when small firms are unable to obtain the finance required to hire workers in advance of intended production: 'Since 40–60 percent of jobs are held in small firms (less than 100 employees), a theory of job creation and unemployment must deal with difficulties in *locating* credit' (2004, p. 945).

In addition to firms obtaining credit from banks, firms can find themselves acting as lenders on credit markets, either in the form of extending credit to other firms to finance accounts receivable or directly on the purchase of short-term debt liabilities. Under these expanded circumstances a contractionary monetary policy that causes interest rates to rise may very well dissuade firms from lending money to other firms (if there are the same types of potential asymmetries of information that are experienced by banks – firms ration credit to each other) or cause them to raise interest rates on those loans to other firms, which may worsen any liquidity problems faced by those firms that are already experiencing reductions in cash flow from reduced sales. Stiglitz and Greenwald suggest that there should be an expanded notion of a money multiplier effect (they refer to it as a *credit multiplier*) which would take into account both the impact that bank lending has on the extension of credit as well as the subsequent effects that intra-firm lending may have on access to credit. As such, these two restrictions on credit may have adverse consequences on output, employment and investment beyond those normally falling within the scope of the traditional money multiplier effect (2003, pp. 184–5).

Once these distributional consequences of credit rationing are brought into the picture, Stiglitz and Weiss conjecture that a perverse response to an expansionary monetary policy might occur – 'an outward shift in the supply of loanable funds could cause an increase in the average interest rate charged borrowers' (Stiglitz and Weiss, 1987, p. 230; see also Stiglitz and Weiss, 1992, p. 184).

Money, credit and prices

The shift in focus from money creation by banks over the course of economic activity to access to credit itself, both from banks and from interfirm lending, sheds new light on the relationship between changes in the amount of high-powered money and changes in the price level. The question addressed by New Keynesian writers has to do with the effects that the availability of credit will have on firms' pricing policies at different stages of the business cycle. There is a general consensus among New Keynesian writers that it is the supply side, in terms of effective supply failures and perhaps what could be called effective supply *successes* that are the preponderant factors in explaining the effects of monetary policies on output and prices:

> [I]n small open economies, weaknesses in economic activity may be more related to supply-side problems than to demand-side problems, so that accordingly it makes sense to focus on policies which operate on the supply side – and which operate in the short run. (Stiglitz and Greenwald, 2003, p. 193)

Suppose there is a monetary contraction which causes an increase in rationed credit and thereby a reduction in economic activity. Under such circumstances it is held that 'the effect of monetary policy [on output] is larger than when credit is not rationed' (Blinder, 1987, p. 351). The inability to gain access to credit by firms affects not only investment activity but also bears heavily on current cash flow exigencies. New Keynesians posit that if prices were to fall in light of a reduction in demand for their products, then in addition to the fall in profits there is also the effect on the firm brought about by a rise in the real value of their debt. Counterintuitive from a traditional neoclassical perspective where contracts are fixed in real terms (indexed to inflation), New Keynesians observe that such debt contracts tend to be fixed in money terms (see Blinder, 1987; Greenwald and Stiglitz, 1993; Stiglitz 2000; Stiglitz and Greenwald 2003). What is most intriguing is that they are baffled as to why the neoclassical tenets are violated:

> [W]hat stops prices from falling so fast that neither the real supply of credit nor real output has to decline, thereby robbing monetary policy of its real effects? . . . The . . . answer has to do with the fact – the unexplained fact – that many long-term contracts without complete indexation exist. We do not have a good explanation for this phenomenon. Neither does anyone else. But that does not imply that the consequences of nominal rigidities should be ignored. (Blinder and Stiglitz, 1983, p. 300)

> A major lacuna in this theory is the failure to explain why debt contracts are denominated in money terms. (Greenwald and Stiglitz, 1993, p. 29)[5]

> [E]conomic activity may depend on the nominal interest rate as well as the real interest rate, thus providing an explanation of one of the more disturbing anomalies in economics. . . . [S]tandard economic theory argues that investment should depend just on real interest rates, not nominal interest rates. Yet empirical studies seem to suggest the contrary. (Stiglitz and Greenwald, 2003, p. 3)

New Keynesian writers suggest that prices may *rise* rather than fall in light of a monetary contraction, flying in the face of another neoclassical conventional wisdom: '[I]f recessions are initiated by declines in supply, rather than by declines in demand, then prices may rise, not fall, as economic activity contracts' (Blinder, 1987, p. 328). Blinder explains this apparently perverse outcome by assuming that a reduction in credit availability will reduce demand for firms' products. Then, given the consequences of effective supply failures, firm supply will fall to a greater extent than demand, implying that excess demand will cause prices to *rise*. The rising prices will cause a reduction in real credit, reducing further the reductions in demand and supply, but with supply falling to a greater extent than demand. In fact, as Greenwald and Stiglitz point out, firms' demand for credit increases as sales fall, and, with the real value of that credit rising as access to credit does not rise, it is necessary for the mark-up of price over marginal cost to rise (1993, p. 29).

Stiglitz and Greenwald (2003) maintain that as output in the economy falls, 'the shadow price of capital increases', causing investment to fall and mark-ups to increase, 'implying that real wages fall *relative* to marginal productivities'. Thus, Blinder summarizes: 'when an economy is credit-constrained, it is subject to a kind of instability owing to inflation' (1987, p. 351).

One last word about this credit channel view of monetary policy seen in the context of credit rationing and fluctuations in effective supply. Just as the consequences of a restrictive monetary policy can be heightened, not because of monetary or interest rate effects but on account of the credit rationing that ensues, so too can the effects of an expansionary monetary policy be greater than posited by either of the traditional approaches. For the 'multiplier effects' of such policies would be greater than what had normally been considered given the greater access to credit both from the banking system and from within the corporate sector itself – there are now not only aggregate demand effects to this policy but aggregate supply effects as well. 'These supply-side effects are particularly worth drawing attention to, because they imply that economic activity can be increased without the threat of inflationary pressures (or in any case, with less of a threat)' (Stiglitz and Greenwald, 2003, p. 192).

Credit rationing – an assessment

The questions broached by the New Keynesian approach offer a degree of realism and insightfulness not often seen among the mainstream. The fact that they have attempted to push beyond the limits of the neoclassical framework by addressing the relationship between balance sheet changes in the financial sector (both in banks proper and with firms serving as providers of credit) and real sector activity (both in production and investment decisions) is laudable. They have come a long way, in their opinion, from the strictly closed framework that the mainstream offers. But should that concession to realism compel us to accept their contention that the economics of information represents a paradigmatic shift in economic theory and policy?

The literature from a post-Keynesian perspective concludes that they have not succeeded in that claim. For a paradigm shift cannot occur so long as they refuse to reject those heuristical devices that are decisively neoclassical. It is the consensus among most post-Keynesian writers that such a shift is possible only if they were to fold the interesting questions that they raise into Keynes's theory of effective demand, which subsumes but does not minimize the important components of what New Keynesians call effective supply. For it is only within this open system of thought that we can understand and identify clearly the sources and implications of questions of employment and pricing, investment *and* decisions to provide liquidity (at the level of financial institutions and the central bank). Left by the wayside must be the mainstream approach in which we think in terms of the microeconomics of markets for labour, capital and credit *then* leading to macroeconomic analyses which rely on those same heuristical frameworks. Any genuine paradigm shift must disavow a methodological individualism that insists on a microfoundation for macroeconomic behaviour.

A New Keynesian economist might object to that characterization, stating that the very idea of credit rationing forces the theorist to move beyond the simple analytics of supply and demand:

> The Law of Supply and Demand is not in fact a law, nor should it be viewed as an assumption needed for competitive analysis. It is rather a result generated by the underlying assumptions that prices have neither sorting nor incentive effects. The usual result of economic theorizing: that prices clear markets, is model specific and is not a general property of markets – unemployment and credit rationing are not phantasms. (Stiglitz and Weiss, 1981, p. 409)

What they fail to recognize is that there is a difference between beginning their inquiry with the language of a market while declaring it to be a failure under specified circumstances versus rejecting the very logic under which the conceptualization of markets and their macroeconomic reflections are admissible, as post-Keynesians would contend. The point is one of the highest importance: given how questions are posed will always lead to conclusions that limit the perceptual field of inquiry. No matter how they object and qualify the issues, the law of supply and demand in a methodological individualist framework in which microfoundations are the decisive mode of reasoning remains their law of motion, their underlying generative mechanism from which all else follows; no paradigm shift has occurred.

It is no wonder, therefore, that the New Keynesian methodology forces the thought process into the allocation of a given quantity of reserves – either allocated fully or rationed – at the micro level (see Rochon, 1999 and Piegay, 1999–2000), while following a logic which must begin with exogenous changes in the quantity of high-powered reserves to allocated loans (rationed or not) to macroeconomic consequences on output and prices:

$$\Delta \text{ monetary policy} \rightarrow \Delta M_{HP} \rightarrow \Delta L \rightarrow \Delta P, \Delta Q$$

And yet New Keynesian writers would not deny that credit rationing on the part of banks results in a money stock that is less than what it would be if all demanders were satisfied at the going rate of interest. They surely recognize that the money stock in this case rises to the extent that the demand for loanable funds is or is not satisfied. Moreover, enough New Keynesian writers have been intimately involved with the conduct of monetary policy, notably Alan Blinder and Ben Bernanke in the USA, to know that a federal funds target as a short-term indicator of monetary policy implies an accommodative (and thus endogenous) policy stance. Thus, with the qualification that suppliers of debt must be creditworthy, New Keynesian economists would not deny the inherent endogeneity of the money stock. And although this is a highly relevant question to post-Keynesian economists, New Keynesians find such questions of money endogeneity to be uninteresting from either a theoretical or a policy perspective because they are invisible within their realm of perception. The closed system nature of their world-view compels them to think only in terms of exogenous changes in high-powered money, their effect on loanable reserves (the asset side of the bank's balance sheet), and possible effects on economic activity (with the emphasis on matters of effective *supply*). Thinking about questions that might emanate from the demand side of the picture, or more aptly where forces of demand and supply interact (Keynes's theory of *effective demand*) simply does not fit.[6]

Post-Keynesian alternatives

> The differences between the two approaches stem ultimately from the difference between information as the basis of decision making, as in New Keynesian economics, and knowledge, as in post-Keynesian economics . . . While New Keynesian economics offers a sophisticated analysis of one aspect of credit creation, that aspect is too narrow to address the full role of credit portrayed by post-Keynesian analysis; nor does it provide a satisfactory monetary theory. (Dow, 1998, pp. 214–15)

The key element in the post-Keynesian critique of the literature on informational asymmetries is that the *information* is something that is known or is knowable (see Dymski, 1993; 1994; 1996; Kregel, 1995; Le Héron, 2002; Piegay, 1999–2000; Rochon, 1999; 2005; van Ees and Garretsen, 1993; and Wolfson, 1996). Information that can be elicited from the unique characteristics of the firm (the productivity of the capital and the competitive price at which the resultant product is sold) allows for the demand for the funds to underwrite those activities to be individuated – they are independent of the actions of any other individual in the economy.

Using the phrase *information* in this fashion leads to two conclusions: (1) we can speak of a unique relationship between a lender (a single bank) and a borrower (a single firm) without thinking of any other banks or firms in the economy; and (2) we are in a position to add up over all individual banks and firms to arrive at *the* credit market for industry as a whole. The first conclusion allows us to think in terms of *a* market for loanable funds, where the only salient factors are the characteristics of the individuals involved (including access to *information*). The second validates the New Keynesian methodology of thinking in terms of microfoundations for macroeconomic activity.

A post-Keynesian alternative to the narrowly defined and therefore closed nature of the New Keynesian system relies on a more open perspective on the relationship between the past, present and the future, especially with regard to the investment decision (the primary factor underlying the demand for money to finance those endeavours). Based on the writings of Keynes (1936) with elaboration by Shackle (see 1955; 1958), and extensive development by Davidson (1972; 1991; 1994), post-Keynesians recognize that this temporal relationship is not known by firms as they calculate the prospective yields of their capital assets. Rather, that knowledge is *uncertain*. *Knowledge* of events in the future may be uncertain either because it is too far ahead to provide any useful information for the present or because the expectations upon which individual decisions are made, and the confidence that entrepreneurs have in those expectations, must be predicated on perceptions of decisions and outcomes made by the collectivity of individuals. With regard to each of these senses in which the focus of attention changes to the uncertain basis of knowledge, Keynes observed:

> The outstanding fact is that the extreme precariousness of the basis of knowledge on which our estimates of prospective yield have to be made. Our knowledge of the factors which will govern the yield of an investment some years hence is usually very slight and often negligible. (1936, p. 149)

> Now prospective yield wholly depends on the expectation of future effective demand in relation to future conditions of supply. (Ibid., p. 212)

The latter statement implies that no individual firm can know the prospective yield on a capital asset independent of what will be supplied and demanded in the aggregate in the future. Then again, what will be demanded and supplied in the aggregate in the future will depend upon the individual decisions to consume and invest that are made today. Now each individual decision depends upon the aggregate of decisions, while the aggregate of decisions depends upon all individual decisions – each presupposes the existence of the other; neither can be reduced to the other. Under such circumstances, the conditions that underlie the demand schedule for a capital good by a firm, which would determine the amount of money it would need to finance that asset, are *uncertain*, in the sense that the prospective yield of that asset cannot be known independent of what is to occur by the organic interaction of all suppliers and demanders in the future. As Kregel concludes:

> It is not that information is incomplete, but that the information that the market requires simply does not exist, could not be discovered . . . Entrepreneurs have to form expectations about values of variables at future dates about which there is no currently existing 'objective' information . . . Since expectations are formed in part on the basis of the functioning of the economy and in part on the 'imagination' of entrepreneurs, they will have both endogenous and exogenous elements. (1995, p. 218)

What Kregel describes is the need for a more open methodology in which decisions both affect and are affected by the organically interdependent relationship between an individual and all individuals, again, where neither can be reduced to the other. Such a new methodology was provided by Keynes in what he called his *theory of effective demand* (see 1936, ch. 3), which defined for him a *monetary economy* whereby

> changing views about the future are capable of influencing the quantity of employment and not merely its direction. But our method of analyzing the economic behaviour of the present under the influence of changing ideas about the future is one which depends on the interaction of supply and demand, and is in this way linked up with our fundamental theory of value. (1936, p. vii)

Keynes defined the point of effective demand to be where aggregate supply equals aggregate demand. Both terms were defined in terms of *expected* proceeds (1936, pp. 24–5). Effective demand is different from the notion of both aggregate demand and supply, because it relates to the expectation that the proceeds received by each firm will reflect the proceeds that will justify their engaging in the productive process to begin with. Thinking in terms of the conditions underlying effective demand causes the mode of analysis to move beyond any form of methodological individualism/microfoundations for macro-economics. Moreover, thinking in terms of a theory of effective demand compels us to think in terms of economic activity occurring in real time, that is cyclically, as compared with the mainstream view that cyclical behaviours are ephemeral and provide no systematic information.

How do these conclusions affect the way we think about the questions of credit rationing and effective supply? First, since the investment decision is now based on the *prospective* yields of capital assets, which are uncertain rather than risky – because they rely on future effective demand – we are not in a position to think about questions of money and finance within a framework of a capital market or loanable funds theory of the rate of interest. Questions of credit rationing may be interesting matters to consider, but they require a framework that is profoundly different from the market-oriented microeconomics of rational banking behaviour. Second, questions of firm behaviour (banks included) must not be seen as independent of conditions of aggregate and effective demand, but rather as responsive to and contextualized in those two notions: while money was always endogenous even within a New Keynesian theory of credit rationing, such questions were invisible because demand for money took a back seat to the portfolio decisions of the banks themselves in light of their lack of knowledge of the ability of demanders to repay their loans. Third, once the methodological individualist/microfoundations approach is abandoned, it is not sufficient to ask the question: what is the impact of changes in the money supply on prices, output and employment? A theory of effective demand requires that it is just as relevant to ask questions about the impact that prices, output and employment have on the demand for money at the level of banks, and central bank responsiveness to those demands, as it is to inquire as to what might be the effects of a policy shift by central banks.

$$\Delta \text{ monetary policy} \longleftrightarrow \Delta M_{HP} \longleftrightarrow \Delta L \longleftrightarrow \Delta P, \Delta Q$$

Money endogeneity is as relevant as, or even more so than, questions about the purported exogeneity of the money stock.

A post-Keynesian perspective on money and credit rationing

Keynes's theory of effective demand was situated within a monetary theory of production, i.e., where contracts are fixed in money rather than real terms. The necessity of fixing contracts in money results from the need to make decisions today based on an uncertain future, recognizing that such decisions will affect some of the variables upon which those decisions are made (see Davidson, 1972). As such, contracting in real terms would be impossible for any individual, whereas contracting in money terms implies more rational decision making in light of an uncertain future. The key element is that not only does a monetary economy require contracts to be fixed in money terms, but there must be institutions created to ensure that employment, output and pricing decisions are monetized. There need to be institutions that can allow for the essential role that money plays in a monetary economy – there need to be both banks (and other financial institutions) and a central bank whose actions and policies allow for the finance and liquidity to be there when it is needed by the economy:

> Credit is the pavement along which production travels; and bankers if they knew their duties, would provide the transport facilities to just the extent that is required in order that the

productive powers of the community can be employed to their full capacity. (Keynes, 1930, p. 220)

There needs to be an inherent capability for an endogenous money supply.

Second, banks, like any other business, must make lending decisions on the basis of an uncertain future – borrowers do not know the prospective yields of their capital assets, nor do banks.[7] Wolfson suggests that

> borrower and lender will have different estimates of the uncertain likelihood that loans can/will be repaid, what he refers to as *asymmetric expectations*: all that is necessary for a theory of credit rationing based on Keynesian uncertainty is that borrower and lender evaluate the future differently – that is, that they have asymmetric expectations. (1996, p. 451)

Rochon (2005) elaborates on this idea when he observes that such expectations are founded on both individual and aggregate circumstances. He states that the expectations of lenders towards the likelihood of firms repaying their loans are therefore dependent upon factors partly unique to the borrower – Wolfson calls it the 'history of repayment' – plus cyclical circumstances that affect all borrowers.

In the same regard, Dow (1996) and Dymski (1998) make reference to the creditworthiness of borrowers within this broader post-Keynesian framework. Dow observes:

> If risk cannot adequately be determined using quantitative methods, the distinction between credit-worthy demand for credit and non-credit-worthy demand takes on heightened significance. In particular, since conventional judgment is more a macro than a micro phenomenon . . ., the issue of credit rationing and bank capitalization ceases to be a purely micro phenomenon. Rationing as a result of conventional judgment as to credit-worthiness may then apply to whole classes of borrowers. Insofar as the banks themselves might fall into such a class under particular market conditions, and find general difficulty in raising capital to back increased lending, rationing of the banks themselves could become a general phenomenon. (Dow, 1996, p. 500)

Dymski makes reference to 'the social construction of creditworthiness' (1998). Instead, knowledge by banks regarding the creditworthiness of potential borrowers (based on the principle of uncertainty that we are using here) has a social context, meaning 'that market opportunities themselves are endogenous and socially constructed at any point in time' (1998, p. 251).

Dow (1996), Dymski (1996), Rochon (1999) and Wolfson (1996) indicate a strong debt to Minsky's ideas on cyclical changes in financial fragility (Minsky, 1986) as reasons why lenders' expectation regarding the likelihood of borrowers ability to repay loans changes over the cycle (see also Fontana, 2004). Expectations thus become endogenous in a more open model of the economy (see Wolfson, 1996, p. 454; and Piegay, 1999–2000, p. 277). As such, one may find that banks might be more wary of lending available reserves when the perception of corporate balance sheets is that they are more financially fragile. Of importance is the extent to which the financial exigencies of corporations (and the nature of what is backing their demand for finance) and the liquidity preferences of banks both affect and are affected by fluctuations in effective demand and cyclical activity (see Monvoisin and Pastoret, 2003).

There is much more that can be addressed regarding the role of money and finance within a post-Keynesian framework than space allows. Two issues that could not be addressed fully are resolutions to the New Keynesian anomaly that contracts appear to be fixed in money, rather than real, terms, and that product prices may actually rise in light of monetary contraction and subsequent credit rationing. With regard to the former, it was one of the most important theoretical components of Keynes's *General Theory* to explain why it was *rational* for money wages and money rates of interest to be the important rates and how they comprised a key element in the theory of effective demand, and the assurance that the amplitude of economic fluctuations was never too great (see especially Davidson, 1972). Explanations of the second issue, from a post-Keynesian perspective within a more open system theory of effective demand, can be found in the writings of Eichner (1973), Gerrard (1989), Sawyer (1992) and Rotheim (1998c).

Final observations
The three conclusions that have been reached are:

1. Contrary to what New Keynesians have written, there is no merit to the assertion that the economics of information, directed here toward matters of credit rationing and failures in the market for loanable funds (emanating from asymmetric information), constitutes a paradigm shift in economic theory and policy. The approach taken by New Keynesian writers relies on the methodological individualism and microfoundations that are quintessentially neoclassical.
2. A true paradigm shift would need to discard the methodological individualist and microfoundations approach of New Keynesian in favour of an open systems approach reflected in Keynes's theory of effective demand. Then we could understand the role of money and credit both as endogenous and exogenous factors: it is expectations, not information, that may suffer from asymmetries.
3. A theory of effective supply suffers as well from the narrow methodological constrictions of its neoclassical roots. What New Keynesian economists hope to extract from analysis of effective supply failures owing to credit rationing simply cannot be plausible given the market-oriented framework upon which they rely. On the other hand, so much of what they hope to achieve in those interesting depictions of the effects of financial constraints on firm and bank behaviours do fit nicely within the open effective demand framework.

Notes
1. See Mankiw and Romer (1991) and Rotheim (1998a).
2. Stiglitz and Weiss (1981) make it clear that the theory of credit rationing identifies a situation of equilibrium, not temporary disequilibrium (p. 393).
3. It is not always clear whether Stiglitz and Weiss are assuming that the adverse selection effect is something that occurs in reality or in the minds of banks. Take, for example, the following statement: 'When the interest rate is raised slightly above r_1, the mix of applicants changes dramatically: all low risk applicants withdraw' (p. 397). Here, they seem to be implying that this adverse selection effect is actually occurring among potential borrowers.
4. 'That some loans are not repaid is central. A theory of monetary policy which pays no attention to bankruptcy and default is like *Hamlet* without the Prince of Denmark, and is likely to – and in the East Asia crisis, did – lead to drastically erroneous policies' (Stiglitz and Greenwald, 2003, p. 3; see also Greenwald and Stiglitz, 1993, p. 24).
5. See also Blinder (1977).
6. See Lavoie (2004), p. 18.
7. Keynes, of course, made reference to both borrower's and lender's risk in *The General Theory* (1936, p. 144). See also, Lavoie (1996) and Rochon (2005).

References

Blinder, A. (1977), 'Indexing the economy through financial intermediation', in Brunner, K. and Meltzer A. (eds), *Carnegie-Rochester Conference Series on Public Policy*, supplement, *Journal of Monetary Economics*, 5, 173–9.

Blinder, A. (1987), 'Credit rationing and effective supply failures', *Economic Journal*, June, 327–52.

Blinder, A. and Stiglitz, J. (1983), 'Money, credit constraints, and economic activity', *American Economic Review*, 297–302.

Davidson, P. (1972), *Money and the Real World*, London: Macmillan.

Davidson, P. (1991), 'Is probability theory relevant for uncertainty? A Post Keynesian perspective', *Journal of Economic Perspectives*, Winter, 129–44.

Davidson, P. (1994). *Post Keynesian Macroeconomic Theory*, Aldershot, UK and Brookfield, US: Edward Elgar.

Dow, S. (1996), 'Horizontalism: a critique', *Cambridge Journal of Economics*, July, 497–508.

Dow, S. (1998), 'Knowledge, information and credit creation', in Rotheim (1998a), 214–26.

Dymski, G. (1988), 'A Keynesian theory of bank behavior', *Journal of Post Keynesian Economics*, Summer, 499–526.

Dymski, G. (1993). 'Keynesian uncertainty and asymmetric information: complementary or contradictory?', *Journal of Post Keynesian Economics*, **16**(1), 49–54.

Dymski, G. (1994). 'Fundamental uncertainty, asymmetric information, and financial structure: "New" versus "Post" Keynesian microfoundations', in Dymski, G. and Pollin, R. (eds), *New Perspectives in Monetary Macroeconomics*, Ann Arbor, MI: University of Michigan Press, 77–103.

Dymski, G. (1996). 'Basic choices in Keynesian models of credit', in Deleplace, G. and Nell, E. (eds), *Money in Motion*, London: Macmillan.

Dymski, G. (1998), 'Disembodied risk or the social construction of creditworthiness?', in Rotheim (1998a), pp. 241–61.

Eichner, A. (1973), 'The theory of the determination of the mark-up under oligopoly', *Economic Journal*, 1184–200.

Fontana, G. (2004). 'Rethinking endogenous money: a constructive interpretation of the debate between horizontalists and structuralists', *Metroeconomica*, **55**(4), 367–85.

Friedman, M. (1970), *A Theoretical Framework for Monetary Analysis*, *Journal of Political Economy*, March/April, 193–238.

Gerrard, W. (1989), *Theory of the Capitalist Economy*, London: Blackwell.

Greenwald, B. and Stiglitz, J. (1993), 'New and Old Keynesians', *Journal of Economic Perspectives*, Winter, 23–44.

Hodgman, D. (1960), 'Credit risk and credit rationing', *Quarterly Journal of Economics*, May, 258–78.

Jaffe, D. and Russell, T. (1976), 'Imperfect information, uncertainty, and credit rationing', *Quarterly Journal of Economics*, November, 651–66.

Keynes (1930), *A Treatise on Money*, 2 vols. Reprinted as Vols V and VI, *The Collected Writings of J.M. Keynes*, London: St Martin's Press, 1971.

Keynes (1936), *The General Theory of Employment, Interest, and Money*. Reprinted as Vol VII, *The Collected Writings of J.M. Keynes*, Cambridge: Cambridge University Press, 1973.

Kregel, J. (1995), 'Keynes and the New Keynesians on the role of uncertainty and information', *Nouvelles perspectives de la macroéconomie: mélanges en l'honneur d'Alain Barrère*, Paris: Sorbonne.

Lavoie, M. (1996), 'Horizontalism, structuralism, liquidity preference and the principle of increasing risk', *Scottish Journal of Political Economy*, **43**(3), 275–300.

Lavoie, M. (2004), 'A Post-Keynesian amendment to the New Consensus on monetary policy', working paper, University of Ottawa, pp. 1–23.

Le Héron, E. (2002), 'La préférence pour la liquidité des banques: une analyse post-keynésienne du comportement bancaire', *Les Cahiers Lillois d'Économie et de Sociologie*.

Mankiw, N.G. and Romer, P. (1991), *New Keynesian Economics*, 2 vols, Cambridge, MA: MIT Press.

Minsky, H. (1986), *Stabilizing an Unstable Economy*, New Haven, CT: Yale University Press.

Monvoisin, V. and Pastoret, C. (2003), 'Endogenous money, banks and the revival of liquidity preference', in Rochon and Rossi (eds) (2003), pp. 18–40.

Piegay, P. (1999–2000), 'The New and Post Keynesian analyses of bank behavior: consensus and disagreement', *Journal of Post Keynesian Economics*, Winter, 265–83.

Rochon, L.P. (1999), *Credit, Money, and Production*, Cheltenham, UK and Northampton, MA, USA: Edward Elgar.

Rochon, L.P. (2005), 'Endogenous money, central banks and the banking system', manuscipt.

Rochon, L.P. and Rossi, S. (eds) (2003), *Modern Theories of Money: The Nature and Role of Money in Capitalist Economies*, Cheltenham, UK and Northampton, MA, USA: Edward Elgar.

Rotheim, R. (1998a), *New Keynesian Economics/Post Keynesian Alternatives*, London: Routledge.

Rotheim, R. (1998b), 'New Keynesian macroeconomics and markets', in Rotheim (1998a), pp. 51–70.

Rotheim, R. (1998c), 'On sticky prices: A Post Keynesian perspective', in Arestis, P. (ed.), *Method, Theory and Policy in Keynes: Essays in Honour of Paul Davidson*, vol. 3, Cheltenham, UK and Lyme, USA: Edward Elgar, pp. 147–74.

Sawyer, M. (1992), 'The nature and role of the market', *Social Concept*, 25–45.

Shackle, G. (1955), *Uncertainty in Economics*, Cambridge: Cambridge University Press.

Shackle, G. (1958), *Time in Economics*, Amsterdam: North-Holland.

Stiglitz, J. (2000), 'The contributions of the economics of information to twentieth century economics', *Quarterly Journal of Economics*, November, 1441–78.

Stiglitz, J. (2002), 'Information and the change in the paradigm in economics', *American Economic Review*, June, 460–501.

Stiglitz, J. and Greenwald, B. (2003), *Towards a New Paradigm in Monetary Economics*, Cambridge: Cambridge University Press.

Stiglitz, J. and Weiss, M. (1981), 'Credit rationing with markets with imperfect competition', *American Economic Review*, **71**, 22–44.

Stiglitz, J. and Weiss, M. (1987), 'Credit rationing: reply', *American Economic Review*, **77**(1), 228–31.

Stiglitz, J. and Weiss, M. (1992), 'Asymmetric information in credit markets and its implications for macroeconomics', *Oxford Economic Papers*, **44**, 694–724.

Van Ees, H. and Garretsen, H. (1993), 'Financial markets and the complementarity of asymmetric information and fundamental uncertainty', *Journal of Post Keynesian Economics*, **18**(1), 37–48.

Wasmer, E. and Weil, P. (2004), 'The macroeconomics of labor and capital market imperfections', *American Economic Review*, September, 944–63.

Wolfson, M. (1996), 'A Post Keynesian theory of credit rationing', *Journal of Post Keynesian Economics*, **18**(3), spring, 443–70.

20 Liquidity preference theory
Jörg Bibow

To ditch or to build on it?

The theory of liquidity preference is probably the single most controversial of the core constituents of *The General Theory*. Keynes presented a 'liquidity [preference] theory of interest', a theory that is supposed to fill the vacuum left by what he regarded as the flawed 'classical [savings] theory of interest'. In the early post-*General Theory* literature, the notion of liquidity preference quickly became a synonym for the demand for money. Together with a constant stock of money, liquidity preference was the factor that determined the rate of interest in the money market of Hicks's seminal IS–LM model. The novelty of Keynes's contribution was widely seen in the speculative motive for the demand of money only. And his revolutionary claim regarding the flawed classical theory of interest that needed replacement seemed ill founded when Hicks (1939) declared that liquidity preference and classical (loanable funds) theories were 'equivalent'.

Within the broader context of developments in postwar monetary and macroeconomic thought, this was but one element in weaving (or 'synthesizing') Keynes's supposedly 'general' theory into the essentially unshattered neoclassical mainstream by relegating the relevance of his insights to special circumstances that could potentially arise in the short run if money wages were sticky (Modigliani, 1944). Correspondingly, in policy matters, monetary policy was stylized as a short-run tool that could help stabilize the economy by controlling the supply of money – with the money neutrality postulate firmly upheld as far as the long run is concerned. Friedman thought that Keynes's liquidity trap concerns were of little practical relevance. Especially with a steady growth in the money stock, the money demand function would be sufficiently stable to allow self-adjusting market forces to stay on target. According to his vision there should be no interest rate manipulations by central bankers as the markets, merely anchored by steady base growth but not otherwise under any policy guidance, would grind out whatever productivity and thrift might require at any time (Friedman, 1960; 1968).

Kaldor's (1982) defence against the monetarist avalanche was as much a rejection of the view that while the money stock could be effectively controlled, macro policies could not be applied to deliberately stabilize the economy, as it was a critique of Keynes's liquidity preference theory which had inspired Friedman's monetary thought. Kaldor argued that the monetary authorities controlled the short-term rate of interest but had no control over 'the' money stock, and that Keynes was wrong in *The General Theory* to give such an impression and make liquidity preference theory a building block in his attack on the classics. Kaldor's critique of the new monetary orthodoxy has found many followers among post-Keynesians, many of whom today regard liquidity preference theory as a cul de sac and obstacle to an alternative monetary theory.

This is a regrettable misapprehension of liquidity preference theory. I argue that liquidity preference theory provides a suitable analytical framework for investigating the role of monetary policy and the financial system, offering insights that are of great relevance today, in both theory and practice.

Filling the gap – the liquidity (preference) theory of interest

It is crucial to remember that Keynes diagnosed the theory of interest as the fatal flaw in the (neo)classical orthodoxy he was attacking. In *The General Theory*, he emphasized that decisions to spend or not to spend must not be confused with the separate and subsequent decision to either hold wealth in the form of money or some other asset. Not denying that the rate of interest affects decisions to invest and consume, his point was that the classics got it wrong in allocating the determination of the rate of interest at the level of *spending/saving decisions*. Instead, the rate of interest – while being one determinant of effective demand – is 'determined *exogenously* with respect to the income generation process', as Pasinetti (1974, p. 47) put it.

The proper place of the theory of interest was at the level of *portfolio decisions*, Keynes argued. To him it seemed a purely logical step to require that at any time interest rates must be such that the general public's desire to hold money ('liquidity *par excellence*') rather than other financial instruments ceases at the margin given the amount of liquidity the banking system decides to provide:

> [T]he rate of interest at any time, being the reward for parting with liquidity, is a measure of the unwillingness of those who possess money to part with their liquid control over it. . . . It is the 'price' which equilibrates the desire to hold wealth in the form of cash with the available quantity of cash (*JMK* 7, p. 167).[1]

Keynes argued that he was simply stating the monetary principle from which to start in order to fill the gap left by the flawed classical theory of interest: 'And in stating what it is, I follow the books on arithmetic and accept the accuracy of what is taught in preparatory schools' (*JMK* 14, p. 215).

The 'finance motive debate' shed some important light on the matter. In reply to his loanable funds critics, Keynes acknowledged that in *The General Theory* he had not considered that 'an accumulation of unexecuted or incompletely executed investment decisions may occasion for the time being an extra special demand for cash' (*JMK* 14, p. 208). As a solution to the problem of providing the *extra finance*, therefore, what is needed, according to Keynes, is a 'technique to bridge this gap between the time when the *decision* to invest is taken and the time when the correlative investment and saving actually occur' (ibid., p. 208).

The crucial point is that the finance motive is a motive for the demand for money and that the need to secure 'finance' for any investment decision planned to be carried out *precedes* the actual investment and saving flows with which his loanable funds critics were preoccupied. Keynes's following remark neatly depicts his critics' confusion between saving and money or the 'loanable funds fallacy':

> Increased investment will always be accompanied by increased saving, but it can never be preceded by it. Dishoarding and credit expansion provides not an *alternative* to increased saving, but a necessary preparation for it. It is the parent, not the twin, of increased saving. (*JMK* 14, p. 281)

Accordingly, the vision of capitalism underlying *The General Theory* is one of finance rather than saving as the precondition for entrepreneurial investment activity. While this was equally true for his earlier *Treatise on Money* as well, it was probably due to the primary focus in the later work on the forces that 'determined the level of output and employment at any time' that the monetary implications (or requirements) of continuing *growth* in aggregate spending and economic activity were not fully spelt out. In the finance motive debate, Keynes then referred to this crucial point as the 'coping-stone' of the liquidity preference theory of interest, which would buttress his proposed theory against the savings theory of interest (cf. *JMK* 14, p. 220).

Whereas the finance motive debate focused on the rise-in-investment case, an earlier debate on the same matter that followed the publication of the *Treatise on Money* had focused on the case of a rise in thrift. In that earlier 'buckets-in-the-well' controversy Keynes had already proved his critics wrong on their idea that a rise in thrift would *directly and immediately* depress interest rates. Turning back to the earlier version of liquidity preference theory has at least two advantages. First, the *Treatise* apparatus was designed to investigate disequilibrium processes as characterizing business cycles – and the loanable funds issue concerns the disequilibrium adjustment process of the market rate of interest in response to changes in productivity and thrift. Second, Keynes analysed the role of the banking system as provider of liquidity in far more detail than in his later book – when the whole question of monetary policy control and endogenous money hinges on bank behaviour.

The loanable funds fallacy

On the first, the loanable funds question, Keynes's *Treatise* analysis pinpoints that an unforeseen rise in thrift implies a corresponding revenue shortfall on the part of the firms confronted with the rise in thrift, i.e. drop in sales. No matter whether they accumulate unplanned inventories or cut price, firms' cash flow falls short of expectations, and exactly by the amount of the rise in thrift. Essentially, then, saving does not lead to a rise in wealth, but a redistribution in wealth. Keynes's analysis makes it clear that loanable funds theorists are mistaken in focusing on one side of the transaction only, namely, the savers who may either hoard (hold deposits) or supply their saving in the loanable funds market. This overlooks that – by logical necessity – distressed firms, too, will be in the loanable funds market to somehow cover their cash-flow shortfall experienced in the current period in which households – unexpectedly – saved more. Interest rates may change in either direction owing to this change-in-distribution effect, as portfolio preferences of the parties concerned do not need to match. Interest rates may actually rise, though – falsifying loanable funds theory!

The drop in sales may well induce further adjustments in business and consumer behaviour and thus influence developments in subsequent periods. For instance, firms may conclude that the rise in thrift and drop in sales was not just a one-off event but might perhaps herald worse to come, and cut production accordingly. A deflationary cumulative process may thus be set in motion. But at which point would it end? The 'banana plantation parable' of the *Treatise*, in particular, shows that Keynes had not fully grasped at that time that a cumulative process of falling production, incomes and spending that might arise from such a thrift campaign could end before the complete collapse of production and incomes. In other words, he had not yet comprehended what he later dubbed the 'fundamental psychological law' that 'men are disposed, as a rule and on the average, to increase their consumption as their income increases, but not by as much as the increase in their income' (*JMK* 7, p. 96), which, as a practical rule, prevented the economic system from being wildly unstable and, intellectually, was a key insight in Keynes's development towards the theory of effective demand.

A related issue is that in marked contrast to the prominent role of mistaken expectations in the *Treatise*, short-term expectations of producers are generally assumed to be correct in *The General Theory*. In conjunction with the principle of effective demand, correct short-term expectations imply that producers can avoid the revenue shortfall associated with a *foreseen* drop in sales by a timely scale-back in production. This time round, then, it is savers' aspirations that get disappointed by being correctly anticipated: 'Saving will not even materialize; it will be frustrated if, quite independently, a corresponding demand to invest is not being exerted' (Pasinetti, 1997, p. 202). Neither is any correctly anticipated drop in sales of consumption goods likely to stimulate investment; quite the opposite. Nor is any supposed increase in the supply of loanable funds going to depress interest rates so as to stimulate investment in this way, as loanable funds proponents would have it. For the 'savers' have nothing to show for their 'planned savings' that got frustrated by being anticipated.

Whether unanticipated, as in the *Treatise on Money*, or correctly anticipated, as in *The General Theory*, outside the classical corn economy it is simply fallacious to consider saving as a source of funds that could finance investment. Instead, in monetary production economies, it is money, either existing hoards of it or as newly produced by banks (through their purchases of assets), that allows production of real things to go ahead.

The Keynes mechanism

There is one other way in which interest rates can be affected by a rise in thrift, though, even if *indirectly* only, and still move in the right direction. In the context of the finance motive debate Keynes expressed the point as follows:

> If there is no change in the liquidity position, the public can save *ex ante* and *ex post* and *ex* anything else until they are blue in the face, without alleviating the problem [i.e. the demand for *money*, not *saving*] in the least – *unless, indeed, the result of their efforts is to lower the scale of activity to what it was before.* (*JMK* 14, p. 222; emphasis added)

At issue here is the 'Keynes mechanism', which may be triggered not by any rise in thrift as such, but by the resulting falling off in the scale of economic activity. For it depends on the (planned) scale of economic activity what degree of pressure gets exerted on the 'pool of liquidity' provided by the banking system at any time.

The Keynes mechanism featured prominently in both the *Treatise on Money* and *The General Theory*. In practice, the *Treatise* perspective on mistaken sales forecasts and unplanned inventory adjustments may be highly relevant. On the financial side, the corresponding adjustments are likely to feature bank loans as working capital finance. From a purely theoretical viewpoint, however, Keynes chose to abstract from any 'haggling of the market' in *The General Theory* and focused on the equilibrium position as determined by the principle of effective demand. In this case, producers can avoid the initial run-up in inventories and recourse to working capital loans which often characterize the onset of a slump, but may reduce their demand for working capital loans in line with falling sales right away.

Endogenous money theorists rightly stress that *loans make deposits*. According to this view, though, money moves in parallel with economic activity. If, in a recession, firms manage to adjust their indebtedness to banks roughly in line with their shrinking business, the size of the banks' balance sheets would tend to shrink *pari passu*. At least, this would occur if banks did nothing else but *passively* accommodated firms' varying working capital requirements. Money would then be *endogenous*, purely credit-demand-driven.

Notice that this vision of banking describes bank behaviour as purely passive. The extreme 'horizontalist' position has it that banks, on the basis of prearranged credit lines, perfectly elastically meet any changes in credit demand. This possibility cannot be ruled out *a priori*. But how probable is this kind of business conduct? Clearly, one alternative course of action would be for banks to start to panic and claw back on their business, by enforcing tighter credit requirements and selling assets in particular. More generally, however, if banks are not overwhelmed by fears and uncertainties themselves, another course of action for them is to try to compensate for the falling off in loan demand by expanding their business in other directions. For instance, faced with weak loan demand banks might buy financial instruments such as bonds instead, especially if they expect rising bond prices, which, in turn, is not unlikely if they anticipate a monetary policy reaction to the incipient recession.

This pinpoints a key contrast between the endogenous money view and Keynes's 'constant-money-stock-assumption' (CMSA) of *The General Theory*. Clearly, for the stock of money to remain constant when the demand for working capital loans is falling off, for instance, banks must expand their business activities in other directions. In particular, they may decide to buy more bonds, thereby driving down bond yields. *The CMSA presupposes bank behaviour of this sort, whether policy-controlled interest rates are adjusted or not (yet)*. Textbook representations *à la* IS–LM feature a substitution between money held to satisfy the transactions motive (as a function of income) and money held to satisfy the speculative motive (as a function of the rate of interest). Since banks issue their liabilities by buying assets, ignoring the substitution taking place on the asset side of banks' balance sheet tells at best only part of the story. It may actually miss out the true underlying driving force – featuring active bank behaviour. As Keynes stressed, 'in general, the banking system holds the key position from a lower to a higher scale of activity' (*JMK* 14, p. 222).

Analytically speaking, the Keynes mechanism is driven by the banks' profit motive; it presupposes both agile behaviour on the part of banks and unchanged liquidity preference of the general public. The Keynes mechanism describes an *indirect* interest rate channel featuring a liquidizing effect caused by a tendency on the part of banks to try to prevent a falling-off in profits due to slack business in any one particular direction by expanding their activities in alternative ones instead – and vice versa. This should at least tend to lessen the deflationary effects of increased thriftiness. The tendency of interest rates to fall would not be due to any increased supply of saving offered on the loanable funds market, though, but to an increased supply of liquidity relative to the scale of economic activity.

While defining the rate of interest in *The General Theory* as the price which equilibrates the desire to hold wealth in the form of money with the available liquidity and focusing the analysis on the motives behind the 'unwillingness of those who possess money to part with their liquid control over it' (*JMK* 7, p. 167), the finance motive debate led up to a more symmetric statement of the liquidity preference theory of the rate of interest, featuring the 'interplay of the terms on which the public desires to become more or less liquid and those on which the banking system is ready to become more or less unliquid'

(*JMK* 14, p. 219). The crucial role of the banking system was thus moved back into the limelight. The finance motive brings to the forefront the importance of the behaviour of the banking system and shows that liquidity preference theory is also a theory of financial intermediation. Yet, at any moment in time a certain pool of liquidity is provided by the banking system and, when taken in conjunction with the demand for liquidity by non-banks, liquidity preference theory collapses into a theory of the rate of interest, as one of the determinants of the level of economic activity at that time.

Notice, however, that – essentially – the theory only spells out the equilibrium condition for interest rates and asset prices, namely that they must be such that all existing assets are willingly held at current prices, including the banking system, which must be 'satisfied' with its balance sheet position at those rates. The theory does not explain any particular equilibrium level of interest rates and asset prices, though. It neither explains why the general public's liquidity preference (or, propensity to hoard) is what it is at any time, nor why the banking system provides a certain amount of liquidity at any time, and neither more nor less.

Presumably, this is what Hicks's (1939) 'bootstrap' critique referred to. What this critique overlooks is that Keynes's analysis in the *Treatise on Money* and *The General Theory* undermined productivity and thrift as the supposed real anchors of the rate of interest in neoclassical and loanable fund theories. For Keynes's analysis denied the working of the 'loanable funds mechanism', while featuring the 'Keynes mechanism' as one driving force behind interest rate *changes* instead. The rate of interest was thus decoupled from the real sphere, which the classics believed would uniquely determine its equilibrium level. Turning the classics' vision upside down, Keynes's analysis showed that it is the real sphere that has to accommodate itself to whatever rate of interest the financial system might come up with. This is not some unique equilibrium level of interest allowing the system to automatically adjust to its unique long-run full employment equilibrium, just *any* level of interest and asset prices which happens to satisfy views and conventions held in financial markets at any time.

Keynes's vision of monetary policy and financial markets

The neoclassical mainstream had a hard time accepting the liquidity preference part of Keynes's claimed revolution in economics – and thus the essence of the Keynesian revolution. Letting go of those real forces of productivity and thrift as unique anchors of the general equilibrium system of equations proved too hard a nut to crack for a profession under the spell of the 'veil of money' doctrine. To them liquidity preference theory seemed to, at best, add some interesting practical considerations to the otherwise unscratched structures of their real analytical building.

Therefore, Keynes was at pains to point out that the primary role of liquidity preference theory was to fill the gap left by the *flawed* classical theory of interest, referring to his innovation as a piece of pure logic. In truth, however, liquidity preference theory is much more than that. It was Keynes the brilliant mind and theorist who diagnosed the fatal flaw in the orthodox system. But Keynes the practising financial market player with his in-depth experience and understanding of the working of the financial system also added some flesh to the theoretical skeleton.

Keynes's analysis showed that it is the real economy that has to live with and accommodate itself to whatever terms the financial system might come up with. The terms of finance determined by the financial system in whatever ways condition the level of incomes and employment actually attained. The market adjustment mechanisms supposed to do the trick according to the classics were found either lacking (namely, the loanable funds mechanism) or impractical and risky (namely, downward wage flexibility) as far as the – supposedly – *automatic* attainment of macroeconomic equilibrium is concerned.

Therefore, the question was *how* economic policy should best be organized and applied to deliberately manage the economy with the aim of securing satisfactory macroeconomic performance. To Keynes this issue was not a yes or no question. For in his perception the real world was such that so-called market economies were *managed* economies anyway – the *laissez-faire* ideal of an automatically functioning free market economy was pure fiction. In particular, then and now, there is no way around the fact that real-world central banks conduct interest rate policies.

In Keynes's view, the failure to achieve satisfactory macroeconomic performance was generally due to inappropriate policy arrangements (the 'barbarous relic', for instance) and ignorance (the 'Treasury view' and loanable funds beliefs, for instance). It is most telling that right after diagnosing the conventional nature of the rate of interest – a convention that can prove durable *at any level* – Keynes turns to the role of the authorities:

> But it may fluctuate for decades about a level which is chronically too high for full employment; – particularly if it is the prevailing opinion that the rate of interest is self-adjusting, so that the level established by convention is thought to be rooted in objective grounds much stronger than convention, the failure of employment to attain an optimum level being in no way associated, in the minds either of the public or of authority, with the prevalence of an inappropriate range of rates of interest'. (*JMK* 7, pp. 203–4)

A good starting point is thus to acknowledge that interest rates do not automatically attain their unique equilibrium levels by some magic market mechanism, but are rooted in whatever beliefs may guide financial market participants' behaviour in conjunction with the authorities' policies (and whatever views may guide these).

The liquidity preference theory of bank behaviour

The 'excess-bearish factor' encapsulates the *Treatise* version of liquidity preference theory. It concerns the interaction between the demand for, and the supply of, money – determining the 'market rate of interest'. The portfolio decisions not only of the general public, but also of the banks, enter explicitly into play, where both parties' portfolio decisions are seen as being based upon a balancing of 'relative attractions' of the various forms in which wealth may be held (including expectations about future securities prices, which may be 'bullish' or 'bearish' in nature and of varying degrees). It is made explicit here that the banks may *decide* to adjust their portfolios, either in size and/or composition, both over the cycle as well as in the event of sudden changes in the 'state of bearishness' of the general public, for instance. The outcome, i.e. the stock of money in existence at any time, always depends on the banks' portfolio decisions.

For instance, the banking system of the *Treatise* may facilitate a changing degree of diversity of opinion within the general public ('two views') by providing advances ('financial loans') to the 'bulls' who therewith buy out the 'bears', the latter being content, for the time being, to hold more savings deposits at rising securities prices. Furthermore, the banks themselves may, perhaps, disagree with the public and take a varying amount of securities off the market (at some price). In particular, only to the extent that the banking system does *not* meet the changing requirements on the part of the public will such changes affect securities prices, the '*excess*-bearish factor', which includes the possibility that the banking system not only fails to compensate for, but might even aggravate, such changes. The excess-bearish factor represents a theory of the 'market rate of interest' in terms closely similar to the liquidity preference schedule of *The General Theory*, albeit featuring the general public *and* the banking system the role of which is not hidden behind the assumption of an 'exogenous' quantity of money (*JMK* 5, p. 128).

Essentially, expressed in Wicksellian terms, monetary factors work through their impact on the 'market rate of interest', a departure from the 'natural rate' of which sets off saving–investment *disequilibria* and, hence, profit inflations (or deflations). The authorities should thus aim at making the market rate of interest match the natural rate. Yet the monetary authorities' control over the market rate of interest is not taken for granted in the *Treatise*. Keynes not only identified the various motives for the public's demand for money by distinguishing various types of deposits provided by banks to meet these motives, but also offers an analysis of the process of supply of these deposits along liquidity preference lines: the *Treatise* features a liquidity preference theory of bank behaviour.

Importantly, Keynes's vision of banking business extended well beyond the mere provision of working capital finance; itself being procyclical. One may think of Keynes's banks either as 'universal banks' or consider that hedge funds, for instance, rely on banks for their leveraging too. According to Keynes, the banking system has a 'dual function' (cf. *JMK* 6, pp. 310–11), including a role in the financing of fixed investment (be it directly or through underwriting the liquidity of other financial intermediaries and markets).

One aspect stressed by Keynes is that banks are *not* driven by their depositors, as the traditional deposits-make-loans view would have it. Instead, he diagnosed an important element of inherent instability due to the interdependence of banks that leads to a 'tendency towards sympathetic movement on the part of the individual elements within a banking system' (*JMK* 5, p. 23). Without any central anchor, the system's overall stance would just be whatever 'average behaviour' of banks (not depositors!) happens to be.

Another aspect concerns the 'interchangeability of non-reserve bank assets'. This aspect featured prominently in the Keynes mechanism discussed further above and represents the core of Keynes's liquidity preference theory of bank behaviour. Banks are pictured as *actively* managing their balance sheets. In deciding about the form of their lending, or the division of their resources in different forms of investment available to them, they balance profitability considerations as against liquidity (i.e. market risk) considerations. In an uncertain world, moreover, this balancing job represents a 'never-ceasing problem', since the strength of various considerations is continuously varying over time with changing circumstances:

> what bankers are ordinarily deciding is, not *how much* they will lend in the aggregate – this is mainly settled for them by the state of their reserves – but in *what forms* they will lend – in what proportions they will divide their resources between the different kinds of investment which are open to them. (*JMK* 6, p. 59)

Keynes also offered some explanations for these fluctuations in banks' portfolio proportions. In particular, these fluctuations may be due to variations in the banks' customers' *demand for advances*. Keynes viewed banks as applying judgement to the issue of whether or not to accommodate their customers' changing requirements. Distinguishing between trade customers and 'speculative movement[s]', he pointed out that banks' judgement appears to concern both microeconomic and macroeconomic issues, and that banks' own liquidity preference may change too. Most importantly, even to the extent that banks accommodate the variations in their customers' demand for advances, this would at best make one component of their overall balance sheet *endogenous*. For in Keynes's view banks would try to compensate such endogenous variations in their loan business by employing their resources in alternative directions (cf. *JMK* 6, pp. 59–60).

Keynes's key question is how a central bank can best frame and use 'means of establishing an unchallengeable centralised control over [the banks'] aggregate behaviour' (ibid., p. 190), and thereby over the market rate of interest. Keynes is particularly interested in methods of control that yield *direct* influence over *longer-term* rates of interest. He distinguished between customary ways of making bank rate 'effective', i.e. securing control over short-term rates, and open market operations directed at steering longer-term rates too. To some extent the latter provided an additional method of securing control over the system. But Keynes stressed that short-term and longer-term rates were related and that the term structure of interest rates was largely driven by bank behaviour.

In applying his liquidity preference theory of bank behaviour to the varying proportions of short-term and long-term securities in banks' portfolios (and the related issue of the yield curve), Keynes explicitly referred to the banks' profit motive and concern about their reputation as being both behind their individual behaviour as well as the element of self-fulfilling prophecy in banks' credit creation that is related to the inherent instability in banking referred to above (cf. *JMK* 6, p. 320).

Just as it is due to the banks' concern about their own profitability – and hence their capital base – that they respond to a falling-off in profitability in any particular form of lending, either due to slack demand (business cycle) and/or market yields obtainable (term structure), by looking for alternative kinds of investment. It is by playing on banks' own profit motive, then, that the central bank will normally be able to draw the banking system in the desired direction as the

> member banks will soon begin, if only to maintain their profits, to second the efforts of the central bank by themselves buying securities. This means that the price of bonds will rise unless there are many persons to be found who, as they see the prices of long-term bonds rising, prefer to sell them and hold the proceeds liquid at a very low rate of interest. (*JMK* 6, p. 333)

Notice here that this remark features the liquidity preference of the general public as satisfied by the banking system as a whole. For Keynes also addressed the possibility that the central bank may have to shoulder the task alone.

Follow your leader – or not

This was in his most illuminating discussion of situations where 'the normal and orthodox methods by which a central bank can use its powers for easing (or stiffening) the credit situation' fail to work. Extreme situations can develop (like an 'obstinate persistence of a slump') that are characterized by increased uncertainty and depressed financial sentiment and the emergence of a 'very wide and quite unusual gap between the ideas of borrowers and of lenders in the market for long-term' (*JMK* 6, p. 334), with the result that banks may refuse to second the efforts of the central bank. As alluded to in his advice, the central bank should then be under duty to take recourse to 'extraordinary methods', namely carrying out open market operations in long-term securities *à outrance*, that is, '*up to a price far beyond what it considers to be the long-period norm*' (ibid.).

Keynes did not elaborate on what the central bank might consider to be 'the long-period norm' on this occasion, how it comes about, and whether it is some sort of *unique* norm. Apart from the possibility of a serious impairment of the capital base of banks (reflecting *past* asset price drops and frozen loans), banks' refusal to 'second the efforts of the central bank' would seem to reflect their own liquidity preference in view of *prospective* losses they perceive as likely to result if they followed suit. In particular, banks may refuse to engage themselves beyond what *they* consider the long-period norm for fear that a future reversal of positions may involve a 'serious financial loss'. In other words, the expectation of a renewed future rise in interest rates prevents them from expanding their holdings of long-term securities – a liquidity trap prototype. Keynes had more to say on this coordination problem between the central bank and banks in *The General Theory*.

Expectations management and liquidity traps
In fact, in *The General Theory* Keynes provided the theoretical blueprint for steering market expectations in line with policy intentions as a key part of effective monetary policy conduct, much discussed today under the headings of policy communication and credibility. This advance in practical policy matters has to be seen in the light of the breakthrough represented by the theory of effective demand and the evolution of liquidity preference theory between the two works. The former stroke of genius irreparably undermined the Wicksellian notion of the 'natural rate of interest', uniquely determined by the legendary real forces of productivity and thrift. With the anchor gone, the rate of interest was left in the air. And as the market rate of interest itself attained the pivotal role as the centre of gravitation, liquidity preference theory too assumed a new role: as a theory of interest. Hence money was seen as ultimately 'ruling the roost' of real activity and accumulation.

While the substance of liquidity preference theory remained essentially unchanged, Keynes presented a greatly simplified version of it in *The General Theory*, particularly as far as bank behaviour was concerned. Essentially, the excess-bearish factor, the element his critics had most difficulties with, was set on neutral by means of the CMSA. Yet the part played by liquidity preference is at the same time made even clearer: the rate of interest is established at any time at that level at which the desire for extra liquidity vanishes at the margin; an *attempt* to become more liquid changes the rate of interest forthwith. The new truncated excess-bearish version simplifies Keynes's analysis without distracting from the essence of his theory of effective demand, namely, that it is spending, and investment spending in particular, that is driving the system.

In this regard, the CMSA makes it clear that, for instance, an increase in the level of economic activity may affect interest rates *indirectly* simply due to the changing requirements of the industrial circulation (the transactions motive), *if* the banking system does not duly enlarge the pool of liquidity. This shows that purely *monetary* factors condition the equilibrium level of *real* activity. They do so not only at the new higher level of activity (perhaps prompted by a rise in the marginal efficiency of capital) which is sustainable even at higher interest rates, but also at the initial level of economic activity. By implication, there is no unique long-period equilibrium, independent of the 'banking policy'. With another banking policy, the long-period equilibrium would probably be different too.

The issue of controlling bank behaviour and the market rate of interest thus appeared in a different light too. With the rate of interest rooted in convention rather than anything real and unique, the question arose to what extent market conventions may be subjected to deliberate management. Again, government interventions in the market such as interest rate policies by central banks are a fact of life anyway. And bank rate policy itself was of no concern to Keynes since the 'short-rate of interest is easily controlled by the monetary authority' (*JMK* 7, p. 203), in both theory and common practice. While the short rate affects bank behaviour and other interest rates and asset prices, the real issue was whether monetary policy could be made more effective by using tools beyond simply setting bank rate. Keynes distinguished direct effects due to market dealings and changes in liquidity from an expectational channel.

Central to Keynes's theory of the determination of interest rates is the speculative motive for the demand for money, defined as 'the object of securing profit from knowing better than the market what the future will bring forth' (*JMK* 7, p. 170). The speculative motive is also seen as central to the working of open market operations: 'it is by playing on the speculative-motive that monetary management . . . is brought to bear on the economic system' (ibid., p. 196). For the interest-elasticity of 'the' liquidity preference schedule is largely due to the speculative motive. However, analytically speaking, 'the' liquidity preference schedule is based on some given state of expectations. Expectations are seen as an integral part of monetary management, since expectations about future monetary policy feature as a chief factor in moulding 'the' given state of expectations. Keynes thus argues that open market operations actually work through two channels: 'they may not only change the volume of money, but may also give rise to changed expectations concerning the future policy of the central bank or of the government' (ibid., p. 197).

It is thus *not* that Keynes believed in some *stable* and *unique* liquidity preference schedule. Open market operations can hardly fail immediately to affect the prices of securities dealt in to some degree. For 'in normal circumstances the banking system is in fact always able to purchase (or sell) bonds in exchange for cash by bidding the price of bonds up (or down) in the market by a modest amount' (ibid.). But there may be rather narrow limits to playing on the speculative motive by moving interest rates away from what is considered a 'fairly safe rate' – *in some given state of expectations.*

Therefore, in order to be fully effective, open market policies directed at longer-term securities must lead to a change the state of expectations in the desired direction. In Keynes's view, full effectiveness largely depends on the *credibility* of the actions undertaken, and the institution undertaking them – in particular, whether monetary policy 'strikes public opinion as being experimental in character or easily liable to change', or whether it 'appeals to public opinion as being reasonable and practicable and in the public interest, rooted in strong conviction, and promoted by an authority unlikely to be superseded' (*JMK* 7, p. 203). Again, if there is a monetary policy at all, the monetary authorities cannot help but greatly influence expectations about future policy anyway. The only question is whether they succeed in aligning market expectations with policy intentions and thus marshal the markets support of policy.

For example, in the 1930s, the task was to steer the conventional view downwards. And, by and large, Keynes ventured, 'precisely because the convention is not rooted in secure knowledge, it will not always be unduly resistant to a modest measure of persistence and consistency of purpose by the monetary authority' (ibid., p. 204). The British experience after the departure from the gold standard in September 1931, i.e. the relaxation of the external constraint which featured in the *Treatise*, followed by the successful War Loan conversion in 1932, seems to have encouraged this judgement. Keynes used this example to illustrate his case in *The General Theory*. '[M]odest falls' to which public opinion can be 'fairly rapidly accustomed' are distinguished there from 'major movements . . . effected by a series of discontinuous jumps'. The former would appear to be the direct result of open market purchases, playing – within limits – on the speculative motive in a given state of expectations. The minor movements so achieved successfully prepared the ground for the major ones, the 'series of discontinuous jumps', corresponding to *shifts* in the liquidity function of the public (ibid.).

Is there a limit to such policies? Keynes repeatedly refers to what may be seen as some *absolute floor* below which interest rates, seemingly, could never fall. But he believed that: 'whilst this limiting case might become practically important in future, I know of no example of it hitherto' (ibid., p. 207). In fact, the point he is making about the limitations of monetary management is not at all restricted to this hypothetical absolute floor. The problem Keynes described exists at *any* level of interest: if open market purchases drive up securities prices, their running yields so reduced will compensate for *less* perceived risk of a renewed future rise in interest. Yet, in a given state of expectations, this risk *rises* the further the rate of interest deviates from what is considered a 'fairly safe level' in that state of expectations. *Ceteris paribus* investors prefer to move into a more liquid position – the trade-off which provides the basis for the authority's playing on the speculative motive. A limit is reached when selling pressure due to securities holders' move into cash fully offsets the upward price pressure due to open market trades. At that point the central bank has lost effective control: the system is in *a* liquidity trap. This condition may arise at *any* level of interest. There is correspondingly a *multiplicity* of liquidity traps.

This problem would not arise, however, if the authorities managed to shift the state of expectations in the desired direction. The market participants' assessments of risk of capital losses largely depend on their expectations of future rates of interest. This risk would not rise with falling yields if participants trusted that lower yields would stay low for some time. Best of all, views about the fairly safe level of interest fall together in line with market yields and a new convention as to the appropriate rate of interest gets established. Securities would then willingly be held at higher prices even without any increase in cash (at least as far as the speculative motive is concerned).

In practice, open market purchases of securities may at the same time move market yields directly, thereby *ceteris paribus* enlarging the liquidity of the system correspondingly (liquidity channel), and successfully steer the convention itself downwards too (expectational channel). In this case, the increased liquidity so provided would not actually be required to make good for any rise in perceived market risk, i.e. to particularly satisfy the speculative motive, but to balance the reduced spread (opportunity cost of holding cash) instead, i.e. to satisfy the demand for liquidity more generally. But Keynes's theoretical observations also include the possibility that the state of expectations may move in the wrong way. In that case the expectational channel may *counteract*, and possibly more than fully, any effect on interest rates coming through the liquidity channel. More generally, then, one may consider policy communication as the key tool directed at steering market expectations in line with policy intentions, backed up by the possibility of actually carrying out open market operations if that threat is held credible by the markets.

To summarize: due to the insight that 'the' long-period norm is established by *some* convention Keynes became far more alert to the complexity of influence of monetary policies on interest rates. In theory, the problem is that the convention the financial system comes up with may be wrong – and the economy get stuck in an unemployment equilibrium as a consequence. In practice, 'the' convention is moulded largely by monetary policy itself anyway, but the authority may fail to change it when needed – namely for failure of convincing the banks to follow suit.

This pinpoints the essence of Keynes's liquidity preference theory as applied to the theory of monetary policy, including the management of expectations.

A vanishing role for money and banks, and liquidity preference theory?

The pivotal role of banks as providers of liquidity is to be seen in the fact that under normal conditions the central bank, while underwriting the liquidity of the financial system, provides an ever smaller share of what is considered 'liquidity *par excellence*' by the general public and its institutional investment agents (be it pension funds or hedge funds). Satisfying an enlarged liquidity preference of the general public will be no issue as long as the banks 'second the efforts of the central bank', Keynes argued. Actually, this need not occur in response to policy changes but is likely to happen in anticipation of it, particularly if policy communication works properly. Two-way interaction between markets and the central bank is involved here.

I emphasized above that the 'Keynes mechanism' – and active bank behaviour more generally! – is at work at any given monetary stance. Surely banks' incentive to take more bonds off the market when their loan demand is falling off will be enhanced should they anticipate that the central bank will cut the short-term rate in reaction to a weakening economy too. In this way, as is sometimes observed, the bond market partly does the job for the central bank, and the central bank seems to follow the markets, seemingly just signing off the markets' 'policy'.

Actually, however, the bonds markets will only do so without bank support if the liquidity preference schedule smoothly adjusts accordingly, which, in turn, depends on the expectation management and credibility of the central bank. Markets strive for profits, but the markets can only properly do the central bank's job if it is fairly safe to anticipate the central bank's moves, which is equally true for the banks in so far as the system requires enhanced liquidity provision in moving to lower interest rates. Notice that the role of banks includes the possibility that the banks themselves may be key drivers in markets, enhancing the general public's demand for liquidity by driving up securities prices.

By contrast, the burden of liquidity provision would rest on the central bank's balance sheet alone if the banks declined to second its efforts, a refusal which may either be due to an impaired capital base or to the perceived riskiness of following suit. For one thing, an impaired capital base may be the legacy of erroneously following a monetary policy course that turned out ill guided. For another, the perceived riskiness of following the central bank depends on whether market expectations are aligned with policy intentions – whether the anticipated course of policy is perceived sustainable by the markets.

Markets are forward-looking and all the time on the watch to anticipate policy anyhow. So there is always the risk that the markets may either misread policy if the central bank fails to get its message across. Or the markets may disapprove of it, anticipating that some particular policy course will turn out unsustainable, particularly if the markets went along with it. If a policy is perceived as unsustainable (and a reversal thus seems likely), seconding the efforts of the leader would not be in the banks' best interest. In fact, betting against the central bank may seem more profitable instead. This, once again, underlines that from the central bank's perspective managing market expectations is key to policy effectiveness. For causing market confusion or even provoking widespread market opposition may seriously disrupt the implementation of policy. Essentially, liquidity traps represent *communication failures* between the central bank and its clients, banks. A liquidity trap arises when the monetary authority – for lack of power and/or credibility – fails to communicate convincingly with the markets. Importantly, such potential complications are not restricted to the bond market.

In expounding his liquidity preference theory of interest in *The General Theory*, Keynes focused on debt markets, describing the central bank as a 'dealer in money and debts' (*JMK* 7, p. 205). Compared to the *Treatise* where Keynes referred more broadly to 'securities' as an alternative to bank deposits, he now emphasized that equities – as distinct from debts – were more closely related to the marginal efficiency of capital and 'animal spirits' too. This clarified that 'investment depends on a comparison between the marginal efficiency of capital and the rate of interest' (ibid., p. 151, n. 1), and it rightly denied any unique and stable relationship between debt and equity markets. None the less, Keynes's thoughtful account of 'spot-the-convention-type' of asset-market play in chapter 12 is clearly relevant to securities and derivative markets in general, including foreign exchange and property markets etc. Furthermore, as is clear from chapter 17 in particular, liquidity preference theory is a theory of asset prices more generally too.

Keynes argued there that it is the rate of interest on money which 'rules the roost' by setting 'the standard to which the marginal efficiency of a capital-asset must attain if it is to be newly produced' (ibid., p. 222). As regards his key concern in the book, he observed that

> unemployment develops . . . because people want the moon; – men cannot be employed when the object of desire (i.e. money) is something which cannot be produced and the demand for which cannot be readily choked off. There is no remedy but to persuade the public that green cheese is practically the same thing and to have a green cheese factory (i.e. a central bank) under public control. (Ibid., p. 235)

The point is that while controlling the short-term rate of interest is an easy thing to do in both theory and practice, the problem of monetary control does not end with the endogenous supply of reserves at that rate.

Short-term interest rates as directly controlled by the central bank affect asset prices in the economy both via arbitrage as well as market expectations, the latter channel being more complex and far less easily controlled. Given the background of a constantly changing competitive environment of financial innovation and re-regulation, liquidity preference theory offers a conceptual framework that allows proper assessment of the profound role of the financial system in monetary production economies – its role being that of providing liquidity and finance rather than saving, and on terms decided in a complex two-way interaction between markets and the authorities, terms to which the real economy must adapt itself – possibly with unacceptable macroeconomic outcomes.

If Keynes's vision needs updating, it is in the area of consumer finance and consumption spending. Keynes focused on entrepreneurs and investment as prime movers behind capitalism. Today, debt-financed consumer spending has become another key mover too.[2] This neither diminishes the relevance of the theory of effective demand and analytical framework of *The General Theory* nor the applicability of liquidity preference theory, though. Quite the opposite.

Some concluding observations on horizontalist heterodoxy, modern Taylor-rule orthodoxy and money neutrality

Post-Keynesian endogenous money proponents deserve high credit for stressing that 'loans make deposits' (rather than the other way round) and that real-world central banks control short-term interest rates (rather than monetary aggregates). Regrettably, starting from these sound observations, followers have often drawn conclusions that are true only under special conditions. In particular, the whole story about monetary policy and all that would seem to end with setting the short-term rate of interest. Banks passively meet any credit demand, money is endogenous, and money demand non-existent. Liquidity preference theory is worse than useless as it prevents reaching these insights, or so it may have seemed.

Yet pushing endogenous money in this corner represents a gross trivialization of monetary policy, banking and finance. From a liquidity preference theoretical perspective this describes no more than a primitive special case that does not yield any insights of interest beyond those profound propositions started out from. The point is: endogenous money is not the end of the story; it is just the starting point. Kaldor was right in stressing the role of financial innovation, but he failed to see how this relates to the behaviour of banks and other financial market players in liquidity preference theory. Another Cambridge economist, Richard Kahn, clearly understood the role of bank behaviour in liquidity preference theory:

> Other things equal, a larger quantity of money means lower interest rates, because it means that the banking system is taking a larger quantity of securities off the market, is assisting in greater measure in financing the holding of securities, and is reducing the extent to which securities have to be issued on the market in order to secure finance. . . . If the quantity of money is increased, this means that the banks have increased their assets, and in doing so they will have bid up the prices of securities, i.e. lowered rates of interest. (Kahn [1958] 1972, pp. 146–7)

It is thus of interest that the mainstream has recently shown some serious interest in financial market phenomena and instabilities that are hard to square with the 'efficient market' view, broadly under the heading of 'behavioural finance'. It is of no less interest that the mainstream has meanwhile largely converted to endogenous money, with monetary policy and macroeconomic modelling being recast in terms of interest rate reaction functions *à la* Taylor's rule. Without wishing to repeat our above critique, this approach too assumes that financial market expectations are automatically fully aligned with the intended course of policy so that the short-term rate is a good measure of the central bank's control over the financial system and the economy. Moreover, issues such as monetary and fiscal policy interaction, exchange rate developments and the state of the financial system are only taken into account indirectly through their effects on inflation and the output gap.

And yet one cannot fail to acknowledge that the modern mainstream theory of monetary policy has made some important progress towards Keynes's vision. Recall that Taylor's rule (as a generic form of inflation targeting) prescribes that the central bank should set its policy instrument (i.e. short-term interest rate) according to:

$$i^T = r^e + \pi^* + \gamma_1(\pi_t - \pi^*) + \gamma_2(y_t) \tag{20.1}$$

In this, i^T refers to the central bank's (nominal) target rate of interest. The three factors supposed to be considered when setting the 'Taylor rate' are: first, the equilibrium real rate of interest, r^e, second, an equilibrium or target rate of inflation, π^*, and, third, deviations from the target inflation rate and capacity output, where y_t is an output gap measure and γ_1 and γ_2 are feedback parameters measuring the strength of policy response to inflation and output, respectively.

Taylor's 'rule' is *not* a non-reactive rule for Friedman-style monetary arrangement. Instead, it follows the reaction function approach, requiring continuous adjustments in the policy instrument aimed at keeping the system in equilibrium through deliberate management. Furthermore, the rule would seem to at least partly incorporate the wisdom of three giants of monetary theory: first, Fisher's hypothesis concerning nominal and real interest rates; second, Wicksell's fundamental insight that it is not the absolute level of interest which matters, but the relative level (or 'spread') compared to some equilibrium rate of interest, and, third, Keynes's key result that monetary policy is of real importance to the level of employment too (output gap).

But this still leaves plenty of room for interpreting this approach along either Wicksellian or Keynesian lines – with the mainstream opting mainly for the former (see Woodford, 2001). Importantly, there is no substantial disagreement on the role of price stability in all this. Disagreement mainly arises when it comes to employment. Critical issues concern the equilibrium real interest rate and the output gap measure, neither of which are directly observable, but estimates for both of which are crucial to policy assessments by means of Taylor's rule. Keynes's key insight here was that there is no unique equilibrium rate of interest but a '*different* natural rate of interest for each hypothetical level of employment . . . in the sense that the system will be in equilibrium with that rate of interest and that level of employment' (*JMK* 7, p. 242).

The issue here is that the neutral rate is not only changing over time, but also, at any time, partly a legacy of past monetary policies. For instance, if a central bank successfully steered an economy around some predetermined 'natural rate of unemployment', *ex post* measurement by standard statistical tools would show that 'the' natural rate of employment was exactly that while 'the' equilibrium real rate of interest appearing in Taylor's rule may correspondingly be estimated as the historical average over that period of time. The point is: all of this is based on the *postulate* of money neutrality – and the statistical tools conveniently 'prove' the postulate by assumption. The same kind of proof could have been provided if monetary policy had been different, with unemployment fluctuating around some other 'natural' level. In fact, whichever course monetary policy adopts, the particular monetary policy adopted will shape the course of output and prices and, hence, tomorrow's policy environment too. And whatever course of policy and history may unfold, a reasonably good fit for *some* Taylor rule – including *some* average real interest rate! – can then be found to perhaps 'prove' that money was neutral, even though it wasn't.

As any serious economist knows, monetary policy's *long-run* real effects mainly arise from its impact on the capital stock. Kahn ([1958], 1972, p. 139) aptly warned against fighting inflation by causing unemployment:

> The economic waste involved in such a policy is particularly great if demand is regulated by restricting productive investment, as will be the main result of relying on monetary policy. Not only is there the loss of potential investment. But the growth of productivity is thereby curtailed, thus narrowing the limit on the permissible rate of rise in wages and increasing the amount of unemployment required to secure observance of the limit.

Surprisingly, when it comes to monetary policy in practice, central bankers who seemingly all share the conventional money neutrality conviction may still view the real world through rather different lenses – and act correspondingly different too. For instance, Federal Reserve Governor Ben Bernanke (2002) argued against the idea of pre-emptive tightening in 1997, as this 'would have throttled a great deal of technological progress and sustainable growth in productivity and output'. By contrast, the ECB's chief economist Otmar Issing does not miss any opportunity to assert that an exclusive focus on price stability is the best contribution monetary policy can possibly make to long-run economic growth too. After four years of domestic demand stagnation, Mr Issing simply declared that the eurozone's potential growth trend should be adjusted downwards (hint: so as to match actual dismal performance and 'measure away' the looming negative output gap for which the ECB routinely rejects any responsibility). Both central banks use standard statistical tools and follow conventional standards of economic 'science'. Money is neutral in either world of thought, it seems – but never in the real world, for sure!

No other than Milton Friedman lectured Mr Issing on the relevance of the money neutrality postulate in this world by declaring himself baffled by Mr Issing's suggestion that standard monetary neutrality propositions would be among the few results a prudent central banker can get comfort from. No such luck for central bank politicians; Friedman (2002) explained in such memorable words that we may leave it to *two* giants of monetary theory to conclude the whole matter, and this chapter too:

> Taken seriously, monetary neutrality means that central bankers are irrelevant: real magnitudes – which are what ultimately matter to people – go their own way, independently of what the central banker does. Central bankers are important insofar as money is not neutral and does have real effects. Neutrality propositions give little if any guide to effective central bank behaviour under such circumstances. Perhaps they offer comfort to central bankers by implying that all mistakes will average out in that mythical long run in which Keynes assured us 'we are all dead'. Keynes [*Tract on Monetary Reform*, 1923] went on, 'Economists [central bankers] set themselves too easy, too useless a task if in tempestuous seasons they can only tell us that when the storm is long past the ocean is flat again.'

Notes

1. Significant confusion exists in the literature as to the meaning of cash and money in Keynes's theory. Being an active financial market player himself, Keynes used the term 'cash' not as referring to notes and coins, but in the markets' sense as ready liquidity at hand. More generally, he explained that it 'is often convenient in practice to include in *money* time-deposits with banks and, occasionally, even such instruments as (e.g.) treasury bills. As a rule; I shall, as in my *Treatise on Money*, assume that money is co-extensive with bank deposits' (*JMK* 7, p. 167, n. 1). All references to the *Collected Writings of John Maynard Keynes* will hereafter be referred to by '*JMK*' followed by the volume and page numbers.

2. This is not to say that Keynes had nothing to say on this issue at all. On 'windfall changes in capital-values' see *JMK* 7, pp. 92–3 and 319. In today's context, adding property prices and mortgage finance does not diminish the importance of such concerns, but enhances it.

References

Bernanke, B.S. (2002), 'Asset-price "bubbles" and monetary policy', New York 15 October, *BIS Review* 59/2002.
Friedman, M. (1960), *A Program for Monetary Stability*, New York: Fordham University Press.
Friedman, M. (1968), 'The role of monetary policy', *American Economic Review*, **58**(1), 1–17.
Friedman, M. (2002), 'Comment on Gaspar and Issing', *Australian Economic Papers*, **41**(4), 366–8.
Hicks, J.R. (1939), *Value and Capital*, Oxford: Clarendon Press.
Kahn, R.F. ([1958] 1972), [Radcliffe] *Report of Committee on the Working of the Monetary System*, London: HMSO.
Kaldor, N. (1982), *The Scourge of Monetarism*, Oxford: Oxford University Press.
Keynes, J.M. (1971–89), *The Collected Writings of John Maynard Keynes* [*JMK*], 30 vols, London: Macmillan for the Royal Economic Society.
Modigliani, F. (1944), 'Liquidity preference and the theory of interest and money', *Econometrica*, **12**(1), 45–88.
Pasinetti, L.L. (1974), *Growth and Income Distribution – Essays in Economic Theory*, Cambridge: Cambridge University Press.
Pasinetti, L.L. (1997), 'The marginal efficiency of investment', in Harcourt, G.C. and Riach, P. (eds), *A 'Second Edition' of The General Theory* London: Routledge.
Woodford, M. (2001), *Interest and Prices. Foundations of a Theory of Monetary Policy*, Princeton, NJ: Princeton University Press.

21 Financial liberalization and the relationship between finance and growth
Philip Arestis

Introduction[1]

The relationship between financial development and economic growth has received a great deal of attention throughout the modern history of economics. Its roots can be traced in Lydia of Asia Minor, where the first money was in evidence. The first signs of public debate, however, on the relationship between finance and growth, and indeed on experiments with free banking, can be located in Rome in the year AD 33. In that year there was probably the first classic case of public panic and run on the banks. The Romans debated intensely and fiercely at that time the possibility of placing a hitherto free banking system under the control of the government. Since then, of course, a great number of economists have dealt with the issue. An early and intellectual development came from Bagehot (1873), in his classic *Lombard Street*, where he emphasized the critical importance of the banking system in economic growth and highlighted circumstances when banks could actively spur innovation and future growth by identifying and funding productive investments. The work of Schumpeter (1911) should also be mentioned. He argued that financial services are paramount in promoting economic growth. In this view production requires credit to materialize, and one 'can only become an entrepreneur by previously becoming a debtor . . . What [the entrepreneur] first wants is credit. Before he requires any goods whatever, he requires purchasing power. He is the typical debtor in capitalist society' (p. 102). In this process, the banker is the key agent. Schumpeter (1911) is very explicit on this score: 'The banker, therefore, is not so much primarily the middleman in the commodity "purchasing power" as a *producer* of this commodity . . . He is the ephor of the exchange economy' (p. 74).

Keynes (1930), in his *A Treatise on Money*, also argued for the importance of the banking sector in economic growth. He suggested that bank credit 'is the pavement along which production travels, and the bankers if they knew their duty, would provide the transport facilities to just the extent that is required in order that the productive powers of the community can be employed at their full capacity' (II, p. 220). In the same spirit Robinson (1952) argued that financial development follows growth, and articulated this causality argument by suggesting that 'where enterprise leads, finance follows' (p. 86). Both, however, recognized this as a function of current institutional structure, which is not necessarily given. In fact, Keynes (1936) later supported an alternative structure that included direct government control of investment.

Although growth may be constrained by credit creation in less developed financial systems, in more sophisticated systems finance is viewed as endogenous, responding to demand requirements. This line of argument suggests that the more developed a financial system is, the higher the likelihood of growth causing finance. In Robinson's (1952) view, then, financial development follows growth or, perhaps, the causation may be bidirectional. However, McKinnon (1973) and Shaw (1973), building on the work of Schumpeter (chiefly 1911), propounded the 'financial liberalization' thesis, arguing that government restrictions on the banking system restrain the quantity and quality of investment (see, for example, Arestis and Demetriades, 1998, for further details). More recently the endogenous growth literature has suggested that financial intermediation has a positive effect on steady-state growth (see Pagano, 1993, for a survey), and that government intervention in the financial system has a negative effect on the equilibrium growth rate (King and Levine, 1993b). These developments can be considered as an antidote to the thesis put forward by Modigliani and Miller (1958) that the way firms finance themselves is irrelevant (their 'irrelevance propositions'), which is consistent with the perception of financial markets as entities independent from the rest of the economy, so that finance and growth are unrelated. Despite severe doubts on the relevance of the Modigliani and Miller theorem, some economists still would argue that finance and growth are unrelated. A good example of this view is Lucas (1988), who argues that economists 'badly over-stress' the role of the financial system, thereby reinforcing the difficulties of agreeing on the link and its direction between finance and growth.

This chapter aims to explore the relationship between financial development and growth from the perspective of evaluation of the effects of financial liberalization. Since the focus is on financial liberalization, a short review of certain related issues is in order. It used to be the case that banking, with banks as the first major lenders, along with rights of private ownership of investment, led to control of real investment by bank lenders. In many parts of today's world only government and banks direct much of the real investment.[2] Projects live or die by bank decision as to willingness to finance. In the G7 nations, however, in addition to government and banking, investment is directed by managers of retirement funds (both public and private), insurance companies investing their reserves, along with many other financial institutions with accumulated reserves. Individuals, via their self-directed pension and retirement funds, do not have much impact in this; they place money with financial institutions which in turn place the money as they think fit. This institutional framework has been facilitated by various pieces of accumulated legislation, such as those creating tax-deferred retirement accounts, and tax-deferred insurance reserves, along with many others. The result is a variety of professional managers responsible for facilitating real investment whose performance is measured by institutionally determined financial standards. So now there is a combination of public, commercial and managerial institutions, directing real investment, each with its own set of financial objectives, and which can be competing and/or operating at cross-purposes. Failing to recognize that positive financial outcomes are not necessarily positive real outcomes has serious consequences. Many of these considerations fall under financial liberalization. However, lacking in the financial liberalization literature is a cost–benefit analysis of the real costs of the financial sectors, which results from the incentives induced by the institutional structure that surrounds finance and are inherent in today's real investment activity.

The financial liberalization thesis is introduced in the section that follows. Its theory and policy implications are explored in a subsequent section. The problematic nature of financial liberalization is then explored under a number of headings. A final section summarizes and concludes.

The financial liberalization thesis

This chapter attempts to demonstrate the problematic nature of 'market liberalization' by concentrating on an area where renewed interest has resurfaced: financial markets. More precisely, the focus of this contribution will be on the setting of financial prices by central banks, especially in developing countries, a fairly common practice in the 1950s and 1960s, which was challenged by Goldsmith (1969) in the late 1960s, and by McKinnon (1973) and Shaw (1973) in the early 1970s. They ascribed the poor performance of investment and growth in developing countries to interest rate ceilings, high reserve requirements and quantitative restrictions in the credit allocation mechanism. These restrictions were sources of 'financial repression', the main symptoms of which were low savings, credit rationing and low investment. They propounded instead the thesis that has come to be known as 'financial liberalization', which can be succinctly summarized as amounting to 'freeing' financial markets from any intervention and letting the market determine the allocation of credit.[3]

However, left out of consideration were other policy options selected by government that preceded these policies; for example, the general case was that of various combinations of foreign fixed exchange rates and governments incurring debt in external currencies. Many of the financial restrictions subsequently imposed were designed to help sustain the exchange rate regime and support the external debt. This combination obviated otherwise available government policy responses (such as government deficit spending of local currency) to support investment and consumption at full employment levels. Instead, financial liberalization was proposed in the context of fixed exchange rates and external debt. It should, thus, have been no surprise that a variety of currency and banking crises followed the attempts at financial liberalization (see, for example, Arestis and Glickman, 2002). One might qualify this straightaway by suggesting that this analysis is conducted under a given institutional structure as mandated by government, and that policy options can be selected that inhibit investment. With direct government investment always an option, and accounting that recognizes government investment as such, government can always alleviate lack of investment, although typically it would be a different form of investment. It is, thus, true that government can 'allow' markets to direct real investment. The history of banking, however, as the policy makers in both developing and developed countries adopted the essentials of the financial liberalization thesis and pursued corresponding policies, tells a rather sad story. It actually points to two striking findings.

The first is that over the past 30 years or so, financial and banking crises have been unusually frequent and severe, especially in developing countries with foreign fixed exchange rate policies and external debt, both relative to the experience of developed countries and to the experience of the preceding three decades. The magnitude of the crises is clearly indicated by the fact that as much as over two-thirds of the IMF member countries experienced significant banking sector problems during the period from 1980 to today (see, for example, Arestis and Glickman, 2002). In Africa, in Asia, and in the transition economies of Central and Eastern Europe, over 90 per cent of the IMF country members suffered at least one serious bout of banking difficulties over the period. The severity of the crises can be highlighted by the fact that at least a dozen developing-country episodes where bank balance sheet losses and/or public sector financial resolution costs of these banking crises amounted to 10 per cent or more of GDP. While industrial countries have had some sizeable banking crises of their own over the period (Spain, 1977–85; three Nordic countries in the late 1980s/early 1990s; the US saving and loan débâcle, 1984–91; and the recent Japanese bad loan problem[4]), the frequency and scale of crises have, on the whole, been lower than in the developing world.

The second important finding is that beyond the financial costs of banking crises for the local economies involved, they exacerbate downturns in economic activity, thereby imposing substantial real economic costs. Banks in developing countries hold the lion's share of financial assets, meaning that they are the main holders of shares, etc., operate the payments system, provide liquidity to financial markets, and are major purchasers of government bonds. In addition, bank liabilities have been growing much faster in developing countries over the past two decades than economic activity. Moreover, the increasing weight and integration of developing and emerging economies in international financial markets have resulted in spillover effects to industrialized countries. There is, thus, an increased risk that banking crises in developing economies will have unfavourable repercussions on industrial countries. A very disturbing aspect of the crises discussed in this section is that they spill over to the real economy where real output and investment are lost. This is exacerbated by the fact that the latter are not accompanied by appropriate policy responses to sustain aggregate demand, output and employment, when the exposure to which we have just referred materializes. Governments could have allowed real output to be sustained in spite of bank 'financial' difficulties, and in spite of losses by shareholders, lenders, etc. In fact, governments have allowed banking crises to alter the 'quantity' of new investment and real output, when those governments have had the option all along to allow growth to continue. More seriously, though, is the cost in terms of real output resulting from these crises. Table 21.1 makes the point very well. Such loss in many countries was staggering, reaching over 60 per cent in some cases, followed by substantially reduced output and employment.

We wish to argue that this experience is not unrelated to the financial liberalization policies pursued by countries that adopted the principles of the thesis in the context of their existing institutional structure. This we do by looking at a number of problems entailed in the thesis and at the evidence that can be adduced. We begin with a brief summary of the main propositions of the financial liberalization thesis before we turn our attention to its problematic nature.

Financial liberalization: theory and policy implications

A number of writers question the wisdom of financial repression, arguing that it has detrimental effects on the real economy. Goldsmith (1969) argued that the main impact of financial repression was the effect on the efficiency of capital. McKinnon (1973) and Shaw (1973) stressed two other channels: first, financial repression affects how efficiently savings are allocated to investment; and second, through its effect on the return to savings, it also affects the equilibrium level of savings and investment. In this framework, therefore, investment suffers not only in quantity but also in quality terms since bankers do not ration the available funds according to the marginal productivity of investment projects but according to their own discretion. Under these conditions the financial sector is likely to stagnate. The low return on bank deposits encourages savers to hold their savings in the form of unproductive assets such as land, rather than the potentially productive bank deposits. Similarly, high reserve requirements restrict the supply of bank lending even

Table 21.1   Estimated length of crisis, gross output loss and recovery time

		Years	As percentage of GDP
Argentina	1980–82	4	16.6
Argentina	1995–96	3	11.9
Australia	1989	1	0
Brazil	1994	0	1
Bulgaria	1996–97	3	20.4
Chile	1981–88	9	45.5
Colombia	1982–85	5	65.1
Czech Republic	1989	1	0
Ecuador	1996	1	0.9
Egypt	1991–94	5	6.5
Finland	1991–96	7	23.1
France	1994	1	0
Ghana	1982	2	6.6
Hungary	1991–92	3	13.8
Indonesia	1992–present	9	42.3
Indonesia	1997–present	4	33.0
Japan	1992–present	9	27.7
Malaysia	1985–87	4	13.7
Malaysia	1997–present	4	22.8
Mexico	1994	2	9.6
New Zealand	1987–92	7	18.5
Norway	1987–93	8	19.6
Paraguay	1995	1	0
Philippines	1983–86	5	25.7
Philippines	1998–present	3	7.5
Poland	1992	1	0
Senegal	1988	1	0
Slovenia	1992	2	2.1
South Korea	1997–98	3	16.5
Spain	1977	1	0
Sri Lanka	1989–90	3	0.5
Sweden	1991–92	3	6.5
Thailand	1983	2	8.7
Thailand	1997–present	4	31.5
Turkey	1982	1	0
Turkey	1994	2	9.1
United States	1981–82	3	5.4
Uruguay	1981–85	6	41.7
Venezuela	1994–96	4	14.1

Source: Honohan and Klingebiel (2000).

further while directed credit programmes distort the allocation of credit since political priorities are, in general, not determined by the marginal productivity of different types of capital.

The policy implications of this analysis are quite straightforward: remove interest rate ceilings, reduce reserve requirements and abolish directed credit programmes. In short, liberalize financial markets and let the free market determine the allocation of credit, where it is assumed that there will be a 'free market' with just a few banks, thereby ignoring issues of oligopoly and, of course, of credit rationing type of problems as in Stiglitz and Weiss (1981). With the real rate of interest adjusting to its equilibrium level, at which savings and investment are assumed to be in balance, low-yielding investment projects would be eliminated, so that the overall efficiency of investment would be enhanced. Also, as the real rate of interest increases, saving and the total real supply of credit increase, which induces a higher volume of investment. Economic growth would, therefore, be stimulated not only through the increased investment but also due to an increase in the average productivity of capital. Moreover, the effects of lower reserve requirements reinforce the effects of higher saving on the supply of bank lending, while the abolition of directed credit programmes would lead to an even more efficient allocation of credit, thereby stimulating further the average productivity of capital.

Even though the financial liberalization thesis encountered increasing scepticism over the years, it nevertheless had a relatively early impact on development policy through the work of the IMF and the World Bank which, perhaps in their traditional role as promoters of what were claimed to be free market conditions, were keen to encourage financial liberalization policies in developing countries as part of more general reforms or stabilization programmes. When events following the implementation of financial liberalization prescriptions did not confirm their theoretical premises, there occurred a revision of the main tenets of the thesis. Initially, the response of the proponents of the financial liberalization thesis was to argue that where liberalization failed it was because of the existence of implicit or explicit deposit insurance coupled with inadequate banking supervision and macroeconomic instability (for example, McKinnon, 1988a; 1988b; 1991; Villanueva and Mirakhor, 1990; World Bank, 1989). Those conditions were conducive to excessive risk-taking by the banks, which can lead to 'too high' real interest rates, bankruptcies of firms and bank failures. That led to the introduction of new elements into the analysis of the financial liberalization thesis in the form of preconditions, which would have to be satisfied before reforms would be contemplated and implemented. The financial liberalization analysis led to recommendations, which included 'adequate banking supervision', aiming to ensure that banks had a well-diversified loan portfolio, 'macroeconomic stability', which refers to low and stable inflation and a sustainable fiscal deficit, and the sequencing of financial reforms. Gradual financial liberalization is to be preferred. In this gradual process a 'sequencing of financial liberalization' (for example, Edwards, 1989; McKinnon, 1991) is recommended. Employing credibility arguments, Calvo (1988) and Rodrik (1987) suggest a narrow focus of reforms with financial liberalization left as last. Successful reform of the real sector came to be seen as a prerequisite to financial reform. Thus financial repression would have to be maintained during the first stage of economic liberalization.

A further development took place where another dimension was recognized. This was based on the possibility that different aspects of reform programmes might work at cross-purposes, disrupting the real sector in the process. This is precisely what Sachs (1988) labelled as 'competition of instruments'. Such conflict was thought to occur when abrupt increases in interest rates cause the exchange rate to appreciate rapidly thus damaging the real sector. Sequencing becomes important again. It is thus suggested that liberalization of the 'foreign' markets should take place after liberalization of domestic financial markets. In this context, proponents suggest caution in 'sequencing' in the sense of gradual financial liberalization, emphasizing the required preconditions for successful financial reform. The preconditions include the achievement of stability in the broader macroeconomic environment and adequate bank supervision within which financial reforms were to be undertaken (Cho and Khatkhate, 1989; McKinnon, 1988b; Sachs, 1988; Villanueva and Mirakhor, 1990). It is also argued by the proponents that the authorities should move more aggressively on financial reform in good times and more slowly when borrowers' net worth is reduced by negative shocks, such as recessions and losses due to terms of trade (see also World Bank, 1989). Caprio et al. (1994) reviewed the financial reforms in a number of primarily developing countries and concluded that managing the reform process rather than adopting a *laissez-faire* approach was important, and that sequencing along with the initial conditions in finance and macroeconomic stability were critical elements in implementing successfully financial reforms. All these modifications, however, indicate that there is no doubt that the proponents of the financial liberalization thesis do not even contemplate abandoning it. No amount of revision has changed the objective of the thesis, which is to pursue the *optimal* path to financial liberalization, free from any political, i.e. state, intervention.

Still another financial liberalization development is related to the emergence of the 'new growth' theory (i.e. the endogenous growth model). This development incorporates the role of financial factors within the framework of new growth theory, with financial intermediation considered as an endogenous process. A two-way causal relationship between financial intermediation and growth is thought to exist. The growth process encourages higher participation in the financial markets, thereby facilitating the establishment and promotion of financial intermediaries. The latter enable a more efficient allocation of funds for investment projects, which promote investment itself and enhance growth (Greenwood and Jovanovic, 1990). Furthermore, in such models financial development can affect growth not only by raising the saving rate but also by raising the amount of saving funnelled into investment and/or raising the social marginal productivity of capital. With few exceptions (for example, Easterly, 1993) the endogenous growth literature views government intervention in the financial system as distortionary and predicts that it has a negative effect on the equilibrium growth rate. Increasing taxes on financial intermediaries is seen as equivalent to taxes on innovative activity, which lowers the equilibrium growth rate. Imposing credit ceilings reduces individual incentives to invest in innovative activity, which retards the growth of the economy (King and Levine, 1993b).

New growth theory suggests that there can be self-sustaining growth without exogenous technical progress. Generally, constant returns to scale at the firm level, with increasing returns overall, are assumed. The efficiency of individual firms, however, is made a function of aggregate capital stock. Capital accumulation triggers a learning process which, being a public good, raises efficiency in the economy. It is possible to show that within this framework financial intermediation can have not only level effects, but also growth effects (Pagano, 1993). In general terms, financial markets enable agents to share both endowment risks (such as health hazards) and rate-of-return risk (such as that due to the volatility of stock returns) through diversification. They channel funds from people who save to those who dissave in the form of consumer credit and mortgage loans. If the loan supply falls short of demand, some households are liquidity-constrained, so that current resources limit their consumption and savings increase. There is, however, an important difference between the financial liberalization and the endogenous growth theory theses. As Singh (1997) argues, the endogenous growth theory proponents argue for deliberate and fast development of stock markets, especially in developing countries. By contrast, the financial liberalization advocates view stock market development as either unimportant or at best as a slow evolutionary process (Fry, 1997).

The most recent development includes '*structural* characteristics of finance, such as the relative importance of banks and securities markets and *infrastructural and institutional* prerequisites, such as the legal and informational environment as well as the regulatory style' (Honohan, 2004, pp. 1–2). This discussion has stemmed from that on whether 'financial structure matters'. The well-known debate on bank-based and capital-market-based financial systems has recently been followed by empirical investigation that concludes in the negative (Arestis et al., 2004, review these developments). This has led to two further developments that might be termed the 'financial services' view (Levine, 1997; see also Arestis et al., 2004), and the finance and law view (La Porta et al., 1998; see also Levine, 1999). The financial services view attempts to minimize the importance of the distinction between bank-based and market-based financial systems. It is financial services themselves that are by far more important than the form of their delivery. In the financial services view, the issue is not the source of finance. It is rather the creation of an environment where financial services are soundly and efficiently provided. The emphasis is on the creation of better-functioning banks and markets rather than on the type of financial structure. The evidence produced to support this view is based on panel and cross-section studies, and demonstrates that financial structure is irrelevant to economic growth. However, these multi-country studies are also subject to a number of concerns, summarized in Arestis et al. (2004). Using time series and accounting for heterogeneity of coefficients across countries, it is demonstrated by Arestis et al. that 'financial structure does matter'. The finance and law view maintains that the role of the legal system in creating a growth-promoting financial sector, with legal rights and enforcement mechanisms, facilitates both markets and intermediaries. It is, thereby, argued that this is a much better way of studying financial systems than concentrating on bank-based or market-based systems. This view, however, does not quite accord with the facts. For it is the case that while the degree of financial development has changed over the last 100 years or so, legal origins in each country have not changed by much and with the frequency that the degree of financial development has changed.

We wish to argue in the rest of this chapter that there are a number of issues in these arguments that are critical in the development of the financial liberalization thesis. We argue that these propositions are not problem-free. They are, in fact, so problematic that they leave the thesis without serious theoretical and empirical foundations.

Problems with financial liberalization

This section summarizes a number of critical issues of the financial liberalization thesis (for more details see Arestis and Demetriades, 1998; Arestis, 2004). They are:

- sequencing;
- causality;
- free banking leads to stability of the financial system;
- financial liberalization enhances economic growth;
- savings causes investment;
- absence of serious distributional effects as interest rates change;
- financial liberalization is pro-poor;
- no role for speculation;
- favourable financial policies.

We proceed now to discuss these critical issues briefly.

Sequencing
Sequencing does not salvage the financial liberalization thesis for the simple reason that it depends on the assumption that financial markets clear, while the goods markets do not. But in the presence of asymmetric information, financial markets too are marred by so-called imperfections. But even where the 'correct' sequencing took place (e.g. Chile), where trade liberalization had taken place before financial liberalization, not much success can be reported (Lal, 1987). The opposite is also true, namely that in those cases, like Uruguay, where the 'reverse' sequencing took place, financial liberalization before trade liberalization, the experience was very much the same as in Chile (Grabel, 1995).

Stiglitz (2000) highlights difficulties with the sequencing literature in explaining the South East Asian crisis. South East Asian countries had very strong macroeconomic fundamentals, along with sound systems of banking regulation and supervision. Thus reasonable economic policies and sound financial institutions were in place; high growth rates for long periods with low inflation rates were also evident. Still the South East Asian financial crisis of 1997–98 was not prevented. Stiglitz (ibid.) emphasizes the destabilizing implications of short-term capital flows to conclude that 'there is not only no case for capital market liberalization . . . there is a fairly compelling case *against* full liberalization' (p. 1076). More recent research on sequencing produced similar results. For example, Kaminsky and Schmuckler (2003), when discussing relevant findings, conclude that 'the ordering of liberalization does not matter in general. Opening the capital account or the stock market first does not have a different effect than opening the domestic financial sector first' (p. 31).

Causality
The difficulty of establishing the link between financial development and economic growth was first identified by Patrick (1966) and further developed by McKinnon (1988a), who argued that 'Although a higher rate of financial growth is positively correlated with successful real growth, Patrick's (1966) problem remains unresolved: What is the cause and what is the effect? Is finance a leading sector in economic development, or does it simply follow growth in real output which is generated elsewhere?' (p. 390).

The relationship between financial development and economic growth is, therefore, a controversial issue, which could potentially be resolved by resorting to theoretical arguments backed up by convincing empirical evidence. A recent attempt to explore this aspect of the debate has been attempted by King and Levine (1993a), who have argued that

Schumpeter (1911) may very well have been 'right' to suggest that financial intermediaries promote economic development. Using data for a number of countries, covering the period 1960 to 1989, they find that 'higher levels of financial development are significantly and robustly correlated with faster current and future rates of economic growth, physical capital accumulation and economic efficiency improvements' (King and Levine, 1993a, pp. 717–18). From these results the authors conclude that the link between growth and financial development is not just a contemporaneous correlation and that 'finance seems importantly to lead economic growth' (ibid., p. 730). They thus show that the level of financial intermediation is a good predictor of long-run rates of economic growth, capital accumulation and productivity improvements.

It has been shown elsewhere (Arestis and Demetriades, 1997) that although King and Levine (1993a) attempted to tackle in an ingenious way an issue that has plagued the empirical literature on the relationship between finance and development for a long time, their causal interpretation could be improved further. Once the contemporaneous correlation between the main financial indicator and economic growth has been accounted for, there is no longer any evidence to suggest that financial development helps predict future growth. Furthermore, the cross-section nature of the King and Levine (1993a) data set cannot address the question of the link between finance and growth in a satisfactory way. To perform such a task, time series data and a time series approach are required, as for example in Granger (1988), among others.

Free banking leads to stability of the financial system
The underlying assumption of the thesis is that market forces do produce stability in the banking and financial systems, as they do in other sections of the economy. At the limit, since there would be no possibility of government bailouts in free banking, any hint of imprudence would cause customers to shift to competitors. Consequently, the market discipline would be stronger the larger the number of independent note issuers. We have argued elsewhere (Arestis and Demetriades, 1998) that even in the most frequently discussed cases of free banking, the system may either have worked because of support emanating from outside the system itself, or it was simply marred by serious problems. The upshot is that banking systems should be regulated (Dow, 1996). Further serious theoretical drawbacks, which spring from two sources, *asymmetric information* and *uncertainty*, are particularly acute in a free banking system.

Asymmetric Information   This drawback originates from the new-Keynesian notions of asymmetric information (see, for example, Stiglitz and Weiss, 1981), which leads to two types of problems: *adverse selection* and *moral hazard*. Adverse selection refers to cases when more creditworthy borrowers are drawn to other means of finance, usually at lower costs, leaving only the lesser creditworthy borrowers for the banking system. The problem here is the unsupported assumption that banks don't have 'absolute' credit standards, but instead are willing to take the best credits from the available customer base to fill out their loan portfolio desires, even if they are very high risk. Moral hazard refers to banks being put in a position where the managers have no risk of loss yet a possibility of gain. For example, an unregulated bank may have a management team that receives a bonus based on profits. It might be to their personal advantage to put some very high-risk, high-yield five-year securities in the bank's portfolio if they could accrue the interest earned for, say,

12 months, and be paid bonuses based on the accrued interest, even if the securities had a high risk of subsequent default.

Uncertainty   It can be argued that in the presence of uncertainty in the loan market, changes in the rate of interest alone do not guarantee clearance of the loan market (Basu, 2002). The fact that banks do not maintain a uniform credit standard for all borrowers, rather than market imperfections, allows discriminatory lending policy by the banks. Consequently, the variation in access to the loan market for different borrowers is predicated on the credit standard borrowers can offer. Under these circumstances, free banking and liberalization of the loan markets do not guarantee that flexibility in interest rate variation would establish the 'equilibriating' characteristic assumed by the financial liberalization thesis.

Financial liberalization enhances economic growth

In demonstrating that a positive relationship exists between financial liberalization and economic development, the thesis under scrutiny ignores a number of aspects, which are of significant importance. We discuss two such aspects: *hedge effects and curb markets* first, followed by the *lack of perfect competition* aspect.

Hedge effects and curb markets   This critique emanates from the structuralist theory (Taylor, 1983; Van Wijnbergen, 1983). It suggests that higher interest rates from financial liberalization might leave unchanged or, indeed, reduce the total supply of funds. This is due to hedge effects, which may not materialize, in which case the total supply of funds may not be affected, or to curb effects, which may reduce it. Hedge effects are due to substitution of hedge assets; gold and land are the most obvious examples, for bank deposits brought about by higher interest rates. However, it should be readily conceded that both the hedge and curb effects have not been unambiguously empirically validated (Ghate, 1992).

Lack of perfect competition   The McKinnon and Shaw type of models are based on the unrealistic assumption of perfect competition, which is particularly arbitrary in the case of less developed countries (LDCs). For it is true to argue that perfect competition is 'always and everywhere' unrealistic and impossible in all countries and markets, but especially so perhaps in credit markets. Given, then, that banking sectors are undoubtedly rather oligopolistic, the result of financial liberalization could very well be the monopoly result whereby the decrease in loans and the increase in the real interest rate are higher magnitudes than that under perfect competition. This result may occur for reasons that have to do with the possibility of inadequate regulation over banking practices, which leads to undue risk-taking, especially in the presence of deposit insurance. Under such circumstances the banks are beneficiaries of an unfair bet against the government: if the projects they have financed do well they make a lot of profit, if they do badly they rely on the government to rescue them. Such a situation has been termed 'upward financial repression'.

Relationship between savings and investment

In the McKinnon/Shaw model savings precedes investment. But savings can only fund investment, i.e. it can only facilitate the finance of investment. Savings cannot *finance* capital accumulation; this is done by the banking sector, which provides loans for invest-ment without necessitating increases in the volume of deposits. With a credit-creating financial system, it is banks, and not savers, that finance investment. Consequently, it is finance, and not savings, along with entrepreneurial long-term expectations, that are the prerequisites to capital accumulation. Savings, none the less, has a different, and import-ant, role to play, which is to achieve and maintain the financial stability of the growing economy (Studart, 1995). A second problem with the McKinnon/Shaw model is the related assumption that deposits create loans. In modern banking systems, including most developing countries, loans create deposits, not the other way round.[5]

Interest rate changes and distribution of income
The financial liberalization thesis does not pay much attention to distributional effects of changes in interest rates. As a result, the contributions initiated on this issue have been rather small, both theoretical and quantitative. Fry (1995) surveys the limited work that has been conducted on this issue, to conclude that 'financial repression and the ensuing credit rationing worsen income distribution and increase industrial concentra-tion' (p. 205). Consequently, financial liberalization and the ensuing freeing of credit markets improves income distribution and reduces industrial concentration, due to widened access to finance and decreased degree of credit market segmentation. This benefits small firms because it avoids subsidizing priority sectors, which leads to market segmentation, an obvious characteristic of the financial repression case, which hits them harshly.

There are, however, more important and significant effects, which are ignored by the financial liberalization thesis. We turn to these effects next.

Pricing: demand-determined and cost-determined sectors   We begin with pricing in the modern economy (Kalecki, 1971). There is the competitive sector, essentially agriculture and raw materials. In this sector prices are determined by supply and demand, as in the neoclassical tradition. This is a 'demand-determined' price sector. The other sector, which is dominant, is the 'cost-determined' price sector, manufacturing and services, where prices are set at some stable mark-up over average variable costs. Prices are, thus, admin-istered on the basis of some expected normal rate of capacity utilization through a mark-up process over normal average variable costs, sufficient to cover fixed costs, dividends and the internal finance of planned investment expenditures. Thus the mark-up is chosen to produce a level of retained profits, after depreciation, interest and dividend payments, sufficient to provide for the required internal finance as dictated by planned investment expenditure. The price leaders effectively set the market price as just described, so as to yield their target profits. The rest follow the price leaders and they may have higher or lower average costs, and hence lower or higher mark-ups and net profits. Interest is a cost and must be passed on if firms are to achieve their profit targets to finance their invest-ment plans. The bigger the size of the firm, the easier it is for it to pass on the increase in interest rates. It follows that increases in interest rates hit the small-sized firms particu-larly hard. The latter suffer in the same way as the 'demand-determined' price firms. They absorb interest rate changes in the case of demand-determined price firms in the short run. In the long run, interest rate changes may be expected to be passed on in prices if the profit rate is to remain unchanged.

Savings: 'small' and 'big' firms   There is a further important redistributional effect, which we may discuss by also referring to the distinction between 'cost-determined' and 'demand-determined' price sectors. An important difference in this respect is that the 'demand-determined' price firms, the small firms such as farming and small retailing, save very little; generally, they are net borrowers. Small firms, therefore, are very sensitive to interest rate changes. 'Cost-determined' price firms, that is big firms, by contrast, possess a preponderant amount of savings. They prefer to have too much rather than too little savings, which gives them independence from lenders and enables them to substitute capital for labour, if need be. It is internally created funds that are utilized for investment purposes, so that these firms are insulated from capital markets. It follows that high interest rates hit the 'small' firms rather harshly, but leave the 'big' firms fairly unscathed. The weak, therefore, are victimized. An undesirable distributional effect is thus created which promotes sectoral inequalities. It also retards socially desirable sectors, as for example the case with the housing sector, which has a high propensity to borrow.

Household, government and financial sectors   The extent to which the household sector is affected by interest rate changes depends crucially on the size of their debt/asset ratio. The higher this ratio, the more adversely the household sector will be affected from an increase in the rate of interest. The wealthy receive a large proportion of their income from interest payments, but they can also maintain a higher debt/asset ratio too. Similar redistributional effects of increases in interest rates apply in the case of governments. But there is another problem with the government sector. To the extent that their debt/asset ratio incorporates a substantial proportion in foreign debt, global increases in interest rates can have serious redistributional effects across countries. This analysis clearly corroborates Keynes's (1973) argument that increases in interest rates enhance the degree of income inequality substantially. This inequality suggests that monetary policy that aims to sustain high levels of interest rates entails a certain degree of moral responsibility. We have argued this for the case of developing economies where in addition to the redistributional issues there is also, in many cases, the awkward problem of external debt. For higher interest rates at a global level are accompanied by an increase in third world debt, which implies redistributional effects across countries. It is also the case that with financial liberalization higher-income groups are in a better position than lower-income groups. The importance of the ethical issues that cannot be exaggerated (Arestis and Demetriades, 1995). It is also for this reason that we would support interest rate policies that aim at *a stable and permanently low level of interest rates.*

Financial liberalization is pro-poor
The proponents have argued that financial liberalization mobilizes savings and allocates capital to more productive uses, both of which help increase the amount of physical capital and its productivity. Financial liberalization, therefore, increases economic growth, which reduces poverty. Fry (1995), when surveying the limited work on this issue, concludes that 'financial repression and the ensuing credit rationing worsen income distribution and increase industrial concentration' (p. 205). By implication, then, financial liberalization and the ensuing freeing of credit markets improve income distribution and poverty. None the less, one would expect the economic and institutional changes brought about by a financial liberalization package to have a more complex effect on the living

conditions of the poor than merely through the presumed growth channel and the simplistic view summarized by Fry (1995). Arestis and Caner (2004) investigate two further channels of interest, in addition to the growth channel to which we have just alluded: the crises channel and the access to credit and financial services channel.

In some countries, financial markets were liberalized prematurely due to a failure to recognize their imperfect characteristics, and in many other cases all those attempts led to financial crises (Arestis and Glickman, 2002). It is possible that the poor might be more severely affected by such crises. The channel that we label the crisis channel works via the changes in the macroeconomic dynamics, increasing volatility and vulnerability to financial crises following liberalization. The second channel proposed in Arestis and Caner (2004) concentrates on the possible changes in poverty caused by better access to credit and financial services that financial liberalization is expected to yield. To the extent that a liberalization programme increases the financial resources available to the previously disadvantaged and to the extent that the poverty problem is related to lack of consumption-smoothing mechanisms, there is room for financial liberalization to help alleviate poverty. The main conclusion reached in Arestis and Caner (2004) is that there is still no clear understanding of the mechanisms underlying the way moving from financial repression to a liberalized regime influences different segments of the population and, in particular, the poor. A straightforward application of the standard liberalization policies without taking any measures to protect the initially disadvantaged groups of the population from potential losses can worsen the living conditions of these groups.

The role of speculation
Financial liberalization induces two types of speculative pressures: expectations-induced and competition-coerced, both of which contribute to the increased presence of short-term, high-risk speculative transactions in the economy and to the increased vulnerability to financial crises. The first emanate from expectations-induced pressures to pursue speculative transactions in view of the euphoria created by financial liberalization. Given the proliferation of speculative opportunities, this euphoria rewards those speculators who have short time horizons and punish the investors with a long-term view. Keynes (1936) in the famous chapter 12 is very sharp-tongued:

> As the organisation of investment markets improves, the risk of the predominance of speculation . . . increase . . . Speculators may do no harm as bubbles on a steady stream of enterprise . . . a serious situation can develop . . . when enterprise becomes the bubble on a whirlpool of speculation. When the capital development of a country becomes the by-product of the activities of a casino, the job is likely to be ill-done . . . It is usually agreed that casinos, in the public interest, be inaccessible and expensive. (pp. 158–9; see Arestis et al., 2001, for evidence supportive of these arguments.)

The competition-coerced type of pressures emanate from the pressures on non-financial corporations which may feel compelled to enter the financial markets in view of higher returns, induced by financial liberalization, by borrowing to finance short-term financial speculation. A critical manifestation of this possibility is increasing borrowing to finance short-term financial speculation. Lenders in their turn may feel compelled to provide this type of finance, essentially because of fear of loss of market share (Minsky, 1986). An undesirable implication of these types of pressures is that economies are forced to bear a greater degree of 'ambient' risk and thus uncertainty with financial liberalization than without it (Grabel, 1995). This may very well lead to a reduced volume of real-sector investment (Federer, 1993), while exerting upward pressures on interest rates in view of the higher risk.

The types of speculation just referred to are particularly acute in the case of stock markets. The related developments that have taken place recently, and were discussed earlier, enhance the importance of speculation in the stock markets. These stock market developments represent a source of macroeconomic instability in that stock market financial assets are highly liquid and volatile, thus making the financial system more fragile rather than less fragile (Arestis et al., 2001), consequently encouraging short-termism at the cost of long-term growth. Financial liberalization, therefore, is less likely to enhance long-term growth prospects, especially of developing countries. Additionally, dependence on external inflows, which have produced stock market expansion particularly in developing countries, erodes policy autonomy, and, in the case of a fixed exchange rate policy, it forces monetary authorities to maintain high interest rates to sustain investor confidence and greed. There is also the argument that external financial liberalization may lead to a reduction in the rate of return as a result of increased capital flows which reduces the domestic saving rate. Domestic institutions may face competition from foreign institutions that leads to excessive pressure on them and eventually to their bankruptcy.[6]

Financial policies
A broad literature has established that the financial sector in an economy can be important in determining the average productivity of capital, itself being one of the main channels of economic growth. The screening and monitoring of investment projects, which the financial system routinely engages in, are likely to help boost the efficiency of investment (Pagano, 1993). A growing body of literature demonstrates that the development of the financial system has positive effects on (i) the long-run rate of economic growth or (ii) the volume or efficiency of investment (Fry, 1995). However, the causal nature of this relationship is now known to exhibit considerable variation across countries, which indicates that institutional factors or policies may play a critical role in determining how the process of financial development affects economic growth (Arestis and Demetriades, 1997). The importance of institutional factors is confirmed by Demirgüç-Kunt and Detragiache (1998), who demonstrate that institutional quality is inversely related to the incidence of financial fragility that usually follows episodes of financial liberalization. The relevance of financial liberalization policies is highlighted by Arestis et al. (2002), who demonstrate that the direct effects of financial repression in some developing countries are much larger than, and in some instances opposite to, those emanating from changes in the real interest rate.

Arestis et al. (2003) provide a novel assessment of the effects of several types of financial policies on the average productivity of capital in 14 countries, including both developed and developing countries. Specifically, they utilize a new data set on financial restraints, capital adequacy requirements and restrictions on capital flows in these countries, for a period of 40 years. Modern panel–time series methods are employed to examine the effects of these policies on the productivity of capital, controlling for financial development, employment and capital. Their findings suggest that the effects of these policies vary considerably across countries, probably reflecting institutional differences.

They also demonstrate that the main predictions of the financial liberalization literature do not receive adequate empirical support, a result that may reflect the prevalence of financial market imperfections. In contrast, their findings provide significant support to the thesis, currently gaining increasing support among international policy makers, that some form of financial restraints may indeed have positive effects on economic efficiency. These results are very much within the spirit of Stiglitz's (1998) proposition that

> there are a host of regulations, including restrictions on interest rates or lending to certain sectors (such as speculative real estate), that may enhance the stability of the financial system and thereby increase the efficiency of the economy. Although there may be a trade-off between short-run efficiency and this stability, the costs of instability are so great that long-run gains to the economy more than offset any short-run losses. (p. 33)

An interesting aspect that relates closely to this discussion is the distinction between flexible and fixed foreign exchange rates, which has not always featured in the discussion of financial liberalization, and that of policy in particular, as intensely as it deserves. Omitted is the recognition that the core policy of fixed exchange rates and external government debt requires what was deemed as 'financial repressive' policies for purposes of macroeconomic stability. Financial liberalizing in these circumstances promotes instability. Clearly, 'foreign markets' liberalization implies a freely foreign exchange rate system. But then the discussion often confuses the two systems. It is ignored that under the fixed exchange rate system availability of the reserve currency, however important it may be, is limited, and that interest rates are market determined, while with floating exchange rates banking is not reserve constrained and the interest rate is set by the central bank. This can have clear and significant implications for financial liberalization in general, and financial liberalization policy in particular.

Summary and conclusions

We have identified in this contribution a number of key theoretical propositions of the financial liberalization thesis, and have suggested that they are marred by serious difficulties. We have also selectively indicated where operative assumptions are flawed and others are omitted. Furthermore, and as we have shown elsewhere (see, for example, Arestis, 2004), the available empirical evidence does not offer much support to the thesis either. Space limitations preclude detailed discussion of the empirical evidence. Suffice to say, though, that in Arestis and Demetriades (1997) and Arestis (2004) we review two types of evidence: experience of individual countries, which went through financial liberalization, and evidence based on econometric investigation. It is clear from this review that no convincing empirical evidence has been provided in support of the propositions of the financial liberalization hypothesis. A recent IMF study (Favara, 2003) fails to establish significant coefficients on financial variables in instrumented growth regressions. Interestingly enough, Rousseau and Wachtel (2001) report that in high-inflation countries the possible effects of finance on growth weaken substantially. These contributions add to the unconvincing empirical support of the financial liberalization thesis.

Ultimately, then, Stiglitz (1998) is surely right to suggest that the financial liberalization thesis is 'based on an ideological commitment to an idealised conception of markets that is grounded neither in fact nor in economic theory' (p. 20). Indeed, we would strongly suggest that when financial liberalization is viewed in this way, it falls under the rubric of 'innocent fraud', as used in Galbraith (2004). Namely, the current structure is somehow a 'natural' phenomenon, rather than the direct result of specific laws, institutions and policies of government. In fact, the mainstream debate begins with assumptions regarding institutional structure that are but policy options subject to review. Or, as Galbraith argues, there is 'a continuing divergence between approved belief – what I have called elsewhere conventional wisdom – and the reality' (p. ix). Ultimately, and unsurprisingly, though, what really emerges is that 'it is the reality that counts' (p. ix). It is precisely these aspects that this chapter has attempted to explore.

Notes

1. I am grateful to Warren Mosler and Malcolm Sawyer for extensive and helpful comments. All remaining errors, omissions and ambiguities are, of course, entirely my responsibility.
2. The sentence beginning with 'it used to be that banking . . .' refers to the early periods of banking as we know it today. Furthermore, the argument that banks, by decisions on whether or not to grant a loan, simply means that they can effectively determine which proposed investment takes place and which does not. There is no more to the 'control of real investment', and certainly it does not refer to a more direct involvement than just whether banks accept or refuse a loan request.
3. It ought to be noted that the statement 'letting the market determine' the outcome, as though the market were some natural phenomenon, is not unproblematic. What typically happens is that it is the banks that determine the allocation of credit, and they are often relatively few in number, an argument that is reinforced in what follows in this chapter.
4. It ought to be noted that in Japan the banking 'cost' did not hurt real output all that much, since banks were actually 'open for business' all along. Real output lagged for other reasons, mainly due to a shortage of aggregate demand.
5. It is worth noting in the context of the argument in the text that the liquidity preference of the banks is very important (Chick and Dow, 2002), as well as the ability of the banking sector to innovate, with liability management being a good example (Arestis and Howells, 1996).
6. A relevant study is that of Weller (2001), who concludes that in a number of countries there was a widening gap between credit expansion and industrial expansion after financial liberalization, a result that is interpreted as an indication of more speculative financing.

References

Arestis, P. (2004), 'Washington consensus and financial liberalisation', *Journal of Post Keynesian Economics*, **27**(2), 251–71.

Arestis, P. and Caner, A. (2004), 'Financial liberalization and poverty: Channels of influence', Working Papers Series No. 411, Levy Economics Institute of Bard College, Annandale-on-Hudson, New York.

Arestis, P. and Demetriades, O.P. (1995), 'The ethics of interest rate liberalisation in developing economies', in S.F. Frowen and F.P. McHugh (eds), *Financial Decision-Making and Moral Responsibility*, London: Macmillan.

Arestis, P. and Demetriades, O.P. (1997), 'Financial development and economic growth: Assessing the evidence', *Economic Journal*, **107**(442), 783–99.

Arestis, P. and Demetriades, O.P. (1998), 'Financial liberalization: Myth or reality?', ch. 11 in P. Arestis (ed.), *Method, Theory and Policy in Keynes: Essays in Honour of Paul Davidson, Volume Three*, Cheltenham, UK and Lyme, USA: Edward Elgar.

Arestis, P. and Glickman, M. (2002), 'Financial crisis in South East Asia: Dispelling illusion the Minskyan way', *Cambridge Journal of Economics*, **26**(2), 237–60. Reprinted in R.E. Allen (ed.), *The International Library of Writings on the New Global Economy: The Political Economy of Financial Crises*, Cheltenham, UK and Northampton, MA, USA: Edward Elgar, 2004.

Arestis, P. and Howells, P. (1996), 'Theoretical reflections on endogenous money: the problem with "Convenience Lending"', *Cambridge Journal of Economics*, **20**(5), 539–51.

Arestis, P., Demetriades, O.P. and Luintel, K.B. (2001), 'Financial development and economic growth: The role of stock markets', *Journal of Money, Credit, and Banking*, **33**(1), 16–41.

Arestis, P., Demetriades, O.P. and Fattouh, B. (2003), 'Financial policies and the aggregate productivity of the capital stock', *Eastern Economic Journal*, **29**(2), 217–42.

Arestis, P., Luintel, A.D. and Luintel, K.B. (2004), 'Does financial structure matter?', Working Papers Series No. 399, Levy Economics Institute of Bard College, Annandale-on-Hudson, New York.

Bagehot, W. (1873), *Lombard Street: A Description of the Money Market*, London: John Murray.

Basu, S. (2002), *Financial Liberalization and Intervention: A New Analysis of Credit Rationing*, Cheltenham, UK and Northampton, MA, USA: Edward Elgar.

Calvo, G. (1988), 'Servicing the public debt: the role of expectations', *American Economic Review*, **78**, 647–61.

Caprio, G. Jr, Atiyas, I. and Hanson, J.A. (eds) (1994), *Financial Reform: Theory and Experience*, Cambridge: Cambridge University Press.

Chick, V. and Dow, S. (2002), 'Monetary policy with endogenous money and liquidity preference: a nondualistic treatment', *Journal of Post Keynesian Economics*, **24**(4), 587–607.

Cho, Y.-J. and Khatkhate, D. (1989), 'Lessons of financial liberalisation in Asia: a comparative study', World Bank Discussion Papers, No. 50.

Demirgüç-Kunt, A. and Detragiache, E. (1998), 'Financial liberalisation and financial fragility', International Monetary Fund, Working Paper, 98/83.

Dow, C.S. (1996), 'Why the banking system should be regulated', *Economic Journal*, **106**(436), 698–707.

Easterly, W.R. (1993), 'How much do distortions affect growth?', *Journal of Monetary Economics*, **32**(2), 187–212.

Edwards, S. (1989), 'On the sequencing of structural reforms', Working Paper, No. 70, OECD Department of Economics and Statistics.

Favara, Giovanni (2003), 'An empirical assessment of the relationship between finance and growth', IMF Working Paper, No. 03/123, Washington, DC: International Monetary Fund.

Federer, P. (1993), 'The impact of uncertainty on aggregate investment spending', *Journal of Money, Credit, and Banking*, **25**(1), 30–45.

Fry, M.J. (1995), *Money, Interest and Banking in Economic Development*, London: Johns Hopkins University Press.

Fry, M.J. (1997), 'In favour of financial liberalisation', *Economic Journal*, **107**(442), 754–70.

Galbraith, J.K. (2004), *The Economics of Innocent Fraud: Truth for Our Time*, Boston, MA and New York: Houghton Mifflin.

Ghate, P. (1992), 'Interaction between the formal and informal financial sectors', *World Development*, **20**(6), 859–72.

Goldsmith, R.W. (1969), *Financial Structure and Development*, New Haven, CT: Yale University Press.

Grabel, I. (1995), 'Speculation-led economic development: a post-Keynesian interpretation of financial liberalization programs', *International Review of Applied Economics*, **9**(2), 127–49.

Granger, C.W.J. (1988), 'Causality, cointegration and control', *Journal of Economic Dynamics and Control*, **12**(2/3), 551–59.

Greenwood, J. and Jovanovic, B. (1990), 'Financial development, growth and the distribution of income', *Journal of Political Economy*, **98**, 1076–108.

Honohan, P. (2004), 'Financial development, growth and poverty: how close are the links?', ch. 1 in G.A.E. Goodhart (ed.), *Financial Development and Economic Growth: Explaining the Links*, Basingstoke: Palgrave Macmillan.

Honohan, P. and Klingebiel, D. (2000), 'Controlling fiscal costs of banking crises', Mimeo, Washington, DC: World Bank.

Kalecki, M. (1971), 'Costs and prices', ch. 5 in M. Kalecki (ed.), *Selected Essays on the Dynamics of the Capitalist Economy, 1933–1970*, Cambridge: Cambridge University Press.

Kaminsky, G.L. and Schmuckler, S.L. (2003), 'Short-run pain, long-run gain: The effects of financial liberalization', IMF Working Paper WP/03/34, Washington, DC: International Monetary Fund.

Keynes, J.M. (1930), *A Treatise on Money*, London: Macmillan.

Keynes, J.M. (1936), *The General Theory of Employment, Interest and Money*, London: Macmillan.

Keynes, J.M. (1973), *The General Theory and After, Collected Writings*, Vol. XIV, London: Macmillan.

King, R.G. and Levine, R. (1993a), 'Finance and growth: Schumpeter might be right', *Quarterly Journal of Economics*, **VIII**, 717–37.

King, R.G. and Levine, R. (1993b), 'Finance, entrepreneurship, and growth: theory and evidence', *Journal of Monetary Economics*, **32**(3), 513–42.

Lal, D. (1987), 'The political economy of economic liberalization', *World Bank Economic Review*, **1**(2), 273–99.

La Porta, R., Lopez-de-Silanes, F., Shleifer, A. and Vishny, R.W. (1998), 'Law and finance', *Journal of Political Economy*, **106**(6), 1113–55.

Levine, R. (1997), 'Financial development and economic growth: views and agenda', *Journal of Economic Literature*, **35**, 688–726.

Levine, R. (1999), 'Law, finance, and economic growth', *Journal of Financial Intermediation*, **8**(1–2), 8–35.

Lucas, R.E. (1988), 'On the mechanics of economic development', *Journal of Monetary Economics*, **22**(1), 3–42.

Minsky, H.P. (1986), *Stabilizing an Unstable Economy*, New Haven, CT: Yale University Press.

McKinnon, R.I. (1973), *Money and Capital in Economic Development*, Washington, DC: Brookings Institution.

McKinnon, R.I. (1988a), 'Financial liberalisation in retrospect: interest rate policies in LDCs', in G. Ranis and T.P. Schultz (eds), *The State of Development Economics*, Oxford: Basil Blackwell.

McKinnon, R.I. (1988b), 'Financial liberalisation and economic development: a reassessment of interest-rate policies in Asia and Latin America', Occasional Papers, No. 6, International Centre for Economic Growth.

McKinnon, R. (1991), *The Order of Economic Liberalization: Financial Control in the Transition to a Market Economy*, Baltimore, MD: Johns Hopkins University Press.

Modigliani, F. and Miller, M.H. (1958), 'The cost of capital, corporation finance and the theory of investment', *American Economic Review*, **48**(2), 261–97.

Pagano, M. (1993), 'Financial markets and growth: an overview', *European Economic Review*, **37**(2–3), 613–22.

Patrick, H. (1966), 'Financial development and economic growth in underdeveloped countries', *Economic Development and Cultural Change*, **14**, 174–89.

Robinson, J. (1952), 'The generalisation of the general theory', in J. Robinson (ed.), *The Rate of Interest and Other Essays*, London: Macmillan.

Rodrik, D. (1987), 'Trade and capital account liberalization in a Keynesian economy', *Journal of International Economics*, **44**(1), 113–29.

Rousseau, P.L. and Wachtel, P. (2001), 'Inflation, financial development and growth', in T. Negishi, R. Ramachandran and K. Mino (eds), *Economic Theory, Dynamics and Markets: Essays in Honor of Ryuzo Sato*, Boston, MA: Kluwer, pp. 309–24.

Sachs, J. (1988), 'Conditionality, debt relief and the developing countries' debt crisis', in J. Sachs (ed.), *Developing Country Debt and Economic Performance*, Chicago, IL: University of Chicago Press.

Schumpeter, J. (1911), *The Theory of Economic Development: An Inquiry into Profits, Capital, Credit, Interest and Business Cycle*, Cambridge, MA: Harvard University Press.

Shaw, E.S. (1973), *Financial Deepening in Economic Development*, New York: Oxford University Press.

Singh, A. (1997), 'Stock markets, financial liberalisation and economic development', *Economic Journal*, **107**(442), 771–82.

Stiglitz, J.E. (1998), 'The role of the state in financial markets', in M. Bruno and B. Pleskovic (eds), *Proceedings of the World Bank Annual Conference on Development Economics*, Washington, DC: World Bank, pp. 19–52.

Stiglitz, J.E. (2000), 'Capital market liberalization, economic growth and instability', *World Development*, **28**(6), 1075–86.

Stiglitz, J.E. and Weiss, A. (1981), 'Credit rationing in markets with imperfect information', *American Economic Review*, **71**(3), 393–410.

Studart, R. (1995), *Investment Finance in Economic Development*, London: Routledge.

Taylor, L. (1983), *Structuralist Macroeconomics: Applicable Models for the Third World*, New York: Basic Books.

Van Wijnbergen, S. (1983), 'Interest rate management in LDCs', *Journal of Monetary Economics*, **12**, 433–52.

Villanueva, D. and Mirakhor, A. (1990), 'Interest rate policies, stabilisation and bank supervision in developing countries: Strategies for financial reform', IMF Working Papers, WP/90/8.

Weller, C.E. (2001), 'Financial crises after financial liberalization: exceptional circumstances or structural weakness?', *Journal of Development Studies*, **38**(1), 98–127.

World Bank (1989), *World Development Report*, Oxford: Oxford University Press.

22 Deregulation
Dorene Isenberg[1]

Deregulation is a concept that is imbued with theoretical, ideological, political, historical and policy implications. As a concept it implies that regulation in the financial sector had already occurred and it now needs to be reversed. So to understand deregulation, it is first important to understand regulation. Effectively, for some predetermined reason financial markets were viewed as being unable to produce the optimal allocation, stability, efficiency and equity results that neoclassical economics proposes, so behavioral and operational rules were imposed by the government on the financial markets and institutions. These regulations did not supplant markets, but altered them so that when they operated, their outcomes would be as close to optimal as possible. The process of deregulation then implies the lifting of the governmentally determined rules and allowing markets to operate freely. It also implies that deregulation creates markets that produce optimal outcomes automatically. These implications produce a view of a market as a process of price-making and quantity-determining that is a-politically, a-culturally, a-geographically and a-historically constructed, which markets are not (Hodgson, 1988). If markets are imbued with political, cultural, geographical and historical attributes, then the processes of regulation and deregulation need to be seen as less diametrically opposed.

This chapter will begin by introducing the theoretical foundations of the debates over deregulation; then it will use the case of the USA to explain the process of deregulation. The historical nature of this chapter should not be taken to mean that this process has been completed. It has not. As the chapter will show, the process is ongoing. And, given the advancement of the current neoliberal paradigm, deregulation continues to be a process working through globalization to affect both developed and developing countries. Many argue that the integration of global financial markets is the reason that the financial disruption in the currency market for the Thai baht in 1997 was able to produce financial and economic crises across Asia and work its way to the other side of the world to disrupt financial activities in South America and Russia. The impacts from these changes are not simply theoretical.

Theoretical views: regulation or not?

The importance of the controversy over financial regulation was recognized by the *Economic Journal* which in 1996 dedicated a section to airing the sides in this debate. Three sides were aired: free banking, deposit insurance only, and regulation that must include a lender of last resort. Central to this discussion are two questions: (1) what is the nature of money in a capitalist market system? and (2) how do banks behave in a capitalist market system? Kevin Dowd (1996) argues for free banking. He posits that if one agrees that *laissez-faire* is in general a desirable economic approach, then this structure should also be desirable for the financial sector. This is the free banking stance: no role for government in markets.

Dowd addresses the money question by making the assumption that a commodity-based money would need to be introduced into the economy, and it would become the 'anchor' to the monetary system (Dowd, 1996, p. 680). In effect, he is proposing a return to a gold standard. Bank liabilities would be the circulating medium; they would always be convertible into the 'anchor' commodity at a fixed exchange rate. He assumes that this commodity's value will not change, and any changes in the size of this 'money' supply will be reflected in proportional changes in prices in the economic system. Effectively, money does not matter in the operation of the economy.

This type of money, as Dow (1996) notes, is not currently in use in any nation-state. Additionally, a commodity-based money anchors the economy by not expanding in step with the growth in production. It puts 'natural' limitations on the growth in the productive system which is antithetical to the nature of capitalism. Capitalism's *raison d'être* is expansion. Credit money is by design a money that is appropriate to the capitalist system. It is also prone to expansions and contractions that not only affect prices, but also affect the level of operation of the economy. It produces instability and uncertainty.

In his address to the second question, Dowd states that free markets function best without the help of a government or central bank. He argues that central banks and deposit insurance, specifically, and regulators, in general, create the problems that they are supposed to remedy. His argument focuses on the behavior of market actors – bank depositors and bank managers – and reasons that they will act in their own best interest if by doing so will effect outcomes that are efficient and macroeconomically stabilizing (Dowd, 1996, pp. 681–2). Supporters of deposit insurance argue that it is supposed to safeguard depositors against the failures of excessively risk-taking managers and the unforeseen downturns in macroeconomic activity that are known to affect banks negatively. Dowd argues that banks without this insurance safeguard will act rationally by holding the level of capital that is necessary to safeguard deposits, and that, contrarily, banks will hold less capital – thus putting their deposits at more risk – when they have deposit insurance. In other words, deposit insurance creates a moral hazard. Finally, his argument extends to the lender of last resort (LLR). He posits that having an LLR will produce the same effect of increased risk-taking by managers because they understand that the depositors will be bailed out by the central bank should the bank become insolvent.

Benston and Kaufman (1996) hold a view about bank regulation that is similar to Dowd's. Instead of trying to reorganize the existing capitalist system as Dowd does, they argue that one needs to focus 'on how banks should be regulated in an existing non-laissez faire structure to achieve the best of both worlds' (ibid., p. 688). In their article they do not address the nature of money, but they agree that bank regulation and an LLR create moral hazard. Effectively, they see that these interventions can create bank failures with very large losses which only publicly provided insurance can absorb. Ultimately, they argue that government can play an important prudential role, and it must, because its intervention creates the problems.

Their argument takes the form of asking how bank regulation can aid in producing an optimal allocation of resources by redressing the violations of assumptions that produce competitive market systems. They think that banking regulation could improve outcomes in two areas: administrative efficiency and market externalities (ibid.). In their discussion of administrative efficiency, however, Benston and Kaufman argue that the government's record on monitoring banks' risk-taking is not enviable and that the central bank has a questionable record implementing policies that stabilizes money supply changes (ibid., p. 689). Then in their discussion of externalities, they argue that bank money provides a positive externality in being accepted as money. Government intervention, however, does nothing to reduce the uncertainties associated with money, and central bank policies may increases the possibility of losses due to the policies' propensity to incite inflation (ibid., pp. 691–2).

These views lead them to conclude that 'the only efficiency justification for government-provided deposit insurance is credible absorption of government-imposed losses' (ibid., p. 689). They indicate that private insurance could not provide a competitive, therefore credible, product. It would not be able to absorb the potential losses. Their final point is that bank regulation should be limited to imposing capital requirements large enough to absorb banks' possible losses (p. 694). This action, they note, would have happened automatically had not the government intervened (p. 696).

The final perspective on banking regulation is captured by Dow (1996), a post-Keynesian, who views banking as an industry that produces a public good: moneyness.[2] From this perspective, money is a process, not any particular financial asset, and its behavior is dependent on the institutional structures produced by the government and markets. Money is credit money. By its nature, the process that creates moneyness and is integral to maintaining its liquidity arises in banks, so banks must function so as to maintain people's confidence in them, and also in moneyness. Since this view of money emerges from a capitalist market economy, some of the basic characteristics of capitalism also affect moneyness: uncertainty and economic activity's cyclicality. Both uncertainty (not statistical risk) and cyclicality can affect the confidence with which people demand and hold money. A change in confidence can alter money's liquidity and value. To maintain this confidence, 'society adopts conventions as a basis for expectation formation, and supported by the state, creates elements of stability to aid decision-making (see Hodgson, 1988)' (Dow, 1996, p. 699). Additionally, a central bank through its LLR activity adds to that confidence and stability. Dow notes that banks' cyclical lending patterns, which could ultimately induce their own insolvency, will not hinder money's liquidity because the central bank will intervene. The institutional origination of money and its grounding in a capitalist economy mean that bank regulation and supervision can act as 'elements of stability'. Government, therefore, can intervene to prudentially regulate banks so that money can confidently continue to function as a medium of exchange, unit of account and store of value.

Dow's institutionally grounded post-Keynesian view lays the foundation for an alternative understanding of how money arises from and is endogenous to a capitalist economy, and why bank regulation is necessary. It stands in contrast to the other two neoclassically based arguments which have a vision of money that is exogenous to the economic process. This means that in Dowd's argument money is a commodity whose value is determined by supply and demand in its own market: uncertainty and liquidity are not problematic. While bank liabilities may operate as one kind of money, they are always convertible into the commodity form at a fixed exchange rate, so their liquidity and value are assured (Dowd, 1996, p. 680). Dow notes that this type of money is increasingly less common, and further that Dowd's notion of banks having an option not to convert their liabilities into the money commodity would mean loss of confidence in the moneyness of bank liabilities and, therefore, in banks' stability. She argues that Benston and Kaufman's modification of free banking, which includes deposit insurance but not an LLR, would rely on market decisions to provide additional reserves to needy – illiquid, but not insolvent – banks. Yet, 'it has not been demonstrated that the allocation of reserves by the market would be based on better knowledge than that available to a central bank with a supervisory apparatus' (1996, p. 702). And, when in an economic expansion the unrealistic expectations of asset values are held in common throughout the banking system, the ravages from Minsky's (1982b) systemic financial fragility would best be countered by an infusion of liquidity. This type of systemic intervention is the usual purview of a central bank (Dow, 1996, p. 702).

These theoretical differences in conceptualizing money undergird the different views of bank regulation. The regulated financial sector that draws from Dow's understanding of a capitalist economy emerged for many countries out of the turbulence of the Great Depression. In the post-Great Depression period, confidence in market decision-making was low because the financial sector had been implicated in causing and/or lengthening the depression. The reconstruction of the financial sector after the Great Depression was a response to and an attempt to learn from those financial weaknesses that had devastated economies worldwide. The financial and economic stability that these regulations produced is also important in understanding the reasons for their fall from favor. The regulatory structure was central to the production of sustained domestic economic activity which increased the confidence in the stability of the banking system and money's liquidity. Additionally, the integration of the regulated domestic financial sector with the international financial structures of the Bretton Woods agreement produced a stable world financial structure into the 1970s. At the end of this period, inflation led to economic disruptions that challenged the effectiveness of traditional Keynesian policies. The combination of the economic problems and this ostensible failure of Keynes's theory opened the door to deregulation.

If the process of deregulation that began in earnest in the 1970s is to be understood, then it needs to be investigated within a national context. The manner in which deregulation in each nation-state proceeded is different even though the market forces that pushed for it may have been very similar. For this particular investigation of deregulation, I shall use the case of the USA. It was one of the first nation-states to deregulate, and because of its powerful role in global politics and economics, it has been one of the major forces and models for deregulation.

Deregulation in the post-World War II USA
Theoretical structures
The foundation of this historically and nation-specific analysis of deregulation depends upon the theoretical insights of the Social Structure of Accumulation (SSA) (Bowles et al., 1984) and Minsky's financial instability hypothesis (FIH) (1982a and 1982b). These views synchronize with Dow's Keynesian approach and are appropriate to analyzing the post-World War II US economy. They argue for a view of the capitalist system in which cyclical fluctuations are endogenous; money matters; and political and economic institutions can have an impact on the operation of the nation-state. They complement each other as evolutionary theories that understand the behavior of a capitalist economy as being historically grounded, institutionally based, and dependent upon its class relations. Each approach depends upon historical context as the frame for its analysis. In the SSA, historical context allows the various sets of capital, labor and citizen relationships to vary through time. The path of economic change, then, depends upon the interaction of the

current institutional structures with the prevailing capital–labor–citizen relations. Minsky's FIH uses historical context to show how the decisions made by both financial institutions and firms to finance investment can affect the accumulation process and the level of economic activity. At any particular historical moment firms and financial institutions have attained a level of financial stability that is reflective of their analysis of borrowers' and lenders' risk, and the level of economic activity in the current phase of the business cycle. As the expansion phase of the business cycle extends, the use of debt rises, and risk assessments show a reduced perception of the level of risk as the confidence from the expansion climbs. This reduced perception of risk, working in concert with the increased level of debt finance, means that the level of potential financial instability has risen. How quickly the economy moves to a financially unstable position and whether financial instability results in an economic downturn depends upon the economy's growth rate, its institutional structure, and its financial regulation, supervision and policy.

Production's structure
The USA experienced some mild recessions in the years right after World War II ended, but overall the period from 1945 to 1973 is called the Golden Age because of its effectively high and stable rates of growth. The annual growth rate averaged 4.3 percent while the rate of investment averaged 4.7 percent. These growth rates were accompanied by an average unemployment rate of 4.3 percent and an annual inflation rate of about 2.0 percent. The process of converting from a war- into a 'peace'-time economy did not produce the expected postwar recession. The transition was smoothed by wartime savings that financed 'pent-up' consumer demand, by the governmental expenditures on the Korean War, which perpetuated the war economy, and by Europe's Marshall-Plan-financed expenditures. Effective aggregate demand kept the economy operating close to its level of full employment.

Drawing upon the SSA analysis allows us to see that the Golden Age's high and stable growth rates resulted from the institutional arrangements between capital, labor, the citizen and the state (Bowles et al., 1989). The major manufacturing sectors were provided with a set of contractual international relationships, e.g. fixed exchange rates, that stabilized trade and a set of domestic agreements with organized labor that produced a manageable labor force, a procedure to 'set' wages and, therefore, the distribution of income. Additionally, the state had taken on new foreign and domestic roles in which it assumed responsibility for maintaining a level of aggregate demand sufficient to avoid anything but mild business cycles; a military presence that would sustain the *Pax Americana*; and a set of domestic policies that advocated for the poor and promoted a readjustment to the skewed US income distribution.

Financial structure
The US financial structure in the post-World War II era had been developed in response to the Great Depression. The New Deal financial legislation passed by Congress aimed at reintroducing confidence into the depository system so that it could concentrate on fulfilling its goal: financing economic growth. An integral part of confidence-building in the sector was functional as well as prudential regulation. First, functional regulation took the form of segmented markets that distributed deposits to the different depository institutions. Each depository institution was specialized by its type of deposit and lending

activity. This segmentation provided a dedicated conduit by which credit was allocated to particular industries. Then, price competition for deposit funds between like depository institutions was dampened through the use of deposit rate ceilings. Regulation Q mandated non-interest-bearing demand deposits and low-interest-bearing time deposit rates which acted to keep borrowers' rates low. Finally, 'firewalls' between depository and non-depository institutions were established to separate the highly speculative activity of non-depository institutions from the credit apparatus that was fundamental to the growth of the economy (Dymski, 1990). Functional regulation, more than prudential regulation, sculpted the shape of the financial sector. Providers of finance were divided into three basic credit conduits: freely functioning financial markets organized primarily by investment banks that provided long-term capital funds, e.g. plant and equipment; commercial banks for short-term commercial funds, e.g. operating capital; and savings and loans for long-term residential finance, e.g. mortgages. The creation of the regulated financial sector was, in effect, an industrial policy that carved the financial sector into regulated markets that made credit decisions based on an understanding that the success of their borrowers, the industrial and commercial sectors and homebuyers, was fundamental to the success of the lenders, the commercial banks and savings and loan associations.

This functional financial structure was a direct response to the fear of financial fragility, collapse and contagion that was created by the Great Depression. The segmentation of deposits and loans by type of institution was a conscious measure to dampen competition and the spread of any problem between the different types of depository institutions. This separation produced liability and asset sides of each type of depository institution that were unique. Commercial banks specialized in demand deposits on the liability side and short-term commercial and industrial loans on the asset side. They were limited to offering non-interest-bearing demand deposits and savings deposits. Savings and loans (S&Ls) specialized in passbook savings accounts on the liability side and home mortgages on the asset side. Their time deposits rates were not limited by Regulation Q until 1966, at which point they were usually about one-fourth percentage point higher than the commercial banks' time deposits. Since the different depository institutions did not have major asset or liability overlaps, competition between these depository institutions was at a minimum and a crisis in one institution or type of asset was not easily communicated to other types of institutions or assets.

This functional structure produced a segmented financial market in which lenders were constrained to work with particular borrowers. The borrowers, however, were not mandated to obtain loans from the depository institutions, and they often had other possibilities: internal finance or trade credit. Lenders, on the other hand, had nowhere else to turn for their assets. They operated within prescribed credit markets; their borrowers were, in effect, legislated. So while both borrowers and lenders were linked together, the lender was even more dependent upon the borrower than the reverse. As long as each side remained mutually dependent, this set of relationships operated in a mutually beneficial symbiotic way.

The prudential regulation enacted because of the Great Depression included depositors' insurance and an enhanced interventionary role for the Federal Reserve. The insurance limited depositors' risk and, therefore, reduced the possibility of a financial collapse due to bank runs. All depository institutions regardless of their charter status had to be insured. Not all depository institutions, however, could be or were members of the

Federal Reserve, but all of them did have some Fed-like regulator and supervisor. This regulator was responsible for implementing and maintaining a regular examination schedule of its institutions to assure the proper operation of the depository institutions and to guard against fraudulent activities. Additionally, it was up to this regulator to assure the deposit institutions' access to liquidity and, in the final instance, the Federal Reserve was the lender of last resort. This responsibility went beyond the provision of liquidity. If a member bank was experiencing solvency problems, then the Fed would have to decide what the impact of its insolvency would be on the economy. If the institution were too important to fail, then the Federal Reserve was there to organize a bailout.

The US economy's operation

The theoretical arguments posed by Dowd and by Benston and Kaufman imply that the moral hazard produced by the regulations should have produced cyclical economic activity between 1945 and 1970 in the USA. Overall, the experience was one of strong stable financial institutions and expansions that outpaced recessions. In the initial postwar years, when there was a spike in inflation or an increase in credit demand during a business cycle expansion, the financial institutions never experienced duress. The structures of the financial sector and the production sector were well suited to interact with each other. The financial sector promoted the flow of finance and the social structure of production turned it into economic growth. Yet this idyllic set of relationships did not last forever. To understand what forces were instrumental in producing the move towards deregulation, it is necessary to understand what happened in the intervening years.

The 1950s

The 1950s economy was replete with business cycles. Economic activity was strong over the decade, with 4.1 percent average annual growth rate, but punctuated with recessions in 1953–54 and 1957–58. The Federal Reserve was actively engaged in using countercyclical monetary policies to stimulate economic activity, but it also had its eye on inflation which seemed to have adopted a new postwar behavioral pattern (Campagna, 1987, p. 272). The volatility of economic activity – four years of growth rates higher than 7 percent and four years of growth rates 2 percent or less – could have pushed financial institutions into untenable positions, but none was negatively affected.

While the commercial banks were not destabilized by the recessions of the 1950s, they were not without challenges. The corporations did not want to deposit their operating funds into non-interest-bearing deposit accounts. Together with the securities dealers they quietly produced the repurchase agreement (RP) market. This innovation meant that funds were withdrawn from the banks, creating a drain on their primary source of finance for loans. The large banks soon became active participants in the RP market, which allowed them to recoup the corporate deposits and, at the same time, they facilitated the corporations' activities in the RP market (Dymski, 1990). Along with their search for a return on their deposits, corporations were looking for cheaper short-term finance. By the end of the decade, they realized that deficit corporations could borrow from surplus corporations without a bank as an intermediary. This move on the part of large corporations into corporate paper (CP) was a challenge to the most fundamental source of banks' profits, commercial lending (Dymski, 1990). While banks maintained their lending to the small and medium-sized enterprises, this transformation in credit demand was indicative of the problem produced when only one side in a financial relationship is regulated. The banks were legislated to lend to the commercial sector, but commerce was not mandated by regulation to borrow from the banks.

The S&Ls did not experience any major changes on their demand or asset side. The Housing Act of 1954, passed as a part of a stimulative fiscal policy, eased mortgage requirements under Federal Housing Administration (FHA) financing. Smaller down-payments and longer terms to maturity made it easier for potential homebuyers to pur-chase homes, which they did. FHA housing starts increased by 10 percent between 1953 and 1954 and under Vetesan's Administration (VA) the increase was almost 100 percent (Campagna, 1987, p. 242).

The depository institutions handled the macroeconomic activity and changes in demand of the 1950s quite easily. The impact from financial innovations was minor, espe-cially when compared to the innovations that emerged in the 1960s, the era of liability management and 'go-go' banking.

The 1960s
In the 1960s the US economy experienced its longest and strongest expansion to date since the Great Depression. During this expansion, the economy grew on average at an annual rate of over 5 percent fueled by investment expenditures, the Kennedy–Johnson invest-ment tax credit, and government expenditures on the military and Great Society pro-grams. To maintain this pace of activity, firms increasingly relied on debt finance. Borrowers, as they searched for lenders, were also seeking cheaper ways to finance their expenditures. The commercial banks, constrained by their regulations, yet pushed by demand, were unable to attract more deposits by changing their deposit rates, so they innovated. By the end of the decade, pushed by excess demand, loss of borrowers to other financiers, and the Fed's tight monetary policy, they realized that a new dynamic was at work. The banks were being driven to innovate and their regulators legitimated their changes. Once introduced, these new assets and liabilities began to tear at the threads that had woven the sector together.

Innovations and the crunch
The first set of banking innovations in this period was in response to the heavy demand for bank loans. Given the regulation of their liabilities – deposit rates and required reserves – the banks, when they wanted to increase their loanable funds, could not simply raise the interest rate paid on deposits. The development of negotiable certificates of deposit (CDs), the Eurodollar market, and bank holding company-issued commercial paper (CP) were the most important supply-side innovations of this period. CDs, which were created in 1961, were deposits, but there was no limitation on their deposit rates and they had no reserve requirements. These attributes meant they could offer competitive rates, a first since the introduction of Regulation Q (Dymski, 1990; Wolfson, 1994). This competitiveness meant that Regulation Q could no longer guarantee the competitive advantage of the S&Ls' time deposit rate. Now, the commercial banks could compete against the S&Ls for savers' deposits. They could also attract funds that might have gone to another commercial bank or a non-depository institution. Finally, it meant that the segmented markets, which had dampened the depository institutions' intra-market competition, were bridged.

After the Fed brought CDs under the regulatory roof, the Eurodollar market was developed as a substitute. Eurodollars were dollar accounts held in the foreign branches of American banks. The excess reserves from these accounts were lent to the American branch of the bank. The interbank lending market in the USA was constrained by the level of excess reserves in the system, so by repatriating foreign dollar-deposits reserves as liabilities, the US banking system was able to expand its supply of credit.[3]

In 1969 another important 'new' source of bank funds emerged: bank holding company-issued CP. The 1956 Bank Holding Company Act had limited multi-bank holding companies' activities, but not those of one-bank holding companies. In 1969, when the Fed applied a 10 percent required reserve to Eurodollar liabilities, the one-bank holding companies moved to supplant those lost reserves with CP. The holding company did this by issuing CP and then used the funds to purchase a loan portfolio from its affiliated bank. Banks received an infusion of new reserves in exchange for their loans and circumvented the Fed's regulation and tight monetary policy (Dymski, 1990, p. 11).

The second set of changes in this period affected the banks' designated borrowers, their demand side. Large corporations with access to capital markets were increasingly issuing their own short-term debt to finance working capital (Federal Reserve, 1969). The impact of this change on the commercial banks during the late 1960s, when credit demand was high, was minimal. The banks, however, understood that the industrial sector – their legislated market – was finding and using other lenders. This innovation, unlike the others, was not introduced by the commercial banks, but by their customers. Given their regulated status, the banks understood the potential impact of this change on their market and future.

The final innovation in this period changed the shape of competition. A Eurodollar loan along with expanding the domestic supply of credit was a loan from one bank to another. Rather than lending directly to an industrial borrower who would purchase working capital, this was a loan that was internal to the set of depository institutions. It was a finance-to-finance relationship that added another layer of debt – increased leverage – to the credit creation process. It was also a transaction that initially circumvented the rule of the Federal Reserve and its regulations. Eurodollars increased the efficiency of the now internationalizing financial system, for unused reserves were recycled. In addition to this efficiency, however, more risk was added to the financial system. Two layers – the deposit and the Eurodollar loan – rather than one, formed the foundation for the retail loan. This layering also linked the depository institutions together, which meant that liquidity or solvency problems at one institution could be communicated to the other. The preponderance of banking innovations was starting to challenge the regulated structure of finance.

The S&Ls experienced the 1960s differently. There was no housing market boom to compare to the rise in demand for bank loans, nor was there a move toward asset or liability innovation. No challenges by the same types of changes comparable to those of the banks occurred. S&Ls did, however, experience the fallout from the 'hot' credit market. They were caught in the first post-Great Depression credit crunch.

The credit crunch was the end product of the interaction between the high market-determined deposit rates on CDs and the regulated deposit rates on time deposits. The banks were offering CDs with market-determined deposit rates. These rates were higher than those offered on S&Ls' time deposits, which resulted in disintermediation from the

S&Ls. The S&Ls' time deposit rates were not regulated, but they were less than the banks' CD rates because the S&Ls' assets, home mortgages, had low interest rates. The S&Ls had to keep their costs below their revenues and, in so doing, they lost their deposits. Funds initially flew into CDs. The banks also experienced some disintermediation problems as they competed with other short-term market instruments. Their negotiable short-term CD rate was regulated by the Fed. As market interest rates rose, bank CDs were not rolled over, which meant that these funds left the banking system – disintermediation. This loss of funds from the depository institutions led to a reduction in bank reserves, bank credit and the money supply. Additionally, it roiled the tax-exempt bond market. To keep further financial disruption from occurring, the Federal Reserve reversed its tight monetary policy and opened its discount window to all banks that needed funds to maintain their financial positions (Wolfson, 1994: 36–9). Disintermediation, coupled with the reduced inflows of savings deposits into the S&Ls, posed major problems for the S&Ls and was a strong contrast with the experience of the banks. On average, the total interest-bearing deposits of banks rose at the rate of 15 percent between 1962 and 1965. This growth compares unfavorably to the growth in non-bank deposits – funds in S&Ls, and mutual savings banks – which topped 11.9 percent in 1963, fell to 10.9 percent in 1964, continued its decline to 8 percent in 1965, and at the end of the third quarter in 1966 only achieved a growth of 3.1 percent (Federal Reserve, 1966: 1748). On average, the S&Ls paid 1.33 percent above the commercial banks' deposit rate from 1957 through 1961. This spread fell to, on average, 0.88 percent between 1962 and 1965 (ibid.: 1745). Even with their deposit rate advantage, the S&Ls were losing deposits. Without a growth comparable to the banks', the growth in S&Ls' assets would also fall behind the banks'. Asymmetrical innovation and deposit growth rates should have been warning signs to their regulators. The banks and S&Ls were no longer traveling along symmetrical and segmented paths.

While the disintermediation and credit crunch of 1966 did not produce a financial crisis, it did signal that tight monetary policy, the inflation-fighting prescription, was not conducive to the healthy activity of regulated depository institutions. In the 1950s, the rate of return on assets (ROA) on S&Ls and commercial banks was relatively equal. In 1962, S&Ls' ROA was 0.80 percent. In 1966 it fell to 0.41 percent, and in 1967 it touched its lowest point in the decade, 0.36 percent. These figures compare with the commercial banks' ROA of 0.82, 0.73 and 0.81 percent, respectively (Isenberg, 2000: 256). The banks operating under a regulator which allowed innovation were able to adapt to changes that had negative impacts on them. Their ROAs show that their adaptations were successful. The S&Ls, on the other hand, did not want to change their instruments or market structure. Their ROAs indicate how the changes in the economy and the financial innovations worked against them. They wanted the stability of the regulated financial sector to return and the old structure to be maintained.

International banking

Cutting across these decades was the development of international banking activities. International financial markets and banks were a source of new banking ideas for the operation of US banks. In the 1950s a few large banks followed their multinational borrowers abroad so that they could continue to meet the needs of these clients. 'In 1950, the seven US banks operating abroad had 95 foreign branches. By 1965, 13 US banks had

211 branches overseas with nearly $9 billion in assets, up from $3.5 billion five years earlier' (Moffitt, 1983, p. 44). The operation of commercial banks overseas stood in strong contrast to the prescribed activities of US banks at home. They had no reserve requirements, no Regulation Q, no deposit insurance premiums, and a broader array of financial activities from which to choose – investment banking being most prominent. US banks moved into this new structure eagerly and found that it enhanced their bottom line. Given these positive foreign experiences, this private cost-reducing and asset-expanding financial structure figured largely in the industrial and regulatory changes that large commercial banks promoted in the 1970s.

One of the most important financial instruments of the 1960s, Eurodollars, set up many domestic banks to become active in international banking. International banking was the source of numerous 'shell' banks in the Caribbean. Unlike the London branches of domestic banks, these were banks in name only. They were created to be an address that would allow US banks the same circumvention of regulations as a London branch would, but at far less cost. Loans were booked out of these offices, but their real use was for the Eurocurrency market and foreign exchange trades. With the fixed exchange rate system of Bretton Woods, banks rarely lost on currency speculation (D'Arista, 1976: 924). With the introduction of flexible exchange rates in 1973, their insulation from loss was no longer guaranteed.[4]

Just as commercial banks' engagement in the foreign exchange market increased the risk in the financial sector, it also signaled a change in the banks' relationship to their traditional activities. Unlike a loan, which generates a return from the interest rate charged, foreign exchange trades generate income from the fees charged on each transaction and from any gains made by capital appreciation. This was not an activity that fostered economic growth by connecting lenders and borrowers. Instead, it downplayed the banks' role as a depository institution and as an intermediary between savers and borrowers. It developed new roles for the bank: intermediary between buyers and sellers of financial assets – foreign currencies – and speculator. Given the transformations that the commercial banks would undergo in the future, these activities were prescient.

These changes in the financial sector – new markets, instruments, crises – were not limited to the financial side of the economy. The industrial sector's structure was also being challenged.

Dissolving industrial and international structures

Bowles et al. (1984; 1989) have argued that all four pieces of the SSA came under pressure by the end of the 1960s. The *Pax Americana*, which they exemplify by terms-of-trade figures, had turned against the USA. Instead of the ratio of the import deflator to the export deflator remaining less than 1, its value throughout the 1950s, it rose to over 1 in the early 1960s (1984: 83). Along with the decline in the terms of trade, other important factors, like the Bretton Woods institutions and arrangements that underpinned the strength of the US dollar were disintegrating. Additionally, the Vietnam War was eating away at the government's budget and the nation's conscience.

The capital–labor accord had been constructed at a point in time when unions reflected a power structure that admitted primarily white men into their halls. The overlooked groups were now raising their voices and shouting to get in and get even. Additionally, the power of the corporation over the workforce was in decline. The unemployment rate by the end of the 1960s hovered just above 3 percent, and it had been falling throughout the expansion. The fear of job loss was waning (1984, pp. 90–91). The capital–citizen accord came under pressure to address the civil rights of groups of Americans that previously had been dismissed. Additionally, the poor and their advocates pushed for a redistribution of the national income via governmental programs since even the 'fully employed' economy failed to eradicate poverty. Along with wanting more butter, some groups in the USA wanted more guns. The Vietnam War produced an increase in the government's expenditures, but given its unpopularity, it had to be deficit financed. The public and private sectors' demand for debt finance and the Fed's tight monetary policies fueled domestic inflation and increased interest rates.

Finally, the intercapitalist rivalry that had been moderated through functional regulation in the financial sector and the USA's commanding role in international trade began to heat up. Changes in the operations of financial institutions due to their international activities and to heavy credit demand rendered the old rules of operation dysfunctional. The functional regulation of the financial sector that made it subservient to the industrial sector was being challenged and changed by financial innovations. On the industrial side, the dominant role of US producers in the US market was contested as the countries that had been decimated after World War II became economically viable competitors. Imports began to take the place of domestically produced goods. This transformation is best seen in how fuel-efficient Japanese autos first introduced to the US market in the 1970s dominated the auto market by the early 1980s. The solidity of the SSA by the end of the 1960s could be compared to an ice cube that had started to melt. The changes that each of these sets of relationships had experienced meant that the domestic and international structures that had set the parameters for market coordination in the post-World War II era were no longer in force.

By the end of the 1960s the New Deal institutions, programs, economic structures and power relationships were still dominant, but challenged. Douglas Dillion and Robert Roosa, bankers in the Kennedy administration, had been advocating the deregulation of Western European capital markets. They argued that liberalized markets would function more smoothly and efficiently, and thereby produce better information and better decisions. In the early 1960s their views were not believed to merit further investigation, but the Federal Reserve's overt agreement to keep Eurodollars free of reserve requirements and the Kennedy–Johnson governments' support for opening up and continuing this offshore market were signs of the changing times (Dickens, 1990; Helleiner, 1994).

Change begins: studies on deregulation

The emergence of persistent inflation in the 1970s had ignited a vast amount of discussion about stabilization policy. The traditional Keynesian prescriptions were not effective, so classical ideas along with several non-traditional theories were debated. These ideas, along with the political punch of the banks and their borrowers, made the 1970s a period of turmoil and change. As the USA moved into the 1970s, facing persistent inflation, an unpopular war outside its borders, social dissent within its borders, and a collapsing international monetary framework which mirrored a rearrangement of international economic and political power, a presidential commission and a House of Representatives subcommittee were formed to analyze financial restructuring. President Richard Nixon's Commission on Financial Structure and Regulation (informally known as the Hunt

Commission) and the House of Representatives Subcommittee on Financial Institutions, Supervision, Regulation, and Insurance (known as the FINE Study) dove head first into the debates over financial regulation, market structure and competition.

The ostensible reason for the presidential commission was the 'saving' of the S&Ls. Their operations had been disrupted by the Fed's tight monetary policies. Between 1966 and 1973 they experienced three rounds of disintermediation, and the housing industry was quite disturbed. Congress on several different occasions – 1968, 1970 and 1973 – proposed non-intermediated ways for meeting and satisfying the demand for home mortgages. 'In 1970, Senator William Proxmire promoted legislation that would require "the Federal Reserve to lend directly to the housing industry"' (Dickens, 1996, p. 120). In 1968 and again in 1973, Representatives Barrett and Sullivan introduced legislation that mandated making federal-funded mortgages directly available to prospective home-buyers at a 6.5 percent interest rate when S&Ls were unable to satisfy the demand (US House of Representatives, 1973, pp. 644–5). These proposals were never more than that, but they showed the representatives' dissatisfaction with the current arrangement and 'threatened' the existing financial institutions with replacement if appropriate changes were not adopted.

The more likely reason for this commission was to begin the process of financial liberalization which the commercial banks strongly supported. Understanding the commission's mandate, knowing the economic interests and connections of its members, and understanding how the commercial banks' successes in the 1960s provided them with economic and political power provide strong support for this particular view.[5] The commission's mandate was to

> focus primarily on problems relating to commercial banks, mutual savings banks, savings and loan associations, credit unions, private pension plans and reserve life insurance companies. For these institutions, the Commission elected to study in detail their functional specialization, the effects of deposit rate regulations, chartering and branching, problems of deposit insurance, reserves and taxation, the effects of regulations on mortgage markets and residential construction, competitive problems and the framework of the financial regulatory agencies. (Report of the President's Commission on Financial Structure and Regulation, 1971, p. 2)

The S&Ls were only one component in the regulated financial sector of this period. Yet the commission's mandate to look at the problems relating to all the financial institutions, not just the S&Ls' problems, indicates that the investigation was about more than just the S&Ls' problems.

The members of the Hunt Commission came from the academy, the homebuilding industry, the industrial sector, a union, and from a cross-section of the financial sector. The weighting of this representation is, however, indicative of the distribution of opinions. The breadth of the representation which matched its mandate, and its weighting towards commercial banks (three representatives) and their borrowers (three representatives) rather than the S&Ls (two representatives) and their borrowers (one representative), again implies that this commission was about more than housing sector problems.

Finally, the economic success of the commercial banks was outstripping that of the S&Ls. In each year of the 1950s except for one, the S&Ls had an ROA higher than the commercial banks. Starting in 1960, this relationship was reversed. The S&Ls' ROAs fell to between 0.4 and 0.6 percent while the commercial banks' ROAs only dipped below 0.8

once in the 1960s (Isenberg, 2000, p. 255). These returns show the effects of the changing US industrial sectors. While the housing sector grew during the 1960s, the emergence of consumer culture, expansion of consumer credit, and introduction of credit cards opened up major markets for the commercial banks. The growth of the 1960s was transformed into successful growth in their assets.

Deregulation begins

In 1971, the Hunt Commission was completed, and in 1975, the FINE Study was issued. The changes proposed in both supported the creation of a financial sector in which participants would be actors in a prudentially regulated market that was imperfectly competitive rather than a functionally and prudentially regulated market. The proposals in these reports to remove the 'protective' regulations responsible for producing the specialized, segmented-market depository institutions meant that the committees thought that nothing less than a complete overhaul of the current system would be sufficient to their task. In effect, functional regulation should be eradicated.

The reports determined that the best type of depository institutions for the emerging US economy was market-based financial institutions with undifferentiated products and services. Since both the commercial banks and the thrifts had been protected from inter-market competition, the protection that had made each type of institution unique had to be dropped. Following from this thinking, the reports proposed that all institutions with transaction accounts would be subject to the same reserve requirements; Regulation Q would be phased out; and markets would determine deposit rates. This meant that all depository institutions could compete against each other using both prices and products. Interstate branching, which had been legislated out of existence in 1927, was also encouraged. The homogenization of products and services meant that the protected status accorded to housing finance would no longer exist, so to insure housing finance availability, various incentives, such as tax credits, were proposed. Suggestions for a new set of universal prudential regulations were made to promote stability in this openly competitive environment. And, the array of depository institution-specific regulators should be rationalized. Most important in this context was the desire to separate the Fed from its regulatory functions so that its sole responsibility would be making US monetary policy.

In 1973, soon-to-step-down President Richard Nixon submitted a bill to the House of Representatives, 'A Program for Reform of our Financial System'. This bill was the legislative kick-off in the drive for financial liberalization. Nixon opened his program by stating:

> Our country depends on a strong, efficient and flexible financial system to promote sound economic growth, including the provision of adequate funds for housing. Such a system is one which allows financial institutions to adapt to the changing needs of borrowers and lenders, large and small, and is free to make full use of technological innovations . . . Events during the last decade, however, have revealed significant defects in the operations of our financial institutions . . . The inflexibility of our financial system can be directly attributed to the methods used by the Government to direct credit flows – methods designed to meet the depressed economic conditions of the 1930's but poorly suited to cope with the expansionary conditions of the past decade (p. 1).

His words were a direct condemnation of the functional regulation that had fostered the strong growth of the USA through most of the post-World War II period. The idea underlying these proposed changes was to implement a 'level playing field' on which each depository institution would be able to compete on its merits. The operation of the market and its decisions were being portrayed as stable, efficient, effective and adaptable. Gone was the view of the market that had emerged during the cataclysmic Great Depression.

By 1974, the large commercial banks were lobbying strongly for financial liberalization. They were the major supporters of deregulation (Adams, 1973; First National City Bank, 1972; Schott, 1972; Smith, 1973). The FINE study was not yet complete, but the banks had already heavily invested in the type of market assets and activities that both the FINE Study and the Hunt Report proposed. As detailed earlier, the commercial banks had been able to alter their sources of funds, expand their operations both geographically and through new products and services, and reshape the contours of their competitive terrain. Their innovations had allowed them to prevail over the usually negative impact of inflation while the S&Ls were held to their traditional financial roles by their regulators and their powerful borrowers. Banks had also engaged in international banking. D'Arista (1976, p. 892) reported that for 12 very large banks operating overseas, between 1971 and 1975, their earnings from foreign activities made up an increasingly large amount of their total income: 1971, 22.7 percent; 1972, 33.9 percent; 1973, 41.5 percent; 1974, 42.6 percent; and 1975, 63 percent. Along with their international operations came the Eurodollar market, the development of the foreign exchange market, opaque lending arrangements – guarantees and lines of credit – and the new borrowers, real-estate investment trusts. The banks saw their future and it had very little to do with traditional corporate lending and everything to do with making their own decisions about new products and risk-taking. They had already shown how successfully they could innovate when it was allowed, and they were chafing at the regulatory bit that continued to subjugate them to industry. Financial liberalization would legitimate what they were already doing and set them on the road to continued innovation and expansion.

The S&Ls did not greet the proposals of this commission and study with the same sense of affirmation as the commercial banks did. Rather than saving the S&Ls, which was ostensibly the reason for these commissions and studies, these changes were seen as producing exactly the opposite result. The S&Ls never supported any of the legislation that proposed a 'leveling of the playing field' approach to financial re-regulation (Camp, 1973; Scott, 1973; Isenberg, 2000). They supported a re-regulation that would have maintained their special status – segmented markets – but expanded the assets in which they could invest. Their idea was to construct a 'family finance' center in which consumer and housing loans were made available. By including consumer finance in their portfolio, they could enter the short end of the market which would diversify their holdings and introduce them to a new expanding part of the credit market. In addition, the S&Ls' regulator, the Federal Home Loan Bank Board (FHLBB), proposed mortgage pooling to provide a stabilized flow of long term funds to the S&Ls (Carlson, 1973).

Standing alongside the FHLBB and the S&Ls was the housing industry. The housing industry needed the S&Ls in a way that the large corporations did not need the banks. The financial assets offered by the S&Ls were not available in another form in the financial market; there was no perfect substitute for a mortgage. This lack of alternatives kept the home builders, homebuyers and S&Ls allied by their mutual interests and produced a lobbying effort to support the S&Ls' proposals for re-regulation.

President Nixon's introduction of legislation in 1973 was the initial move towards codifying the existent financial innovations and laying the groundwork for more to come.

The Congress was not easily as convinced as the President to take a particular side in this economic and financial restructuring. Restructuring bills were introduced in 1974, 1976, 1977 and 1979. It took until 1980 to pass what became the first in the series of six major pieces of deregulatory legislation. The Depository Institutions Deregulation and Monetary Control Act of 1980 (DIDMCA) set the theoretical and institutional tone for rest of the Acts that would combine to almost completely eradicate the changes introduced after the Great Depression.

The deregulation of the 1980s and 1990s

Financial deregulation was spasmodically implemented across the 20 years between 1980 and 2000. The six major pieces of US legislation in conjunction with the Basel Accord of 1988 both deconstructed and re-regulated the US financial sector. Unlike the 'free banking' model suggested by Dowd or the depository insurance model of Benston and Kaufman, this deregulation process constructed a financial sector that still relied upon a central bank which was responsible for acting as a lender of last resort, governmentally backed deposit insurance, asset-side incentives that differentiated between depository institutions, tax differentials, and a broad set of guidelines about community investing. The deregulation aspect of these legislative Acts stripped most of the functional regulation out of the sector and modified some of the prudential regulations. Overall, the motivation was to rely more upon market decision-making for financial asset prices and quantities and less upon regulator decision-making.

DIDMCA and the Garn–St Germain Act of 1982 led the way to deregulation (Cooper and Fraser, 1986). Most importantly, these Acts erased the segmented markets on both the asset and liability sides of depository institutions. On the liability side, Regulation Q was to be phased out over six years and depository institutions would then be free to pay a market-determined deposit rate on their funds or not. Each depository institution was also free to determine which types of deposits it wanted to offer. The combination of these two changes meant that the depository institutions could compete against the powerful money market mutual funds. It also meant that banks and thrifts would compete against each other and the market for funds. No longer would commercial banks and S&Ls necessarily be differentiated by their types of deposits or loans. The cost differential which had been deposit-linked was also eradicated by making all depository institutions offering transaction accounts subject to the same reserve requirements. Institution size made a difference initially in these requirements, but not the type of depository institution or chartering body or membership in the Federal Reserve System. On the asset side, state usury laws were nullified: lending rates on mortgages, business loans and agricultural loans no longer had ceilings. The S&Ls and mutual savings banks were allowed to offer short-term loans: consumer loans and business loans, respectively. This alteration in lending knocked down the final wall in the segmented market. Now, depository institutions could provide the same services – demand and time deposits – with competing deposit rates and they could also compete against each other by offering the same types of loans. The final component, which was an attempt to attract more funds to the depository institutions, extended the coverage of deposit insurance from $40 000 to $100 000.

In addition to these changes, the Garn–St Germain Act expanded the asset side of the thrift institutions' activities. More of their assets, 55 percent, could be invested in commercial lending: commercial real estate; commercial loans; and leasing. At the same time it extended thrift activity in commercial lending, it reduced the level of permitted activity in consumer loans. And, finally, it made some major changes in how regulators could deal with troubled depository institutions. After 1980 there was a swift rise in the number of S&Ls that were experiencing liquidity as well as solvency problems. The new rules relaxed the requirements about who could purchase a failing institution and how the regulators could aid illiquid institutions. These latter rule changes were seen as a necessity because of the large number of illiquid thrifts, but later legislation would decide with 20–20 hindsight that some of these changes exacerbated the thrifts' problems.

Chronologically, the Basel Capital Accord of 1988 was the next important aspect of deregulation. This regulation was introduced by the Bank for International Settlements (BIS), which was working with the important central banks of the developed countries. Given the rising level of uncertainty as financial institutions altered their products and processes, BIS and the money-center central banks agreed that a standardized risk-based assessment of loans would reduce the level of uncertainty. The explosive innovation of this 1980s – new assets, new liabilities and new types of lending activities – meant that institutions were in an experimental moment. There was no historical knowledge about the new assets, competitors, or types of competition to guide regulators or actors. Determination of credit, interest rate, liquidity and exchange rate risks are inaccurate at the best of times (Dow, 1996). In periods of change and confusion such determinations are at best misleading. Cutting across the turbulence, the Basel Accord constructed a categorical index of depository assets and assigned a credit risk weight to each one. Depending upon the risk weight, a certain amount of capital had to be held as a 'reserve' against the asset. The highest risk weight mandated an 8 percent capital reserve. These capital requirements were higher than those imposed in the USA's central bank, but they were phased in over a four-year period.

The turmoil brought on by the interaction of innovation, macroeconomic policies and activities, deregulation, and historically determined assets of the S&Ls and commercial banks ended in a landslide of thrifts' and banks' bankruptcies. Both the S&Ls and the banks failed to adapt smoothly to all the changes of the decade. In the case of the S&Ls, the deregulation that they as an industry had not supported pushed them towards collapse. As for the banks, they had welcomed deregulation and the chance to innovate, but the vagaries of markets, lemon loans, high-risk gambles and some fraud also pushed them to the brink.

The next two pieces of legislation were drafted to reconfigure the S&Ls, again, and redefine the rules for banks' deposit insurance. By 1989 Congress agreed that the failures of the S&Ls had to be addressed systematically. It passed the Financial Institutions Reform, Recovery, and Enforcement Act (FIRREA), which legislated new regulations and a new regulator, disposed of the old regulator and insurer as well as the assets of the bankrupt S&Ls, and imposed new asset and liability regulations. The shape of the new S&L looked very similar to the pre-deregulation S&L. FIRREA re-established mortgage instruments as the primary S&L assets (70 percent of tangible assets) and reduced their other riskier assets, commercial real estate and junk bonds (Laderman, 1990). To further address their balance sheet risk, capital standards were raised. The Federal Deposit Insurance Corporation Improvement Act of 1991 (FIDICIA) addressed the stress that bank failures were causing the Federal Deposit Insurance Corporation (FDIC). In the six years between 1987 and 1992, more than 1000 banks were resolved at a cost to the Bank

Insurance Fund (a subsidiary of FDIC) of about $30 billion, which more than exhausted the $18 billion reserve in the deposit insurance system (CBO, 1994). The legislation introduced new requirements about when and how to resolve a troubled bank. Additionally, it revamped the insurance premium. Risk-based analysis was introduced by the Basel Accord and FIDICIA extended that program by mandating that risk-based insurance premia should replace the flat rates.

The final two pieces of legislation, the Interstate Banking and Branching Efficiency Act of 1994 (IBBEA) and the Gramm–Leach–Bliley Act of 1999 (GLBA), reignited the deregulation process. The first of these bills completed the vision of a deregulated financial sector as manifested in the Hunt Report and FINE Study by allowing interstate branching. Since the 1927 McFadden Act, banks were restricted to branching operations within their state. Several regional pacts concluded in the 1980s circumvented this restriction; however, most banking and branching was still intrastate. By repealing this restriction, potential markets for deposits, loans and other financial services were expanded. This removal of geographical restrictions meant that competition among already established banks would rise. The second bill took another very significant step: it repealed the Glass–Steagall Act of 1933. Glass–Steagall had separated investment from commercial banking. This combination had been indicted in the early post-Great Depression era as a cause of the depth and duration of the Depression. The 1933 Act had been considered fundamental to the maintenance of the financial health of the US financial sector and economy. The GLBA authorized commercial and investment banks to integrate using a financial holding company (FHC) structure. Under the auspices of an FHC the segmentation and firewalls of the post-Great Depression regulated market were erased. Now the FHC can underwrite and deal securities as well as accept deposits and underwrite insurance. Commercial banks are once again allowed 'to hold equity in firms for the purpose of eventual resale' (Furlong, 2000). The GLBA maintains the same regulators as before with the same purview.

Changing the rules of operation in the US financial sector was not easy. Neither the political nor the economic climate was supportive of it in the first 30 years after the Great Depression. Even in the 1970s after the Hunt Report and the FINE Study were published, it took ten years to fight through the passage of the first piece of deregulatory legislation. And then, it took 20 more years to persuade legislators to rescind the primary elements of functional regulation. Prudential regulations persist. While many of the regulatory elements that Dow's theoretical vision would propose as necessary to stabilize a systemically unstable financial sector have been deconstructed, neither the 'free' banking view of Dowd nor the minimalist regulation and insurance view proposed by Benston and Kaufman have been constructed. Given the ongoing theoretical tension in how the capitalist system operates, the institutional nature of markets, and the indeterminacy about the impacts of deregulation, it is unlikely that the process of deregulation will ever produce those outcomes.

Notes

1. This description of deregulation draws heavily upon ideas that were published in two articles: Isenberg (2000; 2003).
2. Corrigan (1982; 2000) makes a similar argument that banks are 'special' because they produce liabilities that are accepted as money. Even with the proliferation of close-money substitutes, it is still only depository institutions that produce this liability that is 'payable on demand at par and readily transferable to third parties'.

Additionally, it is only banks that remain as the back-up source of liquidity for the other parts of the economy – financial and non-financial.

3. In 1969, when the Fed implemented a tight monetary policy to combat inflation, market interest rates rose above CD rates. The banks used Eurodollars to minimize the effect on their pool of total purchased funds, and therefore, their ability to supply credit was retained (Wolfson, 1994, p. 179).

4. How much exposure did US banks have in this market? It was unknown. Congress had asked in 1973 that foreign exchange transactions be reported to the US Treasury. In 1976, they were still perfecting the form on which these transactions were to be recorded (D'Arista, 1976, p. 877).

5. Lane Kirkland, representative from the AFLCIO, refused to sign the commission's report and wrote in his dissenting statement: 'Besides avoiding the social priority area, it would appear that the net effect of the Commission recommendations would be to channel funds out of the housing market as well as to raise the cost of mortgage money – especially during a tight credit market.

   'The Commission recommendations that would eliminate interest rate ceilings on deposits, widen the functions of thrift institutions and allow interest rates on mortgages to escalate would have a harmful effect on the housing market.' Unfortunately, his analysis came true, for affordable housing has become one of the dominant problems plaguing the USA since the 1980s.

References

Adams, Eugene (1973), Chairman of the Board, First National Bank of Denver and President, American Bankers Association, letter to Jack Carlon, Assistant to the Director for Economic Policy, Office of Management and Budget, 16 October. William E. Simon Papers, Special Collections, David Biship Skillman Library, Lafayette College, Easton, PA.

Benston, George and George Kaufman (1996), 'The appropriate role of bank regulation', *Economic Journal*, **106**(May), 688–97.

Bowles, Samuel, David Gordon and Thomas Weisskopf (1984), *Beyond the Wasteland*. Garden City, NY: Anchor Press.

Bowles, Samuel, David Gordon and Thomas Weisskopf (1989), 'Business ascendancy and economic impasse: a structural retrospective on conservative economics, 1979–1987', *Journal of Economic Perspectives*, **3**(1), 107–34.

Camp, Carl (1973), Acting Director of Federal Home Loan Bank Board, letter to Roy Ash, Director, Office of Management and Budget, 4 May. William E. Simon Papers, Special Collections, David Bishop Skillman Library, Lafayette College, Easton, PA.

Campagna, Anthony (1987), *US National Economic Policy 1971–1985*, New York: Praeger.

Carlson, Jack (1973), Economic Policy Division, Office of Management of the Budget, memo on FHLBB proposal for pooling mortgages, 31 August. William E. Simon Papers, Special Collections, David Bishop Skillman Library, Lafayette College, Easton, PA.

Congressional Budget Office, Congress of the United States (1994), 'The changing business of banking: a study of failed banks from 1987 to 1992', www.cbo.gov/ftpdocs/49xx/doc4915/doc30_part2.pdf

Cooper, S. Kerry and Donald R. Fraser (1986), *Banking Deregulation and the New Competition in Financial Services*, New York: Ballinger.

Corrigan, Gerald (1982), 'Are banks special?', Annual Report Essay, http://minneapolisfed.org/pubs/ar/ar1982.cfm

Corrigan, Gerald (2000), 'Are banks special? A revisitation', Annual Report Essay, http://minneapolisfed.org/pubs/region/00-03/corrigan.cfm

D'Arista, Jane (1976), 'US banks abroad', in *Financial Institutions and the Nation's Economy*, Compendium of Papers Prepared for the FINE Study, Committee on Banking, Currency, and Housing. US House of Representative, 94th Congress, Second Session, Book II, Washington, DC.

Dickens, Edwin (1990), 'Financial crises, innovation and federal reserve control of the stock of money', *Contributions to Political Economy*, **9**, 1–16.

Dickens, Edwin (1996), 'The Federal Reserve's low interest rate policy of 1970–72: determinants and constraints', *Review of Radical Political Economy*, **28**(3), 115–25.

Dow, Sheila (1996), 'Why the banking system should be regulated', *Economic Journal*, **106**(May), 698–707.

Dowd, Kevin (1996), 'The case for financial *laissez-faire*,' *Economic Journal*, **106**(May), 679–87.

Dymski, Gary (1990), 'The structure and regulation of the US banking system from the Great Depression to the present day', unpublished manuscript.

Federal Reserve (1966), 'Time deposits and finacial flows', *Bulletin*, **52**(12), 1739–52.

Federal Reserve (1969), 'Changes in corporate financing patterns', *Bulletin*, **55**(12), 911–18.

First National City Bank (1972), 'The Hunt Report – an agenda for counter-reformation', *Monthly Economic Letter*, July, 7–12.

Furlong, Fred (2000), 'The Gramm–Leach–Bliley Act and financial integration', *FRBSF Economic Letter*, 31 March, www.frbsf.org/econrsrch/wklyltr/2000/312000-10.html

Helleiner, Eric (1994), *States and the Reemergence of Global Finance: From Bretton Woods to the 1990s*, Ithaca, NY: Cornell University Press.

Hodgson, Geoffrey (1988), *Economics and Institutions*, Philadelphia, PA: University of Pennsylvania Press.

Isenberg, Dorene (2000), 'The political economy of financial reform: The origins of the US deregulation of 1980 and 1982', in Robert Pollin (ed.), *Capitalism, Socialism, and Radical Political Economy*, Cheltenham, UK and Northampton, MA, USA: Edward Elgar, pp. 247–69.

Isenberg, Dorene (2003), 'The national origin of financial liberalization: The case of the United States', in P. Arestis, M. Baddeley and J. McCombie (eds), *Globalisation, Regionalism and Economic Activity*, Cheltenham, UK and Northampton, MA, USA: Edward Elgar, pp. 182–209.

Laderman, Elizabeth (1990), 'FIRREA and the future of thrifts', *FRBSF Economic Letter*, Federal Reserve Bank of San Francisco, 19 Jan.

Minsky, Hyman (1982a), *Can 'It' Happen Again?* Armonk, NY: M.E. Sharpe.

Minsky, Hyman (1982b), 'The financial instability hypothesis: Capitalist processes and the behavior of the economy', in Charles Kindleberg and J. Laffargue (eds), *Financial Crises: Theory History and Policy*, Cambridge: Cambridge University Press.

Moffitt, Michael (1983), *The World's Money: International Banking from Bretton Woods to the Brink of Insolvency*, New York: Simon and Schuster.

Report of the President's Commission on Financial Structure and Regulation, December 1971, Washington, DC: USGPO.

Schott, Francis (1972), 'A qualified "yes" to the Hunt Commission Report', *Bankers Magazine*, Summer, 91–5.

Scott, Tom (1973), 'State of Tom B. Scott, Chairman, Legislative Committee, United States savings and loan league', *US House of Representatives*, Part 1.

Smith, Tynan (1973), Secretary of the Board, Board of Governors of the Federal Reserve, letter to Deputy Secretary, William E. Simon, 5 April, William E. Simon Papers, Special Collections, David Bishop Skillman Library, Lafayette College, Easton, PA.

US House of Representatives (1973), *The Credit Crunch and Reform of Financial Institutions*, Hearings, Committee on Banking and Currency, 93rd Congress, first session, parts 1 and 2.

Wolfson, Martin (1994), *Financial Crises*. 2nd edn. Armonk, NY: M.E. Sharpe.

23 Banking and financial crises
Gary A. Dymski

1. Introduction

The past 25 years have witnessed an endless succession of financial crises. A partial list includes the 1980s Latin American debt crisis, the 1980s US savings-and-loan crisis, the 1990s Japanese banking crisis, the 1994–95 Mexican banking and currency crisis, the 1997–98 East Asian financial crisis, the 1998–99 Russia/Brazil currency crisis, the 2000–2001 Turkish currency crisis, and the 2001–2002 Argentine currency and banking crisis.[1] The global economy has been ever prone to financial crises (Kindleberger, 1978), but never with this pace and depth. Why now? What is special about this period, and what do heterodox economists have to say about these events? Global financial deregulation and liberalization are clearly defining characteristics of the current period – but what is the connection between these phenomena and the landscape of financial and banking crises?

This chapter delineates and contrasts orthodox and heterodox approaches to finance and banking and to contemporary financial crises. In the orthodox view, globalization and liberalization are exposing weaknesses in developing nations' regulatory frameworks, forcing the abandonment of non-market mechanisms for allocating credit, and expanding the set of assets whose prices are moved in part by uninformed and panicky traders. This said, the social damage caused by financial crises in this period is temporary, part of the price to be paid for the transition in developing nations from state-led to market-led growth.

In the heterodox view, by contrast, the liberalization and marketization girdling the world is often dictated by strong-armed interventions by the International Monetary Fund and the World Bank. State-led mechanisms for allocating credit are not flawless; but market-led credit flows will not invariably improve allocations, while widening the scope for financial instability. Much of the fuel for these crises has been provided by structural macroeconomic contradictions, and these have been worsened, not ameliorated, by official institutions' interventions. A semi-orthodox dissent has also emerged (Stiglitz, 2003); indeed, the lines of debate are shifting, as new crises emerge and play out in real time.

This chapter is necessarily selective regarding both the crisis episodes (the extended banking crisis in Japan is not discussed here) and the three heterodox theoretical approaches that are covered here (post-Keynesian, structural Keynesian, and post-Walrasian). Section 2 introduces orthodox and heterodox conceptualizations of money and credit; section 3 delineates different approaches to banking and financial crisis. Section 4 summarizes events through the 1980s, focusing on the Latin American debt crisis and US banking crises; section 5 reviews crises in the 1990s and 2000s, with special attention to the East Asian crisis. Section 6 concludes.

2. Orthodox and heterodox approaches to money and finance

Orthodox economic theory can be defined as the conception that economic outcomes can be satisfactorily explained by identifying the strategic and non-strategic interactions of goal-seeking agents. The highest feasible levels of social welfare will arise when these agents can freely interact in competitive markets. There are few economists who use the purely competitive ideal of the Walrasian general equilibrium as their operative model for understanding social dynamics; however, there are many for whom the Walrasian ideal of perfect competition and complete information acts as a frame of reference and an evaluative criterion. A standard methodological convention in orthodox theory is to deviate only when necessary from Walrasian assumptions; theoretical results are understood in relation to this benchmark case.

Each variant of heterodox theory identifies one or more axes of real-world economic and, in most cases, social processes that are ruled out in the core orthodox vision. Some heterodox economists focus on gender inequality or on racial inequality, others on the impacts of real time and uncertainty, others on class conflicts, still others on unequal relations between global South and North. In this sense, heterodox theory can be defined by its 'unity in difference', in Lawson's phrase (2005, p. 2). The key point of difference is the absence of a pre-analytical commitment to the idea that market coordination accurately allocates social resources.

Money and credit relations
Money and credit have special characteristics as goods. Contemporary money is 'fiat' (intrinsically non-valuable) money, whose worth depends largely on the policies and efficacy of the state that has issued it. Credit, in turn, is intrinsically heterogeneous, since it is extended by banks and non-banks to borrowers with different degrees of risk; its volume depends in turn on the willingness of lenders to lend, on borrowers' degree of desperation or desire, and on regulators' willingness and ability to control lenders' behaviour. Economic theory must account for these characteristics, directly or by implication.

In the orthodox approach, economic agents see through the veil of fiat money's nominal amount and evaluate its worth based on what it can buy. Changes in the amount of money issued by government have no affect on this capacity; consequently money is 'neutral', in the long run if not in the short run. So if sober-minded central bankers manage financial aggregates and markets in a sober way, agents in markets will be able to properly evaluate price signals and price risk, and crises can be minimized or avoided. Orthodox theories view banking institutions, in turn, as consensual arrangements that unambiguously increase welfare. Consider the two most influential orthodox banking frameworks: Diamond (1984) views banks as exploiting economies of scale in monitoring borrower performance – hence as 'delegated monitors'. Diamond and Dybvig (1983), in turn, show how banks can arise as devices for enhancing liquidity and providing insurance.

In contrast with orthodox theory, heterodox theorists of money and financial relations generally contend that financial processes are a key source of contemporary economic crises. They emphasize one of several critical elements – missing information, uncertainty, or socioeconomic conflict – that can lead to unstable, irrational, or unfair financial processes.

Many economists have emphasized the impact of Keynesian uncertainty on investment and on financial markets, developing ideas that Keynes set out vividly in the *General Theory* (1936, especially chs 5 and 12; 1937).[2] When agents must make decisions whose outcomes are fundamentally unknowable, confidence and conventional beliefs become crucial in decision-making.[3] Decisions about asset-holding and investment – and hence asset markets – are then especially unstable. And since longer-term investment and asset decisions support aggregate demand and shape productive capacity, 'Keynesian' uncertainty plays a significant role in macroeconomic dynamics.

Uncertainty in this sense necessarily gives rise to the possibility of speculation in asset markets. Asset speculation can be defined in one of two ways: in one definition, it occurs when an agent buys an asset in the hope that it can be sold at a return greater than its inherent value; in the second, it occurs when an agent buys an asset in the hope that its price will rise at a rate significantly faster than that of assets (or commodities) as a whole. In a Keynesian-uncertain environment, one can buy an asset and hope that it will be overvalued by conventional opinion – leading to the prospect of speculative gain. In effect, the gap between one's own judgement and conventional opinion, or even shifts in conventional opinion itself, can make speculation in asset markets a reasonable course of action.

The next two heterodox approaches discussed here represent different embodiments of conflict theory. Generally, conflict theory involves an assertion that key social actors – for example, members of capitalist (firm-owning) and worker (labour-providing) classes, men and women, financial capitalists and 'productive' capitalists, and so on – have competing and disputed claims over the distribution of social product and/or over social planning, production, or investment processes. These claims cannot be resolved in a socially neutral way; instead, they are settled by the exercise of social power.

The Keynesian structural macroeconomic approach to money and credit builds on the pioneering insights of Edmar Bacha and Hollis Chenery; it was developed by economists such as William Darity, Amitava Dutt, Bill Gibson, Nora Lustig and especially Lance Taylor (1983; 2004). This approach focuses on the challenges of growth in the global South by incorporating Keynesian, Sraffian and Kaleckian features into formal, aggregate macroeconomic models that emphasize intranational income distribution and the structure of global trade and finance relations. Money and finance relations do not always play a decisive role in these models, but they may. This approach highlights the potential for sectoral 'gaps', which can arise because of both resource limitations and structural handicaps (Taylor, 1994a). Financial gaps, in particular, can arise because of investment–savings imbalances, current and capital account imbalances, and government fiscal imbalances. Such financial gaps can lead to hyperinflation, debt crises, credit starvation, or economic stagnation.

Models developed within the structural Keynesian approach emphasize social conflicts of two kinds: intranational class or distributional conflict, and/or conflicts among national economies. Emerging in the 1980s, another strand of heterodox theory emphasizes conflict at the microeconomic level. Bowles et al. (1983), among others, argue that labour–capital conflict was at the heart of the historical development of the twentieth-century US economy. This conflict, over the terms and conditions of labour extraction, is conditioned by and spills over into other social arenas. Bowles and Gintis (1993; 2000; Bowles, 1985) undertake theoretical investigations that attribute this labour–capital conflict to the contested nature of market exchange in the presence of principal–agent conflict. Generalizing this finding to credit as well as labour markets, these authors argue that taking contested exchange seriously suggests the need for economic theory to be more socially embedded and to pay explicit attention to the political aspects of economic exchange.

While these heterodox concepts were being developed, Joseph Stiglitz and others were also developing principal–agent models of credit and labour markets which emphasized not unevenly distributed power, but unevenly distributed (asymmetric) information.[4] Asymmetric information models of the credit market assert that borrowers may know more than lenders about their competence or their plans for using and repaying loaned funds. Lenders' optimal response is to ration credit and/or to use signalling mechanisms to screen borrowers; but no single equilibrium exists (Stiglitz and Weiss, 1981). In suggesting the indeterminacy of market mechanisms, and the possibility of chronically inefficient outcomes, these models and their makers wander far from orthodox core values. Stiglitz and his frequent co-author Bruce Greenwald argue that an information-intensive model should replace the Walrasian model as the general paradigm in monetary economics (Stiglitz and Greenwald, 2003), if not in economics *per se* (Greenwald and Stiglitz, 1989). In effect, theirs is a 'semi-orthodox' perspective.[5]

3.   Orthodox and heterodox approaches to banking and financial crises

Orthodox theory, as we have seen, views the equilibria in banking and financial markets as sets of welfare-enhancing optimal contracts. Financial development enhances these markets' scope, liquidity and depth, and thus facilitates growth.[6] A crisis then arises when either the choice-enhancing or welfare-enhancing characteristics of these markets are damaged through some external interference. The older versions of orthodox monetary theory – especially monetarism – advocated steady monetary policy that avoids extremes. On one side, a government using inflationary monetary policy to increase its control over resources (Friedman, 1971) can go too far and trigger excessive price increases, disrupting the economy's orderly price-signalling process. On the other, monetary authorities' failure to provide reserves to a faltering economy can lead to debt deflation, as in the 1930s (Friedman and Schwartz, 1963).

This older orthodox tradition emphasizes that crises occur when financial processes are destabilized due to governmental interference. In newer orthodox writings, crisis occurs when agents are blocked from achieving optimal financial contracts. A situation such as that described by Friedman – unstable or inappropriate monetary policy – is interpreted as making it more expensive to make contracts on financial markets or causing financial markets to shut down altogether. Credit markets involving smaller borrowers, who depend on costly intermediation by banks, are especially prone to these two problems. For example, Bernanke (1983) argues that intermediated credit markets' slowdown contributed to the Great Depression; and Mankiw (1986) argues that intermediated markets can cease to exist in some equilibrium states. Perverse incentives for rent-seeking or gains-taking by regulators captured by regulated industries (Kaufman, 1990) can also lead to credit-market malfunctioning.

The newer orthodox literature suggests relying on appropriate regulation and oversight to avoid financial and banking crises. Incomplete and asymmetric information creates multiple equilibria; to avoid crises (bad equilibria) due to greedy borrowers or risk-loving managers, market regulation must establish and maintain discipline in markets that involve risk-taking and credit commitments.

How, in contrast, do economists use heterodox theory to view financial crises? There are some systematic differences common to all the heterodox approaches discussed above. First, they all view the economy as a fragile latticework of structural debtor–creditor relations, whose sustainability depends on maintaining either debt–income ratios (the post-Keynesian approach), stock–flow balances (the structural Keynesian approach), or social-power balances (the contested-exchange approach). Second, none of these hetero-dox approaches views the economic system as being governable in any real sense by monetary authorities or other regulators. In the post-Keynesian approach, the theory of endogenous money asserts that lenders can and will make as many loan commitments as they are able; in the structural Keynesian approach, the volume of money and credit is determined by factors outside national authorities' control; in the contested-exchange approach, profit-maximizing agents make their own bargains on their own terms. Third, all the heterodox approaches view information as only one dimension that agents consider in making financial decisions. Further, the degree of belief in this information can vary.

Many heterodox analyses have explored financial crises in the context of the business cycle. Money, credit and banking relations are fundamental to both Marx's and Keynes's conceptions of capitalist crisis and business cycles (Crotty, 1985; Itoh and Lapavitsas, 1999). Hyman Minsky (1975; 1982; 1986) set out a vision of a financially driven business cycle that synthesizes Keynes's insights into uncertainty and investment with those of Irving Fisher (1933) on debt deflation.

At the centre of Minsky's vision is the financial instability hypothesis. This hypothesis suggests that financial fragility will emerge endogenously in the economy. Rising debt levels relative to income, together with unsustainable asset prices, lead to a collapse in investment and asset prices, causing a possibly precipitous economic downturn. So financial and banking crises arise endogenously in Minsky's vision of contemporary cap-italism. The rise of what Minsky called 'money market capitalism' (Whalen, 1997) and ongoing technological change transform the patterns and incidence of financial instabil-ity and crises, but make them no less inevitable. The central bank's reactions to these crises define the contemporary business cycle. In the absence of adequate intervention, debt deflations occur, devastating household solvency and business viability. With timely lender-of-last-resort interventions and countercyclical public spending, however, asset-price collapses are avoided, at the price of a 'big government' and a chronic tendency toward price inflation.

While Minsky builds his ideas around a stylized business cycle model, he does not specify the equations of a model. Further, his writings specify only incompletely how microfoundational behaviours and macroeconomic dynamics intersect (Crotty, 1990). Focused as he was on his core ideas, he was, in Isaiah Berlin's expression, a hedgehog and not a fox (Dymski and Pollin, 1993). For example, Minsky's notion that speculative invest-ment and finance rise in the business cycle upswing can be explained as due to Keynesian uncertainty (Wolfson, 1996). But it can also be attributed to cognitive dissonance – 'disaster myopia' (Guttentag and Herring, 1984) – among investors, to 'noise' caused by uninformed traders (Black, 1986), or to disruptions in monitoring and pooling mech-anisms used by lenders to offset asymmetric information (Bernanke, 1983; Mankiw, 1986). So the agents becoming more financially fragile can be understood as either ratio-nal and informed, rational but uninformed, arational, or irrational.

Economists working in the structural Keynesian approach have, unlike Minsky, devel-oped formal models incorporating different features of his ideas into an aggregate macro-economic setting. The breakthrough paper in this area was that by Taylor and O'Connell (1985). These authors note that Minsky's vision is 'microeconomically detailed and institutional' and hence 'beyond the reach of mere algebra' (p. 871). In their model, accu-mulation depends on the gap between the expected profit rate and the interest rate (firms' cost of funds); whether this gap is maintained depends partly on whether rentiers hold their portfolios in firms' liabilities (thus reducing interest rates) or flee to money (thus driving up interest rates and firms' cost of funds) and generate a crisis.[7]

Delli Gatti and Gallegati (1990), in turn, develop an IS–LM model in which financial crisis can arise due to the lack of pre-coordination between the price of capital assets and the supply price of investment goods. The latter price is fixed by firms' pricing-decision rules, and the former by equilibrium in the money market. The degree of leverage by firms and feedback effects between anticipated profits and investment can lead the economy to an unsustainable peak, beyond which it collapses into crisis. Delli Gatti et al. (1994) show how this simple framework readily leads to complex dynamics, especially when linearity assumptions are relaxed.[8] Jarsulic (1988; 1989; 1990) shows how bank behaviour can cause cyclical behaviour due to interactions with demand factors; financial constraints on investment, in combination with the debt–capital ratio, determine growth dynamics. Palley (1994) develops a model that combines features of Kaldor's business cycle theory with Minsky's insights into financial fragility. This model differs from the others mentioned here because it focuses on consumer debt. Consumer debt both expands consumption possibilities but also, over time, constrains economic growth as debt burdens become more onerous.

Interestingly, in all these models expectational errors are not crucial. In all these cases, mutually inconsistent sectoral interconnections generate unstable outcomes and financial crises. Money is not 'neutral', a common feature of Keynesian models; and this non-neutrality in structural Keynesian models is embodied in the inconsistent, interlocking interactions among financial and non-financial markets. These models also suggest, in contrast to the orthodox framework, that market liquidity is endogenous and unreliable – market depth changes quickly when agents become fearful or firms become overleveraged (or both).

While the frameworks reviewed thus far depict closed economies, open economy aspects of financial fragility are centrally important (Minsky, 1995; Wolfson, 2002). Lance Taylor, whose work with O'Connell had launched the literature on closed economy formal Minsky models, helped create a formal structural open economy model of financial crisis, focusing on currency markets. Krugman and Taylor (1978) developed a Keynesian model specifying conditions under which currency depreciation can lead to reduced national output – that is, imports exceed exports, consumption propensities from profits and wages differ, and government revenues rise with devaluation. This result, which asserts that structural factors can impact economic output, flies in the face of conventional theory, according to which devaluations increase output growth by stimulating exports.

But then, what happens to governments that attempt to avoid currency depreciation? Krugman (1979) answers this question. He shows that there are limits to any government's ability to defend its currency through open market operations and foreign exchange market interventions; when those limits are reached, the government must devalue. Speculation may not take the form of a one-time attack, but instead may ebb and flow over a period of time before the government loses its last reserves and its ability to defend itself. Krugman's model is not explicitly Keynesian, but is structural; in effect, it suggests that when a nation's macroeconomic structure is unsustainable in the medium run, speculators can start a currency crisis (and trigger a banking crisis) in the short run by making payment demands that precipitate a currency collapse.

A description of the unfolding of crisis has not been developed in the contested-exchange approach. The equilibrium and evolutionary models (Bowles, 2004) used in this approach describe scenarios of allocative inefficiency, not crisis processes. For example, Bowles (2004, pp. 312–20) illustrates credit-market inefficiency by describing a situation of exclusion that closely resembles Mankiw's (1986) scenario of credit crisis. Bowles's discussion emphasizes the exercise of power in markets, wherein strong agents victimize those who are weak and lack options; if not countered, this leads to the institutionalization of systematic social differences in wealth.[9]

4.   Financial crises from Bretton Woods to the Latin American debt crisis

The USA became the financial hegemon with the establishment of the Bretton Woods system of fixed exchange rates in the 1940s. For some years thereafter, nominal and real interest rates were low and stable, and macroeconomic growth was relatively steady. Indeed, in the higher-income countries, this period has been called a 'golden age' of capitalism. Tight regulation of banks combined with central-bank vigilance minimized worries about banking crises and about the destabilizing consequences of cross-border lending. By the mid-1960s, this calm and crisis-free situation (in higher-income countries) was breaking down. The USA experienced a credit crunch in 1966 (Wray, 1999). This encouraged Minsky to develop his ideas about the endogenous emergence of financial fragility in periods of tranquility (Minsky, 1975; 1995). From that point on, financial crises emerged as recurrent events in economic dynamics (Wojnilower, 1980; Wolfson, 1994).

The end of the Bretton Woods dollar-standard system in 1973 then exposed nations and firms to exchange risk for the first time in four decades. With the reemergence of exchange-rate volatility, some economists began to monitor and theorize financial disruptions across borders (Krugman and Taylor, 1978; Krugman, 1979). Kindleberger (1978) demonstrated that financial instability – for the explanation of which he largely drew on Minsky – crossed national borders.

The end of the Bretton Woods system was followed in short order by two oil price shocks, which led to stagflation and high interest rates. The emergence of innovative financial instruments such as money-market mutual funds created new savings options for middle-market households and firms. The withdrawal of below-market-rate funds from the US banking system – in a process termed disintermediation – exposed US banks and savings and loans to liquidity and default risk (Dymski, 1988). Larger corporate borrowers began to raise short-term and long-term funds in direct credit markets, bypassing banks. Banks had to seek out new loan customers.

Meanwhile, national restrictions on international capital movements were lifted: floating exchange rates created 'the overwhelming need to hedge against the costs that fluctuating exchange rates imposed upon the private sector' (Eatwell and Taylor, 2000, p. 2). Banks found their new loan customers by recycling the revenues of oil exporters, especially to oil-importing nations. They also channelled funds to the 'oil-patch' states of the USA, especially Texas, which experienced an oil boom.

All the elements were in place for a three-pronged banking and financial crisis. The first prong involved the savings and loan associations (thrifts). Many thrifts became insolvent in the early 1980s, squeezed between the long-term low-interest mortgage loans in their asset portfolios, the loss of substantial volumes of long-term savings, and rising short-term borrowing costs. Stronger institutions absorbed weak and failing thrifts, with the federal government providing substantial subsidies to offset acquired firms' money-losing mortgage portfolios. Many of the banking firms acquiring these thrifts expanded aggressively into oil-rich states. An extended process of bank and thrift deregulation was initiated. The rapidly growing secondary markets for mortgage debt created new mechanisms for reducing mismatches between risk-taking and risk-bearing. Regulatory oversight and the enforcement of anti-trust law in the financial realm were weakened.

The precipitous drop of global oil prices in the mid-1980s burst the oil-patch bubble and triggered the second prong of the decade's banking crisis. Many large banks in oil-patch states failed, leading to the next phase of the US bank merger wave (Dymski, 1999). Many investments and speculative schemes launched by deregulated thrifts came crashing to earth in a sea of lawsuits. A 1999 US savings-and-loan bailout bill provided for the public recapitalization and (re)privatization of the new wave of failed thrifts (Jaffee, 1989).

Economic theoretical and policy analysis of the thrift and oil-patch banking crisis was dominated by the self-appointed 'Shadow Financial Regulatory Committee' (Benston et al., 1986; Kane, 1989; Kaufman, 1990; White, 1989). This 'Committee' attributed the thrift crisis to realized moral hazard: deposit insurance removes depositors' incentives to discipline intermediaries whose managers or boards take undue risks. The prescription is orthodox policy – continued deregulation and more limited, though more effective, bank regulation.[10]

There was little or no direct response to these arguments by heterodox theorists. Most agreed with journalist Martin Mayer (1990) that this crisis resulted both from the US banking system's structural crisis (Warf and Cox, 1996) and from a systemic, government-financed plundering of the public purse (Glasberg and Skidmore, 1998). Economists and social researchers who had been developing a critical analysis of credit-market discrimination and redlining (Squires, 1992) viewed the thrift crisis and bailout as an assertion of power by large financial institutions and their political allies.

The third prong of the 1980s banking crisis also had its roots in the 1970s. Oil-market disruptions created the need for 'petrodollar recycling'. Large banks made up for the domestic loan-market customers they lost to the direct credit market by lending aggressively to Latin America (especially Argentina, Brazil and Mexico). In an era of rapidly escalating prices for exhaustible resources, this sovereign lending (loans backed by national governments) seemed eminently justified by these nations' resources and growth prospects. As Citibank's Walter Wriston put it, countries don't go bankrupt (Mayer, 1999).

Competitive pressures among megabanks, together with these lenders' 'disaster myopia' (Guttentag and Herring, 1986) led to a rapid build-up of bank loans to Latin America.[11] This lending momentum came to a sudden stop with Mexico's August 1982 debt moratorium, which triggered the first international debt crisis in 50 years. This period's unprecedented nominal interest rates, combined with global stagnation, generated debt renegotiations and adjustment programmes throughout Latin America (Cline, 1984; 1996).

The principal–agent model of credit markets under asymmetric information, which was applied to the thrift crisis, was used to interpret this situation as well. The paradigmatic orthodox model is Eaton et al. (1986). The borrower country is the (unitary) agent, and the lending bank the principal. The borrower country compares the relative utility of repaying its debt and of defaulting; as a rational agent, it defaults when the utility from default is larger. These authors agree with Wriston that 'the resources of the debtor are likely to be adequate to repay the loans regardless' (1986, p. 485). The debt 'crisis' of non-payment is thus due to inadequate debtor effort – that is, to realized moral hazard. The solution is to improve regulatory oversight, and to increase non-payment penalties until these exceed the value of the principal lent. These authors conclude, 'it is surprising that there has been as much lending to developing countries as there has been, not that there is not more' (p. 512).

Using a microfoundational optimization model to interpret this situation necessitates a severely restricted view of events. The possibility of 'disaster myopia' is dismissed out of hand, since lenders and borrowers are viewed as fully rational; also ignored are com-petitive pressures among credit suppliers. Credit risk is treated in a simplified way: its insti-tutional and historical determinants are set aside. Further, treating borrowers as unitary agents with complete control over national wealth abstracts from the political constraints on states in the real world.

Some heterodox accounts of this crisis were developed, most rooted in the structural Keynesian approach. Darity and Horn (1988) developed an overlending model in which developing nations are locked out of primary markets, except in periods of excess liquid-ity. The late 1970s and early 1980s were such a period; during that time the multinational banks 'pushed' credit on to less developed countries because of their competition for market share (Joint ECLAC, 1989). In this framework, the root of the Latin American debt crisis is uneven global development and market segmentation, not borrower recalcitrance. Taylor (1986) sets out a North–South structural model of this crisis. Dymski and Pastor (1990) develop a labour-extraction model of the causes of the crisis: repayment to exter-nal lenders may be problematic because it requires the regressive redistribution of national income; this, in turn, threatens both the legitimacy of political leaders and the continued worker effort on which national output depends. Marcel and Palma (1988) explore the strategic motivations of UK banks and of global North governments in the build-up of Latin American debt, and then the game-theoretic outcomes once the crisis hit. Structural models of the consequences of this debt crisis for macro-management in Latin America were developed by Taylor (1985) and Ros and Rodriguez (1987), among others.

5.   Global financial crises in the 1990s

By the end of the 1980s, Latin America was adrift in its 'lost decade' – stagnation accom-panied by hyperinflation, devaluation and regressive redistribution. None the less, the attractions of lending to developing countries soon beckoned again. Sachs (1989), for example, asserted that developing countries could avoid renewed debt crisis by adopting proper macroeconomic policies. Large-scale financial flows resumed. According to Bank for International Settlements data, cross-border lending to East Asia increased after 1984, rising to a peak of $534 billion in 1997. Lending to the transition economies of Europe also grew, from $134 billion in 1990 to a high of $275 billion in 2000. After 1990, cross-border lending to Latin America also recovered: the nominal value of claims on Latin America grew in every year except one after 1990, from $250 billion in 1990 to $746 billion in 2001.

Mexico became a favoured locus for capital inflows because of the financial liberaliza-tion and renewed prospects for foreign investment under the 1992 North American Free Trade Agreement. The Mexican currency crisis of 1994–95 consequently came as a rude shock. The run on the peso both exposed credit-related problems in Mexican banks, and precipitated a jump in credit risk and defaults, especially among small and medium enterprises. The Mexican government was forced to subsidize selloffs of leading Mexican banks to offshore owners.

Mishkin (1999) summarizes the events of this crisis, and observes that the 'overriding lesson is that the dynamics of financial crises in emerging market countries differ from those in industrialized countries because institutional features of their debt markets differ' (p. 1521). Calomiris (1999) disagrees; he argues that 'the novelty of the Mexican crisis may be overstated' (p. 1458); in his view, its new aspects were its surprisingly large (adverse) spillovers for the external debt of Brazil and Argentina.[12] In their paper on the 'tequila' crisis, Calvo et al. (1996) emphasized the need for policies protecting borrower countries – especially the maintenance of adequate reserves and provisions for orderly workouts. Stronger measures, such as exchange and capital controls, are rejected. Goldstein et al. (2000), in turn, argued for 'early warning systems' for investors and creditors. Both suggestions anticipate that enhancing information and guarantees will suffice to limit contagion and bandwagon effects.

This calming prognosis was contained in a World Bank report on capital flows to developing nations (World Bank, 1997), which reviews both the Latin American and 'tequila' crises. This report admits that financial opening and cross-border financial flows entail macroeconomic and financial risks; however, these risks are manageable and are outweighed by prospective efficiency and output gains.

Controversies about orthodox views of finance, development and crisis
The oubreak of the 'tequila' crisis so soon after the Latin American crisis led to an extended debate about financial crises and about financial aspects of development.[13] One aspect of this reconsideration was new work on whether financial liberalization aimed at financial deepening would promote growth. McKinnon (1989), a central proponent of financial deepening, argued from recent experience that financial liberalization does not always enhance growth. Other critical examinations of the links between finance and growth soon followed (Wachtel, 2003).

This scepticism about the finance–growth link has then extended to what type of institutional arrangements for credit and finance best promote development. The contrast between the crises-prone, stagnant condition of nations with liberalized financial systems and the steady growth of nations with closed financial systems suggested that institutions matter, and that 'one size doesn't fit all'. Stiglitz (1996) in particular asserted that the East Asian financial system was a key to this region's superior growth, a conclusion also reached in the structural Keynesian perspective (Singh, 1996) (though not universally accepted: Krugman, 1994).

The fact that the 'tequila' crisis was such a surprise had resonance for formal macro models of currency crisis. Obstfeld (1986) had authored and co-authored a series of papers showing how currency crises could arise through 'rational speculative bubbles'. This approach was termed the second-generation model (SGM) of currency crises (Obstfeld, 1994), in contrast to the 'fundamentalist' or first-generation model (FGM) of Krugman (1979). The SGM showed that non-linearities in the behaviours and beliefs of agents in capital, credit and currency markets were sufficient to generate currency crises, especially when macroeconomic fundamentals fall into a 'grey area'.[14] The SGM thus raises the possibility, common to non-linear systems, that small changes in beliefs and fundamentals can unleash cumulative cascades and set off contagion effects in other countries. In effect, the FGM looked to the interaction between financial market behaviours and economic macrostructures and balances; the SGM looks primarily to agents' beliefs and self-reinforcing actions.

The SGM has become more prominent: the move from FGM to SGM parallels the shift from aggregate Keynesian to representative-agent models in macroeconomic theory. For example, Calvo (1987) shows that the cases of Mexico and Argentina in the Latin American crisis can be explained as consistent equilibria (the SGM view); the structural imbalance view (FGM) may give a misleading interpretation of what the policy choices are. In his view, it is imperative to penetrate to deeper structural circumstances, which means 'rather than continuing the search for ad hoc models that yield the desired results, our understanding might be better served by examining a simple monetary model with solid microeconomic foundations' (p. 21).

The Asian financial crisis and its aftermath

As noted, East and Southeast Asia were favoured venues for cross-border debt flows in the 1990s. The Asian financial crisis, like the 'tequila' crisis, was a surprise. It hit the global financial system like an iceberg: from its beginning in Indonesia and Thailand in May 1997, it spread over the next eight months to South Korea and the Philippines, among other nations; eventually, it led to speculative attacks on Brazil, Russia and Turkey, among other nations.

The Asian financial crisis, coming on the heels of the 'tequila' crisis, has shaken economists' ideas about financial crises even more. For one thing, neither the FGM nor the SGM fit the East Asian case (Bustelo, 1998). For another, the same analytical framework that had been used to celebrate East Asia's rapid growth was immediately deployed to explain its collapse. Krugman (1998) argued that rampant moral hazard in Asia's state-controlled banking systems was the root cause of this crisis. Stiglitz himself strongly defended the prerogative of developing nations to regulate markets and maintain independent (including non-neoliberal) strategies (Stiglitz, 1998; 2000). In an essay that aims at developing a consensus orthodox view, Corsetti et al. (1999) acknowledge that speculation and contagion effects were important, but asserted that moral hazard and poorly designed economic policies triggered these effects. This paper's support for both the FGM and the SGM demonstrates the vast scope of this crisis, and the ambiguous line between historical experience and theoretical interpretation. There is similar confusion regarding policy implications of the Asian crisis. The International Monetary Fund (1998) argues that borrower nations were vulnerable because their financial systems had too little competition and inadequate regulation. The World Bank (1999) attributes financial crises not just to inadequate regulation, but to international capital-market imperfections, which can lead to contagion effects, liquidity crises and panics.[15]

The Asian crisis certainly provides further empirical evidence that contagion effects matter and that financial liberalization and crisis are linked. For example, Demirgüç-Kunt and Detragiache (1998) find that financial liberalization increases the probability of banking crisis, and that financial crises' contagion effects are large and costly. Hardy and Pazarbaşioğlu (1999) find that variables capturing the vulnerability of the banking and corporate sector predict subsequent crises, but macroeconomic variables do not.

Williamson and Mahar (1998) find that financial liberalization and financial crises coincide. Agénor's empirical survey (2001) finds that financial integration is generating efficiency losses due to patterns of unduly concentrated and procyclical lending in some nations, combined with credit starvation in others.

Heterodox explanations also proliferated. A number of papers combined Keynesian and conflict perspectives in institutional analyses arguing that external and not internal factors – the stagnant global economy, global speculators and the concentration of financial power in the global North – had triggered the crisis (see, for example, Chang et al., 1998; Wade, 1998; Wade and Veneroso, 1998). This fed the idea that external factors – such as the stagnant global macroeconomy, unstable global financial markets, the power of Wall Street, and IMF policies – had played the key role. Kregel (1998) and Arestis and Glickman (2002) show that the Asian crisis can be understood as an outbreak of Minskyian financial instability.

In the Keynesian structuralist and Minskyian approaches, the Asian financial crisis, like the Latin American and 'tequila' crises, are not exogenous – and preventable – events, due to noise traders or to unwise governmental policies; nor do crises afflict only economies with weak 'fundamentals'. These crises arise endogenously because of forces that are intrinsic to the global economy. A Minsky crisis can affect an economy of any size. Eatwell and Taylor (2000) take to its logical conclusion the Keynesian structuralist analysis of the dilemmas facing any one nation. They point to the inescapability for developing nations of the 'trilemma', wherein liberalized capital markets, a fixed exchange rate, and an independent monetary or fiscal policy are not mutually consistent. The trilemma tends to generate cycles: capital inflows spill over to the macroeconomy via the financial system, worsening the current account, and leading to an increased interest rate, and thence to heightened financial fragility and risks. Structural contradictions, not moral hazards, drive this scenario.

6.   Conclusion

A ceaseless string of banking and financial crises has led even economists using orthodox models to become more sceptical about liberalized financial flows. For example, Espinosa-Vega et al. (2000) argue that developing economies may grow faster if they impose some restrictions on cross-border capital movements; and Calvo (1999) has accused Wall Street of being a 'carrier'. Substantial energy is being devoted to developing forecasting models that can warn of the possibility of financial crises in advance; see Kaminsky et al. (2003) and the references therein.[16]

The Asian crisis has led to more, not less, confusion among economists committed to orthodox models about what design principles should guide model-building and policy formation. For example, Chang and Majnoni (2002) show that whether contagion effects or fundamentals generate financial crises (that is, whether FGM or SGM factors dominate) depends on whether the fundamentals are 'weak'. Investigations using orthodox frameworks are ham-strung in addressing contemporary financial crises. Since these models use Walrasian equilibrium as an index of how markets are *supposed* to work, they are reluctant to drop it as a benchmark. At the same time, recent experience makes them uneasy about this reference point. And whereas experience dictates that financial crises are complex and often globe-girdling phenomena, so that 'thick' and 'approximate' models will be more appropriate than 'thin' and 'narrow' ones, the conventions of orthodox model-building favour thin and narrow. In consequence, orthodox debates proceed uncertainly, with participants sometimes talking past one other. The consensus remains that more financial liberalization and market-opening is needed, as long as these markets' regulation is sufficiently reformed. Proper regulation – and perhaps accurate early-warning systems – can remove the tendencies toward crisis from real-world financial systems; the problem is akin to removing a thorn from a foot.

A more troubling interpretation based on post-Keynesian and structuralist Keynesian approaches is available. As noted above, financial crises are endogenous in contemporary macroeconomies, especially in global South economies operating under significant structural imbalances. The Mexican crisis is not anomalous; virtually any developing nation that becomes a favoured offshore investment/loan target will, by virtue of accepting capital inflows, create the macroeconomic circumstances that will later justify speculative runs on its currency. The questions that have to be faced are these: how to restructure global flows of goods and services to minimize the size of such crises, how to build appropriate recovery and reconstruction mechanisms, and how to build macro and micro structures that permit equitable growth throughout the planet.

These questions are perhaps beyond the reach of economists. In the meantime, dialogue and communication are crucial. Some economists have constructed models that combine orthodox tools with heterodox insights, so as to counter orthodox arguments. To take one example, Bustelo and Olivié (1999) assert that contrary to conventional theory, liberalizing markets may increase interest rates and shrink the available pool of credit supply; the reason is that any distortions intrinsic to the formerly closed economy (due to asymmetric information or weak contract enforcement) will be more pronounced (and possibly heavily punished) in the global-market environment. This sort of dialogue is surely the guiding intention of Bowles and Gintis's recent formal explorations of the links between the distribution of rights and power (for example, Bowles and Gintis, 2000), the productivity of enterprises (and the safety of loans), and fairness in market outcomes.

New and innovative analytical directions are also crucially important. Bischi et al. (2004) show how financial instability can evolve under asymmetric information, using an agent-based computational model. Downe (1987) combines ways of inserting post-Walrasian insights into a Minskyian framework. More innovative analytical, empirical and institutional analysis on the basis of heterodox insights is urgent. Further asset-market crises loom ahead. The core elements of heterodox monetary theory – the challenge offered up by Keynesian uncertainty and its consequences, the inescapability of structural contradictions in the global South and of its macroeconomies' structural interconnections to the global North, and the centrality of social power in market exchanges between parties with different levels of global recourse – should be central considerations in efforts to counter such crises and to construct pro-growth, pro-equity policy alternatives for the real world.

Notes

1. Caprio and Klingebiel (2003), in a survey extending only through the mid-1990s, identify 117 different financial crises globally since the late 1970s.
2. Hamouda and Harcourt (1988) identify a commitment to Keynesian uncertainty as a defining characteristic of one of three branches of post-Keynesian theory.
3. Keynesian uncertainty exists when a current decision will generate outcomes later in time which cannot be known in advance, and which cannot be reliably predicted on the basis of a statistical distribution of past values for similar decisions (Davidson, 1978; Cardim de Carvalho, 1988).
4. Compare Bowles (1985) with Shapiro and Stiglitz (1984).

5. Greenwald and Stiglitz (1993) write: 'we believe that the focus [in Keynesian theory] should be on how imperfections in information limit, and sometimes even eliminate, the markets which distribute risk in modern economies . . . amplify shocks . . . and . . . when translated to the labor market and combined with information and other problems . . . can give rise to high levels of unemployment' (pp. 42–3). One might expect that asymmetric-information theorists would coalesce with heterodox microfoundational theorists. This has happened to only a small extent. For example, Stiglitz (1993) wrote of Bowles and Gintis (1993) that its emphasis on power is inappropriate, and that its central insights could be well expressed in information-theoretic terms.

6. For a detailed analysis of the relationship between financial liberalization and growth, see the chapter by Philip Arestis in this volume (Chapter 21).

7. Similar models were suggested by Lavoie (1986/87) and Semmler (1987). Skott (1994) proposes a model with more explicitly Kaleckian features. This outpouring of work led Taylor (1994b) to propose an 'etiology' of macrodynamic work on the Minskyian framework. Taylor (2004, chs 8 and 9) provides a lucid summary of the use of Keynes's and Minsky's insights in structuralist models.

8. Nasica (2000) also explores non-linear extensions of the Minsky framework, in which investment and finance generate recurrent financial crises.

9. Interestingly, Stiglitz and Weiss describe credit-market exclusion in their 1981 paper (their 'redlining' scenario) without discussing this situation's allocative inefficiency. Some members of the 'Shadow Financial Regulatory Committee' have staked out a far more aggressive response to this heterodox argument: White (1993) and Benston (1999) attack policies mandating public reporting or social accountability in banking, such as the Community Reinvestment Act.

10. For example, Benston argues that financial intermediaries' 'specialness for public policy is now limited to fraud and deposit insurance' (2004, p. 13) – precisely what Fama (1980) concludes about banks in efficient financial markets.

11. Vos (1994) observes that overlending is especially likely when overseas lending markets are oligopolistic, banks are competing for market share, and lenders underassess risks.

12. In Argentina, for example, the Mexican currency crisis eroded financial confidence in the Argentine banking system (Carrizosa et al., 1996).

13. The Eaton and Taylor (1986) survey of literature on the Latin American debt crisis, covering a dizzying and mutually inconsistent array of methods and models, foreshadows this theoretical storm.

14. Masson and Agénor (1996) suggest the peso crisis was generated more by SGM-like than by FGM-like factors.

15. Cardim de Carvalho (2000–2001) offers a scathing critique of IMF strategy in the Asian crisis.

16. Grabel (2003) has pointed out that these models are inconsistent and contradictory, and thus provide no safety.

References

Agénor, Pierre-Richard (2001), 'Benefits and costs of international financial integration: theory and facts', Policy Research Working Paper 2699, Washington, DC: The World Bank, October.

Arestis, Philip and Murray Glickman (2002), 'Financial crisis in Southeast Asia: dispelling illusion the Minskian way', *Cambridge Journal of Economics*, **26**, 237–60.

Benston, George J. (1999), 'The Community Reinvestment Act: looking for discrimination that isn't there', *Policy Analysis*, **354**, Washington, DC: Cato Institute.

Benston George J. (2004), 'What's special about banks?', *Financial Review*, **39**(1), 13–33.

Benston, George J., Robert A. Eisenbeis, Paul M. Horvitz, Edward J. Kane and George G. Kaufman (1986), *Perspectives on Safe and Sound Banking: Past, Present, and Future*, Boston, MA: MIT Press.

Bernanke, Ben S. (1983), 'Nonmonetary effects of the financial crisis in the propagation of the great depression', *American Economic Review*, **73**(3), 257–76.

Bischi, Gian Italo, Domenico Delli Gatti and Mauro Gallegati (2004), 'Financial conditions, strategic interaction and complex dynamics: a game-theoretic model of financially driven fluctuations', *Journal of Economic Behavior and Organization*, **53**(2), 145–71.

Black, Fischer (1986), 'Noise', *Journal of Finance*, **41**(3), 529–43.

Bowles, Samuel (1985), 'The production process in a competitive economy: Walrasian, neo-Hobbesian, and Marxian models', *American Economic Review*, **75**(1), 16–36.

Bowles, Samuel (2004), *Microeconomics: Behavior, Institutions, and Evolution*, Princeton, NJ: Princeton University Press.

Bowles, Samuel and Herbert Gintis (1993), 'The revenge of Homo Economicus: contested exchange and the revival of political economy', *Journal of Economic Perspectives*, **VII**(Winter), 83–102.

Bowles, Samuel and Herbert Gintis (2000), 'Walrasian economics in retrospect', *Quarterly Journal of Economics*, **115**(4), 1411–39.

Bowles, Samuel, David M. Gordon and Thomas E. Weisskopf (1983), *Beyond the Waste Land: A Democratic Alternative to Economic Decline*, New York: Doubleday.

Bustelo, Pablo (1998), 'The East Asian financial crisis: an analytical survey', ICEI Working Paper 10/1998, October. Madrid, Instituto Complutense de Estudios Internacionales.

Bustelo, Pablo and Iliana Olivié (1999), 'Economic globalisation and financial crises: some lessons from East Asia', *The Indian Journal of Quantitative Economics*, **14**(1), 29–49.

Calomiris, Charles W. (1999), 'Lessons from the tequila crisis for successful financial liberalization', *Journal of Banking and Finance*, **23**, 1457–61.

Calvo, Guillermo (1987), 'Balance-of-payments crises in a cash-in-advance economy', *Journal of Money, Credit, and Banking*, **19**(1), 19–32.

Calvo, Guillermo (1999), 'Contagion in emerging markets: when *Wall Street* is a carrier', mimeo, 2 May, College Park, MD: University of Maryland.

Calvo, Guillermo, Morris Goldstein and Eduard Hochreiter (eds) (1996), *Private Capital Flows to Emerging Market after the Mexican Crisis*, Washington, DC: Institute for International Economics.

Caprio, Jr, Gerard and Daniela Klingebiel (2003), 'Episodes of systemic and borderline financial crises', World Bank, Washington, DC, unpublished.

Cardim de Carvalho, Fernando J. (1988), 'Keynes on probability, uncertainty, and decision making', *Journal of Post Keynesian Economics*, **11**(1), 66–81.

Cardim de Carvalho, Fernando J. (2000–2001), 'The IMF as crisis manager: an assessment of the strategy in Asia and of its criticisms', *Journal of Post Keynesian Economics*, **23**(2), 235–66.

Carrizosa, Mauricio, Danny M. Leipziger and Hemant Shah (1996), 'The tequila effect and Argentina's banking reform', *Finance & Development*, **33**(1), 22–5.

Chang, Ha-Joon, Hong-Jae Park and Chul Gyue Yoo (1998), 'Interpreting the Korean crisis: Financial liberalisation, industrial policy, and corporate governance', *Cambridge Journal of Economics*, **22**(6), 735–46.

Chang, Roberto and Giovanni Majnoni (2002), 'Financial crises: fundamentals, beliefs, and financial contagion', *European Economic Review*, **46**, 801–8.

Cline, William R. (1984), *International Debt: Systemic Risk and Policy Response*, Washington, DC: Institute for International Economics.

Cline, William (1996), *International Debt Reexamined*, Washington, DC: Institute for International Economics.

Corsetti, Giancarlo, Paolo Presenti and Nouriel Roubini (1999), 'What caused the Asian currency and financial crisis?', *Japan and the World Economy*, **11**, 305–73.

Crotty, James (1985), 'The centrality of money, credit, and financial intermediation in Marx's crisis theory', in Steven Resnick and Richard Wolff (eds), *Rethinking Marxism*, New York: Autonomedia.

Crotty, James (1990), 'Owner–manager conflict and financial theories of investment instability: a critical assessment of Keynes, Tobin, and Minsky', *Journal of Post Keynesian Economics*, **12**(4), 519–42.

Darity, William, Jr and Bobbie L. Horn (1988), *The Loan Pushers: The Role of Commercial Banks in the International Debt Crisis*, Cambridge, MA: Ballinger,

Davidson, Paul (1978), *Money and the Real World*, 2nd edn. London: Macmillan.

Delli Gatti, Domenico and Mauro Gallegati (1990), 'Financial instability, income distribution, and the stock market', *Journal of Post Keynesian Economics*, **12**(3), 356–74.

Delli Gatti, Domenico, Mauro Gallegati and Laura Gardini (1994), 'Complex dynamics in a simple macroeconomic model with financing constraints', in Gary A. Dymski and Robert Pollin (eds), *New Perspectives in Monetary Macroeconomics Explorations in the Tradition of Hyman P. Minsky*, Ann Arbor, MI: University of Michigan Press, pp. 51–76.

Demirgüç-Kunt, Asly and Enrica Detragiache (1998), 'The determinants of banking crises in developing and developed countries', *IMF Staff Papers*, **45**, 81–109.

Diamond, Douglas W. (1984), 'Financial intermediation and delegated monitoring', *Review of Economic Studies*, **51**(3), 393–414.

Diamond, Douglas W. and Philip H. Dybvig (1983), 'Bank runs, deposit insurance, and liquidity', *Journal of Political Economy*, **91**(3), 401–19.

Downe, Edward A. (1987), 'Minsky's model of financial fragility: a suggested addition', *Journal of Post Keynesian Economics*, **9**(3), 440–54.

Dymski, Gary A. (1988), 'A Keynesian theory of bank behavior', *Journal of Post Keynesian Economics*, **10**(4), 499–526.

Dymski, Gary A. (1999), *The Bank Merger Wave: The Economic Causes and Social Consequences of Financial Consolidation*. Armonk, NY: M.E. Sharpe.

Dymski, Gary A. and Manuel Pastor, Jr (1990), 'Debt crisis and class conflict in Latin America', *Review of Radical Political Economics*, **22**(1), 155–78.

Dymski, Gary A. and Robert Pollin (1993), 'Hyman Minsky as hedgehog: the power of the Wall Street paradigm', in Steven Fazzari and Dimitri B. Papadimitriou (eds), *Financial Conditions and Macroeconomic Performance: Essays in Honor of Hyman P. Minsky*, Armonk, NY: M.E. Sharpe.

Eaton, Jonathan and Lance Taylor (1986), 'Developing country finance and debt', *Journal of Development Economics*, **22**, 209–65.

Eaton, Jonathan, Mark Gersovitz and Joseph Stiglitz (1986), 'The pure theory of country risk', *European Economic Review*, **30**, 481–513.

Eatwell, John and Lance Taylor (2000), *Global Finance at Risk*, New York: New Press.

Espinosa-Vega, Marco A., Bruce D. Smith and Chong K. Yip (2000), 'Barriers to international capital flows: when, why, how big, and for whom?', Federal Reserve Bank of Atlanta Working Paper 2000-16.

Fama, Eugene F. (1980), 'Banking in the theory of finance', *Journal of Monetary Economics*, **6**(1), 39–57.

Fisher, Irving (1933), 'The debt-deflation theory of great depressions', *Econometrica*, **1**, 337–57.

Friedman, Milton (1971), 'Government revenue from inflation', *Journal of Political Economy*, **79**(4), 846–56.

Friedman, Milton and Anna J. Schwartz (1963), *A Monetary History of the United States, 1867–1960*, Princeton, NJ: Princeton University Press.

Glasberg, Davita Silfen and Dan Skidmore (1998), 'The dialectics of white-collar crime: the anatomy of the savings and loan crisis and the case of Silverado Banking, Savings and Loan Association', *American Journal of Economics and Sociology*, **57**(4), 423–49.

Goldstein, Morris, Graciela Kaminsky and Carman Reinhart (2000), *Assessing Financial Vulnerability. An Early Warning System for Emerging Markets*, Washington, DC: Institute for International Economics.

Grabel, Ilene (2003), 'Predicting financial crises in developing economies: astronomy or astrology?', *Eastern Economic Journal*, **29**(2), 243–59.

Greenwald, Bruce and Joseph E. Stiglitz (1989), 'Toward a theory of rigidities', *American Economic Review*, **79**(2), 364–9.

Greenwald, Bruce and Joseph E. Stiglitz (1993), 'New and old Keynesians', *Journal of Economic Perspectives*, **7**(1), 23–44.

Guttentag, Jack M. and Richard Herring (1984), 'Credit rationing and financial disorder', *Journal of Finance*, **39**(5), 1359–82.

Guttentag, Jack M. and Richard J. Herring (1986), *Disaster Myopia in International Banking, Essays in International Economics*, **164**.

Hamouda, Omar F. and Geoffrey C. Harcourt (1988), 'Post Keynesianism: from criticism to coherence', *Bulletin of Economic Research*, **40**, 1–33.

Hardy, Daniel C. and Ceyla Pazarbaşioğlu (1999), 'Determinants and leading indicators of banking crises: further evidence', *IMF Staff Papers*, **46**(3), 247–58.

International Monetary Fund (1998), 'The IMF's response to the Asian crisis', Washington, DC: International Monetary Fund.

Itoh, Makoto and Costas Lapavitsas (1999), *Political Economy of Money and Finance*, London: Macmillan.

Jaffee, Dwight (1989), 'Symposium on federal deposit insurance for S&L institutions', *Journal of Economic Perspectives*, **3**(4), 3–10.

Jarsulic, Marc (1988), 'Financial instability and income distribution', *Journal of Economic Issues*, **22**(2), 545–53.

Jarsulic, Marc (1989), 'Endogenous credit and endogenous business cycles', *Journal of Post Keynesian Economics*, **12**(1), 35–48.

Jarsulic, Marc (1990), 'Debt and macro stability', *Eastern Economic Journal*, **16**(2), 91–100.

Joint ECLAC/United Nations Center on Transnational Corporations (1989), *Transnational Bank Behavior and the International Debt Crisis*, Estudios e Informes de la CEPAL. Santiago, Chile: Economic Commission for Latin America and the Caribbean, United Nations.

Kaminsky, Graciela L., Carmen M. Reinhart and Carlos A. Végh (2003), 'The unholy trinity of financial contagion', *Journal of Economic Perspectives*, **17**(4), 51–74.

Kane, Edward J. (1989), 'The high cost of incompletely funding the FSLIC shortage of explicit capital', *Journal of Economic Perspectives*, **3**(4), 31–48.

Kaufman, George G. (ed.) (1990), *Restructuring the American Financial System*, Norwell, MA: Kluwer Academic.

Keynes, John Maynard (1936), *The General Theory of Employment, Interest, and Prices*, London: Macmillan.

Keynes, John Maynard (1937), 'General theory of employment', *Quarterly Journal of Economics*, **51**(2), 209–23.

Kindleberger, Charles P. (1978), *Manias, Panics, and Crashes*, New York: Basic Books.

Kregel, Jan (1998), 'Yes, "it" did happen again – a Minsky crisis happened in Asia', Working Paper 234, Jerome Levy Economics Institute, April.

Krugman, Paul (1979), 'A model of balance of payments crises', *Journal of Money, Credit, and Banking*, **3**(1/2), 311–25.

Krugman, Paul (1994), 'The myth of Asia's miracle', *Foreign Affairs*, **73**(6), 62–78.

Krugman, Paul (1998), 'What happened to Asia?', Working Paper, MIT Department of Economics.

Krugman, Paul and Lance Taylor (1978), 'Contractionary effects of devaluation', *Journal of International Economics*, **8**(3), 445–56.

Lavoie, Marc (1986/87), 'Systemic financial fragility: A simplified view', *Journal of Post Keynesian Economics*, **9**(2), 258–66.

Lawson, Tony (1988), 'Probability and uncertainty in economic analysis', *Journal of Post Keynesian Economics*, **11**(1), 38–65.

Lawson, Tony (2005), 'The nature of heterodox economics', mimeo, Cambridge University.

Mankiw, N. Gregory (1986), 'The allocation of credit and financial collapse', *Quarterly Journal of Economics*, **101**(3), 455–70.

Marcel, Mario and Gabriel Palma (1988), 'Third World debt and its effects on the British economy: a Southern view of economic mismanagement in the North', *Cambridge Journal of Economics*, **12**(3), 361–400.

Masson, Paul R. and Pierre-Richard Agénor (1996), 'The Mexican peso crisis – overview and analysis of credibility factors', Working Paper 96/6, Washington, DC: International Monetary Fund.

Mayer, Martin (1990), *The Greatest-Ever Bank Robbery: The Collapse of the Savings and Loan Industry*, New York: Scribner.

Mayer, Martin (1999), 'The ratings game', *The International Economy*, Washington, DC: Brookings Institution.

McKinnon, Ronald (1989), 'Financial liberalization and economic development: a reassessment of interest-rate policies in Asia and Latin America', *Oxford Review of Economic Policy*, **5**(4), 29–54.

Minsky, Hyman P. (1975), *John Maynard Keynes*, New York: Columbia University Press.

Minsky, Hyman P. (1982), *Can 'It' Happen Again? Essays on Instability and Finance*, Armonk, NY: M.E. Sharpe.

Minsky, Hyman P. (1986), *Stabilizing an Unstable Economy*, New Haven, CT: Yale University Press.

Minsky, Hyman P. (1995), 'Longer waves in financial relations: financial factors in the more severe depressions II', *Journal of Economic Issues*, **29**(1), 83–96.

Mishkin, Frederic S. (1999), 'Lessons from the tequila crisis', *Journal of Banking and Finance*, **23**, 1521–33.

Nasica, Eric (2000), *Finance, Investment and Economic Fluctuations: An Analysis in the Tradition of Hyman P. Minsky*, Translated by Cecile Dangel, Cheltenham, UK and Northampton, MA, USA: Edward Elgar.

Obstfeld, Maurice (1986), 'Rational and self-fulfilling balance-of-payments crises', *American Economic Review*, **76**(1), 72–81.

Obstfeld, Maurice (1994), 'The logic of currency crises', Working Paper No. 4640, Cambridge, MA: National Bureau of Economic Research.

Palley, Thomas J. (1994), 'Debt, aggregate demand, and the business cycle: an analysis in the spirit of Kaldor and Minsky', *Journal of Post Keynesian Economics*, **16**(3), 371–90.

Ros, Jaime and Gonzalo Rodriguez (1987), 'Mexico: study on the financial crisis, the adjustment policies and agricultural development', *CEPAL Review*, **33**, 145–55.

Sachs, Jeffrey (ed.) (1989), *Developing Country Debt and the World Economy*, Chicago, IL: University of Chicago Press for the National Bureau of Economic Research.

Semmler, Willi (1987), 'A macroeconomic limit cycle with financial perturbations', *Journal of Economic Behavior and Organization*, **8**(3), 469–95.

Shapiro, Carl and Joseph E. Stiglitz (1984), 'Equilibrium unemployment as a worker discipline device', *American Economic Review*, **74**(3), 433–44.

Singh, Ajit (1996), 'Savings, investment and the corporation in the East Asian miracle', *East Asian Development: Lessons for a New Global Environment*, Study No. 9, Geneva: United Nations Conference on Trade and Development.

Skott, Peter (1994), 'On the modelling of systemic financial fragility', in Amitava Dutt (ed.), *New Directions in Analytical Political Economy*, Aldershot, UK and Brookfield, US: Edward Elgar, pp. 49–76.

Squires, Gregory D. (ed.) (1992), *From Redlining to Reinvestment: Community Responses to Urban Disinvestment*, Philadelphia, PA:Temple University Press.

Stiglitz, Joseph E. (1993), 'Post Walrasian and post Marxian economics', *Journal of Economic Perspectives*, **7**(1), 109–14.

Stiglitz, Joseph E. (1996), 'Some lessons from the East Asian miracle', *World Bank Research Observer*, **11**(2), 151–77.

Stiglitz, Joseph E. (1998), 'Sound finance and sustainable development in Asia', Washington, DC: The World Bank.

Stiglitz, Joseph E. (2000), 'Capital market liberalization, economic growth, and instability', *World Development*, **28**(6), 1075–86.

Stiglitz, Joseph E. (2003), *Globalization and Its Discontents*. New York: W.W. Norton.

Stiglitz, Joseph E. and Andrew Weiss (1981), 'Credit rationing in markets with imperfect information', *American Economic Review*, **71**(3), 393–410.

Stiglitz, Joseph E. and Bruce Greenwald (2003), *Towards a New Paradigm in Monetary Economics*, Cambridge: Cambridge University Press.

Taylor, Lance (1983), *Structuralist Macroeconomics: Applicable Models for the Third World*, New York: Basic Books.

Taylor, Lance (1985), 'The crisis and thereafter: macroeconomic policy problems in Mexico', in Peggy B. Musgrave (ed.), *Mexico and the United States: Studies in Economic Interaction*, Boulder, CO: Westview Press, pp. 147–70.

Taylor, Lance (1986), 'Debt crisis: North–South, North–North, and in between', in Michael P. Claudon (ed.), *World Debt Crisis: International Lending on Trial*, Cambridge, MA: Ballinger, pp. 227–47.

Taylor, Lance (1994a), 'Gap models', *Journal of Development Economics*, **45**, 17–34.

Taylor, Lance (1994b), 'Financial fragility: is an etiology at hand?', in Gary A. Dymski and Robert Pollin (eds), *New Perspectives in Monetary Macroeconomics: Explorations in the Tradion of Hyman P. Minsky*. Ann Arbor, MI: University of Michigan Press, pp. 21–50.

Taylor, Lance (2004), *Reconstructing Macroeconomics*, Cambridge, MA: Harvard University Press.

Taylor, Lance and Stephen A. O'Connell (1985), 'A Minsky crisis', *Quarterly Journal of Economics*, **100**(5), 871–85.

Vos, Rob (1994), *Debt and Adjustment in the World Economy*, New York: St Martin's Press.

Wachtel, Paul (2003), 'How much do we really know about growth and finance?', *Economic Review*, first quarter, Federal Reserve Bank of Atlanta, 33–47.

Wade, Robert (1998), 'Gestalt shift: From "miracle" to "cronyism" in the Asian crisis', *Cambridge Journal of Economics*, **22**(6), 693–706.

Wade, Robert and Frank Veneroso (1998), 'The Asian crisis: the high debt model vs. the Wall Street–Treasury–IMF complex', *New Left Review*, No. 228.

Warf, Barney and Joseph C. Cox (1986), 'Spatial dimensions of the savings and loan crisis', *Growth and Change*, **27**(2), 135–55.

Whalen, Charles J. (1997), 'Money-manager capitalism and the end of shared prosperity', *Journal of Economic Issues*, **31**(2), 517–25.

White, Lawrence J. (1989), 'The reform of federal deposit insurance', *Journal of Economic Perspectives*, **3**(4), 11–30.

White, Lawrence J. (1993), 'The Community Reinvestment Act: good intentions headed in the wrong direction', Working Paper, New York University, Leonard N. Stern School of Business, Department of Economics.

Williamson, John and Molly Mahar (1998), 'A survey of financial liberalization', Essay in International Finance No. 211, Princeton, NJ: Princeton University.

Wojnilower, Albert M. (1980), 'The central role of credit crunches in recent financial history', *Brookings Papers on Economic Activity*, 277–326.

Wolfson, Martin H. (1994), *Financial Crises: Understanding the Postwar U.S. Experience*, Armonk, NY: M.E. Sharpe.

Wolfson, Martin H. (2002), 'Minsky's theory of financial crises in a global context', *Journal of Economic Issues*, **36**(2), 393–400.

World Bank (1997), *Private Capital Flows to Developing Countries: The Road to Financial Integration*, Oxford: Oxford University Press for the World Bank.

World Bank (1999), *Global Economic Prospects for Developing Countries 1998/99: Beyond Financial Crisis*, Washington, DC: World Bank.

Wray, L. Randall (1999), 'The 1966 financial crisis: financial instability or political economy?', *Review of Political Economy*, **11**(4), 415–25.

24 A post-Keynesian analysis of financial crisis in the developing world and directions for reform
Ilene Grabel[1]

1. Introduction

The Mexican crisis of 1994–95 was the first in a series of currency and financial crises that have unfortunately become a recurrent feature of life in the developing world over the last ten years. Former International Monetary Fund Managing Director Michel Camdessus had it right when he dubbed the Mexican débâcle the 'first financial crisis of the twenty-first century'. Shortly thereafter, financial crises emerged in numerous developing countries in rather close succession to one another. The most serious and perhaps surprising currency and financial crises of the last decade took place in the East Asian 'miracle economies' during 1997–98. Turkey, Brazil, Poland, Russia and Argentina were also parties to rather severe financial instability in this same period.

The East Asian crises stimulated an outpouring of research by heterodox economists, particularly by post-Keynesians (e.g. Arestis and Glickman, 2002; Chang, 1998; Crotty and Dymski, 1998; Crotty and Epstein, 1999; Grabel, 1999; 2003c; Palma, 1998; Singh, 1999; Taylor, 1998; Wade, 1998).[2] This is because heterodox economists found in the events in East Asia strong support for their case that neoliberal financial reform is fundamentally inappropriate for developing countries in so far as it introduces important types of currency and financial risk. These risks can and often do culminate in currency and financial crises.

When many of the world's fastest-growing economies in Asia collapsed, neoliberal economists tried to explain what had gone wrong in the very economies that they had earlier termed miracles. In the Asian crisis countries, neoliberals discovered new – yet somehow deeply rooted – patterns of cronyism, unsustainable speculation and indebtedness, and misguided government intervention. This type of explanation was remarkably similar to the one previously advanced in the context of the Mexican financial crisis. That crisis was also dismissed as an aberration stemming from the country's 'exceptional features'. Neoliberals had earlier cited economic mismanagement, corruption and political instability as underlying causes of the Mexican crisis. Several years later, neoliberals explained the Russian crisis as a by-product of the country's rampant corruption, tax evasion and governmental mismanagement. The Brazilian crisis was seen as the outcome of the government's futile effort to fix the value of the currency and its uncertain commitment to neoliberal reform. And finally, the Argentine currency board went from saviour to demon in the months leading up to its collapse when it and the economy encountered difficulties too serious and too public for even the most ardent neoliberals to ignore.[3]

Neoliberals rely on the benefit of a conveniently short memory in accounting for the recurrent financial crises in developing countries. Economies that pre-crisis are favorites of the international financial community are uniformly recast post-crisis as tinderboxes with serious and glaring deficiencies. The revisionist account of the Argentine crisis (like that of the earlier crises in Mexico, Asia, Russia, Brazil and Turkey) is seriously misguided. In my view, these crises do not stem from the exceptional features of any particular country (though this is not to suggest that they have identical etiologies). Instead, the crises stem from the serious currency and financial risks that are introduced by the neoliberal financial model.

In this chapter I examine analytically the reasons why neoliberal financial reform increases the likelihood of currency and financial crisis in developing countries. Then I discuss several strategies that policymakers can employ to mitigate these risks. Finally, I discuss the policy lessons that derive from this research.

2.   The risks associated with neoliberal financial reform

Over the last quarter of a century, neoliberal economists have been pressing for radical reform of all sectors of developing economies. A centrepiece of the neoliberal reform programme over this period is financial reform. Neoliberal financial reform entails promoting market over state mediation of internal and external financial flows. It also entails eliminating myriad avenues of state influence and control over financial flows (so that, for example, currency values are determined by market forces instead of being fixed by governments, bank loans are allocated based on rate-of-return criteria rather than by government fiat, foreign investors have the opportunity to purchase the assets of domestic firms through outright takeovers or through the purchase of their shares on the country's stock market, and domestic savers and investors can hold their portfolios outside of the country if they choose to do so).

Neoliberal financial reform introduces five distinct, interrelated risks to developing economies. The realization of these risks (and the unique interaction thereof) is at the root of the currency and financial crises that have occurred in the developing world over the last decade. I term these risks currency, flight, fragility, contagion and sovereignty risk. These risks – and the factors that aggravate them – are summarized in Table 24.1.

2.1   Currency risk

Currency risk refers to the possibility that a country's currency may experience a precipitous decline in value following investors' decisions to sell their holdings. This risk is an attribute of any type of exchange rate regime, provided the government maintains full currency convertibility. Note that a convertible currency is defined as a currency that holders may freely exchange for any other currency regardless of the purpose of conversion or the identity of the holder. In practice this means that the central bank pledges to buy or sell unlimited amounts of the domestic currency (and if the exchange rate is fixed, this commitment extends to guaranteeing the price).

That floating exchange rates introduce currency risk is rather obvious. But as Friedman emphasized in 1953, and as events in East Asia and Argentina have underscored, pegging a currency does not eliminate currency risk.[4] If a currency peg is not economically sustainable because the government lacks resources sufficient to protect it, then investors will 'play chicken' with the government in a game that governments ultimately lose. Thus, merely establishing a fixed or pegged exchange rate will not insulate a country from the risk of currency collapse (even if it delays the collapse for some time).

Developing economies confront much more severe currency risk than do wealthier economies for two reasons. First, governments in developing economies are unlikely to

Table 24.1   The risks associated with neoliberal financial reform in developing countries

Type of risk	Definition	Aggravated by
Currency	Risk that a country's currency may collapse following investors' decisions to sell their holdings	• Reserve inadequacy • Inability to organize multilateral rescues • Currency convertibility • Investor herding • Developing economy status
Flight	Risk that holders of liquid financial assets will seek to sell their holdings, thereby causing significant declines in asset/collateral values and increasing economy's ambient risk	• Investor herding • Developing-economy status • Currency convertibility • Absence of mechanisms to manage capital flows
Fragility	Risk that the economy's private and public borrowers are vulnerable to internal or external shocks that jeopardize their ability to meet current obligations	• Locational and maturity mismatch • Volatility of collateral values • Global financial integration • Absence/inadequacy of measures to manage investment, lending and borrowing decisions
Contagion	Risk that a country will fall victim to financial and macroeconomic instability that originates elsewhere	• Financial openness • Extent of currency, flight and fragility risk
Sovereignty	Risk that a government will face constraints on its ability to pursue independent economic/social policies once it confronts a financial crisis	• Developing economy status • Absence/inadequacy of measures to constrain currency, flight, fragility, and contagion risk

hold sufficient reserves to protect the value of their currency should they confront a generalized investor exit. An initial exit from the currency is therefore likely to trigger a panic that deepens investors' concerns about reserve adequacy. An exception would be those cases where a developing economy maintains a currency board (see Grabel, 2000). However, the collapse of the Argentine currency board several years ago demonstrates that merely fixing the exchange rate through a currency board – absent controls on international capital flows – does not insulate the domestic economy from currency, flight, fragility or sovereignty risks. Second, developing-economy governments are rarely (if ever) able to orchestrate multilateral currency rescues or pooling of official reserves, as are wealthier countries.

2.2   Flight risk
Flight risk refers to the likelihood that holders of liquid financial assets will seek to sell their holdings *en masse*, thereby causing significant declines in asset values and

increasing ambient risk in the macroeconomy. By acting on fears of capital losses, investors create a self-fulfilling prophecy. To the extent that declining asset values have spillover effects to other sectors, the realization of flight risk can aggravate currency risk and render the economy vulnerable to a financial crisis. If, for instance, stock portfolios serve as loan collateral, an investor flight from the equity market can induce bank distress, as was the case in East Asia.

Flight risk is also most severe in developing economies because of the likelihood of investor herding. In this context investors are less confident about the integrity of the information they receive, and they perceive greater political and economic risks. Moreover, since investors tend to see developing economies in an undifferentiated fashion, these countries are more vulnerable to generalized investor exits. There is simply no analogue to the 'tequila effect' or the 'Asian flu' among wealthier economies: if investors sour on Japan, this does not make it likely that they will become pessimistic about Germany or the USA (indeed, the reverse is more likely).

Flight risk is most severe when governments fail to restrict the inflow of liquid, short-term capital flows that are subject to rapid reversal. The elimination of such restrictive measures (known as capital controls) has been a key feature of the neoliberal reform agenda of the last 25 years. In this context, policymakers in many developing countries have no means to manage inflows of capital that that are subject to rapid reversal.

2.3   Fragility risk

Fragility risk refers to the vulnerability of an economy's private and public borrowers to internal or external shocks that jeopardize their ability to meet current obligations. Fragility risk arises in a number of ways. First, borrowers might finance long-term obligations with short-term credit, causing 'maturity mismatch' (or what economist Hyman Minsky called 'Ponzi financing'). The prevalence of Ponzi finance patterns in an economy increases the ambient risk level, and hence increases the likelihood of financial crisis. Ponzi borrowers are highly vulnerable to any changes in interest rates (either domestically or internationally, depending on the source of credit), and to changes in the supply of credit.

Second, borrowers might contract debts that are repayable in foreign currency, causing locational mismatch. This leaves borrowers vulnerable to currency depreciation or devaluation that may frustrate debt repayment because it raises the costs of servicing external debts. Or, as in the case of Argentina before the collapse of its currency board, the severe locational mismatch of its external debt portfolio left the country essentially unable to devalue its currency despite the severe costs borne by the tradable goods sector.

Third, if much of the economy's private investment is financed with capital that is highly subject to flight risk, then the economy is vulnerable to fragility risk as well. This is because the viability of investment projects becomes directly dependent on the continued availability and price of unstable capital. In addition, this dependence renders collateral values, upon which the supply of domestic and foreign lending depends, more volatile. Hence capital flight reduces the creditworthiness of borrowers just when they are most in need of funds.

Fourth and finally, fragility risk is introduced whenever economic actors finance their projects with highly risky, non-transparent financial instruments, such as derivatives or off-balance-sheet activities, more generally. For example, in the case of derivatives the sudden necessity to meet collateral requirements often requires the selling of some other securities (often not in an area yet hit by turmoil).[5] This forced selling spreads turmoil to other sectors of the financial system, and ultimately can lead to difficulties in the economy as a whole.

Fragility risk is, to some extent, unavoidable. But the degree to which the decisions of economic actors can induce fragility risk depends very much on whether the institutional and regulatory climate allows or even encourages the adoption of risky strategies. If regulatory bodies do not seek to coordinate the volume, allocation, and/or prudence of lending and investing decisions, then there will exist no mechanisms to dampen maturity or locational mismatches, or the impulse to overborrow, overlend or overinvest. Global financial integration magnifies the possibilities for over-exuberance (and introduces currency-induced fragility) by providing domestic agents with access to external sources of finance.

2.4 Contagion risk

Contagion risk refers to the threat that a country will fall victim to financial and macro-economic instability that originates elsewhere. While global financial integration is the carrier of contagion risk, its severity depends on the extent of currency, flight and fragility risk that characterize the economy. Countries can reduce their contagion risk by managing their degree of financial integration and by reducing their vulnerability to currency, flight and fragility risks.

2.5 Sovereignty risk

Sovereignty risk refers to the danger that a government will face constraints on its ability to pursue independent economic and social policies once it confronts a financial crisis. The constraint on policy autonomy can be introduced for numerous reasons.

First, governments may be forced to pursue contractionary economic policies (namely, restrictive monetary and/or fiscal policy) during financial crises in order to slow investor flight. This is because many central banks and governments try to stem investor flight by raising interest rates and cutting social spending in so far as both are thought to induce inflationary pressures that reduce the real rate of return on investment. Moreover, following a crisis, a particularly contractionary policy regime may be seen as necessary to induce investors to return to the country. This is because it is assumed that the return of foreign investment to the country after a financial crisis depends on the availability of a risk premium. While investors are not dictating policy *per se*, governments may find their ability to pursue expansionary monetary and/or fiscal policy severely constrained when they are seeking to reverse investor flight.

Second, and more directly, developing economies face constraints on their sovereignty when they receive external assistance from powerful countries such as the USA or from multilateral institutions such as the International Monetary Fund. Assistance comes at the price of having critical domestic policy decisions vetted by the external actors that provide support.

Although sovereignty risk stems from the structural position of developing economies in the world economy, this does not imply that this risk is unmanageable. The adoption of measures to constrain currency, flight, fragility and contagion risk all render the possibility of financial crisis less likely (or reduce its severity should it occur), and thereby buttress policy sovereignty.

2.6 Risk interactions
These distinct risks are deeply interrelated. The realization of currency risk can induce investor flight, and inaugurate a vicious cycle of further currency decline, flight and increased fragility. Should these circumstances develop into a full-fledged crisis, policy sovereignty is compromised. In this context, other countries may face contagion. The severity of the contagion risk depends in turn on the degree of global financial integration, the degree to which investors can and do herd out of developing economies, and the extent to which countries have measures in place that constrain currency, flight and contagion risks.

These risk interactions capture well the dynamics of the currency and financial crises that have occurred over the last decade.[6] I am not, however, proposing a strict temporal model of risk interaction. Analytically, the key point is that the construction of neoliberal financial systems in developing countries introduces the constellation of risks presented here. The weight of each risk varies from country to country. The precise triggering mechanism is ultimately unimportant and usually unpredictable. Similarly, the particular characteristics of an individual country (for example, the level of democracy or corruption) do not themselves induce a vulnerability to crisis. Vulnerability to currency and financial crisis is created instead by the specific and interacting risks of the neoliberal financial model.

3.   Policies that can reduce the risks of neoliberal financial reform
I now turn to prescriptive matters. In what follows I consider three strategies for curtailing the risks of neoliberal finance, and thereby for reducing the potential for currency and financial crisis. The strategies to be discussed are as follows: 'tripwires' and 'speed bumps', restrictions on currency convertibility, and the Chilean model.[7]

3.1 'Trip wires' and 'speed bumps'
Grabel (1999) presents in preliminary form a proposal for 'trip wires and speed bumps'. Recent research develops and extends this proposal a great deal (see Grabel, 2004; 2003a; 2003c). The strategy of coupling trip wires and speed bumps involves the development of a set of targeted, graduated policies (i.e. speed bumps) that are activated whenever particular vulnerabilities in the economy are revealed by trip wires.

The trip wire–speed bump strategy is rather straightforward. Trip wires must be appropriately sensitive to subtle changes in the risk environment and adjustable. Sensitive trip wires would allow policymakers to activate graduated speed bumps at the earliest sign of heightened risk, well before conditions for investor panic had materialized (cf. Neftci, 1998; Taylor, 1998). It would be the task of policymakers within their own countries to establish appropriate thresholds for each trip wire, taking into account the country's particular characteristics (e.g. size, level of financial development, regulatory capacity) and its unique vulnerabilities (e.g. existing conditions in the domestic banking system, stock market, corporate sector, etc.). Critical values for trip wires and the calibration of speed bumps would be revised over time in light of experience, changes in the economy, and improvements in institutional and regulatory capacity.

When a trip wire indicates that a country is approaching trouble in some particular domain (such as new short-term external debt to GDP has increased over a short period of time), policymakers could then immediately take steps to prevent crisis by activating speed bumps. Speed bumps would target the type of risk that is developing with a graduated series of mitigation measures that compel changes in financing and investment strategies and/or dampen market liquidity.

Examples of trip wires   Currency risk can be evidenced by the ratio of official reserves to total short-term external obligations (the sum of accumulated foreign portfolio investment and short-term hard-currency-denominated foreign borrowing), and the ratio of official reserves to the current account deficit.

A proxy for maturity mismatch could be given by the ratio of short-term debt to long-term debt (with foreign-currency-denominated obligations receiving a greater weight in the calculation). Locational mismatch that induces fragility risk could be evidenced by the ratio of foreign-currency-denominated debt (with short-term obligations receiving a greater weight in the calculation) to domestic-currency-denominated debt.

An indicator of lender flight risk is the ratio of official reserves to private and bi-/multilateral foreign-currency-denominated debt (with short-term obligations receiving a greater weight in the calculation). Vulnerability to the flight of portfolio investment can be measured by the ratio of total accumulated foreign portfolio investment to gross equity market capitalization or gross domestic capital formation.

A trip wire for cross-border contagion risk task might function in the following manner. A trip wire is activated in 'country A' whenever crisis conditions emerge in 'country B' or whenever speed bumps are implemented in 'country B,' assuming that policymakers in country A have reason to expect that investors would view countries A and B in a similar light (correctly or incorrectly).

Note that the risk that arises from off-balance-sheet activities such as derivatives is not amenable to trip wires precisely because data on these activities are not readily available. For this reason, it is my view that these activities have no place in developing economies because they introduce far too much financial risk (e.g. foreign exchange exposure) to financial systems that are already quite vulnerable. Indeed, research on the East Asian crisis illuminates the important role that off-balance-sheet activities played in the crisis (see Dodd, 2001; Neftci, 1998; Kregel, 1998). Thus financial regulators in developing countries might consider banning the use of these activities altogether. An alternative direction for policy towards derivatives is to mandate their transparency, such that these transactions appear on firm balance sheets. See Dodd (2002) for discussion of transparency and other aspects of prudential financial regulation *vis-à-vis* derivatives in developing economies. With transparency it would be reasonable to think about the development of appropriate trip wires (and speed bumps) for derivatives.

Speed bumps   Trip wires could indicate to policymakers and investors whether a country approached high levels of currency risk or particular types of fragility or flight risk. The speed bump mechanism provides policymakers with a means to manage measurable risks, and in doing so, reduces the possibility that these risks will culminate in a national financial crisis. Speed bumps affect investor behaviour *directly* (e.g. by forcing them to unwind risky positions, by providing them with incentives to adopt prudent financing strategies, etc.) and *indirectly* (by reducing their anxiety about the future). Together, their effects mitigate the likelihood of crisis. Those countries that have trip wires and speed bumps in place would also be less vulnerable to cross-country contagion because they would face lower levels of risk themselves.

Speed bumps for currency risk   Currency risk can be managed through activation of speed bumps that limit the fluctuation of the domestic currency value or that restrict currency convertibility in a variety of ways. The fluctuation of the domestic currency might be managed through a short-term programme of sterilized intervention. The government can also activate a policy of selective currency convertibility, if trip wires illuminated the emergence of currency risk. Specifically, a speed bump might allow the currency to be convertible for current account transactions only. It is important to note that the IMF's Articles of Agreement (specifically Article 8) provide for this type of select-ive convertibility.

Another type of speed bump might allow the government to curtail (but not eliminate) the possibility that non-residents will speculate against the domestic currency by control-ling their access to it. This can be accomplished by preventing domestic banks from lending to non-residents and/or by preventing non-residents from maintaining bank accounts in the country. The Malaysian government took precisely these steps in the after-math of the Asian financial crisis. It restricted foreigners' access to the domestic currency via restrictions on bank lending and bank account maintenance and by declaring cur-rency held outside the country inconvertible.

Speed bumps for lender flight risk   Policymakers would monitor a trip wire that measures the economy's vulnerability to the cessation of foreign lending. If the trip wire approached an announced threshold, policymakers could then activate a graduated speed bump that precluded new inflows of foreign loans (particularly those with a dangerous maturity and/or locational profile) until circumstances improved.

Alternatively, a speed bump might rely upon the tax system to discourage domestic borrowers from incurring new foreign debt obligations whenever trip wires indicated that it would be desirable to slow the pace of new foreign borrowing.[8] In this scenario, domestic borrowers might pay a fee to the government or the central bank equal to a certain percentage of any foreign loan undertaken. This surcharge might vary based on the structure of the loan, such that loans that involve a locational or maturity mismatch incur a higher surcharge. Surcharges might also vary based on the level of indebtedness of the particular borrower involved, such that borrowers who already hold large foreign debt obligations face higher surcharges than do less indebted borrowers. This tax-based approach would encourage borrowers to use (untaxed) domestic sources of finance. Surcharges might also vary according to the type of activity that was being financed by foreign loans. For instance, borrowers might be eli-gible for a partial rebate on foreign loan surcharges when loans are used to finance export-oriented production.

Note that policymakers in Chile and Colombia employed several types of tax-based policies to discourage foreign borrowing during much of the 1990s. Consistent with the trip wire–speed bump approach, the level and scope of these taxes were adjusted as domestic and international economic conditions changed. For instance, in Chile, foreign loans faced a tax of 1.2 percent per year (payable by the borrower), and all foreign debts and indeed all foreign financial investments in the country faced a non-interest-bearing reserve requirement tax during this time. In Colombia, foreign loans with relatively short maturities faced a reserve requirement tax of 47 percent, and foreign borrowing related to real-estate transactions was simply prohibited.[9]

Speed bumps for portfolio investment flight risk   If a trip wire revealed that a country was particularly vulnerable to the reversal of portfolio investment inflows, a graduated series of speed bumps would slow the entrance of new inflows until the ratio falls either because domestic capital formation or gross equity market capitalization increased sufficiently or because foreign portfolio investment falls. Thus a speed bump on portfolio investment would slow unsustainable financing patterns until a larger proportion of any increase in investment could be financed domestically. I emphasize the importance of speed bumps governing inflows of portfolio investment because they exert their effects at times when the economy is attractive to foreign investors, and so are not as likely as outflow restrictions to trigger investor panic. Though not a substitute for outflow controls, inflow restrictions also reduce the frequency with which outflow controls must be used, and their magnitude.[10]

Consistent with the trip wire–speed bump approach, Malaysian authorities twice imposed temporary, stringent restrictions over portfolio investment in the 1990s. The first such effort was in early 1994. At that time, the Malaysian economy received dramatic increases in the volume of private capital inflows (including, but not limited to, portfolio investment). Policymakers were concerned that these inflows were feeding an unsustainable speculative boom in real estate and stock prices and were creating pressures on the domestic currency. In this context, policymakers implemented stringent, temporary inflow controls. These measures included restrictions on the maintenance of domestic-currency-denominated deposits and borrowing by foreign banks, controls on the foreign exchange exposure of domestic banks and large firms, and prohibitions on the sale of domestic money market securities with a maturity of less than one year to foreigners. Reaction to these measures was rapid and dramatic, so much so the that authorities were able to dismantle them as planned in under a year (as they achieved their goals during this time). The immediate, powerful reaction to these temporary controls underscores the potential of speed bumps to stem incipient difficulties successfully.

The Malaysian government again implemented stringent controls over capital inflows and outflows in 1998 during the East Asian crisis. This effort involved restrictions on foreign access to the domestic currency, on international transfer and trading of the currency, and on the convertibility of currency held outside the country. The government also established a fixed value for the domestic currency, closed the secondary market in equities, and prohibited non-residents from selling local equities held for less than one year. By numerous accounts, these rather stringent measures prevented the further financial implosion of the country – a notable achievement since the country was also gripped by a severe political and social crisis during this time. Comparing the situation of Malaysia to other countries that were party to the East Asian crisis, studies find that the country's capital controls were responsible for the faster recovery of its economy and stock market as well as the smaller reductions in employment and wages (Kaplan and Rodrik, 2001). The latter achievements were possible because capital controls provided the government with the ability to implement reflationary economic and social policies uninhibited by the threat of additional capital flight or IMF disapproval.

As discussed in the context of speed bumps on foreign borrowing, policymakers in Chile and Colombia adjusted restrictions on portfolio investment during much of the 1990s as domestic and international circumstances warranted. Consistent with the trip wire–speed bump approach, many other developing countries (such as China and India) have adjusted their restrictions on portfolio investment as circumstances warranted. (For details, see Grabel, 2003c; Epstein et al., 2004; Chang and Grabel, 2004: ch. 9.)

Speed bumps for fragility risks   The fragility risk that stems from excessive reliance on inflows of international portfolio investment or foreign loans could be curtailed by the speed bumps that focus on these types of flight risks (see above). The fragility risk from locational and/or maturity mismatch could be mitigated by a graduated series of speed bumps that requires borrowers to reduce their extent of locational or maturity mismatch by unwinding these activities, or by imposing surcharges or ceilings on them whenever trip wires revealed the early emergence of these vulnerabilities. Recall that speed bumps for off-balance-sheet activities necessitate legislating their transparency.

Speed bumps for cross-border contagion risks   A trip wire–speed bump programme that reduces currency, flight and fragility risks would render an individual economy far less vulnerable to cross-border contagion. This is because well-functioning trip wires and speed bumps would reduce levels of financial risk in the economy, and, as a consequence, mollify anxious investors. Moreover, trip wires and speed bumps would increase the resilience of an economy to a speculative attack were it nevertheless to materialize.[11] This certainly helps to account for the resiliency of the Chilean, Malaysian and other economies during recent financial crises.

3.2   Restrictions on currency convertibility

A convertible currency is a currency that holders may freely exchange for any other currency regardless of the purpose of conversion or the identity of the holder. Today over 150 countries maintain fully convertible currencies. Developing economies have been pressed to adopt full convertibility much earlier in their development than did Western Europe and Japan. Had the East Asian crisis not intervened, the IMF was poised to modify its Articles of Agreement to make the maintenance of full convertibility and an open capital account preconditions for membership.

Historical and contemporary experience demonstrates that there is a variety of means by which currency convertibility can be managed (see, e.g., Grabel, 2003c; Epstein et al., 2004; Chang and Grabel, 2004: ch. 11). As discussed above (section 3.1), the government can maintain currency convertibility for current account transactions but impose controls on capital account transactions. The government can manage convertibility by requiring that those seeking access to the currency apply for a foreign exchange licence. This method allows authorities to influence the pace of currency exchanges and distinguish among transactions based on the degree of currency and financial risk associated with the transaction. The government can also suspend foreign exchange licensing (or convertibility, generally) as a type of speed bump. The government can also control non-resident access to the domestic currency by restricting domestic bank lending to non-residents and/or by preventing non-residents from maintaining bank accounts in the country.

Maintenance of unrestricted currency convertibility in developing economies is highly problematic from the perspective of financial stability. Investors cannot move their money freely between countries unless they can easily convert capital from one currency into another. But the practice of currency conversion and the exit from assets denominated in the domestic currency places currencies under pressure to depreciate. For this reason, unrestricted convertibility introduces currency, flight and currency-induced fragility risks.

Currencies that are not convertible cannot be placed under pressure to depreciate because there are substantial obstacles to investors' acquiring them in the first place. Moreover, to the extent that investors are able to acquire the currency (or assets denominated in it), their ability to liquidate these holdings is ultimately restricted. Thus the likelihood of a currency collapse is trivial because the currency cannot be attacked. The greater are the restrictions on convertibility, the smaller is the scope for currency risk.

Restricting currency convertibility can curtail flight risk. Restricting convertibility can effectively discourage foreign investors from even buying the kinds of domestic assets that are most prone to flight risk because these holdings cannot be readily converted to their own national currency. To the extent that these restrictions do not discourage foreign investors from purchasing assets subject to flight risk, they nevertheless undermine their ability to liquidate these investments and take their proceeds out of the country. Convertibility restrictions also reduce the ability of domestic investors to engage in flight.

Convertibility restrictions also reduce currency-induced fragility risk. This measure reduces the possibility that currency depreciation will lead to an unexpected increase in debt-service costs. Restricting convertibility does not reduce the fragility risk induced by the adoption of risky financing strategies, such as those involving maturity mismatch.

By reducing the overall risk of financial crisis, currency convertibility restrictions can reduce sovereignty risk. This measure protects policy autonomy by slowing the rate of depletion of foreign exchange reserves, thereby giving the government time to implement changes in economic policy without being forced to do so by pressures against the currency (Eichengreen et al., 1995). Finally, convertibility restrictions can reduce a country's vulnerability to contagion by rendering the economy overall less vulnerable to financial crisis. In so far as investors know that the economy is less vulnerable to crisis, they are less likely to engage in actions that induce contagion via a 'guilt by association' effect.

Note that countries that did not maintain convertible currencies such as China, India and Taiwan were largely unaffected by the crisis in so far as it was impossible for them to experience a currency collapse (and related currency-induced fragility risk) and the risk of investor flight was minimal. Investors had little reason to fear a collapse of currency and/or asset values in these countries, and they therefore behaved accordingly. These experiences suggest that had a greater number of countries taken steps to reduce currency and flight risks (by restricting convertibility or via other means), there may not have been so many ready sites for contagion.

Restrictions on currency convertibility alone did not inoculate China, India and Taiwan from the Asian crisis. The restrictions did, however, curtail the risks (and investor perceptions thereof) to which these economies were exposed. It is noteworthy that a study of capital account regimes by IMF staff concludes that despite the efficiency costs and some evasion of Chinese and Indian capital account restrictions, these restrictions are among the factors that can be credited with the performance of these economies during the Asian crisis (Ariyoshi et al., 2000: pp. 16–17, 31–4).

There are, of course, costs associated with maintaining convertibility restrictions (and, indeed, any financial restrictions). These costs may be contained if convertibility restrictions are strengthened or activated only when trip wires reveal a vulnerability to crisis. Speed bumps notwithstanding, the potential costs of convertibility restrictions must be weighed against the actual, significant costs of crisis. Critics may also counter that convertibility restrictions reduce growth by raising capital costs. But the effects on capital costs and growth in any one country depends very much on whether other economies maintain such restrictions, and whether the hurdle rate is reduced by the reduction in the vulnerability to crisis (see section 4).

3.3   The Chilean model

In the aftermath of the Asian crisis, a great deal of attention was focused on the 'Chilean model', a term that refers to a policy regime that Chilean and Colombian authorities began to implement in June 1991 and September 1993, respectively. The model has since been dismantled. But the model (particularly the more effective variant in Chile) deserves careful examination in view of its record of success and its potential as a tool of crisis prevention.

Financial integration in Chile was regulated through a number of complementary measures. From June 1991 through early 2000, authorities maintained an exchange rate band that was gradually widened and modestly revalued several times. The monetary effects of the rapid accumulation of international reserves were also largely sterilized. Central to the success of Chilean policies was a multifaceted programme of inflows management. First, foreign loans faced a tax of 1.2 per cent per year. Second, FDI faced a one-year residence requirement. Third, from May 1992 to October 1998, Chilean authorities imposed a non-interest-bearing reserve requirement of 30 per cent on all types of external credits and all foreign financial investments in the country. The required reserves were held at the central bank for one year, regardless of the maturity of the obligation.

The central bank eliminated the management of inflows in several steps beginning in September 1998. This decision was taken because the country confronted a radical reduction in inflows in the post-Asian-crisis environment. Chilean authorities determined that the attraction of foreign capital was a regrettable necessity in light of declining copper prices and a rising current account deficit. Critics of the Chilean model heralded its demise as proof of its failure. But others viewed the dismantling of the model as evidence of its success in so far as the economy had outgrown the need for protections. In my view, the decision to terminate inflows management was imprudent given the substantial risks of unregulated short-term inflows and the risk that Chile could be destabilized by emergent crises in Argentina and Brazil. It would have been far more desirable to maintain the controls at a low level while addressing the current account deficit and the need to attract inflows through other means. Indeed, flexible deployment of the inflows policy was a hallmark of the Chilean model (consistent with trip wires–speed bumps), and it is regrettable that authorities abandoned this course.

The Chilean model represents a highly effective means for managing the risks that often culminate in currency and financial crisis in developing countries. Chilean authorities managed currency risk via a crawling peg complemented by inflows management. Taken together, these measures greatly reduced the likelihood that the currency would appreciate to such a degree as to jeopardize the current account, and the policies made it difficult for investor flight to induce a currency collapse. Indeed, the appreciation of the Chilean currency and the current account deficit (as a share of GDP) were smaller than in other Latin American countries that were also recipients of large capital inflows (Agonsin, 1998). Moreover, the currency never came under attack following the Mexican and Asian crises.

Chilean policies reduced the likelihood of a sudden exit of foreign investors by discouraging those inflows that introduce the highest degree of flight risk. The reserve requirement tax in Chile was designed to discourage such flows by raising the cost of these investments. The Chilean minimum stay policy governing FDI reinforced the strategy of encouraging longer-term investments while also preventing short-term flows disguised as FDI. The reduction in (foreign investor) flight risk complemented efforts to reduce currency risk.

Chilean inflows management also mitigated fragility risk. The regime reduced the opportunity for maturity mismatch by demonstrating an effective bias against short-term, unstable capital inflows. Taxes on foreign borrowing were designed precisely to discourage the financing strategies that introduced so much fragility risk to Asian economies and Mexico.

Numerous empirical studies find that inflows management in Chile played a constructive role in changing the composition and maturity structure (though not the volume) of net capital inflows, particularly after the controls were strengthened in 1994–95 (Ffrench-Davis and Reisen, 1998; LeFort and Budenvich, 1997; Palma, 2000).[12] Following implementation of these policies, the maturity structure of foreign debt lengthened and external financing in general moved from debt to FDI.[13] Moreover, Chile received a larger supply of external finance (relative to GDP) than other countries in the region, and FDI became a much larger proportion of inflows than in many other developing economies.

Some analysts challenge the sanguine assessment of the Chilean model. Edwards (1999) argues that the effectiveness of the model has been exaggerated. However, in a paper published a year later, De Gregorio et al. (2000) conclude that Chilean controls affected the composition and maturity of inflows, though not their volume. The De Gregorio et al. (2000) result is confirmed for Chile in other studies that claim to demonstrate the failure of the model, even though their reported results show just the opposite (Ariyoshi et al., 2000; Valdés-Prieto and Soto, 1998).

Based on the empirical evidence, we conclude that Chilean policies reduced the likelihood of financial crisis by containing currency, fragility and foreign investor flight risk. Policymakers were accordingly insulated from potential challenges to policy sovereignty via reduction in the risk of crisis. Furthermore, policymakers were able to implement growth-oriented policies because the risk of foreign investor flight was curtailed (LeFort and Budenvich, 1997). The Chilean model also reduced the vulnerability to contagion by fostering macroeconomic stability. The transmission effects of the Asian crisis in Chile were quite mild compared to those in other Latin countries (e.g. Brazil), let alone elsewhere. The decline in capital flows in Chile following the Mexican and Asian crises was rather orderly, and did not trigger currency, asset and investment collapse.

4. Lessons for policymakers

The risks and strategies discussed in this chapter suggest the following lessons for policymakers in developing countries.

Lesson 1: Developing countries can balance the challenges and opportunities of financial integration. The strategies discussed in section 3 suggest that there is a variety of means by which policymakers can maintain access to international private capital flows without necessarily increasing their vulnerability to currency and financial crisis. The strategies discussed in section 3 are summarized in Table 24.2.

Table 24.2   Policy menu: options for reducing the risks of neoliberal financial integration

Type of risk	Policies that can reduce this type of risk
Currency	Trip wires and speed bumps; Chilean model; convertibility restrictions
Flight	Same as for currency risk, except note that Chilean model reduces only the risk of foreign investor flight
Fragility	Trip wires and speed bumps (affect only transparent activities); Chilean model; convertibility restrictions (affect only currency-induced fragility)
Contagion	Trip wires and speed bumps; Chilean model; convertibility restrictions
Sovereignty	Same as for contagion risk

Lesson 2: The mantra 'there is no alternative' to neoliberal finance and the risks thereof is simply wrong.[14]   This research suggests that it is the task of policymakers in developing countries to select from among those tools that represent the most appropriate, desirable and feasible means to reduce the specific risks deemed most dangerous to their economy. This means, then, that there is neither a single policy innoculant nor a single policy package that should be applied uniformly.

Lesson 3: A programme of crisis prevention in developing countries necessitates the implementation of a comprehensive and consistent set of complementary policies.   This means that policymakers must pay attention to 'policy complements' because the independent implementation of certain risk-minimizing measures will have undesirable and even perverse effects. Moreover, reliance on a set of complementary policies reduces the necessary severity of any one of its components.

A few examples will illustrate the need for policy complements. Recent experience in East Asia and Argentina demonstrates that efforts to manage currency risk (by maintaining a pegged or a fixed currency value) must be complemented by the management of international private capital inflows. In the absence of measures to control capital inflows, undue pressure will be placed on the currency should the volume and pace of inflows accelerate rapidly.

Implementation of a programme to reduce flight risk by restricting only gross capital outflows (by any number of means) is likely to trigger an investor panic if these policies are not accompanied by measures to manage gross inflows. Indeed, if inflows management policies are well designed so that flight risk is reduced (as in the Chilean model), there may be little need for outflows management.

Conversely, the implementation of some measures can enhance the effectiveness of other measures. For instance, the ability of a trip wire–speed bump regime to reduce flight and currency risk in developing economies will be magnified by the presence of other measures to reduce flight risk, such as the Chilean model of inflows management, and vice versa.

More generally, a policy regime that minimizes a national economy's vulnerability to financial crisis (by managing currency, flight and fragility risks) will reduce sovereignty and contagion risks. Indeed, policy sovereignty and state capacity may actually be enhanced by the protections offered by crisis-prevention policies. This is because policies that diminish vulnerability to crisis can also augment other government initiatives to secure sustained, stable economic development.

Lesson 4: We simply do not know whether implementation of the measures presented in section 3 in one or a few developing countries will increase or reduce the hurdle rate necessary to attract private capital flows.   The hurdle rate (that is, the expected rate of return) necessary to attract foreign investment may increase if investors demand a premium in order to commit funds to an economy in which liquidity or exit options are compromised by the policy regime. But it is just as plausible to assume that the hurdle rate in such economies may be reduced by a policy regime that gives investors less reason to fear that capital losses will be incurred or growth will be sacrificed because of currency risk or a large-scale exit of investors. That foreign investors found Chile and East Asian economies attractive when they had controls in place gives some credence to the latter view (as does investors' continued fascination with China).

Corollary to lesson 4: The hurdle rate for developing countries as a whole would be lower in a world in which all or most developing countries chose from among the policy options discussed here.   It is of course true that developing countries always face a higher hurdle rate than do wealthier economies because of investor concerns about informational adequacy and inflation and political risks. And, as discussed above, it is possible (though not given) that individual economies may face higher hurdle rates by implementing any of the policies considered here. But since there is no absolute hurdle rate for developing countries (in so far as hurdle rates are always derived from a relative comparison of investment options), it is quite reasonable to conclude that developing countries as a whole would find it easier and less costly to attract private capital flows if they reduced their vulnerability to crisis through collective implementation of the policies examined here.

Lesson 5: It is far from certain that efforts to reduce the risks of financial crisis will be frustrated by corruption, waste and evasion and will purchase stability at the cost of growth. Counter to the claims of the new-political economy, corruption, waste and evasion occur under both liberal and illiberal regimes. The policies considered here may well introduce *new* forms of corruption and waste. But it is by no means certain that the *volume* of these activities will be greater under an illiberal regime. The frequently invoked problem of policy evasion, too, is a red herring. Some actors will evade policy under any regime. Evasion, however, does not imply policy failure. The experiences of India, China, Chile and Colombia, for example, suggest that financial controls have been highly effective despite some evasion. It is nevertheless imperative that the particular controls adopted be consistent with national conditions, including state capacity (per lesson 2).

On the matter of economic growth, a tradeoff between stability and growth has not been established, though critics of financial controls often implicitly assume that is has. Certainly the experiences of Chile and China (and South Korea during the *dirigiste* era) cast strong doubt on the growth–stability tradeoff. More generally, if foreign investors value stability and predictability (especially in the post-Asian-crisis environment), countries with well-functioning financial controls might have a comparative advantage in attracting capital inflows. Finally, it is important always to weigh the *actual* costs of instability and crisis against the *potential* costs of slower, sustainable growth.

In conclusion, this chapter has explored the link between neoliberal financial reform and currency and financial crises in developing countries. It has also exposed the fallacy of the argument that crises are an inherent feature of the financial landscape of developing countries. With appropriate political will, policymakers can implement measures that effectively manage the challenges and opportunities of global financial integration. Recent events in East Asia, Argentina, Brazil and Russia (among other countries) have revealed the costs of poorly specified programmes of neoliberal financial reform. In the post-Asian-crisis context, and in the context of growing scepticism about the neoliberal form of globalization, we might perhaps be cautiously optimistic about the prospects for serious discussion of the need to manage financial integration in developing countries.

Notes

1. This chapter draws on several of my previous papers, especially Grabel (1996; 2002; 2003a; 2003b; 2003c; 2003d; 2004).
2. Grabel (1996) examines the contribution of neoliberal financial reform to the Mexican financial crisis.
3. Note that a currency board is an institution charged with maintaining a fixed rate of exchange between the domestic currency and a hard foreign currency, such as the US dollar, and with restricting any growth in the domestic money supply to the receipt of additional holdings of the hard foreign currency. Note also that the International Monetary Fund and consultants to the institution previously invoked the success of the Argentine currency board in efforts to export the arrangement to other countries (and indeed, it was exported to Estonia, Bulgaria, Bosnia and Herzegovina, among other places).
4. See Grabel (2000; 2003b) on currency boards.
5. I thank Randall Dodd for raising this point.
6. On the Mexican and East Asian crises, see Grabel (1996 and 1999, respectively).
7. See Grabel (2003c) for a thorough assessment of these and other policies to prevent financial crisis. See also Crotty and Epstein (1996) for discussion of numerous types of capital controls, and see Epstein et al. (2004) for discussion of broader capital management techniques in developing countries.
8. Tax-based speed bumps on foreign borrowing are discussed in Chang and Grabel (2004: ch. 9).
9. See Grabel (2003c; 2003d) for further details on tax-based policies in Chile and Colombia; and see Epstein et al. (2004) for details on policies toward foreign borrowing in other developing countries.
10. However, outflow controls can play a useful role in some circumstances as suggested by Malaysia's experience in 1998.
11. The reduction in financial risks associated with trip wires and speed bumps would also increase the economy's resilience to external shocks.
12. These studies also find that leakages from these regulations had no macroeconomic significance.
13. FDI is not unproblematic, however. It can and has introduced sovereignty risk (Grabel, 1996).
14. Chang and Grabel (2004) present alternatives to neoliberal policy in developing countries in a range of policy domains.

References

Agonsin, M. (1998), 'Capital inflows and investment performance: Chile in the 1990s', in Ffrench-Davis, R. and Reisen, H. (eds), *Capital Flows and Investment Performance*, Paris: UN/ECLAC Development Centre of the OECD.
Arestis, P. and Glickman, M. (2002), 'Financial crisis in Southeast Asia: dispelling illusion the Minskyian way', *Cambridge Journal of Economics*, **26**, 237–60.
Ariyoshi, A., Habermeier, K., Laurens, B., Otker-Robe, I., Canales-Kriljenko, J. and Kirilenko, A. (2000), *Country Experience with the Use and Liberalization of Capital Controls*, Washington, DC: IMF.
Chang, H.-J. (1998), 'Korea: the misunderstood crisis', *World Development*, **26**(8), 1555–61.
Chang, H.-J. and Grabel, I. (2004), *Reclaiming Development: An Alternative Policy Manual*, London and New York: Zed Books.
Crotty, J. and Dymski, G. (1998), 'Can the global neoliberal regime survive victory in Asia?', *International Papers in Political Economy*, **5**(2).
Crotty, J. and Epstein, G. (1996), 'In defence of capital controls', in Panitch, L. (ed.), *Are There Alternatives? Socialist Register*, London: Merlin Press.
Crotty, J. and Epstein, G. (1999), 'A defense of capital controls in light of the Asian financial crisis', *Journal of Economic Issues*, **33**(2), 118–49.

De Gregorio, J., Edwards, S. and Valdés, R. (2000), 'Controls on capital inflows: do they work?', *Journal of Development Economics*, **63**, 59–83.

Dodd, R. (2001), 'The role of derivatives in the East Asian financial crisis', Derivatives Study Center/Financial Policy Forum, Special policy report 1, 14 August, www.financialpolicy.org.

Dodd, R. (2002), 'Derivatives, the shape of international capital flows and the virtues of prudential regulation', WIDER Discussion Paper 93.

Edwards, S. (1999), 'How effective are capital controls?', *Journal of Economic Perspectives*, **13**(4), 65–84.

Eichengreen, B., Rose, A. and Wyplosz, C. (1995), 'Exchange market mayhem: the antecedents and aftermath of speculative attacks', *Economic Policy*, **21**(2), 249–312.

Epstein, G., Grabel, I. and Jomo, K.S. (2004), 'Capital management techniques in developing countries: an assessment of experiences from the 1990's and lessons for the future', prepared for the XVIth Technical Group Meeting of the Group of Twenty-four in Port of Spain, Trinidad and Tobago, 13–14 February 2003. Published as G24 Discussion Paper No. 27, March 2004, United Nations, New York and Geneva.

Ffrench-Davis, R. and Reisen, H. (eds) (1998), *Capital Flows and Investment Performance*, Paris: UN/ECLAC Development Centre of the OECD.

Grabel, I. (1996), 'Marketing the Third World: the contradictions of portfolio investment in the global economy', *World Development*, **24**(11), 1761–76.

Grabel, I. (1999), 'Rejecting exceptionalism: reinterpreting the Asian financial crises', in Michie, J. and Grieve Smith, J. (eds), *Global Instability: The Political Economy of World Economic Governance*, London: Routledge, pp. 37–67.

Grabel, I. (2000), 'The political economy of "policy credibility": the new-classical macroeconomics and the remaking of emerging economies', *Cambridge Journal of Economics*, **24**(1), 317–36.

Grabel, I. (2002), 'Neoliberal finance and crisis in the developing world', *Monthly Review*, **53**(11), 34–46.

Grabel, I. (2003a), 'Predicting financial crisis in developing economies: astronomy or astrology?', *Eastern Economics Journal*, **29**(2), 245–60.

Grabel, I. (2003b), 'Ideology, power and the rise of independent monetary institutions in emerging economies', in J. Kirshner (ed.), *Monetary Orders: Ambiguous Economics, Ubiquitous Politics*, Ithaca, NY: Cornell University Press, pp. 25–52.

Grabel, I. (2003c), 'Averting crisis: assessing measures to manage financial integration in emerging economies', *Cambridge Journal of Economics*, **27**, 317–36.

Grabel, I. (2003d), 'International private capital flows and developing countries', in H.-J. Chang (ed.), *Rethinking Development Economics*, London: Anthem Press, pp. 325–45.

Grabel, I. (2004), 'Trip wires and speed bumps: managing financial risks and reducing the potential for financial crises in developing economies', prepared for the XVIIIth Technical Group Meeting of the G-24 in Geneva, Switzerland, 8–9 March 2004. Published as G24 Discussion Paper No. 33, November, United Nations and Geneva.

Kaplan, E. and Rodrik, D. (2001), 'Did the Malaysian capital controls work?', *NBER working Paper No. 8142*.

Kregel, J. (1998), 'Derivatives and global capital flows: applications to Asia', *Cambridge Journal of Economics*, **22**, 677–92.

LeFort, V.G. and Budenvich, C. (1997), 'Capital-account regulations and macroeconomic policy: two Latin American experiences', *International Monetary and Financial Issues for the 1990s*, Research papers from the Group of Twenty-four, Vol. VIII.

Neftci, S. (1998), 'FX short positions, balance sheets and financial turbulence: an interpretation of the Asian financial crisis', Center for Economic Policy Analysis Working Paper No. 11, New School University.

Palma, G. (2000), 'The three routes to financial crises: the need for capital controls', mimeo, Faculty of Economics and Politics, Cambridge University.

Palma, G. (1998), 'Three and a half cycles of mania, panic and (asymmetric) crash', *Cambridge Journal of Economics*, **22**(6), 789–808.

Singh, A. (1999), '"Asian capitalism" and the financial crisis', in *Global Instability: The Political Economy of World Economic Governance*, London: Routledge, pp. 9–36.

Taylor, L. (1998), 'Capital market crises: liberalization, fixed exchange rates and market-driven destabilization', *Cambridge Journal of Economics*, **22**(6), 663–76.

Valdés-Prieto, S. and Soto, M. (1998), 'The effectiveness of capital controls: theory and evidence from Chile', *Empirica*, **25**(2), 133–64.

Wade, R. (1998), 'The Asian debt-and-development crisis of 1997–?: causes and consequences', *World Development*, **26**(8), 1535–53.

25 Financial bubbles
Mark Hayes*

> The a priori assumptions of rational markets and consequently the impossibility of destabilising speculation are difficult to sustain with any extensive reading of economic history. The pages of history are strewn with language, admittedly imprecise and possibly hyperbolic, that allows no other interpretation than occasional irrational markets and destabilising speculation. Here are some phrases culled from the literature: *manias . . . insane land speculation . . . financial orgies . . . frenzies . . . feverish speculation . . . epidemic desire to become rich quick . . . wishful thinking . . . intoxicated investors . . . turning a blind eye . . . people without ears to hear or eyes to see . . . investors living in a fool's paradise . . . easy credibility . . . overconfidence . . . overspeculation . . . overtrading . . . a raging appetite . . . a craze . . . a mad rush to expand.* (Kindleberger, 2000: 24–5, original emphasis)

> Before economists relegate a speculative event to the inexplicable or bubble category, we must exhaust all reasonable economic explanations . . . the business of economists is to find clever fundamental market explanations for events; and our methodology should always require that we search intensively for market fundamental explanations before clutching the 'bubble' last resort . . . from our current perspective, [the] irrational speculation [of 1719–20] probably looked a lot like a normal day in a pit of the Board of Trade. (Garber, 1990: 35)

1. Introduction

This chapter advances a post-Keynesian perspective on 'financial bubbles', a topic of considerable research interest and policy relevance. This can be seen as supporting Kindleberger against Garber in their contrasting views of the nature and significance of bubbles, set out in the above quotations. The source of their conflict is profound, and corresponds ultimately to different conceptions of the role of time in economic theory. This fault-line in economics was first identified by Keynes in *The General Theory* (1973 [1936], *CW* VII, hereafter *GT*). The analysis leads in turn to a consideration of Keynes's distinctive approach to policy on speculation.

The chapter does not offer a detailed survey of particular theories or empirical investigations, nor of the rich literary evidence surrounding some of the most dramatic episodes in economic history, all of which can be found elsewhere.[1] The following three sections consider in turn the theory, empirical evidence and policy questions relating to financial bubbles.

2. Questioning the fundamentals

The division between the currently orthodox and the post-Keynesian alternative views of financial bubbles centres on the concept of 'fundamental value', or 'fundamentals' for short. Orthodox theory depends on fundamentals, even when they serve only as a benchmark for departures from rational behaviour, and the very notion of rationality is bound up with them. So fundamental (!) is this issue that a fairly abstract preliminary discussion is necessary if we are to make sense of the competing and contradictory claims about bubbles that abound in the literature.

Clarity of thought in this matter is best arrived at, I suggest, by distinguishing the market price of an investment or financial claim q_t from its fundamental value in prospect (*ex ante*) q_t^* and its fundamental value in retrospect (*ex post*) q_t^{**}; q_t^* is an expectation of the outcome q_t^{**}. This taxonomy will prove helpful in discussing, on the one hand, theories of departures of market prices from fundamental value, and on the other, the nature of fundamental value itself. Note that both the market price q_t and the *ex post* fundamental value q_t^{**} are observable. It is in the nature of financial assets that they are traded on well-organized markets with well-defined competitive prices, so that q_t can easily be observed. *Ex post* fundamental value q_t^{**} can also in principle be observed, although it is a subject for accountants, and even then, only for those with a peculiarly academic and historical bent. For it is in principle possible, if of little or no commercial importance, to identify the market interest rates and the money yield of an asset over the course of its economic life, and so the price q_t^{**} that would have warranted the holding of the asset at any time as an alternative to a debt, given perfect foresight.[2] By contrast, the *ex ante* fundamental value q_t^* is intrinsically unobservable, except in the case of fixed annuities, and we shall find in due course that this unobservability presents an insuperable problem.

2.1   Fixed annuities

We set out from common ground, the case in which $q_t = q_t^* = q_t^{**}$. The market price in equilibrium of a claim to a series of fixed future money receipts (a 'fixed annuity') is the net present value of the series, which can be expressed as:

$$q_t = q_t^* = q_t^{**} = \sum_{1}^{N} d_{t+i} \frac{1}{(1 + R_{t+i})} \tag{25.1}$$

where N is the number of discrete time periods over which the series extends, d_{t+i} is the receipt due at time $t+i$, and R_{t+i} is the interest on a loan of a unit of money at time t for i periods. The three qs, with and without asterisks, are equivalent because both d_{t+i} and R_{t+i} are known at any time, given a market for fixed-rate debts of comparable maturities. Equation (25.1) can be simplified by the assumptions that the stream of future receipts is a perpetual annuity growing in each period at a constant rate g and that the rate of interest in each period is a constant r, to give:

$$q_t = \frac{d_{t+1}}{(r - g)}, \text{ such that } (r > g) \tag{25.2}$$

which looks very much like the standard dividend discount model for the valuation of equity securities. However, it is a considerable leap from the equilibrium price of fixed annuities to the market prices of financial assets in general, and the various assumptions required to make such a leap represent the heart of the controversy.

If, as an alternative to holding the claim to maturity, an investor can transfer the claim at an earlier date (including the next period), the relation between the present and future market prices q_t and q_{t+1} is, in equilibrium, given by the 'no arbitrage opportunity' condition:

$$q_t = \frac{d_{t+1} + q_{t+1}}{(1 + R_{t+1})} \tag{25.3}$$

where today's asset price equals the net present value of the sum of tomorrow's dividend and tomorrow's asset price. Of immediate relevance to bubbles is the possibility that market prices q_t may not represent fundamental value in the sense of equation (25.1) even though equation (25.3) holds, so that we can have $q_t \neq q_t^* = q_t^{**}$ if $q_{t+1} \neq q_{t+1}^* = q_{t+1}^{**}$. This situation arises because equation (25.1) is not the only solution of the first-order difference equation (25.3), since the general solution is:

$$q_t = \sum_{1}^{N} d_{t+i} \frac{1}{(1 + R_{t+i})} + B_t = q^* + B_t = q^{**} + B_t \qquad (25.4)$$

where B_t is of the form $B_0(1 + R_{t+i})$, $B_0 > 0$, a 'bubble term'. Equation (25.4) describes a 'deterministic bubble' which implies prices rise *ad infinitum*; any sustained departure from the *ex ante* fundamental value q_t^*, i.e. for $B_{t+1} > 0$, requires a departure from 'rationality' to extrapolate from any initial 'displacement' to indefinite future growth.

A historical example of a bubble in the value of a fixed annuity, something along the lines of equation (25.4), is the famous South Sea Bubble of 1720 (Carswell, 1960). Unlike the case of John Law's Mississippi Bubble, it was public knowledge that the commercial rights to the South Sea trade were rendered of no immediate value from the start by the Spanish War of 1718. The core of the South Sea scheme was the offer to privatize the national debt, by swapping a variety of existing forms of government debt (fixed annuities) trading at a heavy discount in poorly organized markets, for a single class of equity shares trading in a unified market. The resulting improvement in market liquidity provided a one-off gain in value to holders of existing debt, in line with the actual post-Bubble share price; the Bank of England itself competed unsuccessfully to offer the Treasury a similar scheme. The progression from this initial gain ($B_0 > 0$) to a continuing bubble was brought about and sustained only by the direct manipulation of the share price by the company itself to keep B_t moving up.

2.2 Rational expectations and the efficient markets hypothesis
It is a small but significant step from equation (25.3) to the 'rational expectations hypothesis' and the claim that rational, well-informed agents do not make systematic errors in forming their expectations. This is expressed by incorporating into (25.3) an expected value operator (to be scrutinized closely in the next section):

$$q_t = E_t \left[\frac{d_{t+1} + q_{t+1}}{(1 + R_{t+1})} \right] \qquad (25.5)$$

and by substitution and the use of the 'law of iterated expectations', that $E_t[E_{t+1}[q_{t+2}]] = E_t[q_{t+2}]$, one solution of the first-order difference equation (25.5) in q_t looks very like equation (25.1) with the addition of the expectations operator:

$$q_t = q_t^* = E_t \left[\sum_{1}^{N} d_{t+i} \frac{1}{(1 + R_{t+i})} \right] \qquad (25.6)$$

Equation (25.6) states that q_t^* is the expected value of the prospective yield, in turn assumed to be a stochastic variable with a random disturbance term. This crucial assumption takes the only source of uncertainty to be the disturbance term, of which the expected value is zero, so that equations (25.1) and (25.6) are otherwise equivalent. If the disturbance term is normally distributed, uncertainty becomes synonymous with variance or 'volatility'. Equations (25.1) and (25.6) are indeed equivalent in the case of a fixed annuity, where $E_t[d_{t+i}] \equiv d_{t+i}$ and $q_t^* = q_t^{**}$.

The general solution of equation (25.4) also includes the stochastic 'rational bubble':

$$q_t = E_t\left[\sum_1^N d_{t+i} \frac{1}{(1 + R_{t+i})}\right] + E_t\left[\frac{B_{t+1}}{(1 + R_{t+1})(1 - p)}\right] = q_t^* + E_t\left[\frac{B_{t+1}}{(1 + R_{t+1})(1 - p)}\right] \quad (25.7)$$

where p is the frequency probability of the bubble bursting in the next period. Continued equilibrium requires that B_t grow at an ever-increasing rate, as the frequency probability of the bubble surviving to period n, $(1 - p)^n$, tends to zero as $n \to \infty$. In the case of a perpetual fixed annuity such as the South Sea case, uncertainty applies only to the duration of the bubble, so that in equation (25.7) $q_t^* = q_t^{**}$: there is no uncertainty about the value of the annuity $d_{t+1} d_{t+N}$, or the discount rate.

In the absence of a bubble, equation (25.6) represents the efficient markets hypothesis (EMH) that $q_t = q_t^*$, i.e. observed prices in competitive financial markets represent *ex ante* fundamental values.[3] Behavioural finance and complexity theory (see section 3) identify investor psychology and the limits of arbitrage as systematic sources of divergence from fundamental value, but the critique now offered here, following Keynes, raises the prior question whether market prices of assets other than fixed annuities can ever represent an accurate expectation of fundamental value.

In a theory of competitive equilibrium, the prospective yield of a capital good represents a set of expected equilibrium prices and outputs reflecting supply and demand at future dates. To sustain the EMH requires one of two assumptions, either

EMH-A   *the world behaves as if complete futures and insurance markets extend to the horizon of long-term expectation; or*

EMH-B   *a process of trial and error leads to a convergence of expectations on their equilibrium values.*

EMH-B implies EMH-A, while EMH-A is sufficient on its own, if no more than an assertion, given the absence of the required markets. It is an understanding that the world is such as to make both these assumptions invalid that leads Keynes to write

> Or, perhaps, we might make our line of division between the theory of stationary equilibrium and the theory of shifting equilibrium – meaning by the latter the theory of a system in which changing views about the future are capable of influencing the present situation. *For the importance of money essentially flows from its being a link between the present and the future.* We can consider what distribution of resources between different uses will be consistent with equilibrium under the influence of normal economic motives in a world in which our views concerning the future are fixed and reliable in all respects; – with a further division, perhaps, between an economy which is unchanging and one subject to change, but where all things are foreseen from the beginning. Or we can pass from this simplified propaedeutic to the problems of the real world in which our previous expectations are liable to disappointment and expectations concerning the future affect what we do today. (*GT*, pp. 293–4, original emphasis)

Keynes draws a sharp distinction between the states of short-term and long-term expectation, which govern production and investment decisions respectively. He would arguably be quite prepared to accept the two EMH assumptions as complements in the case of short-term expectation: in practice, entrepreneurs correct their expectations by trial and error in circumstances which are usually stable over short production periods (EMH-B); and thus for analytical purposes it is acceptable to assume rational short-term expectations (EMH-A):

> Entrepreneurs have to endeavour to forecast demand. They do not, as a rule, make wildly wrong forecasts of the equilibrium position. But, as the matter is very complex, they do not get it just right; and they endeavour to approximate to the true position by a method of trial and error. Contracting where they find that they are overshooting their market, expanding where the opposite occurs. It corresponds precisely to the higgling of the market by means of which buyers and sellers endeavour to discover the true equilibrium position of supply and demand. . . . The main point is to distinguish the forces determining the position of equilibrium from the technique of trial and error by means of which the entrepreneur discovers where the position is. . . . *Ex ante* decisions may be decided by trial and error or by judicious foresight, or (as in fact) by both. (*CW* XIV, pp. 182–3)

By contrast, 'it is of the nature of long-term expectations that they cannot be checked at short intervals in the light of realised results' (*GT*, p. 51). The long-term durable nature of capital assets is precisely the problem: if the expectations upon which the investment was based prove mistaken, it is not possible either to reverse the investment today or to go back in time, adjust the original investment decision, and then check the revised results in the present. It is only in a stationary or steady state that adjustments made today might (given stable dynamics) be expected to have the same effect in the future as the same adjustments, made in the past, would have had today. So the convergent feedback mechanism necessary to generate in practice a set of long-term equilibrium prices as the basis of prospective yield is absent in any economy subject to unforeseen change, such as the one we inhabit. It cannot be emphasized enough that it is simply not legitimate to model the real world in terms of long-term equilibrium, because of the irreversible, historical nature of time.

A stationary state with the addition of a stochastic disturbance term and perhaps a deterministic trend (making it a steady state) can be described as an 'ergodic' system (Davidson, 1996). The ergodic hypothesis was originally conceived by Boltzmann in developing the kinetic theory of gases in physical chemistry, to explain the behaviour of macroscopic volumes in terms of the Brownian motion of individual particles. The EMH can be understood as taking markets to generate equilibrium prices in the same way that equilibrium temperatures and pressures are generated by the random collisions of myriads of gas molecules in a closed vessel with a fixed volume. However, the real world is far from stationary, even in a stochastic sense. As Keynes puts it eloquently:

> The outstanding fact is the extreme precariousness of the basis of knowledge on which our estimates of prospective yield have to be made. Our knowledge of the factors which will govern the yield of an investment some years hence is usually very slight and often negligible. If we speak frankly, we have to admit that our basis of knowledge for estimating the yield ten years hence of a railway, a copper mine, a textile factory, the goodwill of a patent medicine, an Atlantic liner, a building in the City of London amounts to little and sometimes to nothing; or even five years hence. (*GT*, p. 149)

By uncertain knowledge, let me explain, I do not mean merely to distinguish what is known for certain from what is only probable. The game of roulette is not subject in this sense to uncertainty . . . Or, again, the expectation of life is only slightly uncertain. Even the weather is only moderately uncertain. The sense in which I am using the term is that in which the prospect of a European war is uncertain, or the price of copper and the rate of interest 20 years hence, or the obsolescence of a new invention, or the position of private wealth owners in the social system in 1970. About these matters there is no scientific basis on which to form any calculable probability whatever. We simply do not know. (*CW* XIV, pp. 113–14)

According to Fama (1970, p. 389), the EMH emerged as a theoretical response to the empirical evidence that stock market prices follow a 'random walk'. A random walk (which also describes Brownian motion) can be expressed as:

$$q_{t+1} = q_t + \varepsilon_{t+1} \tag{25.8}$$

where ε is a random disturbance with zero expected value. This must be carefully distinguished from a stationary stochastic process which represents a disturbance about the equilibrium value (note the asterisk):

$$q_{t+1} = q_t^* + \varepsilon_{t+1} \tag{25.9}$$

If the EMH is to be based on the discovery of the equilibrium position by trial and error (EMH-B), equation (25.9) alone is the appropriate description, and this can be relevant only where q_t^* is constant or predictable within an ergodic system. The literature to date does not appear to have noted that the consistency of the EMH with the random walk of equation (25.8) requires perfect foresight of future equilibrium prices, not as a complement or analytical representation of trial and error, but as an independent condition (EMH-A). For if market prices always represent *ex ante* fundamental equilibrium values, i.e. $q_t = q_t^*$ under EMH-A, then a random walk may be[4] generated as a result of unpredictable shocks to the endowment, technology and tastes which are the parameters taken to determine future general equilibrium prices. However, the possibility of unpredictable shocks to the *parameters* of the system (and thus to q_t^* rather than q_t) conflicts with the assumption of a stationary (ergodic) state required by EMH-B, where expectations and therefore prices can be wrong in the short term, but the underlying equilibrium price stays put and can be discovered by trial and error. The world required by EMH-B does not generate a random walk, but a stationary stochastic process; the futures markets required, if EMH-A is to be more than an assertion, do not exist. Thus although the EMH purports to explain the empirical evidence of a random walk in prices, it can only do so by asserting EMH-A. The random walk cannot itself be offered as evidence in support of EMH-A.

To summarize the argument so far, it is plausible that in competitive equilibrium the market prices of fixed annuities (q_t) represent *ex ante* their fundamental values (q_t^*). Equally, the fundamental value of any past investment can be determined *ex post* at the end of its economic life (q_t^{**}), permitting a historical judgement of the profitability of the initial investment decision. However, the historical nature of time in a world subject to unforeseen change presents insoluble ontological obstacles to the extension of the concept of *ex ante* fundamental value (q_t^*) beyond fixed annuities to financial assets in general. In order to progress beyond this concept, we must consider Keynes's understanding of the nature of long-term expectation.

2.3   The state of long-term expectation

Keynes's approach to long-term expectation is informed by his understanding of probability. He treats classical frequentist probability theory (implicit in the rational expectations hypothesis) as a special case within a branch of philosophical logic that deals with arguments that are doubtful, but neither demonstrably certain nor logically impossible. He understands probability as an argument or logical relation between one set of propositions (the conclusions) and another set (the evidence). Mathematics deals with analytic relations between propositions that must be either true or false. In matters of metaphysics, science and conduct, an argument is considered 'probable' to the extent that it warrants a degree of rational belief. Such a probability relation is objective, in the sense that any rational judge would reach the same conclusion upon the same evidence. Probability is not in general numerical, as in frequentist theory, but arguments can be, and often are, compared. An archetypal case is the verdict reached in a court of law.

Although Keynes treats investors as forming single-valued expectations of prospective yield, these estimates bear a complex relation to the 'bundle of vague and more various possibilities which actually make up their state of expectation when they reach their decisions' (*GT*, p. 24, fn. 3), a relation which cannot be reduced to 'actuarial' calculations based on relative frequency. The following paragraphs endeavour to express in the symbols of Keynes's *Treatise on Probability* (1973, *CW* VIII) the substantive content of section II and the first paragraph of section IV of *GT* chapter 12 (*GT*, pp. 148–9, 152), with a view to clarifying precisely the nature of the flaw in the concept of *ex ante* fundamental value.

Using Keynes's terminology, I propose that the *ex ante* expectation q_t^* of the *ex post* outcome q_t^{**} is the value of q_t^* which satisfies:

$$(q_t^{**} \geq q_t^*)|\Omega_t = (q_t^{**} \leq q_t^*)|\Omega_t \tag{25.10}$$

where this expression means that the probability (in Keynes's sense) that the outcome q_t^{**} lies at or above the expectation q_t^* equals the probability that the outcome lies at or below the expectation, given the available evidence Ω_t, including relevant propositions for and against each conclusion.[5] Ω_t is a subset of $\tilde{\Omega}$, the complete 'perfect foresight' information set from which q_t^{**} might be known with certainty, i.e. $q_t^{**}|\tilde{\Omega} = 1$.

The 'expected value' $E[x]$ of classical probability theory is in similar fashion given by the centre of gravity of the population relative frequency density function[6] $\varphi(x)$ such that:

$$E[x] = \int_{-\infty}^{+\infty} x\varphi(x)dx \tag{25.11}$$

whence it follows that:

$$\int_{-\infty}^{E[x]} \varphi(x)dx = \int_{E[x]}^{+\infty} \varphi(x)dx = 0.5 \tag{25.12}$$

Equation (25.12) is the classical equivalent of (25.10), in that q_t^{**} is as likely to fall above $q_t^* = E_t[q_t^{**}]$ as below it, with the difference that, if we *know* $\phi(q_t^{**})$, we *know* that, in the limit, half the 'drawings from the urn' will fall on one side and half on the other of the expected value q_t^*. In Keynes's terms, $q_t^* \mid \varphi(q_t^{**}) = 1$; the *expectation* (although not the actual q_t^{**} itself) is *known* with certainty (as opposed to merely probable in Keynes's sense) as soon as the frequency density function is *known*, since the conclusion follows from the evidence as a matter of strict logical implication: expected value is simply a mathematical transformation of the frequency density function. By contrast, in equation (25.10), the information set Ω_t does not permit conclusive determination of the expectation q_t^* (let alone, *a fortiori*, the actual value q_t^{**}); or put another way, the two sides of equation (25.10) do not 'sum' to unity (although strictly these Keynesian probabilities are not in general of the numerical form necessary for addition).

While each side of equation (25.10) depends on the balance of the evidence for and against each conclusion, the 'weight' of the argument for the expectation q_t^* depends on the relation between the available information Ω_t and the complete information $\bar{\Omega}$. Although no numerical comparison is possible between Ω_t and $\bar{\Omega}$, it is clear that if Ω_t is very scant, little confidence will be placed in the expectation; while if $\Omega_t = \bar{\Omega}$, there will be complete certainty and therefore absolute confidence. Thus the degree of confidence in the expectation q_t^* will depend, although not by a numerical functional relation, upon the weight of the evidence in Ω_t relative to the complete information set $\bar{\Omega}$, which in practice can only be known in retrospect.

From this we can see that the rational expectations hypothesis replaces the assumption of perfect foresight with the only slightly weaker assumption of knowledge of an objective frequency distribution. If we follow EMH-B, that this knowledge can be acquired by discovery in an ergodic system, every addition to the information set Ω_t will improve confidence in the expectation q_t^*, in the sense of reducing its standard error as the sample size increases. In the more general Keynesian case, an addition to the information set Ω_t need not conform to the distribution of previous information in such a well-behaved manner, so that the expectation may fluctuate dramatically. Even if there is considerable weight behind a given expectation, confidence may be shaken by the addition of unexpected bad news; the knowledge that we know so little about the future always haunts us.

In the presence of such fundamental or intractable uncertainty, and in the context of highly liquid investment markets, it is only *rational* to pay more attention to tomorrow's market price q_{t+1} than to tentative and unreliable expectations of fundamental value q_t^*. At this point we must put aside fundamentals and concern ourselves with the proximate determinants of actual market prices. What really matters, I suggest, is not equation (25.10) but the rather different:

$$(q_{t+1} \geq q_t(1 + R_{t+1}))\mid\Omega_t = (q_{t+1} \leq q_t(1 + R_{t+1}))\mid\Omega_t \tag{25.13}$$

which expresses in terms of Keynesian probabilities that tomorrow's price is judged as likely to exceed as to fall short of today's price plus interest; or putting it another way, that the bullish tendency is balanced by the bearish (where these tendencies may exist together in the mind of the same investor or separately among different investors). Information in Ω_t which would not be relevant evidence for the purposes of (25.10), such as the intentions of other investors, must now dominate consideration of fundamentals. Indeed, the *only* thing that matters (ignoring transactions costs, etc.) is the intentions of other investors, so that individual opinions matter only in so far as they contribute to 'average' opinion. If particular investors ('bears') believe the market is overpriced, they should sell today and buy back tomorrow, even if their long-term intention is to hold the asset for its economic life. There may be serious-minded investors in the market whose intentions reflect a model such as equation (25.2), employing information about current dividends or earnings together with expected growth and interest rates, yet it is still their immediate intentions in the form of arbitrage operations that matter, and not the accuracy of their model, which can only be established long after the event. As Keynes points out in detail in *GT*, chapter 12, the real business of the professional investor must, perforce, be the study of market sentiment, in which the study of fundamental value is at best a minority option. The solution of equation (25.13) thus provides us with a formal expression of a 'conventional valuation', the price today that balances the bullish and the bearish tendencies in the market as a whole and represents the average opinion or conventional wisdom as to the correct price, given the current information. This price should there-fore continue to prevail until there is change in the information – or, of course, in average opinion.

In normal times, the conventional view of the proper relation between the market price and the current information experiences discontinuous shifts from time to time, perhaps quite frequently. Market prices fluctuate continually, not only as the information set changes, but in line with such changes in conventional valuation. Speculators may do quite well anticipating changes either in the news or in the psychology of the market, but there is no intrinsic reason why they should expect these changes to move in one direc-tion. With the onset of a bubble, the convention becomes, in effect, that the conventional basis of valuation will continually change one way, usually upward. As always, it does not matter whether individual rational investors think the new convention is well founded or insane, provided they believe that it will hold long enough for them 'to beat the gun' and sell before the convention collapses. Nevertheless, as we shall see in section 3, a sustained bubble seems to involve a process of positive feedback based on either a sufficient number of irrational investors with a simple faith in its continuation; or sufficient fuel, in the form of short-term credit against the collateral of the speculative assets themselves, to allow speculators to play Keynes's hard-nosed game of 'Old Maid' among themselves (cf. *GT*, p. 156);[7] or most likely, both ingredients together.

2.4   Conclusions on theory

The concept of *ex ante* fundamental value reaches into every corner of orthodox think-ing about financial markets, yet neglects the self-evident facts that time is irreversible and the world is subject to unforeseen change, which cannot be reduced to a frequency distri-bution. Once it is admitted that *ex ante* fundamental value can have no operational meaning beyond the case of fixed annuities, the concept of rationality must also be reassessed: it has been too easy for orthodoxy to create a false division between rational (meaning objectively optimal) and irrational behaviour. On the contrary, we have seen that conventional valuation is an entirely rational Socratic response to the knowledge of our lack of knowledge of the future, even though conventions must be based on the psy-chology of the market, and only indirectly, at best, on investors' models of fundamental value. This is by no means to deny the existence of irrational behaviour, but the alterna-tive perspective affects the manner in which we approach the evidence of financial bubbles: the question of methodology.

3. Identifying the presence and causes of bubbles and crashes

We are now in a position to consider the methodology of research into the empirical evidence relating to bubbles and crashes in the light of the preceding *a priori* critique of the concept of *ex ante* fundamental value. Three main approaches to empirical research can be found in the literature, here labelled for convenience as: the dominant 'statistical' method of orthodox quantitative analysis; the newly ascendant 'psychological' approach associated with behavioural finance; and the original 'historical' method. The question of practical interest is whether the presence of a bubble can be detected without the hindsight resulting from a subsequent crash, and whether the causes of a bubble and subsequent crash can be identified.

3.1 The statistical method

As noted earlier, the discovery that equity prices tend to follow the random walk of Brownian particles preceded the development of the EMH as an explanation. The main method of testing the EMH was the 'event study' which analysed the price movement before and after a price-sensitive announcement, such as an unexpected earnings increase or drop. These studies largely corroborated the EMH, although they also provide evidence of specific patterns of psychological response. Taken together, the evidence of a random walk and that 'news' is rapidly incorporated in the price is consistent with the EMH that prices reflect fundamental value. However, this evidence is equally consistent with conventional valuation, if the convention is understood to encompass not just the price itself but the 'model', such as a conventional price/earnings ratio. A change in the news may thus affect the price without a change in convention and, as Keynes points out, 'we should not conclude that everything depends on waves of irrational psychology. On the contrary, the state of long-term expectation is often steady' (*GT*, p. 162). The conventional valuations of 'normal times' may be fairly robust and bear some steady relationship to the changing information that becomes available.

Perhaps the decisive empirical test which discriminates between these two hypotheses is the variance bounds test (Shiller, 1981; 2003). The logic of this test is that if prices are a good *ex ante* estimator of fundamental value, the volatility of prices should not exceed the volatility of *ex post* fundamental value. Using US data for 1871–1980, Shiller found that price volatility was at least five times the volatility in fundamental value, rather than less, as the EMH predicts. Much ink has been spilt in an effort to overturn Shiller's claim, motivated presumably by the correct instinct that investors do not normally behave irrationally. Yet if price volatility reflects variation in conventions as well as in the news about technology, preferences and endowment, Shiller's result is fully to be expected, since conventions may change frequently without a descent into irrationality. Furthermore, equity prices will follow a random walk, if news is random and *a fortiori* if changes in conventions are also random.

Shiller's test of the EMH is not sensitive to the exact specification of fundamental value, nor does accurate specification matter for his purposes, whereas his critics must produce a model of fundamental value that predicts observed prices. While this is admitted to be difficult enough, an attempt to model conventional valuation in mathematical terms would seem quixotic. In fact the finance literature on the forecasting of volatility, relevant to the pricing of options and other derivatives, makes little or no reference to fundamentals, and employs an essentially inductive method of seeking to predict future volatility from a transformation of past prices (Poon and Granger, 2003). The notion of 'efficiency' is reduced to the weak form 'no arbitrage opportunity' claim of equation (25.5), that prices are not systematically predictable, rather than that they reflect fundamental value (Malkiel, 2003). This has not deterred cross-disciplinary research between physics and finance from using complexity theory (also known as catastrophe or chaos theory) to model equity prices as the complex outcome of simple processes, popularly illustrated by fractal patterns. These models make no essential use of fundamental values, but depend on 'locally' imitative behaviour by atomistic traders, leading to unplanned emergent outcomes and 'extreme events' such as stock market crashes. This has led to claims of the discovery of distinctive statistical signatures of incipient crashes (robust log-periodic power-law values) which, if valid, would be of considerable predictive value (Sornette, 2003).

The finance literature has in practice abandoned the concept of fundamental value, although it retains the belief that price trends and volatility can be reliably modelled in mathematical terms, given sufficient fire-power. Our *a priori* critique suggests that both *ex ante* fundamental value and inductive mathematical modelling face the insuperable obstacle presented by the nature of time, to which may be added further questions related to human agency and the role of institutions that undermine the atomistic treatment of investors within a stochastic but otherwise deterministic model.

3.2   The psychological approach

'Behavioural finance' theory offers a critique of the EMH on a different tack from the post-Keynesian position, as well as a positive model of investor psychology that provides an explanation of apparently irrational behaviour. A weakness of behavioural finance is its continued adherence to the concept of *ex ante* fundamental value, if only as a reference point. The implication is that any departure from fundamental value is in some sense 'irrational', in contrast to the present argument that conventional valuation may be the only rational response to an unknowable future.

The behavioural finance critique of the EMH centres on the limits to arbitrage by the 'smart money' (i.e. investors with rational expectations) in offsetting irrational trading by 'noise traders' (i.e. investors who trade on the basis of 'non-news' or 'pricing models' with no rational foundation). Risk-averse arbitrageurs will not be able to hold the market to its fundamental value, partly because they are unable to hedge the market as a whole over time; and also because the noise traders may push the market further away from fundamental value before it reverts, while credit costs and limits tend to prevent arbitrageurs from taking longer-term positions. Worse still for the purposes of the EMH, the 'smart money' may egg on, rather than bet against, the 'feedback traders' (i.e. a species of noise trader who buys when prices rise, and sells when they fall), supporting rather than preventing the expansion of a bubble.[8]

The positive contribution of behavioural finance theory lies in providing a basis in investor psychology for the behaviour of noise traders. Drawing upon work in experimental psychology, the observed behaviours of trend-following and of under- and over-reaction to news can be explained in terms of 'conservatism' and 'representativeness' (Shleifer, 2000, pp. 112–30). Conservatism means that investors are slow to revise their expectations, effectively discounting the relevance of individual news items until they are corroborated. This tendency manifests itself in event studies which show that excess returns are recorded for a considerable period (60 days) after the announcement (under-reaction). Conversely, representativeness means that investors form perceptions of particular shares as 'winners' or 'losers' based on a run of good or bad returns, rather than ascribing the observed sequence to chance, and thus rating the shares higher or lower than the EMH would warrant, manifested in lower or higher future returns (over-reaction). Taken together, these two tendencies provide a behavioural foundation for positive feedback, with a run of good returns encouraging bullish expectations, which are then slow to react to disappointment. Behavioural finance theory does not lead to predictive models of stock prices, although simulations can be run which display some of the stylized facts of event studies and historical bubbles (Shleifer, 2000, pp. 140–43, 154–74). The weakness of behavioural finance theory is its continued attachment to fundamental value and the corollary that all departures therefrom are irrational, leaving it unable to discriminate between the conventional valuation of normal times and the mania of the true bubble. There may be scope for research incorporating the insights of behavioural finance into the formation of conventions.

3.3   The historical method

Studies of the signs and causes of bubble and crash from a historical perspective have placed emphasis on features of contemporary accounts which have not, so far at least, been accommodated within mathematical or psychological models. Two examples are the spread of a speculative frenzy to groups of people who had not previously invested in shares at all (not even as 'noise traders'), and the role of credit both as fuel for the bubble and as driver of the ultimate panic (identified by Minsky, 1983 [1977], although not given this particular emphasis by him). Conventional valuation provides a possible theoretical link between these two neglected factors, through the effect of conspicuous realized capital gains on expectations and its unwinding in the free-fall of the crash. The following discussion is intended as an example of how future research might proceed, and the challenge, noted by Spotton and Rowley (1998), lies in translating this insight into a testable, if not necessarily predictive, hypothesis. An alternative hypothesis based on a similar concern with the historical evidence can be found in Spotton-Visano (2002).

Hypothetically, a speculative increase in prices does not necessarily require either trading or cash. If all investors share the same expectations, prices can be marked up without any shares changing hands, so that all make paper profits. If expectations differ, but investors hold only shares and cannot exchange them for other goods (ignoring the question of settlement), speculative trading can take place, prices can rise, and the aggregate portfolio of shares will be redistributed. Traders may gain or lose, but this need not be a zero-sum game; on paper there can be an aggregate profit. The point of this hypothetical argument is to illustrate that 'weight of money' arguments, *per se*, are not credible: price movements can be independent of cash flows 'in and out of the market'. However, new money is indeed required if paper profits are to be realized in cash. This new money can come from the sale of other assets by holders of existing shares and by new investors; from new savings; from buy-backs by companies; or from credit.

The historical method identifies the effect on investor expectations of the conspicuous consumption of new wealth acquired more or less overnight by speculation:

> Luxurious and showy spending rose sharply. The accepted signs of wealth – coaches, jewellery, new clothes – were all in strong demand and their prices rose. But more important was the demand for the other great symbol of personal status – land. Estates . . . went to increasingly high premiums. (Carswell, 1960, p. 146)

> Speculation on a large scale requires a pervasive sense of confidence and optimism and conviction that ordinary people were meant to be rich. (Galbraith, 1973, p. 174)

> There is nothing so disturbing to one's well-being and judgement as to see a friend get rich. (Kindleberger, 2000, p. 15)

> Envy of others who have made more in the stock market than one earned at work in the past year . . . is a painful feeling. (Shiller, 2000, p. 56)

> The frenzy . . . descended to persons in the humblest circumstances, and the farthest removed, by their pursuits, from commercial cares. . . . Not only clerks and labourers, but menial servants, engaged the little sums which they had been laying up for a provision against old age and sickness. (Bagehot, quoted in Kindleberger, 2000, p. 29)

> Yes, many who trade in tulips are riding a horse, have a carriage or a wagon, and during winter, an ice carriage . . . (Quoted by Shiller, 2003, p. 93).

The mania of the bubble, driven by greed and envy, including the simple fear of missing out, has a different quality from the systematic failure to recognize fundamental value, emphasized by behavioural finance. It is tempting to limit the term 'bubble' to describe, not merely a state of speculation or systematic over-reaction, but the peculiar psychological state that characterizes relatively short periods such as May–August 1720 and March 1928–August 1929, although this would leave open the categorization of the longer-term bull markets leading up to 1929, 1987 and 2002.

Although it is a mistake to identify credit as the initial source of a bubble, this argument from conspicuous consumption makes credit in its various forms a key enabler and amplifier, together with the entry of inexperienced investors alongside seasoned speculators. A positive feedback loop is created between conspicuous realized gains and the increases in credit, or inflow of new investors, required to convert speculative profits from paper to cash. Credit is created by a contract to deliver a specified quantity of goods (usually money), and is not limited to the banking system: this includes barter contracts (1637), bills of exchange (1763), part-paid securities and share subscriptions on credit (1720, 1847), transferable property sale contracts or 'binders' (Florida, 1925), broker loans from corporations and individuals, and investment trust bonds and preference shares (1929), and contemporary contracts for differences, spread betting and other derivatives.

When the bubble bursts, it is a dependence on credit that turns a crash into a panic. 'The "mob" didn't sell, it got sold out' in 1929 to meet margin calls on broker loans (Galbraith, 1973, p. 151). Where banks were involved, in the eighteenth and nineteenth centuries, the crash led to failures and a domino effect where otherwise sound investors and concerns, perhaps not involved in the speculation, found themselves insolvent. The linkage of the South Sea crash to the failure of the connected Sword Blade Bank in turn led to multiple bank failures (very nearly including the Bank of England), a collapse in confidence in paper money and a sharp reduction in the effective money supply (Carswell, 1960, pp. 191–9, 202).

The more recent experience in the UK and USA of 1987, 2000 or 2002 is of crash without serious panic (hence the advent of the more neutral term 'correction'). The sharp fall in prices represents a windfall loss with consequences for the long term, indeed, but without widespread immediate insolvency. This isolation of market crashes is the result of the regulation of banking and financial services, yet regulation has not eliminated the bubbles themselves.

4. Implications of bubbles – do they matter and can they be avoided?

What are the implications of financial bubbles for the economy and for policy in the light of these different perspectives? We look in turn at the implications for the banking sector, for personal savings and investment, and for the production of consumption and capital goods. Any case for policy to prevent bubbles must also consider its feasibility and other consequences.

4.1 The banking sector

Banks are torn, more so than other businesses, between the pursuit of profit and the maintenance of solvency, and financial bubbles offer opportunities for profitable lending to speculators as well as the risk of loss for depositors as the value of collateral evaporates in a crash. Modern bank regulators and central banks aim to limit the potential damage from the collapse of a bubble (and other catastrophes, including fraud) to the shareholders alone, and to isolate the losses of a particular bank from its own depositors and those of the banking and payments system as a whole, both nationally and globally. Regulators, like tax authorities, are engaged in a constant game of leap-frog with regulated and (currently) unregulated institutions, driven by profit opportunities continually to create new forms of credit that fall outside regulatory constraints, including 'special purpose vehicles', securitization and the many forms of derivatives. Legislation has become increasingly sophisticated and widely drawn (e.g. UK Financial Services and Markets Act 2000), as has prudential supervision and regulation, including the concepts of capital adequacy enshrined in the international Basle accords.

Recent experience suggests that these efforts to confine losses to shareholders and avoid widespread contagion have been reasonably successful. However, the move in the Basle II proposals to allow larger banks to shift from simple and conservative rules on capital adequacy to sophisticated stochastic risk models rings a warning bell, given a Keynesian understanding of probability. Although the intention of the new proposals is avowedly to detect risks on complex credit instruments that are not covered by the present arrangements, they also allow banks to reduce their capital cover on lending which the models calculate to be 'safer'. As the inappropriately named hedge fund Long-Term Capital Management found to its cost, the models can be wrong (Eichengreen and Mathieson, 1999). Sornette has identified that crashes are statistically 'outliers' that fall well outside the normal confidence limits which underpin calculations of value at risk (VaR), and puts the probability of the 1987 crash at once in 520 million years (Sornette, 2003, p. 16).

Even if banking depositors can be protected, the potential role of banks in promoting bubbles requires scrutiny if the losses from crashes fall not only upon bank shareholders and their speculative borrowers, but on external bystanders, including personal investors and employees. This is a far more difficult area in which to set and enforce specific rules, and there remains much to be said, both on the grounds of externalities and in order to protect depositors against unforeseeable risk, for fire-walls which simply prohibit banks from certain activities in the public interest, although this will invariably be resisted by bank shareholder interests as an interference with free enterprise.

4.2   Personal savings and investment

The historical accounts of the South Sea Bubble and the 1929 crash contain sorry tales of personal bankruptcy and ruin that may be regarded as an unacceptable social cost of bubbles. Investors, already ruined by the loss of their savings, are more likely to find themselves bankrupt if they have speculated on credit. The main response has been to regulate comprehensively the sale of financial services to the personal sector, since 1933 in the USA and since 1986 in the UK. Individual investors are now permitted direct access to the two-edged instruments of speculative leverage such as margin accounts and forward contracts only if they can demonstrate experience and net worth.

The current problems of the UK pensions and life insurance sector are partly the unintended consequences of the shift to a low inflation, low nominal interest rate, environment, as well as of the bull market of the 1990s. Both the US and UK governments have faced the embarrassment of having subsidized individual pension provision for demographic reasons, leading to heavy investment in equity markets at bubble valuations and subsequent losses, at the same time as defined benefit schemes have been squeezed by falling nominal interest rates. Leverage has taken its toll on popular and historically 'safe' with-profit funds, several of which have been forced to switch into bonds at what has proved to be the worst possible time in the aftermath of the 2002 crash, to protect their solvency in relation to accumulated guaranteed bonuses.

4.3   The real economy

Galbraith partly attributes the US Depression of the 1930s to the effect on the consumption of the wealthy of the falls in the equity market, also acknowledged by Keynes (*GT*, p. 93). Our analysis suggests that the consumption effects of bubbles are mixed, since the losses of some investors are matched by the realized gains of others, and the net effect depends upon the aggregate propensity to consume. In his famous passage on 'casino capitalism' (*GT*, p. 159), Keynes deplores the effects of speculation on real investment but weighs these against the advantages of liquidity. Keynes may have conceded too much to the view that equity markets play an important role in the allocation of resources to new investment. The strand of post-Keynesian tradition following Kalecki has emphasized the empirical evidence that real investment is financed by corporate cashflow both directly, and indirectly through corporate borrowing (Meyer and Kuh, 1957; Fazzari and Mott, 1987; Hayes, 2003). New equity issues are dominated by merger and acquisition activity and during bubble periods by sectors such as TMT (technology, media and telecoms) and bio-pharmaceutical. An extensive literature questions the efficiency of the market for corporate control (Tichy, 2001) and the uncritical flood of equity into technology stocks in the late 1990s is, just as in 1720, as likely to have encouraged waste and misallocation as to have supported enterprise and innovation.

This line of argument suggests that financial bubbles are no more relevant to real aggregates than the stock market itself. The case for tolerating bubbles on the grounds of efficient allocation is weak, both because of the evidence against the EMH, and because corporate investment is not dependent on equity markets. Nevertheless the case for preventing bubbles cannot be based on a simple adverse relationship with aggregate consumption and investment, but rather on the distributional consequences of bubbles for personal investors and the direct costs of extreme events such as the risk to the payments system.

4.4   Can bubbles be avoided?

The consensus of those charged with maintaining financial stability appears to be that occasional bubbles are inevitable, but that 'the incidence and severity of crisis can be mitigated through public policy actions', through the adoption of principles and standards for monetary and financial policy aimed at macroeconomic stability, and the protection of the banking system and personal investors through regulation (Clementi, 2000). In favour of this consensus from our perspective is its recognition of the role of credit, and the practical difficulties of distinguishing *ex ante* a speculative bubble from a boom in enterprise. There is no evidence that in the periods ending 1929, 1987 or 2002 monetary policy was unduly lax or contributed directly to the bubble and crash, so that monetary policy appears impotent as far as bubbles are concerned, and is a blunt instrument that affects the real economy more than it does (if at all) the stock market.

Keynes's view was that relatively high transaction costs and stamp duty reduced the influence of the speculative motive on Threadneedle Street relative to Wall Street: the Tobin tax proposal to reduce the volatility of currency markets reflects this view. It is possible that speculation on equity bubbles is more easily deterred, since it is not a bet against government arbitrage that has known technical and political limits. This provides an argument for at least maintaining, if not increasing, the 0.5 per cent stamp duty on UK share transfers, despite the dubious claim (Cruickshank, 2003) that this would reduce real investment. Furthermore, Keynes would have expected that the UK move in 1995 from 14-day accounts to five-day rolling settlement to have reduced speculation as well as settlement risk, although this change did not prevent the 2000 or 2002 crashes.

Keynes's tongue-in-cheek solution for stock market bubbles, by 'marrying' the investor to the asset, might be made workable through a legal requirement that corporate securities listed on recognized investment exchanges could be issued only with a dividend fixed in relation to nominal value (i.e. preference shares), making the equity market only slightly more volatile than the bond market. This would not prevent the issue of ordinary shares as private equity, although the potential gains would be limited to something corresponding to 'fundamental value' rather than being fuelled by public equity issues at bubble prices. Such a restriction would not prevent the issue of preference capital to finance real investment and the emergence of a genuine role for the listed share market in capital allocation. Preference dividends would offer a risk premium over bond interest rates that would make them attractive to long-term diversified investors such as pension funds. Although such a proposal would face fierce political opposition, the EMH provides no theoretical objection, since it implies that financial structure is a matter of indifference. Furthermore, asymmetric information theory claims that 'risky debt' of this sort is the optimal form of capital security (Townsend, 1979). Utopian as this reform might appear, it would lead to greater efficiency and permit less extensive and expensive regulation.

5.   Summary and conclusions

The concept of *ex ante* fundamental value is central both to the efficient markets hypothesis and as a reference point for behavioural finance theory, despite Keynes's critique in *The General Theory*, which remains unanswered. The *ex post* fundamental value of any past investment can in principle be determined in retrospect, and it is plausible that in competitive equilibrium the market prices of fixed annuities represent their *ex ante* fundamental values (the South Sea Bubble notwithstanding). However, the historical nature of time in a world subject to unforeseen change presents insoluble ontological obstacles to the extension of the concept of *ex ante* fundamental value from fixed annuities to equity shares. In the presence of intractable uncertainty, and in the context of highly liquid investment markets, it is only *rational* to pay more attention to tomorrow's market price than to tentative and unreliable estimates of fundamental value. Expectation becomes dominated by the intentions of other investors, and the balance of the bullish and bearish tendency, or average opinion, determines a conventional valuation.

With the onset of a bubble, the convention becomes, in effect, that the conventional basis of valuation will continually move in one direction. Theory and historical evidence suggest that a sustained bubble requires a process of positive feedback driven by naïve investors and speculators. The case against bubbles and crashes hinges upon their distributional consequences for personal investors and the risk they pose to the banking system; bubbles continue to undermine personal provision for pensions and other long-term needs. The public interest may be better served by adopting Keynes's prescription of higher stamp duties and radical reform in the ownership of investments, addressing bubbles at their source as an alternative to further extensive and expensive regulation. Meanwhile, the wise investor will continue to pay close attention to market sentiment.

Notes

*   I am most grateful to Murray Glickman for valuable comments and advice. The usual disclaimer applies.
1. A good starting point, in addition to the references cited in the text, is Camerer (1989) and the Symposium on Bubbles in the *Journal of Economic Perspectives*, Vol. 4, No. 2 (1990), updated by Malkiel (2003) and Shiller (2003).
2. No meaningful definition of 'risk-adjusted' *ex post* fundamental value is possible, since the original risk cannot in general be measured with hindsight from outcomes, as we shall see.
3. The reference here is to the 'strong' EMH (where prices reflect all information available). The 'semi-strong' EMH (where prices reflect all information available to the market) allows for asymmetric information between insiders and outsiders, and the possibility of insider trading profits, while the 'weak' EMH holds only that prices already reflect the information embodied in past prices, leading to a random walk in prices, since new information ('news') is unpredictable.
4. Only 'may be', since the random walk assumes that the shocks are randomly distributed and there is no reason to suppose this to be the case in general, especially with technology.
5. Glickman (1994) notes the need to distinguish the 'propositions' included in Ω_t from 'events' or raw information which are significant only when interpreted. The term 'information set' must be understood accordingly, and not simply as in standard econometric usage.
6. I use 'relative frequency' to distinguish probability based on frequency from Keynesian probability.
7. 'Old Maid' is a card game in which the objective is to pass on to others the one card for which there is not a matching pair and to avoid being left with that card.
8. Temin and Voth (2004) provide a fascinating case study of the success of Hoare's Bank in 'riding the South Sea Bubble'.

References

Camerer, C. (1989), 'Bubbles and fads in asset prices', *Journal of Economic Surveys*, **3**(1), 3–41.
Carswell, J. (1960), *The South Sea Bubble*, London: The Cresset Press.
Clementi, D. (2000), 'Crisis prevention and resolution: two aspects of financial stability', *Financial Stability Review*, no. 9 (December), London, Bank of England.
Cruickshank, D. (2003), 'Urgent action on stamp duty needed to boost economy', press release 26 March, London Stock Exchange.
Davidson, P. (1996), 'Reality and economic theory', *Journal of Post Keynesian Economics*, **18**(4), 477–508
Eichengreen, B. and Mathieson, D. (1999), 'What do we really know about hedge funds?', *Economic Issues*, no. 19, International Monetary Fund.
Fama, E.F. (1970), 'Efficient capital markets: a review of theoretical and empirical work', *Journal of Finance*, **25**(2), 383–417.

Fazzari, S.M. and Mott, T.L. (1987), 'The investment theories of Kalecki and Keynes: an empirical study of firm data, 1970–1982', *Journal of Post Keynesian Economics*, **9**(2), 171–87.

Galbraith, J.K. (1973 [1954]), *The Great Crash 1929*, London: André Deutsch.

Garber, P.M. (1990), 'Famous first bubbles', *Journal of Economic Perspectives*, **4**(2), 35–54.

Glickman, M. (1994), 'The concept of information, intractable uncertainty, and the current state of the "efficient markets" theory: a Post Keynesian view', *Journal of Post Keynesian Economics*, **16**(3), 325–49.

Hayes, M.G. (2003), 'Investment and finance under fundamental uncertainty', unpublished Ph.D. dissertation, University of Sunderland.

Keynes, J.M. (1973 [1936]), *The General Theory of Employment, Interest and Money*. Vol. VII of *Collected Writings of John Maynard Keynes*, London: Macmillan.

Keynes, J.M. (1973 [1921]), *A Treatise on Probability*, Vol. VIII of *Collected Writings of John Maynard Keynes*, London: Macmillan.

Keynes, J.M. (1973), *The General Theory and After*, Vol. XIV of *Collected Writings of John Maynard Keynes*, London: Macmillan.

Kindleberger, C.P. (2000), *Manias, Panics and Crashes*, New York: John Wiley.

Malkiel, B.G. (2003), 'The efficient market hypothesis and its critics', *Journal of Economic Perspectives*, **17**(1), 59–82.

Meyer, J.E. and Kuh, E. (1957), *The Investment Decision: An Empirical Study*, Cambridge, MA: Harvard University Press.

Minsky, H.P. (1983 [1977]), 'The financial instability hypothesis', reprinted in Wood, J.C. (ed.), *John Maynard Keynes – Critical Assessments*, vol. 4, 282–92, London: Croom Helm.

Poon, S.-H. and Granger, C.W.J. (2003), 'Forecasting volatility in financial markets: a review', *Journal of Economic Literature*, **41**, 478–539.

Shleifer, A. (2000), *Inefficient Markets – an Introduction to Behavioral Finance*, Basingstoke: Palgrave Macmillan.

Shiller, R.J. (1981), 'Do stock prices move too much to be justified by subsequent movements in dividends?', *American Economic Review*, **71**(3), 421–36.

Shiller, R.J. (2000), *Irrational Exuberance*, Princeton, NJ and Oxford: Princeton University Press.

Shiller, R.J. (2003), 'From efficient markets theory to behavioral finance', *Journal of Economic Perspectives*, **17**(1), 83–104.

Sornette, D. (2003), 'Critical market crashes', *Physics Reports*, **378**, 1–98.

Spotton, B. and Rowley, R. (1998), 'Efficient markets, fundamentals and crashes', *American Journal of Economics and Sociology*, **57**(4), 663–90.

Spotton-Visano, B. (2002), 'Financial manias and panics', *American Journal of Economics and Sociology*, **61**(4), 801–27.

Temin, P. and Voth, H.-J. (2004), 'Riding the South Sea Bubble', *American Economic Review*, **94**(5), 1654–68.

Tichy, G. (2001), 'What do we know about the success and failure of mergers?', *Journal of Industry, Competition and Trade*, **1**(4), 347–94.

Townsend, R.M. (1979), 'Optimal contracts and competitive markets with costly state verification', *Journal of Economic Theory*, **21**, 265–93.

26 Keynesian uncertainty and money
Giuseppe Fontana

1. Introduction

In the last few decades the economic profession has been making fast progress in recognizing the fundamental importance of uncertainty in explaining economic behaviour. The basic idea is that increasing the realism of the psychological underpinnings of economic theory will generate more powerful theoretical insights and better economic policy (Rabin, 1998). Unfortunately, this new literature does not seem to be aware of the long-standing research programme on Keynesian uncertainty.

Uncertainty is a central theme in the economic and philosophical writings of Keynes. He argued that the orthodox approach in both probability theory and economic theory had limited the analysis to the special cases of certain or probabilistic knowledge. He lamented that the orthodox approach had excluded considerations of the effects of uncertainty on economic behaviour and left economists in ignorance of what was excluded. For this reason he sought to develop a more general theory of probability and of knowledge which could lead to a fuller appreciation of the nature and role of uncertainty in economics.

It is the basic proposition of this chapter that Keynes's theory of probability and knowledge has continuing relevance as a contribution to economic theory. His original analysis and further developments by Post Keynesian scholars provides the foundation for a more general theory of decision-making under uncertainty which can be used to explain several economic phenomena including the long-run demand for a stock of liquid assets and related possibility of involuntary unemployment, as well as the existence of final means of payment and their key role in the working of modern monetary economies.

The structure of the chapter is as follow. Section 2 discusses Keynes's two-dimensional theory of probability and related forms of knowledge. Section 3 deals with the nature of uncertainty in the writings of Keynes and in the subsequent development of Post Keynesian economics. Section 4 considers the intimate link between uncertainty and the existence of money in its dual roles of store of wealth and final means of payment. Section 5 concludes.

2. Keynes on probability theory and knowledge

On probability relations

In *A Treatise on Probability* (1921) Keynes is concerned with the analysis of probability relations, i.e. probabilities are conceived as a relation between a conclusion and certain evidence:

$$p = a|h \tag{26.1}$$

where a is the proposition or conclusion, h the set of premises, and p the degree of belief that is rational to hold in the proposition a given the evidence h. The probability relation (26.1) has two important features. First, it is a logical relation. Just as no place is intrinsically distant in space, no proposition is intrinsically probable. Probabilities are always relative to certain evidence. Given the set of premises h, the logical conclusion a is fixed in an objective way. In the sense important to formal logic, the probability of any conclusion is thus not subject to human caprice (Keynes, 1921, p. 4).

Second, the probability relation (26.1) is a subjective relation. Probabilities are not a property of the external material reality but rather a property of the way individuals think about the external material reality (Lawson, 1988, pp. 42–4). The probability relation (26.1) is thus subjective because individuals have different reasoning powers and different evidence at their disposal. This means that the acquisition of new evidence, say h_1, does not affect the validity of (26.1) but gives rise to the new probability relation $p_1 = a/h_1h$. Continuing with the space analogy, when it is said that a place X is, say, five miles away, the implicit assumption is that X is five miles away from a certain starting point. If the starting point is moved, say, two miles closer to X, the place will be three miles away. To argue that, as a result of further evidence, p is wrong and that p_1 is correct makes as little sense as to argue that the initial opinion that X was five miles away is wrong because the place is now only three miles away. Both of the probabilities are correct relative to their evidence: 'new evidence would give us a new probability, not a fuller knowledge of the old one' (Keynes, 1921, p. 33). In more general terms, it can be argued that probabilities are not an object of knowledge but simply a form of (relational) knowledge. For this reason, Keynes was critical of the realist view of English Empiricists according to which the probability of an event can be discovered or learned with new evidence (Keynes, 1907, p. 18; see also Carabelli, 1985, pp. 155–6; O'Donnell, 1989).

In short, Keynes considered his theory of probability to be both (logically) objective and rational (Lawson, 1985). For any two individuals faced with the same evidence and reasoning powers it is rational to hold the same degree of belief in a given proposition. In this sense the probability of a proposition is objective. Importantly, this objectivity only exists at the level of opinion or knowledge of the external material reality. It is not a property of the external material reality itself (Keynes, 1921, p. 19).

Probability and knowledge
Another fundamental idea discussed by Keynes in *A Treatise on Probability* is the intimate link between probability and knowledge. The probability relation (26.1) is what Keynes calls a 'secondary proposition' and it represents a statement about the 'primary proposition' a. He then goes on to distinguish between knowledge of, and knowledge about, the primary proposition a, the difference being that the former corresponds to certainty of rational belief in a, whereas the latter coincides only with a probable degree of rational belief in the primary proposition a (Keynes, 1921, p. 15).

For Keynes there is a direct link between probability relations and knowledge. Probability relations can lead to a broad variety of degrees of rational belief in the primary proposition or conclusion a. These rational beliefs can be certain in degree, as well as probable or uncertain. In this sense, probability relations lead to a general theory of knowledge.

Table 26.1, row 1, shows four forms of knowledge that can be derived from different degrees of rational belief. Certainty, which describes the highest degree of rational belief, represents a special case in which the set of premises h is known, and also the secondary proposition p asserting a certainty relation between the primary proposition a and the

Table 26.1   Keynes's two-dimensional theory of probability and related forms of knowledge

Forms of knowledge	1. Certainty	2. Risk	3. Uncertainty$_1$	4. Uncertainty$_2$
Degree of rational belief, p	($p = 1$)	($0 < p < 1$)	($0 < p < 1$)	(p non-existent)
Weight of argument, V	High	High	Low	Non-existent

premises h is fully known.[1] In this case the knowledge of a that is implied from h is perfect; that is, $p = 1$. For this reason, certainty represents the upper limit of probable knowledge or 'the maximum probability', in Keynes's words (Keynes, 1921, p. 16). A less-than-certain knowledge prevails when h is known as well as the secondary proposition p, asserting in this case a probability relation between a and h. The degree of rational belief in a is thus positive but lower than the case of certainty. In algebraic terms this means that $0 < p < 1$. The form of knowledge that can be derived in this case is labelled, for no better name, risk. A more radical form of knowledge is uncertainty. Keynes did not explicitly refer to uncertainty in *A Treatise on Probability*. However, several authors have argued that there are two clear notions of uncertainty that arise out of the book, namely (i) uncertainty as probable knowledge based on slight information and (ii) uncertainty as absence of probable knowledge (see, for example, Lawson, 1985, pp. 913–14; Runde, 1991, pp. 130–33; Bellofiore, 1994, pp. 107–16). In the following, the first type of uncertainty is labelled uncertainty$_1$, where the second one is called uncertainty$_2$.

The weight of argument and uncertain knowledge type 1 (uncertainty$_1$)
The first notion of uncertainty that arises out of *A Treatise on Probability* describes situations in which probable knowledge does exist but it based on slight information. This is labelled uncertainty$_1$ in Table 26.1. The cause of this form of uncertain knowledge is to be found not in the probability relation p itself, but rather in the distinct nature of the set of premises h on which knowledge about a is derived. For this reason, the notion of uncertainty$_1$ comes out in conjunction with the discussion of the concept of weight of argument, V.

$$V = V(a|h) \qquad (26.2)$$

In *A Treatise on Probability* Keynes uses three different definitions of weight of argument, namely (i) the absolute amount of relevant evidence (Keynes, 1921, p. 84), (ii) the balance of the absolute amounts of relevant knowledge and relevant ignorance (ibid., p. 77), and (iii) the degree of completeness of information (ibid., p. 345). As Runde has argued, those definitions are not fully consistent and they are open to different interpretations (Runde, 1990, pp. 279–83). For instance, an increase in the amount of relevant evidence will increase the weight of the argument under definition (i), but this is not necessarily the case under definitions (ii) and (iii). If additional evidence indicates that there is more ignorance than individuals previously believed, the degree of completeness of information will decrease, as will the absolute amount of relevant knowledge compared to relevant ignorance. Since under definitions (ii) and (iii) the weight of argument moves in the same direction, in the rest of the chapter the absolute amount of relevant knowledge (compared to relevant ignorance) and the degree of completeness of information will be used interchangeably. In any case, what counts for the purpose of this chapter is that the weight of argument is for Keynes an important part of probability theory (Keynes, 1921, p. 345).

As for the probability relation p, the weight of argument V has also two important features. First, weights are a distinct property of arguments. In other words, the weight of argument is different from the corresponding probability of argument. As the amount of relevant evidence h increases, the magnitude of the probability of the argument p may decrease, increase or stay constant, depending upon whether the new knowledge strengthens or not the unfavourable or favourable evidence. However, independently from changes in p, the new evidence would always affect the degree of completeness of information on which rests the primary proposition a. Thus, as Keynes maintained, 'the weighing of the *amount* of evidence is quite a separate process from the *balancing* of the evidence for and against' (Keynes, 1921, p. 80). The rational degree of belief p and the weight of argument V are two distinct components of his theory of probability.

Second, the weight of argument is an important determinant of practical decision-making. In chapter 26 of *A Treatise on Probability*, titled 'The Application of Probability to Conduct', Keynes restates that the probability relation (26.1) represents the degree of belief p that is rational to hold in the proposition a given the evidence h. Thus, Keynes argues, the probability relation (26.1) tells individuals which degree of belief, in preference to alternative degrees of belief, is rational to hold on the basis of the evidence h. Also, moving slightly from theory to practice, the probability relation (26.1) tells individuals which belief is rational to use as a guide to conduct in preference to alternative beliefs. 'The probable is the hypothesis on which it is rational for us to act' (Keynes, 1921, p. 339). From this perspective, Keynes then concludes that it is rational to be guided in action by probability relations though he is quick to point out that probability relations are only one of the things to be determined, and taken account of, before a course of action is decided. This is an important qualification. The problem with the use of probability relations in practical decision-making is that p is a poor guide to action in the case of a resting on slight information h.[2] It is here that individuals are very much interested not in the logical relation between a and h, but in the degree of completeness of h, i.e. in the balance between the absolute amounts of relevant knowledge and relevant ignorance on which a rests.

It should be now clear why in *A Treatise on Probability* the first type of uncertainty, namely uncertainty$_1$, comes out in conjunction with the discussion of the concept of weight of argument, V. In situations in which probable knowledge does exist but it is based on slight information, the weight of argument becomes the decisive factor for convincing individuals that the probability relation is a reliable guide to action. For this reason Keynes speaks of 'doubtful arguments' (Keynes, 1921, p. 3). The arguments exist but they are doubtful in practice.

It is also worthwhile to note that for Keynes there is a scale of weight of arguments (see Table 26.1, row 2). Depending on the quantity and quality of the evidence h on which rests the primary proposition a, it is possible to discriminate between different degrees of evidential weight (Keynes, 1921, p. 78). At one end there is the case of low weight. In this case the only set of premises h on which the primary proposition a rests is nothing but bare information just sufficient for conceiving a probability relation between a and h. Individuals have no other relevant evidence at their disposal, except the information that there is a logical relationship between *a* and *h*. This is a case of uncertainty₁ in Table 26.1. As the degree of completeness of *h* increases, the weight of argument rises. But how far will it rise? Keynes does not provide a definite answer to this question (ibid., pp. 77–80). Building on this deficiency of evidence, some Keynesian interpreters have argued that unlike the case of probability relations, the weight of arguments is not gradable on a cardinal scale (Kregel, 1987, p. 526; Dequech, 1997, p. 30). It is not feasible to speak, say, of $V = 1$ or $0 < V < 1$ but rather of more or less complete information. For this reason, in Table 26.1, row 2, the weight of argument *V* is measured in terms of high or low. Starting with low *V*, as new relevant evidence reduces the incompleteness of information, individuals feel less uncertain of their knowledge about *a*, and hence less uncertain about using probabilities as a guide to action. Ironically, it follows that the weight of argument is at its maximum level when it becomes irrelevant in practical decision-making. When individuals perceive the set of premises *h* to be sufficiently complete (*V* is high) to imply a rational degree *p* in the primary proposition *a*, *p* becomes prominent and *V* falls into the background. In other words, the weight of argument loses practical relevance when it is high, and probabilities take centre stage as a guide to action. This is the case of certainty and risk in Table 26.1, row 2.

Uncertainty as absence of probabilistic knowledge: uncertainty type 2 (uncertainty₂)
The second notion of uncertainty that comes from *A Treatise on Probability*, uncertainty₂, derives from two cases, namely when probabilities are unknown and when probabilities are numerically incalculable or incomparable. Unknown probabilities lead to (at the best) vague knowledge (Keynes, 1921, p. 34). That is the case when the probability relation can be known but the reasoning power of individuals is so weak as to prevent relating the premises to the conclusion. Unknown probabilities are a theoretical possibility but they do not play any relevant role in *A Treatise on Probability*. They are simply an acknowledgement of the fact that in some circumstances limited human reasoning does not allow individuals to conceive a probability relation. For this reason, unknown probabilities will not be discussed in the rest of this chapter.

More important for Keynes is the case of numerically incalculable or incomparable probabilities (Keynes, 1921, p. 32). In this case uncertainty is not due to limited human reasoning powers. 'It is not the case here that the method of calculation, prescribed by theory, is beyond our powers or too laborious for actual application. *No* method of calculation, however impracticable, has been suggested' (ibid.) Here, the uncertain degree of rational belief in the primary proposition *a* reflects the absolute inconclusive base of the evidence or premises of the probability relation. If the evidence upon which individuals base their belief is *h*, then what individuals know, namely the secondary proposition *p*, is that the primary proposition *a* bears the probability relation of degree *p* to the set of premises *h*; and this knowledge justifies individuals in holding a rational belief of degree *p* in the proposition *a*. The problem with numerically incalculable or incomparable probabilities is that the evidence *h* upon which individuals should base their belief is inconclusive, and hence the secondary proposition *p* cannot either be estimated or be used for comparison with other secondary propositions. For this reason individuals cannot rationally hold any probable degree of belief *p* in the primary proposition *a*, i.e. *p* is simply non-existent. The inconclusiveness of the evidence *h* also means that the weight of argument *V* is non-existent. In Table 26.1, uncertainty₂ is thus described by both *p* and *V* being non-existent. In this case there is either no information at all or whatever evidence is available is far below what is required to give meaning to the logical relation between a and h. For this reason, it also makes little sense to speak of different degree of uncertainty$_2$, as was the case for uncertainty$_1$. Importantly, since for all their practical purposes individuals cannot know probabilities and weight of arguments, uncertainty$_2$ describes the case where individuals show the highest degree of distrust and uneasiness in committing real resources towards economic activities. Uncertainty$_2$ is thus the most radical form of uncertain knowledge. But this does not mean that it is very rare. Interestingly, for Keynes, numerically incalculable or incomparable probabilities are more common than it is usually assumed (Carabelli, 1988, pp. 42–50). In some part of *A Treatise on Probability* Keynes suggests that measurable probabilities rather than incalculable or incomparable probabilities represent a special case of his general theory of probability relations (e.g. Keynes, 1921, pp. 22–3).

In summary, in *A Treatise on Probability* Keynes is concerned with probability relations such as (26.1). But this is only the first dimension of his probability theory. In the same book, Keynes also introduced the notion of weight of argument (26.2). This is the second dimension of his probability theory. Whereas probability relations provide a rational assessment of the relative degree of belief attached to alternative propositions, the weight of argument measures the evidential base of these degrees of belief. Taking together probabilities and weight argument, Keynes's theory of probability relations leads to a general theory of knowledge that includes the cases of certainty, risk, uncertainty$_1$ and uncertainty$_2$ (Fontana and Gerrard, 2004; see also Harcourt, 1992, pp. 235–43).

3. On the nature of uncertainty
Formal logic versus human logic
The previous section has argued that in *A Treatise on Probability* Keynes was concerned with probability relations and thereby developed an original theory of knowledge. In particular, it argued that there are two notions of uncertainty that emerged from his 1921 book, uncertainty$_1$ and uncertainty$_2$. The difference is that in the latter the absolute inconclusiveness of the set of premises h means that a probability relation cannot be conceived, whereas in the former h does exist and does lead to the formation of probability relations, but, given the incompleteness of the set of premises, these probability relations are unreliable as a guide to conduct. But why is there uncertainty$_1$ and uncertainty$_2$ in the first place? In other words, why is the set of premises h incomplete to the point that those probability relations become unreliable? Similarly, why is the set of premises h inconclusive?

In the editorial foreword to *A Treatise on Probability*, Braithwaite hints at a possible explanation for the omission. Braithwaite, a close friend of Keynes from the time he was finishing the book, explains that the main purpose of *A Treatise on Probability* is to argue for probabilities being conceived as a logical relation between a proposition a and a set of premises h (Braithwaite, 1973, p. xxi). The book is thus naturally silent on the nature of the quality and quantity of the set of premises h. Questions about the degree of completeness of the set of premises h or their conclusiveness were not part of the core enquiries of the book. For this reason these questions were at the best only partially answered.

Braithwaite suggests that after 1921 the only publication by Keynes on the subject of probability theory was a short review of *Foundations of Mathematics* by Ramsey (Keynes, 1931). In the paper Ramsey had criticized Keynes for defending the view that probabilities can be numerically incalculable or incomparable. As Gerrard has argued, Keynes rated Ramsey's criticism highly for two reasons (Gerrard, 1992, pp. 86–90; see also Fontana and Gerrard, 1999, pp. 313–16). First, it clarified the proper scope of probability relations. The probability calculus represents the set of rules for ensuring consistency within degrees of belief. As such the probability calculus is subject to formal logic, which is concerned with the set of rules of consistent thought. Thus the proper scope of probability relations is to measure in numerical terms the rationality of the different degrees of belief in a proposition *a* given the evidence *h*. On this point, then, Keynes had to agree with Ramsey that probabilities are always numerically measurable.

Second, Ramsey's criticism pointed the way towards the next area of enquiry in probability theory, namely the basis for the rationality of the different degrees of belief. For Keynes, this is 'part of our human outfit' (Keynes, 1931, p. 338) and for this reason it is beyond the study of formal logic. It is part of human logic. Thus Keynes had now come to accept that in order to defend the possibility of probabilities being incalculable or incomparable, the explanation had to be found not in the rationality of degrees of belief but rather on the evidential basis of these degrees of belief. In other words, Keynes had to concede that *A Treatise on Probability* was mainly a study in formal logic and for this reason the case for incalculable or incomparable probabilities was not justified. That case could only be granted once the nature of the information used to attach probabilities to primary propositions was fully investigated and explained. For this, he had to move from formal logic to human logic, and within human logic the focus of the analysis had to be on the possibility of inconclusiveness of the evidence.

On the nature of the premises of probability relations

In *A Treatise on Probability* Keynes had touched on the issue of the evidential basis of the different degrees of belief when he discussed the weight of argument. Keynes had explained that the weight of arguments is of paramount importance when deciding if probability relations are a reliable guide for practical decision-making. But, as suggested by Braithwaite, the analysis of weight of argument was secondary to the purpose of the book and for this reason it was ambiguous and largely incomplete. However, Braithwaite fails to note that Keynes actually returned to the evidential basis of the different degrees of belief in the second part of his book (e.g. Keynes, 1921, pp. 276–8). In particular, in discussing the nature of the inductive method, Keynes argued that probability relations such as (26.1) can only be fully justified if it can be assumed that the material on which are based is made of 'legal atoms', such that each of these atoms exercises its own separate, independent and invariable effect. If this is the case, then complete information of the material reality under investigation can be easily inferred from partial information of its separate components. In other words, given a number of atomistic elements and their connecting laws, it is possible to infer information about the effects of changes of these elements, without exhaustive evidence of all possible circumstances. Unfortunately Keynes warned that this is not always the case. Not all phenomena are atomic, with the result that probability relations such as (26.1) are not always justified. Thus, notwithstanding the sound comments by Braithwaite, in the final chapters of *A Treatise on Probability* Keynes does suggest that the incompleteness or inconclusiveness of the evidential basis of the different degrees of belief is related to the possibility of the non-atomistic nature of the material reality. As argued by Lawson, this is tantamount to an admission that probability relations, which are a form of knowledge of the external reality, are, via the weight of argument, associated with a particular view of reality itself (Lawson, 2003, pp. 173–7).

Keynes further clarified his view on the non-atomistic nature of the external reality in a biographical essay on Edgeworth in 1926 where he distinguishes natural phenomena from social phenomena, the difference being that whereas the 'atomic hypothesis' works perfectly in the former, it breaks down in the latter (Keynes, 1926). The assumption of a uniform and homogeneous continuum of atomistic material is not necessarily satisfied by social phenomena. This means that when constructing probability relations about social phenomena, the set of premises upon which probability relations are based is in some way unique. The problem then is that if the set of premises is incomplete or inconclusive, there are no connecting laws on which to draw in order to reduce the paucity of information. Similarly, as further evidence arises, individuals may have problems in connecting it with previous information. More than a decade later, Keynes would refer to this argument when reviewing *A Method and Its Application to Investment Activity* by Tinbergen for the *Economic Journal* (Keynes, 1939, p. 315).

In the late 1930s Tinbergen had carried out some pioneering testing on business cycle theories on behalf of the League of Nations. Keynes was asked to comment on a proof copy of the work. From the start Keynes made clear that he was very sceptical about the methodology used by Tinbergen. His main criticism was that Tinbergen had failed to differentiate economics and other social sciences from natural sciences. Tinbergen was mistaken on the nature of the material that is the object of economic investigations. If economic phenomena were the outcome of numerically measurable and independent atomistic factors, then the statistical methods pioneered by Tinbergen could be safely applied in order to discover the causal mechanism behind all past, present and future business cycles. But, Keynes maintained, economic material is not uniform through time, with the result that any generalization of whatever economic statistics are available at a point in time must be very cautious. For this reason Keynes was sceptical of the general validity of the results obtained by Tinbergen. He later reinforced this point in private correspondence with Harrod.

> I also want emphasise strongly the point about economics being a moral science. I mentioned before that it deals with introspection and with values. I might have added that it deals with motives, expectations, psychological uncertainties. One has to be constantly on guard against treating the material as constant and homogenous. It is as though the fall of the apple to the ground depended on the apple's motives, on whether it is worth falling to the ground, and whether the ground wanted the apple to fall, and on mistaken calculations on the part of the apple as to how far it was from the centre of the earth. (Keynes, 1938, p. 300)

The quote is a lucid exemplification for economic analysis of the argument about the non-atomistic nature of material reality, which was first put forward by Keynes in the final chapters of *A Treatise on Probability*. The fall of an apple to the ground is a natural phenomenon and as such the atoms that make the apple are regulated, among other things, by the law of gravity. Once this law is properly understood and formulated, it can be applied to other atomistic environments. More generally, once the components of a natural phenomenon and their connecting laws are discovered, it is possible to use the knowledge derived from that particular phenomenon in order to explain several other natural phenomena. Different is the case for economic phenomena, where motives, expectations, psychological uncertainties play a prominent role. The possibility of generalizations from one phenomenon to another is limited. In this sense, the non-atomistic feature of the social reality, i.e. the lack of 'legal atoms' and 'connecting laws', severely restricts the cases of conclusiveness and completeness of the information upon which to build probability relations about social phenomenon (Coates, 1996; Comin, 1999, ch. 5, especially pp. 127–9).

Davidson and Post Keynesians on uncertainty

Keynes had an enormous influence in economics. Among the different scholars who have found inspiration in his writings there is the so-called group of Post Keynesians. Despite all their differences, several members of this group have devoted great efforts to the development of Keynes's theory of probability and knowledge (Arestis, 1996). This is especially the case of Paul Davidson, who has proposed a theory of involuntary unemployment based on the link between uncertainty and money (e.g. Davidson, 1994). The main tenet of Davidson is that there are two paradigms in economics, namely the economics of a predetermined, immutable and ergodically knowable reality; and the economics of an unknowable, transmutable and non-ergodic reality (e.g. Davidson, 1996). The first paradigm is made up of two groups according to whether full knowledge of reality is obtainable in any case (Group 1) or only in the long run (Group 2). Group 1 includes early-century classical models, rational expectations models and new classical macroeconomic models, where as Group 2 covers boundedly rational models, new Keynesian models as well as standard expected utility models. As for the second paradigm, Davidson refers to the work of Shackle, Old Institutionalist models and modern Post Keynesian monetary models. Since Davidson derives these distinctions in terms of Keynes's writings, it is worth discussing the two economic paradigms in terms of Keynes's general theory of probability and knowledge as summarized in Table 26.1.

The first paradigm describing the economics of a predetermined, immutable and ergodically knowable reality is covered by columns 1 and 2 in Table 26.1. Starting with Group 1, Davidson claims that in these models economic reality is assumed immutable and for this reason economic agents have either full knowledge or probabilistic knowledge of the future. The models in Group 2 are slightly different since they assume that in the short run economic agents have limited reasoning powers. For this reason, knowledge of the future is incomplete or altogether missing. However, since in its essential features external reality is fixed, with time the limited reasoning powers of agents lose relevance. In the long run economic agents will have full knowledge or probabilistic knowledge of the future.

Notwithstanding the strength of Davidson's distinction between the first and the second economic paradigm, the assumption of a predetermined or immutable reality is a sufficient but not a necessary condition for achieving certain or probabilistic knowledge. What it really counts in terms of Keynes's theory of knowledge is that economic agents have adequate evidence at their disposal such that it is rational to hold a positive or unitary degree of belief in a proposition about future outcomes. In other words, immutable reality models are a case, possibly the most compelling case, where information is adequate or complete, i.e. V is high, and the probability of argument p is equal to one or close to one. However, columns 1 and 2 in Table 26.1 also include transmutable reality type of models describing routine economic decisions. In these cases, again, the degree of belief that is rational for agents to hold is equal to one or close to one, and the evidential basis of these degrees of belief is high.

In the classification by Davidson the second paradigm in economics champions the view of an unknowable, transmutable and non-ergodic reality. The basic feature of the works included in this alternative paradigm is that the future can be permanently affected by the actions of economic agents, often in a way that is not even completely foreseeable by the performers of these actions. Using an expression familiar to Shackle, in these works the choice of agents is genuine; choice matters (e.g. Shackle, 1961, pp. 271–2; Fontana, 2001). In other words, agents are allowed to act in unpredictable ways. For this reason, Davidson argues, in these cases agents do not have and can never have any knowledge of the future. They are simply uncertain about the future because, in some profound way, the future is yet to be created.

The case of uncertain knowledge described by Davidson is represented by column 4 in Table 26.1. In this circumstance, because of the inconclusiveness of the evidential base, probability relations are numerically incalculable or incomparable. Probabilities and weight of argument are said to be non-existent. This form of uncertainty is what throughout this chapter has been called uncertainty$_2$. However, this is only one case of uncertain knowledge. In terms of Keynes's theory of knowledge, uncertainty also arises when probability relations do exist, i.e. $0 < p < 1$, but the weight of argument V is low. In Table 26.1 this form of uncertainty is listed in column 3 and has been named uncertainty$_1$. In this circumstance, it is the incompleteness rather than the inconclusiveness of the evidential base of our knowledge that leads to uncertain knowledge.

As indicated in Table 26.1, uncertainty$_1$ and uncertainty$_2$ are two distinct notions of knowledge, but they are strongly connected to each other by their mutual reference to the evidential base of probability relations (see, for an early view of this idea, Kregel, 1987, pp. 526–8). In both cases uncertainty arises because of what Keynes labelled the non-atomistic feature of economic reality. Economic phenomena are the outcome of individual decisions which are taken now and in time to come by economic agents. If the economic reality were atomistic, it could be assumed that all economic agents were identical in respect of their reasoning powers and past experience. It would then be rational to expect that in similar circumstances agents would formulate similar propositions about the future. Economic phenomena will be uniform and homogeneous through time. But the economic reality is not atomistic and economic phenomena are not uniform and homogeneous through time. Economic agents are not the same, as the 'legal atoms' of the falling apple in the previous example are. Agents have different experiences and distinct physical make-up. They have therefore different interpretations of the available evidence, and as a result they will produce different propositions about the future. This means that the evidential base used to assign probability relations is itself invented in the very process of making a decision.

This is as far as the non-atomistic nature of economic reality goes. But this does not mean that economic agents will never be able to form probability relations. Sometimes they will and sometimes they will not. When agents do form probability relations about future events, it means that the degree of completeness of the evidential base is adequate. How adequate is impossible to say in advance and for this reason Post Keynesians speak of low or high weight of argument (Table 26.1, row 2). When the degree of completeness of information is low, probability relations are formed, but individuals are uncertain about the meaning to attach them in practical decision-making. This is the case of uncertainty$_1$. When agents do not form probability relations about future events, it is because the degree of completeness of the evidential base is inadequate. The weight of argument is non-existent; probability relations are non-existent. This is the notion of uncertainty$_2$. The distinction between the two notions of uncertainty is not only a question of semantics. Uncertainty$_1$ and uncertainty$_2$ differ in their operational implications. They lead to two different though complementary types of economic behaviour.

4.   Uncertainty and money

Uncertainty$_2$, money and involuntary unemployment

Post Keynesians are well known for their critical view of recent developments in economics. In particular, they have been in the front line against the modern search for the microeconomic foundations of macroeconomics. They argue that, if anything, it is microeconomics that is in need of macroeconomic foundations (Crotty, 1980; and, especially, Nasica and Kregel, 1999). The paradox is easily explained when the practical implications of the theory of knowledge discussed above are taken into account.

This chapter has argued that there is an intimate link between probability relations, theory of knowledge and individual behaviour. If the probability p is defined as the logical relation between a proposition a, and a set of premises h, then when the set of premises is inconclusive, no probability relation can be formed. In this circumstance, it is said that the weight of argument V is non-existent and p is non-existent. It should also be clear by now that the set of premises could be inconclusive because of the non-atomistic nature of economic reality. But if that is the case, then individuals have no knowledge about the proposition a. They may not even be able to form a proposition a, still less a probability about it. In a word, individuals are simply uncertain. Furthermore, if there is no degree of belief that is rational to hold about the proposition a, then there is nothing to guide individuals in their practical decision-making. There is thus an intimate link between inconclusive evidence, non-existent probability relations, and unreliability of probability relations for practical decision-making. This is the notion of uncertainty described by Davidson. But once uncertainty is recognized as a pervasive feature of individual decision-making, what is left to economic agents? In answering this question, some Post Keynesians have focused their attention on the role of money as a store of wealth. Money is the fundamental macroeconomic institution, a time-machine vehicle, in Davidson's expression, for coping with the uncertainty of individual decision-making. This is the first aspect of the Post Keynesian project of the macroeconomic foundations of microeconomics.

Post Keynesians such as Davidson have contended that if there is anything economic agents are certain about, the uncertainty that characterizes their individual decision-making is that once current economic resources are committed, then it may prove very costly, if not impossible, to alter the initial decision. More precisely, if agents know that given the available evidence there is no degree of belief that is rational to hold in a proposition a about, say, an investment decision, then they know that the proposition a is a completely unreliable guide for their investment decision. In these uncertain circumstances, economic agents may prefer to postpone investing resources and hold liquid assets instead (Hicks, 1982, p. 288; Fontana, 2004). A positive demand for a stock of money is thus the way economic agents cope with their uncertain knowledge about the future. Importantly, uncertainty and the related demand for money are grounded in the non-atomistic nature of economic reality. Therefore both uncertainty and the demand for money are permanent features of economic decision-making.

There are two important properties of liquid assets that are important to mention at this point (Keynes, 1936, ch. 17). Money has (i) a zero or very small elasticity of production, and (ii) a zero or small elasticity of substitution with any other assets that have a high elasticity of production. Taking these two properties together, this means that when there is an increase in the demand for money, the level of employment in the production of money or of any other commodity produced by the use of labour services is not affected (Davidson, 1972, p. 222). In terms of the theory of decision-making discussed above, it follows that when uncertainty$_2$ arises and economic agents prefer to hold money rather than buy good and services, then the consequent decline in the demand for labour services in the commodity sector is not offset by any increase in the demand for labour services in the production of money. In conclusion, uncertainty$_2$ and the related demand for the stock of money have a negative effect on the level of effective demand and employment. For this reason, Keynes and Post Keynesians insist that once uncertainty is recognized as a pervasive feature of individual decision-making, the macroeconomic result follows that the economic system may settle in equilibrium at any level between zero and full employment (Keynes, 1936, p. 235; Kregel, 1976, pp. 213–14).

Uncertainty$_1$, money and the production process
This chapter has argued that uncertainty$_2$ is only one notion of uncertainty that arises from the non-atomistic nature of economic reality. When the evidential base does exist but is inadequate for attaching a rational degree of belief to a proposition, individual economic agents are again in a condition of uncertainty and probabilities are an unreliable guide in their practical decision-making. But, as before, once uncertainty is recognized as a pervasive feature of individual decision-making, what is left to economic agents? In answering this question, some Post Keynesians called 'circuitists' have focused their attention on the role of money as a final means of payment (Fontana and Realfonzo, 2004). In this role, money defines the context in which modern economic activities are carried out. Money as a final means of payment is the essential macroeconomic institution for coping with the uncertainty of individual decision-making in daily production activities. This is the second aspect of the Post Keynesian project of the macroeconomic foundations of microeconomics.

Among the contributions of the circuitists, the work of Graziani is prominent (e.g. Graziani, 1989; 2003). The basic starting point of his work is that Keynes has described the working of a monetary economy. In this regard, Graziani refers to the surviving early drafts of *The General Theory of Employment, Interest and Money* (Keynes, 1936), where Keynes sets out his fundamental differences with classical theory in terms of the distinction between a $C–M–C'$ economy and an $M–C–M'$ economy (Keynes, 1979, p. 81). The $C–M–C'$ economy is a barter economy, in which production is organized on the basis of the real returns to the factors of labour and capital. Production is thus undertaken up to the point at which the agreed shares of the final output to labour and capital are just sufficient to compensate for the marginal disutility of supplying further labour and capital services. In this sense, the $C–M–C'$ economy is a cooperative economy. Individual self-interest and maximization of social welfare are fully consistent. In this economy, the only role of money, if any, is to facilitate the exchange of good and services. Money is only used 'for purposes of transitory convenience' (Keynes, 1979, p. 81). By contrast, the M–C–M' economy is a monetary economy. In this economy, individual behaviour is motivated by monetary objectives. The employment of labour and capital services as well as the exchange of good and services are the means of achieving monetary returns. Production is thus undertaken to achieve monetary, not real, returns. In a very fundamental sense, money defines the context for economic behaviour. Graziani then concludes that in order to understand the working of a monetary economy and how it differs from a barter economy, it is essential to explain how the flow of means of payment is created, how such means circulate and how they are transformed into a stock of money balances (Graziani, 1989; see also Parguez, 1996). In short, the description of a monetary economy calls for an analysis of the monetary circuit.

In its basic representation, a monetary circuit is a stage-by-stage analysis of the interaction between four groups of economic agents, namely the central bank, commercial banks, firms and wage earners (Fontana, 2000, pp. 33–7; Graziani, 2003, pp. 26–31). In the first stage a flow of final means of payments is created as a result of the negotiations between firms and commercial banks in the loans market. If, for simplicity's sake, internal transactions between firms are ignored, the initial demand for loans by firms, the so-called initial finance, is equal to the payment for hiring labour services. Therefore the initial demand for loans by firms depends only on the wage rate and the amount of labour services to be used. Commercial banks set the price of these loans, namely the interest rate on loans, as a mark-up on the short-run nominal interest rate set by the central bank.

In the successive stages firms produce and put on sale goods and services. Consumer commodities are sold to wage earners whereas investment commodities are exchanged between firms. The exchange of goods and services between firms and wage earners sets the process of circulation of the newly created means of payments in motion. In fact, firms are the first recipient of bank loans but as soon as these loans are credited in their bank deposits, they are transferred to wage earners in return for their labour services. Wage earners then decide to allocate their wage income between consumption expenditure, purchases of securities or cash balances. If wage earners spend all their income either on the goods market or the financial market, then firms recover the initial flow of means of payments and are able to repay the whole principal of their bank advances. In this case, at the end of monetary circuit the newly created flow of means of payment is destroyed. The total money stock has not changed but the flow of money has proved essential for the reproduction of the economic system. Alternatively, to the extent that wage earners decide to allocate some of their wage income to increase their balances of bank deposits or notes, then some of the initial flow of means of payments is not recovered by firms. For this reason, firms have to renegotiate a new loan with commercial banks in order to cover the increased money balances by wage earners (see, for a dynamic analysis of this process, Andresen, 2006; Keen, 2005). The conclusions of the analysis above are still valid but with the important qualification that in this case there is a net addition to the total stock of money equal to the amount of the newly created means of payment allocated to bank deposits and notes by wage earners.

An important implication of the circuitist analysis, though a step never made by Graziani and his colleagues, is that the distinction between a barter economy and a monetary economy really falls back on the pervasiveness of the notion of uncertainty[1] described above (Fontana, 2000).[3] Graziani is right to call for an analysis of the monetary circuit. But why is there a demand for a flow of final means of payment in the first place? In other words, why does a monetary circuit occur? The answer is in uncertainty$_1$, which pervades the employment of labour services (and capital services) as well as the exchange of good and services. It is the uncertainty$_1$ of the production process described above that calls for a final means of payment to cope with it. In a world of certainty there is no need for a final means of payment. A worker could offer labour services to a firm at time t, confident in the knowledge that the claim to goods and services in return for these services will be met by a transfer by a trader at time $t + n$, while a firm may extinguish the initial bank debt by selling goods and services at some other time to some other worker or trader. But if there is uncertainty$_1$, the firm may be unable to sell goods and services and the worker could not then be confident that the claim on goods and services would necessarily be met at some future date (Shackle, 1971; Goodhart, 1989, pp. 25–9). It is this possibility of defaulting on obligations that calls for a final means of payment to meet and alleviate the problem of exchanging under conditions of uncertainty$_1$.

5. Conclusions

This chapter has argued that there are two important lessons to be learned from the early works on philosophy by Keynes and its further developments by Post Keynesian economists. First, Keynes and the Post Keynesians have developed a general theory of individual knowledge based on a two-dimensional approach to probability theory, namely probability relations and weight of argument. Probability relations provide a rational assessment of the relative degree of belief attached to alternative propositions, whereas the weight of argument measures the evidential base of these degrees of belief. These two components of probability theory allow for a general theory of individual knowledge which includes the mainstream cases of certainty and risk as well as the non-mainstream case of uncertainty. By allowing for the non-atomistic feature of economic reality and its implications for economic behaviour, Keynes and the Post Keynesians have imposed fewer restrictions than has the mainstream approach on the conceptualization of individual knowledge, and for this reason they were able to elaborate a proper understanding of uncertainty.

Second, the general theory of individual knowledge discussed above is strictly related to the general theory of money developed by Keynes and the Post Keynesian economists. There is an intimate link between so-called uncertainty$_1$ and uncertainty$_2$ on one side, and the roles of money as final means of payment and as store of wealth, on the other. The difference between uncertainty$_1$ and uncertainty$_2$ is that in the latter the absolute inconclusiveness of the evidential base of the degrees of belief means that a probability relation cannot be conceived, whereas in the former some evidential base exists and hence leads to the formation of probability relations, but, given the incompleteness of this evidence, these probability relations are an unreliable guide to conduct. This distinction is important in explaining the competing claims of several Post Keynesian monetary economists. When fundamentalist Post Keynesians such as Paul Davidson argue that uncertainty is the cause of involuntary unemployment, they are actually referring to the causal role of uncertainty$_2$ in order to explain the theory of money as time-machine together with its related possibility of prolonged depressions and mass unemployment. Similarly, when monetary circuit Post Keynesians such as Graziani refer to the natural association between the origin and development of the production process and the creation, circulation and destruction of flows of final means of payment, they are actually referring to the causal role of uncertainty$_1$ in order to explain the monetary context of the production process. Finally, taking the theory of individual knowledge and the theory of money together explains the Post Keynesian claim that the modern search for the microeconomic foundations of macroeconomics is fallacious because, if anything, it is microeconomics that is in need of macroeconomic foundations. Money in its dual role of final means of payment and store of wealth is the fundamental macroeconomic institution for coping with uncertainty in its dual forms of uncertainty$_1$ and uncertainty$_2$ that characterize microeconomic decision-making.

Notes

1. Keynes also discuss the case in which *a* is known directly. For this more controversial form of knowledge see Lawson (1987, pp. 957–63).
2. The probability relation (26.1) is, of course, completely inadequate in the case of inconclusive premises of the probability relation. See next section for a discussion of this case.
3. The possibility of natural disasters does create uncertainty, but this type of uncertainty is exogenous to the economic system and for this reason is not a discriminatory feature of the two types of economies. What distinguishes a monetary economy from a barter economy is the unpredictability of the complex interdependencies of individual choices. This non-atomistic feature of reality characterizes a monetary but not a barter economy.

References

Andresen, T. (2006), 'A critique of a Post Keynesian model of hoarding and an alternative model', *Journal of Economic Behaviour and Organization*, Forthcoming.

Arestis, P. (1996), 'Post-Keynesian economics: Towards coherence', *Cambridge Journal of Economics*, **20**, 111–35.

Bellofiore, R. (1994), 'Poverty of rhetoric: Keynes versus McCloskey', in A. Marzola and F. Silva (eds), *John Maynard Keynes: Language and Method*, Aldershot, UK and Brookfield, US: Edward Elgar, pp. 75–127.

Braithwaite, R.B. (1973), 'Editorial foreword', in J.M. Keynes, *The Collected Writings of J.M. Keynes*, Vol. VIII, London: Macmillan for the Royal Economic Society, pp. xv–xxii.

Carabelli, A. (1985), 'Keynes on cause, chance and possibility', in T. Lawson and H. Pesaran (eds), *Keynes' Economics*, London: Croom Helm, pp. 151–80.

Carabelli, A. (1988), *On Keynes's Method*, London: Macmillan.

Coates, J. (1996), *The Claims of Common Sense: Moore, Wittgenstein, Keynes and the Social Sciences*, Cambridge: Cambridge University Press.

Comin, F.V. (1999), *Common Sense Economics: Essays on the Role of Common Sense in the History of Economic Thought*, University of Cambridge, Ph.D. Dissertation, March.

Crotty, J.R. (1980), 'Post-Keynesian economic theory: An overview and evaluation', *American Economic Review*, Papers and Proceedings, **70**(2), 20–25.

Davidson, P. (1972), *Money and the Real World*, London: Macmillan.

Davidson, P. (1994), *Post Keynesian Macroeconomic Theory*, Aldershot, UK and Brookfield, US: Edward Elgar.

Davidson, P. (1996), 'Reality and economic theory', *Journal of Post Keynesian Economics*, **18**(4), 479–508.

Dequech, D. (1997), 'Uncertainty in a strong sense: meaning and sources', *Economic Issues*, **2**(2), 21–43.

Fontana, G. (2000), 'Post Keynesians and Circuitists on money and uncertainty: an attempt at generality', *Journal of Post Keynesian Economics*, **23**(1), 27–48.

Fontana, G. (2001), 'Keynes on the "nature of economic thinking": the principle of non-neutrality of choice and the principle of non-neutrality of money', *American Journal of Economics and Sociology*, **60**(4), 711–43.

Fontana, G. (2004), 'Hicks on monetary theory and history', *Cambridge Journal of Economics*, **28**(1), 73–88.

Fontana, G. and Gerrard, B. (1999), 'Disequilibrium states and adjustment processes: toward a historical-time analysis of behaviour under uncertainty', *Philosophical Psychology*, **12**(3), 311–24.

Fontana, G. and Gerrard, B. (2004), 'A Post Keynesian theory of decision-making under uncertainty', *Journal of Economic Psychology*, **25**(5), 619–37.

Fontana, G. and Realfonzo, R. (eds) (2004), *The Monetary Theory of Production*, Basingstoke: Palgrave Macmillan.

Gerrard, Bill (1992), 'From a *Treatise on Probability* to the *General Theory*: continuity or change in Keynes's thought?', in B. Gerrard and J.V. Hillard (eds), *The Philosophy and Economics of J.M. Keynes*, Aldershot, UK and Brookfield, US: Edward Elgar, pp. 80–95.

Goodhart, C.A. (1989), *Money, Information and Uncertainty*, London: Macmillan.

Graziani, Augusto (1989), 'The theory of the monetary circuit', *Thames Papers in Political Economy*, Spring, 1–26.

Graziani, A. (2003), *The Monetary Theory of Production*, Cambridge: Cambridge University Press.

Harcourt, G.C. (1992), 'The legacy of Keynes: Theoretical methods and unfinished business', in C. Sardoni (ed.), *On Political Economists and Modern Political Economy: Selected Essays of G.C. Harcourt*, London: Routledge, pp. 235–49. (First published 1987.)

Hicks, J.R. (1982), 'Methods of dynamic analysis', in J. Hicks (ed.), *Money, Interest and Wages: Collected Essays on Economic Theory*, Vol. 2, Oxford: Basil Blackwell, pp. 217–35. (First published 1956.)

Keen, S. (2005), 'A Circuitist model of monetary production', mimeo, University of Western Sydney, Australia.

Keynes, J.M. (1907), 'The Principles of Probability', manuscript, Marshall Library, Cambridge.

Keynes, J.M. (1921), *A Treatise on Probability*, London: Macmillan. (Reprinted in J.M. Keynes, *The Collected Writings of J.M. Keynes*, Vol. VIII, London: Macmillan for the Royal Economic Society, 1973.)

Keynes, J.M. (1926), 'Francis Ysidro Edgeworth 1845–1926', *Economic Journal*, **36**, March. (Reprinted in J.M. Keynes, *The Collected Writings of J.M. Keynes*, Vol. X, *Essays in Biography*, London: Macmillan for the Royal Economic Society, pp. 251–66.)

Keynes, J.M. (1931), 'Ramsey as a philosopher'. (Reprinted in J.M. Keynes, *The Collected Writings of J.M. Keynes*, Vol. X, *Essays in Biography*, London: Macmillan for the Royal Economic Society, pp. 336–9.)

Keynes, J.M. (1936), *The General Theory of Employment, Interest and Money*, London: Macmillan. (Reprinted in J.M. Keynes, *The Collected Writings of J.M. Keynes*, Vol. VII, London: Macmillan for the Royal Economic Society.)

Keynes, J.M. (1937), 'The general theory of employment', *Quarterly Journal of Economics*, **51**, 209–23. (Reprinted in J.M. Keynes, *The Collected Writings of J.M. Keynes*, Vol. XIV, *The General Theory and After: Part II Defence and Development*, London: Macmillan for the Royal Economic Society, pp. 109–23.)

Keynes, J.M. (1938), 'Letter to R.F. Harrod', 16 July. (Reprinted in J.M. Keynes, *The Collected Writings of J.M. Keynes*, Vol. XIV, *The General Theory and After: Part II Defence and Development*, London: Macmillan for the Royal Economic Society, pp. 299–301.)

Keynes, J.M. (1939), 'Professor Tinbergen's method', *Economic Journal*, September. (Reprinted in J.M. Keynes, *The Collected Writings of J.M. Keynes*, Vol. XIV, *The General Theory and After: Part II Defence and Development*, London: Macmillan for the Royal Economic Society, pp. 306–18.)

Keynes, J.M. (1979), 'Towards the *General Theory*'. (Reprinted in J.M. Keynes, *The Collected Writings of J.M. Keynes*, Vol. XXI, *The General Theory and After: A Supplement*, London: Macmillan for the Royal Economic Society, pp. 35–160.)

Kregel, Jan (1976), 'Economic methodology in the face of uncertainty: the modelling methods of Keynes and the Post-Keynesians', *Economic Journal*, **86**, 209–25.

Kregel, J.A. (1987), 'Rational spirits and the Post Keynesian macroeconomic theory of macroeconomics', *De Economist*, **135**(4), 520–32.

Lawson, T. (1985), 'Uncertainty and economic analysis', *Economic Journal*, **95**, 909–27.

Lawson, T. (1987), 'The relative/absolute nature of knowledge and economic analysis', *Economic Journal*, **97**, 951–70.

Lawson, T. (1988), 'Probability and uncertainty in economic analysis', *Journal of Post Keynesian Economics*, **11**(1), 38–65.

Lawson, T. (1997), *Economics and Reality*, London and New York: Routledge.

Lawson, T. (2003), *Reclaiming Reality*, London and New York: Routledge.

Nasica, E. and Kregel, J.A. (1999), 'Alternative analyses of uncertainty and rationality: Keynes and modern economics', in S. Marzetti Dall'Aste Brandolin and R. Scazzieri (eds), *La Probabilità in Keynes: Premesse ed Influenze*, Bologna: Clueb, pp. 115–37.

O'Donnell, R. (1989), *Keynes: Philosophy, Economics and Politics*, London: Macmillan.

Parguez, Alain (1996), 'Beyond scarcity: a reappraisal of the theory of the monetary circuit', in G. Deleplace and E. Nell (eds), *Money in Motion*, London: Macmillan, pp. 155–99.

Rabin, M. (1998), 'Psychology and economics', *Journal of Economic Literature*, **36**, 11–46.

Runde, J. (1990), 'Keynesian uncertainty and the weight of arguments', *Economics and Philosophy*, **6**, 275–92.

Runde, J. (1991), 'Keynesian uncertainty and the instability of beliefs', *Review of Political Economy*, **3**(2), 125–45.

Shackle, G.L.S. (1961), *Decision, Order, and Time in Human Affairs*, Cambridge: Cambridge University Press.

Shackle, G.L.S. (1971), 'Foundations of monetary policy: Discussion paper', in G. Clayton, J.C. Gilbert and R. Sedwick (eds), *Monetary Theory and Monetary Policy in the 1970's*, London: Oxford University Press, pp. 32–4.

27 Speculation, liquidity preference and monetary circulation

Korkut A. Erturk

The objective of this chapter is to give a general overview of the dynamic interaction of industrial and financial circulation, focusing specifically on the macroeconomic effects of asset market speculation in the context of the latter. Much of the emphasis in this discussion is on some of Keynes's arguments in his *Treatise* which had been eclipsed by his much better-known *General Theory* (*GT*). In his latter work, Keynes tried to show the validity of the principle of effective demand even in the turf of the mainstream economists by basing his argument as much as possible on conventional assumptions. He often referred to his *Treatise* on technical details of monetary and financial matters and remarked that his two works complemented each other. But, among his readers in later generations, few had the benefit of any in-depth knowledge of his earlier work. But, also, substantively, the formulation of his 'liquidity preference' argument into a theory of the interest rate and the sharp exchanges with some of his critics on the loanable funds theory made it harder to appreciate the degree of continuity in his thought with the tradition of monetary analysis that emanates from Wicksell, of which the *Treatise* was a part. As he (and his followers) became embroiled in debates with mainstream economists in the aftermath of the *GT*, many of his insights in the *Treatise* were lost or abandoned because they no longer fit easily in the truncated theoretical structure he adopted in his latter work. For later economists, this has made it harder to appreciate, let alone pursue, Keynes's early insights. This chapter errs, if at all, on the other side as it highlights these early insights at the expense of Keynes's formulation of his views in the *GT*.

Wicksell, the quantity theory, and monetary theory of production

In the quantity theory, an exogenous increase in the supply of money leads to a higher price level because agents are thought to bid up commodity prices with their increased money balances. As Wicksell (1906, pp. 159–60) realized, this implies that in the transition period during which money income rises to a higher equilibrium level, total demand has to exceed aggregate supply. In other words, Say's Law could not possibly hold and money has to have 'real' effects in the short run defined as the period of adjustment to a higher position of equilibrium. As he put it, the availability of finance in the form of bank credit to 'deficit units' frees investment from past savings, making it possible for total expenditures to exceed total income, and thus an excess of investment over savings corresponds to an excess supply (demand) of money. By implication, the classical dichotomy does not hold since money is no longer a 'veil' at least in the short run.

Wicksell was also first to realize that the banking system would – as long as it acted in tandem – endogenously expand the money supply by simply extending credit to firms, which returned to them in the form of deposits. Given the banks' ability to create credit money, Wicksell argued that a fall in the money rate of interest below the return on new capital, which he called the natural rate of interest, would give rise to a cumulative process of inflation – assuming that full employment held and output remained fixed. The process could also work in reverse, giving rise to a cumulative process of deflation when the money rate of interest rose above the natural rate. In the 1920s, it was not uncommon to think of recessions as being caused by a natural interest rate that fell (either because of over-investment or for technological reasons) below a constant money rate of interest (Ellis, 1934). In fact, Leijonhufvud (1968; 1981) is convinced that Keynes's central insight is a refinement of this basic Wicksellian idea, in which bear speculation in financial markets prevents the bond rate of interest from falling sufficiently following a fall in the natural rate of interest. As we shall see, however, there was more to Keynes's 'early' contribution.

Writing in the quantity theory tradition, Keynes's main contention in his *A Tract on Monetary Reform* was that price fluctuations over a business cycle were characterized not so much by exogenous shifts in the money supply but rather by systematic changes in the demand for real money balances. He thus argued that any attempt on the part of mone-tary authorities to keep the money supply steady would fail to achieve price stability (*CW*, IV, p. 69). Instead, he argued, the more effective policy would be to aim at changing the money supply to compensate for the systemic shifts taking place in the demand for real-money balances over the credit cycle. If changes in desired money balances had a systemic character, this also meant that the excess of investment over saving could correspond to a fall in demand for money in relation to supply as well. In other words, the increased supply of money which Wicksell argued is the dual of the difference between investment and savings could just as well come about by a fall in demand for money balances through dishoarding rather than a rise in total money supply. Likewise, periods of excess savings would be characterized either by increased monetary hoarding or decreased money supply, or both. The disaggregation of money demand by the type of agent and transac-tion in the *Treatise* was thus motivated in part by Keynes's desire to analyze changes in hoarding over the credit cycle.

Keynes's second novel contribution to the basic Wicksellian theme is the insight that over a credit cycle involving the transition from one position of equilibrium to a higher one, the prices of capital goods vary systematically in relation to those of consumer goods. Later partially revived by Minsky's 'two-price' theory (Kregel, 1992), this view holds that the prices of capital goods are determined in financial markets by profit expect-ations that are reflected – though not always accurately, as we shall see – in securities prices, while consumer goods prices are determined by the relative magnitude of con-sumer demand in relation to the available supply. Thus the very *modus operandi* of mone-tary expansion involves changes in the relative values of capital and consumer goods, and that is why the classical dichotomy, Keynes held, was not viable. The idea is that mone-tary injection has a direct and immediate impact on the prices of financial assets (and thus works quite rapidly on new investment goods), but affects consumer goods prices only indirectly and slowly as the level of activity in the investment sector expands. After the *GT*, this idea all but disappeared as macroeconomics came to be associated with one-commodity models even among Keynesians (Leijonhufvud, 1968, p. 23).

Finally, in the *Treatise*, Keynes then links expected changes in securities prices over the credit cycle to changes in net hoarding – his first innovation – through the variations in the stock demand for financial assets, by what he called the 'state of bearishness'. For instance, a period of early expansion is characterized in his view by excess investment, expected increases in asset prices and falling state of bearishness, and thus net dishoarding. This makes it all the easier for banks to accommodate a rising level of activity without having to raise the money rate of interest. In his approach, speculation about asset price expectations is an integral part of the investment–savings nexus, where changes in the state of bearishness have a direct *quantity* effect first and foremost on the relative size of inactive balances without necessarily causing a change in the rate of interest or asset prices in general.

As argued below, this framework afforded a setting where the effects of market speculation and asset price bubbles on monetary circulation could be discussed directly in a way that became impossible to do in the *GT*. In the reformulated version of the argument in the *GT*, as we shall see, changes in the liquidity preference function lacked any determinate functional link to speculative asset price expectations, with the result that shifts in them were seen to be caused by unexplained – and, by implication, unpredictable – shifts in market psychology. Moreover, whatever shift occurred would have solely a direct *price* effect, causing the rate of interest to vary until the 'aggregate desire to hoard becomes equal to the available cash'. Below, I first discuss Keynes's argument in the *Treatise* and then move on to discuss how some of these insights were lost in the *GT*.

The argument in the *Treatise*

An essential feature of Keynes's argument in the *Treatise* is the contention that the prices of investment goods are subject to forces that are quite different from those that bear on consumer goods prices. Keynes's First Fundamental Equation in the *Treatise* (which gives the prices of consumer goods) derives from an intersectoral balance condition, not much different from the one in Marx's schemes of reproduction. It sets the price of consumer goods equal to the cost of production, adjusted as to whether profits are above or below 'normal'. Price exceeds cost of production, and profits are above normal, when the net supply of consumer goods falls short of demand. Whether the demand for consumer goods is equal to its supply depends on whether the value added in the investment goods sector, what Keynes called 'cost of investment', is equal to savings in both sectors. Thus, with a given cost structure and level of savings, the price of consumer goods varies with the level of activity in the investment goods sector. By contrast, the price of investment goods does not directly depend on the relative magnitudes of investment and savings. Profit expectations, along with the state of bearishness and behavior of the banking system, determine the price of securities, which in turn reflects the demand price for new investment goods. A positive difference between the demand price of investment goods thus determined and the cost of producing them gives rise to windfall profits, stimulating an increase in the level of activity in this sector. A higher level of activity, i.e., cost of investment (value added) in the investment sector, in turn, raises the demand for consumer goods and gives rise – with a constant level of savings – to windfall profits in the consumer goods sector as well. Thus the direction of causation in Keynes's account of the credit cycle runs from financial conditions, interpreted broadly, to the price of securities (and thus the demand price of investment goods), and from windfall profits thus determined and the change in the level of activity that causes to the total demand for consumer goods.

Setting off a debate that keeps recurring to this day, Robertson (1931) objected to Keynes's employment of two separate principles to determine, respectively, the investment and consumer goods prices. He argued that Keynes could insulate the price level of new investment goods from changes in the flow of savings only because he was assuming that over-saving was associated with hoarding and under-saving with dishoarding. This argument was only partially true because it misspecified the real issue of contention between them. The very logic of the Quantity Equation as an accounting identity, as Wicksell laid bare, requires that a reduction in monetary income (over-saving) involve a reduced monetary circulation. This can come about either through a fall in the total quantity of money or increased hoarding, or some combination of the two. Thus, if the quantity of total money is not decreasing, over-saving has to be associated with an increase in net hoarding, and thus a fall in the overall velocity for the broad money supply. Otherwise, over-saving and thus a fall in monetary income could not have occurred.[1] So there was something to Robertson's objection. But the real contentious issue in his criticism was whether or not this increase in inactive balances (hoarding) would also translate into excess demand for financial assets. If it did, as Robertson seems to have argued, then, clearly, the price of securities (and thus that of new investment goods) could not be determined independently of savings as Keynes suggested. Thus Keynes's 'two-price' theory was (or should have been) the central issue in this debate.

In his rebuttal of Robertson, Keynes argued that a situation of over-saving involves windfall losses for a class of entrepreneurs who would be forced to liquidate a part of their asset positions in order to be able to meet their current financial obligations that could no longer be covered by sale proceeds (*CW*, XIII, pp. 219–36). Thus the increased demand for financial assets, if indeed inactive balances caused that, would be balanced by the increased supply coming from those entrepreneurs running down their reserves of financial assets to compensate for their windfall losses. In other words, the increase of wealth savers' experience at the end of the period would be matched by the decrease of wealth experienced by entrepreneurs facing windfall losses. The prices of financial assets would then remain basically unchanged, provided that the state of bearishness of savers is not significantly different from that of entrepreneurs. While this argument is plausible, it might have detracted attention from the real issue.

For Keynes's stronger argument is of course the broader justification for his 'two-price' theory, which he also restated in his rebuttal (*CW*, XIII, p. 220). In the language of modern finance theory, this can perhaps be put more succinctly. The price of an asset is determined solely by its expected future price, independently of its current flows of supply and demand, if these flows are dwarfed by speculative stocks that are *very* large. Thus the impact of 'outside' supply and demand on the current price can be only indirect, through its influence, if any, on the expected future price of the asset in question.[2] In a nutshell, this was the gist of Keynes's argument in justification of his 'two-price' theory. Already in the *Treatise*, Keynes had made a distinction between the decision to save in the sense of non-consumption, and the decision on how to dispose of what is not consumed, and remarked that the main consideration in making the latter decision is the current and expected future asset prices, which also influenced how all financial wealth was held. Because the marginal increase in financial wealth, equal to the savings used to purchase securities, was 'trifling' in magnitude compared to the total stock of wealth, expectations about the future asset prices were much more important than the marginal increase in the demand for financial assets. The way he put it, the 'excess bearish' factor, an inverse index of the stock demand for securities, reflected the public's demand for inactive balances (saving deposits) given their expectations (and degree of their confidence in them) about future asset prices, and the current asset prices changed accordingly to the extent that the banking sector chose not to accommodate the changes in the public's demand for saving deposits (inactive balances). In other words, with a given banking sector policy, future asset price expectations governed the current prices of securities (and thus those of investment goods), reflecting in part profit expectations in the real economy along with the other considerations summarized under Keynes's famous 'beauty contest' analogy in the *GT* (see below).

Quite aware of the important role the 'two-price' view played in Keynes's overall scheme, Leijonhufvud (1968; 1981, ch. 7) gives a similar, though a narrower, account of Keynes's argument in support of it.[3] He holds that, even as early as in the *Treatise*, Keynes explained why the interest rate fails to equilibrate investment and savings, by referring to *bear* speculation that results from the inelastic expectations speculators hold about the future bond prices following a fall in the *natural* rate, which prevents the current bond rate from adjusting downward. A falling *natural* rate of interest means a rising price of newly issued financial assets whose supply decreases in relation to its demand with the falling off of investment demand. Because the *bear* speculators satisfy the excess demand of savers for financial assets, thinking that the asset price increase is only temporary, the long bond rate cannot fall to the level of the *natural* rate. In other words, the expected future asset prices determine the current interest rate independently of the supply and demand flows. As remarked before, however, there is more to Keynes's argument in the *Treatise* than Leijonhufvud's account suggests. The inelastic expectations, on which Leijonhufvud places such great emphasis, preclude both destabilizing speculation and asset price bubbles that played an important part in the argument in the *Treatise*, to which I turn next.

Asset price speculation in the *Treatise*
In Keynes's discussion of credit cycle dynamics, in early expansion the rising level of activity does not typically lead to a higher interest rate even with a constant total money supply, because of a falling state of bearishness (dishoarding). Optimistic asset price expectations cause the overall size of inactive balances – which Keynes took to be the index of the state of bearishness – to steadily decrease. This configuration, a decreasing volume of inactive balances (bear position) at a time of rising security prices, is what Keynes called a 'bull market with a consensus of opinion', which is one of the four types of speculative markets he defined in connection with the different phases of a credit cycle (*CW*, V, p. 226). Corresponding to late expansion, he held, is a 'bull market with a difference of opinion' which is characterized by a rising bear position at a time of increasing security prices. In early expansion, the preponderance of market opinion holds that security prices have not risen sufficiently, while in late expansion the increasing bear position means that an ever-rising segment of the market begins to think that security prices have risen more than sufficiently. Similarly, early recession is characterized by a 'bear market with a consensus', and again Keynes distinguishes this from a 'bear market with a division of opinion'. The former involves a rising bear position at a time of falling security prices and the latter a decreasing bear position when security prices are still falling. In the former, the predominant market opinion holds that security prices have not fallen sufficiently and in the latter that they have fallen more than sufficiently.

From the point of view of the orthodox theory of finance, it does not make any sense to say that security prices have increased or decreased more, or less, than *sufficiently* if no new information has emerged at a given point in time. For, if securities are thought to be undervalued, then arbitrageurs would continue to buy them until their prices are bid up to a level that is no longer considered low. Likewise, if securities are thought to be overvalued, again, arbitrage would bring their value down to a level consistent with what is considered to be their 'true' value. Thus, at a given point in time characterized by a given information set, the prevailing asset prices must be the best estimates of fundamental values.[4]

However, Keynes's approach in the *Treatise* is consistent with the modern 'noise trader' (or the so-called *behavioral*) approach to finance, which holds that *riskless* arbitrage is not effective in relation to the prices of shares or bonds as a whole and severely limited even when it comes to the relative prices of individual assets (Shleifer and Summers, 1990; Shleifer and Vishny, 1997). According to this view, even when it is assumed that arbitrageurs know what fundamental values are, they face no *riskless* arbitrage opportunities when actual prices deviate from their true values. For with a finite time horizon, arbitrageurs face two kinds of risk: when they, say, sell overvalued assets short it is possible that by the time they are supposed to liquidate their position (i) the economy can grow so rapidly that the true values increase, or, more importantly, (ii) the asset prices might be even more overpriced. In both cases, arbitrageurs would be experiencing heavy losses. Thus the fear of loss would limit the initial positions the arbitrageurs take and thus prevent them from driving prices down in any significant way. Moreover, if we drop the assumption that arbitrageurs know what the true values are, the risk of loss they face is higher, and the compensatory shift in demand for the undervalued securities smaller.

In the *Treatise*, in a vein very similar to the modern behavioral approach, Keynes remarks that when prices deviate from their 'true' values, no automatic mechanism exists in the short run to check their deviation. *Opinion*, or what we would today call *noise* (Black, 1986), moves prices. 'If everyone agrees that securities are worth more, and if everyone is a "bull" in the sense of preferring securities at a rising price to increasing his savings deposits, there is no limit to the rise in price of securities and no effective check arises from a shortage of money' (*CW*, V, p. 229). However, as prices continue to rise, a 'bear' position begins to develop, and that is what can eventually check the rise in prices. '[I]n proportion as the prevailing opinion comes to seem unreasonable to more cautious people, the "other view" will tend to develop, with the result of an increase in the "bear" position' (ibid., pp. 228–9).

In Keynes's discussion in the *Treatise*, the rise of the bear position at a time when security prices are rising plays an important role in explaining the turning point of a business cycle expansion. In his view, 'it is astonishing . . . how large a change in the earnings bill can be looked after by the banking system without an apparent breach in its principles and traditions' (ibid., p. 272). Yet the banking system's ability to accommodate a rising level of production is typically impaired at some point during a business cycle expansion. That happens typically not because the banking sector is held back by the central bank or faces some intrinsic difficulty, but because the financial sentiment falters. The trigger can have a myriad of immediate causes but the underlying reason is almost invariably the fact that the actual performance of profits, though they might still be rising, falls short of the high expectations that are already capitalized in asset prices. As the view that the market might be overvalued begins to take hold, the bear position develops, and 'the tendency of the financial circulation to increase, on the top of the increase in the industrial circulation . . . break[s] the back of the banking system and cause it at long last to impose a rate of interest, which is not only fully equal to the natural rate but, very likely in the changed circumstances, well above it' (ibid.).

In a similar manner, a declining bear position during a business upswing prevents the interest rate from rising with increasing levels of activity. Again, *stock* decisions dominate *flow* decisions. It can, stylistically, be thought that in a given accounting period the amount by which the net increase in new securities issued by firms (investment) exceeds the net increase in demand for such securities by savers (savings) is purchased by those speculators who, expecting securities' prices to rise, draw down saving deposits in the aggregate. In fact, if the bullish sentiment is strong enough, the prices of securities can even rise, implying that the bond rate might actually decrease rather than increase. Thus, independently of the policy of the banking system, an increase in investment in excess of saving need not put any downward pressure on asset prices.

The 'beauty contest'

Ever since Friedman (1953) argued that destabilizing speculation would be unprofitable, and, thus, unsustainable in the long run, the mainstream view among economists has been the assumption that speculation as a rule could not be destabilizing. Asset price bubbles were considered highly unlikely if not impossible in a 'normally' functioning market. The intuition behind Friedman's argument rested on a simple view of arbitrage, in which the market comprises smart traders who know the true values and misinformed noise traders. If securities are undervalued, so the argument goes, then the smart traders will continue to buy them until their prices are bid up to their true value. Likewise, if securities are overvalued, smart traders will sell them, bringing their price down to their true value. Indeed, under these conditions, speculation is always stabilizing and profitable. Misinformed noise traders create riskless arbitrage opportunities that smart traders profit from, while making losses themselves. In other words, this implies that the rate of current price change is a function of the difference between the current price and the expected future price, which is by assumption equal to *true* value. In simple terms:

$$\frac{dP}{dt} = j(P^e - P), \tag{27.1}$$

where, P^e, the future expected price, is assumed to be constant ($P^e = \bar{P}$) and equal to the *true* value, and j is the adjustment coefficient indicating the speed with which traders respond to changes in current price. When

$$P > P^e, \text{ then } \frac{dP}{dt} < 0$$

and when

$$P < P^e, \text{ then } \frac{dP}{dt} > 0.$$

The time path of price is given by

$$P(t) = P(0)e^{-ji} + P^e,$$

which clearly cannot be unstable, since the stability condition $j > 0$ is always satisfied because the speed of adjustment is positive by definition.

Undoubtedly, the assumption that smart traders or speculators know with certainty true value is exceedingly unrealistic. But, even under this strong assumption, it does not necessarily follow that the deviation of the current price of an asset from its true value creates a riskless arbitrage opportunity. As mentioned above, speculators who sell over-valued assets short can find that by the time they are supposed to close their position, the true value has increased, or the assets in question have become even more overpriced. Thus, even if the true value is known, it does not follow that it will be equal to the expected future price.

This also takes us very close to a world described in Keynes's (1936, ch. 12) famous 'beauty contest' analogy, where speculators base their expectations of future asset prices not only on what they think the true value is, but, more importantly, on what they think the average opinion about the true value is. In other words, *noise* is at least as important as information about true values in causing asset price changes, rendering the resale price uncertain. Because traders typically lack a terminal value from which to bakwardize, they must not only form higher-order expectations (i.e., on what others think others think) but also decide how much weight to assign to them relative to what they themselves think the true value is (Hirota and Sunder, 2003). Since no direct information exists on others' higher-order expectations, traders have to infer that from a *technical* analysis of market trends, i.e., basically, the recent and current price changes.

For instance, if traders observe that the price of an asset (or an asset group) which they think is already overvalued is still rising in price, they are led to surmise that either their opinion about the true value is wrong or that the price increase indicates a bubble, i.e., a self-sustained rise in price on account of noise trading driven by the average opinion thinking that the average opinion thinks the price will keep on rising. In either case, the current price changes are likely to gain in importance in how traders form their expectations about the future price, for it becomes either a proxy for the higher-order expectations or a corrective on opinions about the true value, or some combination of both. If so, the crucial variable that determines whether speculation is stabilizing or not very much depends on the relative weight traders assign to their higher-order expectations (i.e., what they think others think others think) relative to their own assessment of what the true value is. To the extent that they do, they become more responsive to the current price change in forming their expectations about the future price. In Kaldor's (1939) formulation, whether speculation is stabilizing or not in this setting depends on the elasticity of future price expectations with respect to present price changes.[5]

If indeed the expected future price can be thought to comprise two parts, then we can write:

$$P^e = \bar{P} + \sigma \frac{dP}{dt}, \tag{27.2}$$

where $\bar{P}$ is what the true value is believed to be (and is assumed constant for simplicity), and σ is the coefficient of elasticity of expectations about the future price with respect to the current changes in price.

Plugging (27.2) into (27.1) gives:

$$\frac{dP}{dt} = j\left[\bar{P} + \sigma\frac{dP}{dt} - P\right],$$

and rearranging we get:

$$\frac{dP}{dt} + \frac{j}{1 - \sigma j}\bar{P} = \frac{j}{1 - \sigma j}\bar{P},$$

which, in turn, yields the following time path of price:

$$P(t) = [P(0) - \bar{P}]e^{\frac{j}{1-\sigma j}t} + \bar{P}$$

The stability condition, $\sigma < 1/j$, shows that stability depends on both the elasticity of expectations and the reaction speed. If the reaction speed is assumed instantaneous ($j = 1$), as Kaldor seems to have implicitly assumed, a less than unitary elasticity of expectations ($\sigma < 1$) ensures stability. In other words, destabilizing speculation can give rise to an asset price bubble only if traders revise their expected future price proportionally more than the change in current price. However, when the reaction speed is slower ($j < 1$), the threshold value of σ exceeds unity.

One would expect both the reaction speed (j) and the elasticity of expectations (σ) to respond to changes in market opinion as to the degree to which asset prices are misaligned. As remarked above, if traders observe that the actual price is well above what they think the true value is and still rising, they either begin to lose confidence in their own opinion on what is reasonable or think that asset price increases have acquired the character of a bubble. In either case, an increasing number of traders who might think alike will either leave the market or become much more responsive to current price movements in forming expectations about the future price – either *naïvely* as noise traders or *smartly* as speculators are presumed to do. In this setting, unlike what Friedman foresaw, successful (*read* rational) speculators are those who engage in 'trend' speculation, where they act like noise traders themselves in the short run, trying to feed the bubble rather than help deflate it (De Long et al., 1990).[6] Because the successful speculative strategy entails jumping on the bandwagon of noise traders and knowing when to get off while the rest ride on, this might also imply a rising reaction speed.[7] Thus, any sustained trend of a current price increase from what the market opinion generally holds to be the true value, whatever the cause, is likely to raise both the elasticity of expectations and the reaction speed. While this does not explain how initially prices become misaligned, it suggests that speculation can become destabilizing once price deviations exceed in size and duration a certain threshold. Keynes's argument seems to assume that during the upswing, actual profits cannot increase at an increasing rate, while asset prices often will. Thus, sooner or later, optimistic expectations, and thus the asset prices that they underlie, outstrip the actual performance of profits. The latter, though still rising, eventually fall short of the former, but the bullish sentiment tends to persist.

Thus, Keynes's discussion, in his *Treatise*, on how asset prices behave over the business cycle seems to presuppose that speculation can be both stabilizing and destabilizing, depending on the phase of the cycle. As discussed in the previous section, Keynes argues that agents form expectations about the trend value of asset prices, and the weighted average of these opinions tend to shift over the course of a business cycle expansion, which are then reflected in the changing size of the bear position in the economy. He stylistically divides the expansion phase of a business cycle into two parts, where the preponderance of market opinion holds that asset prices are alternately undervalued and overvalued during the early and late periods of the cycle. While speculation is stabilizing in the former period, it becomes destabilizing during late expansion, giving rise to a bubble. The latter period owes its existence, and is prolonged in duration, to the extent that the banking system expands the money supply by recycling the *bear* funds (bank deposits of those who have sold securities short) to those who still have a *bullish* sentiment that asset prices will continue to rise. If investment is still in excess of savings and output is thus expanding, it must be that the total money supply is increasing more than the increase in net hoarding.

Mean reversion in asset prices brings the expansion to an end. As suggested, the bear position develops in direct proportion to the deviation of actual prices from *true* values, and sets the stage for an abrupt fall in asset prices that can be triggered by any adverse piece of *news* (Zeeman, 1974).[8] Once asset prices start falling, Keynes argued that they will overshoot in the opposite direction, touching off a 'bear market with a consensus of opinion'. With a contracting level of activity, the demand for liquidity rises on account of expectations that asset prices will continue to fall, offsetting at least in part the fall in transactions demand. Thus, whatever monetary relief there is in the form of a lower rate of interest rate to output contraction is likely to come about more on account of changed expectations about asset prices having hit bottom than because of a lower transactions demand associated with the reduced level of activity. Once the opinion that asset prices have fallen more than sufficiently gains strength, the bear position begins to fall even when asset prices might still be falling. On the other hand, a more tranquil financial environment where a set of institutions anchor agents' expectations could militate against wide fluctuations in asset prices by inculcating the belief that asset price misalignments are unlikely to become large. In that situation, a more gradual adjustment might be plausible, where the elasticity of expectations might negatively react to the perceived magnitude of the asset price misalignments over a longer period of time, as Kaldor (1939) thought was likely.

'Two-price' theory and the *GT*

While Hicks (1937) arguably stood Keynes's *GT* on its head in his famous review article, he also appears to have identified quite clearly what was unique about his theory. This was in his opinion the notion that an increase in expenditures and income did not necessarily put an upward pressure on the interest rate. Hicks called this Keynes's 'special theory', and distinguished it from the *GT*, which in his view was closer to orthodoxy since Keynes's argument there implied that – as his IS–LM formulation he believed made evident – an increase in expenditure led to a rise in the interest rate, all other things being equal (p. 152). The 'special theory' Hicks was referring to is but the essential feature of the 'two-price' theory, whereby asset prices are determined independently of investment and saving flows.

According to Hicks's yardstick, Keynes's argument in his *Treatise* was already more 'Keynesian' than the *GT*. In the earlier work, it was not just the elastic money supply that kept the interest rate in check, but more importantly the fact that the state of bearishness (stock demand for financial assets) varied as a function of speculative expectations about asset price misalignments, exerting a *quantity* effect on inactive balances. As discussed in detail above, the bear position typically fell in the early phase of a business cycle expansion with optimistic asset price expectations, compensating the upward pressure put on the interest rate by the rising level of expenditure and income. Likewise, the period of late expansion was associated with the rising preponderance of market opinion that held that asset prices are excessive in relation to the actual earning performance of firms. That, in turn, caused the bear position to rise, making it harder for the banking system to accommodate rising levels of output without an increase in the interest rate.

On the face of it, translating the argument in the *Treatise* into the terminology of the *GT* seems to amount to the simple proposition that the liquidity preference schedule shifts down (up) when the marginal efficiency of capital shifts up (down) on account of more optimistic (pessimistic) expectations. In fact, Keynes appears to have made such a connection himself.[9] On closer examination, however, the suggested translation of the argument into the language of the *GT* is not as straightforward as it first appears. For one, in the *GT*, Keynes centered his whole argument of liquidity preference on the expected variations in the price of loan capital, and delineated the variations in share prices as a separate issue to be dealt with under the marginal efficiency of capital.[10] Asset price changes that would be brought about by changes in the interest rate, resulting from shifts in the portfolio choice between bonds and money, then became the focus of analysis. But this also made it harder to conceptualize the macroeconomic effects of asset prices the market opinion held to be misaligned.

For the very concept of the marginal efficiency of capital, which as Keynes stresses is *fixed* by market valuation, implicitly precludes the notion of an asset price bubble. Note that if the marginal efficiency of capital shifts up on account of higher expectations of future profitability that are *justified*, then the initial increase in asset prices will cease to be excessive when actual investment and profits increase. Yet it is not clear how this case would be distinguished from a situation where the higher profit expectations are somehow *unjustified* or that the increase in asset prices is 'excessive' in relation to these expectations, all other things again being equal. If investment rises with the higher marginal efficiency of capital as it should and the multiplier is what it is in both cases, then it is unclear how one could define market overvaluation, barring capacity or employment constraints.

Whether actual return on investment turns out to be less than or equal to what was expected, Keynes assumes that the expected rate of return on capital adjusts to the interest rate in equilibrium through variations in the scale of investment (Keynes, 1936, p. 178). As Keynes put it after the *GT*,

> the necessity of equalizing the advantages of the choice between owning loans and assets requires that the rate of interest should be equal to the marginal efficiency of capital. But this does not tell us at what level the equality will be effective. The orthodox theory regards the efficiency of capital as setting the pace . . . Thus, instead of the marginal efficiency of capital determining the rate of interest, it is truer (though not a full statement of the case) to say that it is the rate of interest which determines the marginal efficiency of capital. (*CW*, XIV, pp. 122–3)

This formulation, combined with the shift to equilibrium analysis, left no room for the shifts in market opinion about asset price misalignments to play any role in the argument. The whole issue was then put on the back burner as Keynes defined his short term in terms of a given set of long-term expectations, which was understood to mean that future profit expectations that underlay equity prices were assumed constant within his short period. This placed the whole emphasis on the present value of this expected future stream of profits that changed with the money rate of interest.

Second, in the reformulated version of his liquidity preference argument as a theory of the interest rate, Keynes remarks that 'what matters is not the absolute level of r [the interest rate] but the degree of its divergence from what is considered a fairly safe level of r, having regard to those calculations of probability which are being relied on' (Keynes 1936, p. 202). Although Keynes accepts that this 'safe' rate can itself vary from time to time, he takes this to be the exception rather than the rule. Thus, if the safe rate is expected to remain unchanged, he remarks that every decrease (increase) in the current interest rate increases the expectation that bond prices will fall (rise) in the future, and thus raising (lowering) 'the risk of illiquidity'. As Kaldor (1939) later elaborated, in this situation even a very small change in bond prices would be sufficient to induce speculators to buy the new bonds firms issue, since they would be expecting the bond prices to rise in the future, as long as their expectations with respect to the long rate remained inelastic.[11]

Note that here the bearish (bullish) sentiment now refers to the heightened (reduced) sense of risk associated with illiquidity, as the focus of the argument moves from shifts in the liquidity preference function as a whole to variations in the demand for liquidity when the said function remains unchanged. By contrast, when Keynes refers to a shift in liquidity preference as a result of the collapse in the marginal efficiency of capital in his chapter on the trade cycle – referred to above – he means a shift in the whole schedule and presumably a change in what is considered a safe rate as well. But, if the liquidity preference varies with shifts in the marginal efficiency of capital, it is harder to derive an interest-elastic money demand schedule on the basis of the speculative motive, for it is then less plausible that expectations about the 'safe' rate are inelastic. In this setting, the only type of as asset price bubble that can ever occur is that in bond prices, caused potentially by an aggressively expansionary monetary policy that brings about too steep a fall in the current rate of interest in relation to the 'safe' rate. The *liquidity trap* that can result in this instance is reminiscent of Keynes's *bull market with a division of opinion* in the *Treatise*, though, its scope is much more limited.

After the *GT*

The 'finance' debate that broke out after the publication of the *GT* was essentially a continuation of the disagreement Robertson had with Keynes in 1931. Above, I argued that this exchange was in fact about two separate issues – one, about consistency in macro accounting and, the other, on economic behavior – that were entangled together, and suggested that the former detracted attention from the more important disagreement with respect to the latter involving Keynes's 'two-price' theory. The 'accounting debate' almost completely crowded out the other one after the *GT*, where Keynes redefined investment and savings and insisted that they were separate but always equal. Agreement first had to be reached on expressing 'investment–saving' disequilibrium in terms of the discrepancies between *intended* and *actual* magnitudes, with all the attending confusion about what *intended* savings meant, but otherwise it was the old 'accounting debate' all over again. In 1931, the issue was the connection between excess savings and increased hoarding (i.e., in the absence of a fall in the money supply); after the *GT*, it became a debate about what the corollary of an increase in 'intended' investment was. A rise in the money supply was ruled out by assumption and 'dishoarding' had an immediate price effect by definition. Thus, this time around, the whole debate could only be framed from the 'money demand' side and focus on the pressure an increase in planned expenditures would exert on the interest rate. In his exchanges with his critics, including Robertson among others, Keynes (1937a; 1937b; 1937c; 1938) had to concede that a rise in planned investment would also raise the demand for money prior to its execution, and, thus, all other things being equal, the interest rate. He emphasized banks' overdraft facilities to argue that this effect on the interest rate would not amount to much in practice. Decades later, in another round of 'finance' debate an article by Asimakopulos (1983) set off, it was in a similar vein accepted that additional bank finance would be required until the multiplier process worked itself out, generating enough savings to equal the higher level of investment (Chick, 1983; 1997).

Thus, in both debates, the increased 'planned' expenditures were linked to a prospective increase in the money supply, but that did little to bring into focus the more important debate about economic behavior. On the contrary, the focus on the accounting problem in both has placed the emphasis on the so-called finance demand as a separate motivation to hold money, and that appears to have weakened the essential aspect of Keynes's 'two-price' theory. In Davidson's (1978) well-known incorporation of the idea into the IS–LM model, an increase in planned investment not only shifts up the IS schedule but the LM schedule as well, causing the interest rate to go up faster and sooner whenever the level of activity rose. Of course, the verbal explanation of why the interest rate rises was very different from Robertson's 'loanable funds' account, but the end result was the same in obliterating whatever remained intact from 'Keynes' special theory'. One outcome of this, it appears, was to dampen interest in liquidity preference among heterodox economists. Keynes's disciples at Cambridge had found little of interest in the *Treatise* and by and large ignored monetary theory all along anyway (Kregel, 1985), while others who retained an interest came to believe that liquidity preference was an irrelevant diversion once an elastic money supply was not ruled out by assumption as Keynes did (Kaldor, 1981; 1982; Dow and Dow, 1989; Lavoie, 1992, ch. 4).[12] Those who tried to retain a role for liquidity preference (Kregel, 1988; Wray, 1990), tended to shift its emphasis away from monetary circulation on to its impact on the structure of asset prices (Wells, 1983; Kregel, 1984–85; Mott, 1985–86), reviving a line of thought that went back to Townshend (1937) and Boulding (1944).[13]

As the 'two-price' view was thus lost sight of, Minsky (1975) had to re-emphasize that Keynes was essentially about 'an investment theory of fluctuations in real demand and a financial theory of fluctuations in real investment' (p. 57). In re-emphasizing the essential feature of the 'two-price' view, he remarked that changing views about the future influence the present through their impact on the current asset prices, which in turn determine the profitability of producing investment goods with a given cost structure in the present period. Any decision to acquire real capital assets, as he was keen to emphasize, is inherently a speculative one as it bequeaths the firm a certain liability structure that gives rise to cash flow obligations far into the future, while generating future earnings that are never certain. Yet, despite his emphasis on the speculative character of investment decisions, Minsky paid little attention to asset price speculation *per se*, ignoring asset price bubbles and their macroeconomic effects on monetary circulation. Perhaps this was

understandable. His views were formed during the era of financial regulation, when speculation 'could do no harm as bubbles on a steady stream of enterprise', unlike the present
era when Keynes's old warning that the situation 'is serious when enterprise becomes the
bubble on a whirlpool of speculation' rings true again.

Conclusion

This chapter has highlighted Keynes's early insights on asset price speculation and its link
to monetary circulation perhaps at the risk of downplaying the importance of the *GT*.
A part of Keynes's analysis in the *Treatise* which emphasized the importance of financial
conditions and asset prices in determining firms' investment decisions was later revived
by Minsky,[14] but another part about the way self-sustained biases in asset price expectations in financial markets exerted their influence over the business cycle was mainly forgotten. In his famous *Quarterly Journal of Economics* article, Keynes (1937a) talked about
how people tend to fall back on conventions in forming expectations about an uncertain
future in financial markets, and emphasized how valuations can change drastically and
violently because doubts of panic have a life of their own close to the surface. In the
Treatise, the changing size of the bear position was the very index of what was brewing
under the surface, of what he called the 'other view'. It provided a convenient setting for
analyzing the macroeconomic effects of asset prices the preponderance of market opinion
held to be misaligned in a way that became impossible to do in the *GT* for at least two
main reasons. First, the reformulation of liquidity preference as a theory of the interest
rate ruled out by assumption that changes in the 'bear' sentiment could have first and foremost *quantity* effects on the size of inactive money balances. Second, separating the determination of prices of assets from those of debts, Keynes defined his 'short period' in terms
of a given set of expectations with respect to firms' future earnings expectations. While
this had the advantage of highlighting the potential of economic policy – to the extent
interest rates could be controlled – in influencing asset prices, it at the same time made it
harder to conceptualize the macroeconomic effects of speculation and asset prices the
market opinion held to be misaligned. Finally, any hint of an interaction between liquidity preference and marginal efficiency of capital was further weakened as the focus of the
former has over time moved away from shifts in the function as a whole to variations in
the demand for liquidity when the said function remained unchanged. Then, as the
interest elasticity of the transaction demand (Tobin, 1956; 1958; Baumol, 1952) soon took
center stage, whatever link that still existed between liquidity preference in the *GT* and the
'state of bearishness' argument of the *Treatise* was completely lost. Asset price speculation no longer had any foothold in Keynesian macroeconomic theory. Thus, paradoxically, despite its strong emphasis on unpredictable shifts in market psychology, the *GT*
unleashed a process of intellectual evolution where at the end it became harder to say
anything determinate about the monetary effects of market speculation and asset price
misalignments.

Notes

1. In his haste to make the point that excess savings and increased hoarding were not one and the same,
    Keynes appears to have caused confusion by insisting that over-saving had no particular relation to
    increased inactive balances unless the banking sector chose to supply a higher amount of saving deposits,
    without however indicating that what he took as his *default* case was an endogenous fall in the supply of
    money. Technically, however, excess savings can be associated with neither a fall in the money supply nor

increased net hoarding in a given period if 'non-GDP' transactions increase inordinately relative to those on the currently produced output, but this cannot be generally the case.

2. Ironically, the 'efficient market hypothesis', which the detractors of Keynes were quick to embrace, also presupposes that the current asset prices are solely determined by their expected future prices independently of outside supply and demand.

3. As Cottrell (1994) remarks in his review of Littleboy (1990), Leijonhufvud (1968; 1981, ch. 7) has two very different interpretations of Keynes in his works, where one is a neo-Walrasian variation on Clower's notion of effective demand, and the other is a theory of intertemporal investment – saving disequilibrium caused by bear speculation. The discussion here refers solely to the latter interpretation. On Leijonhufvud's work, see also Cottrell and Lawlor (1991).

4. The more elaborate support for this position is based on 'the efficient market hypothesis', which has gained currency among economists after Samuelson's (1965) 'proof' that in a market that is *efficient* in appropriating all available information, stock prices should exhibit a random walk and Fama's (1965) demonstration that they almost actually do. But neither proposition is any longer considered valid in the contemporary finance literature. Empirically, it is shown that stock prices do not exhibit random walk, and theoretically it is shown that *unforeseeable* prices are neither necessary nor sufficient for *rationally* determined stock prices. See, among others, Lo and MacKinlay (1999), Bossaerts (2002) and Shleifer (2000).

5. See also Hicks (1946, pp. 205–6).

6. In the modern finance literature on asset price bubbles, the emphasis, until recently, was on rational traders' risk aversion, which was thought to prevent them from eliminating noise-driven price movements. However, the focus has been shifting to 'trend' speculation as the winning strategy for speculators, a fact well known to market participants all along (Soros, 1987; Temin and Voth, 2004).

7. I owe this point to a suggestion by Amit Bhaduri.

8. In an interesting finding, Cutler et al. (1991) report positive autocorrelation at high frequencies and negative serial correlation at longer time horizons exceeding 14 months for a broad class of financial assets, including stocks, bonds and foreign exchange from around the world.

9. In chapter 22 of the *GT*, the liquidity preference schedule shifts up only after the marginal efficiency of capital collapses, setting off a downturn. In Keynes (1937a), there is more a sense of an ongoing interaction between the two schedules when he writes, 'When a pessimistic view taken about future yields, that is no reason why there should be a diminished propensity to hoard. Indeed, the conditions which aggravate the one factor tend, as a rule, to aggravate the other. For the same circumstances which lead to pessimistic views about future yields are apt to increase the propensity to hoard' (*CW*, XIV, p. 118).

10. 'Whilst liquidity-preference due to the speculative-motive corresponds to what in my *Treatise on Money* I called "the state of bearishness", it is by no means the same thing. For "bearishness" is there defined as the functional relationship, not between the rate of interest (or price of debts) and the quantity of money, but between the price of assets and debts, taken together, and the quantity of money. This treatment, however, involved a confusion between results due to a change in the rate of interest and those due to a change in the schedule of the marginal efficiency of capital, which I hope I have here avoided' (Keynes, 1936, pp. 173–4).

11. In my view, Leijonhufvud (1968; 1981) erroneously reads this aspect of the argument in the *GT* into the *Treatise*.

12. Kaldor (1982, p. 26) was to retort, 'liquidity preference turns out to have been a bit of a red herring'.

13. For more recent attempts at reconciling liquidity preference with endogenous money, see also Dow and Chick (2002) and Brown (2003–4).

14. Though, oddly enough, Minsky never mentions the *Treatise* as the source of his 'two-price' theory in any of his writings that I am aware of. However, this connection is emphasized in Kregel (1992), referred to above.

References

Asimakopulos, A. (1983). 'Kalecki and Keynes on finance, investment and savings', *Cambridge Journal of Economics*, **7**, 221–33.

Baumol, W.J. (1952). 'The transaction demand for cash: an inventory-theoretic approach', *Quarterly Journal of Economics*, **7**, 545–56.

Black, F. (1986). 'Noise', *Journal of Finance*, **41**, 529–43.

Bossaerts, P. (2002). *The Paradox of Asset Pricing*, Princeton, NJ: Princeton University Press.

Boulding, K. (1944). 'A liquidity preference theory of market prices', *Economica*, **11**, 55–63.

Brown, C. (2003–4). 'Toward a reconcilement of endogenous money and liquidity preference', *Journal of Post Keynesian Economics*, **26**, 325–39.

Chick, V. (1997). 'The multiplier and finance', in G.C. Harcourt and P.A. Riach (eds), *A 'Second Edition' of The General Theory*, Vol. 1, London: Routledge.

Chick, V. (1983). *Macroeconomics After Keynes*, Cambridge, MA: The MIT Press.

Cottrell, A. (1994). 'Reconciling Leijonhufvud and the Post Keynesians', *Research in the History of Economic Thought and Methodology'*, **12**, 223–32.

Cottrell, A. and M.S. Lawlor (1991). '"Natural rate" mutations: Keynes, Leijonhufvud and the Wicksell connection', *History of Political Economy*, **23**(4), 625–43.

Cutler, D., J. Porteba and L. Summers (1991). 'Speculative dynamics', *Review of Economic Studies*, **58**(3), 529–46.

Davidson, P. (1978). *Money and the Real World*, London: Macmillan.

De Long, J.B., A. Schleifer, L. Summers and R. Waldmann (1990a). 'Noise trader risk in financial markets', *Journal of Political Economy*, **98**(4), 703–38.

Dow, S. and V. Chick (2002). 'Monetary policy with endogenous money and liquidity preference: a nondualistic treatment', *Journal of Post Keynesian Economics*, **24**, 587–607.

Dow, A. and S. Dow (1989). 'Endogenous money creation and idle balances', in J. Pheby (ed.), *New Directions in Post-Keynesian Economics*, Aldershot, UK and Brookfield, US: Edward Elgar, pp. 147–64.

Ellis, H. (1934). *German Monetary Theory, 1905–33*, Cambridge, MA: Harvard University Press.

Fama, E. (1965). 'The behavior of stock market prices', *Journal of Business*, **38**, 34–105.

Friedman, M. (1953). 'The case for flexible exchange rates', *Essays in Positive Economics*, Chicago, IL: Chicago University Press.

Hicks, J.R. (1937). 'Mr. Keynes and the "classics": a suggested interpretation', *Econometrica*, **5**, 147–59.

Hicks, J.R. (1946). *Value and Capital: An Inquiry into Some Fundamental Principles of Economic Theory*, 2nd edn, Oxford: Oxford University Press.

Hirota, S. and S. Sunder (2003). 'Price bubbles sans dividend anchors: evidence from laboratory stock markets', Working Paper. Posted at: http://www.som.yale.edu/faculty/Sunder/research.html

Kaldor, N. (1982). *The Scourge of Monetarism*, Oxford: Oxford University Press.

Kaldor, N. (1981). *Origins of the New Monetarism*, Cardiff: University College Cardiff Press.

Kaldor, N. (1939). 'Speculation and economic stability', *The Review of Economic Studies*, **7**, October, 1–27.

Keynes, J.M. (1964) [1936]. *The General Theory of Employment, Interest, and Money*, New York: Harcourt Brace Jovanovich.

Keynes, J.M. (1973) [1923]. *A Tract on Monetary Reform*, in D.E. Moggridge (ed.), *Collected Writings of J.M. Keynes (CW)*, Vol. IV, London: Macmillan for The Royal Economic Society.

Keynes, J.M. (1973) [1930]. *A Treatise on Money*, Vol. I, in D.E. Moggridge (ed.), *Collected Writings of J.M. Keynes (CW)*, Vol. V, London: Macmillan for The Royal Economic Society.

Keynes, J.M (1973). *Collected Works of J.M. Keynes*, Vols XIII, XIV and XXIX, edited by D.E. Moggridge, London: Macmillan for The Royal Economic Society.

Keynes, J.M. (1938). 'Mr. Keynes on "Finance"', *Economic Journal*, **48**, 318–22.

Keynes, J.M. (1937a). 'General theory of employment', *Quarterly Journal of Economics*, **51**, 209–23.

Keynes, J.M. (1937b). 'Alternative theories of the rate of interest', *Economic Journal*, **47**, 241–52.

Keynes, J.M. (1937c). '"Ex-ante" theory of the rate of interest', *Economic Journal*, **48**, 663–9.

Kregel, J. (1992). 'Minsky's "two price" theory of financial instability and monetary policy: discounting versus open market intervention', in F. Steven and D.B. Papadimitriou (eds), *Financial Conditions and Macroeconomic Performance: Essays in honor of Hyman P. Minsky*, Armonk, NY and London: M.E. Sharpe, 85–103.

Kregel, J. (1984–85). 'Constraints on the expansion of output and employment: real or monetary?', *Journal of Post Keynesian Economics*, **7**, 139–52.

Kregel, J. (1985). 'Hamlet without the Prince: Cambridge macroeconomics without money', *American Economic Review*, Papers and Proceedings, **75**, 133–9.

Kregel, J. (1988). 'The multiplier and liquidity preference: two sides of the theory of effective demand', in A. Barrere (ed.), *The Foundations of Keynesian Analysis*, New York: St Martin Press.

Lavoie, M. (1992). *Foundations of Post-Keynesian Economic Analysis*, Aldershot, UK and Brookfield, US: Edward Elgar.

Leijonhufvud, A. (1981). 'The Wicksell connection', ch. 8 in *Information and Coordination*, New York: Oxford University Press.

Leijonhufvud, A. (1968). *Keynesian Economics and the Economics of Keynes*, New York: Oxford University Press.

Littleboy, B. (1990). *On Interpreting Keynes: A Study in Reconciliation*, London and New York: Routledge.

Lo, A.W. and A.C. MacKinlay (1999). *A Non-Random Walk Down Wall Street*, Princeton, NJ: Princeton University Press.

Minsky, H. (1975). *John Maynard Keynes*, New York: Columbia University Press.

Mott, T. (1985–86). 'Towards a post-Keynesian formulation of liquidity preference', *Journal of Post Keynesian Economics*, **8**, 222–32.

Robertson, D.H. (1931). 'Mr. Keynes' theory of money', *Economic Journal*, **41**, September, 395–411.

Samuelson, P. (1965). 'Proof that properly anticipated prices fluctuate randomly', *Industrial Management Review*, Spring, **6**, 41–9.

Shleifer, A. (2000). *Inefficient Markets. An Introduction to Behavioral Finance*, Oxford: Oxford University Press.
Shleifer, A. and L.H. Summers (1990). 'Noise trader approach to finance', *Journal of Economic Perspectives*, **4**(2), 19–33.
Shleifer, A. and R. Vishny (1997). 'The limits of arbitrage', *Journal of Finance*, **52**(1), 35–55.
Soros, G. (1987). *The Alchemy of Finance: Reading the Mind of the Market*, New York: Simon & Schuster.
Temin, P. and H. Voth (2004). 'Riding the South Sea Bubble', CEPR Discussion Paper 4221.
Tobin, J. (1956). 'The interest-elasticity of the demand for cash', *Review of Economics and Statistics*, **38**, 241–7.
Tobin, J. (1958). 'Liquidity preference as behavior toward risk', *Review of Economic Studies*, **67**, 65–86.
Townshend, H. (1937). 'Liquidity premium and the theory of value', *Economic Journal*, **47**, 157–69.
Wells, P. (1983). 'A Post Keynesian view of liquidity preference and the demand for money', *Journal of Post Keynesian Economics*, **5**, 523–36.
Wicksell, K. (1906). *Lectures on Political Economy*, Vol. 2, New York: A.M. Kelley.
Wray, L.R. (1990). *Money and Credit in Capitalist Economies: The Endogenous Money Approach*, Aldershot, UK and Brookfield, US: Edward Elgar.
Zeeman, E.C. (1974). 'On the unstable behaviour of stock exchanges', *Journal of Mathematical Economics*, **1**, 39–49.

28 Money and inflation
Matías Vernengo

John Maynard Keynes once said that according to Lenin there is no surer way of overturning a society than to degrade its currency. Inflationary processes, it is clear, can be very disruptive in the short run, even if they do not cause revolutions. But they also have long-lasting effects. Fernand Braudel believed that price revolutions represented the strongest secular pattern in modern history. In fact, over the past eight centuries, the world economy has experienced four major price revolutions whose inflationary forces ultimately transformed economic and social structures. These four price revolutions took place approximately in the late-medieval period, from 1180 to 1350, after the age of great discoveries in the sixteenth century, from 1470 to 1650, during the Industrial Revolution era, from 1730 to 1815, and during the twentieth century, from the 1890s to the 1980s (Hackett Fischer, 1996).

Not only inflationary processes come in long waves of steady and low inflation, but also every so often bouts of high inflation and hyperinflation occur. In other words, there are several types of inflationary processes. However, high inflation and hyperinflation are relatively rare events associated with severe crises, wars and situations when the state apparatus collapses.

Two analytical distinctions are useful to understand different explanations of inflationary processes of all types. First, and more importantly, theories can be seen as cost-push or demand-pull theories of inflation. The former theories emphasize the role of wage and input increases, that is, supply forces, in generating inflation, while the latter imply that scarcity and demand forces are the main causes of inflation. Second, the distinction between exogenous and endogenous money supply is important for a proper taxonomy of inflation theories (see the chapters on endogenous money in this volume). This second analytical cut results from the fact that there is a clear empirical connection between inflation and monetary stock measures.

This chapter will deal with the various explanations for inflation and the relation between inflation and money, and a tentative taxonomy is presented at the end.[1] The rest of the chapter is divided into four sections. The following section deals with the historical record, both related to long-term trends (i.e. price revolutions) and the short-lived (from a *longue durée* perspective) but devastating hyperinflations. The two following sections discuss the major theoretical explanations of inflationary phenomena using the two analytical distinctions explained above. Finally we pull the results together for an evaluation of the dominant view on money and inflation and the main counter points from a heterodox perspective.

Inflationary processes in historical perspective

Price revolutions are often neglected by economists, but have been central for economic historians. The conventional wisdom among economists is that monetarist views are the dominant interpretation of those long-term processes. This is particularly the case with the sixteenth-century price revolution, which is the one associated with the first clear expositions of the quantity theory of money (Arestis and Howells, 2001–2). But, in general, historians stress the real causes of inflation based on neo-Malthusian models that emphasize demographical forces, in which money is endogenous.

Price revolutions begin in periods of prosperity, and end in periods of crises. The classic demographic or real model, essentially based on a Malthusian insight, was developed by Postan (1973) and used to explain the behavior of the later-medieval western European economy, and in particular the behavior of price movements. Postan argued that population growth and a relatively static agrarian technology led unavoidably to diminishing returns. Diminishing returns, in turn, drove grain prices up during the long thirteenth century (1180–1350), at a rate estimated by Postan to be around 0.5 percent per year. Symmetrically, population decline during the fourteenth and fifteenth centuries, caused by terrible famines, epidemics and wars, led to a fall in grain prices. In Postan's framework monetary changes played no role in late-medieval price movements or in any of the changes that the economy underwent during the late Middle Ages, for that matter.

Hackett Fisher (1996, p. 72) argues that the prime mover in the following price revolution was the 'revival of population growth, which placed heavy pressure on material resources'. Monetarist-inclined authors emphasize the silver and copper mining boom in Central Europe in the 1460s – before the discovery and inflow of American bullion – as a major factor ending the European bullion famine (e.g. Munro, 2003). Hence monetary factors would be central in explaining the sixteenth-century inflation. The price revolution of the sixteenth century is well known among economists, and Earl Hamilton's (1934) is the classic interpretation, putting emphasis on the effects on prices of American gold and silver inflows. When the price revolution became evident, several explanations were developed. Jean Bodin and the authors of the Salamanca School – Martin de Azpilcueta and Tomás de Mercado more prominently – are usually credited with formulating the first clear version of the quantity theory of money (QTM).[2]

Hackett Fisher (1996, p. 84) suggests that the great inflation created such demand for monetary medium that even 'old mines were reopened at heavy expense'. Arestis and Howells (2001–2) emphasize the role of endogenous money in the realist neo-Malthusian tradition. In the neo-Malthusian view, bad harvests, famine, disease and war – in particular the Thirty Years War (1618–48) – led to a reversion of demographical trends and to the end of the second price revolution.

The price revolution of the eighteenth century started in the 1730s. The flow of the recently discovered Brazilian gold in Minas Gerais to London via Lisbon is seen by bullionists as the initial cause of rising price trends (Vilar, 1960). It is in this period that David Hume (1752) produces his famous defense of the quantity theory of money, and the specie flow mechanism, according to which inflation resulted from increases in gold inflows related to trade surpluses. On the other hand, population trends – a decline in age at marriage and a subsequent increase in the fertility ratios – suggests that demographical forces were also at play. However, the eighteenth-century price revolution is ultimately famous for the debates that it provoked in England in the late eighteenth century and early nineteenth century, known as the bullionist debates.

David Ricardo is usually described as the main bullionist (defenders of the 1810 Bullion report) author and a champion of the view that inflation was caused by the overissue of bank notes by the Bank of England during the suspension period (1797–1821), in which bank notes were not convertible to gold. Green (1992) notes that the classical authors believed in some variation of the labor theory of value and, hence, concluded that the price of commodities depended on technical conditions of production (labor embodied or commanded) for a given wage level (subsistence). Hence the price of gold – the numeraire – would also be determined by the technical conditions of production in that sector.

However, if the relative price of gold is determined in that way, the prices of all other commodities in terms of gold cannot be determined by the quantity of gold. Prices in terms of the standard (gold) must be determined by the costs of production of gold, so that causality is reversed and the quantity of money is endogenously determined. Green (1992, p. 56) refers to this classical view of endogenous money as the Law of Monetary Circulation. According to this Law, even though in the long run money supply is endogenously determined, in the short run – when market prices deviate from normal prices – exogenous changes in the money supply may affect prices. The main opponent of the bullionist view of the eighteenth century inflation was the economist and price historian Thomas Tooke – the leader of the Banking School. According to Tooke (1844, p. 123) 'the prices of commodities do not depend upon the quantity of money indicated by the amount of bank notes, nor upon the amount of the whole of the circulating medium; but . . . on the contrary, the amount of the circulating medium is the consequence of prices'. Prices increased, still according to Tooke, as a result of bad harvests, the depreciation of the external value of the currency that increased the price of imported goods, and higher interest rates, which led to higher financial costs. Reversal of these trends in the post-Napoleonic War period thus explains the deflationary forces in action, and the end of the price revolution.

The last price revolution starts with the end of the Great Depression of 1873–96, the year of William Jennings Bryan's populist bid for the presidency in the USA, based on his attack on the gold standard, and his defense of a bimetallic monetary system. While conventional views would emphasize the role of the discovery of new sources of bullion in South Africa, alternative views would emphasize the importance of distributive conflicts in the inflationary process. Adherence to the gold standard, and the demonetization of silver, meant that money was scarce, and led to deflationary forces, which in turn hurt debtors (mid-western and southern farmers) and benefited eastern industrialists and bankers (the Robber Barons). The agrarian revolt and the rise of populist and progressive movements – which led to the regulation of monopolies, the passing of an income tax, the creation of a central bank and a series of other reforms – turned the tide and generated inflationary pressures. The importance of these events is that for the first occasion in modern times it became clear that inflation could result from disputes over the proverbial pie. Distributive conflict would become central for several explanations of inflation in the twentieth century.

Distributive conflict may very well have had a role in the inflationary surge in the USA, but it was ultimately an American phenomena. Hackett Fisher (1996, p. 186) argues that the twentieth-century price revolution has structural causes related to rising living standards, a public health revolution that led to rising population, and institutional changes that led to what Heilbronner referred to as 'floors without ceilings'. The rise of corporations, and the development of a more regulated economy, with increasing participation of governments, led to an upward bias in prices. Thus Robinson (1971) famously argued that 'the general price level has become a political problem'.

Distributive conflict and political disruption were particularly important in the discussion of inflation in the 1960s. Conventional wisdom presumes that the inflationary pressures were brought about by the expansionary fiscal policies in the USA, and the propagation of these inflationary pressures through the international system (Laidler and Parkin, 1975). The increasingly expansionary fiscal policies of the 1960s – resulting both from the Vietnam War and the Great Society experiment of the Kennedy–Johnson administrations – led to growing balance of payments deficits. The US deficits were initially considered instrumental for the working of the international monetary system that was desperately in need of dollars to obtain the essential imports of capital goods needed for reconstruction. However, by the late 1960s the accumulation of idle dollar balances started to put pressure on the money supply of the rest of world, leading to inflation. That is, according to the monetarist logic, inflation was caused by the US fiscal and monetary policies, and transmitted to the world as a result of the system of fixed parities.

An alternative explanation for the inflationary pressures of the 1960s is possible, though. The Golden Age accumulation regime implied a commitment to full employment and the creation of a safety net for unemployed workers. Additionally, the imposition of capital controls and the cheap money policies – which led to low real rates of interest – implied a favorable environment for workers. Parties with strong ties to the labor movement were in power in several western countries, and this was tolerated, to a great extent, since it was considered a form of reducing the dangers of the Soviet menace. Further, full employment tended to increase the bargaining power of the working class.

In this environment, workers' pressures for higher nominal wages were usually accommodated. For a given real rate of interest, and a fixed nominal exchange rate, the only effect of rising wages would be higher prices. In sum, inflation was the result of wage pressures – cost-push – rather than the expansionary fiscal and monetary policies – demand-pull (Coutts et al., 1976). Note, however, that for a good part of the Golden Age, wages increased at the same pace as productivity, and hence had a negligible inflationary impact. Thus the inflationary process of the 1960s and 1970s seems to be related to the increases in taxes (passed to prices), competitive depreciations (more prominently after 1973), and supply-side shocks, notably the two oil shocks of the 1970s. Stabilization and the end of this last price revolution would not be related then to fiscal consolidation, but to the fall in the prices of commodities, and the weakening of the labor movement (Kaldor, 1976; Eisner, 1989).

It is worth noting that the quantity theory tradition faces an important conundrum. If exogenous increases in money supply are the ultimate cause of inflation, then a *diabolus ex machina* is the culprit for increasing the money supply (Hackett Fisher, 1996, p. 83). Corrupt and incompetent politicians are the main suspects. This explanation of the ulterior causes of inflation is one that emphasizes the role of individuals at the expense of the structural constraints faced by them. Alternative theories are less dependent on methodological individualist premises, and on the moral and intellectual qualities of politicians to explain inflationary processes.

Our brief description of the historical record of money and inflation cannot leave out hyperinflationary processes. The most famous episode of hyperinflation is the post-World War I German case. Historians, says Ferguson (1995, p. 19), have essentially followed two interpretations of the German hyperinflation. The first was offered in the 1930s by the Italian economist Bresciani-Turroni (1931), who blamed poor monetary and fiscal policy and argued that the inflation had predominantly negative consequences (Câmara Neto and Vernengo, 2004). However, recent scholarship among historians, Ferguson admits, has emphasized alternative views of inflation (e.g. Kindleberger, 1984; Holtfrereich, 1986; Burdekin and Burkett, 1996).

The view according to which deficit spending was the main cause of German inflation was named the English or allied view by Bresciani-Turroni (1931, p. 46). The allied view corresponds to what today would be called monetarist, and was later formalized by Cagan (1956). In this view, the burden imposed by the internal war debt, the payment of pensions to war veterans, widows and orphans, the reconstruction of the few devastated regions, and the process of war demobilization was too heavy for the young Weimar Republic and the leftist Social Democrat government to carry. In addition, the incapacity to raise fiscal revenues implied that the increasing fiscal spending had to be financed by the Reichsbank.

One of the crucial characteristics of the monetarist interpretation of inflation is that the rise in money supply precedes the rise in the price level. Also, given the dominance of purchasing power parity as the explanation of exchange rate determination in that period, the rise in the domestic price level precedes and causes the depreciation of the Deutschmark. There is a chain of causality that runs from the exogenous money supply to the price level and then to the exchange rate.

For Bresciani-Turroni, the solution to the inflationary problem was simply to cut the fiscal deficit. Once the principles of sound finance were re-established, the price level would be stabilized. The German government was then to blame. Still, as noted by Merkin (1982, p. 25), among the defenders of the quantity theory of money there was a certain degree of acceptance that in reality the rise in the price level preceded the increase in the quantity of money, and, hence, expectations of future money supply increases played a role.

The German officials who had to deal with the day-to-day problems of running an economy under hyperinflationary conditions saw the problem, not surprisingly, from a different perspective. The most notorious defender of the so-called balance of payments theory was Helfferich (1927). This view was named the German view by Bresciani-Turroni (1931, p. 47).

The disruption of the war led the German government to regulate the foreign exchange 'by way of a direct control of all foreign payments and credits' (Helfferich, 1927, p. 259). However, 'as the collapse of the German nation shows, the force of circumstances proved more powerful than any policy of exchange control' (ibid., p. 262). That is, trade deficits led to depreciation despite the control of the German authorities. As correctly noted by Ellis (1934, p. 224), 'the balance theory takes as its point of departure the decline of German exports'. Helfferich argued that the permanent unfavorable trade balance, caused by the war and the impositions of Versailles, led to depreciation. This was the root of German problems. For him, contrary to the widely held conception, not inflation but the depreciation of the mark was the beginning of this chain of cause and effect. Inflation is not the cause of the increase of prices and of the depreciation of the mark, but the depreciation of the mark is the cause of the increase of prices and of the paper mark issues (Bresciani-Turroni, 1931, p. 45).

In other words, causality runs from the exchange rate to the price level. This means that the rise in the price level cannot be related to the increase in the money supply. Graham (1930) defended Helfferich's position in what was to become, up to the publication of Bresciani's book in English, the most influential view of the German hyperinflation.

Graham (1930, p. 172) argues that 'the proximate . . . chain of causation, up to August 1920 at least, and perhaps at other times, ran from exchange rates to prices to volume of circulating medium rather than in the reverse direction'. According to the balance of payments view it is not possible to stabilize the economy without stabilizing the exchange rate. This was only possible if foreign reserves were available. The renegotiation of reparations in 1922 and the loans obtained through the Dawes Plan in 1924 allowed the stable foreign value of the rentemark to be maintained.

It is clear that some notion of passive or endogenous money is present in the work of the defenders of the balance of payments theory. Yet, as Robinson (1938, p. 74) noted, there was no explanation of the role of wages in the inflationary process. In her words, 'neither exchange depreciation nor a budget deficit can account for inflation by itself. But if the rise in money wages is brought into the story, the part which each plays can be clearly seen'. As correctly pointed out by Robinson, there is an inverse relation between the real wage and the exchange rate, so that depreciation leads to a decline in the real wage. If workers resist the fall in the real wage, because tradables are an important component of the wage basket, for example, then domestic costs will increase, and so will prices. That is, distributive conflict is an essential part of the hyperinflation story. Robinson's reformulation of the German view provided a sound basis for alternative explanations of hyperinflation.

Quantity theorists and the balance of payments school are the two main groups with opposing views on the German hyperinflation. Cagan (1956) developed the typical monetarist view on the basis of the quantitativist or monetarist analysis. On the other hand, the balance of payments school argues that reparations and depreciation are the cause of hyperinflation. Robinson introduces the notion of wage/foreign exchange spirals and distributive conflict. Variations of these two views remain the canonical interpretation of hyperinflationary processes.

The quantity theory and all that
In the old quantity theory tradition (e.g. Friedman, 1956) inflation results from a simple exogenous increase in money supply – in which the money was thrown from an *ad hoc* but memorable helicopter. In modern versions (e.g. Friedman, 1968) an output–inflation tradeoff and the policymakers' intention to maintain full employment are the essential force behind inflation. The older version proclaims that inflation is always a monetary phenomenon, while the modern version affirms that monetary policy determines inflation in the long run, but in the short run it has effects on the level of unemployment. The existence of a tradeoff between inflation and unemployment, and the willingness of governments to exploit it, are seen as the main explanations for the existence of persistent inflation in developed countries.

Wicksell's classic *Interest and Prices* (1898) still provides the best starting point for the understanding of conventional wisdom on inflation.[3] Wicksell distinguished between the natural rate of interest ($R*$) and the monetary or bank rate of interest (R). The former was determined by the marginal productivity of capital (I) and the intertemporal decisions of consumption (leading to savings S), along the lines of what became known as the loanable funds theory. The monetary rate was determined by bank decisions. That is, banks supplied credit (M) at the chosen rate of interest (R), according to money demand (L). Monetary equilibrium occurred when the two rates coincided (see Figure 28.1).

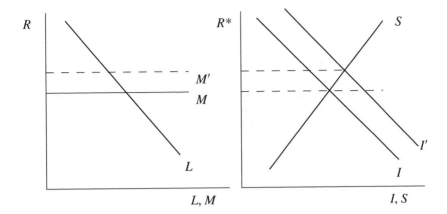

Figure 28.1   Monetary equilibrium

The natural rate is the gravitational center around which the bank rate fluctuates. Real and monetary shocks could cause deviations of the bank rate from equilibrium.

In a pure credit economy, in which all payments are made through bookkeeping entries as in the gyro system, there is no money in circulation. Wicksell presumes that in such a system the banking sector will provide credit on demand. Hence, money is endogenous. Following Wicksell, one can assume that a positive productivity shock raises the natural rate of interest (see Figure 28.1), and that banks maintain the initial monetary rate. Thus, with a low bank rate, investment exceeds savings and once the system reaches full employment prices will go up. In a gyro system the process can go on forever, and the resulting process is termed the cumulative process of inflation. In a normal economy, however, continuous lending will reduce bank reserves, and as a result banks will be forced to increase the monetary bank until a new equilibrium is reached. Inflation results from a bank rate that is too low, as much as deflation (and temporary unemployment) from a bank rate that is too high.[4]

The low bank rate implies overinvestment, and the need for additional savings. The inflationary process, by reducing the ability of consumers to spend, provides the additional forced savings. In this view, then, inflation acts as a tax that provides the additional resources needed to finance investment. Keynes (1923) provided an inflation-tax model of inflation. His long struggle to escape from the quantity theory tradition did not lead to an abandonment of either the notion of demand-pull inflation or exogenous money supply. Keynes (1940) turned once again to discuss inflation. At full employment output, if aggregate demand rises, output cannot follow because of supply constraints. Note that excess demand would mean that the level of output that would be determined by the multiplier process would be higher than the full employment level, and, thus, the market-clearing level of output is not achievable. The difference between the market-clearing and full employment output is the inflationary gap. As nominal wages lag behind good prices in adjustment, the rise in prices will therefore lead to a reduction in the real wage and a redistribution of income away from wage-earners. Further, as workers have greater propensities to consume than capitalists, the redistribution of income induced by the inflationary gap would lead to lower aggregate demand and close the gap. The process is similar to the Wicksellian forced savings effect, emphasizing the role of income distribution instead.

The predominance of the full employment objective as the main target of macroeconomic policy and the widespread use of Keynesian policies in the post-World War II period implied that eventual tradeoffs between full employment and inflation became more visible. The Phillips curve implies that there is an empirical relationship between inflation and the level of unemployment, and that there is a level of unemployment at which prices are stable. Friedman (1968, p. 7) named that rate of unemployment the natural rate, as an explicit analogy with the Wicksellian natural rate of interest, since both imply that whenever the interest rate or the unemployment rate are at their natural level, prices will be stable.

The Keynesian rationalization for the Phillips curve suggests that the rate of change in money wages is a function of excess demand in the labor market. Further, the unemployment rate has a negative correlation with the rate of change in money wages since the latter represents excess supply in the labor market. Also, the rate of change in prices is given by the difference in the rate of change in money wages minus the rate of change of productivity. Formally

$$\frac{\dot{w}}{w} = f\frac{(N_d - N_s)}{N_s} \tag{28.1}$$

$$\frac{\dot{p}}{p} = \frac{\dot{w}}{w} - \frac{\dot{\lambda}}{\lambda} \tag{28.2}$$

where dots on top represent changes in levels, w is the money wage, N_d and N_s are labor demand and supply respectively, p is the price level, and λ is labor productivity.

Yet the experience of the 1960s, in which macroeconomic policies were used to stabilize the business cycle, brought serious doubts about the stability of the Phillips relation. Friedman (1968) and Phelps (1967) anticipated the breakdown of the Phillips curve, suggesting that the relation had only short-term validity, and that in the long run there is no tradeoff between inflation and unemployment. Friedman argued that inflationary expectations were relevant for wage bargaining. Hence the original Phillips equation had to be augmented to incorporate expectations. The monetarist version of the expectations-augmented Phillips curve can be written as

$$\pi = \pi_{-1} - \beta(u - u_n) \tag{28.3}$$

where π is inflation, π_{-1} is the previous period inflation, u is the rate of unemployment and u_n is the natural rate, also know as the non-accelerating inflation rate of unemployment (NAIRU). Equation (28.3) assumes that economic agents are backward looking and that they form expectations about the future using information about the past.

A positive monetary shock has short-term effects on the level of activity because of backward-looking expectations formation. In Figure 28.2 that situation is represented by a movement from point 1 to 2 along the original Phillips curve. In Friedman's story money illusion would lead to an increase of labor supply, and higher output, but as information disseminates, the economy returns to the natural rate, shifting the Phillips curve up, and

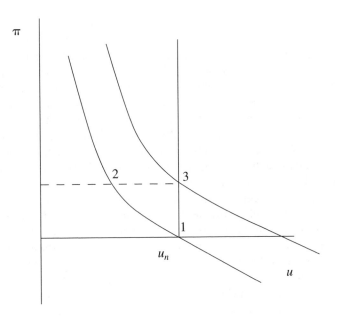

Figure 28.2   The Phillips curve

returning to equilibrium at point 3. The only way government can maintain a level of unemployment below its natural level is by accelerating inflation.

The rational expectations revolution of the 1970s took some of Friedman's conclusions to the extreme. Lucas (1972), using the view that information is costly, argued that producers faced with a monetary shock would have a signal extraction problem, and would not adjust prices fully. Hence, lack of information or other source of price rigidities would allow the existence of a short-run tradeoff and the possibility that governments could exploit, for political gain, the advantages of lower levels of unemployment. One must note that in Lucas's model agents form expectations rationally and the Phillips curve is rewritten as

$$\pi = E\pi_{t+1} - \beta(u - u_n) \qquad (28.4)$$

where backward-looking inflation is replaced by forward-looking expectations, i.e. the expectations of inflation in the next period. In the absence of imperfect information, and when the economy is at the natural level, inflation is a random walk. This proposition generated important results, within the mainstream, related to the effects of expectations on inflation and stabilization processes, in particular the question of dynamic inconsistency (see Chapter 14 on monetary policy in this volume).

Dynamic inconsistency implies severe difficulties in bringing down inflation. The public knows that the government has an incentive to renege on its promises after the public sets its expectations, and therefore does not believe in the disinflation announcement. Hence a strong and credible commitment to low inflation is seen as a precondition of avoiding long and deep recessions during stabilization. Goodfriend and King (2004) suggest that the Volcker disinflation was costly in terms of output because it was highly incredible.

A simple solution to which many countries have resorted to solve the dynamic incon-sistency problem is to peg their currencies to that of a low-inflation-level country. By pegging the exchange rate, the government intends to reduce inflation by importing credi-bility from abroad (Giavazzi and Pagano, 1988). This has been behind the process of dol-larization or fixed exchange rate stabilization programs in several developing countries (Vernengo, 2006). Once again, given that the government has an incentive to break its promises and devalue the currency to stimulate exports and the domestic output, it follows that stabilization will only succeed if it is credible. Price stability requires that central banks build a reputation as stalwart defenders of low inflation (Ball, 1994).

Further, a fully credible disinflation, according to Ball (1994), may very well lead to an economic boom. The cause of the boom is related to the forward-looking behavior of firms. If firms believe in the central bank's announcement of a stabilization program, then they should reduce prices well before the actual money supply is reduced. The consequent increase in real balance would have positive wealth effects leading to increased consump-tion, higher output and lower unemployment. As noted by Mankiw (2000, p. 14), the main problem is that 'credible disinflations cause booms . . . but actual disinflations cause recessions'. The main response to this problem has been to admit that there are no per-fectly credible stabilizations. Another solution is to assume that economic agents are more myopic than has been presumed since the rational expectations revolution. Roberts (1997) questions the rational expectations model and uses backward-looking adaptive expect-ations instead. Finally, and more interestingly, Gordon (1996) and Staiger et al. (1997) argue for hysteresis and the notion that the natural rate moves sluggishly towards the actual unemployment rate. In this case, if contractionary monetary policy leads to a short-run reduction of unemployment below its natural level, the natural level will per-manently increase. A variable natural rate also implies that governments have real incen-tives to maintain the economy close to full employment, even at the expense of a bit of inflation.

It is usually assumed that in developed countries the incentives associated with the maintenance of full employment, and the existence of an inflation–unemployment tradeoff, should be seen as the main causes of inflation. However, in developing countries the lack of organized fiscal institutions and the need to collect inflationary tax through the power of seigniorage are seen as the main cause of inflation within the mainstream of the profession. The canonical model is based on Cagan's explanation of the German hyper-inflation. The model assumes that the government borrows from the central bank, which monetizes government debt. Causality runs from fiscal deficits to money emissions.

Seigniorage is defined as the real value of the increase in the money base, and in steady state is assumed to be equal to the government deficit. We have

$$S = \frac{D}{p} = \frac{\dot{M}}{p} \tag{28.5}$$

where S is seigniorage, D is the public sector's nominal deficit, p the price level and M is money supply. Hence, seigniorage is equal to the real deficit (d), which can be rewritten as

$$d = \frac{\dot{M}}{M}\frac{M}{p} = g_m \times m \tag{28.6}$$

where g_m is the rate of growth of money supply and m represents the real money balances. By definition the rate of growth of real money balances is given by the rate of change in nominal balances minus the rate of change in prices, i.e. inflation. Therefore we have

$$\frac{\dot{m}}{m} = g_m - \pi \qquad (28.7)$$

Substituting (28.6) into (28.7) we obtain the following:

$$d = g_m m = \dot{m} + m\pi \qquad (28.8)$$

that is, seigniorage is divided into two components: the variation of the real stock of money, and the loss of value of the current money stock resulting from inflation, also known as the inflation tax. Furthermore, in the case of a steady state, when $\dot{m}$ equals zero, seigniorage would be equivalent to the inflation tax.

At low levels of inflation, seigniorage and the inflation tax are low. Initially, as inflation goes up, the tax revenue also increases, because the increase in inflation acts as an increase of the marginal tax rate. However, as the rate of inflation increases, economic agents reduce their cash holdings, and the tax base is reduced. Eventually, at very high levels of inflation, an additional increase in inflation will lead to a reduction of inflation tax revenues. This is illustrated by the inverse-U-shaped inflation-tax Laffer curve in Figure 28.3.

If we abstract from the Olivera–Tanzi effect – according to which an increase in inflation leads to a reduction in tax revenues because of lags between the tax generating act and collection – the real deficit can be represented as a horizontal line (see Figure 28.3).[5] Equilibrium is given at the intercept of the real deficit and the inflation-tax Laffer curve.[6]

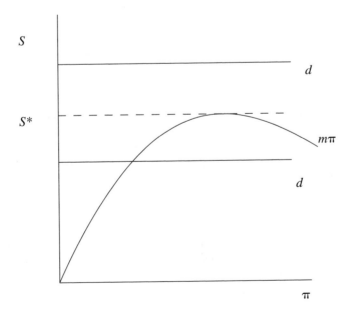

Figure 28.3   Inflation-tax Laffer curve

Hyperinflation occurs when the public sector's financial needs as represented by the real deficit exceed the maximum feasible amount of seigniorage S^*. In that case, $d > S^*$ and real money balances increase without limit.

A more complete model would allow for government debt, reducing the role of deficits in financing government spending. However, most models impose an upper limit on governments' abilities to borrow, in which case borrowing only delays the day of reckoning (Sargent and Wallace, 1981). Once it is noted that the government is overborrowing, the central bank will be forced to buy unwanted government bonds and deficits will become the norm again. Further, in this case borrowing will lead to increases in debt-servicing requirements, and inflation tax revenues will be needed to pay current expenses and the additional interest rate burden. Ultimately stabilization requires that governments reduce their need for inflation tax revenues. The task is easier when economic agents find the government's promise to reduce inflation tax credible (Sargent, 1982).

A structural view of inflation

This section describes briefly the main alternatives to the dominant monetarist theories of inflation, according to which inflation is always a monetary phenomenon. There are three main alternative schools of thought that provided relevant contributions to inflation theory, namely: the Marxists; the post-Keynesians; and the structuralists, who include a latter-day subdivision, usually referred to as inertialists or neo-structuralists.[7] According to all heterodox traditions inflation is essentially the result of a conflict over the distribution of income. Conflict over income shares arises in several social environments, between capital and labor, between landowners and peasants, between different groups of workers, between producers in different sectors or the economy, such as those that produce tradables and those that produce for the domestic market.

The Marxist model developed by Rowthorn (1977) assumes that conflict is a direct function of effective demand, which in turn depends on the exogenous money supply.[8] In this view inflation increases profits by reducing the real purchasing power of workers, since the latter are not able to protect themselves against it. The main difference between Rowthorn's model and the conventional monetarist story is that excess demand affects the balance of power between workers and capitalists, and only indirectly the price level. In the monetarist approach demand affects prices directly.[9]

Post-Keynesian authors have constructed conflict models of inflation in which excess demand is not a relevant component of the explanation. Further, in these models the money supply is endogenous. In other words, inflation reflects only the inconsistency of the desired mark-up of firms and the target real wage that workers consider fair. However, most post-Keynesian models have neglected open economy considerations. Open economy matters have been central to structuralists.

Latin American structuralists also emphasize the role of distributive conflict within a cost-push approach. But, given the recurring balance of payments problems of the region, structuralist authors have paid more attention to balance of payments constraints.[10] Noyola (1956) and Sunkel (1958) are generally regarded as the seminal contributions to the structuralist theory of inflation. According to the structuralist view, inflation has its origins in the supply side. In that sense, excess demand caused by fiscal deficits is irrelevant. In particular, the inelasticity of food supply that results from the concentrated structure of land ownership is seen as the major cause of inflation (Cardoso, 1981).[11]

Also, the structural dependency of capital imports, and the lack of foreign reserves, means that developing countries have recurrent balance of payments problems. Currency depreciation is endemic, with or without foreign exchange controls or other types of capital controls. Hence depreciation is also seen as an essential part of the inflationary problem.

In that sense, the structure of land ownership and the dependence on foreign exchange are seen as the central problems that spark social conflict, ultimately resolved by inflation. Shocks to the terms of trade provide the spark that ignites the inflationary process. Structuralists emphasize both the shocks that initiate inflation and the propagation mechanism that maintains it. It must be noted that some structuralists, in particular Noyola (1956) and Furtado (1959), argue that the propagation of inflation is the result of incompatible income claims. If after an inflationary shock a group is dissatisfied with its income share, it will try to pass its losses to another group. Further, for structuralists inflation is not a monetary phenomenon, and results from real disequilibria. Hence monetary policy is a passive element in the inflationary process. The notion that monetary policy is passive is close to the post-Keynesian view on the endogeneity of the money supply as developed by Kaldor (1982) and Moore (1988).

Finally, neo-structuralists also provided an alternative view to monetarism. In particular, the experience with wage indexation, and the failure of austerity measures to bring down inflation during the 1970s, led many authors to argue that inflation was mainly inertial.[12] The precursors of the idea of inertial inflation were Simonsen (1970) and Pazos (1972). Bresser Pereira and Nakano (1983), Arida and Lara-Resende (1985) and Lopes (1986) were the key contributions to the notion of inertial inflation. These authors called for a 'heterodox shock', by which they meant extreme price controls; that is, prices should be frozen completely to avoid inertia. Given their distrust in orthodox policies, the inertialist authors became known as neo-structuralists.

A simple model that catches some elements of all the above-mentioned contributions can be sketched out.[13] The Kaleckian notion of differential prices for agricultural and manufacturing goods is central to the model. Inflation is defined as the weighted average of inflation in both sectors.

$$\pi_t = \rho \pi_{At} + (1 - \rho) \pi_{Mt} \tag{28.9}$$

where π_{At} and π_{Mt} refer to agricultural and manufacturing inflation respectively. Further, it is assumed that firms form prices as a mark-up on variable costs in Kaleckian fashion, and as a result inflation in the manufacturing sector is a linear combination of changes in input prices such as wages, and the prices of imported inputs and the firm's degree of monopoly, reflected in its ability to increase the mark-up. This is represented as

$$\pi_{Mt} = \phi \omega_t + \sigma \varepsilon_t + \tau^* \tag{28.10}$$

where ω_t is wage inflation, ε_t is the exchange rate depreciation, and τ^* represents a change in the mark-up. Finally, wage indexation introduces an element of inertia in the system. Formally

$$\pi_t = \pi_{t-1} + \omega^* \tag{28.11}$$

where ω^* represents a wage push factor that reflects the workers' willingness to increase wages above past inflation. Solving for inflation, we obtain

$$\pi_t = (1 - \rho)\phi\, \pi_{t-1} + [\rho\, \pi_{At} + \sigma(1 - \rho)\, \varepsilon_t] + (1 - \rho)\phi(\omega^* + \tau^*/\phi) \qquad (28.12)$$

Inflation is the result of three factors: inertia, a series of changes in relative prices (agricultural goods, imported inputs), changes in wages above indexation, and changes in mark-ups in the fix-price sector that reflect distributive conflict.

The first term shows that inertia depends on the share of manufacturing goods in the consumption basket, and the share of wages in producing those goods. For simplicity it was assumed that wages were fully indexed to past inflation. Alternatively one could argue that inertia may result from staggered forward-looking wage contracts, or that indexation is less than perfect and wages recover only a share of past inflation. Inertia is essential in the explanation of persistently high inflation that never leads to full-fledged hyperinflation. This was typical of the Latin American experience. An important effect of indexation is that a shortening of the period of indexation leads to acceleration of inflation.

Although under certain circumstances inflation may very well be fundamentally inertial, it is clear that other forces are relevant. For structuralist authors inflation is an inevitable companion of the process of development. Industrialization implies profound changes in the structure of production, reducing the size of the agricultural sector, increasing the demand for imported intermediary and capital goods. The process of development, thus, increases the possible sources of supply-side constraints on the economy. The increase in manufacturing production may come at the expense of the agricultural sector's ability to produce foodstuffs for domestic consumption. In that case, the relative scarcity of agricultural goods would lead to higher prices. More importantly, by increasing the price of foodstuffs, industrialization may lead to a reduction of the real wage. Real wage resistance would then lead to wage–price spirals that propagate through the indexation mechanism. In sum, a supply-side shock generates a process of chronic inflation.

Structuralists and post-Keynesians see balance of payments constraints as the main limitation to growth and development. External shocks affect the cost structure and may change the income distribution equilibrium of the economy. Relatively appreciated exchange rates allow developing countries to import the essential intermediary and capital goods necessary for the development process. As a windfall gain appreciated, exchange rates tend to reduce inflationary pressures. However, inability to obtain enough foreign exchange to close the balance of payments – to maintain a current account balance sufficient for the requirements of servicing foreign debt, and hence avoiding default – tends to force developing countries to devalue their currencies.

In the same vein as the increase in agricultural prices, devaluation affects prices directly, and to the extent that imported goods are part of the wage basket, or affect the prices of goods in the wage basket, the real wage will tend to fall. Once again wage resistance will lead to further hikes in prices, and foreign exchange–wage spirals will ensue. Propagation mechanisms will lead to a process of chronic inflation.

Finally, according to the model above, inflation depends on the distributive conflict expression. Prices may increase because workers and capitalists are not satisfied with their respective shares of the pie. These inconsistent claims are represented by increases in wages above the indexation norm, or increases of prices by firms above what would be required by increases in the prices of inputs. In other words, the economy is divided between workers and capitalists, who try to increase their share of total income at the expense of each other. The profit share is positively related to the degree of monopoly as represented by the mark-up. Hence, whenever the actual share of profits falls below the target share, firms will increase domestic prices.

For heterodox economists, monetary policy and fiscal policy have limited effects on inflation, even though both can be very strong instruments to affect the level of activity. Controlling inflation is ultimately associated with the elimination of inertia, by promoting the eradication of indexation of wage contracts, the reduction of the effects of supply-side shocks which may be achieved, to some extent, with price controls and foreign exchange controls, and, last but not least, by some sort of social pact that placates the distributive conflict.

Heterodox authors have challenged conventional wisdom, and put forward a view of inflation based on distributive conflict, supply-side shocks and propagation mechanisms. Endogenous money more often than not complements the accepted view among heterodox authors. Stabilization relies on incomes policies rather than macroeconomic austerity. Traditionally the institutional arrangements such as a national-level collective wage-bargaining system were essential for wage-setting practices that reduced inflationary tendencies. The increase in labor market flexibility and the dismantling of labor market institutions makes this type of incomes policy less likely. Also, international financial deregulation, and the ensuing exchange rate volatility, makes the possibilities of inflationary shocks greater. This is a paradoxical result, since according to the mainstream view one of the main reasons for both policies, labor flexibility and financial deregulation, was to control inflation.

Concluding remarks

It was suggested that two organizing principles were essential to clarify diverse views about inflation. Figure 28.4 organizes theories according to the adoption of a demand-pull or cost-push view of inflation, on the one hand, and the adoption of an exogenous or endogenous view of money supply, on the other.

The principal diagonal contains the traditional views regarding inflation. It is clear that the defenders of the old quantity theory tradition from the Salamanca School onwards until recent monetarists, including those using the Phillips curve, would fall into the upper-left quadrant. Keynes's inflation gap model would also fall into that quadrant, but qualified by the fact that his arguments were applied to a war period context. The exact reverse positions taken by most heterodox schools are grouped in the lower-right quadrant.

The secondary diagonal contains the, at least until now, out of the ordinary views on inflation. In the lower-left quadrant we find the real views of inflation that emphasize excess demand and endogenous money. This is a strong view among economic historians,[14] and increasingly so among macroeconomists who embrace some variation of the post-Wicksellian view of the economy. For Wicksell, the real business cycle authors, and the so-called new neoclassical synthesis[15] – which incorporates New Keynesian rigidities into a real business cycle model – real shocks explain economic fluctuations, including price fluctuations, and hence money becomes endogenous.

The upper-right quadrant is perhaps the oddest of all. Marxists authors may be seen as arguing that excess demand, by pushing the economy beyond the NAIRU, leads to

	Demand-pull	Cost-push
Exogenous money	Salamanca school Quantity theory of money Keynes's inflation gap Phillips curve models	Marxists Neo-Chartalists
Endogenous money	Neo-Malthusian model Wicksell's cumulative process Real business cycle New neoclassical synthesis	Balance of payments school Structuralists Scandinavian model Post-Keynesians Inertialists

Figure 28.4   Classification of theories of inflation

increasing bargaining power for workers, and eventually the tighter labor market would generate higher wages and inflation. However, the NAIRU does not represent a natural or full employment barrier; it is a social construct that depends on the nature of labor institutions and reflects class conflict. In that respect, inflation can also be seen as arising from cost-push pressures in the labor market. Hence, even though Marxist could be bumped into the upper-left quadrant, they fit better the one chosen above.

Finally, neo-Chartalists (see Chapter 5 on tax-driven money in this volume) who believe that money is a creature of the state, fall into the upper-right quadrant. It should be noted that Chartalists' position regarding money is controversial, but it seems that their views imply that the monetary authority controls exogenously the money supply, and that the means of payment are multiplied by the banking sector.

The most significant feature to emerge from Figure 28.4 is that all orthodox schools of thought are on the left side, while all the heterodox are on the right side. This suggests that the most important dichotomy is the one associated with the demand-pull versus cost-push divide. This result seems to emphasize that the main distinction between conventional wisdom and all unorthodox views of inflation depends on whether some extraneous element forces inflation into a system that would otherwise work perfectly, generally in the form of governments' excessive money printing, or if social conflicts and structural limitations are ultimately resolved by inflation, typically by allowing costs to increase.

Not surprisingly, orthodox research has concentrated on explanations for governments' inflationary behavior. Government behavior, in turn, is usually justified in terms of short-term electoral gains. In this respect, by introducing political variables into the discussion of economic outcomes, inflation theory became a branch of the so-called new political economy. It is the external political process that contaminates the well-functioning market economy. In contrast, alternative theories have emphasized the old classical political economy tradition according to which distribution is determined by social variables and historically developed institutions. In that context the creative impulse of history is the conflict of antagonistic forces in the productive arena. Inflation is then seen as the vector solution by which some conflicts generated in the process of economic development are accommodated. In the end, heterodox economists argue that the internal contradictions of the functioning of a market economy are essential to understanding inflationary processes.

Notes

1. Similar, if somewhat different, efforts have been made by Moore (1978) and Wray (2001).
2. On the Salamanca School see Grice-Hutchinson (1952), and Popescu (1997).
3. See Leijonhufvud (1997) and Woodford (2003) for Wicksell's influence.
4. Wicksell's analysis prefigures modern discussions on monetary policy. The interest rate rather than money supply is the instrument of policy, and in order to maintain price stability the central authority must equalize the bank rate to its long-term equilibrium level, i.e. the natural rate. For a comparison with modern conventional views on monetary policy see Clarida et al. (1999).
5. The Olivera–Tanzi effect was first noted by Olivera (1967) and independently described later by Tanzi (1977).
6. Two equilibria are possible, one with low inflation and one with high inflation. Stability depends upon economic agents' expectation formation (Heymann and Leijonhufvud, 1995, p. 21). In particular perfect foresight implies multiple equilibria.
7. The discussion is by no means conclusive. Some views are inevitably left out. References to other schools, such as the Scandinavian, the neo-Chartalist and the German balance of payments schools can be found in the notes. Taylor (2004) presents a discussion of structuralist views of inflation that can be seen as broadly encompassing the views of heterodox economists.
8. Bowles (1985) similarly argues for a heterodox version of the natural rate of unemployment. The non-accelerating inflation rate of unemployment (NAIRU) reflects the effects of excess labor demand on the bargaining power of workers. The neoclassical natural rate is a full employment one, while for Marxists the NAIRU is not (Pollin, 1999). Post-Keynesian authors have been more critical of the NAIRU, in particular the fact that both the natural rate and the NAIRU presume that the level of employment is a supply side phenomenon, rather than the result of demand decisions. Sawyer (1999), while emphasizing the role of capacity constraints as possible inflation barriers, argues against the NAIRU and the notion of employment determination as a labor market phenomenon.
9. Desai (1973) and more recently Screpanti (1997) are also important contributions to the Marxist theory of inflation.
10. On Latin American structuralists, and also the German balance of payments school, inflation theories, see Câmara and Vernengo (2004).
11. Canavese (1982) shows that there is a similarity between Latin American structuralists' views and the Scandinavian model of inflation. Both models can be seen as a formalization of the notion that different sectors have different rates of productivity growth. On the Scandinavian model see Frisch (1977).
12. Some post-Keynesian authors also emphasized the role of expectations in producing price inertia, rather than the role of contracts (e.g. Frenkel, 1979; Tavares and Belluzzo, 1984; Carvalho, 1993).
13. Heymann and Leijonhufvud (1995, pp. 29–34) provide a clever version of what may be termed the canonical heterodox model of inflation. A modified version is presented here.
14. The neo-Malthusian view that is dominant among historians emphasizes demand-led inflation. Note, however, that if instead of stressing the role of population dynamics on demand, one accentuates the impact of demographics on the relative strength of the labor class and consequently on wage dynamics, one would have a position that is closer to heterodox interpretations of inflation.
15. On the new neoclassical synthesis see Goodfriend and King (1997).

References

Arestis, Philip and Peter Howells (2001–2), 'The 1520–1640 "Great Inflation": an early controversy on the nature of money', *Journal of Post Keynesian Economics*, **24**(2), 181–203.

Arida, Persio and Andre Lara-Resende (1985), 'Inertial inflation and monetary reform in Brazil', In John Williamson (ed.), *Inflation and Indexation*, Washington, DC: Institute for International Economics, pp. 27–45.

Ball, Laurence (1994), 'Credible disinflation with staggered price setting', *American Economic Review*, **84**, 282–9.

Bowles, Samuel (1985), 'The production process in a competitive economy: Walrasian, neo-Hobbesian, and Marxian Models', *American Economic Review*, **75**(1), 16–36.

Bresciani-Turroni, Constantino (1931), *The Economics of Inflation: A Study of Currency Depreciation in Post-War Germany*. London: Allen & Unwin, Ltd., 1937.

Bresser Pereira, Luiz Carlos and Yoshiaki Nakano (1983), 'Fatores aceleradores, mantenedores, e sancionadores da inflação', *Anais do X Encontro Nacional de Economia*, Belém: ANPEC.

Bresser Pereira, Luiz Carlos and Yoshiaki Nakano (1987), *The Theory of Inertial Inflation: The Foundation of Economic Reform in Brazil & Argentina*. Boulder, CO: Lynne Rienner Publishers.

Burdekin, Richard and Paul Burkett (1996), *Distributional Conflict and Inflation: Theoretical and Historical Perspectives*. London: Macmillan.

Cagan, Phillip (1956), 'The monetary dynamics of hyperinflation', in Milton Friedman (ed.), *Studies in the Quantity Theory of Money*. Chicago, IL: Chicago University Press, pp. 25–117.

Câmara Neto, Alcino F. and Matías Vernengo (2004), 'Allied, German and Latin theories of inflation', in L. Randall Wray and Mathew Forstater (eds), *Contemporary Post Keynesian Analysis*. Cheltenham, UK and Northampton, MA, USA: Edward Elgar, pp. 172–84.

Canavese, Alfredo (1982), 'The structuralist explanation in the theory of inflation', *World Development*, **10**(7), 523–9.

Cardoso, Eliana (1981), 'Food supply and inflation', *Journal of Development Economics*, **8**(3), 269–84.

Carvalho, Fernando (1993), 'Strato-inflation and high inflation: the Brazilian experience', *Cambridge Journal of Economics*, **17** (1), 63–78.

Clarida, Richard, Jordi Gali and Mark Gertler (1999), 'The science of monetary policy: a New Keynesian perspective', *Journal of Economic Literature*, **37**(4), 1661–707.

Coutts, Ken, Roger Tarling and Frank Wilkinson (1976), 'Wage bargaining and the inflation process', *Economic Policy Review*, No. 2, Cambridge, Department of Applied Economics.

Desai, Meghnad (1973), 'Growth cycles and inflation in a model of class struggle', *Journal of Economic Theory*, **6**(6), 427–45.

Eisner, Robert (1989), 'Budget deficits: Rhetoric and reality', *Journal of Economic Perspectives*, **3**(3), 73–93.

Ellis, Howard (1934), *German Monetary Theory: 1905–1933*. Cambridge, MA: Harvard University Press.

Ferguson, Niall (1995), *Paper & Iron: Hamburg Business and German Politics in the Era of Inflation, 1897–1927*. Cambridge and New York: Cambridge University Press.

Frenkel, Roberto (1979), 'Decisiones de precio en alta inflación', *Estudios CEDES*, Buenos Aires.

Friedman, Milton (1956), 'The quantity theory of money: a restatement', in *Studies in the Quantity Theory of Money*. Chicago, IL: Chicago University Press, pp. 3–21.

Friedman, Milton (1968), 'The role of monetary policy', *American Economic Review*, **58**(1), 1–17.

Frisch, Helmut (1977), 'The Scandinavian model of inflation: a generalization and empirical evidence', *Atlantic Economic Journal*, December.

Furtado, Celso (1959), *The Economic Growth of Brazil*. Berkeley, CA: University of California Press, 1963.

Giavazzi, Francesco and Marco Pagano (1988), 'The advantage of tying one's hands', *European Economic Review*, **32**, June, 1055–82.

Goodfriend, Marvin and Robert King (1997), 'The new neoclassical synthesis and the role of monetary policy', *NBER Macroeconomics Annual*, 231–83.

Goodfriend, Marvin and Robert King (2004), 'The incredible Volcker disinflation', *Carnegie–Rochester Conference Series on Public Policy*, November.

Gordon, Robert J. (1996), 'The time-varying NAIRU and its implications for economic policy', NBER Working Papers, No. 5735, National Bureau for Economic Research, August.

Graham, Frank (1930), *Exchange, Prices, and Production in Hyperinflation: Germany, 1920–1923*. Princeton, NY: Princeton University Press.

Green, Roy (1992), *Classical Theories of Money, Output and Inflation*. London: St Martin's Press.

Grice-Hutchinson, Marjorie (1952), *The School of Salamanca: Readings in Spanish Monetary Theory, 1544–1605*. Oxford: Oxford University Press.

Hackett Fisher, David (1996), *The Great Wave: Price Revolutions and the Rhythm of History*. Oxford: Oxford University Press, 1999.

Hamilton, Earl (1934), *American Treasure and the Price Revolution in Spain, 1501–1650*. Cambridge, MA: Harvard University Press.

Helfferich, Karl (1927), *Money*. New York: The Adelphi Company.

Heymann, Daniel and Axel Leijonhufvud (1995), *High Inflation*. Oxford: Clarendom Press.

Holtfrerich, Carl-Ludwig (1986), *The German Inflation, 1914–1923: Causes and Effects in International Perspective*. Berlin: Walter de Gruyter.

Hume, David (1752), 'Of Money', in Eugene Rotwein (ed.), *Writings on Economics*. London: Nelson, 1955.

Kaldor, Nicholas (1976), 'Inflation and recession in the world economy', in Fernando Targetti and Anthony P. Thirlwall (eds), *The Essential Kaldor*. London: Duckworth, 1989, pp. 516–32.

Kaldor, Nicholas (1982), *The Scourge of Monetarism*. Oxford: Oxford University Press.

Keynes, John M. (1923), *A Tract on Monetary Reform. The Collected Writings of John Maynard Keynes*, Vol. IV. London and Cambridge: Macmillan and Cambridge University Press, 1971.

Keynes, John M. (1940), *How to Pay for the War*. London: Macmillan.

Kindleberger, Charles (1984), 'A structural view of the German inflation', in Gerald D. Feldman, Carl L. Holtfrereich, Gerhard Ritter and Peter Witt, *The Experience of Inflation*. Berlin and New York: de Gruyter, pp. 10–33.

Laidler, David and Michael Parkin (1975), 'Inflation: A survey', *Economic Journal*, **85**(December), 741–809.
Leijonhufvud, Axel (1997), 'The Wicksellian heritage', *Economic Notes*, **26**(1), 1–10.
Lopes, Francisco (1986), *O Choque Heterodoxo*. Rio de Janeiro: Campus.
Lucas Jr, Robert (1972), 'Expectations and the neutrality of money', *Journal of Economic Theory*, **2**(April), 103–23.
Mankiw, Gregory (2000), 'The inexorable and mysterious tradeoff between inflation and unemployment', Harvard Institute of Economic Research, Discussion Paper No. 1905.
Merkin, Gerard (1982), 'Towards a theory of the German inflation: Some preliminary observations', in Gerald D. Feldman, Carl L. Holtfrerich, Gerhard Ritter and Peter Witt (eds), *Die Deutsche Inflation: Eine Zwischenbilanz*, Berlin: Walter de Gruyter.
Moore, Basil (1978), 'Monetary factors', in Alfred Eichner (ed.), *A Guide to Post Keynesian Economics*. Armonk, NY: M.E. Sharpe, pp. 120–38.
Moore, Basil (1988), *Horizontalists and Verticalists*. Cambridge: Cambridge University Press.
Munro, John (2003), 'The monetary origins of the "price revolution" before the influx of Spanish-American treasure: The South German silver–copper trades, merchant-banking and Venetian commerce, 1470–1540', in Dennis Flynn, Arturo Giraldez and Richard von Glahn (eds), *Global Connections and Monetary History, 1470–1800*. Aldershot: Ashgate Publishing.
Noyola, Juan (1956), 'El desarrollo económico y la inflación en México y otros países Latinoamericanos', *Investigación Económica*, **XVI**(4), 603–16.
Olivera, Julio (1967), "Money, prices and fiscal lags: A note on the dynamics of inflation', *Banca Nazionale del Lavoro Quarterly Review*, **20**, 258–67.
Pazos, Felipe (1972), *Chronic Inflation in Latin America*. New York: Praeger Publishers.
Phelps, Edmund (1967), 'Phillips curves, expectations of inflation and optimal unemployment over time,' *Economica*, **34**(135), 254–81.
Pollin, Robert (1999), 'Class conflict and the "natural rate of unemployment"', *Challenge*, **42**(6), 103–11.
Popescu, Oreste (1997), *Studies in the History of Latin American Economic Thought*. London: Routledge.
Postan, Michael M. (1973), *Essays on Medieval Agriculture and General Problems of the Medieval Economy*. Cambridge: Cambridge University Press.
Ricardo, David (1817), *The Principles of Political Economy and Taxation*. Edited by Piero Sraffa with the collaboration of Maurice Dobb. Cambridge: Cambridge University Press, 1951–73.
Roberts, John (1997), 'Is inflation sticky?', *Journal of Monetary Economics*, **39**, 173–96.
Robinson, Joan (1938), 'The economics of hyper-inflation', in *Collected Economic Papers*, Vol. 1. Oxford: Basil Blackwell, 1966.
Robinson, Joan (1971), *Economic Heresies*. New York: Basic Books.
Rowthorn, Robert (1977), 'Conflict, inflation and money', *Cambridge Journal of Economics*, **1**, 215–29.
Sargent, Thomas (1982), 'The ends of four big inflations', in Robert Hall (ed.), *Inflation: Causes and Effects*. Chicago, IL: Chicago University Press, pp. 41–97.
Sargent, Thomas and Neil Wallace (1981), 'Some unpleasant monetarist arithmetic', *Federal Reserve Bank of Minneapolis Quarterly Review*, Autumn, 1–17.
Sawyer, Malcolm (1999), 'The NAIRU: A critical appraisal', *International Papers in Political Economy*, **7**(2), 1–39.
Screpanti, Ernesto (1997), 'Wages, inflation, and employment: A dynamic model', *Quaderni del Dipartimento di Economia Politica*, Università di Siena, No. 217.
Simonsen, Mario H. (1970), *Inflação: Gradualismo x Tratamento de Choque*. Rio de Janeiro: Apec.
Staiger, Douglas, James H. Stock and Mark W. Watson (1997), 'The NAIRU, unemployment and monetary policy', *Journal of Economic Perspectives*, **11**(1), 33–50.
Sunkel, Osvaldo (1958), 'Inflation in Chile: An unorthodox approach', *International Economic Papers*, **10**, 1960.
Tanzi, Vito (1977), 'Inflation, lags in collection and the real value of tax revenue', *IMF Staff Papers*, **34**, 711–38.
Tavares, Maria Conceição and Luiz G. Belluzzo (1984), 'Uma reflexão sobre a natureza da inflação contemporânea', in José Marcio Rego (ed.), *Inflação Inercial: Teorias sobre Inflação e o Plano Cruzado*. Rio de Janeiro: Paz e Terra, 1986.
Taylor, Lance (2004), *Reconstructing Macroeconomics*. Cambridge, MA: Harvard University Press.
Tooke, Thomas (1844), *An Inquiry into the Currency Principle; the Connection of the Currency with Prices, and the Expediency of a Separation of Issue from Banking*. London: Longman, Brown, Green, and Longmans.
Vernengo, Matías (2006), 'Monetary arrangements in a globalizing world: an introduction', in Matías Vernengo (ed.), *Monetary Integration and Dollarization: No Panacea*. Cheltenham, UK and Northampton, MA, USA: Edward Elgar, pp. 1–9.
Vilar, Pierre (1960), *A History of Gold and Money, 1450–1920*. London: Verso, 1991.
Wicksell, Knut (1898), *Interest and Prices*. London: Macmillan, 1936.
Woodford, Michael (2003), *Interest and Prices: Foundations of a Theory of Monetary Policy*. Princeton, NJ: Princeton University Press.
Wray, L. Randall (2001), 'Money and inflation', in Richard Holt and Steven Pressman (eds), *A New Guide to Post Keynesian Economics*. London: Routledge.

29 Interest and money: the property explanation
Gunnar Heinsohn and Otto Steiger

1. The property-induced economy versus possession-based production systems

An economic theory deserving that name is wanting because economists have never come to terms with *property* but always confused it with *possession*, which they mislabelled 'property'. What is the difference between these two concepts? The *rules* of possession, individual and/or collective, determine who, in what manner, at what time and place, to what extent and by exclusion of whom, may physically *use* a good or resource and change its substance and form. It is not possessory rules, existing already in animal systems, that bring about economic activity, but the man-made institution of property. Property-induced activities can only endure if they are followed by a legal system safeguarding them. Since sooner or later the civil law required for this task is guarded over by institutions, which form a major sphere of the state's operations, it may appear as if the state itself is the progenitor of the economy and everything that comes with it.

The property operations encapsulated in law comprise the *rights*: (i) to *burden* property titles in issuing money against interest; (ii) to *encumber* these titles as *collateral* for obtaining money; (iii) to alienate or *exchange*, including sale and lease; and (iv) to *enforce*. Property rights do not replace the rules of possession but are added to them, thereby transforming traditional rules into codified rights too. Thus individual *rules* become *private* rights subject only to law but no longer to seigniority.

Taking the term 'property' as the starting-point of our approach to interest and money (Heinsohn, 1984 [1982]; Heinsohn and Steiger, 2006a [1996]; 2003 [2000]; 2006b; 2007) implies that not exchange of goods but operations enabled by property lead to interest and money – a money that, for being genuine, must always be a *creditor's money*. In the history of economic thought, from the time of Aristotle to our days, the analysis of money has always been tied to markets. According to this view, apart from the world of Robinson Crusoe, as soon as two individuals meet they make *barter* exchanges, thereby creating the market. When the number of individuals increases, the problems of the double coincidence of wants and of transaction costs arise. To facilitate barter and to reduce transaction costs, a special standard good will be selected as numeraire – money that allows the barter-exchange relations to be expressed numerically. 'In much of economics, markets appear as a natural given; if there is a good, then there is a market' (Loasby, 2000, p. 299). And, one could continue, if there are more than two persons who want to exchange their goods on the market, then money will develop. But who actually creates the money and how is it related to markets?

Like the derivation of money from markets, in mainstream economics the rate of interest is also derived from barter exchange, although on intertemporal markets. According to the neoclassical time preference theory of interest, present consumption of real-income goods is valued more highly than their future consumption and, therefore, the loss of consumption today is compensated by a savings premium: the commodity or *real* rate of interest. With the notable exception of Keynes, who always stressed that the rate of interest is a *monetary* rate, money and interest, in their derivation from the market, are disconnected.

Rules of possession exist in all social organizations. We label a tribe or a feudal estate a 'system' rather than a 'society' because the latter term is reserved for one peculiar type of social organization – the system based on property. In the property *society* private persons are not subject to power relations but freely bonded by *contract*. All other social systems are not societies but have to be termed either *communities* (tribal systems) or *seigniorities* (feudal/socialist politburo systems).

What is the essence of any contract in the property-based society? In the primary contracts, the debt and sales contracts, the contracting partners must have property. It is either burdened and encumbered (debt contract) or alienated (sales contract). In the secondary contracts, lease and employment contracts, at least one contracting partner has to be a proprietor too.

The most explicit school stressing the contract basis of the economy, post-Keynesianism, locates the essence of any contract in the dimension of time, the period which passes between the present and an uncertain, non-probabilistic future (Davidson, 2005, p. 461). Being devoid of economic institutions and, therefore, unaware of property, post-Keynesians do not see that time passes in every human realm without, however, everywhere leading to contracts too.

Of course, economists of all times and schools make use of the term 'property' relentlessly. Yet they never even realize that the institution of property does not exhibit its peculiarity in the sphere of physical goods and resources. When analysing the essentials of the economy one has to disregard this sphere and focus on the intangible elements of property, especially burdening. As a right, property is not physically related to the sphere of goods and resources but transforms rules of possession into rights. As the Romans knew, *proprietas in iure, possessio in facto est*. The non-physical *de iure* capacity carries the potential of generating interest and money. Why?

Property economics has to answer what it regards as economic theory's core question: what is the loss that has to be compensated by interest? Property economics accepts neither a temporary loss of goods, as in neoclassical economics, nor Keynes's temporary loss of money as the cause of interest. When money – as an *anonymized, notified* claim to *assets* of its issuing proprietor – is created in a collateralized credit contract, the interest causing loss is the loss of unrestricted power over property of the issuer. The immaterial yield which only accrues from unburdened assets, property economics calls the *property premium*.

Both in the money-creating and the money-forwarding credit contract, assets have to be burdened and encumbered. Burdening not only entails encumbrance as a claim to specified property titles. Every economic agent also bears a charge over his unencumbered titles because as a creditor this 'own capital', his net worth, has to compensate for shortfalls of his debtor. The net worth indicates a surplus of the creditor's assets over his liabilities. It serves as a buffer for a bad loan. Only the pure *rentier* has his property titles not only unencumbered but unburdened too.

In the *credit contract*, both partners have to be proprietors. With a creditor's burdening, and not only starting with a debtor's encumbrance which, as opposed to burdening, entails specified and recorded exposure to *foreclosure*, the property is already blocked; that is, the property premium is temporarily given up. Thus it cannot be further burdened or encumbered. The *encumbrance* of the debtor's property enables the creditor to secure the issue of money notes and, thereby, their circulation. The *burdening* of his own property enables the creditor to back his issue of notes and their circulation in case of bad loans. The money-creating creditor is compensated for his burdening with the *rate of interest*, while the money-receiving debtor is compensated for his encumbrance with the money notes' *liquidity premium*. Money's capacity to finally settle contracts, that is, the transfer of property in sales or its redemption in dissolving credit, is due to its being a claim to property of its issuer (Heinsohn, 2006).

In a *sales contract*, both contracting partners are proprietors who act as creditors and debtors and who mutually transfer property. The seller enters the contract as a proprietor who owes the delivery of a commodity or an asset and has a claim on money, while the buyer enters the contract as a debtor of money and has a claim to the delivery.

In a *lease contract*, property is not transferred but the proprietor transfers his possessory rights to the leaseholder who in this capacity acts only as possessor. In an *employment contract* a labourer does not enter as a proprietor because his labour can neither be sold nor burdened. He is only a possessor of his labour which he transfers to an employer, a proprietor or another possessor, e.g. a leaseholder, in exchange for wages paid in money. The labourer is ready to leave a surplus to his employer because, in contrast to a debtor, the contract gives him access to money without paying interest and encumbering property. The employer is ready to forward the money, because the surplus left to him can be transformed into the interest charged for the loan incurred to pay the labourer. For this he has to pledge property in advance, which he, and not the labourer, will lose if he cannot fulfil his credit contract.

The yield of property premium arises whenever property titles are grafted on to possession of resources and goods, including means of production, thereby transforming them into *assets* – and *commodities*. Therefore, the right to possession depends on the right to property. A proprietor can physically use an asset or a commodity but also lease it to a different person. In both cases the *de facto* right of possession is executed as a derivative of the *de jure* right to property and must, therefore, be formalized as a *de jure* contract.

Property rights are man-made. They usually emerge discontinuously through uprisings against command systems or by imposing the laws of property on newly conquered territories which up to then, as tribal or feudal systems, had known only rules of possession.

Property economics does not use the term ownership because it is ambiguous, meaning both property and possession. To this very day, it remains difficult to find a brief appropriate term for the Latin *proprietas* in English. Occasionally, overkill combinations such as 'private property ownership' are employed to evade the vagueness of English. Yet a closer look at such attempts reveals just another definition of possession. 'Ownership relates to a *possessory* interest in a property. This is the right to exert control over the *uses* of property to the exclusion of others' (Bellerue, 1995, p. 1; emphases added).

In such definitions burdening as the essential of property is not even mentioned. Therefore it is not understood that economic activity is tied to property titles which always revolutionize the possessory world of production. Of course, production as such will not disappear when property is abolished. However, in this case individuals are thrown back on to the non-economic lowlands of possession. Although it was seen early on that a grave difference of wealth existed in the seventeenth century between the kingdom of England

and the empires of Mexico and Peru conquered by the Spanish, the reason for this difference – property in England but merely possession in the Aztec and Inca monarchies – was not discovered.

> Nations of the *Americans* . . . are rich in Land and poor in the Comforts of Life. . . . And a King of a large and fruitful territory there feeds, lodges and is clad less worth than a day Labourer in *England*. / The Peruvians . . ., though they made use of gold and silver as ornaments, had no coined money of any kind. Their whole commerce was carried on by barter, and there was accordingly scarce any division of labour among them. (Locke, 1967 [1690], p. 314 f. / Smith, 1976 [1776], I, p. 221)

To explain the differences in wealth one has to return to the difference between possession and property because, as history shows, individuals can organize their material reproduction in three quite distinctive systems, of which only the property-based society is occupied with an economy. Reproduction means the production, distribution, consumption and, occasionally, the accumulation of goods necessary for survival. These three types are:

1. *The customary or tribal community*   This system collectively regulates production, distribution and consumption of goods and resources for its non-free members by *reciprocity*, that is, by mutually supportive provision of goods and resources. Though belonging to an intertemporal set of activity, they do not form loans in kind. The goods handed over neither generate interest and money nor can they be encumbered. There exist *no* independent institutions of law where the community's members can file a suit to enforce the rules of reciprocity. Only possession is known. It exists in the form of common and individual rules – not private rights – to the physical use of goods and resources, including their returns and alienation, which are regulated by custom.

2. *The command or feudal/socialist seigniority*   This regulates production, distribution, consumption and, occasionally, accumulation by *coercive* orders. Planned levies are extracted from a class of non-free individuals, serfs or serflike workers who are entitled to rations. Again, the rations must not be confused with a credit in kind generating interest and being employable as collateral. It goes without saying that in the command system too there exist no independent institutions of law where individuals can sue for rations. Again, only possession is known and exists in the form of common and individual rules set by aristocrats or politburos.

3. *The property-based society*   This system abolishes most of the traditional rules of reciprocity and command. For its *free* members, the society organizes production, distribution, consumption and accumulation by *interest and money* generated through credit contracts based on collateralized property. Independent courts of law enforce their fulfilment. In addition to property, possession, of course, continues to exist, albeit no longer regulated by mere rules, but by rights. Both rights of possession and property can be assigned to one and the same person or to different persons. They exist in the form of common and *private* rights.

The difference between customary and command systems on the one hand, and the property-based society on the other, is a principal and not a gradual one. Tribal or

Table 29.1   Distinctions between possession-based systems and the property-based society

Possession-based systems with mere reproduction	Property-based society with economic activities
Possession is the basis of material reproduction in animal systems as well as in human systems based on reciprocity (tribal *community*) or command (feudal/socialist *seigniority*), in which property is missing. *Only* possession exists. The informally, respectively arbitrarily, set rules determine who, in what manner, at what time and place, to what extent and by exclusion of whom, may *physically use goods* and *resources* and change their substance and form	**Property** is the basis of material reproduction in the property *society* ('capitalism', 'market economy', 'monetary economy'), where it transforms rules of possession into rights of property. Property exists *in addition* to possession
Possessory rules refer to the *non-legal* material use or control of *goods* and *resources* including the returns thereon and their alienation. Alienation here does not mean exchange in the form of sale and lease but only gifts, assignments and – occasionally – inheritance. *Per se* these rules are not capable of generating a genuine economy, with interest and money as its most obvious characteristics. Ironically, mainstream economics applies the term 'property rights' to mere possessory rules. These rules exist in the form of common and *individual* – exclusive – rules	**Property rights** are *de jure* claims. They entitle their holders to immaterial (non-physical) capacities which first constitute economic activities: (i) to *burden* property titles in issuing money against interest; (ii) to *encumber* these titles as collateral for obtaining money as capital; (iii) to alienate or *exchange* including sale and lease; and (iv) to *enforce*. Property rights transform possessory rules into **possessory rights** regulated by law. Thus individual rules become *private* rights. Property rights transform goods and resources into saleable *commodities* and saleable and rentable *assets*
Means of regulating material reproduction: production, distribution, consumption and occasional accumulation	**Means of regulating material reproduction:** production, distribution, consumption and accumulation
'Inborn instincts' (animal kingdom), custom and reciprocity (tribal community), and commands or plans (feudal/socialist seigniority) as *power* relations of *non-free* persons are the non-legal rules of reproduction. Independent courts of law are absent	Credit, sales, lease and employment contracts form a legally determined network of rights between *free*, private individuals on markets necessary for reproduction. Independent courts of law overrule custom and power relations
Burdening and encumbrance of property titles, interest and money, assets and liabilities, credit and banks, prices and markets are as much absent as the advantage seeking *homo oeconomicus*. The rules of reciprocity (tribe) or command (nobility, 'proletariat's avant-garde') determine the production of goods and their distribution for individual consumption, for common	The power to burden and encumber property offers an immaterial yield, the *property premium*. By burdening property for issuing *money notes* – 'notated' titles to property – in a credit contract, both lender and borrower have to give up their respective property premium; that is, they temporarily lose the freedom to burden, encumber or sell it. The encumbrance of the borrower's for property secures the lender's claims and, thereby, the *circulation* of the notes.

Table 29.1   (continued)

Possession-based systems with mere reproduction	Property-based society with economic activities
storage, and – occasionally – for common production goods or means of production. Therefore, storage and *accumulation requires previous savings* or a lower level of individual consumption. Exchange of goods is not a primary task. When exchanged at all, they serve to strengthen *loyalty. Interest-free* intertemporal lending of goods to overcome individual difficulties is bound to the obligation of mutual assistance. Common difficulties are resolved by handing out rations that are to be replenished later, either voluntarily (tribal community) or by command (feudal seigniority). Possession-based systems are forced to develop a *social safety* net for its members, although this can be achieved on a very low material level only	The burdening of the lender's *own capital*, the net worth of his property, enables him to withdraw from circulation the notes that have not been paid back, and also to *redeem* the notes. The lender is compensated for his burdening with *interest*, the borrower for his encumbrance with the money notes' immaterial yield, the *liquidity premium*. Their capacity to finally settle contracts, that is, to finally sell or release property, is due to the fact that money itself is a title to property of its creator. During the period of the loan, lender and borrower continue the physical use of the possessory side of their burdened assets. Since money is a *derivate of assets* (property), and not of goods (possession), *accumulation* can start *without previous savings*. Although needed, *no social safety net* can be developed from within the property-based society

Source: Heinsohn and Steiger (2006b), pp. 26–8.

aboriginal, feudal as well as socialist systems may run undisturbed for very long periods of time without any significant growth and development. Even today, though in marginal environments, tribes still foray on a stone age level. The very definition of underdevelopment in 80 per cent of the world's population is tied to the missing institution of property (Steiger, 2006a, p. 197).

The distinction between rights of property and rights of possession is not related to different classes or individuals. Every asset belongs to a proprietor and a possessor – a fundamental insight missing in the theory of property rights or new institutional economics (Steiger, 2006a, pp. 194–6). The difference is between the rights of the proprietor and those of the possessor, and not necessarily between the classes or individuals to whom the rights are assigned. In the case of land, the right of property, the right to its burdening and alienation, and the right of possession, the right to till the land, can be assigned to one and the same individual. But both rights can also be assigned to different individuals, for example when the landlord rents the land to a tenant.

Whereas in possession-based systems resources are only assigned to physical use, in the property-based society they are put to an *economic* use. 'Economic' means more than efficiency or optimality of barter exchanges. In each social structure human beings – and even animal species – may try to handle resources with as little waste as possible or, to use the mainstream definition of economics, to create an optimal relation between ends and scarce means of alternative uses of goods and resources exchanged according to individual preferences. To translate such universal propensities of living creatures into axioms of an eternal *homo oeconomicus* is a task that can never be solved in the barter paradigm of mainstream economics. A genuine economy does not show the advantage-oriented behaviour of an unfettered *homo oeconomicus*, but is the offspring of the institution of property which forces every human being – be he altruistic or selfish – to obey its laws.

The property-based society can no longer employ instruments of power to regulate the use of resources. Even those still bearing noble or royal names are subject to lawgivers, judges and bailiffs who defend, oversee or enforce legal titles to property to which possession titles are subjugated. Thereby, the order of property law is explicitly blind to the world of goods and the rules of status and privilege dominating command and reciprocity systems. Whoever continues with the acquisition of resources by following traditional rules will find himself in violation of property law; and he can no longer excuse himself with loyalty relations of kinship or vassalage. Only the strict exclusion of customary or command types of access to resources property can give birth to genuine economic activity. The most vital business operations arise out of evading overindebtedness, that is, an *economically* inflicted loss of property. An economic defence of property takes place beyond the legal means by which property is shielded against criminal offence.

The entirely non-physical business operations of property's free saleability and leaseability and, especially, its free burdening and free encumbrance, provide the matter demanding an economic theory in the full sense. All these capacities of property are employed without resorting to its possession side. They arise out of the property premium which remains hidden to a scholarly approach focused on physical uses only. Property is an abstract thing, a legal title. One cannot see, smell, hear, taste or touch it.

Activities observed in history's three different systems of material reproduction – tribes, feudalism, property – are mixed together in mainstream economics, which frequently even places them in an evolutionary continuum. Property economics, however, can clarify for what type of human association economics concepts are appropriate. Resources, for example, become assets only in the property-based society. Possession as an eternal and universal concept exists in all three types of human association. This has caused a great deal of confusion. Yet it is property alone that first forces possession into an economic use.

Because of the very absence of property in customary and command systems, no genuinely economic terms and notions are encountered (see Malinowski, 1961 [1922]; 1935; Polanyi, 1957 [1944]): property, interest, money and liquidity premium; assets and collateral; credit, capital and profit; value and price; commodities and markets. If these concepts are shackled to mere possessional activities, without ever even asking whether they are related to property, economists can do justice neither to reciprocity and command systems nor to the property-based economy.

2.   The core of property economics

A title to property never comes naturally. It can only be brought about by a legal act, not by a certain tendency in human nature – an act that by definition is intangible and initially does not alter the possessional state of resources. By whatever means property is created, it immediately carries a property premium. What is the meaning of this premium on assets? It is a non-physical yield of the potential to burden. It allows its proprietors to enter into contracts –as both creditors and debtors. While only unburdened property is a free asset, burdening turns the asset into a 'liability' that, however, is not necessarily encumbered. An unburdened asset entails the capacity of a creditor to issue notified titles to his property, his own capital or net worth. An unencumbered asset entails the capacity of a debtor to borrow money notes by pledging property as collateral, thereby not only burdening but also encumbering it.

In principle, every proprietor can issue anonymized claims against his assets, which then take the form of transferable documents redeemable in the issuer's property. However, in the history of property, both in antiquity and early modern times, only those creditors survived as issuers of money notes who, as solvent proprietors with a high ratio of own capital, established credit banks (Heinsohn and Steiger, 2006a [1996], pp. 264–76; 2003 [2000], p. 504; 2006b, pp. 117–19).

By burdening its capital in the money-issuing contract, the credit bank gives up the immaterial property premium in exchange for an additional amount of money promised by its debtor: *the rate of interest*. In other words, interest is accounted for by the bank's loss of property premium. To secure the refunding of the loan, the borrower too has to encumber assets. Thereby, his loss of property premium is turned into a *liquidity premium* attached to the money notes he receives. As long as the debtor fulfils his obligations, the bank is not allowed to touch the collateral, for example by using it for redemption of its notes. This has to be done by the bank's own capital.

It goes without saying that Keynes's liquidity premium or monetary theory of the rate of interest does not take into account the rate of interest charged by the bank of issue. This primary rate of interest has nothing whatsoever to do with giving up liquidity premium because it can arise only *after* liquidity has been created by the bank of issue, nowadays the central bank, to its debtor, nowadays its counterparty commercial bank. Once the commercial bank gives up the money received from the central bank in a loan forwarded to a non-bank, of course, its liquidity premium can be transformed into interest. Yet this rate follows the primary rate charged by the creator of money.

In the money-creating contract, creditor and debtor retain their physical possessions and their material returns. It is their property side, which is simultaneously burdened to guarantee the circulation of money and to secure the contract. Therefore, goods are never transferred in a loan contract as the time preference theory of the rate of interest suggests, and which Keynes is right to criticize, albeit for a wrong reason. The rate of interest is, indeed, a monetary rate. But it arises in the process of creation of a creditor's money and not from the giving up of liquidity by some owner of money. Thus interest is not the price for giving up liquidity but the price for burdening property by the creator of money (Heinsohn and Steiger, 2005, pp. 75–8).

The creation of money cannot be separated from the process of loaning it to a proprietor–debtor. Both the issuing of money notes and the establishment of a loan contract occur *uno actu*. Therefore, one has to distinguish between *two* documents in the creation of money: (i) the interest-bearing document secured by debtor's collateral, and (ii) the non-interest-bearing document, the money notes. The first document is the debt contract by which the second document is simultaneously issued and loaned as money proper. Thus, *money is created in a debt contract but is not itself a debt*.

The existence of these two documents is not revealed in the balance sheet of the modern central bank, which classifies bank notes as 'liabilities', thereby hiding its essential liability to return assets, for example in a repurchase contract with a commercial bank. This obliqueness in the balance sheet of the central bank has caused great confusion. It led, in the 1960s, to the 'new view' of money, heralded by Gurley and Shaw (1960), challenging the 'old view' that money is a part of the net wealth of the community. In accordance with the central bank's balance sheet, the challengers claim that the old view only holds for commodity money but not for fiat money. This modern money is seen as a debt to its issuer and an asset for its borrower. Therefore, for the economy as a whole, the net worth of money is supposed to be zero. Against this conviction, Pesek and Saving (1967, p. 143) tried to revitalize the old view also for fiat money. Modern money is not a debt, but net worth. 'Bank notes are an item of net wealth leased to the private sector.'

Property economics can demonstrate that Pesek and Saving are correct, albeit for the wrong reason. They treat the credit creation of bank notes like the lease of newly produced machinery. Yet, when the bank of issue creates money, it does not add to its net worth like the producer of a new machine. Money is never a net worth to its creator but only to its borrower. But what, then, is the debt of the bank of issue? Not its bank notes but its liability to release assets to holders of the notes when presented. It is because of this liability only that it can be stated: '*Federal Reserve notes* are [correctly: imply] claims on the assets of the issuing Federal Reserve bank' (US Treasury, 2006, p. 2). However, when the borrower adds to his net worth the newly created money, he incurs a liability to the bank of issue. Does that not offset his net worth? What is not seen in the borrower's balance sheet is that part of his property he has to encumber to help the money loaned to be created. Money is a net worth because it activates property which, thereby, is collateralized and even risked but not reduced.

The net worth is not eliminated again when the loan is paid back. To become able to refund, the borrower first has to employ the money advanced. Mere financial transactions aside, the borrower has to become a producer, for example, of a machine for himself, for sale or for lease. In any case, net wealth is added to the community.

Of course, money can also be created by buying property titles outright on the open market. But in such a case, the problem arises that, in order to control the circulation of money, titles regularly have to be sold outright. However, this is nothing but a poor imitation of the credit issue of money which automatically guarantees its reflux as, for example, in the form of bills of exchange, the preferred method of central banks in former times. Today's preferred method of repurchase agreements has the advantage that the risk of depreciation rests with the counterparty of the central bank, while in outright transactions it stays with the bank itself.

The bank of issue cannot help but establish its own standard, the *money of account*, in the very moment it issues notes or *money proper*. This standard must reckon the notes in terms of an abstract unit, necessary for denominating their amount in the debt contract in which they are created. It must not be confused with a standard of measurement, which is derived from a standard physical good as unit of account or numeraire as in neoclassical theory.

The question as to where the idea of a money of account comes from has been intriguingly answered by Keynes (1971 [1930], pp. 4 and 10–12) by resorting to Knapp's (1924 [1905]) state theory of money. Since 'millennia', and in order to raise taxes, Keynes believes, tribal communities and feudal states needed a money of account. In reality, however, private pre-bank issuers of money living in the property-based societies of antiquity were the first to establish credit contracts. 'The [private] credit contract as a legal document, collateral and charging of a rate of interest most probably have been practised before the emergence of [state] temple banks' (Bogaert, 1966, p. 66).

In the feudal palace systems preceding those property-based societies there was no money standard by which values could be compared: items were just counted, weighed, or measured as they stood. In contrast, in the property societies of both antiquity and modern times, private proprietors, by forming credit banks, were the first to issue money as coins (antiquity) and coins and bank notes (modern times). And in *this* process of issuing money, they used the already existing terms for standards of measurement – especially weights – of the preceding feudal systems as mere labels for the newly established money of account, for example the pound in early modern times.

How is money theorized for this period? In the history of monetary thought two views can be discerned: one that points in the direction of the theory of a creditor's money, and another, which carries the flaws of a debtor's money. The former theory starts with James Steuart (1767) and his emphasis on the role of the credit bank as a bank of issuing bank notes, while the latter can be derived from Keynes's state theory of money. It is Steuart, not Keynes, who first correctly ties the money of account to the credit contract.

Steuart, who originally coined the term 'money of accompt' (1805 [1761], p. 205), sees the bank of issue as a credit bank whose notes are without 'material use' because they receive their value from property, not from bullion. Thus it is not a bank of deposit whose notes, according to a still popular thesis, originate from the receipts written by goldsmiths for gold valuables deposited with them. The first bank notes are issued for the proprietors of the credit bank who, with their capital in the bank, are responsible for the security of the notes. 'Men of *property* . . . form a stock which may consist indifferently of any species of property. . . . The security of such paper stands alone upon the original capital of the bank' (1767, II, p. 150 f.; emphasis added). As soon as the non-bank public recognizes the acceptability of that paper, it becomes interested to loan such notes. For such loans the bank asks for good securities. Therefore, the security on which the bank's notes stand is not only its own capital but also property titles pledged as collateral by its debtors.

Unlike most theorists of central banking (Steiger, 2006b, pp. 196–206), Steuart is aware that the business of creating money is a risky one. People do not understand how banks of issue 'should ever be at a *loss* for money, as they have a mint of their own, which requires nothing but paper and ink to create millions. But if they consider the principles of banking, they will find that every note' not issued against good securities 'is neither more nor less, than a partial spending either of their *capital*, or profits on the bank' (Steuart, 1767, II, p. 151 f.; emphases added).

Although Steuart cannot explain the rate of interest, he can show why people are ready to pay interest. Why does one proprietor become a creditor who issues money to gain interest, while another proprietor encumbers property and pays interest? Would it not be smarter for the potential borrower to issue money against his own property, thereby obtaining notes without paying interest? However, as long as a debtor obtains money through a loan from someone else, he is free from the obligation to redeem the notes with his property, whereby he would lose his possession too. A debtor pays interest because only a credit bank of issue is able to guarantee the circulation of the notes (Steuart, 1767, II, p. 131 f.), which, according to property economics, implies the bank's capabilities: (i) to let the debtor keep the possessory side of his collateral and, simultaneously, (ii) not to take away its property side but only to enforce its temporary encumbrance.

Keynes falls behind Steuart's insight that bank notes are a creditor's money which derives its acceptability from the capital of the bank of issue and the good securities of its debtors. Keynes knows that so-called 'bank money' must not be confused with money proper because it only means the acknowledgement of a debt. At the same time, however, he maintains that the state is an agent that can declare its debt as money proper in the form of '*representative money*' (Keynes, 1971 [1930], p. 6; emphasis added). What is Keynes's mistake? He confuses the mutual netting of claims, which makes the use of money redundant, with the substitution of money for claims, which he wrongly calls bank *money*. Within banking operations this netting of liabilities is generally feasible without any problem: a creditor's claims for money can be netted off with claims for money against third parties instead of payment. However, the liability does *not* substitute *money* in this case but a clearing of liabilities is simply substituted for the *payment* of money.

Therefore it comes as no surprise that Keynes's analysis of the creation of money sees central bank money, state money and bank money 'on the same footing'. The state's representative money is seen as an asset of the central bank which it can use to create central bank money. State and central bank money alike are held by the member banks as reserves against their deposits, which he calls 'member bank money'. All three categories constitute, when held by the public, 'the aggregate of current money' (Keynes, 1971 [1930], p. 8 f.).

No wonder that, by identifying money proper with a debtor's money, Keynes (1936, p. 200; emphasis added) supports 'the *government printing money*', that is the financing of current state expenditure by central bank credit. He is convinced that the government can undertake expenditures *prior* to their financing.

> With modern representative money and a modern banking system, we know that the necessary 'finance' can be created by a series of 'book' or 'paper' transactions. The Treasury can 'pay' in effect by 'book' entries, and the book entry can be transformed into a regular loan at a much later date. (Keynes, 1982 [1939], p. 140; for more detail see Stadermann and Steiger, 2006)

In the same fashion, James Tobin (1963, p. 415) believes that 'governments . . . can . . . create means of payment to finance their own purchases of goods and services'. It goes without saying that such financing has very often destroyed monetary systems, most strikingly in highly developed economies, for example in Germany (during and after World War I and during the Hitler government, 1933–45) and Argentina (during the Peron government, 1946–51; see Steiger, 2005, pp. 184–6). Nowadays, therefore, such a creation of money is forbidden for all central banks deserving that name. As shown above, Keynes's analysis of the creation of money simply confuses debt titles, which a creditor offers out of his stock of claims against debtors, with debt titles offered directly by a debtor.

If debtors could go with their own IOUs directly to the central bank, the money handed over to them would, indeed, be a debtor's money. Since collateral and own capital in the creation of money remain strangers to post-Keynesians no less than to Keynes himself, this school too cannot help but endorse a debtor's money (see especially Wray, 1998).

Unlike Keynes, post-Keynesian monetary theory is not interested in the monetary explanation of the rate of interest. Interest is merely regarded as an exogenous rate set by the central bank as a parameter of monetary policy. Another Keynesian school, the German Monetary Keynesians (see especially Riese, 1986), aim to combine Keynes's liquidity premium theory of the rate of interest with the creation of money by the central bank. Since they too are unaware of collateralized property and own capital as a decisive cause of the scarcity of a creditor's money, they believe that money is created out of nothing (Riese, 2000, p. 491). Therefore, they believe, money can only be kept scarce by a rate of interest invented by the central bank for this very purpose. But how do Monetary Keynesians explain interest?

They regard the central bank as the only institution in the monetary economy that is not exposed to creditor's risk because it supposedly can produce the very liquidity the lack of which causes illiquidity. This would imply that the bank wields the peculiar power to produce money as an asset for itself over which it has two options: (i) holding the asset money, or (ii) parting with it in a loan contract. In the loan, Monetary Keynesians argue, the central bank is 'parting with the asset "money"' (Riese, 2000, p. 493), thereby giving up the liquidity premium simultaneously produced with the asset itself.

Like Pesek and Saving, Monetary Keynesians do not know that notes issued by a central bank cannot serve as an asset for the bank itself. Therefore, notes flowing back to the bank of their issue are always booked out. Central bank notes are claims to assets of the bank of issue. The notes are created only on behalf of commercial banks, which in exchange – besides interest – have to deliver debt titles not issued by themselves. Therefore, as a creditor's money, money proper is always a derivative of assets.

It may be added here that models of a central bank with no liquidity constraints are not only found in Monetary Keynesianism. Most recently, three ECB (European Central Bank) staff members have developed such a model on 'the strong assumption that the central bank is "liquidity unconstrained"' (Bindseil et al., 2004, p. 13). The authors can neither comprehend the key role of the capital of the central bank as a buffer against defaulting counterparties nor as a liquidity constraint. All they can see is the meltdown of 'central bank credibility', when a central bank runs out of own capital by permanently making losses (ibid., p. 23 f.).

Unlike the Keynesian schools, neoclassical theory has never advanced to the concept of a money of account necessary for a creditor's money. In the neoclassical model of a barter economy, the good chosen as *unit of account* is assigned the price 1 and serves thereby as the nominal anchor for the prices of all other goods. However, this anchor can only help to express their exchange ratios or relative prices. In the property-based economy, the bank of issue does not need a standard good. It issues – denominated in its money of account – money notes as claims to its assets. *Uno actu* with the credit bank's setting a money of account by granting a loan, all property titles receive prices in this standard and are, thereby, nominal or *money prices*. To refund the money loan, the borrower has to start a production whose quantities have to be priced in these values. Thus he turns into a monetary producer who must try to sell his commodities against money proper; that is, he must try to establish a *market*. Therefore, the market is not an ever-present place where goods are exchanged with the help of a standard good to the mutual benefit of their possessors, as neoclassical economics suggests, but an institution constituted by indebted producers to earn sales contracts for money.

To pay interest on the loan, the debtor must be able to generate a value surplus in his monetary production, the rate of *profit*, to be realized by the same sales contract. Thus interest-generated profit creates additional net worth, the *accumulation* of real assets, so characteristic of the property-based economy. Unlike in mere possession-based systems, this mechanism does not depend on a previous accumulation of saved goods.

The activation of property titles brings about economic activities in contrast to those of mere producers. Their activation leads to their intertemporal employment between credit partners. In a loan contract the lender, who blocks his property but retains its possessional side and continues to use it, faces a borrower, who receives money proper, which implies an anonymous claim to its issuer and which is backed by the lender's property. In turn, the borrower has to accept a specified claim of the lender as liability to refund what he has received in a fixed term. To secure the specified claim the borrower has to block his property as collateral and to accept the lender's privilege to enforcement in case of default.

Even if no specified collateral is mentioned in the case of a so-called secure debtor, this does not imply that credit is given without good security. The very definition of a secure debtor is, of course, that the quality of his assets is beyond doubt. 'The furnishing of security makes scrutiny of the general solvency of the borrower unnecessary' (Hawtrey, 1970 [1932], p. 126). It goes without saying that, in a contract with a secure debtor, the creditor never abstains from his right to enforce. However, the less secure a debtor, the more specific his collateral has to be. And in the case of a so-called open credit, the contract is secured by the property of the creditor alone.

The main question of property economics regarding the loss which has to be compensated by interest has to be answered with the loss of the money-creating creditor's property premium. Interest, thus, is not a compensation for a loss of goods of the creditor as in neoclassical theory. Furthermore, interest is not a compensation for the fact that the creditor is not allowed to touch the right of the debtor to continue with the use of the possessional side of his collateral. The debtor, after all, does not put up goods or resources (possession) as collateral, but assets (property). In the ancient institution of *antichresis*, in which the creditor is permitted to use the possessional side of his debtor's collateralized property, the yield going to the creditor only means that it is cleared with his demand for interest, not that he abstains from interest. Finally, the rate of interest does not compensate the loss of liquidity premium as in Keynesian theory because, in this explanation, the creditor only abstains from money which has already been created against interest and, therefore, cannot explain the rate of interest itself.

Collateral covers not only the debtor's inability to refund but also his failure to pay interest. This does not mean, however, that the demand for collateral derives from securing interest. Therefore, by putting up collateral the debtor cannot entice the creditor to abstain from interest.

Securities used as collateral in a credit contract are not risk free. There always exists a hierarchy of risk of property titles stretching from prime land over real capital goods and tradable assets up to contracted income. Their rank plays a role in the determination only of the *level* of the rate of interest. Therefore the level of the *pure* rate of interest, as determined by the level of the property premium, can be raised by a risk premium, which reflects the rank in this hierarchy of the types of security furnished. It goes without saying that this additional charge must not be confused with the property premium.

The credit contract, of course, requires from the debtor collateral with at least the same value as the money notes forwarded to him by the creditor. Thus the issuer's property titles together with the debtor's are the first to be denominated in the money of account, the standard set by the creditor. The *pricing* itself takes place in the market emerging for these titles, the so-called capital market. The degree to which the creditor's titles are demanded for redemption and the debtor's titles are capable of fulfilling the obligations to refund and to pay interest determines the levels of their money prices in a first round.

Credit contracts are expressed neither in an already existing standard good nor in a standard arbitrarily set by the 'monetary authority'. The money of account stands for the valuation of property titles which exist beyond, and in addition to, goods. Their burdening and encumbrance or non-burdening and non-encumbrance stimulates or limits economic activity. A money of account cannot arise independently of these titles. This was sensed in Hawtrey's (1930, p. 545) famous phrase that debt contracts are not defined in terms of money but 'money must be defined in terms of debt'.

The debt titles preceding money proper refute the real bills doctrine. An excessive supply of bank notes, according to this view, can never occur as long as banks restrict themselves to loans secured by real bills, that is, goods already produced. Its famous fallacy does not lie in the search for a limitation of the issue of bank notes. The flaw is due to the lack of understanding that a limit set by existing goods stands in obvious contradiction to the fact that the money forwarded against the bills comes before the goods' production. This misunderstanding can be explained by the disregard of what a bank actually relies upon when it accepts bills. It relies upon the property of all the bills' endorsers against which it can make up for its loss when the bill has to be protested for want of payment.

The triviality that assets permanently undergo market valuations can never disqualify them as securities. The problems these oscillations may create for the stability of the value of money cannot be abolished by simply eliminating collateral in the money-creating process. There is no alternative to collateralized property. Rather, the possible devaluation of assets is taken into account by the money-creating creditor who carefully selects low-risk securities and secures riskier ones with appropriate own capital.

3. The working of the property-based economy

Property economics demonstrates that interest and money cannot be understood without the institution of property and its yield of property premium. How does property bring about the peculiar elements of the economy: an entrepreneur's production of commodities and the market, capital, profit and accumulation, free wage labour and technical progress, as well as business cycles with boom and crisis?

We start with the *entrepreneur* as the decisive debtor in the economy. In an interest-bearing and collateralized contract denominated in a money of account, he has received money proper. With this money he has *uno actu* obtained its liquidity premium which empowers him to finally transfer or redeem property, that is, to settle contractual obligations. As soon as money is created, the liquidity premium can be transferred to all forms of assets which are not money and which, therefore, cannot finally discharge contracts – from demand deposits over tradable financial assets to real assets. The ease of the re-transformability of the different forms of assets into money determines the level of their liquidity premium or the degree of their liquidity.

In a first step, the entrepreneur has to organize a monetary production of goods, that is, money-priced quantities, by buying likewise moneyed quantities of means of production and by contracting labourers for money wages. Only by going through the money advanced do the means of production acquire the character of real or capital assets. *Capital* itself, therefore, is always an advance of property-born money. Thus, no pre-existing goods, of whose consumption somebody has to abstain from by saving, must be made available so that real assets can emerge. Thus the formation of capital assets is not limited by goods or resources but by the readiness with which proprietors collateralize property, that is, forego property premium.

In a second step, the indebted producer also has to sell the money-priced goods, commodities, in sales contracts on the *market* to raise at least the money to fulfil his obligations to refund and to pay interest. To cover interest, the producer must be able to generate a net worth of money to his creditors, the rate of *profit* on the loaned capital. This statement must not be confused with the popular thesis that investment in capital assets is due to already existing profits, that is, *financed* by profits. This may occur, of course, but in this case the entrepreneur has to calculate the opportunity cost of not investing the profit in interest-bearing titles. Only if the producer is able to create profit above the interest on the loan will his investment turn into a net worth of real assets to himself, that is, *accumulation*.

The potential for profits can be enhanced by *competition*, which means, besides the introduction of innovative products, first of all an entrepreneur's search for and application of *technical progress* in the form of labour-saving techniques of production. Why labour-saving methods and not methods that save money for capital assets? Money paid as wages in an employment contract that, like the credit contract, must always be fulfilled, however without any guarantee of entering a sales contract, is irredeemably lost, while money paid for real assets can to some extent be redeemed because, unlike the labourers, they are the producer's property. Furthermore, capital assets can be acquired on credit, thereby, other than labour, not requiring the full cash outlay.

Accumulation consists of real assets always denominated in the money of account. The condition for the generation of these assets is the potential and the *willingness* to burden property, that is, to risk it by giving up property premium, p. This risk will be incurred when the expected rate of profit, r, is above the market rate of interest, i, where i is always equal to p and the liquidity premium, l, but i not necessarily equal to r. Therefore, equilibrium in the economy is, in contrast to the Monetary Keynesian approach (Riese, 1986), not determined by

$$l = i = r \qquad (29.1)$$

but the condition for equilibrium becomes

$$p = i = l = r \qquad (29.2)$$

At first glance, these equilibrium conditions seem to differ only in that the property premium is not taken into account by Monetary Keynesians. For them, giving up money, that is, l, is the decisive economic operation that leads to i and, thereby, forces r into being. In property economics, however, giving up p is the crucial step which allows for the emergence of i and money proper. The money, in turn, supplies the indebted entrepreneur with l, the giving up of which enables him to acquire the capital – advanced as money – to start a monetary production with the potential for r. Of course, the giving up of l can also be used in a subsequent loan to achieve interest above the money creation rate of interest. Consequently, instead of a single market rate of interest, i, property economics distinguishes between the rate of interest of the central bank, i_{cb}, and that of its counterparty commercial bank, i_b. Furthermore, instead of a single liquidity premium l, property economics distinguishes between the liquidity premium of the commercial bank, l_b, and that of the indebted entrepreneur, l_e. However, by this differentiation the economy's equilibrium does not change, because all the different rates of interest and liquidity premia have to be equal in equilibrium:

$$p = i_{cb} = l_b = i_b = l_e = r \qquad (29.3)$$

Equation (29.3) clearly demonstrates that liquidity premium is not a yield of the creator of money but a yield of the agent who borrows the money or acquires it in any other way.

Accumulation is not a one-way street. It can be accelerated or slowed down, or even turned into stagnation, by and in the wake of *business cycles*. To explain the latter, property economics focuses on collateral as a measure of an indebted producer's *creditworthiness* as well as the willingness of the entrepreneur to go into debt and, thereby, risk his property. The good securities debtors have to pledge to get access to credit have no eternal value but are, as assets – R – subject to market valuation. This is determined by the expected rate of profit and the market rate of interest. According to Fisher's (1930, p. 54 f.) well-known formula,

$$i = r / R \qquad (29.4)$$

R increases (decreases) when r rises (falls) and/or i falls (rises). A *boom*, therefore, starts as soon as the value of financial assets that can be pledged as collateral rises, because it increases both the creditworthiness of debtors and their willingness to become indebted. Correspondingly, a *recession* occurs, and eventually may lead to a *crisis*, by a devaluation of property titles pledged as collateral, with the risk of turning debts into bad loans. Good securities, then, are more scarce than ever.

The dependence of the value of assets not only on the rate of profit but also on the rate of interest is not recognized in Fisher's (1930, p. 54 f.) famous example of the apple orchard, with which he wants to overcome the naïve productivity theory of capital value. The value of the plantation, Fisher believes, is determined by the value of its return and not the other way round. However, this determination depends on a presupposed rate of interest, which makes the value of the orchard the discounted value of its expected return. In other words, the rate of interest is equal to the relation between the value of the orchard's crops and the value of the orchard itself, r/R. Fisher, however, does not recognize that the value of the orchard is inversely related to the rate of interest. Therefore, not the value of the orchard's return but the rate of interest is the source of the value of the orchard.

A *crisis* is always characterized by a devaluation of assets pledged as collateral, thereby reducing the debtors' creditworthiness. The sums owed are fixed, whereas the value of securing collateral may undercut them. The property premium soars, and so does the rate of interest and the liquidity premium. *Panics* may occur. The rise of liquidity premium does not cause but only reflects the crisis. Banks as creditors are left with insufficiently secured claims, while banks as debtors cannot take flight from the fixed contracts with their depositors.

Attempts to refinance at the central bank are hampered because in a crisis good securities are wanting. Interventions to turn the tide are mostly useless because the central bank cannot supply the missing securities. Since no one can reduce property premia by showering collateral over the agents, the crisis has its way.

References

Bellerue, Albert R. (1995). 'Private property ownership', *The Freeman* (a publication of the Foundation for Economic Education), **45**(1), www.libertyhaven.com/personalfreedomissues/freespeechorcivilliberties/ownership.html (last visit: 16 April 2006), pp. 1–5.

Bindseil, Ulrich, Andres Manzanares and Benedict Weller (2004). 'The role of central bank capital revisited', ECB Working Paper Series, No. 392, September.

Bogaert, Raymond (1966). *Les origines antiques de la banque de dépôt: Une mise au point accompagnée d'une esquisse des opérations de banque en Mésopotamie*. Leiden: A.W. Sijthoff.

Davidson, Paul (2005). 'The Post Keynesian school', in Brian Snowdon and Howard A. Vane, *Modern Macroeconomics: Its Origins, Development and Current State*. Cheltenham, UK and Northampton, MA, USA: Edward Elgar, pp. 451–73.

Fisher, Irving (1930). *The Theory of Interest as Determined by Impatience to Spend Income and Opportunity to Invest It*. New York: Macmillan.

Gurley, John G. and Edward S. Shaw (1960). *Money in a Theory of Finance*. Washington, DC: Brookings Institution.

Hawtrey, Ralph G. (1930). 'Credit', in *Encyclopedia of the Social Sciences*. New York: Macmillan, vol. 3, pp. 545–50.

Hawtrey, Ralph G. (1970 [1932]). *The Art of Central Banking*. London: Frank Cass & Co.

Heinsohn, Gunnar (1984 [1982]). *Privateigentum, Patriarchat, Geldwirtschaft: Eine sozialtheoretische Rekonstruktion zur Antike*. Frankfurt am Main: Suhrkamp.

Heinsohn, Gunnar (2006). 'Where does the market come from? Why the controversy between the "substantivist" Polanyi school and the "formalist" neoclassical protagonists of an eternal and universal market was never solved', in Otto Steiger (ed.), *Property Economics: Property Rights, Creditor's Money and the Foundations of the Economy*. Marburg: Metropolis, forthcoming.

Heinsohn, Gunnar and Otto Steiger (2003 [2000]). 'The property theory of interest and money'; reprint, with corrections and additions, in Geoffrey M. Hodgson (ed.), *Recent Developments in Institutional Economics*. Cheltenham, UK and Northampton, MA, USA: Edward Elgar, pp. 484–517.

Heinsohn, Gunnar and Otto Steiger (2005). 'Alternative theories of the rate of interest: a reconsideration', in Guiseppe Fontana and Riccardo Realfonzo (eds), *The Monetary Theory of Production: Tradition and New Perspectives (Essays Dedicated to and in Honour of Augusto Graziani)*. London and New York: Palgrave Macmillan, pp. 67–81.

Heinsohn, Gunnar and Otto Steiger (2006a [1996]). *Eigentum, Zins und Geld: Ungelöste Rätsel der Wirtschaftswissenschaft*, 4th, corrected and reset edn. Marburg: Metropolis.

Heinsohn, Gunnar and Otto Steiger (2006b). *Eigentumsökonomik*. Marburg: Metropolis.

Heinsohn, Gunnar and Otto Steiger (2007). *Property, Interest and Money: Foundations of Economic Theory*. London: Routledge, forthcoming.

Keynes, John Maynard (1936). *The General Theory of Employment, Interest and Money*. London: Macmillan.

Keynes, John Maynard (1971 [1930]). *A Treatise on Money – Volume 1: The Pure Theory of Money*. In *The Collected Writings of John Maynard Keynes*, Vol. V. London: Macmillan.

Keynes, John Maynard (1982 [1939]). 'Government loan policy and the rate of interest' (Memorandum of 29 May to the Chancellor of the Exchequer, with a copy to the Governor of the Bank of England), in *The Collected Writings of John Maynard Keynes – Volume XXI: Activities 1931–1939: World Crises and Policies in Britain and America*. London: Macmillan, pp. 534–46.

Knapp, Georg Friedrich (1924 [1905]). *The State Theory of Money*, abridged translation from the 4th German edn of 1923. London: Macmillan.

Loasby, Brian J. (2000). 'Market institutions and economic evolution', *Journal of Evolutionary Economics*, **10**(3), pp. 297–309.

Locke, John (1967 [1690]). *The Second Treatise of Government: An Essay Concerning the True Original, Extent, and End of Civil Government*, in John Locke, *Two Treatises of Government*, ed. P. Laslett, 2nd edn. Cambridge: Cambridge University Press, pp. 283–446.

Malinowski, Bronislaw (1935). *Coral Gardens and Their Magic: A Study of the Methods of Tilling the Soil and of Agriculture Rites in the Trobriand Islands – Volume I: The Description of Gardening*. London: G. Allen & Unwin.

Malinowski, Bronislaw (1961 [1922]). *Argonauts of the Western Pacific: An Account of Native Enterprise and Adventure in the Archipelagoes of Melanesian New Guinea*. New impression New York: E.P. Dutton.

Pesek, Boris P. and Thomas R. Saving (1967). *Money, Wealth, and Economic Theory*. New York and London: Macmillan.

Polanyi, Karl (1957 [1944]). *The Great Transformation: The Political and Economic Orgins of Our Time*. Reprint, Boston: Beacon Press.

Riese, Hajo (1986). *Theorie der Inflation*. Tübingen: J.C.B. Mohr (P. Siebeck).

Riese, Hajo (2000). 'Geld – die unverstandene Kategorie der Nationalökonomie', *Ethik und Sozialwissenschaften: Streitforum für Erwägungskultur*, **11**(4), pp. 487–98.

Smith, Adam (1976 [1776]). *An Inquiry into the Nature and Causes of the Wealth of Nations*, Vol. I, Glasgow edition by Ronald H. Campbell and Andrew S. Skinner. Oxford: Clarendon Press.

Stadermann, Hans-Joachim and Otto Steiger (2006). 'John Maynard Keynes and the theory of the monetary economy', in Jürgen Backhaus (ed.), *The Founders of Modern Economics: The Maastricht Lectures in Political Economy*. Cheltenham, UK and Northampton, MA, USA: Edward Elgar, forthcoming.

Steiger, Otto (2005). 'Schuldnergeld: der wunde Punkt in der keynesianischen Staatstheorie des Geldes'. in Gerhard Huber, Hagen Krämer and Heinz D. Kurz (eds), *Einkommensverteilung, technischer Fortschritt und struktureller Wandel: Festschrift für Peter Kalmbach*. Marburg: Metropolis, pp. 169–88.

Steiger, Otto (2006a). 'Property economics versus new institutional economics: Alternative foundations of how to trigger economic development', *Journal of Economic Issues*, **40**(1), pp. 183–208.

Steiger, Otto (2006b). 'The endogeneity of money and the Eurosystem', in Mark Setterfield (ed.), *Complexity, Endogenous Money and Macoeconomic Theory: Essays in Honor of Basil Moore*. Cheltenham, UK and Northampton, MA, USA: Edward Elgar, pp. 150–69.

Steuart, James (1805 [1761]). *A Dissertation upon the Doctrine and Principles of Money, Applied to the German Coin*, in James Steuart, *The Works, Political, Metaphysical, and Chronological by the Late Sir James Steuart*. London: D.T. Cadell & W. Davies, Vol. V, pp. 171–265.

Steuart, James (1767). *An Inquiry into the Principles of Political Oeconomy: Being an Essay on the Science of Domestic Policy in Free Nations*, Vol. I, London: A. Millar & T. Cadell.

Tobin, James (1963). 'Commercial banks as creators of "Money" ', in Dean Carson (ed.), *Banking and Monetary Studies*. Homewood, IL: Irwin.

US Treasury (2006). 'Fact sheets: Currency & coins', www.treas.gov/education/fact-sheets/currency/distribution.shtml (last visit: 6 March), pp. 1–3.

Wray, L. Randall (1998). *Understanding Modern Money: The Key to Full Employment and Price Stability*. Cheltenham, UK and Lyme, USA: Edward Elgar.

Index